FIRST EDITIONS:
A GUIDE TO IDENTIFICATION

FIRST EDITIONS:
A GUIDE TO IDENTIFICATION

Statements of selected North American,
British Commonwealth, and Irish publishers on
their methods of designating first editions

FOURTH EDITION

Edited by
Edward N. Zempel
and Linda A. Verkler

The Spoon River Press

Published by
The Spoon River Press
P. O. Box 3635
Peoria, Illinois 61612-3635

ISBN 0-930358-18-X

Manufactured in the United States of America

INTRODUCTION

When the predecessor of this book was first published in 1977, *Publishers Weekly* in a review of *A First Edition?* stated, "Each publisher's reply is quoted verbatim . . . each is from the horse's mouth." That has been the premise on which all editions of this reference have been based. All of the information in this book has been obtained *from the publishers themselves.*

Because the information has been obtained directly from the publishers—at intervals over a period of sixty or more years in some cases—this book provides a unique and valuable resource for the collector of modern first editions. There is no other book like it.

This new and expanded fourth edition of *First Editions: A Guide to Identification* has a complex history. Essentially, it is a compilation of publishers' statements regarding their methods of designating a 'first edition.' For some, the term 'first edition' has an unclear meaning. To most librarians, bibliographers, and book collectors, however, it means 'the first printing or first impression of a first edition.' Here, a printing or impression is considered to be all the copies of a book printed in one continuous operation from a single makeready.

In this reference are assembled and coordinated the publishers' statements previously published in seven books, all now out of print. Each of these books was a standard reference for bibliographers, librarians, book dealers, and book collectors. As well as holding updated statements, this book, then, holds the statements from the first, second, and third editions of H.S. Boutell's *First Editions of To-day and How to Tell Them.* It contains also the publishers' statements from *A First Edition?*, published in 1977, and from the first edition of *First Editions: A Guide to Identification*, published in 1984, the second edition of *First Editions: A Guide to Identification*, published in 1989, and the third edition of *First Editions: A Guide to Identification*, published in 1995. The last four books were compiled and edited by the editors of the book at hand. A brief publishing history of each of these books may help the reader appreciate the way in which the information is here presented.

The first edition of Boutell's valuable reference was published in 1928. It held verbatim statements from American and British publishers regarding their methods of designating their first impressions. As Boutell stated in his introductory note:

> Generally speaking, the collector of first editions is really a collector of first impressions, a first impression being a book from the first lot struck off the presses, and a first edition comprising all books which remain the same in content and in format as the first impression. A second impression is a second printing. A second edition postulates some alteration of text or format. But these terms are, unfortunately, not strictly adhered to.

Revised and enlarged, Boutell's book was published in a second edition in 1937. The third edition, again a revision and enlargement of the previous edition, was published in 1949. A fourth edition was published in 1965. All of these editions are now out of print.

As well as including the publishers' statements from the first three editions of Boutell's *First Editions of To-day and How to Tell Them*, this book contains also publishers' statements from three other books: *A First Edition? Statements of selected North American, British Commonwealth, and Irish publishers on their methods of designating first editions* and the first, second, and third editions of *First Editions: A Guide to Identification*. Each of these books was compiled and edited by Edward N. Zempel and Linda A. Verkler, the editors of the work at hand.

A First Edition? was published in 1977. This book, which was a work separate from the various editions of Boutell's work, held statements from over 550 publishers.

The first edition of *First Editions: A Guide to Identification* held statements from over 1,000 publishers. As well as containing the information in the first three editions of the Boutell references and *A First Edition?*, it contained statements from many publishers outlining their 1960 practice of designation. It also held publishers' statements from 1981 or 1982. The statements regarding 1960 practices were gathered to fill a gap that might otherwise have resulted in an inventory of publishers' designation practices. The 1981 and 1982 statements were included to update and, in some cases, expand previous statements.

The second edition of *First Editions: A Guide to Identification* included statements from nearly 1,700 publishers and publishers' imprints. It included publishers' statements for 1988 or 1989. As well as including all of the information in the first edition of *First Editions: A Guide to Identification*, it was expanded to include statements from over 550 publishers and publisher's imprints not listed in the first edition of *First Editions: A Guide to Identification*.

The third edition of *First Editions: A Guide to Identification* included statements from over 2,900 publishers and publishers' imprints. As well as including all of the statements from the second edition, it included statements from over 1,200 publishers and publishers' imprints not appearing in the previous edition.

This new, fourth, edition of *First Editions: A Guide to Identification* has again been expanded to include statements from over 4,200 publishers and publishers' imprints. It includes statements from over 1,300 publishers and publishers' imprints not appearing in the previous edition.

Publishers' statements have, with a few exceptions, been obtained from English-language publishers. Publishers' statements are dated by year. Often the reader is referred to another statement (for example, 1937 Statement: *See* 1928 Statement). In several instances, the publisher providing a statement made insubstantial revisions to their earlier statement, sometimes adding the valuable information regarding when a particular designation practice was begun.

Nearly all of the statements in this book are set within quotation marks. Such statements were printed as received or as they appeared when published verbatim in the first three editions of Boutell's reference, in *A First Edition?*, or in the first, second, or third editions of *First Editions: A Guide to Identification*.

A few statements in this book bear no quotation marks. These statements were abstracted from information provided by the publisher. Information was presented in this fashion *only* when the publisher did not provide a formal statement (but provided information from which one could be prepared) or when the publisher did not wish their statement to be printed verbatim. Every statement, however, was prepared with the *full cooperation and participation of the publisher*.

With a few exceptions, publishers listed in this book were drawn from those in the United States, the British Commonwealth, and the Republic of Ireland. All publishers other than those from the United States are identified by country. In the case of some publishers with identical names, the city is sometimes given. Publishers are listed alphabetically. Note, though, that the names of some publishers may not be alphabetized as you think they should be. This occurs mainly with publishers (usually in the United Kingdom) that have taken a name that includes the surnames of the founders of the joined publishing houses. In such cases, if you don't find the publisher under the last name, look under the first. Generally, changes in the style of a company's name are reflected in this book. We have taken great pains to present each company's name exactly as the company stated it. In a few cases, this may help you distinguish the printing designation practices of one publisher from those of another with a nearly identical name.

One of the strengths of the previous editions of *First Editions: A Guide to Identification* was thought to be its inclusion of the first printing designations of so many small publishers. That interest was retained and amplified in compiling the statements for the present edition. With the consolidation of the publishing industry, many companies have disappeared through mergers or acquisitions. Others have failed. For readers interested in such companies, this book may provide the only record of the ways in which they designated the various printings and editions.

This fourth edition includes a brief primer on identifying book club editions through 1995. This section, "Identifying Book Club Editions," is at the end of the book, immediately after the publishers' statements.

We would like to express our appreciation to the publishers who responded to our queries. Again, their patience was equal to our persistence. Statements from over 4,200 publishers and publishers' imprints are included in this reference. As will be seen from the statements published herein, this book presents a wide inventory of publishers' verbatim statements regarding their methods for designating their first printings.

There is no book like this one. It is a unique resource.

A

A & B PUBLISHERS GROUP

2001 Statement: "We state both 'First edition' and 'First printing' on the copyright page. We also set a number string on the copyright page. The lowest number indicates the printing."

A CAPPELA PUBLISHING
(Florida)

2000 Statement: " 'First Edition 10 9 8 7 6 5 4 3 2 1 © copyright 2000 A Cappela Publishing' appears on a first edition. Subsequent editions are identified, on the copyright page."

A CAPPELLA BOOKS

1993, 2000 Statements: *See* 1993 Statement of Chicago Review Press

AAAI PRESS

2001 Statement: "From 1989 to 2000, first editions bore no designation. Printings of subsequent editions were so designated (i.e. 'second printing,' etc.). In 2000 we began to identify printings with a list of Arabic numerals in descending order (i.e. 10 9 8 7 6 5 4 3 2 1). A first printing will have a '1' while it will be missing from subsequent printings."

ABACUS (UNITED KINGDOM)

1988 Statement: *See* 1988 Statement of Sphere Books Limited (United Kingdom)
2001 Statement: *See* 2001 Statement of Little, Brown and Company (United Kingdom)

ABARIS BOOKS, INC.

1988 Statement: "We have very short press runs (1,000-3,000). Most of our titles are art reference books. The 2nd edition is marked 'Second Edition' and so on for all later editions."
1993, 2000 Statements: *See* 1988 Statement

ABBEVILLE

2000 Statement: *See* 2000 Statement of Abbeville Press, Inc.

ABBEVILLE KIDS

2000 Statement: *See* 2000 Statement of Abbeville Press, Inc.

ABBEVILLE PRESS, INC.

1981 Statement: "For the most part, we simply print 'first edition' on the copyright page of books we expect will go into subsequent printings or revisions. We have no policy on this."

1988 Statement: "Our first printings bear the words 'First edition' on the copyright page. Subsequent printings are identified by number: e.g., 'Second printing.' Revisions are identified as 'Second edition,' and reprints are indicated as above."

1994, 2000 Statements: *See* 1988 Statement

ABC (UNITED KINGDOM)

1994 Statement: "Our practice is to print the following notice on the page preceding the title page:

First published in 19XX by ABC, All Books for Children,

a division of The All Children's Company Ltd,

33 Museum Street, London WC1A 1LD

Printed and bound in XXXX

"To designate a second or subsequent reprinting, it is customary to delete the corresponding number from the sequence from one to ten following the copyright information.

"These practices are followed in our imprints with a slight change to the copyright information as follows:

First edition published in Great Britain by ABC

This edition published in 19XX by SoftbABCks,

an imprint of ABC, All Books for Children . . . etc."

ABC-CLIO

1994 Statement: "ABC-CLIO generally employs a standard, two-part impression line on the copyright page to designate first printings and later impressions. The first part indicates the year of publication; the second part indicates the number of the impression. A book printed for the first time in 1995 would have an impression line like the following:

99 98 97 96 95 5 4 3 2 1

"If, for example, a second printing of the book were to occur in 1997, the new impression line would be as follows:

99 98 97 5 4 3 2

"In the past ABC-CLIO has sometimes printed books with an impression line showing only the number of the printing but not the year."

2000 Statement: *See* 1994 Statement

ABELARD-SCHUMAN LIMITED (UNITED KINGDOM)

1976 Statement: "We do not identify first editions in any special way but indicate a reprint on the copyright page."

1988 Statement: *See* 1981 Statement of Blackie and Son Limited (United Kingdom)

ABELEXPRESS

2000 Statement: "We have never made the effort of designating a first printing or distinguishing the first printing from any later printings. Effective 1/1/01 we will identify the first printing of a first edition by the following number line: 01 02 03 04 05 8 7 6 5 4 3 2 1, where the righthand-most digit is the printing, and the lefthand-most digit is the year of that printing."

ABINGDON PRESS

1937 Statement: "First editions of Abingdon Press publications can be identified by examining the copyright page. There does not appear on the bottom of the copyright page of first editions a statement as to the number of the edition and when printed. This statement does not appear until the second edition and thereafter."

See also Abingdon-Cokesbury Press

1981 Statement: "We distinguish between first editions and revised editions by designating 'Revised' or 'Revised and Enlarged,' but we have no system for designating the various printings of a book."

1988 Statement: "We distinguish between first editions and revised editions by designating 'Revised' or 'Revised and Enlarged.' Reprints are identified on copyright page beginning with the second printing. This new method of designating reprints was begun around 1983."

ABINGDON-COKESBURY PRESS

(Abingdon Press, The Stockton Press, and Cokesbury Press were merged in 1940 to form Abingdon-Cokesbury Press.)

1947 Statement: "Quite some time ago we discontinued using identifying marks for the first printings of our books. We found that they served no useful purpose and were the source of considerable trouble and some unnecessary cost.

"A few first printings may have been identified by showing 'First Edition' on the copyright page in late 1940 or early 1941. We have given very little attention to this matter and long since have decided that identifying first printings is of no value except in very special publications."

ABLEX PUBLISHING

2000 Statement: *See* 2000 Statement of Greenwood Publishing Group Inc.

ABRADALE

2001 Statement: *See* 2001 Statement of Harry N. Abrams, Inc.

WILLIAM ABRAHAMS

1988 Statement: *See* 1988 Statement of E. P. Dutton & Co., Inc.

HARRY N. ABRAMS, INC.

1976 Statement: "I'm afraid we have had no special policies about citing editions. When we've done it, it's been mostly on textbooks. We are now tending more toward putting First Edition on the copyright page. Again, mostly on textbooks (*History of Art* by Janson, for one) we give printings and their dates."

1988 Statement: "I'm afraid we have had no special policies about citing editions. When we've done it, it's been mostly on textbooks."

1993 Statement: "We do not usually indicate first editions on our trade books. Textbooks always identify revisions, and usually specify first and subsequent editions. For the most part, first printings are not distinguished from subsequent reprints if no changes have been made."

2001 Statement: *See* 1993 Statement

BEN ABRAMSON, PUBLISHER
1947 Statement: *See* Argus Books, Inc.

ABZ BOOKS (CANADA)
1995, 2000 Statements: *See* 1995 Statement of Townson Publishing Co., Ltd. (Canada)

THE ACADEMIC & ARTS PRESS
2000 Statement: "I publish only literary limited editions and do not reprint. Therefore any title published under one of my imprints (Scrooge's Ledger, The Academic & Arts Press, Rocky Mountain Creative Arts Journal & Books, or Blue Light Books) is a first edition."

ACADEMIC PRESS
A Harcourt Science and Technology Company
2001 Statement: *See* 1981 Statement of Academic Press, Inc.

ACADEMIC PRESS, INC.
1981 Statement: "Identification of a first edition is actually achieved by the absence of a qualifying notation. This compares with subsequent editions, which always carry (e.g.) 'Second Edition' on the half-title and title page as well as anywhere on the case or jacket where the title appears.

"The copyright page carries a line that appears as follows:

80 81 82 83 84 85 9 8 7 6 5 4 3 2 1

"The far left gives the year and the far right the number of the printing. A book that had no specific Edition designation and that carried the above line as is would clearly be a copy from the first printing of the first edition. Subsequent printings would have the far right digit deleted and as many of the far left numbers as appropriate. For instance, a book whose title had no edition designation and a line that appeared

81 82 83 84 9 8 7 6 5

would be the fifth printing, done in 1981.

"The edition designation policy has been in effect since the founding of the company. The printing designation has changed several times. In earlier years it was the practice to say (e.g.) 'Fifth Printing, 1965' on the title page. During the years from about 1972 through 1976, we designated printings by a vertical column of numbers in the gutter margin on the last page of the book to carry any printing (usually being the last page of the index). That column appeared as follows:

A   5
B   6

C	7
D	8
E	9
F	0
G	1
H	2
I	3
J	4

"The column displayed would indicate that the first printing (A) was done in 1975. Subsequent printings would drop the top letter and/or numeral as appropriate. This system depends on looking at the copyright page to determine the applicable decade. All Academic Press books that appeared during those years carry that form of designation, but subsequent printings of those titles have been converted to the horizontal designation on the title page as described previously.

"Other imprints of Academic Press follow the same policies."

1988, 1993 Statements: *See* 1981 Statement

2001 Statement: *See* 2001 Statement of Academic Press, A Harcourt Science and Technology Company

ACADEMIC PRESS INC (LONDON) LIMITED (UNITED KINGDOM)

1976 Statement: "We do not have any special method of identifying first editions of our titles."

1981 Statement: *See* 1976 Statement

ACADEMIC PRESS LTD (UNITED KINGDOM)

1981, 1994, 2001 Statements: *See* 1976 Statement of Academic Press Inc (London) Limited (United Kingdom)

ACADEMY CHICAGO PUBLISHERS

1988 Statement: "Academy Chicago Publishers do not identify the first editions of their original properties in any special way—no 'First Edition' notations are used. However, when we do a second printing we usually state that and include the date for this new edition. If a copyright page does not say 'Second printing' on it then you may assume it is the first printing of the first edition and the only one extant.

"This policy has been used [since] . . . the company has been in business."

1993, 2000 Statements: *See* 1988 Statement

ACADEMY EDITIONS (UNITED KINGDOM)

1976 Statement: "Our first editions carry the following statement on the title verso:

First published in Great Britain in 19.. by Academy Editions

Following reprints have in addition: Reprinted in 19..

New editions are similarly indicated with: Second edition 19.."

1981, 1988 Statements: *See* 1976 Statement

ACCESS GUIDES
1993 Statement: *See* 1993 Statement of HarperCollins Publishers
2001 Statement: *See* 2001 Statement of Access Travel

ACCESS TRAVEL
2001 Statement: *See* 2001 Statement of HarperCollinsPublishers

ACE
1995 Statement: *See* 1995 Statement of The Berkley Publishing Group
2000 Statement: *See* 2000 Statement of The Berkley Publishing Group

ACE/PUTNAM
1989 Statement: *See* 1989 Statement of G. P. Putnam's Sons

ACETO BOOKMEN
2001 Statement: "We do not designate First Editions since most of our publications are reprints of original material with a new full name index."

BERNARD ACKERMAN, INC.
(In July, 1946, became Beechhurst Press, Inc.)
See Beechhurst Press, Inc.

ACME PRESS
2000 Statement: "We identify the first printing of a first edition by the statement First printing: (date) [and] the following number line: 10 9 8 7 6 5 4 3 2 1 (the smallest number in the line is the current printing); we do both on each printing. Second printing (e.g.) would say First printing: (date 1), Second printing: (date 2)."

ACORN BOOKS
2000 Statement: "Regarding your query about first editions, Acorn Books prints 10 9 8 7 6 5 4 3 2 1 on the copyright page of first editions. With the printing of subsequent editions, we remove the number on the right for each reprinting, e.g., a second edition copyright page would have 10 9 8 7 6 5 4 3 2."

ACORN EDITIONS (UNITED KINGDOM)
2000 Statement: *See* 2000 Statement of The Lutterworth Press (United Kingdom)

ACORN MUSIC PRESS
2001 Statement: *See* 2001 Statement of Music Sales Corp

ACROPOLIS BOOKS LTD.
1976 Statement: "We only indicate those printings or editions after the first."
1981, 1988 Statements: *See* 1976 Statement

ACS BOOKS (AMERICAN CHEMICAL SOCIETY)
1988 Statement: "We do not designate first printings or first editions. For subsequent printings we indicate the number of the printing and the year. This

is placed on the bottom of the copyright page, which is the reverse side of the title page."
1993 Statement: *See* 1988 Statement

ACS PUBLICATIONS INC.

1988 Statement: "We print the date of publication on the copyright page. We do not explicitly identify a first edition although sometimes we do include 'First Printing, month, year' on that page.

"Whenever we reprint a book, whether new material is added or not, we add 'First printing, month, year' and 'Second printing, month, year', ('Third printing, month, year') etc. Some books have 'Revised' on the title page to indicate a substantial revision that would warrant a new ISBN."
1993 Statement: "We identify a first edition by printing the publication date on the copyright page, and also the words 'First Printing.' Whenever we reprint the book, whether new material is added or not, we list each subsequent printing with the date, e.g.: 'First Printing, month, year' and under that, 'Second Printing, month, year,' and so on, to include the current printing. If a book has been substantially revised, warranting a new ISBN, we also print 'Revised' on the cover and on the title page."

ACTA PUBLICATIONS

2001 Statement: "We identify the first printing of a first edition by printing: ...8 7 6 5 4 3 2 1."

THE ACTINIC PRESS (UNITED KINGDOM)

1976, 1981 Statements: *See* 1976, 1981 Statements of J. Garnet Miller Ltd. (United Kingdom)
1994, 2000 Statements: *See* 1994 Statement of Cressrelles Publishing Company Ltd (United Kingdom)

ADASTRA PRESS

1993 Statement: "All Adastra first editions have a Colophon at the back of the book stating, minimally, the print run and dates of production. Most also give the name of the type used and the trade name of the paper stocks used. Additionally, it is noted on the copyright page 'First Edition.' Some early titles used 'Limited Edition.' Titles that have gone into successive printings carry the following notice on the Copyright page:

First printing (month) (year)
Second printing (month) (year)
etc."

2001 Statement: *See* 1993 Statement

ADDICUS BOOKS

2001 Statement: "We identify first editions on our copyright pages with the line of numerals 10 9 8 7 6 5 4 3 2 1. After the first edition, we delete the '1,' indicating a second edition."

ADDISON HOUSE, PUBLISHERS
1976 Statement: "I am afraid that our first edition is probably the same thing as a first printing as most of our books will not warrant change over the years."

ADDISON-WESLEY PUBLISHERS LIMITED (UNITED KINGDOM)
1994 Statement: "The first edition of a book is designated by the line: First printed 199x.

"Any reprint and subsequent edition information is then added as on the copyright of the title verso.

"This has been followed in the UK since 1986. Previously the copyright line was the only information given on the year of publication."

ADDISON-WESLEY PUBLISHING COMPANY
1976 Statement: "Our present method of identification on printings is merely an alphabetical and numerical code. This applies to both our children's books and to our adult trade books. For instance, on the copyright page of a new book the code would be listed:

ABCDEFGHIJK 7987

(this indicates a first printing in the year 1977)

"As each reprint is done, one letter of the alphabet is dropped and the last number if in a different year. For instance, a second printing would have

BCDEFGHIJK 798

(a second printing in 1978)

"We do not indicate 'first edition,' 'second edition.' Some of our earlier children's books have 'first printing,' 'second printing,' etc. Some have no designation whatsoever."

1981, 1989 Statements: *See* 1976 Statement

ADIRONDACK MOUNTAIN CLUB
1988 Statement: "We do not always indicate First Edition on the copyright page, but *lack* of identification marks them as such.

"All future printings and/or editions are noted on the copyright page."

1995 Statement: "Most of our books distinguish the first edition by saying so, usually on the copyright page. Subsequent printings are indicated as well, for example, 'Second edition 1991, revised 1994.' Some earlier first editions do not explicitly state 'first edition,' but subsequent new editions and print-ings are noted as such."

2001 Statement: "Since 1994 we have identified first printings by setting the numbers 1 2 3 4 5 6 7 8 9 10 at the bottom of the copyright page. With the second printing—a reissue of the book—we remove the number 1, and so on for successive printings (as per the *Chicago Manual of Style*). Thus we do not identify first editions, except by implication, until the second and sub-sequent editions, when we include a listing on the copyright page citing First Edition and the date, Second Edition and the date, etc. The last printing in that list notes reprint dates as well and, because guidebooks are a significant part of our titles list, whether or not the printing included revisions (for ex., First Edition . . . 1994, Second Edition . . . 1998, rev. 2000). On a related note, new editions (as opposed to reprints) are issued when 10% or more of the book is in need of revision."

ADLARD-COLES LTD. (UNITED KINGDOM)
1976, 1981, 1988 Statements: *See* 1976, 1981, 1988 Statements of Granada Publishing Limited (United Kingdom)

ADLARD COLES NAUTICAL (UNITED KINGDOM)
1994 Statement: *See* 1994 Statement of A & C Black (Publishers) Limited (United Kingdom)
2000 Statement: *See* 2000 Statement of A & C Black (Publishers) Limited (United Kingdom)

ADRENALINE BOOKS
2001 Statement: *See* 2001 Statement of Avalon Publishing Group Incorporated

ADVENTURE PUBLICATIONS
2001 Statement: "We do not identify a first printing or any printing after the first printing on the copyright page."

ADVENTURE TRAILS PUBLICATIONS
1947 Statement: "We seem to have no standard rule for first editions, except that they are limited in number, and three of them have been hand numbered.

"The first edition of *The Vengeance of the Vixen*, for instance, was limited to 1500 copies, numbered by hand. Of *How the Eggplant Came To Be* there were only 1000 copies of the first edition, numbered. There were two thousand copies of *Peanuts* printed in the first edition, hand numbered. There were 1500 copies of *Chiquito* printed and the number is mentioned in the first edition. The second edition of *The Vengeance of the Vixen* is marked 'second edition.' "

ADVENTURES UNLIMITED PRESS
2001 Statement: "We do not identify first editions. We only identify second editions, etc."

THE ADVOCADO PRESS
1995 Statement: "A first edition, first printing is distinguished by there being no designation on the verso. Any further printings will be designated by number, with year (e.g., Second printing 1995). A further edition would be designated with number and year (e.g., Second edition 1995), with no further designation for the first printing of that edition, and printing and year given for further printings (e.g., Second edition 1995 Second printing 1996)."

ADVOCATE HOUSE
2000 Statement: *See* 2000 Statement of A Cappela Publishing

AEGEAN PUBLISHING COMPANY

2000 Statement: "Our first editions are marked by the fact that the copyright page bears no printing or edition notice, whereas in subsequent editions the dates of subsequent editions and/or printings appear."

AEOLUS PRESS, INC

2000 Statement: "We identify the first printing of a first edition by 'First Edition, First Printing, month, year' on copyright page."

AERIAL FICTION

2000 Statement: *See* 2000 Statement of Farrar, Straus & Giroux, Inc.

AERIE

1994 Statement: *See* 1994 Statement of TOR

AEROFAX (UNITED KINGDOM)

2001 Statement: *See* 2001 Statement of Midland Publishing (United Kingdom)

AFRICAN WAYS PUBLISHING

2000 Statement: "We identify the sequence of publications by the string of numbers on the copyright page 1 2 3 4 5 6 7 8 9 0. The numeral to the left indicates the number of the issue."

AFRICANA PUBLISHING COMPANY

See Holmes and Meier Publishers, Inc.

AGATHON BOOKS

2000 Statement: "We identify the first printing of a first edition by the statement: 'first printing of first edition, month, day, year.' "

AGATHON PRESS, INC.

1988 Statement: "No special designation for first printing."

AGREKA BOOKS

2001 Statement: "We identify the first printing of a first edition by "First Edition'; if [there are] subsequent printings, we either show 'Second Printing' or we revise and show as 'Revised Edition.' "

AHMANSON MURPHY FINE ARTS IMPRINT

2000 Statement: *See* 2000 Statement of University of California Press

AHSAHTA PRESS

1988 Statement: "Our practice of designating different printings and editions has remained constant since our founding in 1974. First editions contain simply the copyright notice. Subsequent printings contain the following notice, '(X) Printing, (Month) (Year),' beneath the original copyright notice. If substantial revisions (corrections, deletions, additions) are made, we note '(X) Printing, (Month) (Year),' beneath the original copyright."

1993, 2001 Statements: *See* 1988 Statement

AIRAVATA PRESS
2000 Statement: *See* 2000 Statement of Blue Dolphin Publishing Inc.

AIRLIFE PUBLISHING LIMITED (UNITED KINGDOM)
1994 Statement: "On the copyright pages of our books we print 'First published in the UK in (year) by Airlife Publishing Limited.'

"In the case of our subsidiary imprints we would print 'First published in the UK in (year) by (name) an imprint of Airlife Publishing Limited.' The various imprints of Airlife Publishing are Swan Hill Press, Waterline, Chatsworth Library.

"If the book had not been originated by us but had been bought in from an overseas publisher, we would place under this information 'First published in USA (or country) by (publisher).' "
2000 Statement: *See* 1994 Statement

AIVIA PRESS
1995 Statement: "First printings are designated 'FIRST EDITION' on the copyright page, along with the numbers 10 through 2. On second printings, 'FIRST EDITION' is deleted. On third printings, the 2 is deleted, and so on. We have always employed this method."

AKROS PUBLICATIONS (UNITED KINGDOM)
1995 Statement: "Our first books under the Akros Publications imprint, e.g., SOUNDINGS. Poems by Alastair Mackie, published in 1966, gave the name and address:
Akros Publications
14 Parklands Avenue, Penwortham, Preston.
The only date was on the author's copyright line—1966.

"In 1967, we used the form that has become our stock imprint:
First published 1967
Akros Publications [followed by publisher's address]

"We have not been consistent, always. Also we have published several books in limited editions and used various forms including:
This first edition published by
AKROS PUBLICATIONS
14 Parklands Avenue, Penwortham
Preston, Lancashire, England
is limited to three hundred numbered copies.
The first fifty copies are signed by the author.
This copy is number:
"The date was on the copyright line.

"We have had few second editions or reprints. One was a reprint of a 1968 limited edition and read
Second edition
reprinted January 1969.

"Another form for a reprint was:
First published October 1974
Second edition November 1974

AKROS PUBLICATIONS
14 Parklands Avenue, Penwortham, Preston
Lancashire, England."

ALAMO SQUARE PRESS
1995 Statement: "We use 1 2 3 4 5 6 7 8 9 0. When reprinted, we delete figure 1, etc., insert 2nd, 3rd, etc., printing on copyright page."

ALASKA GEOGRAPHIC SOCIETY
2000 Statement: "First editions bear only the copyright (©2000, e.g.); subsequent editions are marked with date and number of printing."

ALASKA NATIVE LANGUAGE CENTER
2001 Statement: "We identify the first printing of a first edition by 'First Printing (year).' "

ALASKA NORTHWEST BOOKS
1993 Statement: *See* 1988 Statement of Graphic Arts Center Publishing Company

ALASKA NORTHWEST PUBLISHING COMPANY
1976 Statement: "I'm not sure how regular we've been until the last couple of years, but our current method of designating first editions is not to designate them. A second printing will be marked:
First printing, date
Second printing, date
And so on until we do a revised edition. Then it's
Revised edition, date
Second printing, revised edition, date."
1981, 1988 Statements: *See* 1976 Statement

ALBA HOUSE
1988 Statement: "We print a strip of code numbers on the copyright page to designate the printing. For a first printing it reads:
1 2 3 4 5 6 7 8 9 10"
1993, 2000 Statements: *See* 1988 Statement

ALBATROSS BOOKS PTY LTD (AUSTRALIA)
1994 Statement: "First print of first edition says 'First edition' and the year. Subsequent printings say 'second edition,' etc., followed by the year in each case, or 'reprinted,' followed by a list of years."
2001 Statement: Out of business at the end of 1999.

ALBYN PRESS LTD (UNITED KINGDOM)
2000 Statement: *See* 2000 Statement of The Albyn Press (United Kingdom)

THE ALBYN PRESS (UNITED KINGDOM)
1947 Statement: "Regarding our method of indicating first and subsequent printings of our books, we have to say that this information is contained on the reverse of the title page and reads—

First published 19..
By The Albyn Press
42 Frederick Street
Edinburgh, 2
"Subsequent printings are noted beneath this as—
Reprinted . . . .
New Edition. . . ."

1994, 2000 Statements: *See* 1947 Statement

ALEF DESIGN GROUP

2001 Statement: "We do not identify a first printing or any printing after the first printing on the copyright page."

ALETHEIA PUBLICATIONS, INC.

2000 Statement: "We identify the first printing of a first edition by the following number line: 10 9 8 7 6 5 4 3 2 1."

ALETHEIA PUBLISHING (AUSTRALIA)

1994 Statement: "The current practice is to set the information out as follows:

First Edition . . . March 1990
David Holden 1990
ISBN 0 77316 76130

"In the past, the first edition did not contain any clear statement to the effect that it was a first edition. In the future it is very likely that the above format which began in 1990 will remain."

ALFRED PUBLISHING CO., INC.

1988 Statement: "First editions are not marked in any particular way. Usually, when second and further editions are issued of the same title, they are so marked."

1995, 2000 Statements: *See* 1988 Statement

ALGONQUIN BOOKS OF CHAPEL HILL

2001 Statement: "We state 'First edition' on the copyright page. We also identify the first printing of a first edition by a number line, the lowest number indicating the printing. In addition, we remove 'First edition' from the copyright page at the second printing (and for subsequent reprints). We have a new imprint as of Spring 2001, Shannon Ravenel Books, which follows the same procedure."

ALICEJAMES BOOKS

1981 Statement: "We do not identify first editions as such. We designate second printings by the words 'Second Printing' and the date. We have not changed our method of identification."

1988, 1993, 2000 Statements: *See* 1981 Statement

IAN ALLAN PUBLISHING (UNITED KINGDOM)

1994 Statement: "Currently, all Ian Allan titles state simply 'First published 19xx.' Subsequent reprints and new editions are listed under the 'First published 19xx.' This applies to all our imprints. This form has been adopted since the early 1970s. Before that date it was slightly inconsistent. Sometimes simply a date was used and on other occasions the company adopted the form '© xxxx 19xx.' Occasionally books were undated, but their publication date can be determined through a code. A book has been published for collectors in the UK detailing the 'abc' series. There is a problem with a number of annual publications (such as 'Railways Restored' 1994/95) where we identify the book as 'First published,' even though it may be the umpteenth edition published as all are dated and it is, consequently, the first edition of the volume published that year."

2000 Statement: *See* 1994 Statement

PHILIP ALLAN & CO., LTD. (UNITED KINGDOM)
(Out of business.)

1937 Statement: "It is our practice to put the date of publication of any book either on the title page or on the back of the title page. If the book is reprinted, the date of the reprint appears on the back of the title page beneath the date of the first printing. Subsequent editions and reprints are similarly printed on the back of the title page."

ALLELUIA PRESS

1995 Statement: "All our books are identified as follows: on colophon,
logo and date
typeface
typesetter
(Run) .... constituting
original edition"

2000 Statement: *See* 1995 Statement

ALLEN PUBLISHING

1995 Statement: "Our only method is to examine the biblio on the reverse of the title page. This always reads in the order.
  First published in 1995 (or other date)
by ALLEN PUBLISHING
33 W. Lancaster Avenue, Ardmore, PA 19003
Printed in USA (or other country)
by Book Crafters (or other printer)
All rights reserved

"In the event of a second or subsequent impression being published that fact and the date would also be given on the reverse of the title page as follows:
Second impression March 1995
Third impression March 1995."

J. A. ALLEN & CO. LTD. (UNITED KINGDOM)

1976 Statement: "Please be advised it is our custom to indicate the date of original publication on the verso of the title page. Where there is a new edition or reprint, it will be indicated below the original copyright notice."

1981, 1988 Statements: *See* 1976 Statement

1994 Statement: "Published in Great Britain by J.A. Allen & Co Ltd, 1 Lower Grosvenor Place, London SW1W 0EL. © J.A. Allen (Date of first publication) or © Author (Date of first publication). Subsequent reprints are listed as Reprinted (year) or New Edition (year). This information appears on the titlepage verso."

2000 Statement: "We were bought by Robert Hale Ltd in 1999. Otherwise, the information on title page verso is the same [as the 1994 Statement]."

See also 2000 Statement of Robert Hale Limited (United Kingdom)

W. H. ALLEN & CO., LTD. (UNITED KINGDOM)

1976 Statement: "This Company does not have any special method of identifying first editions. So far as I can ascertain, the Company, which dates back to the eighteenth century, has never used any identifying designation."

1981 Statement: *See* 1976 Statement

See also 1989 Statement of W. H. Allen & Co., PLC (United Kingdom)

W. H. ALLEN & CO., PLC (UNITED KINGDOM)

1989 Statement: "I can only confirm the [1976 and 1981] statements [of W. H. Allen & Co., Ltd.]. However, a first edition could probably be recognised by the absence of a notice saying 'Reprinted 19XX.' "

ALLEN & UNWIN AUSTRALIA PTY. LTD. (AUSTRALIA)

1988 Statement: "All first editions of our books are printed with copyright notice and date (© author 1988) and the words 'first published in 1988.' Reprints and second editions also have the words 'reprinted' or 'second edition' with the date.

"This method of designation has been standard practice for many years and is applied to all imprints and subsidiaries."

("Since our company became independent in 1990, it is now known simply as Allen & Unwin Pty Ltd.")

ALLEN & UNWIN PTY. LTD. (AUSTRALIA)

1994 Statement: "We have in fact now changed our system for reprints, whereby the word 'Reprinted' does not appear, and instead we list the numbers 10 back to 1 on the imprint page, removing numbers in order as the book is reprinted. New editions however are of course specifically referred to."

2000 Statement: *See* 1994 Statement

GEORGE ALLEN & UNWIN, LTD. (UNITED KINGDOM)

1928 Statement: "It is our practice in the first edition to print the words 'First Published in . . . ' (the year of issue) and in subsequent impressions or editions to add the additional dates."

1937 Statement: "It is our practice in the first edition to print the words 'First Published in . . . .' (the year of issue) and in subsequent impressions or editions to add the additional dates. With translations we give the original title, date and place of publication.

"We began using our present method of identifying first printings about 1914."

1947 Statement: *See* 1937 Statement

Statement for 1960: "We can confirm that between 1949 and 1976 the bibliographic designation of first printings was the same [as that given in the 1976 statement]."

GEORGE ALLEN & UNWIN (PUBLISHERS) LTD (UNITED KINGDOM)

1976 Statement: "We identify all our books on the back of the title page by a bibliographical note which declares the date of first publication. Subsequent impressions or editions are noted as and when they occur. A first edition, by which is normally meant a first impression of a first edition will have only a single line entry of first publication with the appropriate date."

1981 Statement: "We have not changed the method by which we denote the first edition of a work and it is still as printed in the original edition of your book."

1988 Statement: *See* 1988 Statement of Unwin Hyman, Limited (United Kingdom)

ALLIANCE BOOK CORPORATION

(Established 1938. Out of business prior to 1949. Ziff-Davis Publishing Co. acquired their publications.)

1949 Statement: *See* Ziff-Davis Publishing Company

ALLIED PUBLISHING GROUP

2000 Statement: "We do not identify first editions per se and everything is copyrighted by year only."

ALLWORTH PRESS

2001 Statement: "We identify the first printing of a first edition by the following number line: 05 04 03 02 01 00 5 4 3 2 1. Subsequent revised editions of a title are identified as revised edition, third edition, fourth edition, etc. The specific year and printing of each edition is indicated on the copyright page by the number line shown above."

ALMOND PRESS (UNITED KINGDOM)

2001 Statement: *See* 2001 Statement of Sheffield Academic Press (United Kingdom)

ALMS HOUSE PRESS

2001 Statement: "We do not identify a first printing; we do identify subsequent printings."

ALOES BOOKS (UNITED KINGDOM)

1976 Statement: "We don't have a hard or fast rule on editions. We hardly ever mention state of printing, merely if it's our second print & so on."

1981 Statement: "We try to be concise on this point and not clutter up the colophon with facts that would tend to make the book an object and not a thing to read. We do clarify if the piece has appeared elsewhere in magazine or book format. If we are lucky enough to go into a second printing then the cover usually carries this information now. In the past some reprints have just had colour changes or board changes for the cover."

ALPHA (UNITED KINGDOM)
2000 Statement: *See* 2000 Statement of The Paternoster Press Ltd. (United Kingdom)

ALPHA BEAT PRESS
1995 Statement: "We distinguish our first editions from subsequent editions by stating: 2nd printing, 3rd printing, etc. on our publisher's page. We began designating subsequent printings in 1989."

ALPHA PUBLICATIONS OF AMERICA INC.
2001 Statement: "We do not identify first printings, but subsequent editions are identified by, e.g., 2nd Edition, 3rd Edition, etc."

ALPINE GUILD, INC.
2000 Statement: "Normally, no notation of any kind appears on first printings of first editions."

ALPINE PUBLICATIONS INC.
1993 Statement: "In the past, our only method was to identify the date first printed in the copyright statement. If a book was revised, that would be stated on the copyright page.

"Beginning in 1993, first editions will bear the statement 'First published in 1993 (or other date).' We use 1 2 3 4 5 6 7 8 9 0. When reprinting, we delete figure 1, etc., on the copyright page."
2000 Statement: *See* 1993 Statement

ALTAMIRA PRESS
2001 Statement: "Books published by AltaMira prior to 1999 were coded 98 99 00 4 3 2 1 to indicate date and printing. Since being purchased by Rowan & Littlefield in August 1999, this practice has been discontinued. No statement is given."

ALTAMONT BOOKS
1994 Statement: *See* 1994 Statement of Altamont Press, Inc.

ALTAMONT PRESS, INC.
1994 Statement: "When Lark Books published our first book (*Fiberarts Design Book*) in 1980, we . . . neglected to indicate that it was the first edition. By 1981, we [added] 'First Edition' on the copyright page, and we continued that practice until 1990 when we began the 10, 9, . . . 1 indication."

ALYSON BOOKS
2000 Statement: *See* 2000 Statement of Alyson Publications

ALYSON CLASSICS
2000 Statement: *See* 2000 Statement of Alyson Publications

ALYSON PUBLICATIONS

1988 Statement: "We designate the first printing of a first edition on the copyright page. We have used this method since our founding in 1977."

1993, 2000 Statements: *See* 1988 Statement

ALYSON WONDERLAND

2000 Statement: *See* 2000 Statement of Alyson Publications

AMADOR PUBLISHERS

2000 Statement: "We identify the first printing of a first edition by the statement 'First Printing, (year).' "

AMATEUR WINEMAKER (UNITED KINGDOM)

1994 Statement: *See* 1994 Statement of Argus Books Ltd. (United Kingdom)

AMBER LANE PRESS LTD (UNITED KINGDOM)

1994 Statement: "The main form of identification for first editions is:
   First published in 19— by
   Amber Lane Press Ltd.
   "Subsequent reprints are shown as:
   First published in 19—, reprinted 19—, 19— etc.
   "If the book was previously published by another publisher we acknowledge this as:
   First published (or originally published) in 19— by XYZ
   This edition published in 19—
   by Amber Lane Press Ltd."

2000 Statement: *See* 1994 Statement

AMERICA'S BEST COMICS

2000 Statement: *See* 2000 Statement of DC Comics

AMERICAN AERONAUTICAL ARCHIVES

2001 Statement: *See* 2001 Statement of Markowski International Publishers

THE AMERICAN ALPINE CLUB PRESS

2001 Statement: "The American Alpine Club Press is a small niche publisher of mountaineering and climbing-related titles. While we have been publishing since the 1920s, we are an infrequent publisher of books beyond our two annual publications: The *American Alpine Journal* and *Accidents in North American Mountaineering.*

"Because of our infrequent publishing history, we have not kept one specific policy regarding how first editions and subsequent editions are noted. Some titles will indicate 'first edition' on the copyright page along with the year of publication, while others will not. Generally subsequent editions or printings will indicate that it is not the first edition."

AMERICAN & WORLD GEOGRAPHIC PUBLISHING

1994 Statement: "No designation at all."

AMERICAN ANTIQUARIAN SOCIETY

2001 Statement: "We do not identify a first printing; we do identify subsequent printings."

AMERICAN ASSOCIATION
FOR STATE AND LOCAL HISTORY PRESS

1988 Statement: "First editions of our books are not specifically identified as first editions *on original publication*. We simply use a regulation copyright notice, showing the date of each book's first appearance:

Copyright © 1975

The American Association for State and Local History

All rights reserved . . . Printed in the United States of America

"However, if we publish a *second* edition, we *do*, in the copyright notice for the *second* edition, list and identify the first edition and its date, followed by the dates when the first edition was reprinted, and by the date and identification of the *second* edition:

Copyright © 1975, 1983, by the American Association for State and Local History. All rights reserved . . . Printed in the United States of America . . . .

First Edition published 1975

Second Printing 1976

Third Printing 1978

Fourth Printing 1979

Second Edition, revised and expanded, 1983

"I must confess, at this point, that we're not always scrupulously consistent about including in our 'second edition' notices the printing history for the first edition. Now and again, we leave that out and simply say:

First Edition published 1975

Second Edition, revised and expanded, 1983

"Since the responsibility for seeing that that copy is included on the copyright pages of our second editions has, at various times, been freely passed around among editors, production managers, staff designers, and press directors, it's sometimes difficult to say who okayed these occasional variations, unless we talk with the staff historian. We frown on the inconsistencies, but we do have some."

1993 Statement: "It has been AASLH's usual practice to insert on the copyright page either 'First Edition' or 'First Printing.' Subsequent editions, revisions, or printings would also be so noted and numbered accordingly.

"I cannot tell exactly when this procedure was established, but it appears that this was usual practice from the inception of our publishing program. I also do not believe that it differs greatly from any other method or procedure we might have used."

AMERICAN BAR ASSOCIATION

1993 Statement: "The ABA does not identify first editions, but many of our books (not all, by any means) have printer's keys through which first, second, and subsequent printings can be identified."

AMERICAN BAR FOUNDATION

1988 Statement: "During the years when the American Bar Foundation had a publishing program (1960-86), first editions were not so identified. Only later editions carried any identification as to edition. Second printings, which have been rare, have usually been identified.

"We have no imprints or subsidiaries."

1993 Statement: *See* 1988 Statement

AMERICAN BIOGRAPHICAL INSTITUTE, INC.

1993 Statement: "We identify the first editions of our titles on the spine and title page as 'first edition'; subsequent editions are second edition, third edition, etc."

AMERICAN-CANADIAN PUBLISHERS, INC.

1995, 2000 Statements: *See* 1995 Statement of Rising Tide Press

AMERICAN CATHOLIC PRESS

1993 Statement: "Since our founding in 1967, American Catholic Press has used no special designations for the first printing of a first edition of a book. However, later printings or editions are always designated, for example, by the words, 'Second Edition' or something similar. We have no imprints and subsidiaries."

2001 Statement: *See* 1993 Statement

AMERICAN COUNCIL ON PUBLIC AFFAIRS

1949 Statement: *See* Public Affairs Press

AMERICAN GEOPHYSICAL UNION

2001 Statement: "We do not identify a first printing; we do identify subsequent printings on the copyright page (usually, unless very small quantities are reprinted)."

AMERICAN HISTORY PRESS

1988, 2000 Statements: *See* 1988 Statement of Northwoods Press

AMERICAN INDIAN STUDIES CENTER AT UCLA

2001 Statement: "Our first editions are unmarked. However, additional printings of books published by the American Indian Studies Center at UCLA are identified on the copyright page."

AMERICAN INSTITUTE OF CHEMICAL ENGINEERS

1988 Statement: "The American Institute of Chemical Engineers does not identify first printings, but when a book is reprinted it carries a line on the reverse of the title page that reads, for example, 'Second Printing 1988.' "

1993, 2001 Statements: *See* 1988 Statement

AMERICAN INSTITUTE OF PHYSICS

1988 Statement: "No designation of first printing or first edition is used. If there are later printings or editions, the information is listed on the copyright page with the year of the printing or edition."

AMERICAN JUDICATURE SOCIETY
2001 Statement: "Our policy is to not make any special identification of first editions. However we do identify reprints and new editions so anything not identified as a reprint or new edition is a first edition."

THE AMERICAN LAW INSTITUTE
1993 Statement: "The American Law Institute has never used the designation 'First Edition' or 'First Printing' on its books. We do identify subsequent editions or printings, and so one may generally assume, unless there is an indication to the contrary, that a particular volume is a first printing or a first edition."
2001 Statement: *See* 1993 Statement

AMERICAN LAW INSTITUTE-AMERICAN BAR ASSOCIATION COMMITTEE ON CONTINUING PROFESSIONAL EDUCATION (ALI-ABA)
1993 Statement: *See* 1993 Statement of The American Law Institute

AMERICAN LIBRARY ASSOCIATION
1988 Statement: "We have no written policy concerning the identification of first editions. In answer to your question:
1. We do not state 'first edition' or 'first printing' on the copyright page
2. Printings (up to March of 1988) have been indicated on the copyright page; in the future they will be indicated *only* when corrections are made in the book itself
3. Revised or second, third, etc., editions are always indicated on the copyright page."
1994 Statement: "We have no written policy concerning the identification of first editions. In answer to your question:
1. We do not state 'first edition' or 'first printing' on the copyright page
2. Printings are always indicated on the copyright page by printing number and year
3. Revised or second, third, etc. editions are always indicated on the copyright page."
2001 Statement: *See* 1994 Statement

AMERICAN LIVING PRESS
2000 Statement: "We do not use the phrase 'First Printing' but second and subsequent editions are always marked. Dates of original publishing are included in printing of each book."

AMERICAN MALACOLOGISTS, INC.
1995 Statement: "[We] have had no particular way of designating first printings. Second or revised printings are so noted on copyright page."

AMERICAN MARITIME LIBRARY
2000 Statement: *See* 2000 Statement of Mystic Seaport Museum

AMERICAN MATHEMATICAL SOCIETY

1993 Statement: "With regard to your query, the American Mathematical Society includes the following reprint notice on the bottom of the copyright page of our books:

10 9 8 7 6 5 4 3 2 1 97 96 95 94 93

"If the number 1 shows as a last number on the right of the first group, the book is a first printing."

2001 Statement: *See* 1993 Statement

AMERICAN PHILOSOPHICAL SOCIETY

1988 Statement: "The American Philosophical Society does not identify first editions. We do, however, specify second editions or reprintings. We have no subsidiaries."

1993, 2001 Statements: *See* 1988 Statement

AMERICAN POETRY AND LITERATURE PRESS

1988 Statement: "Our company designates the first printing of a first edition by: 'First Printing'. . . and the date. Subsequent printings are listed: 'Second Printing' . . . and the date, etc.

"A Revised version is designated, 'Second Edition' and the date. There is a clear differentiation between the two terms. A new 'printing' is a reprint. A new 'edition' has to be revised and have changes in it.

"This method of designation was first adopted in 1979. It does not differ from any previously used.

"In designating first printings, imprints and subsidiaries would follow our practices."

1994 Statement: *See* 1988 Statement

AMERICAN PSYCHOLOGICAL ASSOCIATION

1993 Statement: "Since 1990, APA Books has identified the first printing of a first edition with the words 'First Edition' on the copyright page. In subsequent printings, we indicate the number of printing followed by the month and year of the reprint."

AMERICAN SOCIETY OF CIVIL ENGINEERS

1988 Statement: "No special marking of first printing."

1993, 2001 Statements: *See* 1988 Statement

AMERICAN SOCIETY OF PLANT TAXONOMISTS

2001 Statement: "We do not identify a first printing; we do identify subsequent printings on the copyright page."

AMERICAN SOURCE BOOKS

1995 Statement: *See* 1994 Statement of Impact Publishers

2000 Statement: "American Source Books is defunct. It was bought out by Impact Publishers, Inc." *See* 1994 Statement of Impact Publishers

AMERICANA BOOKS

2000 Statement: "We identify the first printing of a first edition by 'First Edition' on the copyright page. The number '1' in the number line indicates a first printing if hardbound. Booklets and softbound issues are published in small runs, as needed, and the number line only changes if the type is reset."

AMETHYST & EMERALD PUBLISHING
2000 Statement: "We identify the first printing of a first edition by the words 'First Printing' followed by the year the book was printed."

AMHERST WRITERS & ARTISTS PRESS, INC.
2000 Statement: "We identify the first printing of a first edition by the words 'First Edition, First printing.' [This] does not apply to our books published prior to 2000. Books published before 2000 contain no designation of first edition."

AMISTAD
2001 Statement: *See* 2001 Statement of HarperCollinsPublishers

AMNESTY INTERNATIONAL (UNITED KINGDOM)
2001 Statement: "We designate a first printing by: 'First published in (year)' as first line on copyright page, followed by copyright © Amnesty International Publications (year). Many Amnesty International national offices publish independently . . . not all follow same practice."

AMPERSAND PRESS
1976 Statement: "The only designation is the date of publication. Subsequent editions or printings would be indicated as such."

AMPHOTO
1976 Statement: "No special way of indicating *first* editions, but *second* & subsequent editions are so noted. Therefore, absence of *any* indication (or of multiple copyright dates) usually indicates a first edition. It may also indicate a reprint *(unrevised)* of the first, but this, too, is usually noted."
1981 Statement: *See* 1976 Statement

AMPTHILL BOOKS
2000 Statement: *See* 2000 Statement of Wyrick & Co.

AMS CHELSEA PUBLISHING
2000 Statement: "Chelsea Publishing Company's titles were purchased by the American Mathematical Society in 1996. The [1993] Statement is still accurate. When AMS reprints Chelsea's books, they carry the AMS ISBN and are given an 'AMS Chelsea Publishing' imprint."
2001 Statement: *See* 2001 Statement of American Mathematical Society

AMSCO PUBLICATIONS
2001 Statement: *See* 2001 Statement of Music Sales Corp

THE ANALYTIC PRESS, INC.
2001 Statement: "We identify the first printing of a first edition by the number line '10 9 8 7 6 5 4 3 2 1.'"

ANAMNESIS PRESS
2000 Statement: "We indicate a first edition by stating so on the copyright page of the book."

ANANSI (CANADA)
See House of Anansi Press Limited (Canada)

ANCESTRY PUBLISHING
2001 Statement: "We identify the first printing of a first edition by a number line on the copyright page. The lowest number indicates the printing."

ANCHORAGE PRESS
1993 Statement: "The first edition is simply designated by the date of publication.

"A second edition is designated as 'Revised Edition' or 'Second Edition,' plus the date. Example: 'Revised Edition, 1987.' "

ANCIENT CITY PRESS
1995 Statement: "In 1981 we began putting 'First Edition' or 'First Edition, First Printing' on the copyright page. Each subsequent printing was identified with 'Second Printing' etc, etc. Within the last 3 years we have switched over to merely putting the print sequence on the copyright page. So the first edition/first printing would just have the '1' in the numeric sequence at the bottom of the copyright page."
2001 Statement: *See* 1995 Statement

ANDERSEN GIANTS (UNITED KINGDOM)
2000 Statement: *See* 2000 Statement of Andersen Press Limited (United Kingdom)

ANDERSEN PRESS LIMITED (UNITED KINGDOM)
1994 Statement: "For our picture books we print a line of descending numbers (10 9 8 7 . . . 1) after the paragraph on printing specifications and copyright. For a first printing all numbers are included. Upon a second printing the last number is wiped out so the line now reads 10 9 8 7 6 5 4 3 2 and for a third printing 10 9 8 7 6 5 4 3 and so on.

"For our fiction titles, the copyright page is prefaced with the first date of publication written out as,
'First published in 19— by
Andersen Press Limited
20 Vauxhall Bridge Road, London.'
"Then, a middle line is included according to various reprints which includes the years of further reprinting: 'Reprinted in 19.., 19...' "
2000 Statement: "For our books we print a line of descending numbers (10 9 8 7 . . . 1) after the paragraph on printing specifications and copyright. For a first printing all numbers are included. Upon a second printing the last number is wiped out so the line now reads 10 9 8 7 6 5 4 3 2 and for a third printing 10 9 8 7 6 5 4 3 and so on."

ANDERSEN YOUNG READERS LIBRARY
(UNITED KINGDOM)

2000 Statement: *See* 2000 Statement of Andersen Press Limited (United Kingdom)

ANDREWS AND McMEEL, INC.

1981 Statement: "I have slightly revised our company's entry in your book *A First Edition?* Please note that the company's name is now Andrews and McMeel, Inc. The entry should read as follows:

"In the normal course of things, we do not consider minor changes sufficient to refer to a new printing as a new edition. Thus, I will refer to first printings and second printings rather than first editions and second editions.

"We have no special identifying mark for a first printing. The only way one could tell a first printing would be the absence of information on subsequent printings. Our present policy is as follows: When a book goes into a second printing we then introduce on to the copyright page the word 'First printing' and the date and 'Second printing' and the date. A new line is added for each subsequent printing. Thus, as I said, a first printing is actually identified by the lack of such a line."

1988 Statement: *See* 1981 Statement

2001 Statement: *See* 2001 Statement of Andrews McMeel Publishing

ANDREWS McMEEL PUBLISHING

2001 Statement: "Andrews McMeel Publishing identifies the number of the printing, year of printing, and printer with a code on the copyright page, e.g., 00 01 02 03 04 XXX 10 9 8 7 6 5 4 3 2 1. The first numbers, 00, on the left signify the year of the printing, the first number on the far right signifies the number of the printing. A three-letter printer code identifies the printer where the XXX occurs. As subsequent printings happen, the printing number on the right is deleted and the year is updated if necessary."

ANGELUS PRESS

2001 Statement: "We identify the first printing by 'First Printing—Month Year', e.g. 'First Printing—April 1998.' We don't identify editions, but only printings. Subsequent printings would say 'Second (or Third or Fourth) Printing—Month, Year', e.g. 'Third Printing May 1997.' These guidelines hold for almost all of our titles; some from late 70s and early 80s may not be identified."

ANGUS & ROBERTSON PUBLISHERS (AUSTRALIA)

1988 Statement: "Angus & Robertson Publishers designates first editions on the imprint page with the words:

First published in Australia by Angus & Robertson Publishers in...
(year of publication)

"If these words are *not* followed by a list of reprint dates, then the reader can assume that the copy he or she holds is the first edition. However, the wording above, which is used to denote the first-ever edition, anywhere in the world, of a particular title, is also used to denote the first *Australian* edition. Because of this ambiguity, the reader can only be absolutely certain that he or she is looking at the first Australian edition, though in the majority of cases it would also be the first edition world-wide."

1994 Statement: *See* 1994 Statement of HarperCollins Publishers (Australia) Pty Limited (Australia)

ANHINGA PRESS

2000 Statement: "We identify the first printing of a first edition by 'First Edition' (on copyright page). [Printings are identified as such:] 'First Edition—Second Printing' (on copyright page)."

ANNICK PRESS (CANADA)

1995 Statement: "We have no specific way of designating first editions. Subsequent or revised editions are designated as such. Therefore, any title without an edition statement is a first edition."

ANTAEUS

See The Ecco Press

ANTHE PUBLICATIONS

2000 Statement: *See* Pella Publishing Co

THE ANTHOENSEN PRESS

1947 Statement: "With very few exceptions there is only one printing of our books. All information about first or subsequent editions can be found in the colophon. There are noted: number of copies; some production details—binding, paper, etc. Also facts like limited editions, numbered editions, date and designer are in the colophon. There are three imprints under which our books might appear: The Southworth Press, up to the year 1934; The Southworth-Anthoensen Press up to the year 1947. Since January of 1947 the Press has become The Anthoensen Press.

"In the rare cases of second editions, type from the first edition (we use letterpress) is always used, though it might be abridged, or differently bound."

ANTHROPOSOPHIC PRESS, INC.

1976 Statement: "Because of the particular nature of our publications, we do not identify editions. Even reprintings, when they have continued for decades, are not noted."

1981 Statement: "For the time being I will retain the policy indicated in the [1976 statement]."

1988 Statement: *See* 1981 Statement

1994 Statement: "Since 1990 Anthroposophic Press and its imprint Lindisfarne Press have identified editions by the customary manner of numbering the first edition: 1 2 3 4 5 6 7 8 9 and then removing a number with each subsequent edition."

2000 Statement: "Since 1990, Anthroposophic Press and now its imprints, Lindisfarne Books and Bell Pond Books have listed a number line on the copyright page of each book 10 9 8 7 6 5 4 3 2 1 and then removing a number for each reprinting. A New Edition receives a new ISBN number and hence has a complete number line."

ANTI–AGING PRESS
1995 Statement: "Anti–Aging Press First Editions can be identified by the Publisher's Cataloging in Publication which will carry the date first published. Printings first, second, etc. are noted. If other than a first edition, the edition will be stated on the verso as 'second edition' etc."

ANTIOCH PUBLISHING CO.
1995 Statement: "We do not state 'First Edition,' etc."

ANTIQUE COLLECTORS' CLUB LTD (UNITED KINGDOM)
1988 Statement: "Our first printings carry the usual copyright line with date of first publication on the reverse of the title page. When a book is reprinted information is added along the lines of—
    First published 1982
    Reprinted 1984, 1986, 1988
The final date always designates the latest printing.
  "Updated editions are also clearly marked such as—
    First edition 1982
    Reprinted 1984, 1985
    Second edition 1986
    Reprinted 1987, 1988
Once again the final date is the latest printing.
  "Where a book originated elsewhere and we are reprinting it, usually as a revised edition, this is also clearly indicated. This represents our current practice, and on checking back there are a few minor variations, but none are significant or likely to lead to confusion. We do not currently use other imprints or have subsidiaries."
2000 Statement: *See* 1988 Statement, but note that they now also publish under the Garden Art Press imprint.

ANTIQUE PUBLICATIONS
2001 Statement: "Our policy is to not make any special identification of first editions. However, we do identify reprints and new editions so anything not identified as a reprint or new edition is a first edition."

ANTONSON PUBLISHING LTD. (CANADA)
1976 Statement: "Our only means of designating a first edition is the listing of 'First Printing' and the date of this first printing. We date each additional printing. Usually, this relates to the year shown for the current copyright. Our dating as indicated above is consistent."

ANVIL PRESS POETRY LTD (UNITED KINGDOM)
1988 Statement: "In our first editions, first printings the year of publication only is stated; in subsequent editions and printings particulars of all editions and printings to date are given."
1994, 2000 Statements: *See* 1988 Statement

AP NATURAL WORLD
2001 Statement: *See* 2001 Statement of Academic Press, A Harcourt Science and Technology Company

AP PROFESSIONAL
1993 Statement: *See* 1981 Statement of Academic Press, Inc.

APERTURE
1988 Statement: *See* 1976 Statement of Aperture, Inc.
1993 Statement: *See* 1993 Statement of Aperture Foundation, Inc.

APERTURE, INC.
1976 Statement: "First printings are usually identified with either 'First Edition' or 'first printing.' Sometimes, as in the case of *Ghana*, the c/r is used for more than one edition. (There is an English edition as well.) We'll omit the printing; but even here, no absolute rule.

"The phrase 'first published in . . . .' usually means that this is *not* the point of first publication—as, 'first published in Great Britain by Smithy' implies that Smithy is not the first publisher of the book, but the book may be simultaneously published in the U.S. and the book was a U.S. creation.

"When reprint numbers are used, the idea is to simply delete the lowest number from the plate (we don't have to make a new plate) for a reprint. When this method is used, the lowest printing number that can be read is the right one."

1981 Statement: *See* 1976 Statement
1988 Statement: *See* Aperture

APERTURE FOUNDATION, INC.
("Aperture now prefers to go by the name Aperture Foundation, Inc. This change took effect around 1985, but was not followed consistently.")
1993 Statement: *See* 1976 Statement of Aperture, Inc.

THE APEX PRESS
2001 Statement: "We do not identify first editions. 2nd and 3rd (etc.) editions are designated appropriately (2nd edition, 3rd edition)."

APOLLOS (UNITED KINGDOM)
1994, 2000 Statements: *See* 1981 Statement of Inter-Varsity Press (United Kingdom)

APPALACHIAN CONSORTIUM
1988 Statement: "First printings have a standard copyright notice and subsequent printings are indicated as:
    Second Printing 19__
    Third Printing, 19__
and so forth."

APPALACHIAN MOUNTAIN CLUB
1988 Statement: "We always designate the edition of the book on the copyright page, whether it is second, third, etc. Printings are indicated by

stone-offs—for example, for the second printing, in 1988, we would stone-off the number 1 (we begin by listing numbers 1-10) and the year 87 (we begin by listing six years). We began using this method of designation years ago, although it's only recently that we've used it consistently."

1993 Statement: *See* 1988 Statement

APPLE KIDS (UNITED KINGDOM)

2001 Statement: *See* 2001 Statement of Apple Press (United Kingdom)

APPLE PRESS (UNITED KINGDOM)

2001 Statement: "We do not identify a first printing; we do identify subsequent printings."

APPLEFORD PUBLISHING GROUP (UNITED KINGDOM)

1994 Statement: "As to first editions, our popular Marcham pamphlets were produced in bulk and do not consistently have dates. The paperbacks have the date of the first edition next to the copyright note in the prelims. A second edition would say as much. Academic hardbacks under the Sutton Courtenay imprint would also have the first edition date next to the copyright, and any subsequent editions would be noted underneath. Our limited editions are never reprinted and state number and publishing date in the prelims."

2000 Statement: *See* 1994 Statement

D. APPLETON & CO
(Merged with Century Co. to form D. Appleton-Century Co., Inc., on May 31, 1933.)

1928 Statement: "Our first editions are designated by a small numeral one in parentheses (1) at the foot of the last page. Later as we reprint the book this numeral is changed according to the number of the reprinting, that is, (2), (3), etc."

See also D. Appleton-Century Company, Inc.

D. APPLETON-CENTURY COMPANY, INC.
(Merged on January 2, 1948, with F. S. Crofts and Co., to form D. Appleton-Century-Crofts, Inc.)

1937 Statement: "Our first editions are designated by a small numeral one in parentheses (1) at the foot of the last page. Later, as we reprint the book, this numeral is changed according to the number of the printing, that is, (2), (3), etc. This numbering was inaugurated by D. Appleton and Company in 1902."

1947 Statement: "The practice of our New York house is to print the figure 1 within brackets at the end of the last printed page on any book issued by them. When a second printing takes place this figure is, of course, changed to the figure 2, etc., etc.

"In addition our New York house invariably dates the title page and the American copyright law requires the year of first publication to be on the back of the title page, in order to preserve the copyright. This numbering was inaugurated by D. Appleton & Company in 1902."

See also D. Appleton-Century-Crofts, Inc.

D. APPLETON-CENTURY-CROFTS, INC.

1948 Statement: "The merger became effective on January 2, 1948. We do not intend to use the Croft's imprint on any of our books. We have revised our colophon to include another 'C' for Crofts. No change will be made in the method of identifying first printings. We shall continue to place the number of the printing on the last page of the book, and all Croft's books will follow our method."

1982 Statement: "We carry a string of numbers: at left, a series of numbers (last two digits of year), slash, then numbers ten to one in that order to right. Farthest left digits represent year of publication or reprint date; farthest right digit is reprint number. Example below.

      82 83 84 85 86 87/10 9 8 7 6 5 4 3 2 1"

1988 Statement: *See* 1988 Statement of Appleton & Lange

APPLETON & LANGE

1988 Statement: "We carry a string of numbers: at left, a series of numbers (last two digits of year), slash, then numbers ten to one in that order to right. Farthest left digits represent year of publication or reprint date; farthest right digit is reprint number. Example below.

      82 83 84 85 86 87/10 9 8 7 6 5 4 3 2 1"

1993 Statement: *See* 1988 Statement

THE APPLETREE PRESS LTD PUBLISHERS (IRELAND)

1981 Statement: "To get right to the heart of the matter the only thing which distinguishes Appletree Press first editions is the absence of any mention of reprints. The one exception is our *Nationality and the Pursuit of National Independence*. The first edition has a black and blue cover, subsequent editions have a straightforward black and white cover."

1988 Statement: "Appletree Press first editions may normally be distinguished by the wording 'First published in (year) by The Appletree Press Ltd.' Subsequent editions may also include this wording but will, in addition, include additional information about more recent editions."

1994, 2001 Statements: *See* 1988 Statement

APPLEZABA PRESS

1994 Statement: "[The first printing of a first edition is identified] by the lack of a statement saying 'second' etc. printing." This method was adopted in 1977.

AQUA QUEST PUBLICATIONS, INC.

1994 Statement: "We identify the first printing of a first edition by the following number line:

      10 9 8 7 6 5 4 3 2 1.

"For each reprint we delete a number from the right."

THE AQUARIAN PRESS LIMITED (UNITED KINGDOM)

1988 Statement: *See* 1988 Statement of Thorsons Publishing Group Ltd. (United Kingdom)

THE AQUILA PUBLISHING COMPANY LIMITED
(UNITED KINGDOM)

1976 Statement: "Our normal practice is to publish books in at least two editions at the same time, occasionally three. These are pamphlet and signed pamphlets (limited edn.) and paperback, hardback (And in most cases signed ltd. hardback). Where a signed edition is published this is taken by the British National Bibliography and the British Library (formerly the publications division of the British Museum) as the first edition, but legally all three (or two) editions are 'first edition.' When we reprint this is always stated in the book, either on the back cover or on the verso title page.

"Where a second edition is concerned this is also shown. The legal definition of an edition as opposed to a reprint/impression is that an edition must be re-set either in its whole, or in important parts. The corrections of errors, or small author's revisions are normally not enough to make this a new edition, so long as these are of a very minor nature. First editions (not anthologies) are always marked as such on the verso title, and Anthologies have this information usually in the form of a codicil to the copyright notice."

1988 Statement: *See* 1976 Statement

ARCADE PUBLISHING

1995, 2000 Statements: *See* 1995 Statement of Little, Brown & Company

ARCADIA

2001 Statement: "As of 2001, we [will] identify the first printing of a first edition by the statement 'First printed in 2001 (or appropriate future date).' Reprints are identified with the line 'Reprinted in (date).' "

ARCADIA HOUSE

1937 Statement: *See* 1937 Statement of Hillman-Curl, Inc.
1947 Statement: *See* 1947 Statement of Samuel Curl, Inc.

ARCANA PUBLISHING

2001 Statement: *See* 2001 Statement of Lotus Press (Twin Lakes, Wisconsin)

ARCH GROVE PRESS

2000 Statement: "We designate second or later editions or printings as such on the copyright page. We do not identify a first edition/printing as such."

DENIS ARCHER (UNITED KINGDOM)

1947 Statement: *See* 1947 Statement of Selwyn & Blount, Ltd. (United Kingdom)

ARCHITECTURAL ASSOCIATION PUBLICATIONS
(UNITED KINGDOM)

2001 Statement: "Architectural Association Publications does not identify first printings. Second editions are identified, together with the date of first printing, on the copyright page."

ARCHITECTURAL BOOK PUBLISHING COMPANY INC.

1988 Statement: "Our first editions do not usually have an indication that they are a first edition.

"However, whenever we have a reprint, we list the date of the new printing on the copyright page and also, if it is a new edition, we also indicate that on the copyright page."

1993 Statement: 1988 Statement

ARCHITECTURAL PRESS

2000 Statement: *See* 2000 Statement of Butterworth-Heinemann

ARCHITECTURAL PRESS (UNITED KINGDOM)

2000 Statement: *See* 2000 Statement of Butterworth-Heinemann

THE ARCHITECTURAL PRESS LTD (UNITED KINGDOM)

1976 Statement: "The form of words is: First published (year) by the Architectural Press, Ltd."

1981 Statement: *See* 1976 Statement

1988 Statement: *See* 1988 Statement of Butterworth Architecture (United Kingdom)

2000 Statement: *See* 2000 Statement of Architectural Press (United Kingdom)

ARCHIVAL FACSIMILES LIMITED (UNITED KINGDOM)

2001 Statement: "Our imprints on the copyright page of each publication state 'First Published in' followed by year.

"Subsequent editions are shown as 'This Edition' followed by year.

"Concerning the facsimile titles, the imprint reads

'First published in' followed by country or city and year (e.g. Venice 1610)

'This edition published in' followed by year

"Translations are shown as

'First published in English in' followed by year

'Originally published in' followed by language, original title, publisher and year

'English translation' followed by the translator's name and year.

"The above applies to our imprint, The Erskine Press."

ARCHON BOOKS

2000 Statement: *See* 2000 Statement of The Shoe String Press, Inc.

ARCHWAY PRESS

1947 Statement: "First editions bear no identification, as such. Subsequent editions bear full identification (i.e., second edition, third edition) and the date of the edition."

ARCTOS PRESS

2000 Statement: "We identify the first printing of a first edition by the following statement: First Edition. In 1997 with our first publication, we did not include any listing to designate a first edition. Since 1998, however, our subsequent books have all listed First Edition on the copyright page."

ARDEN PRESS, INC.

1995 Statement: "We do not indicate that a book is in its first printing of a first edition, and never have . . . . However, we do indicate 'second edition' as well as 'first edition, second printing.' "

2000 Statement: *See* 1995 Statement

ARDIS PUBLISHERS

1994 Statement: First printings are not identified.

ARE PRESS

2001 Statement: "We state 'First printing' on the copyright page."

ARENA (UNITED KINGDOM)

2000 Statement: *See* 2000 Statement of Gower Publishing Limited (United Kingdom)

ARGENTUM (UNITED KINGDOM)

2000 Statement: *See* 2000 Statement of Aurum Press (United Kingdom)

ARGO PRESS

2000 Statement: "We only identify second and subsequent printings, usually with a statement such as 'second printing, [date].' First editions/printings are merely identified as 'First edition, [date].' "

THE ARGUS BOOK SHOP, INC.

1937 Statement: "Later printings are indicated on the verso of the title page in all our publications. We have used this method since 1926."

ARGUS BOOKS, INC.

(Formerly The Argus Book Shop, Inc.)

1937 Statement: "Later printings are indicated on the verso of the title page in all our publications. We have used this method since 1926."

1947 Statement: "When I first began to publish I used the imprint Argus Books. In 1945 when I first moved to New York I used the imprint Ben Abramson, Publisher. Since June of 1946 the imprint has been Argus Books, Inc. In every case of a reprint it is indicated by being marked 'second printing' or 'third printing,' etc."

ARGUS BOOKS LTD. (UNITED KINGDOM)

1994 Statement: "We have no special method of identifying first editions other than to print 'First published by Argus Books 19..' on the title verso page. However, they can be easily identified as subsequent editions would contain information in the form of reprint dates."

ARGUS COMMUNICATIONS

1976 Statement: "Our first printing is coded on the copyright page in the following way: 0 1 2 3 4 5 6 7 8 9. Each time we go back to press one numeral is deleted starting on the left-hand side."

1981 Statement: "Our code has been reversed, as indicated below. I have not been able to determine when the change was initiated.

"Our first printing is coded on the copyright page in the following way: 0 9 8 7 6 5 4 3 2 1. Each time we go back to press one numeral is deleted starting on the right-hand side."

1988 Statement: *See* 1981 Statement

ARIADNE PRESS

2000 Statement: "We do not identify a first printing. Subsequent printings may be identified, as 'second printing' etc."

ARIEL PRESS

1994 Statement: "The first printing of a first edition is indicated by the statement "First Edition, Ariel Press, year."

ARIEL PUBLICATIONS

2001 Statement: *See* 2001 Statement of Music Sales Corp

ARIEL STARR PRODUCTIONS LTD

2001 Statement: "We state 'First printing' on the copyright page."

THE ARION PRESS

1988 Statement: "Almost all of our publications are reprints of classical literature. They are limited in number and never go beyond our first edition. The occasional original work that we publish is marked in no way except by a copyright date."

1993, 2000 Statements: *See* 1988 Statement

ARIS & PHILLIPS LTD. (UNITED KINGDOM)

1988 Statement: "Each book has the copyright notice—including date—on the title verso, with all the bibliographic details. If the book is reprinted without alteration or corrections this is not indicated. Corrected or revised editions are so designated beneath the copyright statement—Second (corrected) edition & date."

1994, 2000 Statements: *See* 1988 Statement

ARJUNA LIBRARY PRESS

1995 Statement: "Broadside pages are . . . hand signed and dated in type as printed with a second, handwritten, date of signature.

"First Edition books are . . . hand signed with a date of signature (handwritten). On the signature page in the back of the book, the date of printing or revision (which is typeset) is accompanied by the designation of First Edition or Proof Edition. Otherwise, a second printing is noted as a New Edition.

"Most signed items and some unsigned items are also marked with a red seal, either symbolic or in the names Arjuna Library or Journal of Regional Criticism. This system has been consistent since the press was founded in 1979."

2001 Statement: "The [1995 Statement] is all true and current. In addition, subsequently to 1998 most items also have an embossed seal . . . . A prior embossing image (from circa 1979) was the image of a bird . . . ."

ARK (UNITED KINGDOM)

1988 Statement: *See* 1988 Statement of Associated Book Publishers (UK) Ltd. (United Kingdom)

ARKANA (UNITED KINGDOM)

1988 Statement: *See* 1988 Statement of Associated Book Publishers (UK) Ltd. (United Kingdom)

ARKANSAS ANCESTORS

2001 Statement: "Arkansas Ancestors, like most very small publishers, seldom reprints an edition; however, when we do, we note that it is a 'second' etc. edition."

ARKANSAS RESEARCH, INC.

2001 Statement: "Until this year (2001) we have not identified first editions; only second editions are so noted. New titles printed in 2001 will have a line of numbers (1 2 3 4 5 etc) under the ISBN designating the printing number."

ARKHAM HOUSE

(Also uses the imprints Mycroft and Moran, and Stanton and Lee.)

1947 Statement: "Arkham House, Mycroft & Moran, Stanton & Lee publish *only* first editions; any book bearing any one of these imprints is automatically a first edition. Most books carry a colophon setting forth the number of books printed."

Statement for 1960: "All Arkham House books are limited (first) editions with the exception of the collected works of H.P. Lovecraft, the subsequent reprintings of which are acknowledged in the end colophon to each volume. This is and always has been the Arkham policy."

ARKHAM HOUSE PUBLISHERS, INC.

1976 Statement: "All Arkham House books are limited (first editions) with the exception of the collected works of H.P. Lovecraft, the subsequent reprintings of which are acknowledged in the end colophon to each volume."

1981 Statement: "Initial pressruns of Arkham House books (from 1980 to the present) are identified by the term 'First Edition' on the copyright page. If a title subsequently is reprinted, the 'First Edition' designation either is removed from the copyright page or is replaced by an appropriate acknowledgement such as 'Second Printing,' 'Third Printing,' et cetera."

1988 Statement: "All Arkham House first editions are designated by the term 'First Edition,' which invariably occupies the final line on our copyright pages (p. iv). Should a book enter subsequent printings, this line will be replaced by 'Second Printing,' 'Third Printing,' or whatever notification is appropriate. With the exception of our collected critical Lovecraft edition, Arkham House seldom reprints its titles."

1993, 2000 Statements: *See* 1988 Statement

ARLEN HOUSE: THE WOMEN'S PRESS (REPUBLIC OF IRELAND)

1981 Statement: "For a first edition we have in the past said simply:

'Published by . . . '
"In subsequent editions we give details of previous editions thus:
'First published under (title, if previous title different) date.
'This revised (if applicable) edition (date).' "
This practice is followed by the imprints of Arlen House.

ARLINGTON HOUSE PUBLISHERS
1976 Statement: "Arlington House does not designate first editions. However, reprints are indicated in the usual manner: Second printing, May 1973, for example."
1981 Statement: Arlington House Publishers now uses a sequence of numbers from 1 through 9. With each new printing, the lowest number is deleted.

ARMADILLO BOOKS
See Armadillo Publishing Corporation

ARMADILLO PUBLISHING CORPORATION
2000 Statement: "Armadillo Books is now Armadillo Publishing Corporation. Our first editions are marked 'First Edition' on the copyright page. Subsequent editions are not designated."

ARMS AND ARMOUR PRESS (UNITED KINGDOM)
1988, 1994 Statements: *See* 1988 Statement of Cassell plc (United Kingdom)

ARNEFOLD (UNITED KINGDOM)
2001 Statement: *See* 2001 Statement of George Mann Books (United Kingdom)

ARNOLD (UNITED KINGDOM)
2001 Statement: *See* 2001 Statement of Hodder Headline (United Kingdom)

EDWARD ARNOLD (UNITED KINGDOM)
1988 Statement: *See* 1937 Statement of Edward Arnold & Co. (United Kingdom)

EDWARD ARNOLD & CO. (UNITED KINGDOM)
1928 Statement: "We do not designate our first editions of books in any special way. If the book reaches a second edition or second impression we designate it as such on the title page as a rule."
1937 Statement: "We do not designate our first editions of books in any special way. If the book reaches a second edition or second impression we designate it as such on the title page or on the reverse of the title."
1947 Statement: *See* 1937 Statement
1988 Statement: *See* 1988 Statement of Edward Arnold (United Kingdom)

A R O PUBLISHING CO
2001 Statement: "We do not identify the first printing on the copyright page, or any printing thereafter."

JASON ARONSON INC.
1994 Statement: "We designate the first printing by number on the copyright page. We list the numbers from left to right, as 10 9 8 7 6 5 4 3 2 1, with 1 being the last number in the case of a first printing."

ARROW (AUSTRALIA)
2000 Statement: *See* 2000 Statement of Transworld Publishers (Australia)

ARROW BOOKS (UNITED KINGDOM)
1994 Statement: *See* 1994 Statement of Random House UK Limited (United Kingdom)
2000 Statement: *See* 2000 Statement of The Random House Group Limited (United Kingdom)

ARROWHEAD BOOKS
1947 Statement: "The first edition of *Bubu of Montparnasse* by Charles-Louis Phillipe is the only one which has the date at the end of T. S. Eliot's preface. The firm which made the plates used for later editions simply dropped the line and we have not reinserted it.

"The first edition of *Bumarap* can be told by the fact that the copyright date was left out on the page behind the title page. It is to be found in each of subsequent editions.

"The first edition of *Waggish Tales* edited by Norman Lockridge has Alexander Woollcott's name at the end of the introduction. It is omitted in the plates. If there are any further editions the name will not be there."

J. W. ARROWSMITH (LONDON), LTD.
(UNITED KINGDOM)
1928 Statement: "Our custom is to put on the back of the title page 'First published in 1928,' or whatever the year may be. Reprints are marked 'First published in 1928—Second impression 1928—' and so on.

"May we take this opportunity of pointing out that the words 'First Edition' are invariably misused. What is meant is 'First Impression' as a First Edition may include 20 or 30 impressions and presumably it is only the first which is of value."
1937, 1947 Statements: *See* 1928 Statement

ART AND EDUCATIONAL PUBLISHERS, LTD.
(UNITED KINGDOM)
1947 Statement: "The first editions of all our publications bear the following imprint, verso title page 'First Published' followed, in some cases, by the month but always by the year, and our full name and address. Subsequent editions or reprints are marked with the reprint date or new edition date. It should be perfectly clear therefrom that an edition that does not bear either the reissue date or a new edition date, is the *first edition*."

ART DIRECTION BOOK CO.
1988 Statement: "We indicate first editions as:
'1st printing July 1978'

and by listing subsequent printings as:
'2nd printing July 1985,' etc."
1993, 2001 Statements: *See* 1988 Statement

ART GALLERY OF WESTERN AUSTRALIA
1995 Statement: "We do not designate a first edition in our books and have never done so. Subsequent printings or editions are identified as such on the reverse of the title page. We do not have any imprints or subsidiaries."

THE ART INSTITUTE OF CHICAGO
1995 Statement: "At The Art Institute of Chicago, we do not designate first printings in our publications, since the vast majority of our titles is never reprinted. We have felt that to say first printing would imply that we planned on a second or third one, which is misleading. In the rare event of a second or subsequent printing, we make sure to list that fact and the date on the copyright page."
2000 Statement: *See* 1995 Statement

ART STAND (UNITED KINGDOM)
1994 Statement: *See* 1988 Statement of Trigon Press (United Kingdom)

THE ART TRADE PRESS, LTD. (UNITED KINGDOM)
1947 Statement: *See* Rockliff Publishing Corporation, Limited (United Kingdom)
2000 Statement: "This company has not had any connection with Rockliff Publishing or Practical Press for over forty years. We are an independent company publishing only *Who's Who in Art.* We can confirm that the edition is still indicated on the reverse of the title page."

ARTABRAS, INC.
1994 Statement: The first printing of a first edition is indicated by the words "First Edition" and the number line 10 9 8 7 6 5 4 3 2 1. The lowest number showing indicates the printing.
2000 Statement: *See* 2000 Statement of Abbeville Press, Inc.

ARTANGEL (UNITED KINGDOM)
2001 Statement: "We do not identify first editions of our books. Only reprints have a reference to the fact that they are a second edition, either by explicitly stating that they are a second edition, or by way of reference to the copyright year. We may refer to two separate copyright years if the second edition comes out in another year."

ARTE PUBLICO PRESS
1994 Statement: The first printing of a first edition is designated by the copyright date alone. Second and subsequent editions are noted, as are reprints. This method does not differ from any previously used.
2000 Statement: "The printings—and dates (years) of those printings—are denoted by a series of numbers at the bottom of the copyright page:

0 1 2 3 4 5 6 7 8 9   0 9 8 7 6 5 4 3 2 1
year of printing   printing

"A '1' at the far right thus denotes a first printing. For the second printing, the '1' would be removed, and so forth.

"Any actual new edition would be noted quite literally on the title page and/or copyright page and/or cover/dust-jacket: 'Revised edition,' or 'Second edition,' et cetera.

"Arte Publico Press in 1994 began an imprint devoted to children's and young-adult books: Piñata Books."

ARTEMIS CREATIONS PUBLISHING
2001 Statement: "We identify the first printing of a first edition by the number line 1 2 3 4 [and] 'First printing.' "

ARTETECH PUBLISHING COMPANY (UNITED KINGDOM)
2001 Statement: "We do not identify a first printing; we do identify subsequent printings."

ARTISTS & ALCHEMISTS PUBLICATIONS
1976 Statement: "The books printed today, that do not say 'first printing'—are a first printing—in the future we will indicate such."
1981 Statement: *See* 1976 Statement

ARUNDEL PRESS
1994 Statement: "None of our books has, to date, gone into a second printing. If one should in the future do so, we will, no doubt, devise an identification system confusing and erratic enough to confuse any bookseller or bibliographer."
2001 Statement: "Still no reprints, but our commitment to complexity and confusion, in that eventuality, remains unshaken."

FRANCIS ASBURY PRESS
2001 Statement: *See* 2001 Statement of Evangel Publishing House

ASCE PRESS
1993, 2001 Statements: *See* 1988 Statement of American Society of Civil Engineers

ASHER-GALLANT PRESS
1988 Statement: "We do not indicate first editions—only second editions—and we do not indicate first or subsequent printings on any titles. This has been our policy since we started publishing in 1977, under the name Caddylak Publishing."

ASHGATE PUBLISHING LTD. (UNITED KINGDOM)
2001 Statement: "We do not identify first printings or first editions, but subsequent editions are identified as such on the copyright page. The only imprint names we use are Ashgate and Variorum."

ASHGROVE PRESS LTD (UNITED KINGDOM)

1994 Statement: The first Ashgrove Press printing of a book not originally published by them will carry the phrase "This edition (date)" on the © page. The first printing of a book of which Ashgrove Press is the original publisher will carry on the © page the phrase "First published (date)."

2000 Statement: *See* 2000 Statement of Ashgrove Publications (United Kingdom)

ASHGROVE PUBLICATIONS (UNITED KINGDOM)

2000 Statement: "Please note that the Ashgrove list has been acquired by Hollydata Publishers Ltd. The title page imprint now reads: Ashgrove Publications.

"The first Ashgrove printing of a book not originally published by them will carry the phrase 'This edition (date)' (or 'this revised edition (date)') on the copyright page. The first printing of a book of which Ashgrove Publications is the original publisher will carry on the copyright page the phrase 'First Edition.' "

ASHMOLEAN MUSEUM (UNITED KINGDOM)

1988 Statement:

"1. The Ashmolean uses no special identification for *first* editions. The date of publication appears:

(i) at the bottom of the title page

(ii) at the bottom of the title page reverse (copyright page)

"2. All subsequent editions are however clearly indicated on the reverse of the title page with the statement

'First published . . . '

'Second edition published . . . '

"3. If an edition is reprinted the statement will read

'First published . . . '

'Second edition published . . . '

'Reprinted . . . '

"4. In every instance the date of publication will appear at the bottom of the title page and at the bottom of the title page reverse with the name and address of the printer."

1994 Statement: *See* 1988 Statement

ASHTON SCHOLASTIC (AUSTRALIA)

1994 Statement: "The first printing of the first edition of our books can be identified because subsequent reprints are indicated on the imprint page. So a book which indicated 'first published 1994' and gave no indications of reprint dates would be a first printing. This practice was formalised in the late '80s, so would not necessarily apply to books published before 1985."

2001 Statement: *See* 2001 Statement of Scholastic Australia (Australia)

ASIA PRESS

See The John Day Co., Inc.

ASM INTERNATIONAL

2001 Statement: "We do not identify a first printing; we do identify subsequent printings."

ASM PRESS

2001 Statement: "We identify the first printing of a first edition by the [lack of a] statement, title designation only. Subsequent editions are designated by edition numbers. *Some* books, primarily textbooks and reference manuals, have the following number line (10 9 8 7 6 5 4 3 2 1) on the copyright page. The last number indicates the *printing*, not edition. Most of our monographs do not have this number line."

ASPECT

2000 Statement: *See* 2000 Statement of Warner Books, Inc.

ASPEN PUBLISHERS, INC.

1988 Statement: "In the absence of any designation regarding edition, one can assume a title is a first edition. Second and subsequent editions are so identified on the cover, spine, and title page of an Aspen book. This has always been our practice."

1995, 2000 Statements: *See* 1988 Statement

ASPHODEL PRESS

2000 Statement: *See* 2000 Statement of Moyer Bell

ASSOCIATED BOOK PUBLISHERS (UK) LTD.
(UNITED KINGDOM)

1988 Statement: "All our books are first editions unless it indicates otherwise on the title verso.

"For your information, we enclose a copy of statement appearing in our imprints, which are as follows: Routledge, Ark, and Arkana.

First published in 19— by
Routledge
a division of Routledge, Chapman and Hall
11 New Fetter Lane, London EC4P 4EE"

ASSOCIATED BOOK PUBLISHERS (UK) LTD.
(SCIENTIFIC AND TECHNICAL DIVISION)
(UNITED KINGDOM)

1988 Statement: "We do not use any particular method to identify first editions of our books. There is a simple statement on the biblio page of when the book was first published. If there is no additional information on either reprints or new editions then the book is a first edition."

ASSOCIATED UNIVERSITY PRESSES

1976 Statement: "In addition to this press (Fairleigh Dickinson University Press) we also administer the affairs of Bucknell University Press, The University of Delaware Press, and the Art Alliance Press. The Presses have no particular means of designating first editions or first printings. However, subsequent editions and printings do carry printing histories."

1981, 1988, 1993 Statements: *See* 1976 Statement
2000 Statement: *See* 1976 Statement but note that presses currently managed are Bucknell University Press, Fairleigh Dickinson University Press, Lehigh University Press, Susquehanna University Press and the University of Delaware Press.

ASSOCIATION OF COLLEGE & RESEARCH LIBRARIES
2001 Statement: "We identify the first printing of a first edition by a number line on the copyright page, the lowest number indicating the printing."

ASSOCIATION OF RESEARCH LIBRARIES
2001 Statement: "We do not identify a first printing or any printing after the first printing on the copyright page. We do identify any revised printings or editions on the copyright page."

ASTRAGAL PRESS
2001 Statement: "We identify the first edition by 'First Edition.' We do not identify printings/reprintings within an edition, but only the number of the edition."

ASTRO ROOM
2000 Statement: *See* 2000 Statement of Hay House Inc

ASYLUM ARTS PUBLISHING
1993 Statement: "Unless otherwise indicated on the copyright page, the books are first editions. Subsequent editions or printings are indicated by the phrase 'second printing,' 'second edition,' 'second revised edition,' etc."

ATHANOR BOOKS
2000 Statement: "We identify the first printing of a first edition by the absence of any reference to subsequent editions. We only list 'second printing/edition' etc. in books that are not first editions."

ATHANOR PRESS
1995 Statement: "All of first editions can be identified by the fact that no claim of second or subsequent edition is given. We do not differentiate first editions except by declaration of an edition other than first."

ATHENEUM PUBLISHERS
1976 Statement: "Atheneum's method of designating a first edition is by clearly indicating such on the copyright page.

"It will invariably be found on the last line on the copyright page, and will say 'First Edition' or 'First American Edition' (the latter in the case of a book which has been issued earlier in a foreign country)."
1981 Statement: *See* 1976 Statement
1989 Statement: *See* 1989 Statement of Macmillan Publishing Co., Inc.
(No longer publishing in 1995.)

ATHLETIC PRESS
1988, 2000 Statements: *See* 1976 Statement of Golden West Books

THE ATHLONE PRESS (UNITED KINGDOM)

1981 Statement: "Since 1st February 1979, the Athlone Press has ceased to be the university press of the University of London and we are now everywhere styled as The Athlone Press. Otherwise, there is no change whatsoever to our wording or practice."

See also The Athlone Press of the University of London (United Kingdom)

1988, 1994, 2000 Statements: *See* 1981 Statement

THE ATHLONE PRESS OF THE UNIVERSITY OF LONDON (UNITED KINGDOM)

1976 Statement: "We add no words to identify first editions of our books. Indeed the absence of description is the identification since all printings subsequent to the first are identified on the verso of the title page. A first edition would therefore bear on the verso of the title page the copyright line © A.N. Other 1976. The second edition would have the words Second Edition on the title page and this information would also be included in the bibliographical details immediately following the copyright line."

See also The Athlone Press (United Kingdom)

ATL PRESS

2001 Statement: "We identify only subsequent editions."

THE ATLANTIC MONTHLY PRESS, INC.

1937 Statement: "On first editions of Atlantic Monthly Press titles beginning with the fall of 1925 (when they appeared under the Little, Brown and Company imprint) the date at the bottom of the title page coincides with the date of publication printed on the copyright page immediately beneath the copyright notice. Later printings are likewise listed on the copyright page, so that reprints are easily distinguishable.

"Prior to the fall of 1925, however, it is not an easy matter to distinguish first editions of our books. In many instances it has been necessary for us to check back on text corrections to be quite sure, as at that time our title pages carried no dates and our copyright pages did not consistently list reprints of our titles. There is therefore no definite ruling one can give, although in general it is safe to say that such copies containing simply the copyright line on the copyright page are first editions."

1947 Statement: *See* 1937 Statement

1976 Statement: The edition (e.g., First Edition or First American Edition) is indicated on the copyright page. Subsequent printings of the edition are listed.

1981 Statement: *See* 1976 Statement

See also Little, Brown and Company

2000 Statement: *See* 2000 Statement of Grove/Atlantic Inc.

ATRIUM (REPUBLIC OF IRELAND)

2001 Statement: *See* 2001 Statement of Cork University Press (Republic of Ireland)

ATTIC PRESS (REPUBLIC OF IRELAND)
2001 Statement: *See* 2001 Statement of Cork University Press (Republic of Ireland)

AUBURN HOUSE
1995, 2000 Statements: *See* 1995 Statement of Greenwood Publishing Group Inc.

AUCKLAND UNIVERSITY PRESS (NEW ZEALAND)
1976 Statement: "First editions are marked e.g. 'First published 1976'; subsequent printings are identified 'Reprinted 1976' or '2nd edition 1976' depending on whether there is new matter or not. We have always used this method."
1981, 1989, 1994, 2000 Statements: *See* 1976 Statement

AUGENER (UNITED KINGDOM)
2001 Statement: *See* 2001 Statement of Stainer & Bell Ltd. (United Kingdom)

AUGSBURG BOOKS
2001 Statement: *See* 2001 Statement of Augsburg Fortress, Publishers

AUGSBURG FORTRESS, PUBLISHERS
2001 Statement: "We do not identify first editions, but only subsequent editions."

AUGUST HOUSE INC, PUBLISHERS
1988 Statement: "First Edition, (year)
10 9 8 7 6 5 4 3 2 1
"With each printing, one number is lifted so that the last number is the number of the printing."
This method of identification was adopted in 1984.
1993, 2000 Statements: *See* 1988 Statement

J. J. AUGUSTIN INCORPORATED, PUBLISHER
1976 Statement: "All our books are first editions. We never reprint."
1981 Statement: *See* 1976 Statement

J. J. AUGUSTIN PUBLISHERS CORPORATION
1947 Statement: "We are somewhat hesitant to give a definite statement of the method used to identify first printings of our books, however as far as we can see from our recent publications and older ones at hand, the first editions show the word Copyright and the year in the front of the book, while books with two or more editions list the different editions or reprints, respectively."

AUNT LUTE BOOKS
1995 Statement: "We indicate a first edition on the copyright page by indicating printings as follows:
10 - 9 - 8 - 7 - 6 - 5 - 4 - 3 - 2 - 1

"Each subsequent printing has one number deleted. 'Second Editions' are so named with a new number sequence.

"1982 was the year we adopted this method. It differs from previous years when we did nothing. We have no imprints or subsidiaries."

AURA IMAGING
2000 Statement: *See* 2000 Statement of Blue Dolphin Publishing Inc.

AURUM PRESS (UNITED KINGDOM)
1988 Statement: "In general we print the date of the first printing on the title-page verso, with dates of subsequent reprintings or new editions where relevant, as in the following example:

First published 1987 by Aurum Press Ltd
Reprinted 1988
New edition 1989"

1994 Statement: *See* 1988 Statement

2000 Statement: "Our present policy as regards designating successive editions of a book is to print, as our former statement, First published 1999 by Aurum Press Ltd. However instead of listing the subsequent reprints we now put the usual dual row of figures (1,2,3,4 etc. followed by a row of years) underneath, and delete numbers as appropriate to signify that the second printing was, for example, done in 2000."

AUSTRALIAN CONSOLIDATED PRESS UK (UNITED KINGDOM)
2001 Statement: "First printings are not identified; subsequent printings are identified as such on the copyright page."

AUTO BOOK PRESS
2001 Statement: *See* 2001 Statement of Coda Publications

AVALON BOOKS
1994 Statement: *See* 1988 Statement of Thomas Bouregy & Co., Inc.
2000 Statement: *See* 2000 Statement of Thomas Bouregy & Co., Inc.

AVALON PRESS LTD. (UNITED KINGDOM)
1947 Statement: "We adopt the same method to identify the first printings of our books as that employed by other leading publishers. The first edition would have the words 'First published 194-' and subsequent editions would have the words 'Second edition 194-' and so on. If the text of a book has been revised the word 'revised' is also inserted."

AVALON PUBLISHING GROUP INCORPORATED
2001 Statement: "Avalon Publishing Group Incorporated was established in 1994 as the parent company of the following imprints: Thunder's Mouth Press (imprint), Adrenaline Books (sub-imprint of TMP), Nation Books (sub-imprint of TMP); Marlowe & Company, Illumina Books (sub-imprint of M&C); Blue Moon Books.

"We designate printings by setting numbers in descending order (9 8 7 6 5 4 3 2 1) on the copyright page. The lowest number indicating the printing, in this example, a first printing. First editions are listed as 'First edition' or by negative implication on the copyright page, which indicates that the first editions bear no special identification. If a title is reissued, then that fact is labeled on the copyright page. This has been our policy since July 2000."

AVE MARIA PRESS

1993 Statement: "We have never specifically designated first editions or first printings. We do usually include a printing history to the copyright page of reprints when the number of copies in print reaches the 25-30,000 level. A note of a new or revised edition is usually made on the cover, or on the copyright page, with or in lieu of a printing history."

2000 Statement: *See* 1993 Statement

AVERY PUBLISHING GROUP, INC.

1995 Statement: The first printing of a first edition is indicated by the number line 10 9 8 7 6 5 4 3 2 1. The lowest number showing indicates the printing.

"A first edition has only one copyright date listed on the copyright page. The editions can be counted by the number of copyright dates listed."

AVIATION BOOK CO.

1994 Statement: "We have no special way of identifying first editions."

AVIATION PUBLISHERS

2001 Statement: *See* 2001 Statement of Markowski International Publishers

AVON

2001 Statement: *See* 2001 Statement of HarperCollinsPublishers

AVON BOOKS

1981 Statement: "Avon designates the first printing of our books by a copyline which appears on the copyright page, 'First Avon Printing, May, 1981' for example. The copyline reflects the imprint of the title. We have five imprints; Avon (mass market books and trade books), Bard (distinguished fiction, mass market size books), Discus (distinguished non-fiction, mass market size also), Flare (young adult titles, mass market) and Camelot (children's books, trade size). The printing line would read, 'First Flare Printing, May, 1981' or whatever is appropriate. This method of designating the first printing has been the one Avon has always used.

"Starting in July, 1981 we will institute a new method for designating second printings and subsequent editions. A line of numbers will be added to the bottom of the copyright page: 10 9 8 7 6 5 4 3 2 1. The last number on the right indicates the current edition. The above example would designate a first edition. A line reading 10 9 8 7 would indicate the book is in its seventh printing. This line of numbers is in addition to the print line, 'First Avon Printing' etc. Previous to July, 1981 we used to designate second editions by an additional line, 'Second Printing, July, 1981.' "

1993 Statement: "Avon Books designates the first printing of our books by a copyline which appears on the copyright page, 'First Avon Books Printing: May 1993' for example. The copyline reflects the imprint of the title. We have five imprints: Avon Books (mass market books and trade books), AvoNova (science fiction and fantasy books, mass market), Avon Flare (young adult titles, mass market), Avon Camelot (children's books, trade size), and Confident Collector (collectibles line, trade size). The printing line would read 'First Avon Flare Printing: May 1993' or whatever is appropriate. This method of designating the first printing has been the one Avon Books has always used.

"In July 1981, we instituted a new method for designating second printings and subsequent editions. A line of numbers was added to the bottom of the copyright page: 10 9 8 7 6 5 4 3 2 1. The last number on the right indicates the current edition. The above example would designate a first edition. A line reading 10 9 8 7 would indicate the book is in its seventh printing. This line of numbers is in addition to the print line, 'First Avon Books Printing' etc. Previous to July 1981, we used to designate second editions by an additional line, 'Second Printing: July 1981.' "

2001 Statement: *See* 2001 Statement of HarperCollinsPublishers

AVON CAMELOT
1993 Statement: *See* 1993 Statement of Avon Books

AVON FLARE
1993 Statement: *See* 1993 Statement of Avon Books

AVONOVA
1993 Statement: *See* 1993 Statement of Avon Books

AVONSTOKE PRESS
1995, 2000 Statements: *See* 1995 Statement of Momentum Books Ltd.

AVOTAYNU INC
2001 Statement: "We do not identify a first printing; we do identify subsequent printings."

AZURE (UNITED KINGDOM)
2000 Statement: *See* 2000 Statement of Society for Promoting Christian Knowledge (United Kingdom)

B

B & B PUBLISHING
1995 Statement: "We distinguish a subsequent edition by printing 'Revised Edition' or 'Second Edition' on the cover."

BABEL HANDBOOKS (AUSTRALIA)
1994 Statement: *See* 1994 Statement of Nimrod Publications (Australia)
2001 Statement: *See* 2001 Statement of Nimrod Publications (Australia)

BABY STEPS PRESS

1995 Statement: "On the copyright page I note which edition it is by writing 'first,' 'second,' etc. and which printing it is by 'first,' 'second, etc."
2001 Statement: *See* 1995 Statement

THE BACCHAE PRESS

1995 Statement: "Both printing and edition are indicated in each book."
2000 Statement: "Printings are stated '1st Printing,' '2nd Printing,' etc."

BACCHUS PRESS LTD.

1995 Statement: "We distinguish the first edition by printing on the back of the title page: 'First Edition.' Subsequent printings would be as follows: Second impression November 199?. If the book is actually a second edition (i.e., substantial changes, updates and revisions) then on the reverse of the title page would be found 'Second Edition.'

"We adopted this method of designation . . . in 1985. That does not differ from any previously used designations."

BACK BAY BOOKS

2000 Statement: *See* 2000 Statement of Warner Books, Inc.

BACK TO EDEN BOOKS

2001 Statement: *See* 2001 Statement of Lotus Press (Twin Lakes, Wisconsin)

BACKBEAT BOOKS

2001 Statement: *See* 2001 Statement of Miller Freeman Inc

BACKCOUNTRY PUBLICATIONS

1988, 1993, 2001 Statements: *See* 1988, 1993, 2001 Statements of The Countryman Press, Inc.

BACKGROUND BOOKS, LTD. (UNITED KINGDOM)

1947 Statement: "First editions of our publications are printed in the following manner, opposite the title page:
     '1st printing 19..'
"Subsequent printings are identified firstly under the heading of '2nd, 3rd, etc. impression' and a second printing is marked in the same manner as the first printing, and so forth."

THE BACKWATERS PRESS

2000 Statement: "We identify the first printing of a first edition by 'First Printing' followed by the number of copies in the press run, and the month and year of publication. We do not use a number line. When additional printings are done, they will say 'Second Printing' the number of copies, and the month and year, etc., for any additional print runs."

BAEN PUBLISHING ENTERPRISES

1988 Statement: "Since inception in 1984 Baen Books has indicated first editions on the copyright page with the phrase 'A Baen Books Original.' First, and all subsequent printings, are also indicated on the copyright page with month and year of the printing."

1993, 2000 Statements: *See* 1988 Statement

BAHÁ'Í PUBLISHING TRUST

1994 Statement: "Since *The Chicago Manual of Style* issued a revised edition in 1982, we have adopted the system it recommends of using two sets of figures to indicate years of publication and dates of impressions. Hence the first group of numbers represents, from right to left, successive years of publication; the second group, a possible future impressions of the book. In addition, we also include a line reading 'first edition' followed by the year or 'first pocket-sized edition' followed by the year.

"Before 1982 we find that first editions were identified in a variety of ways. If first edition or first printing is not included, we rely on the first copyright date as an indication of the date of the first printing."

2000 Statement: *See* 1994 Statement

A & B BAHR & CO

2001 Statement: *See* 2001 Statement of Factor Press

BAILEY BROS. & SWINFEN LTD. (UNITED KINGDOM)

1988 Statement: "For your information our first imprints give the date of publication on the copyright page i.e. the verso. Should the book be reprinted, the date of the reprint would be shown on this page also. We would not put second edition unless the book had been altered or amended in any way, thus we would continue with third, fourth, fifth printing, etc. The new edition would name the date as would the reprints."

2000 Statement: "Bailey Bros & Swinfen Ltd has not published any titles since 1990. The [1988] Statement is accurate for titles published before 1990."

JOHN BAKER (UNITED KINGDOM)

1976, 1981 Statements: *See* 1976, 1981 Statements of Adam and Charles Black Publishers Limited (United Kingdom)

1988 Statement: *See* 1988 Statement of A & C Black (Publishers) Limited (United Kingdom)

BAKER BOOK HOUSE

1989 Statement: "Almost without exception, first editions have no printing notice—just the copyright. All later editions are identified as 'second edition' or as a subsequent printing, e.g., 'second printing.' "

1993, 2000 Statements: *See* 1989 Statement

BAKER BYTES

2000 Statement: *See* 2000 Statement of Baker Book House

BALCH INSTITUTE FOR ETHNIC STUDIES

1988 Statement: *See* 1976 Statement of Associated University Presses

BALL PUBLISHING

1993 Statement: "We identify a first printing of our books by numbers listed on the copyright page. The numbers indicate the printings and the dates. When a title is reprinted the appropriate numbers are deleted to indicate the reprint and the date . . . . We adopted this method in 1992."

2000 Statement: *See* 1993 Statement

BALLANTINE BOOKS

2001 Statement: *See* 2001 Statement of The Ballantine Publishing Group

THE BALLANTINE PUBLISHING GROUP

2001 Statement: "All first editions of Ballantine and Del Rey books carry the words 'First Edition' on the copyright page.

"For first printings of an edition we have a number line that records 10 9 8 7 6 5 4 3 2 1 and we delete a number starting at '1' when it is the second printing of the first edition.

"So a First Edition *first* printing would read:
First Edition: October 2001
10 9 8 7 6 5 4 3 2 1

"So a First Edition *second* printing would read:
First Edition: October 2001
10 9 8 7 6 5 4 3 2

"I know this method was used [at least] as of 1997."
All imprints of The Ballantine Publishing Group follow this method.

BALLENA PRESS

2000 Statement: "[We identify the first printing of a first edition by the words] '1st Printing' at bottom of reverse of title page. Sometimes nothing."

BALLOON (UNITED KINGDOM)

1994 Statement: *See* 1994 Statement of Ladybird Books Ltd (United Kingdom)

ROBERT O. BALLOU, PUBLISHER

1937, 1949 Statements: *See* Jonathan Cape and Robert Ballou, Inc.

FRANCIS BALSOM ASSOCIATES (UNITED KINGDOM)

See FBA Publications

BAMBOO RIDGE PRESS

2000 Statement: "Bamboo Ridge Press indicates which printing a book is in by a string of numbers on the copyright page. If you look at the first number on the *left*, you will know which printing you have in hand. Thus if the first number you see is 1, you have a first printing; if the first number you see is 3, you have a third printing."

BANCROFT PRESS

2000 Statement: "We indicate a first edition by stating 'First Edition' on the copyright page."

BAMBOO RIDGE PRESS

2000 Statement: "Bamboo Ridge Press indicates which printing a book is in by a string of numbers on the copyright page. If you look at the first number on the *left*, you will know which printing you have in hand. Thus if the first number you see is 1, you have a first printing; if the first number you see is 3, you have a third printing."

BANCROFT PRESS

2000 Statement: "We indicate a first edition by stating 'First Edition' on the copyright page."

BANCROFT-SAGE PUBLISHING, INC.

1995 Statement: "I am afraid that our Company has no specific designation for the first printing. Subsequent printings are noted by a line in the intro pages of the books with 'REPRINTED 19—.' "
2001 Statement: *See* 1995 Statement

BANDANNA BOOKS

1995 Statement: "Bandanna Books first editions are not indicated as such in any way. Revised editions are given a different ISBN number on copyright page, and indicated as such on the title page and on the colophon (if there is one). Additional printings are not notated."
2001 Statement: *See* 1995 Statement

BANKS CHANNEL BOOKS

2000 Statement: "The number of a reprint edition is listed on the copyright page."

BANNER BOOKS

2000 Statement: *See* 2000 Statement of University Press of Mississippi

THE BANNER OF TRUTH TRUST PUBLISHERS (UNITED KINGDOM)

1994 Statement: "Our normal practice is simply to print on the title verso, after the copyright notice, the words, 'First published 19...' with the year of subsequent reprintings shown immediately below, i.e. 'Reprinted 19....'

"A number of our books are reprints of much older books and this is a little more problematical as we cannot always be sure of the date of the first edition, or indeed be certain that we are reprinting the first edition. Normally, however, we would print 'First published 18...' followed by the words 'First Banner of Truth edition 19....'

"This method of wording has been used by us since our first book was published in 1958."
2000 Statement: *See* 1994 Statement

BANQUO BOOKS

2000 Statement: *See* 2000 Statement of Woodbridge Press

BANTAM (AUSTRALIA)

2000 Statement: *See* 2000 Statement of Transworld Publishers (Australia)

BANTAM BOOKS

1988 Statement: "Our general policy has been to designate hardcover and paperback printings by the number code 9 8 7 6 5 4 3 2 1—the number on the right indicating which printing.

"No one seems to know when this practice was adopted. It does not differ from any previous designation. This designation is for Bantam Books only."
1993 Statement: *See* 1988 Statement

BANTAM PAPERBACKS (UNITED KINGDOM)

2001 Statement: *See* 2001 Statement of Transworld Publishers Ltd (United Kingdom)

BANTAM PRESS (UNITED KINGDOM)

2001 Statement: *See* 2001 Statement of Transworld Publishers Ltd (United Kingdom)

BANYAN BOOKS, INC.

1976 Statement: "Our first editions carry the copyright notice alone; subsequent editions are noted (2nd printing, 19..), (rev. ed. 19..) as the situations warrant."
1981, 1988, 1994 Statements: *See* 1976 Statement

BANYAN TREE BOOKS

2000 Statement: "No special statement; if there is simply a copyright line without any indication that it is a 2nd or later printing, it is a first edition."

LILIAN BARBER PRESS, INC.

1994 Statement: "We identify subsequent impressions (printings) and editions. E.g. '2nd Impression,' 'Second Edition,' or 'Third Edition, 2nd Impression' etc."

B. McCALL BARBOUR (UNITED KINGDOM)

1994 Statement: First printings are not designated.
2000 Statement: *See* 1994 Statement

BARBOUR & CO., INC.

1994 Statement: "We don't identify first printings in any way."

BARD

See Avon Books

BARD PRESS

1994, 2000 Statements: *See* 1994 Statement of Ten Penny Players, Inc.

BAREFOOT BOOKS

1993 Statement: *See* 1993 Statement of Shambhala Publications, Inc.

ARTHUR BARKER LTD. (UNITED KINGDOM)

1937 Statement: "It is our general practice to print the number of impressions and editions of our books on the reverse side of the title page.

"The first edition of a book merely has 'first published 1936' or whatever the year happens to be. If the book is reprinted we run a line:

'2nd impression June 1936

'3rd impression July 1936,' etc.

"If the author makes any changes between the first printing or second printing, we usually replace '2nd impression' by the words 'revised edition' followed by the date.

"We started this method in 1933."

1949 Statement: *See* 1937 Statement

BARLENMIR HOUSE, PUBLISHERS

1976 Statement: "Barlenmir House's method of identifying first editions in its publications is by identifying 'FIRST EDITION' on the copyright page of the book."

BARN OWL BOOKS (UNITED KINGDOM)

1989 Statement: A first printing is indicated in the copyright page by the phrase "First published (date)."

BARNARD & WESTWOOD, LTD. (UNITED KINGDOM)

1947 Statement: "We use the following method: First printing—we merely show 'Printed by Barnard & Westwood Ltd.' etc. Subsequent printings are shown 'Second Printing,' 'Third Printing,' and so on."

BARNEGAT LIGHT PRESS

2000 Statement: *See* 2000 Statement of Pine Barrens Press

A. S. BARNES AND COMPANY, INC.
(Including Countryman Press.)

1947 Statement: "First printings of our books can be identified as against subsequent printings. In some cases we do print on the copyright page 'Second printing,' 'Third printing,' et cetera; in other cases we don't. It is really impossible for anyone to actually identify whether or not one of our books is a first edition without intimate knowledge."

1976 Statement: "We make no specific identification of first editions or first printings. Subsequent editions and printings do carry a printing history on the copyright page."

1988 Statement: *See* 1976 Statement

BARNES & NOBLE BOOKS

1976 Statement: "To designate a first edition the words First Edition are used on the copyright page, although often a first edition is not designated. The first printing of an edition is indicated as follows on the copyright page:

76 77 78   10 9 8 7 6 5 4 3 2 1

"The second printing is indicated like this:

76 77 78   10 9 8 7 6 5 4 3 2

"The numbers before 10 indicate years.

"Previously printings were listed as follows:

First printing, July, 1964."

BARNES & NOBLE BOOKS (IMPORTS & REPRINTS)

1988 Statement: "Barnes & Noble Books is strictly an importing operation which specializes in academic title in the humanities. Since we get most of our titles from the British Isles we indicate on the verso of the title page 'First published in the U.S. 19—' followed by our company name and address—even though our imprint appears on the book's title page, spine, and jacket.

"We have been importing academic books since 1949 and the above policy has remained the same. It has not changed over the years. When we have found it necessary to reprint a particular volume we always state 'Reprinted 19—' somewhere on the verso which indicates that that particular copy is not a first edition (printing)."

1995 Statement: *See* 1988 Statement

BARRE PUBLISHING CO., INC.

1976 Statement: "Every printing after the first is listed with the edition on the copyright page. (i.e. on the first edition, first printing, the c/r page says only 1st edition; on 2nd printing, '2nd printing' is added to 1st edition). This method does not differ from any previously used."

BARRICADE BOOKS
(New York, New York)

1995 Statement: "Our first printings say 'First Printing' on copyright page."

BARRICADE BOOKS, INC.
(Fort Lee, New Jersey)

1994 Statement: The first printing of a first edition is indicated by the number line 9 8 7 6 5 4 3 2 1. The lowest number showing indicates the printing.

"More recently we've been [stating] 'First Printing.' "

2000 Statement: "We either indicate the first printing of our Barricade Books titles by the words: First Printing, on their copyright pages or by using the numbers 1 2 3 4 5 6 7 8 9 10 on their copyright pages to indicate the number of their printing."

BARRIE & JENKINS (UNITED KINGDOM)

1988 Statement: *See* 1988 Statement of Century Hutchinson Publishing Group Limited (United Kingdom)

1994 Statement: *See* 1994 Statement of Ebury Press (United Kingdom)

M. BARROWS AND COMPANY, INC.

1947 Statement: "First printings are identified in our books by these very words appearing on our copyright page. Later printings are also identified in the same manner. Our method for Village Green Press books is the same."

BARTHOLOMEW BOOKS

1988 Statement: "First editions have no identification. Subsequent editions are noted: second, third, etc. No other method is used."

BASIC BOOKS

1993 Statement: *See* 1981 Statement of Basic Books, Inc. Note the following: "For paperback first editions, we generally reprint the hardcover edition (with any minor corrections). A new set of digits at the bottom of the copyright page is assigned to the first printing of the paperback edition.

"This is our general policy. Our imprints follow this policy. Our current company name is Basic Books, A Division of HarperCollins Publishers, Inc."

BASIC BOOKS, INC.

1981 Statement: "Generally, when we issue a new edition it is because there is new material in the book. The book will then read, for instance, 'second and revised edition,' 'third and revised edition' etc.

"When there is no change in content, the book will be reprinted. Our normal method of indicating which printing we are making is to remove the digits at the bottom of the reverse of the title page one by one starting with the lowest number.

"This has been our general policy."

THE BASILISK PRESS LTD (UNITED KINGDOM)

1988 Statement: "Basilisk books are *not* reprinted. We print an edition of usually 500 copies, and when it is out of print, it is *really* out of print."

B. T. BATSFORD, LTD. (UNITED KINGDOM)

1937 Statement: "In all our publications the date appears either on the verso or recto of title-page, or where this is not included on this leaf it is to be found as preface date. Reprints or revised editions are always clearly shown on the recto of title."

1947 Statement: *See* 1937 Statement

Statement for 1960: "The words 'First published 19..' were still used during the 1960s and we continue this style [in 1981]."

1976 Statement: "First printing of the first edition is designated by the words: First published 19...

"The form which this follows is similar to that which has been Batsford's practice for a good many years now."

1981 Statement: " 'First published 19..' is still our method of designating a first edition. Under this we would insert as appropriate 'New edition 19..', or 'Reprinted 19..' if only minor amendments are made."

1988, 1994, 2001 Statements: *See* 1981 Statement

BATSFORD BRASSEY, INC.

See Brassey's Inc.

BATTERY PRESS, INC.

1988 Statement: "We use standard copyright information to designate first editions. Subsequent printings or reprints are marked."

1993 Statement: *See* 1988 Statement

WILLIAM L. BAUHAN, PUBLISHER

1988 Statement: "As a rule our books do not contain any specific designation on the copyright page that the book is a first edition. Subsequent printings or revised editions are almost invariably so marked. So it would be safe to assume that a book is a first edition unless otherwise marked.

"This house began as Richard R. Smith publishers on Murray Hill, New York City in 1929, and in 1952 Mr. Smith moved the firm to Rindge, New Hampshire. After his death, William L. Bauhan bought the firm in 1959 and moved it that year to Peterborough, N.H. and in 1972 to Dublin, N.H. In 1968 the Smith name was dropped and the present name assumed. Between 1968 and 1972 some books were issued under the imprint 'Noone House.'

"Since taking over the firm, William Bauhan has generally specialized in regional New England titles."

1993 Statement: *See* 1988 Statement

BAY VIEW
2001 Statement: *See* 2001 Statement of Motorbooks International

BAYLOR UNIVERSITY PRESS
1988 Statement: "Our books carry the usual data on the copyright page indicating the date of publication. If we were to reprint a title this would be added to the information already appearing."

1993, 2001 Statements: *See* 1988 Statement

BBC BOOKS (UNITED KINGDOM)
1988, 1994 Statements: *See* 1988 Statement of BBC Enterprises Limited (United Kingdom)

BBC ENTERPRISES LIMITED (UNITED KINGDOM)
1988 Statement: "BBC Books is a division of BBC Enterprises, a wholly owned subsidiary of the British Broadcasting Corporation.

"The BBC started publishing books in approximately 1966/67 and used as its title page imprint 'British Broadcasting Corporation.' The verso to the title page read—

Published by the British Broadcasting Corporation,
35 Marylebone High Street, London W1
First published . . .

"From March 1987 the title page imprint became 'BBC Books' and the verso to the title page read—

Published by BBC Books, A Division of BBC Enterprises Limited,
80 Wood Lane, London W12 0TT.
First published . . . "

1994 Statement: *See* 1988 Statement

BBC WORLDWIDE LIMITED (UNITED KINGDOM)
1995 Statement: "From 1st January 1995 the statement used is as follows:
Published by BBC Books, an imprint of BBC Worldwide Publishing,
BBC Worldwide Limited, Woodlands, 80 Wood Lane, London W12
0TT. First published . . . ."

BEACH HOLME PUBLISHING LIMITED (CANADA)
1993 Statement: "Currently, we designate all first editions as 'First Canadian Edition' with annotations for subsequent printings, i.e. 'Second printing 1993.' The addition of the 'Canadian' is common to all titles even if our

copyright license is not limited strictly to Canada alone. This new method was adopted in 1991.

"Beach Holme Publishers was originally called Press Porcepic Ltd. We changed the name of the company in June 1991."

BEACON HILL PRESS OF KANSAS CITY
1995 Statement: The first printing of a first edition is indicated by the year and the number line 10 9 8 7 6 5 4 3 2 1. The lowest number showing indicates the printing.
2001 Statement: *See* 1995 Statement

BEACON NIGHT LIGHTS
1988 Statement: *See* Beacon Press

BEACON PRESS
1947 Statement: "Nothing to indicate first printing. Subsequent printings carry a note on the copyright page as follows:
First printing, June 1947
—printing, October 1947"
Statement for 1960: "The method of designating first printings in 1960 was the copyright page statement: 'First published by Beacon Press in 1960.' "
1976 Statement: "The method of designating first printings in 1976 was the copyright page statement: 'First published by Beacon Press in 1976.' "
1982 Statement: First printings of both hardcover and paperback editions are designated by the following number code:
9 8 7 6 5 4 3 2 1
The number on the right indicates the printing.
1988 Statement: "First printings of both hardcover and paperback editions are designated by a series of impression numbers. The smallest number indicates the most recent printing.

"We first began to use this modified method in 1987, and it is used as well in our Beacon Night Lights imprint."
1993 Statement: *See* 1988 Statement

BEAR FLAG BOOKS
1988, 1994 Statements: *See* 1988, 1994 Statements of Padre Productions

BEAR STAR PRESS
2000 Statement: "We identify the first printing of a first edition by the statement 'First Edition' or the following number line: 10 9 8 7 6 5 4 3 2 1."

THE BEAR WALLOW PUBLISHING COMPANY
2000 Statement: "All of our books (except *Rendezvous* of which there were 2 printings) have been offered as limited first printings with 1500 copies numbered and the entire edition signed by the author(s). Each first edition is designated '*A Limited First Printing*' with numbers and signatures on the same page. Also, approximately 100-200 copies of the first edition are designated as *Artist* or *Author's Edition* so that the author(s) do not take numbered copies out of the collector's realm."

BEAUFORT BOOKS INC.

1981 Statement: "Our edition code is based on the assumption that a printing run is equivalent to an edition. We use a sequence of numbers on the copyright page running from 1-10. When one edition is completed, a number is deleted. Thus, if a '1' remains, the book is a first edition. If the sequence '2-10' remains but there is no '1,' the book is a second edition. And so on.

"In the case of a true revision, 'revised edition' appears on the copyright page."

1988 Statement: *See* 1981 Statement

BEAUTIFUL AMERICA PUBLISHING COMPANY

1995 Statement: "From our inception, Beautiful America Publishing Company has identified first editions by inserting on the copyright page the phrase, 'First Edition: and the year.' Subsequent printings are differentiated by using the phrase, 'Second Printing, followed by the year.' "

BEDFORD BOOKS, LTD. (UNITED KINGDOM)

1947 Statement: "We are so short of paper that we have only published two books since the war, and they have only gone to press once."

BEECH TREE BOOKS

1994 Statement: *See* 1994 Statement of Tambourine Books

BEECHHURST PRESS, INC.

1947 Statement: "First editions of Beechhurst Press books have no identification marks on the copyright page. Subsequent printings are identified by the words 'Second printing' and the date or 'Third printing' and the date and so forth. Thus the lack of identification on the copyright page would serve to identify the first printing of any of our titles.

"The firm of Bernard Ackerman, Inc., became Beechhurst Press in July, 1946. There was no change in ownership and the policies were continued in effect. Thus the first editions of Ackerman books can be identified in the same way."

THE BEEHIVE PRESS

1976 Statement: "All books are our first editions, unless the book's copyright page specifically states 'Copyright 1972 by The Beehive Press. Reprinted 1976.' "

1981, 1988, 2001 Statements: *See* 1976 Statement

BEEKMAN PUBLISHERS, INC.

1988 Statement: "Our first editions—so far—have been *only* editions. We would designate those editions after the first printing with proper numbering and information. All of our issues are first 'editions.' "

BEHRMAN HOUSE, INC.

1947 Statement: "When we reprint a book we indicate that it is the second or whatever printing. On the first edition we say nothing. In other words, if a book does not refer to any particular printing, you may rightly assume that it is the first printing of the first edition."

FREDERIC C. BEIL PUBLISHER, INC.

1994 Statement: "We print on the copyright page 'First edition' or 'First published in the United States in 19— by Frederic C. Beil, Publisher.' If a subsequent printing includes a textual change, we do not print the aforementioned designations. If we reprint the first edition with no textual changes, however, the 'first edition' designation may still be used."

2001 Statement: *See* 1994 Statement

BEING PUBLICATIONS

1976 Statement: "The act of publication is our method of identifying a first edition; consecutive editions or printings are so marked.

"We have not used any different methods."

1981 Statement: *See* 1976 Statement

1988 Statement: "We're inactive at present."

CHARLES H. BELDING

1988 Statement: *See* 1988 Statement of Graphic Arts Center Publishing Company

BELFRY BOOKS

2000 Statement: *See* 2000 Statement of Toad Hall, Inc.

THE BELKNAP PRESS

1988, 1993, 2001 Statements: *See* 1988, 1993 Statements of Harvard University Press

G. BELL & SONS, LTD. (UNITED KINGDOM)

1928 Statement: "The title page of the first edition carries the year of publication at the foot, and when it is reprinted the month and year are indicated on the reverse of the title page e.g.:

First Published (say) February 1928.

Reprinted (say) July 1928."

1936 Statement: "We only indicate the months when a book is reprinted twice in a year. We have used this method of identifying first printings since the Great War."

1947 Statement: *See* 1936 Statement

1976 Statement: "We do not have any common form of words on the title page verso of our books relating to the first edition. We would assume that the copyright line giving the year would provide the necessary information. Sometimes we add 'First published in (year)', with or without our name following."

BELL BOOKS

1995, 2000 Statements: *See* 1995 Statement of Boyds Mills Press

DAVID WINTON BELL GALLERY (BROWN UNIVERSITY)

1993 Statement: "We do not distinguish or designate the first printing of a first edition. The Bell Gallery has not issued a subsequent edition or printing of any of its publications."

2001 Statement: *See* 1993 Statement

BELL POND BOOKS

2000 Statement: *See* 2000 Statement of Anthroposophic Press, Inc.

BELL SPRINGS PUBLISHING

2000 Statement: "We identify the first printing of a first edition by the statement 'First Edition, First Printing, Month, Year.' We do not use a number line."

BELLEROPHON BOOKS

1988 Statement: "First editions are usually the ones with errors; we do not otherwise distinguish them."

1993, 2001 Statements: *See* 1988 Statement

BELLEVUE PRESS

1976 Statement: "The colophon page of each of our books clearly states the information any collector would wish to know about any one of our books. Here we note printer, designer or artist when the particular book requires such notes, and the size of our published editions, noting how many are reserved for 'signed' copies, how many are published in the trade edition, and if the book is other than a first edition."

1981 Statement: "Your previous entry is quite sufficient for our press, except that it may be added:

"Since 1979 most Bellevue Press books do clearly state *First Edition* on the copyright page. However the colophon page is still the best source for 'edition' information."

BELLWOOD PRESS

(Illinois)

2000 Statement: *See* 2000 Statement of Bahá'í Publishing Trust

BELTON (UNITED KINGDOM)

2001 Statement: *See* 2001 Statement of Stainer & Bell Ltd. (United Kingdom)

R. BEMIS PUBLISHING, LTD.

1994 Statement: *See* 1976 Statement of Mockingbird Books

BENCHMARK PUBLICATIONS INC.

2000 Statement: "The Benchmark Publications Inc. Small Press imprint indicates First Editions three ways:

—the initial copyright date

—the last two digits of the year-date reading high to low, the lowest being the first edition: 05 04 03 02 01 00 (first edition = 00)

—following the print dates at the right, single digits reading high to low indicate editions.

"An edition number changes only if the binding changes or substantial revisions are made."

ERNEST BENN, LTD. (UNITED KINGDOM)

1928 Statement: "We have two forms of designating first editions, (1) a bibliography printed on the back of the title page stating first published in— and then the year. We use this form mostly. (2) is to have no bibliography on the first edition but to put the year of publication on the front of the title page with our imprint.

"We have used this formula since we first started book publishing in 1923."

1937, 1947 Statements: *See* 1928 Statement

Statement for 1960: *See* 1976 Statement

1976 Statement: "We follow standard practice, e.g. that adopted by University Presses in always stating date of first publication. We always differentiate between a straight reprint, usually referred to as a 'Second impression' etc. and where any revision has taken place 'Second (corrected) impression', and major revision as a 'Second edition.' "

1981 Statement: "We always state date of first publication. The first line on the title-verso (copyright page) reads, 'First published 1981 by Ernest Benn Limited.' Thereafter a straight reprint is called 'Second impression,' etc. If a reprint has been lightly revised, we call it 'Second (revised) impression,' etc. A major revision is called 'Second edition,' etc."

BENN TECHNICAL BOOKS (UNITED KINGDOM)

1994 Statement: *See* 1994 Statement of Tolley Publishing Co. Ltd. (United Kingdom)

BENNETT & KITCHEL

2000 Statement: "Our copyright page gives full bibliographical information." First printings are not indicated.

BERGH PUBLISHING, INC.

1988 Statement: "Our first editions are not marked in any way. Should a second one be printed this of course is mentioned on the cover as well as on the impression page."

BERGHAHN BOOKS INC.

2001 Statement: "We do not identify first printings." This applies as well for their imprint, Berghahn Books Ltd.

BERGIN & GARVEY

1995, 2000 Statements: *See* 1995 Statement of Greenwood Publishing Group Inc.

BERGIN & GARVEY PUBLISHERS, INC.

1988 Statement: "Bergin & Garvey Publishers, Inc. uses two indicators of first edition status in its books, both of which are found on p. iv of the front matter, the copyright page:

"1. A printed statement, 'First published by Bergin & Garvey . . . .' In the case of a book first published by another publisher, say, in the UK, the reader must infer that another publication took place, as we would use 'First published in the United States by Bergin & Garvey . . . ,' by looking at the copyright date also.

"2. We use a number code; the left-hand number indicates the year of publication (890 would mean 1988; 90 would mean 1989; etc.) and the right-hand number, the number of the impression (87654321 would mean first printing; 876543 would mean third printing)."

BERKLEY
1995 Statement: *See* 1995 Statement of The Berkley Publishing Group
2000 Statement: *See* 2000 Statement of The Berkley Publishing Group

BERKLEY (AUSTRALIA)
2000 Statement: *See* 2000 Statement of Penguin Books Australia Ltd (Australia)

BERKLEY PRIME CRIME
1995 Statement: *See* 1995 Statement of The Berkley Publishing Group
2000 Statement: *See* 2000 Statement of The Berkley Publishing Group

THE BERKLEY PUBLISHING GROUP
1995 Statement: "The Berkley Publishing Group designates the printing of each title at the bottom of the copyright page with Arabic numerals. A number is deleted from the copyright page every time a title goes back to press. This method was adopted sometime between 1986 and 1988.

"Before the current method was adopted, Berkley and its imprints listed the first edition and each additional edition on the copyright page along with the date of the printing.

"The Berkley Publishing Group consists of the following imprints: Ace, Berkley, Berkley Prime Crime, Boulevard, HPBooks, Jove, Perigee, and Riverhead Books. All of the imprints follow the current method of designating printings. However, when a title is reissued under a different imprint, it is considered a first edition and the print line starts at one. We, then, list the previous edition and its printings under the heading Printing History on the copyright page."

2000 Statement: "Our company does still follow the practice outlined in our [1995 Statement]. In addition, the words 'a division of Penguin Putnam Inc.' should be inserted after 'The Berkley Publishing Group.' "

BERKSHIRE HOUSE PUBLISHERS
1994 Statement: The first printing of a first edition is indicated by the number line 10 9 8 7 6 5 4 3 2 1. The lowest number showing indicates the printing. The statement "First Printing (Month) (Year)" or "First Printing (Year)" is also used.

"Not all of our books are specifically identified as first printings, but we always use the numbering system."
2000 Statement: *See* 1994 Statement

BERLITZ PUBLISHING COMPANY, INC.

1994 Statement: *See* 1994 Statement of Berlitz Publishing Company Ltd (United Kingdom)
2000 Statement: *See* 2000 Statement of Berlitz Publishing Company Ltd (United Kingdom)

BERLITZ PUBLISHING COMPANY LTD (UNITED KINGDOM)

1994 Statement: "Our practice is to print the following on the back of the title page of our pocket guides, with the edition date relevant to that particular edition in **bold**:

Copyright © **1994** Berlitz Publishing Co Ltd, Berlitz House, Peterley Road, Oxford OX4 2TX, England (we are now also including on titles relevant to the US market '. . . and Berlitz Publishing Company Inc, 257, Park Avenue South, New York, New York 10010, USA.') This is followed lower down on the page by the edition number and date—i.e. '1st edition (1994/1995).'

"The first printing of a first edition is designated as above and was adopted in 1992 when we began the launch of our completely redesigned pocket guide series. All guides with this redesigned interior and completely rewritten text, or substantially updated text, are designated as first editions.

"This method does not alter from any previously used, although first editions of the original pocket guide series are few and far between—dating to around 1970!

"For reprints of pocket guides we print the history of the guide in date order, thus an example: 'Copyright © 1992, 1990, 1982 by Berlitz Publishing Co Ltd, Berlitz House, Peterley Road, Oxford OX4 2TX, England.' with further down the page '9th Edition (1992/1993)' and below that 'Updated or revised 1992, 1990, 1989, 1987, 1984, 1982.'

"For our Discover Guide series we print on the back of the title page 'Copyright © **1994** Berlitz Publishing Co Ltd, Berlitz House, Peterley Road, Oxford OX4 2TX, England.' Updated editions will have the relevant dates added, i.e. 'Copyright © 1994, **1995** . . . .'

"For our Travellers series we print on the back of the title page for example:
    'Copyright © Root Publishing Company
    1990, 1991, 1992, 1993'
and further down the page
    'Published by Berlitz Publishing Company Inc.,
    257 Park Avenue South, New York, New York 10010, USA.'

"For our language learning and reference titles, the copyright history is always given and—for first editions—a mention is given lower down 'First edition 19xx' or 'First printing 19xx.' "

2000 Statement: "Our practice is to print the following on the back of the title page of our pocket guides:
    Copyright © [year] Berlitz Publishing Company, Inc.
    400 Alexander Park, Princeton, NJ 08540 USA
    9-13 Grosvenor St., London W1A 3BZ UK
This is followed at the bottom of the page with:

ISBN x-xxxx-xxxx-x
Revised [year] — [First] Printing {Month, Year}
Printed in [country]."

BERNADOTTE BOOKS

1994 Statement: "We use a number string: 1, 2, 3, 4, 5, etc. The lowest number showing indicates the printing."
2000 Statement: "We do not indicate editions or printings."

BERNARDS (PUBLISHERS), LTD. (UNITED KINGDOM)

1947 Statement: "Our bibliographical notices follow the usual English practice, namely:
"First printing will be identified:—
First published—
"Subsequent printings will be identified with the different number of impressions as follows:—
First published—
New Impression—."

BESS PRESS

1988 Statement: "We have no special identification method. The copyright date indicates the first printing. Subsequent editions are also recorded on the copyright page."
1993, 2000 Statements: *See* 1988 Statement

CORNELIA & MICHAEL BESSIE BOOKS

1988 Statement: Cornelia & Michael Bessie Books follow the practices of Harper & Row Publishers Inc., with an additional imprint logo on the title page.
See 1988 Statement of Harper & Row, Publishers, Inc.

BETTER HOMES AND GARDENS BOOKS

1981 Statement: "Better Homes and Gardens Books clearly designates first printings of its first editions with the words 'First Edition. First Printing.' on the book's copyright page (usually the title page or the page following it). Subsequent editions and/or printings are similarly designated, i.e. 'First Edition. Fourth Printing.' or 'Sixth Edition. First Printing.' "
1988 Statement: *See* 1981 Statement
1994 Statement: *See* 1994 Statement of Meredith Books

BEYNCH PRESS PUBLISHING COMPANY

2000 Statement: "We identify the first printing of a first edition by no statement. We start with 'second printing,' 'third printing'; if it is NOT indicated, it is the first printing."

BEYOND WORDS PUBLISHING INC

2001 Statement: "We do not identify a first printing, but we do identify new editions."

THE BHAKTIVEDANTA BOOK TRUST
1976 Statement: "The printing history of our books is printed on the copyright page of each book. If a book says First Printing, then it is a First Edition. There is no indication as to when a book becomes a Second Edition."
1981 Statement: "The printing history of our books is printed on the copyright page of each book. If a book says First Printing, then it is a First Edition. Subsequent printings are always indicated on the copyright page and it is assumed that each new printing involves correcting of any mistakes."
1989, 2000 Statements: *See* 1981 Statement

BICYCLE BOOKS
(Osceola, Wisconsin)
2001 Statement: *See* 2001 Statement of Motorbooks International

BICYCLE BOOKS, INC.
1993 Statement: "We do not designate First Edition. Instead, all subsequent editions and printings are identified by their printing or edition number. (i.e. if doesn't say anything else, it is the first printing of the first edition)."
2001 Statement: *See* 2001 Statement of Van der Plas Publications

THE BIELER PRESS
2000 Statement: "The Bieler Press prints and publishes limited editions, hence no edition identification is provided other than an indication, in the colophon, of its copy limitation. On occasion we have reprinted certain titles for other publishers and, in several instances, reprinted a previous title under our imprint and, in several instances, reprinted a previous title under our imprint and, [in] these cases, this information is provided in the colophon. We have also had trade editions produced of several limited edition titles. Again precedence is provided in the colophon.

"Under our imprint, Bieler Press Monographs, we publish books that are intended to run into several printings and, hopefully, into several editions. Here, first printing of an initial edition is not indicated. Subsequent printings or edition states, however, are clearly indicated as such on the legal or copyright page."

BIELER PRESS MONOGRAPHS
2000 Statement: *See* 2000 Statement of The Bieler Press

BIG SKY
1976 Statement: "I simply say 'First Edition.' "

BIGWATER PUBLISHING
1995 Statement: "A first printing is designated by numbers at the bottom of the copyright page. No designation is made regarding edition. The number farthest to the right shows the printing, with the number farthest to the left showing the year of publication."
2001 Statement: *See* 1995 Statement

BINATIONAL PRESS
2000 Statement: *See* 2000 Statement of San Diego State University Press

BINFORD & MORT

1976 Statement: "When first publishing under the imprint of Metropolitan Press, our company used the star method to indicate the number of the printing—though when changes in text were made, the book was then stated to be a second edition, etc. One star indicated the first reprinting; two stars, the second, and so on.

"Under Binfords & Mort, we have some books listed under the name of the Metropolitan Press books. Now, under Binford & Mort, the printing or edition is so indicated on the copyright page."

1981, 1988, 1993, 2000 Statements: *See* 1976 Statement

BINFORDS & MORT, PUBLISHERS

1947 Statement: "I am afraid that you won't find any mark noting many of our second printings. This was especially true during the war when we couldn't run even one printing all with the same colored cloth for the cover. *Paul Bunyan the Work Giant* was marked with an 'X' as each different printing was made. The first run of that was numbered.

"Our earlier books were published under the firm name of Metropolitan Press."

See also Binford & Mort

JOSEPH J. BINNS, PUBLISHER

1988 Statement: "All first editions are so marked. Other editions, i.e., 2nd, 3rd, etc., are so indicated."

BIRCH BROOK PRESS

1993 Statement: "Birch Brook Press indicates on its copyright page . . . that the publication is a First Edition, though in the case of anthologies using reprinted materials we may not indicate First Edition; and in books limited to a few hundred copies, in a letterpress edition, we may indicate Limited Edition instead of First Edition. Birch Brook Press has been in operation since 1982."

2001 Statement: "On first printings, we indicate First Edition. On subsequent printings, we indicate Second Printing, plus the year."

BIRCH LANE PRESS

1995 Statement: *See* 1995 Statement of Carol Publishing Group

BIRKHÄUSER BOSTON

1993 Statement: "Birkhäuser has adopted the policy of not identifying first editions as such. Subsequent editions carry appropriate identification on the title page as 'second, third, revised and corrected,' or whatever is appropriate.

"The printing number of a given edition is identified by the notation at the bottom of the copyright page '9 8 7 6 5 4 3 2 1' with the last number dropped for subsequent printings.

"This policy has been in effect since the founding of Birkhäuser Boston in 1979."

2000 Statement: *See* 1993 Statement

BIRNBAUM GUIDES
1993 Statement: *See* 1993 Statement of HarperCollins Publishers

BISON BOOKS
1988, 2000 Statements: *See* 1988 Statement of University of Nebraska Press

BITS PRESS
1988 Statement: "Our books—from 1974 to date—are all first editions (and first printings). Should we ever have cause to reprint, the copyright page will show 2d Printing or (if there are changes in the text) 2d Edition, and so on.

"In the cases of a few limited editions (e.g., John Updike, *Five Poems*, 1978) books have been published in two states (e.g., on handmade and on machine-made paper, or in somewhat different bindings) as noted in the colophons. These are all, nonetheless, properly first editions also."

1993 Statement: *See* 1988 Statement

2001 Statement: "With the death of its editor, Robert Wallace, in 1999, Bits Press has suspended publication and is unlikely to resume. This [1988] statement accurately represents Bits' practice throughout its publications."

BITTERSWEET PUBLISHING COMPANY
2001 Statement: "We identify the first printing of a first edition by the statement 'First Printing' followed by the number of copies. This appears on the copyright page."

H. BITTNER AND COMPANY
1947 Statement: "So far, we have not published any second editions."

BKMK PRESS, UNIVERSITY OF MISSOURI-KANSAS CITY
2001 Statement: "We identify the printing by a row of Arabic numerals in descending order, with the number furthest right indicating the printing. In the past, we have indicated second printings followed by the year of second printing. Our editions are assumed to be first editions unless otherwise indicated on copyright page.

"Wallaroo Books, an imprint, also uses Arabic numerals on the copyright page to indicate printing."

A. & C. BLACK, LTD. (UNITED KINGDOM)
1928 Statement: "Subsequent editions and impressions are so noted."

1947 Statement: "*First Editions* of our publications have the date on the title-page only; Second and Reprints have the date of reprint on the title-page and particulars of all printings in a bibliography on the verso.

"The same particulars would apply to the principal books which we publish over the imprint of S. W. Partridge & Co. Prior to our taking over the business, however, Messrs. Partridge had seldom printed a date on the title-pages of their Juveniles, and as some of these have now been selling for a number of years we are not always giving a bibliography on the reverse of title-pages."

Statement for 1960: Following is an example of the copyright page of a book published by A. and C. Black Ltd.

FIRST PUBLISHED IN ONE VOLUME 1955
BY A. AND C. BLACK LTD
4, 5 & 6 SOHO SQUARE LONDON WIV 6AD
THE BOOK IS ALSO AVAILABLE IN FOUR PARTS
FIRST EDITION 1955
SECOND EDITION 1963
THIRD EDITION 1966
REPRINTED 1968 AND 1970
REPRINTED 1972
ISBN 0 7136 0772 6
© 1966 A. & C. BLACK LTD"

A & C BLACK (PUBLISHERS) LIMITED
(UNITED KINGDOM)

1988 Statement: "Our current practice is to designate a first edition by the words 'First published (date)' on the biblio page."

1994 Statement: "There are a number of minor changes that have taken place since 1989, principally the addition of two new imprints, Adlard Coles Nautical and Christopher Helm.

"The basic copyright page layout remains unchanged except that the proper title of the company is A & C Black (Publishers) Ltd. The other imprints use the same form but they list themselves as subsidiaries of A & C Black."

2000 Statement: "A book is a first edition (first printing) if it bears the wording 'First published (date)' on the biblio page, without subsidiary wording such as 'Reprinted (date)' or 'This edition (date)'. All subsidiary imprints follow the same practice. The imprints Adlard Coles Nautical, Christopher Helm, and The Herbert Press are all current and our subsidiary is Christopher Helm (Publishers) Ltd."

ADAM AND CHARLES BLACK PUBLISHERS LIMITED
(UNITED KINGDOM)

1976 Statement: "We designate a first edition by the words 'First edition (date)' on the biblio page. Subsequently we add the words 'Reprinted (date)' or 'Second edition (date)' etc. These methods of identification do not differ from any previously used, and the same practice is followed by books published by John Baker and Dacre Press."

1981 Statement: *See* 1976 Statement

1988 Statement: *See* 1988 Statement of A & C Black (Publishers) Limited (United Kingdom)

BLACK BEAR PUBLICATIONS, USA

2000 Statement: "We do not have a special method for designating a first edition. The Copyright © Black Bear Publications designates both a first edition and a first printing. If subsequent printings are needed, these are identified by the addition of SECOND PRINTING under the copyright notice."

BLACK BELT PRESS

2000 Statement: "We identify the first printing of a first edition by the following number line: 5 4 3 2 1. The last number appearing on the right indicates which edition. The Starrhill Press imprint, for the most part, uses a longer number line but the same identification is true as for Black Belt Press. The Elliott & Clark imprint is no longer used. We are initiating a new imprint in January 2001 which is River City Press. We will use the same id process as listed above."

BLACK DRAGON

1988 Statement: *See* 1981 Statement of Panjandrum Books

BLACK FARM PRESS

(In 1941 combined with The Press of James A. Decker.)
1947 Statement: *See* The Press of James A. Decker

BLACK HERON PRESS

1994 Statement: "We do not identify first printings as a rule. Only in our first books did we."
2000 Statement: *See* 1994 Statement

BLACK ICE BOOKS

1994 Statement: *See* 1994 Statement of Fiction Collective Two
2000 Statement: *See* 2000 Statement of FC2/Black Ice Books

BLACK LACE (UNITED KINGDOM)

1994, 2000 Statements: *See* 1994 Statement of Virgin Publishing Ltd. (United Kingdom)

BLACK SPARROW PRESS

1976 Statement: "The copyright page of first printings carries no identifying notation, but first printings always have a colophon page in the back, and the title pages are in color.

"Reprints have the title page in black and white only, carry no colophon, and are identified as 'Second printing', 'Third printing', etc., on the copyright page.

"For further details see Seamus Cooney's *A Checklist of the First One Hundred Publications of the Black Sparrow Press* (Black Sparrow Press, Los Angeles, 1971), and its projected successor covering the first 250 titles."
1981 Statement: "The copyright page of first printings carries no identifying notation, but first printings always have a colophon page, and the title pages are in color.

"Reprints have the title page in black and white only, carry no colophon, and are identified as 'Second printing,' 'Third printing,' etc., on the copyright page.

"For further details see Seamus Cooney's *A Checklist of the First One Hundred Publications of the Black Sparrow Press* (Black Sparrow Press, Los Angeles, 1971), and its successor covering the first 300 titles, *A Bibliography of the Black Sparrow Press: 1966-1978* (1981)."

1988 Statement: *See* 1981 Statement
1995 Statement: "First printings of first editions are not designated on the copyright page. Title pages are printed in color.

"Later printings are designated on the copyright page. Title pages are printed in black only."
2001 Statement: *See* 1995 Statement

BLACK SQUIRREL BOOKS
1993 Statement: *See* 1981 Statement of Kent State University Press
2000 Statement: *See* 2000 Statement of Kent State University Press

BLACK SWAN (UNITED KINGDOM)
2001 Statement: *See* 2001 Statement of Transworld Publishers Ltd (United Kingdom)

BLACK SWAN BOOKS LTD.
1988 Statement: "Black Swan Books designates a first printing with the following statement which appears on the verso of the titlepage: 'First edition.' Subsequent printings do not have any designation given, nor does, of course, the above statement appear. First printings of a revised edition are designated 'Revised edition.'

"This method of designation has been used by us from the start of our press and the publication of its first book in 1980."
1993 Statement: *See* 1988 Statement

BLACK THISTLE PRESS
2000 Statement: "We say nothing. We identify the 2nd printing on the copyright page, by 'Second printing.' "

BLACK TIE PRESS
1993 Statement: "We designate first editions by inserting 'First Edition' on the bottom of the copyright page of each new title."

BLACKBERRY
1976 Statement: "All Blackberry books are limited first editions. Any future reprint will, of course, be noted in the book next to the copyright notice."

BLACKIE & SON, LTD. (UNITED KINGDOM)
1928 Statement: *See* 1937 Statement of Blackie & Son, Limited (United Kingdom)

BLACKIE & SON, LIMITED (UNITED KINGDOM)
1937 Statement: "It is not possible to give a general rule for the detecting of our first editions.

"In the first editions of our more recent educational works and general publications (exclusive of Reward or Story Books) the date appears on the title-page, and if it is a new edition, it is so stated. The dates of subsequent reprints are noted on the back of the title-page.

"We are afraid it is impossible to say just what date we started using this present method."

1947 Statement: *See* 1937 Statement
Statement for 1960: *See* 1976 Statement of Blackie and Son Limited (United Kingdom)

BLACKIE AND SON LIMITED (UNITED KINGDOM)

1976 Statement: "Since the 1957 Copyright Act our imprint or biblio pages have contained the words, e.g.

© John Hume 1974

First published 1974

and this style may be taken to identify a first edition. Subsequent editions would have this information plus the date of the subsequent edition (be it a reprint, revision or new edition)."
1981 Statement: "The [1976] statement is still accurate and the same practice is followed by all our imprints."
1988 Statement: *See* 1981 Statement

BLACKSTAFF PRESS LTD. (NORTHERN IRELAND)

1981 Statement: "Our current practice in designating editions is to give the copyright symbol, the name of the copyright holder and the date of first printing on the imprint page. In subsequent reprintings, if the material is unaltered, this information remains the same i.e. we do not indicate second or third printings. We do however indicate a new (i.e. altered, enlarged or cut) edition by saying after the copyright line something like 'second edition' or 'new enlarged edition' etc.

"This company has only one imprint, i.e. Blackstaff Press."
1988 Statement: "Our current practice in designating editions is to give the copyright symbol, the name of the copyright holder and the first date of printing. In subsequent reprintings, if the material is unaltered, the information on the copyright line remains the same but we do insert a new line which indicates reprint dates (e.g. Reprinted 1985, 1986, 1987 etc.). We also indicate a new (i.e. altered, enlarged or cut) edition by adding the new date to the copyright lines *as well as* inserting a new line which indicates the new edition (e.g. 'second edition' or 'new enlarged edition' etc.) together with the relevant date.

"This company has only one imprint, i.e. Blackstaff Press."
1994, 2001 Statements: *See* 1988 Statement

BASIL BLACKWELL (UNITED KINGDOM)

1928 Statement: "Our first editions are published without any reference on the title page whatever; all subsequent editions bear the fact on the back of the title page."
1937, 1947 Statements: *See* 1928 Statement
See also Basil Blackwell and Mott, Ltd. (United Kingdom)

BASIL BLACKWELL LIMITED (UNITED KINGDOM)

1988 Statement: "Ten years ago this company was called 'Basil Blackwell and Mott Limited.' About eight years ago it changed its name to 'Basil

Blackwell Publisher Limited.' Finally, four years ago it changed its name to 'Basil Blackwell Limited.' No further changes are planned at present!

"It is certainly our practice to print full copyright and printing history details on the verso of the title page.

"Shakespeare Head Press is an imprint of this company."

2000 Statement: *See* 1988 Statement

See also Basil Blackwell and Mott Limited (United Kingdom)

BASIL BLACKWELL PUBLISHER LIMITED (UNITED KINGDOM)

1988 Statement: *See* 1988 Statement of Basil Blackwell Limited (United Kingdom)

BASIL BLACKWELL AND MOTT, LTD. (UNITED KINGDOM)

1976 Statement: "Before the Universal Copyright Convention of 1957 it was our practice to put the date of publication on either the recto or verso of the title page, but occasionally for reasons of space it was sometimes transferred to the back of the book, but only rarely. Since 1957 of course the international copyright mark and the date of publication appear on the verso of the title page."

1981 Statement: *See* 1976 Statement

1988 Statement: *See* 1988 Statement of Basil Blackwell Limited (United Kingdom)

BLACKWELL SCIENCE, INC

2000 Statement: *See* 2000 Statement of Blackwell Science Ltd (United Kingdom)

BLACKWELL SCIENCE (AUSTRALIA)

1994 Statement: *See* 1976 Statement of Blackwell Scientific Publications Ltd (United Kingdom)

2001 Statement: *See* 2001 Statement of Blackwell Science Asia (United Kingdom)

BLACKWELL SCIENCE ASIA (UNITED KINGDOM)

2001 Statement: "Blackwell Scientific Publications changed its name to Blackwell Science Asia in 1995. [We] do still follow the practice as outlined in [the 1976] Statement of Blackwell Scientific Publications Ltd (United Kingdom)."

BLACKWELL SCIENCE LTD (UNITED KINGDOM)

2000 Statement: "The company has changed names and is now known as Blackwell Science Ltd and Blackwell Science Inc. We have two additional imprints, Fishing News Books and Iowa State University Press that follow the same practice." *See* 1994 Statement of Blackwell Scientific Publications, Inc.

BLACKWELL SCIENTIFIC PUBLICATIONS, INC.
1994 Statement: *See* 1976 Statement of Blackwell Scientific Publications Ltd (United Kingdom)

BLACKWELL SCIENTIFIC PUBLICATIONS LTD (UNITED KINGDOM)
1976 Statement: "The first editions of our books are identifiable as such only by the absence of any reference to later editions on the title page, recto or verso."
1981, 1988, 1994 Statements: *See* 1976 Statement
2000 Statement: *See* 2000 Statement of Blackwell Science Asia (United Kingdom)

WILLIAM BLACKWOOD & SONS, LTD. (UNITED KINGDOM)
1928 Statement: "Although we have no hard and fast rule, our general practice is to omit the notification of the first edition on the first issue of a book, the date of publication appearing below the imprint. Subsequent editions are notified accordingly."
1937, 1947 Statements: *See* 1928 Statement
1976 Statement: "In the case of a title published by William Blackwood & Sons Ltd., the first edition bears the year of publication below the imprint on the title page. For a reprint the year is removed, and below the copyright note on the verso of the title page, the following note is added: 'Reprinted 19...' Subsequent reprints are recorded in the same way.

"I should stress that this is our current practice. In the past, especially with the large number of books published by the firm up to about 60 years ago, the system was not consistent. However, I think it is true to say that in the case of a reprint, the above notation, or something similar, was always used. Thus any book which does not bear a reprint note may be assumed to be a first edition. But there were possibly exceptions, and I believe in the early 19th century it was the fashion to attempt to 'establish' a new writer by claiming that his book was already in its second edition, whereas in fact it was only the first printing. The first book of John Gibson Lockhart, *Peter's Letters to His Kinsfolk*, was I think treated in such a way."
1981 Statement: "In the case of a title published by William Blackwood & Sons Ltd., the first edition bears the year of publication on the verso of the title page. For a reprint, the following note is added: 'Reprinted 19...' Subsequent reprints are recorded in the same way.

"We changed our method in January of [1981]."

JOHN F. BLAIR, PUBLISHER
1994 Statement: "We currently designate a first edition by inserting the edition number and year on the back of the title page. As far as I have been able to determine, this has been our practice since we were founded in 1954."
2000 Statement: *See* 1994 Statement

BLANDFORD PRESS, LTD. (UNITED KINGDOM)

1947 Statement: "It is rather difficult to give you any hard and fast ruling on how to identify the first printings of our books and to differentiate between them and subsequent printings. Whether we give any indications depends very largely on the type of book. With a technical or semi-technical volume we usually indicate the year of publication and the number of the edition. However, with certain general books it has not been possible to do that during recent years on account of paper restrictions, and shortage of materials, and frequently several printings are made, and we usually have no reason to differentiate between the first, second or third printing, and in certain instances would prefer not to.

"This company was established immediately after the first World War in 1919."

Statement for 1960: Following is an example of the relevant portion of the copyright page of a book in its first printing published by Blandford Press, Ltd., in 1960.

> First published in 1960
> © *Copyright 1960 by Blandford Press Ltd.*
> *16 West Central Street, London, W. C. 1*

1976 Statement: First editions are designated by the words: First published 19..

1981 Statement: "I give the wording as it appears in our publications: 'First published in the U.K. 19.. by Blandford Press Link House, West Street, Poole, Dorset, BH15 1LL Copyright © 19.. Blandford Books Ltd.' "

1988, 1994 Statements: *See* 1988 Statement of Cassell plc (United Kingdom)

GEOFFREY BLES, LTD. (UNITED KINGDOM)

1937 Statement: "Our practice is to give the date of the first edition of the book on the title page verso. Subsequent reprints and editions are noted under that, e.g.

FIRST PUBLISHED	FEBRUARY 1933
REPRINTED	MARCH 1933
REPRINTED	APRIL 1933"

1947 Statement: *See* 1937 Statement

BLIND BEGGAR PRESS, INC.

2000 Statement: "We do not identify first editions or first printings. If we do reprint a publication, we label it as 'Second Printing,' 'Third Printing,' etc. and we include the date for the first and current printings."

BLISS PUBLISHING COMPANY, INC.

2000 Statement: "We identify our first editions on the copyright page of each book."

BLOCH PUBLISHING CO., INC.

1947 Statement: "There is no special way to identify the first printings of our books, but we differentiate from the first printing by marking the second and subsequent printings to that effect on the copyright page. When a book is reprinted and revised or enlarged, mention of this is made."

BLOODAXE BOOKS (UNITED KINGDOM)
1988 Statement: "Bloodaxe Books designates a first edition as being 'first published in X year.'

"Editions after the first are indicated by adding 'second edition' and the year. We designate a title to be in its second edition if there have been changes to the text; otherwise we designate it a second impression.

"We do not designate the first printing. This is designated only for second and subsequent printings (which we designate as impressions).

"All markings are on the back of the title page."
2000 Statement: *See* 1988 Statement

BLUE DOLPHIN PUBLISHING INC.
1994 Statement: "We identify the first printings of a first edition by use of press run numbers at bottom of © page i.e. 8 7 6 5 4 3 2 1. A 'second' edition is clearly noted below the © line on © page. A first edition is therefore 'ipso facto.' "
2000 Statement: "We 'sometimes' list the month and year of first press run on the copyright page—(inconsistent)."

BLUE DOVE PRESS
1995 Statement: "[We] say 'First Edition' or 'First American Edition' on the back of the title page."
2000 Statement: " Our imprint, Radiant Summit is now called Laurel Creek Press. The [1995 Statement] is still our policy."

BLUE HERON PUBLISHING
2001 Statement: "We identify the first printing of a first edition by 'First Edition' [and] '9 8 7 6 5 4 3 2 1.' "

BLUE JEANS POETRY
2001 Statement: *See* 2001 Statement of Coda Publications

BLUE LIGHT BOOKS
2000 Statement: *See* 2000 Statement of The Academic & Arts Press

BLUE MOON BOOKS
2001 Statement: *See* 2001 Statement of Avalon Publishing Group Incorporated

BLUE MOUNTAIN ARTS
2001 Statement: *See* 2001 Statement of SPS Studios, Inc.

BLUE MOUNTAIN PRESS
2001 Statement: *See* 2001 Statement of SPS Studios, Inc.

BLUE NOTE PUBLICATIONS
2001 Statement: "We do not make any special identification of first editions. We do identify subsequent editions and reprints."

BLUE POPPY PRESS

1993 Statement: "We use the 10 9 8 7 6 5 4 3 2 1 designation on a first printing of any edition, deleting the 1, 2, 3, etc. in backwards order on subsequent printings. Edition numbers are clearly designated above the copyright on the copyright page. We have always used this method."

2000 Statement: *See* 1993 Statement

BLUE RIBBON BOOKS

2000 Statement: *See* 2000 Statement of Alpine Publications, Inc.

BLUE SKY MARKETING INC

2001 Statement: "We identify the first printing of a first edition by the number line '10 9 8 7 6 5 4 3 2 1.' First editions have not been identified on the book. Second editions are identified on the copyright page and sometimes on the cover."

BLUE STAR PRESS

2000 Statement: "We do not differentiate first edition."

BLUE UNICORN PRESS

2000 Statement: "We identify the first printing of a first edition by the statement 'First Printing, November 2000.' "

BLUE WIND PRESS

1976 Statement: "Undesignated book = first edition, first printing. The words 'Second Printing' mean 'of the first edition.' We sometimes use the following code:

77 78 79 80 5 4 3 2 1

As is it means first printing, 1977. If we do 2nd printing in 1977 we erase the '1.' If we do 2nd printing in 1978 we erase the '1' and the '77.' And so on. As a rule of thumb I consider a 'new' (2nd, 3rd &c) edition one in which the text has been altered. A new cover is simply a new printing to me. But a book retypeset for a new format (size) but with the text unaltered is also a new edition."

1981 Statement: *See* 1976 Statement

1988 Statement: "Undesignated book = first edition, first printing. The words 'Second Printing' mean 'of the first edition.' We sometimes use the following code:

77 78 79 80 5 4 3 2 1

As is it means first printing, 1977. If we do 2nd printing in 1977 we erase the '1.' If we do 2nd printing in 1978 we erase the '1' and the '77.' And so on. However, we didn't always bother. There are some subsequent printings which aren't noted in any way (except the colors on the cover are often slightly different). As a rule of thumb I consider a 'new' (2nd, 3rd &c) edition one in which the text has been altered. But a book retypeset for a new format (size) but with the text unaltered (or with the title page and cover changed) is also a new edition."

2001 Statement: *See* 1988 Statement

BMJ BOOKS (UNITED KINGDOM)

2001 Statement: "Our imprint statement has now changed. BMJ Books is the name for the British Medical Journal Publishing Group's book division, and the statements that appear on the imprint page of our books are now as follows:

"First edition statements:

First published in 2000

By BMJ Books, BMA House, Tavistock Square

"Subsequent editions carry the statement:

First published in 1995

By BMJ Books, BMA House, Tavistock Square,

First Edition 1995

Second edition 2001

"We are no longer distributors for the British Dental Journal Books. These are distributed by Macmillan."

BOA EDITIONS

1981 Statement: "First Editions published by BOA Editions are indicated in the following manner:

"The phrase 'First Edition' appears on the copyright page of the book and the colophon at the end of the book describes the limitations of the various sub-editions of each book, i.e., paper, cloth and specially bound, limited editions signed by the poet.

"Subsequent printings are then indicated on the copyright page: 'Second Printing,' 'Third Printing' etc., generally with a date included."

1993 Statement: "The phrase 'First Edition' appears on the copyright page of the book, in both cloth and paperback editions, since they are published simultaneously. When a sub-edition exists—such as specially bound, limited copies, numbered and signed by the poet—that information has usually been indicated in the colophon at the end of all editions of the title. Later printings have been indicated by, 'Second Printing,' etc.

"In 1993, BOA adopted a standardized system of indicating later printings, and the years of those printings, by using a digit line on the copyright page, i.e.: 96 95 94 93 10 9 8 7 6, although this system was occasionally used prior to 1993."

2000 Statement: *See* 1993 Statement

THE BOBBS-MERRILL COMPANY

1928 Statement: "We are not entirely consistent in our first edition attitude. Whenever we do mark a first edition the distinguishing mark is a bow and arrow at the bottom of the page on which appears the copyright line.

"However, not all of our first editions are marked."

1936 Statement: "We are consistent in our first edition attitude. We print the words 'First Edition' on the copyright page. All of our first editions are so marked."

1947 Statement: *See* 1936 Statement

BOBBS-MERRILL COMPANY, INC.
1981 Statement: "First editions are designated on copyright pages as first printing, second printing, etc."

THE BODLEY HEAD LIMITED (UNITED KINGDOM)
1976 Statement: A first edition is designated by the words: "First published 19.."
1981 Statement: "The only information I can add is that if the text has been published first in another country (say, in USA), we would then describe our first edition as 'first published in Great Britain 19XX.'

"In this case the date of first edition would be included in the copyright line above, on that page."
See also John Lane The Bodley Head, Ltd. (United Kingdom)
1988 Statement: *See* 1981 Statement
1994 Statement: "I'm afraid that we cannot help with your queries as the Bodley Head is no longer publishing."
2000 Statement: *See* 2000 Statement of The Random House Group Limited (United Kingdom)

BODLEY HEAD CHILDRENS BOOKS (UNITED KINGDOM)
2000 Statement: *See* 2000 Statement of The Random House Group Limited (United Kingdom)

BOLCHAZY-CARDUCCI PUBLISHERS
1988 Statement: "We do not indicate 'First Edition.' We use 'Reprint' or 'Second/Third Revised Edition.' "
1993, 2000 Statements: *See* 1988 Statement

THE BOLD STRUMMER LTD
1995 Statement: First printings are usually not so marked. Subsequent printings are usually noted.
2000 Statement: *See* 1995 Statement

ALBERT & CHARLES BONI INC.
1928 Statement: "We run a note on the copyright page of all our books indicating all subsequent printings after the first."
1937 Statement: *See* 1928 Statement

BONI & GAER, INC.
1947 Statement: "We do not put distinguishing marks in our first printings. However, all subsequent printings are marked and therefore it is safe for you to assume that one of our publications with no marks is a first printing."

BONI & LIVERIGHT
1928 Statement: "As a general rule we have no marking on the copyright page of our publications to show our first edition although on subsequent editions we print Second, Third, Fourth, Fifth, Sixth edition, etc. We have had one or two books with first edition marked on the copyright page but this is not our general practice."

1937 Statement: *(Became Horace Liveright, Inc; later, Liveright Publishing Corporation.) See* 1937 Statement of Liveright Publishing Corporation
1947 Statement: *See* 1947 Statement of Liveright Publishing Corporation.

BONUS BOOKS INC.

1994 Statement: "As a rule, Bonus Books, Inc., and Precept Press titles use a number line to indicate number and year of printing, e.g.

98 97 96 95 94 5 4 3 2 1

for the first printing of a book published in 1994.

"We do not identify first editions specifically, but any other edition of a title will be so identified on the title page, e.g. 'Second Edition' or 'Revised Edition.' "
2000 Statement: *See* 1994 Statement

THE BOOK GUILD LIMITED (UNITED KINGDOM)

1988 Statement: "The words 'first published in [date]' indicate that if nothing else is stated then the book is a first edition. This term is used on every one of our books.

"This is standard practice on all of our books and has been from the incept of this Company. We have two other imprints which are *Temple House Books* which is used for all our paper back editions, and *Seagull Books* which is used for specialized local works by prominent people."
1994, 2001 Statements: *See* 1988 Statement

BOOK PEDDLERS

2000 Statement: The first printing of a first edition is identified by the printing number on the verso page, 10 9 8 7 6 5 4 3 2 1.

"Our first printing is our first edition. [We] have always used this system. On occasion we have used '(preview edition)' when printing a small run to act as galleys."

BOOK PRESENTATIONS

1947 Statement: *See* 1947 Statement of Greystone Press

BOOKCRAFT

2000 Statement: *See* 2000 Statement of Deseret Book Company

BOOKMARKS PUBLICATIONS (UNITED KINGDOM)

2001 Statement: "We state 'First printing' on the copyright page."

BOOKS FOR ALL TIMES, INC.

2000 Statement: "We identify the first printing of a first edition by the following statement: First Edition. All other editions are specific: Revised Edition; 2nd Printing, etc."

BOOKS WEST SOUTHWEST

1995 Statement: "We have consistently noted first printing by placement of the year of publication on the title page. For three of our titles there was also a limited, numbered, signed edition issued simultaneously with the trade. Each of these limited editions is clearly designated with a colophon spelling out the limitation and including the signature(s). The existence of a limited edition is not noted in any way on the trade edition."

BOOKSELLERS
2000 Statement: *See* 2000 Statement of The Graduate Group

THE BOOKSTORE PRESS
1976 Statement: "We have no special methods."
1981, 1988 Statements: *See* 1976 Statement

BOREALIS BOOKS
2000 Statement: *See* 2000 Statement of Minnesota Historical Society Press

BOREAS PUBLISHING CO., LTD. (UNITED KINGDOM)
1947 Statement: "The only identification we are using for our publications is the little difference in design of our trade mark, which is on all of our publications.

"Underneath please find our trade mark: The Viking Ship of the first and every additional edition. The first edition has a stem-post at the end of the sail, but the other issues are without it."

1st Edition   Following Editions

THE BORGO PRESS
1981 Statement: "We state 'First Edition—Month, Year' on verso of title page. Subsequent printings are so indicated."

This method does not differ from any previously used. All imprints follow this same method of identification.

1988 Statement: "We state 'First Edition—Month, Year' on verso of title page. Subsequent printings are so indicated.

"Subsequent printings state: 'Second Printing—Month, Year'—or delete first edition statement altogether (no printing or edition statement).

"Reprints of books published originally by other companies state: 'First Borgo Edition—Month, Year.' "

1993 Statement: "Beginning in 1991, we adopted a new method of indicating editions and printings. The first edition of any book we publish will state 'FIRST EDITION' at the bottom of the verso of the title page; subsequent printings substitute the words 'SECOND PRINTING,' 'THIRD PRINTING,' etc. The imprint date on the title page is altered to reflect the year of publication of each printing. Subsequent editions (where some substantial portion of the interior text has been changed) state 'SECOND EDITION,' etc.; further printings of such editions state 'SECOND EDITION—SECOND PRINTING,' etc. Revised editions (where the text has been updated or reset but not substantially reworked) state 'REVISED EDITION,' etc. Facsimile reprints of books previously published by other companies state 'FIRST BORGO EDITION.'

"The Borgo Press now uses seven imprints: Brownstone Books; Burgess & Wickizer; An Emeritus Enterprise Book; R. Reginald, The Borgo Press (in a boxed imprint logo: the words 'R. Reginald' run above the words 'The Borgo Press'); Sidewinder; St. Willibrord's Press; Unicorn & Son, Publishers. Brownstone, Sidewinder (formerly Sun Dance Press), and St. Willibrord's were acquired by purchase. In addition, we use the label 'A Thaddeus Dikty Book' above the Borgo Press title page boxed logo to identify those books acquired and reprinted or reworked from Starmont House, Inc., when it ceased operations on March 1, 1993; the first of these was published last week. In every case, edition and printing information is uniformly presented in all of our books."

2000 Statement: "The Borgo Press went out of business in 1999. Our last book appeared 12/98."

A. BOROUGH BOOKS

2000 Statement: "Our first editions are marked on the copyright page by the year of the copyright only. Later editions state the year and month of each edition."

BOTTOM DOG PRESS

1994 Statement: "First editions not noted, but all subsequent editions are."
2000 Statement: *See* 1994 Statement

BOULEVARD

1995 Statement: *See* 1995 Statement of The Berkley Publishing Group
2000 Statement: *See* 2000 Statement of The Berkley Publishing Group

THOMAS BOUREGY & CO., INC.

1988 Statement: "At this time, the books in our Avalon line have only one edition. If, in the future we were to publish subsequent editions, we would indicate it on the copyright page."
1994 Statement: *See* 1988 Statement
2000 Statement: "Avalon Books which have additional printings beyond the first edition are so indicated on the copyright page."

R. R. BOWKER CO.

1947 Statement: "We have no definite system of specifically indicating first editions of our publications. First editions usually carry only the copyright notice; subsequent editions or printings usually carry information to this effect."
1989 Statement: "We have no definite system of specifically indicating first editions of our publications. First editions usually carry only the copyright notice; subsequent editions or printings may carry information to this effect."

R. R. BOWKER,
(A Division of Reed Elsevier)
1994, 2001 Statements: *See* 1989 Statement of R. R. Bowker Co.

BOXTREE LTD (UNITED KINGDOM)
2000 Statement: *See* 2000 Statement of Pan Macmillan (United Kingdom)

THE BOXWOOD PRESS
1976 Statement: "All of our publications are original (not reprints) and are first editions. Second editions and reprints are so marked."
1981 Statement: "All of our publications are original (not [from other publishers]) and are first editions. Second editions and reprints are so marked."
1988 Statement: *See* 1981 Statement

MARION BOYARS PUBLISHERS, INC.
1981 Statement: The first printing of a first edition is identified by the lack of any notation other than the copyright date. Printings after the first are identified as such.

MARION BOYARS PUBLISHERS LTD
(UNITED KINGDOM)
1994 Statement: The first printing of a first edition is identified by the line "First published in (country) in (date)."
2000 Statement: *See* 1994 Statement

BOYDELL & BREWER, LTD. (UNITED KINGDOM)
1988 Statement: "Our method is to indicate edition and printing on the copyright page with, e.g.:
> First published 1988 by The Boydell Press
> an imprint of Boydell & Brewer Ltd
> [followed by address]

"Our other imprint is D. S. Brewer and we also publish volumes for other organizations such as The Royal Historical Society, The Suffolk Records Society and The Lincoln Record Society; the same method of designation is used for all of these. Absence of a printing statement should indicate first printing, as the reprint history and further edition details are updated at subsequent printings, e.g.:
> Reprinted 1985, 1987
> Second edition 1988

"We are currently tightening up our procedures for including reprint history on the copyright page. To date, absence of reprint details cannot be taken as a wholly reliable indication of first printing."
1994 Statement: "Broadly speaking our practice remains unchanged, except that our copyright-page wording for books published under two imprints (The Boydell Press and D.S. Brewer) has evolved slightly:
From 1989 we stated:
> First published 1989 by The Boydell Press, Woodbridge
> or

First published 1989 by D.S. Brewer, Cambridge
and further down the page we stated:
> The Boydell Press is an imprint of Boydell & Brewer Ltd [followed by our addresses]
> or
> D.S. Brewer is an imprint of Boydell & Brewer Ltd [followed by our address]

"From 1993 we very slightly amended the wording and layout of the first publication statement to:
> First published 1993
> The Boydell Press, Woodbridge
> or
> First published 1993
> D.S. Brewer, Cambridge."

THE BOYDELL PRESS (UNITED KINGDOM)
1988, 1994 Statements: *See* 1988, 1994 Statements of Boydell & Brewer, Ltd. (United Kingdom)

BOYDS MILLS PRESS
1995 Statement: "Boyds Mills Press designates first printing by the numerals 10 9 8 7 6 5 4 3 2 1. For the second printing, the numeral 1 is removed; for the third printing, the numeral 2 is removed, and so on. First editions are labeled as such. This policy also applies to our poetry imprint, Wordsong/Boyds Mills Press. Boyds Mills Press was incorporated in 1990; this policy was put into effect for the Fall 1992 season."
2000 Statement: *See* 1995 Statement

BOYS TOWN PRESS
2000 Statement: "[There is] no identification of first editions published before 1998. In 1998 and after, first editions can be identified by the number line 10 9 8 7 6 5 4 3 2 1 (on the copyright page)."

BRADFORD BOOKS
2000 Statement: *See* 2000 Statement of The MIT Press

THE BRADFORD PRESS
2000 Statement: *See* 2000 Statement of Toad Hall, Inc.

BRADT PUBLICATIONS (UNITED KINGDOM)
1988 Statement: "First edition copyright [author's name] [date]. Subsequent editions: Second edition [date].

"I've been erratic in applying the above rules: one fourth edition went in as copyright Hilary Bradt 1987 with no mention of earlier editions (1974, 1976, 1980). This provoked a reviewer into writing 'Any book which goes into four editions in one year must be worth buying.' I'm endeavoring to be more accurate now."
1994 Statement: "For the last five years all new editions have had the following:

'First published in 199? by Bradt Publications'
or
'First published in 199? by Bradt Publications . . . and The Globe Pequot Press.' "
2000 Statement: *See* 2000 Statement of Bradt Travel Guides (United Kingdom)

BRADT TRAVEL GUIDES (UNITED KINGDOM)
2000 Statement: "With immediate effect, all Bradt guides will have the following: First published in 2000 by 'Bradt Travel Guides'. Please be advised that Bradt Publications has changed its name to Bradt Travel Guides."

ALLEN D. BRAGDON PUBLISHERS, INC.
1993 Statement: "We do not specify a first edition but we do state 'Second edition' or 'revised edition' with copyright notice if a new printing includes at least 15% revision. We do not otherwise indicate the sequence of printings."
2001 Statement: "We do not specify a first edition but we do state 'Second edition' or 'revised edition' with copyright notice if a new printing includes at least 15% revision. We do indicate the sequence of printings with numbers 10 to 1, with last digit removed at each new printing. Brainwaves Books is a new imprint."

BRAINWAVES BOOKS
2001 Statement: *See* 2001 Statement of Allen D. Bragdon Publishers, Inc.

BRANCH REDD BOOKS
2000 Statement: "Varies. Sometimes by identification of 'First Edition' (and number of copies) on colophon page, sometimes not. [We are] a small press specializing in poetry editions . . . of under 500 copies and . . . have never done a second edition . . . . Sometimes joint ventures entail a difference on the copyright/colophon page."

BRANDEIS UNIVERSITY PRESS
1988, 1993 Statements: *See* 1988 Statement of University Press of New England

THE BRANDEN PRESS, INCORPORATED
1976 Statement: "We do not normally designate a first edition of a book unless it is a limited edition. In this case, the details of the limited edition are explained in some detail.
"On the other hand, we frequently indicate on the copyright page the second edition and so forth after the first printing."
1981 Statement: *See* 1976 Statement
1988 Statement: "For the most part, we specify new editions and/or printing on the copyright page."
1993 Statement: *See* 1988 Statement

BRANDYLANE PUBLISHERS, INC.
2000 Statement: "Sorry, we do not identify first editions."

BRANDYWYNE BOOKS
1988 Statement: *See* 1988 Statement of Underwood-Miller

CHARLES T. BRANFORD CO.
1949 Statement: "Our system is simple. The first printing has no particular markings, but subsequent printings are marked, e.g., 'second printing' and the date."

BRASON-SARGAR PUBLICATIONS
2000 Statement: "We identify the first printing of a first edition by the following statement: On the reverse of the title page (on the copyright page) under the Library of Congress Catalog number, is a series of numbers:

"We identify the first printing of a first edition by the following number line:

0 9 8 7 6 5 4 3 2 1 indicates a first printing/first edition.

10 9 8 7 6 5 4 3 2 1 indicates a first printing/first edition.

"It is the number to the right of the series which is the indicator. For example:

10 9 8 7 6 5 4 indicates a fourth printing.

12 11 10 9 8 7 6 5 indicates a fifth printing."

BRASSEY'S INC.
2001 Statement: "Brassey's (US) Inc. changed to Brassey's, Inc. effective 1999. Previously, it was Batsford Brassey, Inc. The [1981 Statement of Macmillan Publishing Co., Inc.] is still correct." *See also* 1993 Statement of Macmillan Publishing Co., Inc.

BRASSEY'S (US) INC.
1993 Statement: *See* 1993 Statement of Macmillan, Inc.
2001 Statement: *See* 2001 Statement of Brassey's Inc.

A KAREN AND MICHAEL BRAZILLER BOOK
2000 Statement: *See* 2000 Statement of Persea Books

BRB PUBLICATIONS, INC
2000 Statement: "We . . . do not designate 1st Edition or First Printing."

NICHOLAS BREALEY PUBLISHING
2001 Statement: "We do not identify a first printing; we do identify subsequent printings."

BRENTANO'S
(Discontinued publishing in 1933.)
1928 Statement: "Up to the end of 1927 all books published by this company had no edition printed on them unless they reached a second edition. This information would be on the back of the title. From January 1st 1928 the words 'First Printed 1928' were substituted and if the book reached a second edition the words 'second impression April 1928 (or . . .).' "

1933 Statement: *See* 1928 Statement

BRENTANO'S, LTD. (UNITED KINGDOM)
(This English house discontinued by Brentano's in 1933.)
1928, 1933 Statements: *See* 1928 Statement of Brentano's

BRETHERICKS
2000 Statement: *See* 2000 Statement of Butterworth-Heinemann

BRETHERICKS (UNITED KINGDOM)
2000 Statement: *See* 2000 Statement of Butterworth-Heinemann (United Kingdom)

BRETHREN PRESS
2000 Statement: "We do not specifically identify first editions, but we indicate second or revised editions on the copyright page. For the first printing of a first edition (and subsequent printings), we use the following number line: 00 99 98 97 96 5 4 3 2 1. This method was adopted in 1992."

D. S. BREWER (UNITED KINGDOM)
1988, 1994 Statements: *See* 1988, 1994 Statements of Boydell & Brewer, Ltd. (United Kingdom)

BREWER & WARREN
(Succeeded Payson Clarke, Ltd, on Jan. 1, 1930. Became Brewer, Warren and Putnam, Inc., in autumn of 1931. Out of business prior to 1937.)
1937 Statement: "We do not put the actual words 'first edition' on the reverse of the title page for the first edition but when we go into the second printing we say 'first printing such and such a date,' 'second printing such and such a date,' therefore, all copies of a book which do not carry such designation may be taken as being 'firsts.' "

BREWER, WARREN AND PUTNAM, INC.
(Succeeded Brewer and Warren in autumn of 1931. Firm was dissolved on December 8, 1932, and publications were taken over by Harcourt, Brace and Co., Inc.)
1937 Statement (by the former company president): "We did not put the actual words 'first edition' on the reverse of the title page for the first edition but when we went into the second printing we said 'first printing such and such a date,' 'second printing such and such a date,' therefore all copies of a book which do not carry such designation may be taken as being 'firsts.' "

BREWIN BOOKS (UNITED KINGDOM)
1994 Statement: "Until about five years ago, we published under the imprint K.A.F. Brewin Books, and our earlier titles carried this imprint, plus the place name of Studley on the title page together with our logo which consists of the letters KAFB superimposed on an antiquarian book . . . . Our current practice is to run the imprint in shortened form 'Brewin Books' together with logo but without place name on the title page. Occasionally only the logo has been used on the title page. It has always been our practice to show a complete

printing and publishing history on the verso of the title page. Our versos also carry details of copyright, ISBNs, and bibliographic details of typesetting, type face, printer and binder."

2000 Statement: "I can confirm that . . . we still use the same practise for identifying editions as indicated in [the 1994 Statement]. Please note that we are now incorporated as a limited company and our correct trading style is 'Brewin Books Limited.' This does not affect imprint in any way."

K.A.F. BREWIN BOOKS (UNITED KINGDOM)
See Brewin Books (United Kingdom)

BRICK ROW PUBLISHING COMPANY LIMITED (NEW ZEALAND)
1994 Statement: "If we publish a book in association with an overseas publisher we indicate:

First published in New Zealand
by Brick Row Publishing Company Ltd
199_.

"It was decided at the beginning of 1994 to indicate 'First Edition' on all subsequent work which we originate—except journals or serial publications."

BRICKHOUSE BOOKS, INC.
2000 Statement: "All our editions are 'first,' i.e. one-time only, with a few exceptions. In those cases, the subsequent editions indicate that they are 2nd, 3rd, etc."

BRIDGE PUBLICATIONS, INC.
1995 Statement: The first printing of a first edition is indicated by the number line 10 9 8 7 6 5 4 3 2 1. The lowest number showing indicates the printing. "First Edition" is also stated.
2000 Statement: *See* 1995 Statement

BRIDGEPOINT
2000 Statement: *See* 2000 Statement of Baker Book House

BRIGHT MOUNTAIN BOOKS, INC.
1993 Statement: "We do not have any way of distinguishing first editions at this time . . . . Aside from the copyright notice, there is no way of distinguishing the first [edition] from the second."
2000 Statement: "We do not have any way of distinguishing first editions. Subsequent printings do not carry publishing history, but revised editions are so noted on the copyright page."

BRIGHTON PUBLICATIONS, INC.
2000 Statement: "On the copyright page we print the words 'First Edition'. When a book is revised it is noted on the copyright page."

BRIMAX (UNITED KINGDOM)
1989 Statement: *See* 1989 Statement of The Octopus Publishing Group PLC (United Kingdom)

BRISTOL CLASSICAL PRESS (UNITED KINGDOM)
2000 Statement: *See* 2000 Statement of Gerald Duckworth and Company Ltd. (United Kingdom)

BRISTOL PUBLISHING ENTERPRISES INC
2000 Statement: "We do not identify first printings as such at all. We never have, under current ownership."

THE BRITISH ACADEMY (UNITED KINGDOM)
1988 Statement: "An impression is likely to be the first printing of the first edition if there is no mention of succeeding printings/editions on the copyright page (though I know of one or two unfortunate exceptions)."
2000 Statement: *See* 1988 Statement

BRITISH BROADCASTING CORPORATION (UNITED KINGDOM)
1988 Statement: *See* 1988 Statement of BBC Enterprises Limited (United Kingdom)

BRITISH DENTAL JOURNAL (UNITED KINGDOM)
1988 Statement: *See* 1988 Statement of British Medical Journal (United Kingdom)
2001 Statement: *See* 2001 Statement of BMJ Books (United Kingdom)

THE BRITISH LIBRARY (UNITED KINGDOM)
1988 Statement: "We give all bibliographical information about our books on the title verso page. Normally we would say 'first published 1988,' or similar, and usually a copyright statement will include the copyright date, i.e., © 1988 The British Library Board. For subsequent editions we state 'reprinted 1988,' or similar."
1994, 2000 Statements: *See* 1988 Statement

BRITISH MEDICAL ASSOCIATION (UNITED KINGDOM)
1988 Statement: *See* 1988 Statement of British Medical Journal (United Kingdom)

BRITISH MEDICAL JOURNAL (UNITED KINGDOM)
1988 Statement: "British Medical Journal books carry the statement:
British Medical Journal 1988
"Subsequent printings or editions carry the statement:
British Medical Journal, 1983, 1988

....
....

First edition 1983
Second impression (with corrections) 1985
Second edition November 1988

"British Medical Association books carry the statement:
British Medical Association 1988
First Printed July 1988
"British Dental Journal books carry the statement:
Published by the British Dental Association
64 Wimpole Street, London W1M 8AL
Papers from the
British Dental Journal
March 19 to June 25, 1988
Copyright British Dental Journal, 1988"
2001 Statement: *See* 2001 Statement of BMJ Books (United Kingdom)

BRITISH MUSEUM (NATURAL HISTORY) (UNITED KINGDOM)

1988 Statement: "It is our practice to include the following on the title verso:
First published . . . (date)
British Museum (Natural History),
Cromwell Road, London SW7 5BD
"This holds good for all our titles."

BRITISH MUSEUM PRESS (UNITED KINGDOM)

1994 Statement: "British Museum Press was created as a division of British Museum Publications Ltd in 1991 and we have used this name as our imprint since then.

"The 1988 statement [of British Museum Publications Ltd (United Kingdom)] still stands, but I would add that where substantive changes have been made we specify revised or 2nd or 3rd edition etc., as appropriate."
2001 Statement: *See* 2001 Statement of The British Museum Press (United Kingdom)

THE BRITISH MUSEUM PRESS (UNITED KINGDOM)

2001 Statement: "The imprint The British Museum Press replaced British Museum Press from the end of 2000.

"Otherwise, the 1994 Statement [of British Museum Press (United Kingdom)] still stands, except that the name British Museum Publications Ltd was itself changed in 1995, since when the Press has been a division of The British Museum Company Ltd; also, our first editions have since 1995 included the words 'First published' and the date of publication."

BRITISH MUSEUM PUBLICATIONS, LTD. (UNITED KINGDOM)

1988 Statement: "Our first editions bear only the copyright date. Subsequent reprintings bear 2nd (or 3rd) impressions with the date or reprinted with the date. This practice, or something very similar, has been in force since the Company was formed in 1973. When reprinting we would normally take the opportunity of making any necessary alterations."
1994 Statement: *See* 1994 Statement of British Museum Press (United Kingdom)

BRITISH YEARBOOKS (UNITED KINGDOM)

1947 Statement: "All Yearbooks published are annual and are marked as such, only in the case of second and third impressions in the same year are these facts recorded in the Prelims."

BROADMAN & HOLMAN PUBLISHERS

1994 Statement: "We do not identify printings."

2000 Statement: "In 1995 [we began] identifying printings."

BROADMAN PRESS

1988 Statement: "We do not identify printings."

(Changed its name to Broadman & Holman Publishers in June, 1993.)

BROADSIDE PRESS

1989 Statement: "Example of 1st Printing:

First Edition

First Printing

Copyright © 1988 by *author's name*

"Example of 2nd Printing:

Copyright © 1973 by *author's name*

First Printing, November 1973

Second Printing, February 1976

"This method was adopted in 1965."

BROCKHAMPTON PRESS (UNITED KINGDOM)

(Name changed to Hodder & Stoughton Children's Books sometime prior to 1976.)

1976 Statement: *See* 1976 Statement of Hodder & Stoughton Limited (United Kingdom)

BROKEN BOULDER PRESS

2000 Statement: "We don't identify first editions or first printings. Second and subsequent editions are identified by the words 'Second Edition,' 'Third Edition,' etc. and the date, underneath the copyright notice; similarly for second and subsequent printings of a given edition."

BROKEN RIFLE PRESS

2000 Statement: "Broken Rifle Press uses the following format: 'First Printing, Year,' 'Second Printing, Year,' etc."

BROMPTON BOOKS

1993 Statement: "Brompton Books does not designate the first edition of our books. Subsequent printings are differentiated by using the phrase 'second printing, month, year etc.' "

BROMPTON PUBLICATIONS (UNITED KINGDOM)

1994, 2000 Statements: *See* 1994 Statement of S.B. Publications (United Kingdom)

THE BRONX COUNTY HISTORICAL SOCIETY

1988 Statement: "A first edition is noted in the Foreword or Preface. Any subsequent editions are noted on the title page."

1993, 2000 Statements: *See* 1988 Statement

BROODING HERON PRESS

1995 Statement: "Brooding Heron Press books are never marked in any way to overtly designate that they are first editions; this is because our current policy is to do *only* first editions. We have no plans to reprint any of our titles. Each of our books has a colophon detailing the particulars of how and when the book was printed. Should we ever change our minds and do a reprinting . . . we would so indicate this fact on the copyright page (i.e., 'Second Printing') and on the colophon page (some remark explaining the reason for the second printing)."

2000 Statement: *See* 1995 Statement

BROOK FARM BOOKS

2000 Statement: "We do not differentiate first editions except by elimination. All subsequent printings specify revised edition, 2nd edition, etc."

BROOKE HOUSE PUBLISHERS, INC.

1976 Statement: "Brooke House books are intended to carry (as an indication of the number of the printing rather than as any indication of edition) a number on the copyright page consisting of an ascending series of ten figures and a descending series of ten figures. The number on the left is the last digit of the year of the printing; the number on the right is the number of the printing. If a printing is made in the same year as the one just before, only the number on the right is deleted in the new printing. E.g., 7890109876 would indicate a 6th printing in 1977. If a 7th printing were to be made, the 6 would be deleted.—A second *edition* would carry some indication, e.g., Revised Edition, Second Edition, etc.; again on the copyright page."

THE BROOKINGS INSTITUTION

1976 Statement: "We do not explicitly identify first editions, because with few exceptions we publish only first editions. We designate printings by a string of numbers on the copyright page, one of which is deleted whenever the book is reprinted, so that the lowest surviving number indicates the printing in hand. Whenever we do publish revised, second, or third, etc., editions, we so label them on the title page, jacket, cover, stamping die, and foreword; successive printings are indicated as I describe above. Instead of the row of numbers we used until [about 1968] the device exemplified by phrases such as 'Second Printing March 1965.' Original printings were not so designated."

1981, 1988, 1993 Statements: *See* 1976 Statement

2000 Statement: *See* 2000 Statement of Brookings Institution Press

BROOKINGS INSTITUTION PRESS

2000 Statement: *See* 1976 Statement of The Brookings Institution. "Our name was changed/adopted [from The Brookings Institution] in 1996."

BROOKLYN BOTANIC GARDEN, INC.
1993 Statement: Subsequent printings are so indicated.
2000 Statement: *See* 1993 Statement

PAUL H BROOKES PUBLISHING CO
2000 Statement: "We don't distinguish first editions or first printings as such. Subsequent printings are identified on the copyright page by a statement to the effect: __th printing, (month), (year). Subsequent editions are numbered as such on a book's cover and title page. This is the only identification we have ever used."

BROOKS-COLE
2000 Statement: *See* 2000 Statement of The Wadsworth Group

BROUDE BROTHERS LIMITED
1993 Statement: "All of Broude Brothers' publications have been produced by offset lithography, and our approach to the definition of an edition therefore follows the concepts in use by descriptive bibliographers for dealing with non-letterpress material.

"We regard an edition as consisting of all copies reproduced from the same (or substantially the same) autography, engraving, and/or computer composition. Printings subsequent to the first may incorporate changes made to the camera copy used for the first printing, but all copies—whether or not they reflect such alterations—are considered as belonging to the same edition. A new edition is created only when we create new camera copy by re-autographing, re-engraving, or re-composing the entire—or almost the entire—work.

"We do not normally indicate when a second or subsequent printing contains alterations if the first printing has been issued under our imprint. If we are issuing a corrected reprint of a title first issued by another publisher, we normally so indicate."
2000 Statement: *See* 1993 Statement

BROWDER SPRINGS BOOKS
2000 Statement: "I've never had a book go into a 2nd printing."

JOHN BROWN BOOKS
2000 Statement: *See* 2000 Statement of Blue Heron Publishing

BROWN, SON & FERGUSON, LTD. (UNITED KINGDOM)
1976 Statement: "In the majority of our publications, on the bibliographical page is always printed either 'First Edition' or 'First Printed,' but in some of our older books which are non technical, and which have been running for 30 to 40 years, the original printing date has not been included."
1981, 1988, 1994, 2000 Statements: *See* 1976 Statement

BROWN THRASHER BOOKS
2000 Statement: *See* 2000 Statement of The University of Georgia Press

BROWN UNIVERSITY PRESS
1988, 1993 Statements: *See* 1988 Statement of University Press of New England

BROWNDEER PRESS
1995 Statement: *See* 1995 Statement of Harcourt Brace and Company

BROWNSTONE BOOKS
1993 Statement: *See* 1993 Statement of The Borgo Press
2000 Statement: *See* 2000 Statement of The Borgo Press

BRUCCOLI CLARK LAYMAN, INC.
1993 Statement: "When we publish a trade book, the First Printing is identified as such."

BRUCE PUBLISHING COMPANY
(Milwaukee, Wisconsin)
1937 Statement: "We follow no regular rule to indicate first editions of books. In the case of trade books, we usually indicate the second and subsequent printings by an appropriate line on the copyright page giving this information."
1947 Statement: *See* 1937 Statement

BRUCE PUBLISHING COMPANY
(St. Paul, Minnesota)
1937 Statement: "The words First printing, Second printing, et cetera, together with notation of the date of printing—7-21-36—are imprinted in 6 point type on the last page of the book in the lower left hand corner. This method has been in use in our printing plant since 1928."

BRUNNER/MAZEL, INC.
1995 Statement: The first printing of a first edition is indicated by the number line 10 9 8 7 6 5 4 3 2 1. The lowest number showing indicates the printing.

BRUNSWICK PUBLISHING
1988 Statement: "If there is any change in the text, the designation will be *Second Edition*; second or subsequent printing of that edition will carry the designation, e.g.: *Second Edition, Second Printing (and the months and the year)*."

BUCHAN PUBLICATIONS
1995 Statement: "We do not designate first printings in our books. We normally do not do 'second printings.' "

BUCKNELL UNIVERSITY PRESS
1976, 1981, 1988, 1993, 2000 Statements: *See* 1976 Statement of Associated University Presses

BUDDHIST STUDY CENTER PRESS
2000 Statement: "We have no policy on identifying first editions."

BUENA BOOKS
2000 Statement: *See* 2000 Statement of Horizon Books

BUGG BOOKS
1989 Statement: *See* 1989 Statement of Price/Stern/Sloan Publishers Inc.

BULFINCH PRESS
1995 Statement: *See* 1995 Statement of Little, Brown & Company
2000 Statement: *See* 2000 Statement of Little, Brown & Company

BULL RUN OF VERMONT, INC.
1995 Statement: "The copyright page of the first editions simply gives the year. The second printing states the first printing date along with Second printing, date, and either 'revised,' 'completely revised,' or nothing at all."
2001 Statement: *See* 1995 Statement

BUR OAK BOOKS
2000 Statement: *See* 2000 Statement of University of Iowa Press

BURD STREET PRESS
1994 Statement: *See* 1994 Statement of White Mane Publishing Co., Inc.

BUREAU OF ECONOMIC GEOLOGY
(The University of Texas at Austin)
1994 Statement: "As publishers of scholarly and technical works of relatively small press runs, we do not designate first printings as such. Usually we note the revised and/or reprinted works by listing the date of such changes on the cover or title page of the work."
2001 Statement: *See* 1994 Statement

BURFORD BOOKS
2000 Statement: "10 9 8 7 6 5 4 3 2 1. If the '1' appears, it's a first edition."

BURGESS & WICKIZER
1993 Statement: *See* 1993 Statement of The Borgo Press
2000 Statement: *See* 2000 Statement of The Borgo Press

BURKE PUBLISHING COMPANY, LTD.
(UNITED KINGDOM)
1976 Statement: "We confirm that our first editions are identified merely by the bye line 'first published . . . .' which appears above the copyright notice in each book we publish.

"The first printing is clearly identified by the fact that no further bibliographical information appears below, whereas on reprints or new editions similar information is printed under this first line, i.e. reprinted plus the date or revised and reprinted plus the date or second edition plus the date, etc."
1981, 1988 Statements: *See* 1976 Statement

BURNHAM PUBLISHERS INC
2000 Statement: "Only those printings and/or editions after the first are indicated.

"Additional printings (or 'impressions') of the first edition are numbered and so identified on the copyright page.

"Subsequent editions (after the first) carry additional copyrights and are clearly identified on the copyright page. We have no secret codes.

"These methods of designation do not differ from any previously used."

BURNING BUSH PUBLICATIONS

2000 Statement: "We will mark first printings in the following way:

©2001 Burning Bush Publications

10 9 8 7 6 5 4 3 2 1

Printed in the United States of America

Burning Bush Publications

Oakland, CA 94613

"Any later printings will be communicated by the dropping of a number. For instance, the second printing will drop the 1, the third the 2, etc.

"A second edition will be acknowledged on the cover and title page as 'Second Edition,' and the numbering—indicating the printing—would return to include all the numbers: 10 9 8 7 6 5 4 3 2 1. Thus a second printing of the second edition would drop the '1', but have 'Second Edition' on the cover and title page."

BURNING CITIES PRESS

1995 Statement: "Burning Cities Press has no particular way of designating first printings. Second or revised printings are so noted."

BURNING DECK PRESS

1981 Statement: "We would indicate a *second printing* by having 'second printing' on the © page."

1988, 2001 Statements: *See* 1981 Statement

BURNS & MAC EACHERN LTD. (CANADA)

1976 Statement: "We don't designate first editions. We do designate as such all subsequent printings and editions."

BURNS & OATES LTD (UNITED KINGDOM)

1994 Statement: "Burns & Oates has always used the following designation for new books and reprints: First published in Great Britain 19XX."

BURNS, OATES & WASHBOURNE, LTD.
(UNITED KINGDOM)

1928 Statement: "We print on the back of the title page of each of our new books:—

First published 19..

"All new editions or new impressions of a work bear this same note with the added information about subsequent editions."

1937 Statement: "We print on the back of the title page of each of our new books:

Made and Printed in Gt. Britain 19..

"All new editions or new impressions of a work state First Edition (or impression) 19.. with the added information about subsequent editions."

1947 Statement: *See* 1937 Statement

THE BUSH PRESS (NEW ZEALAND)

1994 Statement: "All Bush Press books bear the printing history on the verso of the title page, excepting our series of 32-page books, some of which bear the printing history on the inside cover facing the title page and adjacent to the imprint. We adopted this procedure with our first books in 1979 and intend continuing the practice."

2000 Statement: *See* 1994 Statement

BUSINESS BOOKS (UNITED KINGDOM)

2000 Statement: *See* 2000 Statement of The Random House Group Limited (United Kingdom)

BUTTERFIELD PRESS

2000 Statement: "We identify the first printing of a first edition on the copyright page. The words 'First Edition' appear as a separate paragraph."

THORNTON BUTTERWORTH, LTD. (UNITED KINGDOM)

1928 Statement: "It is our habit to place on the back of the title page of all our books the date of first publication, thus: 'First Published . . . 1928.' If the book should be reprinted we add below indented 'Second Impression' and give the date, further reprints are added immediately under. Should another *edition* of the work be issued we add 'Second Edition' with the date not indented ranging with the first line.

First Published 1928
Second Impression July 1928
Third Impression Sept. 1928
Second Edition . . . .Jan. 1929
Fifth Impression Aug. 1929"

1937 Statement: *See* 1928 Statement

BUTTERWORTH & CO (PUBLISHERS) LTD.
(UNITED KINGDOM)

1988 Statement: "We have no particular method of identifying first editions. Unless it states otherwise (e.g., Second Edition) then our book is a first edition—but not necessarily a first publishing of a first edition.

"There is no change from our previous practice. Our imprints and subsidiaries use the same system."

1994 Statement: "I am afraid that our practise is not entirely consistent. There was a period when we gave full printing details of our books on the verso of the title page. Since, however, many of our titles go into tenth and even greater number of editions (particularly when the publications are published for the academic community), we found there was no space for their printing history and, therefore, in many cases, these days we simply print the copyright line showing the date of the copyright of the first or latest edition."

2000 Statement: *See* 2000 Statement of Butterworths Tolley (United Kingdom)

BUTTERWORTH ARCHITECTURE (UNITED KINGDOM)
1988 Statement: *See* 1988 Statement of Butterworth Scientific Ltd. (United Kingdom)

BUTTERWORTH-HEINEMANN
1993 Statement: "Butterworth-Heinemann and its imprints have, since 1983, designated its first printing—and subsequent printings—by the inverse ordering of numbers 10 to 1 at the bottom of our copyright page: 10 9 8 7 6 5 4 3 2 1. When the book is reprinted, the number one is deleted, and so forth for each subsequent printing. Our UK sister company by the same name uses the phrase 'first published' followed by the year and 'reprinted' followed by the year on their copyright page."
2000 Statement: "There has been no change in the way BH designates printings for its US and UK companies. Thus, the statement as provided in [the 1993 Statement] is still valid."

BUTTERWORTH-HEINEMANN (UNITED KINGDOM)
1993, 2000 Statements: *See* 1993 Statement of Butterworth-Heinemann

BUTTERWORTH SCIENTIFIC LTD. (UNITED KINGDOM)
1988 Statement: "The books programme of Architectural Press was taken over by Butterworth Scientific in February 1988 and the new imprint named Butterworth Architecture. The statement used for all Butterworth Scientific first editions, including the Butterworth Architecture and Wright (previously John Wright of Bristol) imprint [is]:
First published, 19..
© Butterworth & Co. (Publishers) Ltd, 19.. "

BUTTERWORTHS (CANADA)
1988 Statement: "At this time Butterworths does not identify a first edition or subsequent printings. However, I enclose a photocopy of information included on our copyright pages in the past.
"As a matter of fact this topic was discussed recently in regard to reprints and we may decide to insert this information in the future."
Photocopy of copyright page shows:
First Published 1954
Second Edition 1958
Third Edition 1963
Fourth Edition 1967
Fifth Edition 1970
First Reprint 1971
Second Reprint 1972
Sixth Edition 1975
Seventh Edition 1980

2000 Statement: "We show current edition info only in each publication. For reprints, we include the reprint number and the year; i.e. Reprint #1 - 2000."

BUTTERWORTHS (UNITED KINGDOM)
2000 Statement: *See* 2000 Statement of Butterworths Tolley (United Kingdom)

BUTTERWORTHS PTY LIMITED (AUSTRALIA)
1988 Statement: "Our first editions do not carry any identification as such. Insofar as I can ascertain, this has always been the case. The imprint page carries a copyright line, for example:

© 1988 Butterworths Pty Limited.

"Subsequent editions carry the words 'Second Edition' or whatever on the cover and title page, while the imprint page sometimes, but not always, includes a history. For example a third edition might state: 'First edition 1970, Second edition 1981' on the imprint."

BUTTERWORTHS TOLLEY (UNITED KINGDOM)
2000 Statement: "Our entries in your publication remain correct in content. You may care to add in the 1994 Statement [of Butterworth & Co Publishers Ltd. (United Kingdom)] after the words 'even greater number of editions', the words 'particularly where the publications are published for the academic community.' We now trade under the name Butterworths Tolley (part of the Reed Elsevier plc group, since 1996) although we use the brands Butterworths and Tolley independently, depending on market, on print on paper publications."

C

C & T PUBLISHING
1994 Statement: "We designate the first printing of a first edition by using the Standard Numerical Listing on the Copyright Page.

"Example for first printing:

10 9 8 7 6 5 4 3 2 1

for second printing:

10 9 8 7 6 5 4 3 2

"We started doing this in 1992. This method of designation does not differ from any previously used."
2000 Statement: *See* 1994 Statement

CADDIS CASE PRESS
2001 Statement: "We do not identify a first printing or any printing after the first printing on the copyright page. Caddis Case Press books are limited edition, fine press books, which are illustrated with original woodblock prints; there is no second printing of the books."

CADDO GAP PRESS

1993 Statement: "On the back of the title page of each book published by Caddo Gap Press we indicate title, author(s), editor(s), publisher address, and copyright information, including the year of first publication. When reprinting any title we add the date of reprinting to the previous information. When publishing a new edition of any title, we also add that information, while retaining the data concerning earlier editions.

"The above has been our procedure since the inception of Caddo Gap Press."

2000 Statement: *See* 1993 Statement

CADDYLAK PUBLISHING

1988, 1993 Statements: *See* 1988 Statement of Asher-Gallant Press

CADENCE JAZZ BOOKS

2000 Statement: "Cadence Jazz Books designates second and subsequent printings with a note to that effect on the copyright page. First editions have no such notice and have only the copyright date listed."

CADMUS EDITIONS

1988 Statement: "'First Edition' on the copyright page indicates the first printing of a first edition; subsequent printings of the edition are so marked on the copyright page. If the book was first published abroad, 'First American Edition' will appear on the copyright page.

"The above method was adopted at the outset of publication by Cadmus Editions and has been consistent throughout."

1993, 2000 Statements: *See* 1988 Statement

JOHN CALDER (PUBLISHERS) LTD (UNITED KINGDOM)

1988 Statement: "All our title pages make it quite clear if it is a first edition, or in the case of translations, a first English edition and the publishing history is added with subsequent reprints.

"Occasionally we do a special de-luxe first edition in advance of the commercial first printing, but this is only for acknowledged authors of classic status and are usually signed by the author."

(The name was changed to Calder Publications Ltd in 1991.)

CALDER PUBLICATIONS LTD (UNITED KINGDOM)

1994, 2000 Statements: *See* 1988 Statement of John Calder (Publishers) Ltd (United Kingdom)

CALIFORNIA INSTITUTE OF PUBLIC AFFAIRS

1989 Statement: "I looked through some of the 100 or so editions that we've published since 1969 and found that while we are always careful to designate following editions (and printings of editions)—on the reverse title page—we have been spotty about marking first editions—no standard practice."

1993, 2000 Statements: *See* 1989 Statement

CALIFORNIA STATE UNIVERSITY PRESS

1988 Statement: "There is no designation of our first edition titles. Only subsequent editions carry the designation 'Second Printing,' 'Third Printing,' and so forth.

"For example, the Copyright page of the 1986 reprint of our 1984 publication of *Frank Lloyd Wright: Letters to Architects* carries the designation: 'Second Printing.' "

1993, 2000 Statements: *See* 1988 Statement

CALLAWAY & KIRK LLC.

2000 Statement: *See* 2000 Statement of Callaway Editions, Inc.

CALLAWAY EDITIONS, INC.

2000 Statement: "Callaway Editions, Inc. identify the first printing of an edition on the copyright page of the book. We identify the first printing of a first edition by the following number line: 10 9 8 7 6 5 4 3 2 1.

"Any subsequent printings would be acknowledged by the dropping of a number. For example, the second printing would drop the 1, the third would drop the 2, etc."

CALLIOPE PRESS

2000 Statement: "We identify the first printing of a first edition by the following statement: 'First Calliope Press Hard Cover Printing' & date. [For our] children's books, we identify the first printing of a first edition by the following number line: 10 9 8 7 6 5 4 3 2 1."

CALYX BOOKS

1995 Statement: "We identify the first printing by the numbers at the bottom of the copyright page. We list the numbers from left to right—if the number 1 still appears it is the first printing. We began this system in 1993."

2000 Statement: *See* 1995 Statement

CAMBRIC PRESS

2000 Statement: "As of 2000, the words 'First edition' appear below © designation."

CAMBRIDGE UNIVERSITY PRESS (AUSTRALIA)

1994, 2000 Statements: *See* 1976 Statement of Cambridge University Press (United Kingdom)

CAMBRIDGE UNIVERSITY PRESS (UNITED KINGDOM)

1928 Statement: "It is our practice to put the date of the publication of any book on the title-page itself. If the book is reprinted, the date of the reprint appears on the title-page and a bibliographical description on the back of the title, e.g.

> First Edition 1922
> Reprinted 1923
> Second Edition 1924."

1937, 1947 Statements: *See* 1928 Statement

1976 Statement: First printings are designated by the statement "First published 19.." on the verso of the title page. Subsequent printings and editions are indicated.

1981, 1988, 1994, 2000 Statements: *See* 1976 Statement

CAMBRIDGE UNIVERSITY PRESS
(NORTH AMERICAN BRANCH)

1993 Statement: "The copyright pages of first editions of our books carry the statement, 'First published' followed by the year. When reprinted, a similar statement, 'Reprinted' followed by the year or years, will appear on the copyright page. Thus a book without the latter notice is a first edition.

"[This] has been our practice for at least the last thirty years."

2000 Statement: *See* 1976 Statement of Cambridge University Press (United Kingdom)

CAMDEN HOUSE BOOKS, INC.

1988 Statement: "For Camden House, Inc., first editions are indicated by the words: 'First edition' on the copyright page."

1993 Statement: *See* 1988 Statement

CAMEL PRESS

2000 Statement: "There are no reprints, as of this date (23 Oct 00). In the event that any may be issued later, they would be clearly marked as 'Second Edition', etc., with the date. Because we use only hand-set metal types and distribute all forms after printing, there would be no 'second printing' of any edition, only entirely new editions."

CAMELOT

1981, 1993 Statements: *See* 1981, 1993 Statements of Avon Books

CAMERON & CO.

1976 Statement: "Our method of designating a first edition is simply to print the words 'First Edition' in the book. Subsequent printings are designated as 'Second Edition,' 'Third Edition,'etc."

1981 Statement: *See* 1976 Statement

1988 Statement: "In the past we used First Printing to designate First Edition. Beginning this year with *Above New York* we will use First Edition 1988 in lieu of First Printing. Subsequent printings will be designated as Second Printing 19—, etc. Revisions will be designated but there will not be Second and Third Editions."

1994, 2000 Statements: *See* 1988 Statement

CAMINO BOOKS

1993 Statement: "We designate the first printing in the copyright page. We list the numbers, on one side, from left to right with the 1 being the first number of the first printing. On the other side we list date of years, which correspond to the printing number.

"We have always used this method.

"This method is used for all books which are published by Camino Books Inc."
2000 Statement: *See* 1993 Statement

CAMINO E.E. & BOOK CO.

1994 Statement: "We . . . have no particular way of designating first printings. Second or revised printings are so noted; 2nd ed, 3rd ed, etc."
2000 Statement: *See* 1994 Statement

CAMPANILE PRESS

2000 Statement: *See* 2000 Statement of San Diego State University Press

CAMPBELL BOOKS (UNITED KINGDOM)

2000 Statement: *See* 2000 Statement of Macmillan Children's Books (United Kingdom)

CANADA LAW BOOK INC. (CANADA)

1995 Statement: "We designate second and subsequent editions of any book on the cover, spine and title page. Books not bearing such a designation are first editions. We have some annual publications which bear the year of publication. In such cases, notice of a first edition would probably be included in the preface to the first annual edition."
2000 Statement: *See* 1995 Statement

CANADIAN INSTITUTE
OF UKRAINIAN STUDIES PRESS (CANADA)

1995 Statement: "We use no particular designation for first printings of first editions. A second or subsequent printing (or impression) is (usually) so designated on the copyright page."
2000 Statement: *See* 1995 Statement

CANDLEWICK PRESS

1993 Statement: "We designate first printings by the numbers on our print line—the numbers one through ten are listed on the line for first editions, and for subsequent printings numbers are deleted, e.g. '1' would be deleted from the print line for a second edition. We have followed this format since . . . Spring 1992. Candlewick Press does not have any imprints or subsidiaries."
2000 Statement: *See* 1993 Statement. "Please note . . . the following addition to the beginning of the statement: We designate first editions by a statement below the copyright line (e.g., 'First edition 20xx'), and designate first printings of first editions by the numbers on our print line . . . ."

CANONGATE (UNITED KINGDOM)

2001 Statement: *See* 2001 Statement of Canongate Books Ltd (United Kingdom)

CANONGATE BOOKS LTD (UNITED KINGDOM)

2001 Statement: "Copyright page indicates where a book is a first edition by stating 'First published in Great Britain by Canongate Books in (year).' If no further bibliographical info is given, it is a first edition. We always acknowledge a previous edition published in another country and/or by another publisher. Subsequent editions are indicated by a line: This edition published in (year), and by the bind line, i.e.: 10 9 8 7 6 5 4 3 2 would indicate second printing."

CANONGATE CLASSICS (UNITED KINGDOM)
2001 Statement: *See* 2001 Statement of Canongate Books Ltd (United Kingdom)

CANONGATE CRIME (UNITED KINGDOM)
2001 Statement: *See* 2001 Statement of Canongate Books Ltd (United Kingdom)

CANOPY BOOKS
2000 Statement: *See* 2000 Statement of Abbeville Press, Inc.

CANTERBURY UNIVERSITY PRESS (NEW ZEALAND)
1994 Statement: "All our first editions carry the simple statement:
    'First published 19XX by Canterbury University Press.'
This has been the case since this Press was founded."
2000 Statement: *See* 1994 Statement

CANTICLE BOOKS
2000 Statement: *See* 2000 Statement of Magnus Press

CANYON COUNTRY PUBLICATIONS
2000 Statement: "It is our practice to indicate on the copyright page with a line thus: 'Second Printing, Third Printing,' etc. This note does not appear on the first edition.
    "Actually, we don't have 'editions' per se, just subsequent printings, perhaps with minor updates."

CAP & GOWN PRESS, INC.
1994 Statement: "No identification of first editions."

JONATHAN CAPE, LTD. (UNITED KINGDOM)
1928 Statement: "Our practice is to print on the back of the title page 'First published 1928' or whatever the year may be. When the book is reprinted without revision or alteration, we add to this 'second impression,' again giving the year. Each printing is thus recorded in like manner in the same place. It follows then that a book published by us which has on the back of the title page 'First published 1928' and no other information with regard to further printings, is, ipso facto, a first edition."
1937, 1947 Statements: *See* 1928 Statement
Statement for 1960: "Cape's practice before the UK acceded to the UCC (27 September 1957) was [stated in the 1982 statement], except that no copyright line was printed. The copyright line (*See* [1982 Statement]) was introduced on 27 September 1957."
1976 Statement: "Jonathan Cape's books show their bibliographic history on the verso of the title page (i.e. page iv or 4). The statement begins: 'First

published 19..' and it is followed by the copyright line: 'Copyright © 19.. by—.' The date in both lines is identical. If the book was first published elsewhere, we then say: 'First published in Great Britain 19..' and the date in the copyright line will be earlier. For example: 'First published in Great Britain 1976' 'Copyright © 1973 by—.' Dates of subsequent reprints, new editions etc., are listed on the same page."

1982 Statement: "Jonathan Cape's books show their bibliographic history on the verso of the title page (i.e. page iv or 4). The statement begins: 'First published 19..' and it is followed by the copyright line: 'Copyright © 19.. by—.' The date in both lines is identical. If the book was first published elsewhere, we then say: 'First published in Great Britain 19..' and the date in the copyright line may be earlier. It will follow exactly the copyright line used in the edition first published elsewhere. For example: 'First published in Great Britain 1976' 'Copyright © 1973 by—.' Dates of subsequent reprints, new editions etc., are listed on the same page."

1988 Statement: "You will be aware that we are now part of Random House UK (as are Chatto and Bodley Head) but we keep our own imprint.

"Our method of designating a first edition is essentially the same as you have in your last edition of the Guide."

1994 Statement: *See* 1988 Statement

2000 Statement: *See* 2000 Statement of The Random House Group Limited (United Kingdom)

JONATHAN CAPE AND ROBERT BALLOU, INC.
(Organized in May, 1932. Out of business at some time prior to 1937.
Succeeded by Robert O. Ballou, Publisher.)

1937 Statement (by Mr. Robert Ballou): "Both Jonathan Cape and Robert Ballou, Inc., and Robert O. Ballou, Publisher, made no particular attempt to distinguish first editions. The first edition usually bore a statement on the reverse of the title page just under the copyright line which read 'First published 19...' But I find on checking back through some of my own publications, that this was omitted as often as used. When it was used the year only was mentioned. On subsequent editions there was usually (or always if my memory is right) a statement of the month and year in which each edition was printed. This was also directly under the copyright notice. Thus the second printing of the trade edition of *Roll Jordan Roll* has this statement under the copyright notice:

First Printing December, 1933
Second Printing January, 1934

I have no copy of the first edition of this book so I cannot tell you how it is marked, but it is probably not marked at all, having simply the copyright notice. As a matter of fact the only two books under my own name (Robert O. Ballou, Publisher) which I ever reprinted were Julia Peterkin's *Roll Jordan Roll*, and Henry Roth's *Call It Sleep*. Each of these had two editions and any copies that are not marked as second printings are firsts. Of course a number of my publications were made up of sheets imported from England and I have no way of knowing, in most cases whether these were sheets from the first edition there or not."

JONATHAN CAPE AND HARRISON SMITH, INC.
(Out of business prior to 1932. This firm divided and was succeeded by: Harrison Smith, Inc., organized in November, 1931, and Jonathan Cape and Robert Ballou, Inc., organized in May, 1932.)
1937 Statement: "Although no strict rule was followed, in general it will be found that unless books are marked 'Second printing,' they are first editions."

JONATHAN CAPE CHILDRENS BOOKS (UNITED KINGDOM)
1994 Statement: *See* 1994 Statement of Random House UK Limited (United Kingdom)
2000 Statement: *See* 2000 Statement of The Random House Group Limited (United Kingdom)

CAPITOL PUBLISHING COMPANY
1947 Statement: "Our books carry no marks which would distinguish the first edition from the following. The reason for that is that they are picture books for the very young and we did not deem such distinction necessary.

"There is however one exception: *All About Us*, the first title in a new series of books planned by us. In this case the first edition bears no particular imprint whereas the following two editions are defined as such on the copyright page. We intend to continue this practice on the following titles of this series."

CAPRA PRESS
1976 Statement: "We do not designate first editions or first printings, but we do designate successive editions or printings."
1981, 1988, 1993, 2000 Statements: *See* 1976 Statement

CAPTAIN FIDDLE PUBLICATIONS
1993 Statement: "Our first book, *The Fiddler's Almanac*, published in 1985, has either the words 'First Edition, First Printing' or 'First Edition, Second Printing' on the reverse of the title page. Every subsequent book that we have published has included all information on the title page, including: copyright notice, date and city of publication, ISBN, author, and the words 'First Edition, Second Printing' or 'Second Edition, Third Printing,' etc."
2000 Statement: *See* 1993 Statement

CAPTUS PRESS (CANADA)
1995 Statement: "We are publishers of academic and professional books and do not especially designate our first editions. Subsequent and revised editions, however, are noted on the title page of the books."
2000 Statement: *See* 1995 Statement

CAPTUS UNIVERSITY PUBLICATIONS (CANADA)
2000 Statement: *See* 2000 Statement of Captus Press (Canada)

ARISTIDE D. CARATZAS, PUBLISHER
1994 Statement: *See* 1976 Statement of Caratzas Brothers, Publishers

CARATZAS BROTHERS, PUBLISHERS

1976 Statement: "We generally do not have any indication for the first printing of the first edition; subsequent printings of the first edition, or subsequent editions are so indicated on the copyright page and/or the title page (in the case of a second or otherwise revised edition). As we have been in business only for two years there are no past inconsistencies, or few other sins to contend with."

1981 Statement: *See* 1976 Statement

CARCANET NEW PRESS LIMITED (UNITED KINGDOM)

1981 Statement: "We distinguish between two kinds of first edition. The first is the 'absolute' first edition where we are the first publisher of the book in the world. After this, we have the 'first British edition' which means just that—usually a book we have bought in from America. In our books we designate the first printing by the prefix 'first published in 19..' or, for the second category, 'first published in Great Britain in 19..' and then proceed to print the address.

"We have always identified our publications in this fashion. All of the imprints of our company follow this pattern."

1988 Statement: *See* 1988 Statement of Carcanet Press Limited (United Kingdom)

CARCANET PRESS LIMITED (UNITED KINGDOM)

1988 Statement: "[The 1981 statement] remains correct in all particulars apart from the word 'New' which must be removed.

"The dropping of 'New' was not a simple terminate act. At times we had certain titles coming out under the proper 'Carcanet Press' imprint and certain titles from the 'New Press' category. This was entirely a financial distinction."

2000 Statement: *See* 1988 Statement

CARDIFF ACADEMIC PRESS (UNITED KINGDOM)

2001 Statement: "We designate a first printing by © date [which] represents 1st edition, 1st printing. Reprints [are] identified [by] 'Reprinted xyza.' "

CARDINAL (UNITED KINGDOM)

1988 Statement: *See* 1988 Statement of Sphere Books Limited (United Kingdom)

CARDOZA PUBLISHING

1993 Statement: "Cardoza Publishing first editions are identified only by the listing of the copyright date with no additional printing information provided.

"Subsequent printings will be indicated with additional information, as in:

Copyright © 1981 by Avery Cardoza

-All Rights Reserved-

Printing History

First Printing   November 1981

Second Printing   February 1982

Third Printing   July 1982."

WILLIAM CAREY LIBRARY

1976 Statement: "We have no particular way of designating first editions of our books. The copyright page will simply have the copyright notice and date, and the ISBN and Library of Congress Catalog number. However, subsequent printings and editions are designated as 'Second printing, [date],' etc."

1981, 1993 Statements: *See* 1976 Statement

CARLSON PUBLISHING, INC.

1993 Statement: "Alas, we have been inconsistent."

THE CARNATION PRESS

1995 Statement: "Much to our own regret, only one of our books has ever been reprinted. At the time, maybe in a moment of unaccustomed euphoria, we neglected to identify the second edition as such."

2001 Statement: "Sounds cheerful enough, and we really have nothing to add . . . ."

CARNEGIE MELLON UNIVERSITY PRESS

1993 Statement: "Beginning in 1975 the phrase First Edition was indicated on the copyright page. However, in many cases, in subsequent printings, this phrase was not removed. In the cloth bound printings of *Thomas and Beulah* by Rita Dove, for instance, the first edition may be identified only from the dust jacket where the statement 'Winner of the 1987 Pulitzer Prize for Poetry' does not appear. All other cloth-bound volumes in our Poetry Series are true first editions.

"In mid-1992, in the interest of uniformity and clarity, we began to use 10 9 8 7 6 5 4 3 2 1 0. When reprinting, we simply delete the figure 1, etc."

2000 Statement: "With the publication of our first titles in 1975 the phrase 'First Edition' was indicated on the copyright page. Often, in subsequent printings, this phrase was not removed. In mid-1992 we began using a number row on the copyright page of each title; since that time the lowest number indicated on all of our cloth and paperback books is an accurate indication of the particular printing."

CAROL COMMUNICATIONS

1994 Statement: *See* 1988 Statement of Citadel Press Publishers

CAROL PUBLISHING GROUP

1995 Statement: The first printing of a first edition is indicated by the number line 1 2 3 4 5 6 7 8 9 10. The lowest number showing indicates the printing.

CAROLINA ACADEMIC PRESS

1988 Statement: "Second (and subsequent) printings as well as revised editions are indicated on the copyright page."

1994, 2000 Statements: *See* 1988 Statement

CAROLINA WREN PRESS

1995 Statement: "In first editions we list the year of publication. In revised or second editions, we indicate revised or second edition and print the year of publication of the revision or second printing."

CAROLINE HOUSE

1995, 2000 Statements: *See* 1995 Statement of Boyds Mills Press

CAROLINE HOUSE PUBLISHERS

1981 Statement: The copyright page carries the numbers 1 through 10. The lowest number designates the printing. Formerly, no attempt was made to designate a first printing.

CAROLINGIAN PRESS

1976 Statement: "All editions are (to date) first and limited to one."

CAROLRHODA BOOKS, INC.

1976 Statement: "In the past, first printings have been designated by the copyright date alone.

"In subsequent printings, the following was added to the copyright entry.
Second Printing 1977
Third Printing 1979
(and so forth)

"We recently have begun adding a number code to the first printing of each book following the copyright entry.
76 77 78 79 80   10 9 8 7 6 5 4 3 2 1

"When a book is reprinted for the second time, for instance, we remove the '1' and the year of the first printing."

1981 Statement: "In the past, first printings have been designated by the copyright date alone.

"In subsequent printings, the following was added to the copyright entry:
Second Printing 1977
Third Printing 1979
(and so forth)

"We recently have begun adding a number code to the first printing of each book following the copyright entry:

"We now use
1 2 3 4 5 6 7 8 9 10   90 89 88 87 86 85 84 83 82 81

"When a book is reprinted for the second time, for instance, we remove the '1' and the year of the first printing."

All imprints of Carolrhoda Books, Inc. follow the same practice.

1988 Statement: *See* 1981 Statement, but note that the number code to the first printing now follows the CIP (cataloging in publication) data.

1993 Statement: *See* 1988 Statement

2000 Statement: *See* 2000 Statement of Lerner Publishing Group

CAROUSEL PRESS

1995 Statement: "We designate the first printing by numbers at the bottom of the copyright page: 10 is the first number on the left, 1 is the last number on the right. We drop the 1 with the second printing, 2 with the third, etc. We have followed this practice since 1980."

2001 Statement: *See* 1995 Statement

CARPENTER PRESS

1995 Statement: "[We] began designating first editions in 1985 with the publication of Jane Piirto's novel *The Three-Week Trance Diet*. First editions from that title on are designated with the words 'First Edition' on the copyright page. Books published prior to that time have no such designation. Subsequent editions are likewise designated by name, e.g. 'Second Edition' rather than 'Second Printing' for indeed changes are made to both cover and text."

JON CARPENTER PUBLISHING (UNITED KINGDOM)

2001 Statement: "We do not identify a first printing; we do identify subsequent printings."

THE CARRIAGE HOUSE PRESS

1988 Statement: "All Carriage House Press books have a colophon at the back of the book which includes the words 'first edition,' and which gives the number of copies printed in both clothbound and paperback editions."

CARRICK AND EVANS, INC.

(Established 1937. Merged with Lippincott January 8, 1941.)

1948 Statement: "First printings of Carrick and Evans titles were identified by placing the letter 'A' directly beneath the copyright line. On subsequent printings the 'A' was removed."

ROBT. CARRUTHERS & SONS (UNITED KINGDOM)

1976 Statement: "We have no special way of identifying any 'first editions' of the few works we publish. In fact, except for 'The Scottish War of Independence' by Evan M. Barron, they are all 'first editions,' and in its case the second edition is identifiable by its long special introduction, which really makes it more valuable historically and authoritatively than the first! It is also out of print. So in all other cases whatever date may appear with the imprint, or elsewhere, is the date of first publication."

1981 Statement: *See* 1976 Statement

CARSON ENTERPRISES INC

2000 Statement: "We do not designate first printings."

CARSTENS PUBLICATIONS, INC.

1994 Statement: "First printings, with only one or two exceptions, are not so marked. Second and other printings are marked as such, sometimes with printing histories. Second and other editions are so marked, usually with a printing history.

"In a few cases where we acquired rights to a title from another publisher, we do indicate if the work is a First Carstens Printing or a First Carstens Edition."

2000 Statement: *See* 1994 Statement

CARTWHEEL BOOKS
1995 Statement: *See* 1995 Statement of Scholastic, Inc.

FRANK CASS PUBLISHERS (UNITED KINGDOM)
1988 Statement: "This format has been our standard practice for many years:
First published 1987 in Great Britain by
FRANK CASS AND COMPANY LIMITED
Gainsborough House, 11 Gainsborough Road,
London, E11 1RS, England
and in the United States of America by
FRANK CASS AND COMPANY LIMITED
c/o Biblio Distribution Centre
81 Adams Drive, P.O. Box 327, Totowa, NJ. 07511
© 1987 John D. Clarke"
1994 Statement: *See* 1988 Statement
2000 Statement: *See* 1988 Statement, but note that publisher's address now reads: Frank Cass Publishers, Newbury House, 900 Eastern Avenue, London IG2 7HH and Frank Cass Publishers c/o ISBS, 5804 N.E. Hassalo Street, Portland, Oregon 97213-3644.

CASSANDRA BOOKS
1995 Statement: *See* 1995 Statement of Cedar Bay Press

CASSELL & CO (UNITED KINGDOM)
2000 Statement: "Generally speaking, at the present time we are placing on the back of the title page:
"First published in ..."
See also Ward Lock Limited (United Kingdom)

CASSELL & COMPANY, LTD. (UNITED KINGDOM)
1928 Statement: "The date of publication of each book issued by this firm appears on the back of the title page; the publication dates of subsequent editions are added as they occur."
1937, 1947 Statements: *See* 1928 Statement
Statement for 1960: *See* 1976 Statement
1976 Statement: "The only means of identification of first editions of our publications is the statement on page iv (the history page): First published 1976.
"The only departure from this is when the book is not first published in this country in which case our history page reads:
First published in Great Britain 1976
"This has always been our practice."
1981 Statement: *See* 1981 Statement of Cassell Ltd. (United Kingdom)

CASSELL EDUCATIONAL (UNITED KINGDOM)
1994 Statement: *See* 1988 Statement of Cassell plc (United Kingdom)

CASSELL LTD. (UNITED KINGDOM)

1981 Statement: "We have not changed our method of designating the first printing of a first edition. However, please note our new company title. All Trade imprints follow the same policy."

See also Cassell & Company, Ltd. (United Kingdom)

1988 Statement: *See* 1988 Statement of Cassell plc (United Kingdom)

CASSELL PLC (UNITED KINGDOM)

1988 Statement: "All our imprints indicate the print history as
First published 19__
Reprinted 19__, 19__, 19__ . . .
Second Edition 19__
although in the past there will have been some exceptions to this wording."

1994 Statement: *See* 1988 Statement

2000 Statement: *See* 2000 Statement of Cassell & Co (United Kingdom)

CASSELL PUBLISHERS (UNITED KINGDOM)

1994 Statement: *See* 1988 Statement of Cassell plc (United Kingdom)

CASTALIA BOOKMAKERS INC.

1995 Statement: "It is our policy to indicate a first edition, first printing on the back of the title page of each of our publications. We primarily publish small editions. A second printing and all subsequent printings would be identified by number, as would a second and all subsequent editions.

"Several of our titles before 1991 were labeled as first editions only, but each of those titles was a first printing and, to date, there have been no additional printings."

CAT PUBLICATIONS (UNITED KINGDOM)

See Centre for Alternative Technology Publications (United Kingdom)

CATBIRD PRESS

2000 Statement: "[We] use a number line infrequently; otherwise, no identifier."

CATHAY (UNITED KINGDOM)

1989 Statement: *See* 1989 Statement of The Octopus Publishing Group PLC (United Kingdom)

CATHOLIC BIBLE PRESS

1994, 2001 Statements: *See* 1994 Statement of Thomas Nelson Publishers

THE CATHOLIC UNIVERSITY OF AMERICA PRESS

1976 Statement: "Most of the books published by our firm are printed on a one-time basis. However, a few have been reprinted or revised. In the case of reprinting, we merely state on the copyright page: 'reprinted (date).' With a revised edition, we place on the title page either the words 'newly revised edition' or 'revised and enlarged edition,' whichever the case may be."

1981, 1988, 1993 Statements: *See* 1976 Statement

2000 Statement: "First Editions are not specifically identified. Straight reprints are made silently. Subsequent editions are identified on the copyright page."

CAUCASUS WORLD (UNITED KINGDOM)
2001 Statement: *See* 2001 Statement of Curzon Press Ltd (United Kingdom)

CAUSEWAY PRESS LIMITED (UNITED KINGDOM)
1988 Statement: "We indicate a first edition by the words 'First impression' followed by the year of publication. Reprints are indicated by 'Reprinted' followed by the year of the reprint. A second edition is indicated by 'Second edition' followed by the year of that edition. This has been standard policy since the company was formed in 1983."

CAVALIER PRESS (AUSTRALIA)
1981 Statement: *See* 1981 Statement of Widescope International Publishers Pty., Ltd. (Australia)

CAVE BOOKS
1994 Statement: "We do not indicate first editions with anything special, but we do indicate second printings, etc. with the new date(s)."
2000 Statement: *See* 1994 Statement

THE CAXTON PRINTERS, LTD
1937 Statement: "We do not as a rule designate our first editions by printing the words 'First Printing' or 'First Edition' on the back of the title page, but when we make a reprint, we give the date of the first printing and the date of each subsequent printing, on the back of the title page.

"The purchaser of a Caxton book will know, then, that he is getting a first printing, unless there is information indicating that we have made more than one printing, on the back of the title page.

"In the case of books such as Fischer's works, published jointly with Doubleday, Doran, the first edition may be ascertained by examining the bottom of the title page. If our name appears before the name of the cooperating publisher, at the bottom of the title page, the edition is a Caxton first.

"This procedure has been followed since the first book was published by The Caxton Printers."
1947 Statement: *See* 1937 Statement
Statement for 1960: "You are advised that our method of indicating first printings has been uniform since we started publishing books. The method used in 1960 or 50, or 40, or 30, is in accordance with the [1976 statement]. The absence of any information regarding printings on the copyright page indicates a first printing. In the case of additional printings the printings are listed by the number of the printing and the month and year date."
1976 Statement: "All of our first editions are identified by the absence of any information regarding printings on the copyright page.

"In the case of a second printing or second edition etc., you will find on the copyright page a listing of printings or editions such as this:

First Printing July, 1945
Second Printing August, 1947 etc."
1981, 1988, 1993 Statements: *See* 1976 Statement

CEDAR (UNITED KINGDOM)
2000 Statement: *See* 2000 Statement of The Random House Group Limited (United Kingdom)

CEDAR BAY PRESS
1995 Statement: "As a general policy, all books . . . will have the following forms of identification:
On the copyright page the following words shall identify the edition:
　　First Edition (month, year)
　　By CEDAR BAY PRESS
　　P.O. Box 751
　　Beaverton, OR 97975-0751
　　Produced in the United States of America
　　All rights reserved.
　"When reprinted, delete 'First' and in example of the second edition:
　　Second Edition (month, year)
　　By CEDAR BAY PRESS
　　P.O. Box 751
　　Beaverton, OR 97975-0751
　　Produced in the United States of America
　　All rights reserved.
　"Record of a first edition shall be on the copyright page and identified as follows: 1 2 3 4 5 6 7 8 9.
　"When reprinted, delete the number '1' and in example of the second edition: 2 3 4 5 6 7 8 9.
　"[This policy was] formally adopted in 1970 and used either by words only or numbers only previously. All our imprints and subsidiaries follow this same policy."
2000 Statement: *See* 1995 Statement

CELEBRITY PRESS
2000 Statement: *See* 2000 Statement of Hambleton-Hill Publishing, Inc.

CELESTIAL ARTS
1976 Statement: Previously, all printings were listed. As of January 1966, the printing, month, and year are given. A numerical system of one through seven and a series of corresponding dates are given as well:
First Printing, May 1976
1 2 3 4 5 6 7 - 80 79 78 77 76
The first number and the last date designate the printing and date of the current publication.
1981, 1988, 1994, 2000 Statements: *See* 1976 Statement

CELO VALLEY BOOKS
1995 Statement: "We do not usually designate a first edition as such. Occasionally we do so . . . . In these cases we say just that, 'First Edition,' usually on the title page itself."

CELTIC HERITAGE BOOKS
2000 Statement: "We identify the first printing of a first edition usually in the preface."

CENTAUR BOOKS (UNITED KINGDOM)
1994, 2000 Statements: *See* 1994 Statement of Old Vicarage Publications (United Kingdom)

CENTAUR PRESS (UNITED KINGDOM)
1994 Statement: *See* 1976 Statement of Centaur Press, Ltd. (United Kingdom)

CENTAUR PRESS, LTD. (UNITED KINGDOM)
1976 Statement: "Only by omission, as it were. That is to say, a first edition would carry the line (e.g.) © Centaur Press Ltd. 1976.

"A second or subsequent edition would have a line to say so: E.g.,'Second edition 1978.' "

1981, 1988 Statements: *See* 1976 Statement

CENTENNIAL BOOKS
2000 Statement: *See* 2000 Statement of University of California Press

CENTER FOR AFRO-AMERICAN STUDIES PUBLICATIONS
(University of California, Los Angeles)
1994 Statement: "The Center for Afro-American Studies Publications designates our first editions and first printings with the words 'first printing' and the year of publication printed on the copyright page of our books. Subsequent printings are differentiated by using the word 'second printing,' 'third printing,' and so forth, with the corresponding years of publication.

"This method was adopted at the inception of our press, which was in 1979, and has not changed."

CENTER FOR CONTEMPORARY POETRY
1976 Statement: "We only do one edition of 500 copies of each *Voyages*."
1988 Statement: *See* 1976 Statement. Publisher ceased publication with 1979 edition.

CENTER FOR JAPANESE STUDIES
1994 Statement: "The Center for Japanese Studies does not distinguish various printings or impressions of a first edition. The date of publication occasionally appears on the full title page, and the date of copyright always appears on the copyright page. That is all the Center does to define publication. A second edition would indicate such, and the new copyright date and date of publication would appear."
2001 Statement: *See* 1994 Statement

CENTER FOR SOUTHERN FOLKLORE
1976 Statement: "No designation of first printings and/or editions is used. Will be indicated only on printings and/or editions after the first. This hasn't been implemented yet as we are new in publishing."
1981 Statement: *See* 1976 Statement

THE CENTER FOR WESTERN STUDIES
1994 Statement: "The Center for Western Studies usually designates 'First Edition' for all cloth and paper formats of its titles when the release is both a first edition and a first printing. Subsequent printings of the same edition are so designated. Second or revised editions are also so designated. We do attempt to make the very first impression of a title special."
2001 Statement: *See* 1994 Statement

CENTERBROOK PUBLISHING
2000 Statement: *See* 2000 Statement of Centerstream Publishing

CENTERSTREAM PUBLISHING
1994 Statement: "Our practice is to print FIRST EDITION on the title page."
2000 Statement: *See* 1994 Statement

CENTRE FOR ALTERNATIVE TECHNOLOGY PUBLICATIONS (UNITED KINGDOM)
2001 Statement: "First publication of any title is indicated as follows on the copyright page:
" 'First published by The Centre for Alternative Technology Publications in (date) . . .' for those titles originated in the UK; 'First published in Great Britain in (date) . . . ' for those titles published elsewhere in advance of the UK edition. Where the copyright date appears without the above reference a list of printings 1 2 3 4 5 6 7 8 9 is given with full list indicating first edition and later printings as follows: 2 3 4 5 6 7 8 9 etc."

CENTURY (UNITED KINGDOM)
1988 Statement: *See* 1988 Statement of Century Hutchinson Publishing Group Limited (United Kingdom)
1994 Statement: *See* Statement of Random House UK Limited (United Kingdom)
2000 Statement: *See* 2000 Statement of The Random House Group Limited (United Kingdom)

CENTURY BENHAM (UNITED KINGDOM)
1988 Statement: *See* 1988 Statement of Century Hutchinson Publishing Group Limited (United Kingdom)

CENTURY COMPANY
*(Merged with D. Appleton and Co., to form
D. Appleton-Century Co., Inc., on May 31, 1933.)*
1928 Statement: "We have no special mark showing first editions of our publications, except in the case of a few special books. We are planning,

however, in the future to put each printing as made on the back of the title pages of all of our publications."

CENTURY HUTCHINSON PUBLISHING GROUP LIMITED (UNITED KINGDOM)

1988 Statement: "We still follow the procedure as indicated in 1981 by Hutchinson:

"On checking through books published before 1976 it seems that Hutchinson has never included the month in the relevant statement.

"The normal form is: 'First published year (i.e. 1976)'

"However, we sometimes include 'in Great Britain' in the statement, thus: 'First published in Great Britain year (i.e. 1976).'

"This implies that the book has been published somewhere other than in Great Britain in a different year. However, if the overseas edition and our edition are published in the same year, then we use the first version. The edition in question could either be an entirely reset version, or offset from (usually) the US or sometimes the Australian edition with new prelims prepared here, or it could be bought in from the overseas publisher with our prelims substituted in the country of origin. Unfortunately, it is not obvious from the prelims how the book has been produced, although one could probably distinguish an offset or bought-in edition by looking at the text (points of house style, etc.).

"So far as I know all our imprints use this form, certainly those of the General Books division.

"Century & Hutchinson merged in 1984 to become Century Hutchinson. However, there is no Century Hutchinson imprint. We currently use the following imprints for hardcover and trade paperback first editions:

 Century
 Rider
 Century Benham
 Hutchinson
 Hutchinson Children's Books
 Radius
 Barrie & Jenkins
 Muller."

CENTURY PRESS

2000 Statement: "We do not have any method for designating a first edition, except it doesn't say anything. Subsequent editions and printings are designated simply, for example, 'Second printing, 2001', 'Second edition, 2001,' 'Second printing of second edition, 2001' etc."

CEOLFRITH PRESS (UNITED KINGDOM)

1976 Statement: "So far, Ceolfrith Press has only published first editions and this is indicated by simply printing inside the title leaf 'First Edition,' followed by the date.

"However, we also published limited editions of most of our publications (excluding exhibition catalogues) which are numbered and signed by the

authors, poets or artists. The reverse of the title leaf of these editions is also designated as follows:
'This is No . . . of the signed edition' and the numbering is done by hand.

"We also state in our publications how many copies were printed in both ordinary and signed editions."

C E P INC

2000 Statement: *See* 2000 Statement of Paladin Press

W. & R. CHAMBERS, LTD. (UNITED KINGDOM)

1928 Statement: "It is our intention to adopt the plan in future of marking the first impression of our general books 'original edition.' We do not intend to do this in the case of school books."

1936 Statement: "We mark the first impression of all books published by us, including school books, 'Original Edition.' "

1947 Statement: *See* 1936 Statement

1976 Statement: "In all our current publications the first date of publication is usually printed on the reverse of the title page along with the copyright notice. Prior to the institution of the copyright notice we normally put in the date of the latest edition or reprint. However in our early publications very often no date was given and therefore first dates of publication are very difficult to identify."

1981, 1988 Statements: *See* 1976 Statement

CHAMBERS KINGFISHER GRAHAM PUBLISHERS, INC.

1995 Statement: "We identify the first printing of a first edition by the following number line: 2 4 6 8 10 9 7 5 3 1 First American Edition, 19XX."

CHAMELEON (UNITED KINGDOM)

2000 Statement: *See* 2000 Statement of Andre Deutsch (United Kingdom)

CHAMELEONS DRAMASCRIPTS (UNITED KINGDOM)

2000 Statement: *See* 2000 Statement of Ian Henry Publications Limited (United Kingdom)

CHANCELLOR (UNITED KINGDOM)

1989 Statement: *See* 1989 Statement of The Octopus Publishing Group PLC (United Kingdom)

CHANDLER & SHARP PUBLISHERS, INC.

1988 Statement: "We do not designate first printings in any particular way. They are, of course, the first printing run during the year of copyright. Subsequent printings are indicated by number (2nd, 3rd, 4th, etc.) and by year of printing. We have used this method since 1973, when we published our first book. We have no subsidiaries or other imprints."

1993, 2001 Statements: *See* 1988 Statement

CHANTICLEER PRESS

1947 Statement: "First editions of our publications are marked as such on the copyright page, and subsequent editions and reprints are also marked on that page."

1993 Statement: *See* 1947 Statement

CHAOSIUM INC

1994 Statement: "On the inside of each title page, we print the month and date in which a book is printed. We call a new release a new edition if we have made substantive editorial revisions to a book; otherwise it is a new impression. Each time that we release a new edition, we append the month and year on the title page reverse with the new year of release. Thus, the first year listed is always the year of first printing.

"I can not guarantee that we adhered to this policy rigorously, particularly in the early years of this company's existence, but this is now our current policy."

2000 Statement: *See* 1994 Statement

CHAPITEAU PRESS

2000 Statement: "Our first book, published in 1999, did not have any first edition designation. Beginning in 2000, books have 'First Edition' printed on their copyright page. Subsequent printings will be labeled as second printing, third printing, etc., followed by the year."

CHAPMAN (UNITED KINGDOM)

2001 Statement: "We do not identify a first printing; we do identify subsequent printings on the copyright page."

GEOFFREY CHAPMAN (UNITED KINGDOM)

1988, 1994 Statements: *See* 1988 Statement of Cassell plc (United Kingdom)

CHAPMAN AND HALL

1988, 1994 Statements: *See* 1988 Statement of Routledge, Chapman, and Hall, Inc.

CHAPMAN AND HALL (UNITED KINGDOM)

1988 Statement: *See* 1988 Statement of Associated Book Publishers (UK) Ltd. (Scientific and Technical Division) (United Kingdom)

CHAPMAN & HALL, LTD. (UNITED KINGDOM)

1928 Statement: "We do not specify either on the title page or on the back of the title that a first edition is a first edition. When the book is reprinted we generally put a bibliographical note on the back of the title page as follows:—

First Impression March 1928

Second Impression April 1928

and so forth."

1937 Statement: "We do not specify either on the title page or on the back of the title that a first edition is a first edition but all our publications are now dated, technical books bearing the date on the title page and general books carrying the date on the verso. It may therefore be taken that a book carrying dates on the title page is a first edition, as well as books carrying the words 'First published 1936.' Any subsequent reprints or editions are shown in the bibliographical note."

1947 Statement: "There has been little change in our practice of dating books since we supplied you with certain information on this point in 1937. As far as all books on general literature and fiction are concerned, we now show the year of publication on the title page, and in the event of any further editions some mention of this would be made on the verso."

CHAPMANS (UNITED KINGDOM)

1994 Statement: *See* 1994 Statement of The Orion Publishing Group Ltd (United Kingdom)

CHAPTER & VERSE/WELLINGTON LANE PRESS (AUSTRALIA)

2000 Statement: "We have two imprints: Chapter & Verse and Wellington Lane Press. Neither specifically define first editions; we do nominate the year of reprints, however."

CHAPTER TWO (UNITED KINGDOM)

1994 Statement: "Chapter Two titles generally bear the date of publication alongside the copyright notice. First Editions are not so designated but second and third are, so too reprints."

2000 Statement: *See* 1994 Statement, but note that, "this also applies to our English, French and Scandinavian titles."

CHARIOT

1993 Statement: *See* 1993 Statement of Chariot Family Publishing

CHARIOT FAMILY PUBLISHING

1993 Statement: "With the exception of one, all of our imprints, (Chariot, LifeJourney, and Christian Parenting) identify first printings on the copyright page with the words, 'First Printing,' followed by the year. Our Lion imprint uses the words 'First Edition,' followed by the year. I believe this has been the procedure since the late 1970s."

CHARIS PUBLICATIONS

1994, 2000 Statements: *See* 1994 Statement of Servant Publications

DEBORAH CHARLES PUBLICATIONS (UNITED KINGDOM)

2001 Statement: "The year of publication and indication of the year of any subsequent reprinting appears on the copyright page."

THE CHARLES PRESS, PUBLISHERS

1994 Statement: "First editions and first printings are not identified. All subsequent printings and editions are noted as such on verso." ·

CHARLES RIVER BOOKS

1988 Statement: "We usually indicate a second edition on the reverse side of the half title page."

CHARLES RIVER MEDIA

2001 Statement: "We state 'First edition' on the copyright page."

THE CHARLTON PRESS (CANADA)

1995 Statement: "First printing of first edition will simply be a first edition, we very seldom reprint. The second printing will be a second edition. Edition numbers will appear on the title page."

2000 Statement: *See* 1995 Statement

CHARTERED INSTITUTE OF PERSONNEL AND DEVELOPMENT (UNITED KINGDOM)

2001 Statement: "We are now the Chartered Institute of Personnel and Development (as of July 2000), or CIPD. First printing of titles is designated as follows:

©(Author or the Institute) Year
First published Year

Reprints:

©(Author or the Institute) Year
First published Year
Reprinted Year, Year (etc)"

CHATERSON, LIMITED (UNITED KINGDOM)

1947 Statement: "All our books have the date of the first edition on the title page or on the back of the title page. All subsequent editions are listed in addition."

CHATHAM PRESS

1982 Statement: "We use the terminology 'First Edition,' followed by 'First or Second or . . . Printing.' "

1988 Statement: "We use the terminology FIRST EDITION for the first printing only. Follow-up printings have the designation 'First or Second . . . or Printing' or 'Revised Edition . . . Printing.' "

"All subsidiaries and imprints follow this practice."

1993 Statement: *See* 1988 Statement

CHATHAM PUBLISHING (UNITED KINGDOM)

2000 Statement: *See* 2000 Statement of Gerald Duckworth and Company Ltd. (United Kingdom)

CHATSWORTH LIBRARY (UNITED KINGDOM)

1994 Statement: *See* 1994 Statement of Airlife Publishing Limited (United Kingdom)

CHATTO & WINDUS (UNITED KINGDOM)

1928 Statement: "We use no particular distinguishing sign to mark our first editions with."

1937 Statement: *See* 1928 Statement

1947 Statement: "We have no distinguishing mark, but certainly all contemporary work is easily identified by the fact that all books bear the date of publication either on the title-page or the verso of the title, and in the event of a book being reprinted the information as to whether it is a second impression or a new edition is noted in the biblio."

Statement for 1960: "We see that every book carries the date of first publication, and reprints, whether new impressions or new editions, are clearly listed on the verso of the title page."

1976 Statement: *See* 1976 Statement of Chatto & Windus Ltd (United Kingdom)

CHATTO & WINDUS LTD (UNITED KINGDOM)

1976 Statement: "We have no particular method beyond ensuring that every book carries the date of first publication, and reprints, whether new impressions or new editions, are clearly listed on the verso of the title page."

1981, 1988 Statements: *See* 1976 Statement

1994 Statement: *See* 1994 Statement of Random House UK Limited (United Kingdom)

2000 Statement: *See* 2000 Statement of The Random House Group Limited (United Kingdom)

CHATTO & WINDUS/THE HOGARTH PRESS (UNITED KINGDOM)

1995 Statement: *See* 1994 Statement of Random House UK Limited (United Kingdom)

2000 Statement: *See* 2000 Statement of The Random House Group Limited (United Kingdom)

CHECKERBOARD PRESS, INC.

1993 Statement: "In 1986 Rand McNally sold their juvenile division to Macmillan, Inc., who established Checkerboard Press, Inc. Since that time all Checkerboard Press books have had the printing indicated within the copyright by the numbers 0 9 8 7 6 5 4 3 2 1. One number being deleted with each reprinting, thus only the first printing will show all ten numbers. The only exception to this rule is Real Mother Goose, in which Checkerboard Press continues the Rand McNally system of indicating the number of times the book has been reprinted and the year and month of the printing on the copyright page. But Rand McNally did not do this in all their books and in the majority of Rand McNally books taken over by Checkerboard Press there was no way to tell how many times a book had been printed previously, nor how many books had been printed.

"During the 1950s and 60s Rand McNally had indicated in each trade book what print run a particular book came from, but they never did this in their Junior Elf books or other mass market books, and certainly not in any of the books they printed as co-editions, and certainly not in every book that was a trade book."

CHEEVER PUBLISHING, INC.

1994 Statement: The first printing of a first edition is indicated by the statement:
"First Edition

First Printing, Date
Copyright, © year by Cheever Publishing."

CHELSEA GREEN PUBLISHING COMPANY

1988 Statement: "We started in 1984. We have always stated what printing it is. 'First printing, Sept 1987,' for example. Then 'Second printing,' etc. For a paperback reprint, we say 'First paperback printing,' etc. We have no imprints or subsidiaries."

1995 Statement: "Beginning in 1995, we will state the first printing of each book. (For example: First paperback printing: January 1995.)

"Additionally, we use the more modern 'impression line,' 99 98 97 96 95 6 5 4 3 2 1."

2000 Statement: "You might want to update the years (05 04 03 02 01). Otherwise this [1995 Statement] is still accurate."

CHELSEA HOUSE
(Out of business prior to 1949.)

1928 Statement: "So far as the cloth-bound book publication goes so few of the books that we have published have run into more than one edition, that we have not been faced with the necessity of marking first editions in any way."

1937 Statement: *See* 1928 Statement

CHELSEA HOUSE PUBLISHERS

1988 Statement: "We use standard publishers' numbers."
1994, 2000 Statements: *See* 1988 Statement

CHELSEA JUNIORS

2000 Statement: *See* 2000 Statement of Chelsea House Publishers

CHELSEA PRESS

2000 Statement: "Edition and printing information is stated on the copyright page. Subsequent editions or printings would be indicated on this line."

CHELSEA PUBLISHING COMPANY, INC.

1993 Statement: "Chelsea Publishing Company has been in existence for nearly 50 years. In the first few years, we did not designate first editions in any particular way.

"Subsequently, we indicated—in the case of reprints—that it was first published at Such-and-such a City and such-and-such a year.

"In the case of translations and several original publications, a single copyright date would normally indicate a first edition, but not necessarily a first printing of that edition."

2000 Statement: *See* 2000 Statement of AMS Chelsea Publishing

CHEROKEE PUBLISHING COMPANY

1988, 1994 Statements: *See* 1988 Statement of Larlin Corporation
2000 Statement: "We have not been consistent with our identifications of first editions, but we normally use the term 'First Edition' and the coding device as shown on the enclosed sample.

"First Edition
ISBN 0-87797-1144-7
91 90 89 88 10 9 8 7 6 5 4 3 2 1

"For new hardcover titles, we normally employ colored end sheets in the first printing."

CHERRYTREE PRESS LIMITED (UNITED KINGDOM)

1994 Statement: "We began publishing children's information books as Cherrytree Press Ltd in 1988, and although I can't promise that we have strictly adhered to the same wording on every title published, as a general rule, the following wording would appear on the copyright page:

First published (year)
by Cherrytree Press Ltd
a subsidiary of
The Chivers Company Ltd
Windsor Bridge Road
Bath, Avon BA2 3AX.

"There would be no indication of publication date on the title page, and no indication on the copyright page that this was a first edition. However, if the book is reprinted, then the following wording would be added after the final line of the address:

Reprinted (year)
or
Reprinted (year), (year), (year) (twice)."

CHESS ENTERPRISES, INC.

1993 Statement: "We do not in any way identify first editions of our books. Nor do we indicate reprintings of the books from the same plates."
2000 Statement: *See* 1993 Statement

CHESTNUT HILLS PRESS

1994 Statement: *See* 1994 Statement of New Poets Series, Inc.
2000 Statement: *See* 2000 Statement of Brickhouse Books, Inc.

CHICAGO REVIEW PRESS

1993 Statement: A first edition is identified by the phrase "First edition" on the copyright page. On the same page is a string of numbers. The lowest number indicates the printing. A first printing of a first edition would carry the words "First edition" on the copyright page and the lowest number would be 1.
2000 Statement: *See* 1993 Statement

CHILDREN OF MARY

2000 Statement: "We do not state it is the first printing. Second printings on would give the dates of each printing."

CHILDRENS PRESS®

1976 Statement: "Childrens Press® uses the dateline designation. For example:

1 2 3 4 5 6 7 8 9 10 11 12 R 78 77 76 75

"The digits to the left of the letter R (reprint) indicate the printing. The digits to the right of the letter R indicate the year. The above was first printed in 1975. In the following example, in 1975 the title was printed for the 7th time.

7 8 9 10 11 12 13 14 15 16 17 18 19 20 21 22 23 24 25 R 75

"Elk Grove and Golden Gate Junior Books published since we acquired those companies also carry this dateline designation. Titles published prior to our acquisition do not carry any printing designation."

1981 Statement: "Our first printing designation has not changed."

1988, 1993 Statements: *See* 1981 Statement

CHILDRENS PRESS, INC.

1947 Statement: "The reason we did not give a statement of our method of identifying first printings is that we have not identified them in this point. We publish only children's books."

CHILTON BOOK COMPANY

1976 Statement: "Chilton Book Company indicates year of publication and number of printing by a numerical code. First number indicates publication year, last indicates printing. e.g.

7 8 9 0 1 2 3 4 5 6 0 9 8 7 6 5 4 3 2 1
published in 1977   first printing

"Second and additional revised editions are usually noted on both title page and copyright page."

1981, 1988, 1993 Statements: *See* 1976 Statement

CHINA BOOKS & PERIODICALS INC.

1988 Statement: "Historically, China Books has not designated first editions in a consistent manner, though a number of its books do state 'First edition,' or 'First edition' followed by date of publication. However, *later* editions have usually been clearly designated, so it is often safe to conclude that the edition is indeed a first unless otherwise stated. All first editions published after January 1, 1988, will be clearly designated as such."

1993, 2000 Statements: *See* 1988 Statement

CHIRON PRESS

2000 Statement: "Our first editions are usually not identified as such, though we have been printing 'First edition' on the copyright page lately. Subsequent printings are identified on p. 2 (copyright page) such as 'first edition, second printing' or 'second edition,' etc."

CHRISTCHURCH PUBLISHERS LTD. (UNITED KINGDOM)

2000 Statement: *See* 2000 Statement of The Albyn Press (United Kingdom)

CHRISTIAN CLASSICS, INC.

1993 Statement: "We simply indicate on the copyright page of the first printing of all new material the following line: 'First published, date 1993 by Christian Classics, Inc.' We have followed this practice for the last 14 years, the length of time we have operated this company. We have one subsidiary—Wakefield Editions—and follow the same practice."

CHRISTIAN COMMUNITIES
2000 Statement: *See* 2000 Statement of LifeQuest

CHRISTIAN FOCUS PUBLICATIONS (UNITED KINGDOM)
1994 Statement: "We have no special identification of first editions. You would normally be able to tell if a book was a first edition by the fact that on all subsequent editions and printings, it would be noted that the book was reprinted or revised and a date given."
2001 Statement: *See* 1994 Statement

CHRISTIAN MARTYRS' PRESS
2000 Statement: "We do not indicate that a particular work is part of a first printing, but for second or subsequent printings, the information is also carried on the copyright page."

CHRISTIAN PARENTING
1993 Statement: *See* 1993 Statement of Chariot Family Publishing

THE CHRISTIAN SCIENCE PUBLISHING SOCIETY
1994 Statement: "We have no special ways of designating first editions. Our titles are simply dated by copyright."
2001 Statement: "Although our prior 1994 statement was that we do not indicate first editions, in the intervening years we have gone through some changes. We had a General Publications department, which is no longer operational, which between 1996 and 1998 published several books utilizing the Publisher's Cataloging-in-Publication format provided by Quality Books, Inc. At least three of these books indicated '1st ed' following the title line. Without conducting an exhaustive search, it is impossible to state that this practice was followed consistently in every case during the period since 1994. We will be undertaking a review of our policies in this area with respect to future publications."

THE CHRISTOPHER PUBLISHING HOUSE
1947 Statement: "We always state on the title page or copyright page if a book is a second or subsequent edition. All others are first editions."
Statement for 1960: *See* 1982 Statement
1976 Statement: "No set policy, usually second editions and second printings are indicated on copyright page."
1982 Statement: "Same policy on all books from 1910-1982.

"No indication of first edition on copyright page. However, second editions and second printings are usually indicated on copyright page."
1988 Statement: "We always state on the copyright page if a book is a second or subsequent edition. All others are first editions."
1993, 2000 Statements: *See* 1988 Statement

CHRISTOPHER-GORDON PUBLISHERS
1993 Statement: "Christopher-Gordon Publishers indicates the first printing by number at the bottom of the copyright page. We list printings at lower left in descending order from 10. The print year is also listed at the bottom in descending order."
2000 Statement: *See* 1993 Statement

CHRISTOPHERS (UNITED KINGDOM)
1937 Statement: "We always put the date of first publication on the back of the title, thus—
    First published   1923
When the book is reprinted we alter this to—
    First published June   1923
    Reprinted September   1923
    Reprinted October   1928"
1947 Statement: *See* 1937 Statement

CHRISTOPHER'S BOOKS
1976 Statement: "Christopher's Books does not indicate first edition or printing; we have never done a second, but would indicate a second printing or edition if we were to produce one."
1981 Statement: *See* 1976 Statement

CHRONICLE BOOKS
1976 Statement: "Our first editions can be identified by the lack of any edition imprint. Subsequent editions are indicated on the copyright page.

"We specify all subsequent 'printings' after the first one. When it is a 'new edition,' we so specify. So, first printings of the first editions are the only books that do not carry a printing or edition reference."
1981 Statement: *See* 1976 Statement
1988 Statement: "First edition Chronicle Books are indicated on the copyright page. Each book is printed with the numbers 10 9 8 7 6 5 4 3 2 1. With each printing a number is removed from the list. A first edition has the complete list."
1993 Statement: *See* 1988 Statement
2000 Statement: *See* 2000 Statement of Chronicle Books LLC

CHRONICLE BOOKS LLC
2000 Statement: "Our name was changed from Chronicle Books to Chronicle Books LLC in 2000. We still follow the practice outlined in the 1988 Statement of Chronicle Books."

CHURCHILL LIVINGSTONE
1976, 1981, 1993 Statements: *See* 1976 Statement of Longman Inc.

CICERONE PRESS (UNITED KINGDOM)
1994 Statement: "The first printing of first editions of Cicerone books is indicated simply by the copyright mark and the year.

"New printings are indicated by the words 'reprinted 199-' so that you could have, for example, 'copyright 1984, reprinted 1987, 1990, 1993.' A new edition carries the legend 'new edition 199-' and then 'reprinted 199-.' We have always adopted this method in our books from 1969 onwards."

2001 Statement: *See* 1994 Statement

CIPD (UNITED KINGDOM)
See Chartered Institute of Personnel and Development (United Kingdom)

CIRCLET PRESS
2001 Statement: "In our older publications, pre-1995 or so, we did not designate 'First Edition' or 'First Printing,' adding the designation 'Second Printing: (date)' or 'Second Edition: (date),' etc. in subsequent printings.

"Since 1995 we have been designating 'First Edition' or 'First Printing' with the date as shown above. Upon subsequent printings this line is replaced with the appropriate verbiage.

"All Circlet Press and its imprints' publications are categorized in the same way. Circlet Press' imprints include Ultraviolet Library and Circumflex."

CIRCUMFLEX
2001 Statement: *See* 2001 Statement of Circlet Press

CISTERCIAN PUBLICATIONS
1988 Statement: "As a specialized short-run publisher, we do not identify First Editions. Most of our books are First Editions and first printings. When a book is reprinted, the copyright page identifies it as a reprint with the date of the original publication and the reprint date."

1993, 2000 Statements: *See* 1988 Statement

THE CITADEL PRESS
1949 Statement: "Our first printings are sometimes marked so, and at other times are not. However, second printings are always indicated on our original books."

1976 Statement: "It is our normal practice to print the words First Edition on the copyright page."

1982 Statement: "We continue to print First Edition on the copyright page of original titles."

1988 Statement: *See* 1988 Statement of Citadel Press Publishers

CITADEL PRESS PUBLISHERS
1988 Statement: "We no longer print First Edition on the copyright page of our titles. However, second and subsequent printings are indicated by a number code, the lowest number indicating the printing."

1995 Statement: *See* 1995 Statement of Carol Publishing Group

CITIZEN PRESS, LTD. (UNITED KINGDOM)
See Skelton Robinson (United Kingdom)

CITY LIGHTS BOOKS, INC.

1976 Statement: "We don't really have a method. Most of our books state second printing, third printing, etc., but sometimes a new printing has been done without a notice. Usually the absence of any identifying statement would indicate a first printing of a first edition."

1981, 1988, 1995, 2000 Statements: *See* 1976 Statement

CLAITOR'S LAW BOOKS & PUBLISHING DIVISION, INC.

2000 Statement: "We show the date of copyright on the copyright page, and this is a first edition unless noted 2nd ptg 1997, or some such, to show that it is *not* 1st ptg of a 1st edition."

CLAMP DOWN PRESS

2000 Statement: "The statement 'First Edition' is sometimes stated on the copyright page next to the © and author's name. 'First Edition' is *always* stated in the colophon at the end of the book. This same rule applies to subsequent editions (i.e. 'Second Edition' is noted in colophon)."

CLARENDON PRESS (UNITED KINGDOM)

2000 Statement: *See* 2000 Statement of Oxford University Press (United Kingdom)

CLARION (UNITED KINGDOM)

2000 Statement: *See* 2000 Statement of Elliot Right Way Books, Publishers (United Kingdom)

CLARION BOOKS

1993 Statement: "All books published by Clarion Books have a binder's code and a string of numbers at the foot of the copyright notice. First editions will read HOR (or other code, depending on the binder) 10 9 8 7 6 5 4 3 2 1. Numbers are removed from right to left with each subsequent printing. If the book reprints more than ten times, new numbers are put in place. The number that appears on the far right designates which printing we are in. The number of copies in each reprint is not indicated, though this information is available from us should anyone have a legitimate need to know it.

"Clarion Books is a children's book imprint of Houghton Mifflin. To my knowledge, all Houghton Mifflin imprints designate printings as described above. This designation has long been in practice, though I do not know when it was adopted."

2000 Statement: *See* 1993 Statement, but note that the binder code now reads BVG in place of HOR.

CLARITY PRESS

1995 Statement: "No statement identifies first edition. Subsequent editions are identified on cover; subsequent printings are identified on verso title page as second printing (date)."

2000 Statement: *See* 1995 Statement

ARTHUR H. CLARK COMPANY

1976 Statement: "We designate first editions by using only one date on the copyright page. If the edition is a 2nd, it is so stated on the copyright page."
1981, 1988, 1995, 2001 Statements: *See* 1976 Statement

I. E. CLARK PUBLISHER

1994 Statement: "We publish only paperback acting editions of playbooks and have never designated 'first printing.' Subsequent revisions or new editions are so designated by a notation such as '2nd Edition, published 1993' or 'Revised Edition.' "
2001 Statement: *See* 2001 Statement of I. E. Clark Publications

I. E. CLARK PUBLICATIONS

2001 Statement: "We publish only paperback acting editions of playbooks and have never designated 'first printing.' Subsequent revisions or new editions may be designated by a notation such as '2nd Edition, published 1993' or 'Revised Edition.' "

T. & T. CLARK LIMITED (UNITED KINGDOM)

1976 Statement: "All our first editions will have simply the date of publication or 'first printed—.' All subsequent editions will have the date of first, latest and intervening editions clearly set out."
1981, 1988, 1994, 2001 Statements: *See* 1976 Statement

CLARK UNIVERSITY PRESS

1988, 1993 Statements: *See* 1988 Statement of University Press of New England

JAMES CLARKE & CO., LTD. (UNITED KINGDOM)

1988, 1994, 2000 Statements: *See* 1981 Statement of Lutterworth Press (United Kingdom)

CLASSICS WITH A TWIST

2000 Statement: *See* 2000 Statement of Empire Publishing Service

CLAY PUBLISHING CO., LTD. (CANADA)

1976 Statement: All printings after the first are designated by month and year.

CLEAR LIGHT PUBLISHERS

2001 Statement: "We identify the first printing of a first edition by a number line; the lowest number designates the printing."

CLEARWATER PUBLISHING CO., INC.

1976 Statement: "We do not mark our first editions First Edition. Subsequent editions are marked second edition and so on. If the book has no changes, the second printing is considered part of the first edition and is marked, Second Printing."
1981 Statement: *See* 1976 Statement

CLEAVER-HUME PRESS, LTD. (UNITED KINGDOM)

1947 Statement: "We inscribe on the back of the title page of the first edition of a book the date of appearance, e.g. 'First published 1948.' Reprints unaltered are recorded thereunder: 'Reprinted 19..' We reserve the word 'Edition' for a version containing significant revisions, and the dates of successive editions are given in a similar way."

"We believe you will find this coincides with the practice of most serious British publishers."

CLEVELAND STATE UNIVERSITY

1988 Statement: "All of the books we have published have been first editions at the time they were issued. The year of publication is indicated by the copyright date. A couple of our books have gone into a second printing, unchanged, and more may do so in the future; there is no indication in the book that it is a second printing. We have also reprinted some books in an enlarged or revised edition, these editions are so indicated on the acknowledgments page, with additional copyright dates where appropriate. Some of our books have been issued simultaneously in hardcover and paperback editions; these have the same copyright date but different ISBNs on the acknowledgments page. If anyone wishes to apply to us for the particular publication history of a book, we will try to provide it."

CLEVELAND STATE UNIVERSITY POETRY CENTER

1993 Statement: "Since our first publication in 1971, all of the books we have published have been first editions at the time they were issued. The year of publication is indicated by the copyright date. Before 1993 we reprinted several titles without any indication that the copies were second printings. Beginning in 1993 we have added 'Second printing' on page 2 (verso of title page) of otherwise unchanged reprints. We have also reprinted some books in enlarged or revised editions; these editions are so indicated on p. 2, with additional copyright dates where appropriate."

2000 Statement: *See* 1993 Statement. Note the following: "There is no University Press at CSU. We function as a small independent publishing house that is part of the English Department. We publish three different series under three imprints: The CSU Poetry Series, The Cleveland Poets Series, and Imagination Series.

"Any other publishing efforts done by the University are indepedent of our publications and our series. Occasionally, for example, the Art Department will publish a catalogue for a show. We will give them one of our ISBN numbers to use, since we have a current series and they don't, as they publish only occasionally."

CLIFF STREET BOOKS

2001 Statement: *See* 2001 Statement of HarperCollinsPublishers

CLIFFHANGER PRESS

1993 Statement: "As of 1991, the initial printing of our books bears the words 'First Edition' in italics centered toward the bottom of the copyright page."

CLOCK HOUSE PUBLICATIONS (CANADA)

1976 Statement: Editions and printings and their dates are designated on the copyright page.
1993 Statement: *See* 1976 Statement

EDWARD J. CLODE INC.

(Out of business sometime prior to 1949.)

1928 Statement: "There is no way in which it is possible to distinguish any of our first editions from later ones."
1937 Statement: *See* 1928 Statement

CLOSSON PRESS

2000 Statement: "We identify the first printing of a First Edition by adding First Edition to the copyright page. We adopted this policy in 1976 and [have] never done anything differently."

CLOUD, INC.

1947 Statement: "We distinguish the first printing only by an absence of the words 'second edition,' 'third edition,' etc., on the copyright page of the book."

CLOUDBANK

2000 Statement: *See* 2000 Statement of Blue Heron Publishing

CLOUDCAP

1993 Statement: "Later printings are identified 'second,' 'third,' etc. Thus, if no 'printing' is mentioned it is a first."

CLYMER MOTORS

1947 Statement: "On the Historical Motor Scrapbooks, the first edition that was printed in 1944 did not have an index, and only 1,700 of these books were printed. All subsequent printings (we have printed over 150,000) are indexed."

CNW PUBLISHING

2000 Statement: "We identify the first printing of a first edition by 'First Edition' (above the ISBN number)."

COACH HOUSE BOOKS (CANADA)

2001 Statement: *See* 2001 Statement of Coach House Press Inc (Canada)

THE COACH HOUSE PRESS (CANADA)

1976 Statement: "Some books the first edition was numbered by machine. None have said 'First Edition.' Some books had letterpress first editions and offset second or silkscreen and offset. 'Second Printing' and date are usually put in the colophon."

1981 Statement: " 'Second Printing' and date are usually put in the colophon."

COACH HOUSE PRESS INC (CANADA)

1993 Statement: "'Second Printing' (Third, Fourth, etc.) is included on copyright page. Where appropriate, first edition and date are also indicated."

2001 Statement: "First editions from Coach House Books (ISBN 1 55245 as opposed to Coach House Press, ISBN 0 88910) are identified as such on the copyright page by the phrase 'first edition.' In subsequent printings, these words are usually masked out; we have instituted a 'print-on-demand' system for many of our titles (such as *The Farm Show*) which have been reprinted so many times now that keeping track of the printing number is pointless. Revised editions are usually identified as such on the copyright page, and usually have a new ISBN as well. Reprints of Coach House Press titles under the Coach House Books imprint are assigned a new Coach House Books ISBN.

"Regarding ongoing print-on-demand titles, I should add that we do keep very accurate internal records of reprints based on our in-house docket-numbering system. All information regarding titles going into reprint is preserved in both paper and digital form on CD-ROM, and can be viewed at the National Library of Canada."

COACH HOUSE PRESS, INC.

1988 Statement: "Coach House Press, Inc. first editions bear no special markings, and are sometimes re-printed without designation. Since most of our books are production scripts of plays, they receive brief, heavy use and are often discarded."

COASTAL NEW ENGLAND PUBLICATIONS

2000 Statement: *See* 2000 Statement of Harvest Hill Press

COBBETT PRESS, LTD. (UNITED KINGDOM)

1947 Statement: "In general principle we print the date of the first printing or biblio on the verso of the title-page with dates of subsequent re-printings where relevant. While this practice has sometimes been omitted, in general it will be adhered to."

COBBLESMITH

1976 Statement: "We have no special marks."

1981, 1988, 1994, 2000 Statements: *See* 1976 Statement

R. COBDEN-SANDERSON (UNITED KINGDOM)

1928 Statement: "I do not follow any rule in regard to the designation of my first editions. I can only give you examples such as the following:—

First published 1926
Copyright 1926
First published 1925
Second impression May 1925
Third impression October 1925

Fourth impression (cheap edition) September 1927
First published October 1927
Second impression November 1927
First published 1920
Second edition 1920
New and revised edition 1926

"All the above appear on the back of the title page, but sometimes I have the year of publication printed on the title page only."

R. COBDEN-SANDERSON, LTD. (UNITED KINGDOM)
(Formerly R. Cobden-Sanderson; out of business prior to 1949.)
1937 Statement: *See* 1928 Statement of R. Cobden-Sanderson (United Kingdom)

COBRA INSTITUTE
2000 Statement: *See* 2000 Statement of Diane Publishing Co.

CODA PUBLICATIONS
2001 Statement: "We do not identify a first printing (but we do identify printings after the first) on the copyright page."

COE REVIEW PRESS
2000 Statement: "The first printing of a first edition is indicated by the words 'First Edition'. However, we rarely indicate first editions, because we rarely publish a title that we expect to reprint."

COFFEE HOUSE PRESS
1988 Statement: "Presently at Coffee House Press, we have no system of designation for the first editions of our books."
1993 Statement: "To designate first editions of Coffee House Press trade books, we print '10 9 8 7 6 5 4 3 2 1' below the CIP data.

"While we have frequently used this system to designate subsequent printings, effective immediately this is our method of designating first editions.

"Our imprint editions do not follow this practice as we rarely produce reprintings of our letterpress books."
2000 Statement: *See* 1993 Statement

COGITO BOOKS
See 2000 Statement of Medical Physics Publishing Corp

COKESBURY PRESS
(Merged with Abingdon Press August, 1940 and became Abingdon-Cokesbury Press.)
1937 Statement: "Most Cokesbury books carry an edition symbol at the bottom of the copyright page. The first edition carries a symbol 'C'; second editions, the symbol 'O,' and subsequent editions according to the following scheme:

1 2 3 4 5 6 7 8 9 0
COKESBURY P

"A few books in certain classifications carry no edition marks at all. Occasionally a first edition carries the words 'First edition' on the copyright page but this is not our general practice."

COLD SPRING HARBOR LABORATORY PRESS

2001 Statement: "We set a number string on the copyright page. The lowest number indicates the printing, for example: 1 2 3 4 5 6 7. This would indicate a first printing."

COLDWATER PRESS, INC.

1995 Statement: "We distinguish first edition in the following way and on the copyright page: First edition."

2000 Statement: Coldwater Press, Inc. is not now publishing books.

COLLEGE PRESS PUBLISHING CO.

2000 Statement: The first printing of a first edition is identified by: copyright © year of first printing/first edition.

COLLEGIATE PRESS, INC.

(Became Iowa State College Press, sometime prior to 1947.)

COLLIER BOOKS

1989 Statement: *See* 1989 Statement of Macmillan Publishing Co., Inc.

1993 Statement: *See* 1993 Statement of Macmillan, Inc.

REX COLLINGS LIMITED (UNITED KINGDOM)

1976 Statement: "The only information we print in the first edition of any of our publications is the year in which the book is published. This follows the name of the copyright holder (Rex Collings or the author) and appears on the title verso, as:

© REX COLLINGS 1976

"All subsequent editions or reprints carry the impression or edition number in addition to the year of original publication."

1981 Statement: "In general the information you quote is correct. What appears in a first edition is:

First published in Great Britain by Rex Collings,
6 Paddington Street, London W1
© Rex Collings 1981
ISBN . . . .

Reprints are shown:

© Rex Collings 1981
ISBN . . .
Reprinted 1981
Second edition 1982
Reprinted 1982 (twice)
Reprinted 1984
Third edition 1985."

1988 Statement: "We still follow the practice outlined in our 1981 Statement, although a 1988 Statement would show our address as 38 King Street, London, WC2. At present we have no subsidiaries nor imprints."

WILLIAM COLLINS PTY LTD (AUSTRALIA)

1981 Statement: "For the first printing for hardbacks and paperbacks, these are designated in Cataloguing in Publication (CIP) data which is on the reverse of the title page. The line reads:

First published by William Collins Pty Ltd, 19..

This is standard practice for us.

"If the book is a paperback (takeover) the hardback data is given as well as the line

First published in Fontana (our paperback imprint) 19..

"This procedure has been followed for the last 10 years (before that the copyright line for the author would have been the only indication). The change probably came about either in response to a request from the National Library or was initiated in house."

("In 1989 William Collins Pty Limited merged with Angus & Robertson Publishers. The company name subsequently became HarperCollins Publishers (Australia) Pty Limited.")

COLLINS PUBLISHERS SAN FRANCISCO

1993 Statement: *See* 1993 Statement of HarperCollins Publishers

W. COLLINS, SON & CO., LTD. (UNITED KINGDOM)

1928 Statement: *See* 1937 Statement

1937 Statement: "We do not adopt any special method of designating first editions or first impressions. All our books bear on the reverse of the title page the date of publication and the word 'copyright.'

"In case of subsequent publication of a cheaper edition, the date of the original edition and that of the cheap edition are inserted on the back of the title-page.

"We have always used this method of identifying first editions."

1947 Statement: *See* 1937 Statement

1988 Statement: *See* 1988 Statement of William Collins Sons & Co. Ltd. (United Kingdom)

WILLIAM COLLINS SONS & CO. LTD.
(UNITED KINGDOM)

1988 Statement: "We still follow the practice outlined in the [1947] statement of W. Collins, Son & Co., Ltd. (United Kingdom) and all imprints and subsidiaries follow this practice."

See 1947 Statement of W. Collins, Son & Co., Ltd (United Kingdom)

THE COLONIAL WILLIAMSBURG FOUNDATION

1976 Statement: Currently, first printings are not designated. Subsequent printings are so designated; as well as new or revised editions. In the past, second printings, revised editions, etc., were not always designated.

1981, 1988, 1993 Statements: *See* 1976 Statement

COLORADO ASSOCIATED UNIVERSITY PRESS

1976 Statement: "We have no particular method of identifying first editions
.... We are a small operation and seldom reprint."

1981 Statement: "We have no particular method of identifying first editions,
although subsequent editions are always identified by 'Revised Edition,'
'Fourth Edition,' and so on."

1988 Statement: *See* 1981 Statement

COLORADO RAILROAD MUSEUM

1993 Statement: "Most of our publications have been issued in only one
printing. Subsequent printings are indicated by wording on the copyright page
(sometimes on the wraps of softcovers) as 'second printing,' 'revised edition'
or similar wording. One or two merely show an additional copyright date.
Prior editors of our publications were not consistent in this respect."

2000 Statement: *See* 1993 Statement

COLT PRESS
(Paterson, New Jersey)

1947 Statement: "All editions marked in fly sheets of books."

COLUMBIA ALTERNATIVE LIBRARY

2000 Statement: "Subsequent printings either drop a number from the
copyright page '10 9 8 7 6 5 4 3 2 1,' or else will have 'second printing' on
that page."

COLUMBIA UNIVERSITY PRESS

1928 Statement: "No distinction exists in regard to first and other editions
except that there is printed on the title page the date of first printing for the
first editions. On succeeding editions the date is removed from the title page
and the second or third printing is noted on the copyright page."

1936 Statement: "The first printing of any edition is indicated by the
presence of a date with the imprint on the title page. On subsequent printings
the date is removed from the title page, and the information is given on the
copyright page. Revised editions are so noted on the title page, and first or
subsequent printings of such editions are indicated in the same way as they
are indicated for the first editions."

1947 Statement: *See* 1936 Statement

See also King's Crown Press

1976 Statement: "We make a careful distinction between the terms 'printing'
and 'edition'—a 'second printing' is merely a happy reprinting (with errata
corrected) of a book that has sold rather well and is indicated by the disap-
pearance of the '1' from the string of numbers on the copyright page; a 'second
edition' means that the text has been extensively overhauled, perhaps even
chapters added. The latter is indicated by the words 'Second Edition' on the
title page and the dates of the first and second editions on the copyright page."

1988 Statement: "We are no longer putting a date on the title page of our
books. The year of publication is stated in the copyright notice on the
copyright page. Indication of a second (or later) printing of a book can be seen

in a series of digits printed on the copyright page. We are very careful to distinguish a second edition—meaning that the text has been substantially revised or that new chapters have been added or former ones deleted."
1993, 2000 Statements: *See* 1988 Statement

COMMEMORATIVE EDITIONS (AUSTRALIA)
1981 Statement: *See* 1981 Statement of Widescope International Publishers Pty. Ltd. (Australia)

COMMONWEALTH PRESS
1976 Statement: "At CP first editions carry no designation. Second, third, fourth, etc., editions are so designated. We have always used this system."
1981 Statement: "You may repeat [the 1976 Statement]. Also, when we have a top selling book, we include the printing history (month and year of each reprinting)."
1988 Statement: "You may repeat the information supplied SRP in the 1976 and 1981 policy statements, but omitting 'top-selling books include month and year of each reprinting.' "

COMPACT BOOKS
1993 Statement: *See* 1981 Statement of Frederick Fell Publishers, Inc.

COMPARATIVE SEDIMENTOLOGY LAB
2000 Statement: "No second editions of our small serials."

COMPASS EDITIONS
1949 Statement: *See* 1947 Statement of The Press of James A. Decker

COMPASS POINT MYSTERIES
2000 Statement: *See* 2000 Statement of Quincannon Publishing Group

THE COMPASS PRESS
1994 Statement: *See* 1994 Statement of Howells House
2000 Statement: "We do not identify first editions as such, but we identify all subsequent editions and revised editions on jacket, cover, and title page and list each reprinting below copyright date on copyright page."
See also 2000 Statement of Howells House

COMPCARE PUBLISHERS
1993 Statement: "The print number of all our publications has always been indicated by a line of numbers on the copyright page. The numbers are sequential from left to right and are followed by a line of year indicators. Each time we go back to press, the number of the present printing is deleted from the listing and the year indicator is also made current. Therefore, if the number at the far left is 1, it is the first printing."

COMSTOCK BONANZA PRESS
2000 Statement: "At Comstock Bonanza Press we do not always identify the first printing of a first edition (often that's the only printing of a paper-

back), but when we do, we print the words 'First Edition' or 'First Paperback Edition.' These words would not appear in subsequent printings."

COMSTOCK BOOKS
1988 Statement: *See* 1988 Statement of Cornell University Press

COMSTOCK PUBLISHING ASSOCIATES
2000 Statement: *See* 2000 Statement of Cornell University Press

CONARI PRESS
1994 Statement: The first printing of a first edition is indicated by the number line 1 2 3 4 5 6 7 8 9 0. The lowest number showing indicates the printing. "First Edition" is also stated.
2000 Statement: "Please correct to 00 01 02   10 9 8 7 6 5 4 3 2 1. 'First Edition' is not stated."

CONCORDIA PUBLISHING HOUSE
1994 Statement: "We . . . have no particular way of designating first printings. Second or revised printings are so noted."

CONDÉ NAST BOOKS (UNITED KINGDOM)
1994 Statement: *See* 1994 Statement of Ebury Press (United Kingdom)

CONFIDENT COLLECTOR
1993 Statement: *See* 1993 Statement of Avon Books

CONFLUENCE PRESS INC
2001 Statement: "We state 'First edition' on the copyright page. We also use a number string where the lowest number indicates the printing."

CONFRONTATION MAGAZINE PRESS
2000 Statement: "Our first editions are listed by date on the copyright page. Any further printing is listed below the original printing date. Example:
First printing: November 15, 1999
Second printing: May 15, 2000."

CONNECTICUT ACADEMY OF ARTS & SCIENCES
2000 Statement: "We identify the first printing of a first edition by the statement: First published___by the Academy. New Haven Connecticut. Second editions are identified as such."

CONSERVATORY OF AMERICAN LETTERS
1995 Statement: "We do not make any sort of notification for first editions. However all editions and printings after the first are noted on the copyright page."
2000 Statement: "We do not have any method for designating a first edition, except it doesn't say anything. Subsequent editions and printings are designated simply, for example, 'Second printing, 2001', 'Second edition, 2001', 'Second printing of second edition, 2001' etc."

CONSOLIDATED MUSIC PUBLISHERS
2001 Statement: *See* 2001 Statement of Music Sales Corp

CONSTABLE & COMPANY, LIMITED (UNITED KINGDOM)
1928 Statement: "We have no standardised method of designating our first editions, but generally speaking, we put 'First published [date]' on the back of the title-page, and if this appears without any other detail, the book on which it appears is a first edition. Reprints are noted also on the back of the title-page, under the original legend. Please observe that this is merely our usual practice and not a standardised or official method."
1937, 1947 Statements: *See* 1928 Statement
Statement for 1960: *See* 1928 Statement
1982 Statement: "Our practice since 1970 has been to designate a first edition with the words 'First published in Great Britain 0000.' Any further editions have the words 'Reprinted 0000' in addition. If there is no mention of this, the book in question should be a first edition. This has been our usual practice since 1970 but is not a standardised or official method. Prior to 1970 the method indicated in our earlier statement is applicable."
1988 Statement: *See* 1982 Statement
2000 Statement: *See* 2000 Statement of Constable & Robinson Ltd (United Kingdom).

CONSTABLE & ROBINSON LTD (UNITED KINGDOM)
2000 Statement: "Constable & Company, Limited is now called Constable & Robinson Ltd, as of January 2000. No change to the [1988] statement [of Constable & Company, Limited]."
See also Constable & Company, Limited (United Kingdom)

CONTEMPORARY BOOKS
1994 Statement: The first printing of a first edition is indicated by the number line 1 2 3 4 5 6 7 8 9 10. The lowest number showing indicates the printing.

CONTEMPORARY BOOKS INC.
1988 Statement: "Contemporary does nothing to designate first printing and never has."

CONTEMPORARY DRAMA SERVICE
2000 Statement: *See* 2000 Statement of Meriwether Publishing Ltd.

CONTEMPORARY RESEARCH PRESS
2001 Statement: "We state 'First edition' on the copyright page. We also set a number string; the lowest number indicates the printing."

CONTINUUM INTERNATIONAL PUBLISHING GROUP INC
(New York)
2000 Statement: "If the year on top of copyright page matches © year, it's a first edition. This method was adopted in 1980."

CONWAY MARITIME PRESS
2001 Statement: *See* 2001 Statement of Brassey's Inc.

LEO COOPER LTD. (UNITED KINGDOM)

1976, 1981 Statements: *See* 1976, 1981 Statements of Seeley, Service & Cooper Ltd. (United Kingdom)

1989 Statement: *See* 1989 Statement of The Octopus Publishing Group PLC (United Kingdom)

1994 Statement: "Leo Cooper is an imprint of Pen & Sword Books Ltd., 47 Church Street, Barnsley, South Yorks S70 2AS, England. Prior to this arrangement of 1990, he has been associated with Frederick Warne, then Secker & Warburg, William Heinemann and lastly the Octopus Publishing Group. First printings are indicated by the statement 'First published in 19—' and the absence of any note of subsequent printings."

CO-OPERATIVE UNION LTD (UNITED KINGDOM)

1994 Statement: "The imprint Holyoake Books has been in existence since 1986 and since that time our consistent policy has been to print on the back of the title page 'First published in (followed by the month and year).' Subsequent reprints or editions continue to carry the above line but with an additional line stating 'Second edition (year).' "

2001 Statement: *See* 1994 Statement

COPLEY PUBLISHING GROUP

2000 Statement: "Copley Publishing Group does not currently differentiate first printings of first editions."

COPPER BEECH PRESS

1981 Statement: "Since we do paperback books exclusively (perfect bound), we almost never have more than one edition of a single title. When we do, we generally indicate either by a change of cover or by some note after the title page that the imprint is indeed a second printing."

1989, 1993, 2000 Statements: *See* 1981 Statement

COPPER CANYON PRESS

1976 Statement: "Since all our titles to date have been first editions, we make no notice of same. When (this winter) we do make a second printing, it will be so stated on the copyright page. We also do very limited editions signed and hand bound on most titles. These, of course, are distinguished by the poet's signature and by the binding itself."

1981 Statement: "Unless otherwise noted, all Copper Canyon Press books are first editions. When we reprint trade paperbacks from limited signed fine editions, it is so stated in the colophon. Second printings are noted on the copyright page."

1988, 1994 Statements: *See* 1981 Statement

2000 Statement: "Since 1999 Copper Canyon Press has designated the edition on the copyright page using scratch numbers or in writing. Books published before 1999, unless otherwise noted on the copyright page are first editions. In cases of trade paperback reprints of limited fine editions, the edition is noted in the colophon."

CORDILLERA PRESS

1995 Statement: *See* 1995 Statement of Johnson Books
2000 Statement: The Cordillera Press is no longer in operation.

CORGI (UNITED KINGDOM)

2001 Statement: *See* 2001 Statement of Transworld Publishers Ltd (United Kingdom)

CORK UNIVERSITY PRESS (REPUBLIC OF IRELAND)

1988 Statement: "I set out hereunder the present position of the Press in this regard:
  "Our past editions and past printings carry the following wording:
    'First published 19..' on copyright page.
  "If we have a subsequent printing the description used is
    'First published 19..
    Second edition 19...' "
1994 Statement: "Cork University Press uses the following to designate the printing of a first edition:

First Published in YEAR by
Cork University Press
University College
Cork
© AUTHORNAME YEAR
Reprinted YEAR
(if applicable)

This usually appears on the recto of the title-page."
2001 Statement: *See* 1994 Statement. "However, in that time we have expanded. Three years ago we bought Attic Press and have since set up Atrium, as an imprint of Attic. All books published under these two imprints use the same wording as that for Cork University Press titles."

CORMORANT BOOKS INC. (CANADA)

2001 Statement: "In the past, Cormorant Books has not had a policy of identifying first editions. Beginning with the Fall 2001 season, first editions will be identified with the line 'This Cormorant Book is a first edition' on the copyright page. Subsequent editions will be identified by 'Second Edition' etc."

CORNELL MARITIME PRESS

1947 Statement: "No special method of identifying first editions. Copyright date is date of first printing. Subsequent prints so stated under copyright line."
1976 Statement: "We do not use any specific method other than indicating later printings as a Second Printing, etc."
1981 Statement: "Beginning in April of 1980, we have tried to leave as clear a 'bibliographical trail' as we can, although sometimes a paucity of records has made this difficult.

  "As a matter of standard practice, we do give the data about the printing history in each new printing of any book. We don't, however, make any attempt to recite all the details. If we are doing, for example, the third printing of the fourth edition of a work, we would show (on the copyright page) a notice which might read like this:

'First edition, 1960. Fourth edition, 1970; third printing, 1981.'

"We make no effort, you will notice, to indicate when the second and third editions were issued nor the number of printings of any previous edition. But we do indicate in each printing just which one it is."

1988, 1993, 2000 Statements: *See* 1981 Statement

CORNELL UNIVERSITY PRESS

1976 Statement: "A book published by Cornell University is a first edition unless stated otherwise. It is also a first printing unless stated otherwise."

1981, 1988, 1993, 2000 Statements: *See* 1976 Statement

CORNERSTONE PRESS CHICAGO

2001 Statement: "We state 'First printing' on the copyright page. We also use a number string where the lowest number indicates the printing. We follow the *Chicago Manual of Style*."

CORNERSTONE PUBLISHING

1995 Statement: "We do not specifically designate a first printing in our books. However, second or revised printings are so noted in this way on the copyright page. Therefore, by process of elimination, our first printings can be determined. Cornerstone adopted this method of designation in 1992."

CORWIN PRESS, INC.

2001 Statement: "We identify the first printing of a first edition by a number line. The lowest number indicates the printing."

COSMOPOLITAN BOOK COMPANY
(Out of business prior to 1937.)

1928 Statement: "Up to the present time we have published only large editions of popular authors and there has been no cause to designate the first edition. We are changing our policy slightly now and it is possible that we may find it necessary to mark the editions. In this case we will probably print the words 'First Edition' under the copyright notice and remove it on any later printings."

COTEAU BOOKS (CANADA)

2001 Statement: "As a publisher primarily of Canadian fiction, poetry, drama and children's literature, we rarely do any more than the first edition of a book. But we do frequently do more than one printing.

"We don't identify first editions as such. In the year 2000, we started using the countdown numbering system on the copyright page to identify which printing of the first edition the copy in question represents. We count down: 10 9 8 7 6 5 4 3 2 1.

"However, a feature we use to facilitate selling our titles into the American market is to use the following copyright notice on our Fall season books:

(Copyright symbol) (the author) 2000

First US Edition, 2001
"So, in these cases, you could say that the first US edition is clearly identified with a statement."

JOANNA COTLER BOOKS
1993 Statement: *See* 1993 Statement of HarperCollins Publishers
2001 Statement: *See* 2001 Statement of HarperCollinsPublishers

THE COTTAGE PRESS
1993 Statement: "On the copyright page, we note 'First Printing' for the first run. Subsequent runs are marked:
Second Printing
Third Printing, etc."
2001 Statement: *See* 1993 Statement

COTTAGE PUBLICATIONS, INC.
1995 Statement: "We do not identify a first edition in any way within that edition. However, second and subsequent editions are identified both on the front cover and on the copyright page, and we list previous editions consecutively on the copyright page of the second and subsequent editions. We have stopped designating first and subsequent printings of any edition . . . because they have no value to us or to our customers, especially since we sometimes reprint a particular edition several times, depending upon our market demands.

"Our policy identifying second and subsequent editions was initiated in 1986. The policy of not identifying individual printings of editions started in 1990."

COTTONTAIL PUBLICATIONS
2000 Statement: "We do not identify the First Edition by any particular ID. The subsequent printings or editions are identified after the copyright notice."

MICHAEL E. COUGHLIN, PUBLISHER
2000 Statement: "We identify the first printing of a first edition by the statement: 'First edition printed in The United States of America.' "

COUNCIL FOR BRITISH ARCHAEOLOGY
(UNITED KINGDOM)
1988 Statement: We do not specify a first printing or first edition; this is implied if the copyright page simply states: "Published 1988," etc. A further printing will state: "reprinted 1988." A new edition will state, for example: "1st edition 1985," "2nd edition 1988," etc.

"This is the method we have always used, and we have no imprints or subsidiaries."
1994, 2000 Statements: *See* 1988 Statement

COUNCIL FOR INDIAN EDUCATION
2000 Statement: "All First Printing, First Editions have only the copyright date. All other printings and editions have directly below the copyright date the statement 'Fifth printing,' or 'Second edition,' etc."

COUNCIL OAK PUBLISHING CO., INC.

1994 Statement: The first printing of a first edition is indicated by the number line 99 98 97 96 95 94 5 4 3 2 1. The lowest number showing indicates the printing.

"We have not been very consistent on this matter. If there's no edition or impression statement in one of our books, it's probably a first impression, first edition."

2000 Statement: *See* 1994 Statement

COUNCIL PUBLICATIONS

2000 Statement: *See* 2000 Statement of Council for Indian Education

COUNTERPOINT PRESS

2001 Statement: "We state 'First printing' on the copyright page [and] we identify the first printing of a first edition by a number line, the lowest number indicates the printing."

COUNTRY LIFE, LTD. (UNITED KINGDOM)

1937 Statement: "It is our practice not to put the date of publication on the title page but on the back of the title. In subsequent editions the Bibliographical description is added. Thus:

First Published 1934
Second Impression 1935
Second Edition 1936."

1949 Statement: *See* 1937 Statement

1989 Statement: *See* 1989 Statement of The Octopus Publishing Group PLC (United Kingdom)

COUNTRY MUSIC FOUNDATION PRESS

2001 Statement: "We state 'First edition' on the copyright page. We also set a number string, using the lowest number in the string for the printing."

COUNTRYMAN PRESS

(Absorbed by A. S. Barnes and Company, Inc.)
See A. S. Barnes and Company, Inc.

THE COUNTRYMAN PRESS, INC.

1976 Statement: "The Countryman Press does nothing to indicate a first edition in the original printing. On a subsequent printing, there is noted 'second printing' with the date, or 'revised edition.' Anything other would be considered a first edition."

1981 Statement: *See* 1976 Statement

1988 Statement: "Please note that there have been some changes effected since the statement that appeared in 1976. To wit: The Countryman Press is now the parent company for two imprints, Backcountry Publications and Foul Play Press. All titles published have a full colophon on the copyright page listing the designer, compositor, printer, et al. The printing or edition [after the first] is also listed thereon."

1993 Statement: "On the copyright pages of first editions, there is no statement indicating the number of the edition. In the case of second editions, the notation on the copyright page will state either 'revised edition' or 'second edition.' All subsequent editions will state the number of the edition—i.e., third edition, fourth edition, etc. Since 1990, we have been indicating the printing of each edition by a row of numbers on the copyright page, with the lowest number indicating the printing; if, for example, the lowest number is 2, then the book is part of the second printing of that edition."

2001 Statement: "The [1993 Statement] remains the same, but we are now owned by W.W. Norton & Co., Inc., who bought Countryman in 1996."

COUNTRYSIDE BOOKS (UNITED KINGDOM)
2001 Statement: "We state 'First published' on the copyright page. Subsequent printings and editions are then identified on the title verso page."

THE COUNTRYWOMAN'S PRESS
1988, 1994 Statements: *See* 1988, 1994 Statements of Padre Productions

COURIER OF MAINE BOOKS
1976 Statement: "Our first editions and their first printings are designated in no special way. They simply carry on the copyright page a standard copyright notice, the ISBN, and LC number. These methods do not differ from any previously used."

LOUISE COURTEAU, EDITRICE (CANADA)
1995 Statement: "We have no particular way of designating first printings. In the event of a second or subsequent impression being published, that fact would be given on the reverse of the title page as follows:
Second impression   November 1994
Third impression   May 1995."

PASCAL COVICI
(Became Covici, Friede.)
1928 Statement: "Sometimes we print 'first edition' on the reverse of the title page, and sometimes not, but invariably we print 'second printing' on the second issue."

COVICI, FRIEDE, INC.
(Out of business. Publications bought by Crown Publishers.)
1937 Statement: "We do not identify our first editions in any way. However, when a book goes into a second printing we record on the copyright page the date of the first printing and the date of the second printing, etc. In other words, a first edition of Covici, Friede is generally identified by the fact that the copyright page does not designate the edition."

COWARD-McCANN
1993 Statement: *See* 1993 Statement of The Putnam & Grosset Group

COWARD-McCANN, INC.

1937 Statement: "When we first began to publish in 1928, we used to print our colophon on the copyright page of all first editions:

"On second and subsequent editions we omitted the torch part of the colophon and used only the lower half.

"However, we did not continue with this arrangement, so that it is impossible to be certain of our first editions. What is certain though, is that any edition appearing with the colophon without the torch is not a first.

"At present our first editions bear no distinguishing marks. If a book goes into a second or third printing, a note to this effect appears on the copyright page."

1947 Statement: *See* 1937 Statement

COYOTE BOOKS

2000 Statement: "We have used no consistent designation to identify printings or editions."

CRAFTSMAN BOOK COMPANY

1976 Statement: "We make no effort to identify first editions."

1981, 1988, 1994, 2000 Statements: *See* 1976 Statement

ROBERT L CRAGER & CO

2000 Statement: *See* 2000 Statement of Pelican Publishing Company

CRANKY NELL BOOKS

2000 Statement: *See* 2000 Statement of Kane/Miller Book Publishers

CRAZY GAMES

2000 Statement: *See* 2000 Statement of Price Stern Sloan

CRCS PUBLICATIONS

1994 Statement: "We print 'First Edition' on the first edition, but we keep it on all reprints unless a second edition is done."

CREATIVE AGE PRESS, INC.

1947 Statement: "Creative Age Press books which are first printings simply say 'Copyright—' with no reference to a printing of any kind. Subsequent printings, however, carry the legend on the copyright page, 'Second Printing,' 'Third Printing,' etc. Therefore, a rule of thumb which can safely be followed is: if there is no reference to a printing, it is a first; all others identify themselves."

CREATIVE ARTS BOOK CO.

1994 Statement: "We have no indications of first editions."

CREATIVE BOOK CO
2001 Statement: "We do not identify a first printing (but we will from now on). We do identify printings after the first printing on the copyright page."

CREATIVE BOOK PUBLISHING (CANADA)
2001 Statement: "With our titles, there is no indication on a first edition book that it is indeed a first edition. However, reprints indicate what number of reprints have occurred i.e. 3rd Printing; 2nd Printing July 2000, 1st Printing June 1999. Thus, if no indication is given that a book is in its 2nd, 3rd, 4th . . . etc. printing, it is a first edition. This policy has been adopted since Creative Book Publishing became a publishing company. This method has not changed since it was adopted. All of our imprints follow the same guidelines: Creative Publishers, Tuckamore Books, and Killick Press."

CREATIVE HOMEOWNER
2000 Statement: "The first printing of a first edition is identified by the following number line: 10 9 8 7 6 5 4 3 2 1. This method has always been used."

CREATIVE MONOCHROME LTD (UNITED KINGDOM)
2001 Statement: "All books marked 'First Edition' are also First Printing unless qualified to the contrary."

CREATIVE PUBLISHERS (CANADA)
2001 Statement: *See* 2001 Statement of Creative Book Publishing (Canada)

CREATIVE PUBLISHING COMPANY
1988 Statement: "We have always stated the edition and printing. Our first book was published in 1978. If we reprinted a book and added or deleted material, we would indicate that it was a second edition, first printing."
1993 Statement: *See* 1988 Statement

CREEKSTONE (CANADA)
2001 Statement: "We do not identify our first editions as such: however, reprints are identified on the publication page. For example, 'Fourth Printing, March 2001.' "

CRESCENDO
1988 Statement: *See* 1976 Statement of Taplinger Publishing Co., Inc.

THE CRESSET PRESS, INC.
2000 Statement: "We do not make any identification of first editions."

CRESSRELLES PUBLISHING COMPANY LTD. (UNITED KINGDOM)
1994 Statement: A first printing is designated by the phrase "First published in (date)" on the back of the title page.
2000 Statement: *See* 1994 Statement

CRESTLINE
2001 Statement: *See* 2001 Statement of Motorbooks International

CRICKET BOOKS
2001 Statement: "We state 'First edition' on the copyright page."

CRICKETFIELD PRESS
1994 Statement: *See* 1994 Statement of Picton Press

CRISP LEARNING
2001 Statement: *See* 2001 Statement of Crisp Publications Inc

CRISP PUBLICATIONS INC
2001 Statement: "We identify the first printing of a first edition by a number line. The lowest number indicates the printing."

CRITERION BOOKS
1976 Statement: *See* 1976 Statement of Thomas Y. Crowell Company
1981, 1988 Statements: *See* 1981, 1988 Statements of Harper & Row Publishers, Inc.

CROCODILE BOOKS
2001 Statement: *See* 2001 Statement of Interlink Publishing Group Inc

F. S. CROFTS & CO., PUBLISHERS
(Merged with D. Appleton-Century Co., Inc., on January 2, 1948, to become D. Appleton-Century-Crofts, Inc.)
1947 Statement: "The verso of the title page of one of our books, 'Basic Spanish,' will show you how we indicate the printings that are made of our books:—

Copyright, 1939, by F. S. Crofts & Co., Inc.
First printing, April, 1939
* * * * * * * * * * *

* * * * * * * * * * *

Twenty-first printing, September, 1947"

CROSBY LOCKWOOD STAPLES (UNITED KINGDOM)
1976, 1981, 1988 Statements: *See* 1976, 1981, 1988 Statements of Granada Publishing Limited (United Kingdom)

CROSS CULTURAL PUBLICATIONS INC
2001 Statement: "We do not identify 'First Editions.' However, whenever we have a second or subsequent edition, we do indicate that on the title page."

CROSS RIVER PRESS
2000 Statement: *See* 2000 Statement of Abbeville Press, Inc.

THE CROSSING PRESS
1976 Statement: "The only way we designate first editions is the omission of 2nd printing, 3rd printing, so on. (or 2nd edition, 3rd edition). Am I clear? When we rerun a book, we place the date of the rerunning & the words 2nd or 3rd printing or edition."
1981, 1988, 1994 Statements: *See* 1976 Statement
2000 Statement: "We distinguish a 2nd edition only—and rarely."

CROSSROAD/CONTINUUM

1988 Statement: "Our first editions bear no special designation. If, however, a title is reprinted or reissued, that fact is set forth on the copyright page.

"Crossroad/Continuum was established in 1980 as a new independent publishing house, continuing to publish the programs developed by Herder and Herder in the 1960s, Seabury Press in the 1970s, and The Frederick Ungar Publishing Company since 1940. Crossroad/Continuum imprints and subsidiaries follow the same practice."

CROSSROAD/CONTINUUM PUBLISHING GROUP

1988 Statement: *See* 1988 Statement of Crossroad/Continuum

THE CROSSROAD PUBLISHING COMPANY

("Crossroad and Continuum are now separate companies.
Crossroad was established in 1981.")

1994 Statement: "Our first editions bear no special designation. If, however, a title is reprinted or reissued, that fact is set forth on the copyright page."

CROSSROADS BOOKS

1993 Statement: "We are publishers of scholarly works on inter-cultural topics. We also publish general works on cross-cultural matters for the general audience. We do not have special designations for first editions or first printings except the standard statement on the copyright page."

CROSSWAY BOOKS

1993 Statement: "We designate the first printing and all printings by using numbers at the bottom of the copyright page: 1 2 3 4 5 6 7 8 9 0. When we reprint, we delete figure 1, etc."

2000 Statement: *See* 1993 Statement. Note that "special small print runs of books we had out-of-print and brought back in print . . . do not have updated printing statements."

CROSSWAY BOOKS (UNITED KINGDOM)

1994 Statement: "Crossway Books, Nottingham, adopts the form:
First edition 1993
Reprinted 1994."

2000 Statement: *See* 2000 Statement of Inter-Varsity Press (United Kingdom)

THOMAS Y. CROWELL COMPANY

1928 Statement: "Our present practice is not to indicate in any way the first edition. Subsequent printings are so indicated.

"In the absence of the words, Second Printing, Third Printing, etc., it can be safely assumed that without such an inscription the book is a copy of the first edition."

1937 Statement: "Our present practice is not to indicate in any way the first edition. Subsequent printings are so indicated.

"In the absence of the words 'Second Printing,' 'Third Printing,' etc., it can be safely assumed that without such an inscription the book is a copy of the first edition.

"We began using this method about ten years ago."

1947 Statement: "The statement above is still true, although of course the statement that we began using the method about ten years ago needs bringing up to date.

"You might also mention that offset books carry a series of numbers from 1 to 10 at the bottom of the copyright page. Since additions cannot be made to offset plates, the lowest number is rubbed out with each reprinting. Thus the first printing will have all the numbers; the second printing will run from 2 to 10; the third printing from 3 to 10; the fourth from 4 to 10; and so on."

1976 Statement: "On first editions, the numbers 1 2 3 4 5 6 7 8 9 10 appear at the bottom of the page. Each time the book is reprinted, the next number is deleted, thus designating the current printing. A long time ago, I believe the previous method was to say: 'First printing,' 'Second printing,' etc."

1981, 1988 Statements: *See* 1981, 1988 Statements of Harper & Row Publishers, Inc.

CROWN PUBLISHERS

1947 Statement: "In most instances, we make no identification beyond numbering the various printings of each of our books."

Statement for 1960: "[Prior to July, 1979] a first edition, first printing, had absolutely no printing history on it. Reprints were indicated by the printing history."

1976 Statement: *See* Statement for 1960

1981 Statement: "At Crown, the first printing of a first edition is indicated by the printing number '1' (in a descending series starting with '10') and the words 'First Edition.' After the first printing, the words 'First Edition' and the number '1' are deleted. Numbers are deleted with each corresponding reprint, thus, the line '10 9 8 7 6' would indicate the sixth printing.

"The above system is used for all Crown adult, Clarkson N. Potter and Harmony titles produced in-house, and it appears on the copyright page of books published after January 1980.

"Until I joined this company in July 1979, a first edition, first printing, had absolutely no printing history on it. Reprints were indicated by the printing history."

1988 Statement: *See* 1988 Statement of Crown Publishers Inc.

CROWN PUBLISHERS INC.

1988 Statement: "First printings carry the numbers 10 9 8 7 6 5 4 3 2 1 and the words First Edition under the numbers. In subsequent printings, we eliminate each number as needed and the words First Edition are deleted as well.

"This is for Crown, Harmony Books, Clarkson N. Potter, Inc., titles."

1995 Statement: *See* 1988 Statement

CRUCIBLE BOOKS (UNITED KINGDOM)
1988 Statement: *See* 1988 Statement of Thorsons Publishing Group Ltd (United Kingdom)

HARRY CUFF PUBLICATIONS LIMITED (CANADA)
1995 Statement: "Where titles have gone into a second or third printing (or edition), the usual practice has been to indicate same on the copyright page (about 20 titles). However, three of our most popular titles were in the past 'rushed' into a second printing without such notice appearing: *I've Been Working on the Railroad*, *Daughter of Labrador*, and *Art Rockwood's Newfoundland and Labrador Trivia*. With these three titles copies of the first printing are distinguishable only by their covers (which in all cases are noticeably 'darker' in the second printing)."

CULINARY ARTS LTD.
1995 Statement: "We have been publishers of specialty cookbooks since 1983. It is generally our custom to note First Edition on the copyright page. There have been a couple of our books where that was omitted and just the Copyright © (with symbol) and year were shown. We have always noted the year of subsequent printings and also note if it is a revised and/or expanded edition.

"In 1995 we began using a new method of notation as follows:
FIRST EDITION
95 96 97 98 99 - 10 9 8 7 6 5 4 3 2 1
When reprinting we will strike off the First Edition and change the year if appropriate, etc."

JAMES CUMMINS BOOKSELLER
1995 Statement: "We have no particular designation for a first editions, sometimes using 'First Published' on the copyright page and sometimes nothing but our imprint and date of publication. To date we have had only one printing of each of our titles. Our reprints list the first edition publisher's imprint and date of publication, and then include our imprint and date of reprinting on the copyright page. Some of our reprints are strictly limited to a specified number of copies, not to be reprinted by us, and this information is mentioned in our introduction."
2001 Statement: *See* 1995 Statement

CUNE PRESS
2001 Statement: "We identify the first printing of a first edition by no designation or by the words 'First Edition' with a number line.

"Books in second or later printing will always have a printing designation. Third printing will show '10 9 8 7 6 5 4 3'; Second printing will show '10 9 8 7 6 5 4 3 2.'"

CURBSTONE PRESS
1976 Statement: "We designate a first edition by the words 'First Edition' on the copyright page. We make no distinction between 'First Edition' and

'First Printing.' If we print more copies of the same book, it is labelled 'Second Edition.' "
1981 Statement: *See* 1976 Statement
1988 Statement: "We designate a first edition by the words, 'First Edition' on the copyright page. If we print more copies of the same book, it is labelled 'Second Printing.' "
1993, 2000 Statements: *See* 1988 Statement

CURIOUS NELL BOOKS
2000 Statement: *See* 2000 Statement of Kane/Miller Book Publishers

SAMUEL CURL, INC.
(A continuation of Hillman-Curl, Inc., it includes the imprints Arcadia House and Mystery House.)
1947 Statement: "First editions of our publications are distinguished by the lack of any printing notice on the copyright page. Following editions bear the date of the first printing, together with date of new printing, and which printing it is."

CURRENCY PRESS PTY LTD (AUSTRALIA)
1994 Statement: "Our method for identifying first editions and those follow-ing to date has been to state the year in which the book was first published on the verso page and then in subsequent editions, to list the dates of the reprinted versions."
2000 Statement: *See* 1994 Statement

CURRENT BOOKS, INC.
See A. A. Wyn, Inc.

CURRENT MEDICINE, INC.
2001 Statement: "We identify the first printing of a first edition by a number line, using the lowest number to indicate the printing."

CURZON PRESS LTD (UNITED KINGDOM)
2001 Statement: "We identify only editions, not printings; a first edition is so identified on the copyright page. Our imprints are Japan Library and Caucasus World."

CYCLOTOUR GUIDE BOOKS
2001 Statement: "We set a number string on the copyright page. The lowest number indicates the printing, for example: 1 2 3 4 5. This would indicate a first printing."

CYGNET BOOKS (AUSTRALIA)
1988 Statement: *See* 1988 Statement of The University of Western Australia Press (Australia)
2000 Statement: *See* 2000 Statement of University of Western Australia Press (Australia)

CYNIC PRESS

2000 Statement: "We identify the first printing of a first edition by the words 'First Edition.' Chapbooks are all single run, small run editions. They do not necessarily have a separate designation as 'First Edition.' "

CYPRESS HOUSE

2000 Statement: *See* 2000 Statement of QED Press

CYPRESS PRESS

1994 Statement: The first edition of a title is indicated by the words "First Edition" on the copyright page. This method has always been in use.

D

DACRE PRESS (UNITED KINGDOM)

1976 Statement: *See* 1976 Statement of Adam and Charles Black Publishers Limited (United Kingdom)

ANDREW DAKERS, LTD. (UNITED KINGDOM)

1947 Statement: "Our method of identifying first printings of our books and of differentiating subsequent printings, is that of printing on the back of the title page as follows:—

First published January 1945
Reprinted August 1946
Reprinted March 1947 and so on."

DAKOTA PRESS

See 1988 Statement of The University of South Dakota Press

DALKEY ARCHIVE

1988 Statement: "Since 1988, first printings of our books carry a 'First Edition' statement. Our earlier books (1984-87) have only a copyright date, but they can be assumed to be first printings unless a 'Second Printing' notice appears. We have no imprints or subsidiaries."

1993, 2000 Statements: *See* 1988 Statement

DAN RIVER PRESS

1995 Statement: *See* 1995 Statement of Conservatory of American Letters
2000 Statement: "We do not have any method for designating a first edition, except it doesn't say anything. Subsequent editions and printings are designated simply, for example, 'Second printing, 2001', 'Second edition, 2001', 'Second printing of second edition, 2001' etc."

C. W. DANIEL COMPANY (UNITED KINGDOM)

1928 Statement: "Our method of designating first editions of our books is to put 'First published, etc.,' on the back of each title page, and to add to that the dates of all further editions as they are issued."

THE C. W. DANIEL COMPANY, LTD. (UNITED KINGDOM)

1937 Statement: "Our method of designating first editions of our books is to put 'First published,' etc., on the back of each title page, and to add to that the dates of all further editions as they are issued."

1948 Statement: *See* 1937 Statement

1988 Statement: "Our company and subsidiaries still follow the practice [as given in the 1937 Statement]."

1994, 2000 Statements: *See* 1988 Statement

JOHN DANIEL & CO.

2001 Statement: *See* 2001 Statement of Fithian Press

JOHN DANIEL AND COMPANY

1993 Statement: *See* 1988 Statement of John Daniel, Publisher

JOHN DANIEL, PUBLISHER

1988 Statement: "We don't have any uniform practice of designating editions or printings."

2000 Statement: *See* 1988 Statement

DANIEL & DANIEL, PUBLISHERS, INC.

2001 Statement: *See* 2001 Statement of Fithian Press

DARK HORSE COMICS, INC. (CANADA)

2001 Statement: "At Dark Horse Comics, all book editions and printings are indicated on the copyright page. An example of our first-edition designation on books is noted as follows on the copyright page:

First Edition: January 2001
(ISBN)

"Subsequent editions are handled similarly. The month of publication is determined by the earliest possible planned on-sale date for the individual title. In the case of a paperback edition following a first edition in hardcover, 'First Paperback Edition' will be designated, with 'Paperback' struck from subsequent paperback editions. On the rare occasion of a hardcover and softcover edition published simultaneously, both designations will appear on the copyright page.

First Hardcover Edition: (Month YEAR)
(ISBN)
First Paperback edition: (Month YEAR)
(ISBN)

"On subsequent paperback editions, we would strike the hardcover designation entirely and remove 'Paperback' from the edition designation. In the case of a first-edition paperback with an accompanying limited-edition hardcover, the designations are as follows:

First edition: (Month YEAR)
(ISBN)
Limited hardcover edition: (Month YEAR)
(ISBN)

"The limited-edition designation will be struck from future softcover impressions.

"Our printing history on all editions is a simple strikeoff plate, with the previous impression struck before reprinting:

10 9 8 7 6 5 4 3 2 1

Printed in (Country)

"A second printing would appear thusly:

10 9 8 7 6 5 4 3 2

"In the case of a centered text design, the strikeoff plate looks like this:

1 3 5 7 9 10 8 6 4 2

Printed in (Country)

"A second printing would appear thusly:

3 5 7 9 10 8 6 4 2

"We do not indicate dates of individual printings. These practices have been in place at Dark Horse, with minor modifications, since the early Nineties."

DARTMOUTH (UNITED KINGDOM)
2000 Statement: *See* 2000 Statement of Gower Publishing Limited (United Kingdom)

DARTMOUTH COLLEGE
1988, 1993 Statements: *See* 1988 Statement of University Press of New England

THE DARTNELL CORPORATION
1976 Statement: "First printing of a first edition designated by copyright date only. This has always been our standard practice."
1981, 1988, 1993 Statements: *See* 1976 Statement

DARTON LONGMAN & TODD LTD (UNITED KINGDOM)
1994 Statement: "Darton, Longman & Todd designates the first printing of a first edition on the copyright page (the verso of the title page) of the book, saying: 'First published in 19XX by Darton, Longman & Todd' followed by our address.

"As far as I am aware, we have used this method of designation since the company was founded in 1959."
2000 Statement: *See* 1994 Statement

DARWIN BOOKS
2000 Statement: *See* 2000 Statement of The Darwin Press, Inc.

THE DARWIN PRESS, INC.
1993 Statement: "We are publishers of scholarly and educational books and have no particular way of designating first printings. Subsequent or revised printings are so noted."
2000 Statement: *See* 1993 Statement

DAUGHTERS OF ST. PAUL
1976 Statement: "Our first editions may be designated by the copyright date on the page after the title page."

1981 Statement: "Our first editions may be designated by the earliest copyright date on the page after the title page."

MAY DAVENPORT, PUBLISHERS

1994 Statement: "It seems we started out in 1977 with 'First Printings' but have used 'First Editions' on our books on the credit page behind the title page. With subsequent reprints, we have noted, 2nd edition or 2nd printing."

2000 Statement: *See* 1994 Statement

JONATHAN DAVID PUBLISHERS, INC

1988 Statement: "Our first printings are designated by the appearance of the numeral one on the copyright page. The year appears above the numeral. Subsequent printings are indicated by a change in numerals. This has been our practice since 1974."

1994 Statement: "Prior to 1978 we designated the first edition of each of our publications by printing, on the copyright page of the work, the words 'First edition' or 'First printing' followed by the year of publication. Subsequent editions were similarly coded.

"In 1978 we adopted the system of designating the editions of a work by printing the numbers '2 4 6 8 10 9 7 5 3 1' on the copyright page. With each subsequent printing, one of the numbers is deleted. Above these numbers, in a similar format, we indicate the year of the printing."

2000 Statement: *See* 1994 Statement

DAVID & CHARLES (HOLDINGS) LTD.
(UNITED KINGDOM)

1976 Statement: "We only identify first editions by providing the usual '© John Smith 1976' on the back of the title page; any subsequent impressions or editions would be identified as such, with their date. So the absence of any note such as 'second impression' conveys that the book is in fact a first impression."

1981 Statement: *See* 1976 Statement

1988 Statement: *See* 1988 Statement of David & Charles Publishers PLC (United Kingdom)

DAVID & CHARLES PUBLISHERS PLC
(UNITED KINGDOM)

1988 Statement: "Apart from the fact that we are now called David & Charles Publishers PLC, we can confirm that the [1976 Statement of David & Charles (Holdings)] still stands."

See 1976 Statement of David & Charles (Holdings) Ltd. (United Kingdom)

1994 Statement: *See* 1988 Statement

CHRISTOPHER DAVIES PUBLISHERS LTD
(UNITED KINGDOM)

2001 Statement: "We designate a first printing by printing on the imprint page 'Published in [the year]' together with copyright for the same year and name of author. Subsequent reprints have the year date of reprint and are printed on the imprint page. New editions are printed on the imprint page together with date. The 'First edition' is also printed on the imprint page in these circumstances."

PETER DAVIES, LTD. (UNITED KINGDOM)

1928 Statement: "I have no hard and fast method of designating a first edition.

"More often than not a bibliographical note is printed on the verso of the title-page of my publications. It reads: 'First printed in (e.g.) May, 1928.' In case a further edition or impression is issued, there will be an addition to the note, e.g. 'Reprinted, June 1928.' In the absence of any such addition, the book will be a first edition.

"If there is no bibliographical note at all, in which case the date, that is the year, will almost certainly appear on the title-page, then also the book may be taken to be a first edition."

1937, 1947 Statements: *See* 1928 Statement

Statement for 1960: "Our 1976 statement would equally have applied to the situation in 1960 and continues to reflect our current practice. If a book is a first edition it will carry the notice 'First published/First published in Great Britain 19...'

"If it is a reprint or a second or subsequent edition the original notice will be followed by 'Reprinted 19..' or 'Second edition 19..' as appropriate."

1976 Statement: "We have no means of identifying first editions other than the obvious bibliographical information provided on the verso title page of all our books."

1981 Statement: *See* 1976 Statement

F A DAVIS CO

2001 Statement: "We identify the first printing of a first edition by the number line 10 9 8 7 6 5 4 3 2 1."

DAVIS PUBLICATIONS, INC.

1988 Statement: "We do not make any designation. Essentially, we publish an anthology once. If these volumes are subsequently republished, they are done so in hardcover or in omnibus editions and are often prepared and distributed by other publishers who would apply their own policy."

DAVIS PUBLICATIONS, INC.
(Worcester, Massachusetts)

1993 Statement: "We designate a first edition with a standard indicia and statement 'revised' on the copyright pages of subsequent editions."

STEVE DAVIS PUBLISHING

1994 Statement: The first printing of a first edition is indicated by the statement "First Edition."

DAVIS-POYNTER LIMITED (UNITED KINGDOM)

1976 Statement: "We have no particular method of identifying first editions. We use the normal international copyright line, that is the details of copyright holder and date. Any reprints have another date line."

1981 Statement: *See* 1976 Statement

DAW BOOKS, INC.

1981 Statement: "DAW Books includes on the copyright page the designation 'First Printing,' and the month and year of that first release. Below this we print a sequence of numbers from 1 to 9. With each new printing, a number is deleted.

"Thus a first printing would have the number '1' lead off beneath the notice of this 'First Printing.' If the copyright date given on that page is the same as the year of our first printing, then you can be sure that it is also a First Edition.

"It should be noted that DAW Books are published by DAW Books, Inc., a separate corporate entity from New American Library, Inc, which is our co-publisher for marketing, production, and services, but which does not have any proprietary interest in us."

1988, 1993 Statements: *See* 1981 Statement.

2000 Statement: *See* 1981 Statement, but note that Penguin USA is now the co-publisher for marketing, production, and services.

THE DAWN HORSE PRESS

1976 Statement: "We originally published in hard cover, *The Knee of Listening*, by Franklin Jones. To identify our first edition, this first publication was printed by CSA Press, Lakemont, GA 30552. This is the distinguishing characteristic of the first edition of the publication. All our other publications are duly marked, 1st edition, 2nd edition, etc."

1981, 1988 Statements: *See* 1976 Statement

2000 Statement: "Unfortunately, our policy is no longer as concise and straighforward as our 1976, 1981, and 1988 statements. We have published many, many books since then with many unusual edition listings. So no, we do not follow the policy of our last statement.

"In approximately 1989, the Dawn Horse Press began to use the following system to identify first printing or first editions: the first edition of a book is usually not indicated with any edition description, but simply copyrighted in the year it is published. Subsequent editions of the same book will indicate that the new edition supercedes the previous editions (and generally lists all previous editions and their dates)."

DAWNE-LEIGH PUBLICATIONS

1981, 1988 Statements: *See* 1976 Statement of Celestial Arts

DAWSON'S BOOK SHOP

1976 Statement: "We do not identify first editions of our publications since we very seldom reprint our titles. In the few instances when they have been reissued, the later edition is clearly indicated."

1981, 1988, 2001 Statements: *See* 1976 Statement

THE JOHN DAY CO., INC.
(Includes Asia Books; formerly John Day & Company.)

1928 Statement: "This company has adopted the method of designating first editions on the copyright page with a line reading: First published, month, year. Subsequent printings are designated by a line below this reading: second printing, date, third printing, date, etc."

1937 Statement: "For some time now The John Day Company has adopted the following method of distinguishing first editions: On the first printing copyright page appears only the copyright notice: Copyright, 1936, by Richard Roe, and the usual printer's imprint: Printed in the United States of America by The John Smith Printing Company. Lately we have included a paragraph: All rights reserved, including the right to reproduce this book or portions thereof in any form. However, all other printings of the same book may be distinguished by: Second printing, Jan. 1936, Third printing, February, 1936, et cetera, with the proper month inserted.

"You will notice that 'John Day & Co.' is no longer used; when the book is wholly owned by The John Day Company 'The John Day Company, New York' appears on the title page.

"The same method applied to Reynal and Hitchcock; that is, no notice of first printing appears on the first edition, but notices of second, third, and fourth printings being added as is the case. In 1935, The John Day Company was associated with Reynal and Hitchcock, and on the title page of books published under this new association you will find the imprint: 'a John Day Book, Reynal and Hitchcock, New York.' This method of imprinting our books is similar to The Atlantic Monthly Press and Little Brown & Co., with which you may be familiar. On the copyright page of books put out under the joint imprint you will find on both first printing and subsequent printings the words: 'Published by John Day in association with Reynal and Hitchcock.' However, this has no bearing on the edition printings."

See also 1937 Statement of Reynal and Hitchcock, Inc.

1947 Statement: "As of May, 1938, we ceased our relationship with Reynal and Hitchcock, and all new books published since then, and reprintings made since then of older books, have carried no mention of Reynal and Hitchcock.

"Our present title pages carry: 'The John Day Company, New York.' Our copyright pages, on first impressions, carry the following:

Copyright, 1947, by Richard Roe

All rights reserved. This book, or parts thereof, must not be reproduced in any form without permission.

Manufactured in the United States of America.

"On books for which we control the Canadian rights, the copyright page also carries a line reading: 'This book is published on the same day in the Dominion of Canada, by Longmans, Green and Company, Toronto.' In most cases, this last entry does not mean that any copies of the book have been printed in Canada; Longmans, Green and Company act as selling agents for copies of our own edition.

"If the copyright page has no reference to the number of the impression the copy is from the first impression. On subsequent printings, we add 'second impression,' 'third impression,' etc.

"The copyright pages of Asia Books are handled in exactly the same way as John Day books. The only difference is that on certain Oriental books published by John Day, the line 'An Asia Book' is included on the title page the binding, and the jacket."

1976 Statement: *See* 1976 Statement of Thomas Y. Crowell Company

1981, 1988 Statements: *See* 1981, 1988 Statements of Harper and Row Publishers, Inc.

STEPHEN DAYE PRESS
(Became Stephen Daye Press, Inc.
Bought by Frederick Ungar Publishing Co. in 1945.)

1937 Statement: "We mark second editions and second and subsequent printings on copyright page. We do not print the words 'First Edition.' "

1949 Statement: *See* 1937 Statement

THE DAYSPRING PRESS, INC.
1993 Statement: All printings after the first are so indicated.

D.B.A. BOOKS
2000 Statement: "We do not identify first printings of the first editions, only second printing and subsequent ones."

DBS PUBLICATIONS, INC.
1993, 2000 Statements: *See* 1993 Statement of Drama Book Publishers

DC COMICS
2000 Statement: "On our book format publications, we've been listing 'first printing,' 'second printing,' and so on since the formats began in 1986. These notes are usually format specific—i.e., a softcover will not necessarily indicate that there was a prior hardcover.

"On our periodical format publications our practice, in keeping with our industry, was not to identify the rare instances where multiple printings occurred. We began to identify second and later printings with the serial format of *Batman: The Dark Knight Returns* in 1985 and customarily now do so either in the indicia or inside cover, but only when it's a second or later printing.

"Generally, these standards apply to publications of DC Comics (including our eponymous imprint, Vertigo, Paradox Press, WildStorm and America's Best Comics) and E.C. Publications (MAD Magazine and MAD Books)."

JOHN De GRAFF, INC.
1976 Statement: "We do not have an unvarying procedure to identify which of our books are first editions and which ones are reprints.

"Normally a reprint is indicated on the copyright page by 'reprinted and year' but there are occasions like book club printings and oversights when the copyright page is not changed."

1981, 1988 Statements: *See* 1976 Statement

ALDINE de GRUYTER
2001 Statement: "We identify the first printing of a first edition by a number line; the lowest number indicates the printing."

MOUTON de GRUYTER

1994 Statement: "Only second and following editions of de Gruyter books are identified as such, on the title page."
2000 Statement: *See* 1994 Statement

DeVORSS & COMPANY

1988 Statement: "We have no particular system for indicating 'First Edition.' The copyright date would indicate the year of the first edition, and in almost all cases, we indicate on the copyright page the number of printings there have been since the copyright."
1993 Statement: "[We do] not designate a first printing. Second or revised printings are so noted."
2000 Statement: *See* 1993 Statement

DEAN & SON LTD. (UNITED KINGDOM)

1976 Statement: "As we are in the mass children's book market we do not publish special first editions.

"Generally speaking, we do an initial large run and do not reprint except in special circumstances."
1981 Statement: *See* 1976 Statement
1989 Statement: *See* 1989 Statement of The Octopus Publishing Group PLC (United Kingdom)

DEARBORN TRADE
A Kaplan Professional Company

2000 Statement: "The first printing of a first edition is identified on the copyright page, and cover of the work. Subsequent printings and editions are also included on the copyright page."

DECEMBER PRESS

1976 Statement: "We designate only those printings and/or editions after the first, and so far we haven't had any of those."
1981, 1988 Statements: *See* 1976 Statement
1995 Statement: "All December Press publications, with the one exception of *Wicked City*, are first editions. *Wicked City*'s 2nd printing is identified with the key 2 3 4 5 96 95 94 on the copyright page."

IVAN R. DEE, INC. PUBLISHER

1994 Statement: "When we print the first edition of a manuscript which we originate, we ordinarily make no note of it on the copyright page—though we ordinarily note the year of first publication on the title page. In second or subsequent printings of such a book, we ordinarily print 'Second Printing' (or the appropriate number) on the copyright page.

"When we first print a paperback reprint of a book that has earlier appeared in hardcover (published by us or someone else), we ordinarily note on the copyright page that this is our first paperback edition.

"When we print an American edition of a book whose rights we have purchased from an English or other foreign publisher, we ordinarily note

'First American Edition' on the copyright page, or we specify that the English translation is new and copyrighted.

"We have followed this style from the inception of our list in 1989."

2000 Statement: *See* 1994 Statement

DEE-JAY PUBLICATIONS (REPUBLIC OF IRELAND)

1994 Statement: "Our designation for first printing of a first edition is simply contained on the verso of the title page. For example:

First published in Ireland by
DEE-JAY PUBLICATIONS
Enterprise Centre
North Quay
Arklow, Co. Wicklow
Ireland
Copyright...............1992

"Subsequent reprints of the first edition or prints of new editions will carry the information as follows:

First Published 1992
Reprinted 1994

"These lines are inserted between the address and the copyright declaration."

2001 Statement: *See* 1994 Statement. Note, however, that the address is now: Dee-Jay Publications, 2 Meadows Lane, Arklow, Co. Wicklow, Ireland.

DEERTRAIL BOOKS

2000 Statement: "We do not identify the first edition as such. But on the 'copyright page' we state the number of the printing with the date: First printing April 1988; fourth printing July 1999, etc."

DEJHA PUBLISHING

1995 Statement: *See* 1995 Statement of Cedar Bay Press

MARCEL DEKKER, INC.

2000 Statement: "No special designation of first edition. Printing shown by last number at bottom of copyright page."

DEL REY

2001 Statement: *See* 2001 Statement of The Ballantine Publishing Group

DELACORTE PRESS

1976, 1981 Statements: *See* 1976 Statement of Seymour Lawrence Incorporated

1994 Statement: *See* 1994 Statement of Dell Publishing

JAMES LADD DELKIN

1947 Statement: "No mention is made of 'Printing' in the First Edition. Following printings say 'Second Printing,' 'Third Printing,' 'Fourth Printing'—as in the case of my 'Pacific Ocean Handbook.' Indications of 'Revision' or 'Enlargement,' when necessary, are so printed.

"As to my Fine Press Books—none are numbered—and *none have* or will be reprinted in the same format, hence the date will tell the first printing of the material (when and if). (Example: The Grabhorn Press does not reprint editions.)

" 'Flavor of San Francisco' (in its four editions) is indicated only by dates—the material being revised in each issue."

DELL PUBLISHING
1994 Statement: "We identify the first printings of a first edition by the following number line: 10 9 8 7 6 5 4 3 2 1. This is true for Delacorte, Dial Press, Dell, Delta & Dell Trade Paperbacks. We also include the month and year of our publication on the copyright page."

DELL TRADE PAPERBACKS
1994 Statement: *See* 1994 Statement of Dell Publishing

DELLEN PUBLISHING CO
1993 Statement: *See* 1993 Statement of Macmillan, Inc.

DELTA BOOKS
1994 Statement: *See* 1994 Statement of Dell Publishing

DELTA-WEST PUBLISHING INC
2000 Statement: "It is our practice to state on the imprint page 'First Published (date)' and that is how our first edition and all subsequent editions can be identified."

DELTIOLOGISTS OF AMERICA
1995 Statement: "We have no particular method of denoting first editions or first printings. Subsequent editions and printings, however, are so noted on the copyright page in each case."
2001 Statement: *See* 1995 Statement

DEMBNER BOOKS
1988 Statement: "Dembner Books does not designate the first printing of a first edition. When a book goes back to press, we indicate 2nd, 3rd, 4th, etc., printing."

DEMITASSE
2000 Statement: "We do not do anything to denote a first edition . . . because they are handset, handprinted, handbound letterpress books and are only printed once."
See also Coffee House Press

T. S. DENISON & CO., INC.
1976 Statement: "We do very little in this regard. We do designate second, third, fourth, etc., printings on the copyright page, but usually do nothing to designate a first edition other than the standard book # and copyright date. In the publishing of special edition books we assign registration numbers. This is usually a limited printing."

1981 Statement: *See* 1976 Statement

1988 Statement: "We usually do nothing to designate a first edition other than the standard book # and copyright date. In the publishing of special edition books we assign registration numbers. This is usually a limited printing."

1993 Statement: *See* 1988 Statement

DENLINGER'S PUBLISHERS

1976 Statement: "We do not include a statement in our books to identify first editions. We identify second editions or other later editions through inclusion of additional dates in the copyright statement. A single copyright date in one of our books indicates that the book is a first edition.

"Second printings or other later printings are identified through inclusion of the words 'Second Printing' or other later printing on the copyright page."

1981, 1988, 1993, 2001 Statements: *See* 1976 Statement

J. M. DENT (UNITED KINGDOM)

1994, 2001 Statements: *See* 1994 Statement of The Orion Publishing Group Ltd (United Kingdom)

J. M. DENT & SONS, LTD. (UNITED KINGDOM)

1928 Statement: "Our usual practice is to print a date on the title page of a first edition; if a book is reprinted we put a new date on the title page and print on the reverse—'First published so-and-so. Reprinted so-and-so.' Thus you will be able to identify first editions by the absence of any such note on the reverse of the title page."

1936 Statement: "The procedure which we follow for identifying first editions is now slightly different from that of 1928, and I think the following paragraph states the present position.

"Our usual practice is to print on the back of the title page a biblio. note giving the date of publication of the edition. If a book reprints the date of the reprint is added. Thus it may be assumed that if the following line 'First published . . . .' only appears it is a first edition. If it is a reprint of our own first edition the line 'Reprinted . . . .' will be added underneath. If it is the first time that we have published it and it is the reprint of some earlier edition, we print 'First published in this edition . . . .' This applies particularly to reprints of old and established books. This has been our practice since 1929."

1947 Statement: *See* 1936 Statement

Statement for 1960: *See* 1976 Statement

1976 Statement: "We do not have any set formula for identifying our first editions, but these normally carry (on the title verso) the statement 'First published 19...'

"Where a previously published title is to appear for the first time in a new format or series, we usually make the statement 'First published in this edition 19...' "

1981 Statement: *See* 1976 Statement

1989 Statement: *See* 1989 Statement of George Weidenfeld & Nicolson Limited (United Kingdom)

DENT CHILDREN'S BOOKS (UNITED KINGDOM)
1994 Statement: *See* 1994 Statement of The Orion Publishing Group Ltd (United Kingdom)

J. M. DENT PTY LTD (AUSTRALIA)
1989 Statement: *See* 1989 Statement of Houghton Mifflin Australia Pty Ltd (Australia)

DEPARTMENT OF PRIMARY INDUSTRIES (AUSTRALIA)
1994 Statement: "First editions: The wording 'First published [year printed]' appears on the imprint page of first editions. The year of publication also appears at the end of the copyright line on the imprint page.

"Subsequent editions: The wording 'First published [year printed], Second edition [year printed], etc.' appears on the imprint page of subsequent editions. The year of publication of the last edition appears at the end of the copyright line on the imprint page.

"Reprints: The wording 'First published [year printed], Reprinted [year printed], Reprinted with amendments [year printed], etc.' may appear on the imprint page of reprints. All the years of publication are listed at the end of the copyright line on the imprint page.

"We have more or less consistently practised this form of identifying editions over the last five years."
2001 Statement: *See* 1994 Statement

DEPTH CHARGE
1995 Statement: "The way we designate first printings of first editions is simple. On the copyright page the following statement appears:

First Edition published by:

"This is then followed by the name of our press or imprint. We delete this 'First Edition' statement in subsequent printings."

THE DERRYDALE PRESS, INC.
(Went out of business in 1941.)
1937 Statement: "All of our publications are limited editions. This is so stated, together with the number of copies in the edition, either at the end of the book or on the back of the title page. If a second edition of one of our books is issued, it is so noted in the limit notice."
See also Windward House

DESERET BOOK COMPANY
1976 Statement: "We do not make a designation for first edition; however, if the date of publication on the title page is the same as the copyright date, it is a first edition.

"If the book is reprinted, the date of publication on the title page will be changed to correspond to the reprint date. We do not indicate a revised edition unless substantial copy changes are made."
1981 Statement: "Deseret Book company has changed the policy and we will now include the number of each edition of our publications on the title

page. The reason for this is that it is very possible that we would have more than one or two reprints in a year.

"We have begun doing this as of January 1, 1981, and all of our new books reflect this new practice. We will be adding printings on older books as reprints are ordered and as information is available. Unfortunately, some of the records of the past are no longer available, so books that were published before 1975 are almost impossible to bring up to date. Books published since that year will have the printings added as we reprint them."

1988 Statement: "All of our books printed since January 1, 1981, have the month and year of each printing, including the first one, indicted on the copyright page. Thus, 'First printing March 1988' would appear in the first printing, and subsequent printings would be similarly listed below that entry. As books first printed prior to 1981 are reprinted, we try to indicate the dates of prior printings if the information is available; however, some of our records are incomplete, particularly for books published prior to 1975, and this is not always possible.

"If a book is revised, each new printing will have the original publication date as well as the month and year for each reprinting of the revision.

"If a book that has been out of print for several years is brought back into publication, we will similarly indicate both the original printing date and the date of the new printing."

1993 Statement: "Deseret Book has changed its method of indicating first printings since your last publication. In 1990 we adopted the method many publishers now use: a list of numbers at the bottom of the copyright page, with the lowest number deleted each time we reprint. Thus, the first printing will have the numbers 10 9 8 7 6 5 4 3 2 1, and the next printing, or first reprinting, will have the number 1 deleted. For the first printing, the year will always be the copyright date. Thus, book published first in 1993 will have that as the copyright date and the full sequence of ten numbers as above. (Of course, when we have more than 10 reprintings, we add additional numbers as needed.)

"The previous information furnished to you still applies to books published before 1990."

2000 Statement: *See* 1993 Statement

THE DESIGN IMAGE GROUP INC
2000 Statement: "We identify the first printing of a first edition by the words 'First Edition' on copyright and legend page [and] the number line 10 9 8 7 6 5 4 3 2 1."

DESTINY BOOKS
1988, 2000 Statements: *See* 1988 Statement of Inner Traditions International Ltd.

DETSELIG ENTERPRISES LTD. (CANADA)
1988 Statement: "We do not make any special identification of first editions—that is, all of our titles are first editions except when identified otherwise. Second and subsequent reprints are sometimes identified as such.

Our company has not made any changes in this area since it was formed in 1975."

1993, 2000 Statements: *See* 1988 Statement

ANDRE DEUTSCH LTD. (UNITED KINGDOM)

1976 Statement: "Our normal practice is to print our copyright notice on the imprint page (i.e. the reverse of the title page). This will normally read:

First published 19.. by

Andre Deutsch Limited

(etc.)

"If we do a reprint then a further line would be added saying

Second impression 19...

"In other words, the first edition is not identified as such but merely by the absence of any reference to further printings, revised editions, etc."

1981, 1994 Statements: *See* 1976 Statement

2000 Statement: "Our normal practise has not altered much since 1989, however we no longer add an additional line stating 'Second impression 20....'

"We now add a reprint line later on the page and the reprint number can be determined by the lowest number left on the line. [This] example depicts the second reprint: 3 5 7 9 10 8 6 4 2. For the third imprint, the figure 2 would be removed. This policy was implemented in 1997."

THE DEVIL'S MILLHOPPER PRESS

2000 Statement: "Because in the past we have rarely reprinted any books, we have never made a statement. In future editions (beginning with our next release), we will use the following statement: 'First Edition.' "

THE DEVIN-ADAIR COMPANY

1947 Statement: "All books published by us in recent years have carried the notation *second printing* on the copyright page. Otherwise it is assumed that all books are first editions."

Statement for 1960: In 1960, a first printing was designated by the words "First Printing" on the copyright page. Printings subsequent to the first were identified as "Second Printing," etc.

1976 Statement: "In almost all instances the second and subsequent printings carry the notation *second printing* on the copyright page."

1981, 1988 Statements: *See* 1976 Statement

1993 Statement: "All first printings are identified with the term 'First Printing,' and/or 'First Edition.' Subsequent printings are identified as 'Second,' 'Third,' etc. printings. Revised editions . . . are also noted as 'Revised First' or 'Revised Second Edition.' "

2001 Statement: *See* 1993 Statement

DHARMA PUBLISHING

1988 Statement: "In 1975 we began using registration numbers at the bottom of the copyright page. In a first printing, the number 1 appears at the end of a series of numbers. Before this date we noted 'Second edition' or 'Second

Printing,' but very few books were reprinted before 1975. Since then we have kept nearly all of our books in print.

"We are a small, non-profit company dedicated to preserving the Tibetan cultural and religious heritage. We have no other imprints or subsidiaries as of this date."

1993, 2000 Statements: *See* 1988 Statement

MICHAEL di CAPUA BOOKS
1988 Statement: *See* 1988 Statement of Farrar, Straus & Giroux, Inc.
1993 Statement: *See* 1993 Statement of HarperCollins Publishers

DIAL (AUSTRALIA)
2000 Statement: *See* 2000 Statement of Penguin Books Australia Ltd (Australia)

DIAL HOUSE (UNITED KINGDOM)
2000 Statement: *See* 2000 Statement of Ian Allan Publishing (United Kingdom)

THE DIAL PRESS
1976 Statement: "We designate a first printing of a first edition by writing 'First printing 19..' on the copyright page."
1981 Statement: "First printings of first editions at The Dial Press are designated by the words 'First printing' on the copyright page. We add the year for later printings; for example, 'Second printing—1981.' "
1994 Statement: *See* 1994 Statement of Dell Publishing

DIAL PRESS, INC.
(Formerly Lincoln MacVeagh, The Dial Press.)
1937 Statement: "We wish to state that our system is to carry on the title page the year in which the edition is published and on the back of this page, merely a note as to when it was reprinted, such as is done by most publishers."
1947 Statement: *See* 1937 Statement

DIALOGUES ON DANCE
2000 Statement: *See* 2000 Statement of Ommation Press

DIANA PRESS, INC.
1976 Statement: "We do not usually designate first editions—only second editions."

DIANE PUBLISHING CO.
1993 Statement: "We have no particular way of designating the first printing. Second and/or revised printings are so noted."
2000 Statement: *See* 1993 Statement

LOVAT DICKSON, LIMITED (UNITED KINGDOM)
(Taken over by Peter Davies.)
1937 Statement: "It is our practice to print bibliographical data on the reverse of the title page of all our books, in which the date of first publication and subsequent reprints is stated, as follows:
First Published 1934
Second Impression 1935
Third Impression 1936
Lovat Dickson Ltd. 38 Bedford Street London and St. Martin's House
Bond Street Toronto
set and printed in Great Britain
by Billing & Sons Limited Guildford and Esher
Paper made by John Dickson and Company Limited
Bound by G. & J. Kitcat Limited
Set in Monotype Baskerville"

DIDIER, PUBLISHERS
1947 Statement: "With our own publications second and subsequent printings are indicated as such in the front matter of the book."

THE DIETZ PRESS
1947 Statement: "Some of our earlier books contained a statement on the copyright page, 'first edition.' Other first editions of our books have not been imprinted 'first edition.' However, on all subsequent editions we use the imprint 'second printing' or 'second edition.'

"In other words all of the first editions from this press may be identified by the imprint 'first edition' or by no specific edition imprint."

DIGITAL PRESS
2000 Statement: *See* 2000 Statement of Butterworth-Heinemann

DIGITAL PRESS (UNITED KINGDOM)
2000 Statement: *See* 2000 Statement of Butterworth-Heinemann

DILLON PRESS, INC.
1981 Statement: "At present, Dillon Press does not use a method for indicating a first edition. Subsequent printings and revisions are indicated on our copyright page. If such information does not appear there, the book in question is a first edition."
1988 Statement: *See* 1981 Statement

DIME (UNITED KINGDOM)
2000 Statement: *See* 2000 Statement of Tarquin Publications (United Kingdom)

DIMI PRESS
1995 Statement: "The copyright page of every book that we publish says both 'First Edition, First Printing' (or whatever). We have used this method since we began publishing books in 1988."
2000 Statement: *See* 1995 Statement

DINAS (WALES)
2001 Statement: *See* 2001 Statement of Y Lolfa Cyf (Wales)

DIRIGO EDITIONS
1947 Statement: *See* 1947 Statement of Falmouth Publishing House, Inc.

DISCOVERY ENTERPRISES, LTD.
1994 Statement: The first printing of a first edition is indicated by the number line 10 9 8 7 6 5 4 3 2 1. The lowest number showing indicates the printing.

"Following editions are identified as follows: Second Edition (Date); First Edition (Date)."
2000 Statement: *See* 1994 Statement

DISCOVERY HOUSE PUBLISHERS
1994 Statement: The first printing of a first edition is indicated by the number line 10 9 8 7 6 5 4 3 2 1. The lowest number showing indicates the printing.
2000 Statement: *See* 1994 Statement

DISCUS
1981 Statement: *See* 1981 Statement of Avon Books

DISNEY PRESS
1993, 2000 Statements: *See* 1993 Statement of Disney Publishing

DISNEY PUBLISHING
1993 Statement: "First printings of first editions are indicated by running the *entire* line of printing numbers, as follows: 1 3 5 7 9 10 8 6 4 2. This line sets just beneath the line that reads 'First Edition.' To indicate subsequent printings, we delete the number of the previous printing. For example, the second printing of the first edition of a particular title would be denoted by running the printing line as '3 5 7 9 10 8 6 4 2.' For the second edition of a given title, we would run the full line of printing numbers beneath the line that reads 'Second Edition.'

"These methods were established with the inception of the juvenile division (1990) and are used by our two imprints, Disney Press and Hyperion Books for Children, and by our paperback line, Hyperion Paperbacks for Children."
2000 Statement: "Everything in the [1993] Statement looks correct, except the last line in the first paragraph . . . . The term 'Second Edition' isn't one we normally use, so you could probably just delete that from the statement."

DIXIE PRESS
1988, 2000 Statements: *See* 1988 Statement of Pelican Publishing Company

DENNIS DOBSON, LTD. (UNITED KINGDOM)
1947 Statement: "Our books bear the date of their first publication in Great Britain on the verso of the title page. Style as below. Sometimes they have the publication date in Roman figures on the title page itself.
(Title page.)
> DENNIS DOBSON, LTD.
> LONDON—MCMXLVII

(Verso.)
FIRST PUBLISHED IN GREAT BRITAIN IN 1947
BY DENNIS DOBSON, LIMITED
29 GREAT QUEEN STREET
KINGSWAY, LONDON W C 2

1928 Statement: *See* 1937 Statement

1937 Statement: "We have never made a practice of labelling our books as first editions or second editions, etc., in fact, to our mind an edition is not the same thing as a printing. The first seems to us to denote some change in the contents of a book while the second is simply the number of times the book has been put to press. While we do not label our books First Edition or First Printing, we do, as soon as a second printing is ordered, add a notice on the copyright page giving the date of the publication of the book and the date of the second printing. If other printings follow, a third, etc., up to sometimes as many as fifteen, we add the date of each subsequent printing as it is ordered. This has been our practice up to the present time, and has been in use at least since 1925."

1947 Statement: *See* 1937 Statement

Statement for 1960: "I am not absolutely certain how we designated first printings in the books we published in 1960. In some cases we may have printed 'First Edition' or 'First Printing,' and in other cases we may have printed nothing in the first edition, but would print 'Second Printing,' 'Third Printing,' etc., in printings done subsequent to the first edition."

DOCUMENTEXT

1988, 1993, 2000 Statements: *See* 1988 Statement of McPherson & Company

DOCUMENTS OF COLORADO ART

2000 Statement: *See* 2000 Statement of Ocean View Books

DODD, MEAD & CO.

1976 Statement: "We generally do not mark a book's first edition nor do we usually mark second and later printings, although there are exceptions to this practice and there seems to be no consistency about doing so. Naturally, if a second printing is marked, the absence of such notice would indicate a first edition. Any notice of editions would appear as such on the copyright page.

"We would only be certain to mark a second edition if there were changes extensive enough to warrant a change in the copyright notice and the second edition came out in a year different from the first.

"As of December 9, 1976, Dodd, Mead & Company, Inc. has changed its practice regarding the designation of first printings. The new practice is as follows:

"A line of numbers—1 through 10—appears on the copyright page of the first printing of a book. On the second printing, the number 1 is simply blanked out, leaving the first number of the sequence a 2, and so on for each subsequent printing.

"Dodd, Mead will begin this method of printing indication with all new books, the copyright pages for which have yet to be set into type. This includes adult and juvenile titles."

1981 Statement: *See* 1976 Statement

1988 Statement: "A line of numbers—1 through 10—appears on the copyright page of the first printing of a book. On the second printing, the number 1 is simply blanked out as well as the words First Edition, leaving the first number of the sequence a 2, and so on for each subsequent printing.

"On some occasions we delete the number line and say Second Printing, Third Printing, and so forth. This is at my discretion."

DODGE PUBLISHING COMPANY

1937 Statement: "First editions of our books carry the line:
FIRST EDITION
on the copyright page. On subsequent editions this line is eliminated and the month and year of publication is substituted; the number of subsequent printings is listed below that:
PUBLISHED, JANUARY, 1936
THIRD PRINTING. MARCH, 1936"

DOG EAR PRESS

1988 Statement: "To designate the first printing of a first edition, Dog Ear Press books have the words 'First Edition' either on the jacket flaps (earlier books) or on the copyright page (more recent books).

"In addition, the newer books have numbers 10 through 1 in descending order, and subsequent editions remove a number (second edition removes the '1,' etc.)."

2001 Statement: *See* 2001 Statement of Tilbury House, Publishers

DOG-EARED PUBLICATIONS

2000 Statement: "We identify the first printing of a first edition by copyright symbol and year on title page. Subsequent printings or editions are placed on title page also under the copyright information."

THE DOLMEN PRESS LIMITED (REPUBLIC OF IRELAND)

1976 Statement: "We are publishing this autumn (1976) a bibliography of our Press in which all our first editions are identified."

1988, 2000 Statements: *See* 1988 Statement of Colin Smythe Limited, Publishers (United Kingdom)

THE DOLPHIN BOOK CO., LTD. (UNITED KINGDOM)

1976 Statement: "We have no particular identifying method for defining first editions. Only when a second edition is published we state on the verso of the title page the date of the first edition. Otherwise it is understood that the book is a first edition, and we always mention the date of publication."

1994, 2000 Statements: *See* 1976 Statement

DONHEAD PUBLISHING LTD (UNITED KINGDOM)

2001 Statement: "For identification of the first edition of our titles we include the statement, e.g., 'First published in the United Kingdom 1995 by Donhead Publishing' followed by our address. For a second edition we would add 'second edition 1999' to those bibliograhical details. If we are reprinting a book first published by another publisher we would state, e.g., 'First published in 1984 by Hutchinson', followed by their reprint dates, followed by 'Reprinted 1995 by Donhead Publishing.' "

THE DONNING COMPANY/PUBLISHERS

1981 Statement: "We usually do not designate first editions; however, when we do, we simply print 'FIRST EDITION' on the copyright page. We also do a number of limited editions in science fiction art and regional pictorial histories that we designate by printing a signed and numbered bookplate on the end sheet."

1988, 2001 Statements: *See* 1981 Statement

M. A. DONOHUE & COMPANY

1947 Statement: "We have never made it a practice to mark our first editions and are not now doing so. Sometimes there is a little difference between the first and second editions but we have no general rule to follow. Ordinarily we print from plates and all editions are the same. Our lines today consist primarily of children's books and for that reason we operate as we do."

DOODLE ART

2000 Statement: *See* 2000 Statement of Price Stern Sloan

DORAL PUBLISHING, INC.

1993 Statement: "We . . . have no particular way of designating first printings. Each subsequent printing of the same book indicates the reprint number."

2000 Statement: *See* 1993 Statement

GEORGE H. DORAN & CO.
*(Merged with Doubleday, Page, as Doubleday, Doran & Co.
on December 30th, 1927.)*

1927 Statement: "The sign of a first edition of a Doran book is a small round colophon in which the initials 'G H D' appear and which is always placed directly beneath the copyright line.

"Occasionally the colophon is omitted, in which case the words 'First Printing' always appear."

DORCHESTER PUBLISHING CO., INC.

2001 Statement: "We do not identify a first printing or any printing after the first printing on the copyright page."

DORIEL PUBLISHING CO.

1995 Statement: "We indicate the edition by printing on back of title page: First Edition."

DORLING KINDERSLEY LIMITED (UNITED KINGDOM)

1989 Statement: "All titles published in the U.K. by Dorling Kindersley Ltd. indicate the date of first U.K. publication on the copyright page. If nothing else appears on this page, then the volume can be taken to be the first printing of the first edition.

"Subsequent printings are indicated by 'Reprinted...(date).' New editions, for which significant revisions have been made, are indicated by 'Second edition...(date),' 'Third edition...(date),' or whatever.

"Overseas editions of our books—in both English language and foreign languages—are published all over the world by our numerous co-edition partners. They are responsible for the wording of the imprint details and printing history that appears in their editions."

1994 Statement: *See* 1989 Statement

In May, 2000, Dorling Kindersley became part of the Penguin Group.
See 2001 Statement of Penguin Publishing Co Ltd (United Kingdom)

DORLING KINDERSLEY PUBLISHING, INC.

1993 Statement: "Books published by Dorling Kindersley Publishing, Inc., are labeled 'First American edition' on the imprint page, to help distinguish them from books published by Dorling Kindersley Ltd., our British parent company. Our books also carry a number line (2 4 6 8 10 9 7 5 3 1 or similar) to indicate printing; the lowest number is the printing. This method was adopted in 1991."

DORPETE PRESS

2000 Statement: "Our first editions are identified as first printings on the copyright page of each book."

DORRANCE & CO. INC.

1928 Statement: "As a usual thing, First editions are not indicated as such other than by a line giving copyright and year, but when other Editions are got out, full information is given. Take for example, the volume *Record Flights* which we have published this spring. On the Second Edition we had 'copyright 1928. First printing March—Second printing March.' In a special Limited Edition of this book there was printed 'In a limited Edition of five hundred copies, of which this is No...' In the future, in the case of unusual books and rare books, we expect to print 'First Edition' on the First Edition. [This method has been in use since 1920.]"

1937 Statement: *See* 1928 Statement

1947 Statement: "As a usual thing First Editions are not indicated as such other than by a line giving copyright and year, but when other editions follow, full information is given. For example, a Third Edition would be indicated as follows:

> Copyright 1947
> First Printing March
> Second Printing May
> Third Printing June

on the copyright page. If the year of copyright only appears, then we consider the book a First Edition book."

DORSET NATURAL HISTORY
AND ARCHAEOLOGICAL SOCIETY (UNITED KINGDOM)
1988 Statement: "We do not use any designation on our first editions, copyright and date of publication only, but for our rare second editions we put 'reprinted [and date].' Think this is what DNHAS have always done."
2001 Statement: *See* 1988 Statement

THE DORSEY PRESS
1976 Statement: "First editions have only title & author's name on the cover. Second & subsequent editions are identified by placing appropriate designation after the title on the cover & title page.

"First printings & their dates we identify as such by a statement (example: First Printing, January 1976) which appears under the copyright declaration."
1981 Statement: "The second paragraph [of the 1976 statement], is no longer correct. We use a printers' key under the copyright declaration. It may be rendered as follows:
1 2 3 4 5 6 7 8 9 0 K 7 6 5 4 3 2 1
"The first numeral 1 stands for the first printing. When we have a second printing, this numeral 1 is opaqued on the film before plates are made so that the first numeral becomes 2, designating the second printing. The last numeral 1 stands for 1981. When a printing is ordered in 1982, the 1 will be opaqued. This continues until a new edition is published. The letter in the center stands for the printer used to manufacture this book. K is for Kingsport Press, M.V. is for Maple-Vail, etc."

DOUBLEDAY
1988 Statement: "The words First Edition are indicated on the copyright page. On subsequent printings this is removed and the print history line indicating the current printing is added."
1993 Statement: *See* 1988 Statement
2001 Statement: "Doubleday is now a division of Random House Inc. The 1988 Statement is still valid with one exception: the printline is included on the first print as well; on subsequent printings, we remove First Edition and the printline is updated."

DOUBLEDAY (AUSTRALIA)
1988 Statement: *See* 1988 Statement of Transworld Publishers (Australia) Pty Limited (Australia)
2000 Statement: *See* 2000 Statement of Transworld Publishers (Australia)

DOUBLEDAY (UNITED KINGDOM)
2001 Statement: *See* 2001 Statement of Transworld Publishers Ltd (United Kingdom)

DOUBLEDAY & CO., INC.
(Formerly Doubleday, Doran & Co., Inc.)
1947 Statement: "Our method of indicating first editions is the printing of the words 'first edition' beneath the copyright notice which backs up the title page.

"Unfortunately there is no record of the date on which we began to follow this plan. It was many years ago."
1976 Statement: "We designate First Editions on the copyright page thus: FIRST EDITION. On subsequent printings this is removed."
1981 Statement: *See* 1976 Statement
1988 Statement: *See* 1988 Statement of Doubleday

DOUBLEDAY, DORAN & CO., INC.
(Changed name to Doubleday & Co., Inc. December 31, 1945.)
1928 Statement: "We always plan to indicate right under the copyright line on the first printing the fact that the book is the first edition."
1937 Statement: "Our method of indicating first editions is the printing of the words 'first edition' beneath the copyright notice which backs up the title page.

"Unfortunately there is no record of the date on which we began to follow this plan. It was many years ago."

DOUBLEDAY, PAGE & CO.
(Merged with George H. Doran & Co. as Doubleday, Doran & Co., Inc. on December 30th, 1927.)
1927 Statement: "Our method of indicating first editions is the printing of the words 'first edition' beneath the copyright notice which backs up the title page."

DOUBLES
2000 Statement: *See* 2000 Statement of Gryphon Books

ALTON DOUGLAS BOOKS (UNITED KINGDOM)
2000 Statement: *See* 2000 Statement of Brewin Books (United Kingdom)

NOEL DOUGLAS, LTD. (UNITED KINGDOM)
(Out of business prior to 1949.)
1928 Statement: *See* 1937 Statement
1937 Statement: "We designate our first editions by printing the date of publication on the reverse of the title page, as 'published 1928.' Subsequent editions or reprints are added below, as,

published 1928
reprinted 1929
second edition 1930
"This method was adopted about 1926 or 1927."

DOUGLAS-WEST PUBLISHERS, INC.
1976 Statement: "The first copies of a new title are normally designated 'First Printing' or 'First Edition' if we anticipate the title going into several

printings. If the book carries an expensive list price and is likely to become a collector's item, we designate the first printing as 'First Edition.' Most publishers, we find, use the two terms interchangeably; in other words, First Printing or First Edition means the same thing."
1981 Statement: *See* 1976 Statement

DOVER PUBLICATIONS, INC.
1976 Statement: "We do not distinguish in any way between the first and subsequent printings of our publications."
1981, 1988, 1993, 2000 Statements: *See* 1976 Statement

DOWN EAST BOOKS
1988 Statement: "For the past 8 years or so, Down East Books has designated its editions with the number system, the lowest number shown being the current edition. Prior to that it was either First edition or no indication.
"The above applies to imprints and subsidiaries of the Book Division."
1993 Statement: *See* 1988 Statement, but with one correction. "This [1988 Statement] indicates printings, not editions. Unless stated otherwise on the title page, all books are first editions."
2000 Statement: *See* 1993 Statement

DOWN HOME PRESS
1993 Statement: "Down Home Press began publishing in 1989. We use 'First Printing' followed by the month and year to designate first editions."
2001 Statement: *See* 1993 Statement

DOWN THERE PRESS
2000 Statement: "We identify the first printing of a first edition by the number line 10 9 8 7 6 5 4 3 2 1."

DOWNLANDER PUBLISHING (UNITED KINGDOM)
1994 Statement: "We designate a first edition of any poetry work we have published by stating above our logo on the title page 'First published in Great Britain by Downlander Publishing (followed by the year of publication).'
"This has always been our practice since we were formed in 1978."

DOXA PRESS
2000 Statement: *See* 2000 Statement of Religious Education Press

DPI PUBLICATIONS (AUSTRALIA)
See Department of Primary Industries (Australia)

DRAMA BOOK PUBLISHERS
1993 Statement: "Our designation of first editions varied wildly with the production person of the moment. There are no guidelines we could offer that make sense . . . . A little eccentric for publishing perhaps, but it's been grand and continues so."
2000 Statement: *See* 1993 Statement

DRAMA BOOK SPECIALISTS/PUBLISHERS
1993, 2000 Statements: *See* 1993 Statement of Drama Book Publishers

DRAMALINE PUBLICATIONS
2000 Statement: "It is not our practice to differentiate 1st editions."

DRAMATIC LINES PUBLISHERS (UNITED KINGDOM)
2001 Statement: "We state 'First printing' on the copyright page."

THE DRAMATIC PUBLISHING COMPANY
1993 Statement: "The Dramatic Publishing Company first editions bear no special markings and are re-printed without designation. Since most of our books are production scripts of plays, they receive brief, heavy use and are often discarded."
2000 Statement: *See* 1993 Statement

DRAMATISTS PLAY SERVICE, INC.
1988 Statement: "The Dramatists Play Service, Inc. is a play-licensing organization, and we publish our plays in acting editions so that they will be available for production by stock and amateur groups.

"Therefore we do not designate first printings or first editions in any special way. We reprint our titles as needed."
2000 Statement: "Dramatists Play Service, Inc. publishes paperback acting editions of plays which the company licenses for stock and amateur performance. We do not designate first printings or first editions. Titles are reprinted as needed."

DREAMS AND NIGHTMARES
2000 Statement: "We do not indicate first printings or first editions. We indicate later printings with e.g., 'Second printing' and later editions with e.g., 'Second edition' and the appropriate year of publication."

DREENAN PRESS, LTD.
1976 Statement: "All of our book printings, whether first editions or subsequent ones bear the 10 9 8 7 6 5 4 3 2 1 indicators on the copyright page. The last numeral that appears is the number of the printing. E.G. if the copyright page reads 10 9 8 7 6 then the copy is from the sixth printing of that edition.

"Only revised editions (not reprints) bear the info. as to edition and that is on the title page. If no info. appears on title page then it is a first edition."
1981, 1988 Statements: *See* 1976 Statement

MAXWELL DROKE, PUBLISHER
1947 Statement: "On an initial printing of a book we make no particular identification beyond the customary copyright data. As subsequent printings are ordered, these are indicated directly beneath the copyright notice.

"Where a revision of any consequence in any of our backlog texts is made, this is treated as a new edition and is noted below the copyright material."

LINDSAY DRUMMOND, LIMITED (UNITED KINGDOM)

1947 Statement: "A first edition of a book of British origin would contain, usually on the verso of the title page, the words 'First published 1947.' Owing to production delays it is difficult to put a month with any accuracy. In a second printing of the book we would add below the original line 'Second impression' etc. This would imply that there were no radical changes from the first printing. If the book was revised or brought up to date by the inclusion of new material this further printing would be registered as a second edition, with date.

"This is the usual method we adopt, which I believe is the general one, though some publishers use the word 'reprinted' instead of first, second or third impression."

DRY BONES PRESS INC

2000 Statement: "We identify the first printing of a first edition by the statement 'First Edition.' However, we often do print-on-demand, which moots the point."

DUCK EDITIONS (UNITED KINGDOM)

2000 Statement: *See* 2000 Statement of Gerald Duckworth and Company, Ltd. (United Kingdom)

GERALD DUCKWORTH AND COMPANY, LTD.
(UNITED KINGDOM)

1928 Statement: *See* 1937 Statement

1937 Statement: "Our usual custom is to put on the reverse of the title page 'First published, 1928.' In some cases instead of this we put the date at the foot of the title page. In either case a second edition has a definite statement that it is a New Impression or a New Edition on the reverse of the title page.

"We are sorry it is not possible for us to give the date when we first began using this method of identifying first printings."

1947 Statement: "Our usual custom is to put on the reverse of the title page 'First published, 1928.' In some cases instead of this we put the date at the foot of the title page. Second or other revised editions are always proclaimed as such on the reverse of the title page, where the date of the most recent printing is also given."

1982 Statement: "The copyright notice on the verso of the title page includes a year date, which is the date of first publication unless the book contains previously copyrighted material in which case the date of first volume publication is also given."

1988, 1994, 2000 Statements: *See* 1982 Statement

DUELL, SLOAN AND PEARCE, INC.

1947 Statement: "We have not been altogether consistent in our method of indicating editions of our books. In general it is our practice to indicate first impressions of trade books by words 'First Edition,' or by Roman numeral 'I' on reverse of title page. In subsequent printings these are replaced by 'Second Printing' or numeral 'II' respectively, or in cases where texts are revised by 'Second Edition.' In case of a book published in another country prior to, or simultaneously with our edition, we use line 'First American Edition' to indicate this fact."

DUFFIELD & CO.

(Became Duffield & Green, now out of business. Publications purchased by Dodd, Mead & Co., in April, 1934.)

1928 Statement: "We designate our first editions by printing the copyright date on the reverse of title page. Occasionally we insert the phrase 'First edition printed such and such a date,' in cases where the first edition is assumed to be important."

JAMES DUFFY & CO., LTD. (REPUBLIC OF IRELAND)

1976 Statement: "Our only method is to print the year on the cover and inside title. For reprints we put:

First published 1976
Reprinted 1977
Reprinted 1978

"On the reprints we would omit the year on the cover and inside title."

1981 Statement: *See* 1976 Statement

DUFOUR EDITIONS, INC.

1993 Statement: "We do not, nor have we ever, made any special indication of first editions."

2001 Statement: *See* 1993 Statement

DUKE UNIVERSITY PRESS

1947 Statement: "The Duke University Press is a small organization devoted almost wholly to the publication of the results of scholarly research for a limited audience, largely academic. Consequently our editions are small, and we print from type rather than plates. Any book of ours is likely to be a first edition, though it may be a second or third impression. If there are no corrections, often there is no way to tell which impression a particular book comes from. If there have been corrections, a note of this, and of the impression, is to be found on the copyright page. If a demand for a book continues after the type has been melted, we use a photo-offset process to reprint. Here a good eye for type is the only way to tell such a reprint from the original."

1976 Statement: "Although we customarily note a second or later edition or second or later printing as such, we have no particular means of noting a first edition."

1981, 1988, 1993, 2001 Statements: *See* 1976 Statement

DUMBARTON OAKS RESEARCH LIBRARY AND COLLECTION

1993 Statement: "First editions would not carry any specific designation beyond the regular copyright notice and CIP data. Subsequent printings would carry the designation, 'Second Impression, date.' "

DUMONT PRESS

2000 Statement: "We had no more than one printing for each book and therefore never had a need to designate separate editions."

DUNSTER HOUSE BOOKSHOP

1928 Statement: "Our own publications have always had the date in the First edition on the title page. This is the same method as that used by Messrs. Houghton Mifflin Company."

DUQUESNE UNIVERSITY PRESS

1976 Statement: "There has been no consistent method used to identify first editions of Duquesne University Press titles. For the most part, however, first editions can be identified by the notation 'first printing' which, when used, appears on the copyright page. In instances where there is no indication of the edition or number of printings, there is no doubt that the book is a first edition.

"If a book has been revised and a new edition printed, the information is always registered on the title page. The number of printings of the new edition is notated on the copyright page."

1981 Statement: "From 1978 on, the notation 'First Edition' appears on the copyright page. Prior to 1978, there had been no consistent method used to identify first editions of Duquesne University Press titles. For the most part, however, first editions can be identified by the notation 'first printing' which, when used, appears on the copyright page. In instances where there is no indication of the edition or number of printings, there is no doubt that the book is a first edition.

"If a book has been revised and a new edition printed, the information is always registered on the title page. The number of printings of the new edition is notated on the copyright page."

1988, 1994, 2000 Statements: *See* 1981 Statement

OLIVER DURRELL, INC.

1947 Statement: "Unless the copyright page bears a notice of the second or additional printings, the book is a first edition."

DUSTBOOKS

1976 Statement: "We simply print 'First Printing' on reverse of title page."
1981 Statement: "We simply put © date—author and sometimes add '1st printing—date.' Nothing more."
1988, 1993, 2000 Statements: *See* 1981 Statement

DUTTON

1993, 2000 Statements: *See* 1993 Statement of Dutton Signet

DUTTON (AUSTRALIA)

2000 Statement: *See* 2000 Statement of Penguin Books Australia Ltd (Australia)

E. P. DUTTON & CO., INC.

1928 Statement: "Unfortunately we have no definite scheme for identifying First Editions. Recently a copyright notice behind a title-page, on which nothing occurs but that, is an indication it is a first, because when we begin the second printing we mark it on the back."

1936 Statement: "Since 1929 we use the words 'first edition' immediately below our copyright notice for all such books. If the book is reprinted a notice is substituted on the copyright that this is the second or third printing as the case may be."

1947 Statement: *See* 1936 Statement

Statement for 1960: First printings were not indicated.

1976 Statement: First printings are indicated on the copyright page.

1981 Statement: *(E. P. Dutton changed its name to Elsevier-Dutton in 1978. In 1981, the name was changed back to E. P. Dutton.)*

"The first printing of a first edition is designated on the copyright page. Five years ago, we didn't include this information; this is the only difference in our method of identification."

1988 Statement: "The first printing of a first edition is indicated on the copyright page by the words 'First Edition.'

"This is the policy for adult books and our Obelisk, William Abrahams, and Truman Talley subsidiaries."

DUTTON SIGNET
(A Division of Penguin USA)

1993 Statement: "Dutton Signet, a division of Penguin USA, clearly designates on the copyright page first printings of first editions in the imprints Signet, Signet Classic, Mentor, Onyx, Plume, Meridian, Roc, and Dutton.

First Printing, (date)

1 2 3 4 5 6 7 8 9

"Subsequent prints are denoted by the numbers on the above printing line.

"A revised edition would contain the words:

First Printing, Revised Edition, (date)

1 2 3 4 5 6 7 8 9

"When we reprint a book we indicate that it has been previously published by another publisher or by Dutton Signet in another imprint by the following:

First (current imprint name) Printing, (date)

1 2 3 4 5 6 7 8 9."

2000 Statement: *See* 1993 Statement

E

EAGLE GATE

2000 Statement: *See* 2000 Statement of Deseret Book Company

EAGLE PUBLISHING (UNITED KINGDOM)

2001 Statement: "We do not identify a first printing; we do identify subsequent printings as such on the copyright page."

EAGLE'S VIEW PUBLISHING

1993 Statement: "Starting in 1991, all books designate the printing by descending numbers at the bottom of the copyright page with the last number indicating the printing of that book. First printings end with the number 1. 'First Edition' usually appears on the copyright page.

"Prior to 1991 no completely consistent method was used. First printings of first editions usually state 'First Edition' on the copyright page, but this was not always removed if no substantial changes were made for subsequent printings. Books published in another form and revised by Eagle's View usually say Eagle's View Edition, but whether or not it is a first printing is not always indicated. Many of these books were only printed once prior to 1991. Bar codes were added to all books printed after May, 1990."

2000 Statement: *See* 1993 Statement

EAKIN PRESS

1994 Statement: The copyright page carries the words First Edition and a string of numbers. The lowest number indicates the printing.

2000 Statement: *See* 1994 Statement

THE EAKINS PRESS FOUNDATION

1976 Statement: "In fact Eakins publications are not intended to go into editions beyond the first, and consequently no particular mark of identification is accorded the first printing."

1981 Statement: *See* 1976 Statement

EARTH LOVE PUBLISHING HOUSE, LTD.

2000 Statement: "We identify the first printing of a first edition by the following statement: 'First Printing   Year.' "

EARTH MAGIC PRODUCTIONS, INC.

1995 Statement: "Earth Magic Productions, Inc. identifies its first printings by notating the following information on the copyright page, 'First Edition, copyright date [year only], by [the author].' This is the method of designation we have used since . . . 1993."

EARTHSCAN PUBLICATIONS LTD (UNITED KINGDOM)

2001 Statement: "First printings are not identified but subsequent printings are identified as such on the copyright page."

EAST GATE BOOKS

2000 Statement: *See* 2000 Statement of M E Sharpe Inc

THE EAST WOODS PRESS

1981 Statement: "We designate the first printing of a first edition by simply typesetting 'first printing' underneath the copyright information. I believe we have done this with each book during our four years of publication.

"The East Woods Press is the trade name and imprint of Fast & McMillan Publishers, Inc. All books from our company follow the same practices."

1988 Statement: *"The East Woods Press merged with The Globe Pequot Press on October 1, 1986."*

See 1988 Statement of The Globe Pequot Press, Inc.

EASTERN ACORN PRESS
See Eastern National Park & Monument Association
See Eastern National

EASTERN NATIONAL
2000 Statement: *See* 1994 Statement of Eastern National Park & Monument Association. The statement still stands, but note that the name must be amended to read Eastern National.

EASTERN NATIONAL PARK
& MONUMENT ASSOCIATION
1994 Statement: "We always put our edition on the page after the Title page. We usually make the following statement: © 19— Eastern National Park & Monument Association. We were chartered in 1948. Our publication and product development department did not come into its own until 1980. Until 1988 we entitled our edition statement in the following manner: © 19— Eastern Acorn Press, publishing imprint of Eastern National Park & Monument Association."
2000 Statement: *See* 2000 Statement of Eastern National

EASTERN PRESS
1993 Statement: "Our first printing does not give any edition information, but second or third edition or revised edition gives the information at the title page."

EASTERN WASHINGTON STATE HISTORICAL SOCIETY
1994 Statement: "We do not identify a first printing .... If we reprint/revise, etc. it would be indicated as such e.g. 'revised edition.' "
2001 Statement: *See* 1994 Statement

EASTLAND PRESS
2001 Statement: "We identify the first printing of a first edition by a number line, the lowest number indicating the printing."

EASTMAN KODAK COMPANY
1988 Statement: "We do not designate the first printing of first editions."

EBURY PRESS (UNITED KINGDOM)
1994 Statement: "Our practice, to identify the first printing of a first edition, is to print on the verso of the title page the words 'First published 19**.' We then print the numbers one to ten in the following form:
                    1 3 5 7 9 10 8 6 4 2
to provide for subsequent printings to be identified by the deletion of each number in turn.

"There then follow the notice of copyright and a statement about the rights of reproduction, after which we print: 'First published in the United Kingdom in 19** by Ebury Press Limited, Random House, 20 Vauxhall Bridge Road,

London SW1V 2SA,' followed by the names and addresses of our associated companies in Australia, New Zealand and South Africa.

"This practice is followed by all the imprints within Ebury Press, including Vermillion, Stanley Paul, Barrie & Jenkins, and Condé Nast Books.

"We have adhered to this practice since this company was taken over by Random House UK Ltd in 1991. Before that date, we printed the words 'Published by Ebury Press,' followed by 'First impression 19**.' "

2000 Statement: *See* 2000 Statement of The Random House Group Limited (United Kingdom)

EBURY PRESS STATIONERY (UNITED KINGDOM)
1994 Statement: *See* 1994 Statement of Random House UK LImited (United Kingdom)
2000 Statement: *See* 2000 Statement of The Random House Group Limited (United Kingdom)

E. C. PUBLICATIONS
2000 Statement: *See* 2000 Statement of DC Comics

THE ECCO PRESS
1976 Statement: "Starting with our spring, 1977 books, all copyright pages will run the line 'FIRST EDITION' when it is applicable. Previously, we have not run this line. However, if any of our books should go into a second printing, we will run the line 'SECOND EDITION.' "
1981 Statement: "The 1976 statement you have on file for The Ecco Press regarding our designation of first editions is still correct. The line we use to indicate that a book is a first edition is 'First published by The Ecco Press in . . . . (year).' Additional printings are indicated by the following line: 'Second printing . . . .' If any of our books should be reprinted in a new edition, we will indicate this by the line 'Second Edition.' "
1988 Statement: *See* 1981 Statement
1993 Statement: "The previous information up until 1991 is correct. Since 1991, all first printings run the line FIRST EDITION. Additional printings run the line SECOND PRINTING, THIRD PRINTING, etc."
2001 Statement: *See* 2001 Statement of HarperCollinsPublishers

ECLIPSE BOOKS
1993 Statement: "Our first editions usually say either 'First printing' or 'First edition.' We also use 10 9 8 7 6 5 4 3 2 1, wiping the 1 off on the second printing. If *no* indication is given, the work is a first printing; subsequent editions are *always* so indicated."

EDEN PRESS (CANADA)
1988 Statement: "The words 'First Edition' appear on our copyright/ISBN page. This has been done since 1978. Subsequent editions and/or printings are also so marked."

EDEN PUBLISHING
1995 Statement: "We . . . make no particular effort to designate first printings. Second or revised printings are indicated."

EDGE BOOKS
2001 Statement: *See* 2001 Statement of Guantlet Press

EDGEWISE PRESS
2000 Statement: "All first edition and subsequent printings information is indicated on the copyright page."

EDINBURGH (UNITED KINGDOM)
1988, 2000 Statements: *See* 1988 Statement of Edinburgh University Press (United Kingdom)

EDINBURGH UNIVERSITY PRESS (UNITED KINGDOM)
1988 Statement: "Since the introduction and use of ISBNs in the late 1960s, Edinburgh University Press has adopted a style which makes use of the copyright sign followed by the name of the copyright holder (if applicable) and the year of publication, viz.: © N. Author 1988.

"Only when a book reprints is 'First edition' mentioned, viz.:
First published 1984
Reprinted 1986, 1988

"With reference to Edinburgh University Press books (we are the imprint 'Edinburgh'), it can be taken that no reference or mention of 'First edition' means that that particular printing *is* the first."
1994, 2000 Statements: *See* 1988 Statement

EDITIONS D'AFRIQUE DU NORD
2000 Statement: *See* 2000 Statement of Edgewise Press

EDUCATIONAL TECHNOLOGY PUBLICATIONS
1993 Statement: "We state 'First printing: date' in each book. Later, the chronology of printings is given, first printing and date, second and date, etc."
2000 Statement: *See* 1993 Statement

WM. B. EERDMANS PUBLISHING CO.
1976 Statement: "We never explicitly state the appearance of a first edition. The absence of any identifying statement would indicate the first printing of a first edition.

"All other printings of a first edition are indicated as such. Revised editions are explicitly identified."
1981, 1988 Statements: *See* 1976 Statement
1995 Statement: "We do not explicitly identify a first edition as such. We always identify subsequent editions as such, and the absence of that identification indicates a first edition.

"Since 1994 we use two sets of numerals (indicating year and the number of the impression) on the copyright page to indicate the book's publishing history. The first impression of a first edition will be indicated when the year

of the impression is the same as the year of the copyright and the impression numeral is '1.' "
2000 Statement: *See* 1995 Statement

THE EIGHTH MOUNTAIN PRESS

1993 Statement: "The first printing of the first edition can be recognized by the words 'first edition' on the copyright page followed by a series of ten numbers beginning with one. For the second printing, the number one is dropped, so that the numbers go from two to ten, and from then on, the lowest number remaining in the sequence indicates the printing. If it is two, it is the second printing, etc. This is the only method we have ever used."
2001 Statement: *See* 1993 Statement

ELAND BOOKS (UNITED KINGDOM)

1989 Statement: "By and large, nearly all our books are reprints. We like therefore to put 'First published by,' designating the original publisher.

"We then like to put, also on the verso page 'First issued in this edition,' giving the year of issue.

"Occasionally our books are mongrels, some of the material having been published in book form before, some of it being new. We try to indicate where this is the case and usually use the sentence 'First issued in this edition,' again giving the date.

"If we reprint our edition of the book, we like to put in 'Reprinted,' giving the year of the reprint."
2000 Statement: "By and large, nearly all our books are reprints. We like therefore to put 'First published by,' designating the original publisher.

"We then like to put, also on the verso page 'First issued in this edition,' giving the year of issue.

"Occasionally our books are mongrels, some of the material having been published in book form before, some of it being new. We try to indicate where this is the case and usually use the sentence 'First issued in this edition,' again giving the date."

ELDON PRESS, LTD. (UNITED KINGDOM)
(Controlled by Macdonald & Co.)

1937 Statement: "First Editions are marked on the back of the title page
Published by
Eldon Press Ltd.
1934

"For reprints the month of publication is added together with the date of the reprint, as follows.
Published by
Eldon Press Ltd.
December 1934
Second Impression January 1935"
1947 Statement: Publisher supplied sample title page showing present method. This bears on verso:

First published 1947
Second Impression December 1947

ELECTROCHEMICAL SOCIETY INC

2001 Statement: "We do not identify a first printing or any printing after the first printing on the copyright page."

PAUL ELEK PUBLISHERS, LTD. (UNITED KINGDOM)

1947 Statement: "All first editions of our books are printed with copyright notes and date, whereas 'reprints' and 'second editions' always have the words 'reprinted' or 'second edition' and the date."

1976 Statement: "We have no method of identifying first editions."

ELEPHANT PAPERBACKS

2000 Statement: *See* 2000 Statement of Ivan R. Dee, Publisher
See also 2001 Statement of J. S. Sanders

ELEPHANT'S EYE

2000 Statement: *See* 2000 Statement of The Overlook Press

EDWARD ELGAR PUBLISHING INC

2001 Statement: "We do not identify a first printing; we do identify subsequent printings as such on the copyright page."

ELK GROVE BOOKS

1976, 1981, 1988 Statements: *See* 1976 Statement of Childrens Press®

ELLICOTT PRESS

1995 Statement: "Our first editions are designated by the fact that they are not so designated. Subsequent editions and printings are designated on the reverse of the title page."

ELLIOTT & CLARK

See Black Belt Press

ELLIOT RIGHT WAY BOOKS, PUBLISHERS (UNITED KINGDOM)

1946 Statement: "All books were printed with the words 'All rights reserved' on the back of the title page. This practice continued until about 1950."

1950 Statement: "All first editions were printed: 'Copyright, A.G. Elliot' with the year in roman numerals i.e. MCMLVI (1956).

"If it was not a first edition then the words 'reprinted' or 'second edition,' with the date again would appear underneath. This practice continued until 1967."

1967 Statement: "This was the date of our formation as a company, initially as a limited company, and from this date all first editions carried the legend: '© Elliot Right Way Books Limited' followed by the year in roman numerals.

"Later the word 'Limited' was dropped.

"Throughout all these years, the distinguishing feature of a first edition is that it carries no reference to any subsequent edition or printing, whereas any edition which is not a first edition will say so."

1994, 2000 Statements: *See* 1967 Statement

AIDAN ELLIS (UNITED KINGDOM)

1988 Statement: "Date of edition is always indicated on the imprint page."

1994, 2000 Statements: *See* 1988 Statement

ELM PUBLICATIONS (UNITED KINGDOM)

1994 Statement: "For our first editions we usually begin the copyright page:

© Author's name(s), date

Title

First published by in (month) (year)

"Second and subsequent editions are generally marked Second (or third, etc.) Edition on the copyright page with the date, and on the cover."

ELM TREE BOOKS (UNITED KINGDOM)

1988 Statement: *See* 1988 Statement of Hamish Hamilton Ltd. (United Kingdom)

ELM TREE PRESS

See William Edwin Rudge

ELSEVIER

1988 Statement: *See* 1988 Statement of Elsevier Science Publishing Company, Inc.

ELSEVIER SCIENCE PUBLISHING COMPANY, INC.

1988 Statement: "Elsevier Science Publishing Co., Inc., indicates the first printing of a first (or subsequent) edition on the copyright page using the following designation.

Current printing (last digit):

10 9 8 7 6 5 4 3 2 1

"When we reprint a book, we update the copyright page by opaquing the last digit (e.g., for the second printing, we would opaque the '1'). This system was instituted in 1985 and is used for all Elsevier New York imprints (Elsevier, North-Holland, and Medical Examination Publishing Company). Prior to 1985 we did not have a method of indicating the number of the printing of a book.

"We do not state that a book is a first edition; however, subsequent editions are designated on the cover, copyright page, and title page."

1993 Statement: "On behalf of Elsevier Science Publishing Company, Inc., the New York office of Elsevier Science Publishers. We have . . . discontinued the publication of book titles from this office, and therefore have no such policy as you describe."

ELSEVIER-DUTTON PUBLISHING CO., INC.

See 1981 Statement of E. P. Dutton Co., Inc.

ELSP (UNITED KINGDOM)
2001 Statement: *See* 2001 Statement of Ex Libris Press (United Kingdom)

EM PRESS
2001 Statement: "We do not identify a first printing or any printing after the first printing on the copyright page. Limited edition letterpress usually, but not always, individually numbered. The size of the edition is indicated in the colophon."

EMERITUS ENTERPRISES
1993 Statement: *See* 1993 Statement of The Borgo Press
2000 Statement: *See* 2000 Statement of The Borgo Press

EMERSON BOOKS, INC.
1976 Statement: "We make no specific identification mark on our first editions and to the best of my knowledge have never done so.

"We do identify subsequent editions marking each by the number of its printing. For example—
2nd Printing 1943
3rd Printing 1967
"In some instances we eliminate reference to previous printings but always identify with the current printing."
1981, 1994 Statements: *See* 1976 Statement

EMPIRE PUBLISHING
2000 Statement: *See* 2000 Statement of Empire Publishing Service

EMPIRE PUBLISHING SERVICE
2000 Statement: "We do not label First Editions, only second and later. So, if not labeled, it is a first edition."

EMPIRE STATE BOOKS
1988 Statement: *See* 1988 Statement of Heart of the Lakes Publishing

ENCYCLOPAEDIA AFRICANA
2000 Statement: *See* 2000 Statement of Reference Publications, Inc.

ENCYCLOPAEDIA BRITANNICA, INC.
1988 Statement: "As publishers chiefly of encyclopedias and yearbooks, we issue very few first editions. The *Encyclopaedia Britannica* is in its 15th edition (first issued 1974, with annual revised printings); *Compton's Encyclopedia* has, since 1922, referred to each annual revised version as an edition, but they are identified by year of copyright rather than serially numbered. Our yearbooks of course, have only one printing each and one date of issue.

"Our principal book-publishing subsidiary, Merriam-Webster, Inc., of Springfield, Mass., has in recent years used the common practice of indicating serial number and year of printing by a line of type: 12345RMcN888786 indicating a first printing (in 1986), 345RMcN8887 indicating a third printing (in 1987). The imprints 'First Printing' and 'First Edition' are also found."

1993 Statement: "The statement supplied in 1988 still represents the policy of Encyclopaedia Britannica, Inc., except in one particular: in 1993 the company sold Compton's Learning Company, publisher of *Compton's Encyclopedia*, to the Tribune Co. Since 1968 the company has distributed a replica version of the First Edition of the *Encyclopaedia Britannica* that is most easily distinguished from a genuine First Edition by the fact that the photographically reproduced pattern of foxing recurs every 32 pages."

ENRICH BOOKS
1989 Statement: *See* 1989 Statement of Price/Stern/Sloan Publishers Inc.

ENSIGN PRESS
1995 Statement: "We do not do anything spectacular on first runs of first editions. We do note second runs as such; we also of course specifically identify second editions."
2001 Statement: *See* 1995 Statement

ENTERPRISE PUBLICATIONS (AUSTRALIA)
1994 Statement: "Books published by Enterprise Publications are first editions unless the statement 'reprinted in . . . year' is included on the reverse of the title page."

ENTRADA BOOKS
1988 Statement: *See* 1988 Statement of Northland Press

ENTWHISTLE BOOKS
1981 Statement: "We say 'First Printing,' sometimes followed by the month and year."
   This method of identification has not differed from any previously used. All imprints use this method.
1989 Statement: *See* 1981 Statement

EOS
2001 Statement: *See* 2001 Statement of HarperCollinsPublishers

EPM PUBLICATIONS, INC.
1994 Statement: "Starting in 1994, EPM will identify the first printings of our books by inserting on the copyright page the following phrase: 'First Printing, month, year.' Subsequent printings will be identified by using the phrase 'Second Printing (or whichever), month, year.' If the printings are new
. editions bearing change of ISBN and possibly ©, that will also be noted.
   "Some of our earlier books bear the edition number on the cover of the book and/or copyright page."
2000 Statement: *See* 1994 Statement

EPOCH PRESS
2000 Statement: *See* 2000 Statement of Warren H. Green, Inc.

EPWORTH PRESS (UNITED KINGDOM)

1937 Statement: "It is our practice to put the date of the publication of any book on the back of the title-page. If the book is reprinted, the date of the reprint appears on the back of the title-page, e.g.:

First Edition 1922

Reprinted 1923"

1947, 1994, 2000 Statements: *See* 1937 Statement

EQUATION (UNITED KINGDOM)

1988 Statement: *See* 1988 Statement of Thorsons Publishing Group Ltd (United Kingdom)

EQUINOX COOPERATIVE PRESS, INC.

1937 Statement: "Most of our previous books have been limited editions and there was therefore only one printing. The only book on which we have had a second printing is 'Imperial Hearst,' by Ferdinand Lundberg. All subsequent editions carry a line to that effect on the copyright page."

ERESPIN PRESS

1995 Statement: "Erespin Press is and has always been since its founding in 1980, a private press. We have never issued an edition larger than 350 copies, and the usual edition is limited to twelve copies. If any person sees an Erespin Press publication, he sees a first edition. We leave no type standing in galleys and keep no plates for second printings."

2001 Statement: *See* 1995 Statement

PAUL S. ERIKSSON PUBLISHER

1976 Statement: "We customarily make no mention of first editions or first printings. We do make an attempt to print notices on the © page designating which printing of a particular edition it is—after the *first* printing. On new editions, we mention *revisions* only; e.g. © 1971. Revised Edition, 1976."

1981 Statement: "We also now sometimes use the numerical system 10 9 8 7 6 5 4 3 2 showing which *printing* a title is in."

1988 Statement: "We now use the numerical system 10 9 8 7 6 5 4 3 2 showing which *printing* a title is in."

1993 Statement: *See* 1988 Statement

2000 Statement: "Our latest shows only 5 4 3 2 1."

LAWRENCE ERLBAUM ASSOCIATES, INC.

1994 Statement: "We designate first printings of first editions by the use of a number line at the bottom of the copyright page beginning with 10 and ending with 1. With each successive reprint the next number in the line, beginning with the '1,' is deleted."

2000 Statement: *See* 1994 Statement

LAWRENCE ERLBAUM ASSOCIATES, LTD.
(UNITED KINGDOM)

See LEA (United Kingdom)

THE ERNEST PRESS (UNITED KINGDOM)
2001 Statement: "The Ernest Press was established in 1984 with the aim of a) publishing high-quality facsimiles of classic mountaineering titles long out of print and b) bringing out new titles mainly concerned with biographies of notable mountaineers and historical/philosophical surveys of mountaineering. In 1989 we started to publish a series of UK guides for mountain bikers. This year, 2001, we are bringing out the first fiction book.

"All our books show on the bibliographical or title verso page 'Published by The Ernest Press in 19??' and that is the only indication that it is a first edition. Any subsequent reprints or amended editions are so noted on the same title verso page. There has been no variation in this practice since the company was established. All our books are published in Great Britain, though there is no statement to this effect anywhere in the books."

EROS BOOKS
1995, 2000 Statements: *See* 1995 Statement of Cedar Bay Press

EROS COMIX
2000 Statement: *See* 2000 Statement of Fantagraphics Books

EROS PLUS (UNITED KINGDOM)
2000 Statement: *See* 2000 Statement of Titan Books Ltd. (United Kingdom)

THE ERSKINE PRESS (UNITED KINGDOM)
2001 Statement: *See* 2001 Statement of Archival Facsimiles Limited (United Kingdom)

THE ESSEX INSTITUTE
1928 Statement: "It is very unusual for our publications to run to more than one edition and we have not designated the first in any case except by the date. We have designated second editions as such on the title page."
1937, 1947 Statements: *See* 1928 Statement

ESTAMP (UNITED KINGDOM)
2001 Statement: "This company was formed in 1989 to publish artist's handbooks . . . . Dedicated to expanding both the practical and the aesthetic horizons, all books bearing an estamp imprint were carefully chosen, researched and prepared . . . . First printings are not designated as such. Subsequent printings are labelled 'second printing,' etc. All our titles are sold out and some now are collected on the second-hand specialist market.

"estamp closed its publication doors at the beginning of the third millennium, although a few of the titles with small numbers of books remaining continue to be available through their agents, Central Books. The research that estamp undertook concerning the history of print workshops in the UK is lodged in the Tate Gallery Archive, London; and the research on paper is contained in the book *The Book of Fine Paper* by Silvie Turner published in December 1999 by Thames & Hudson."

ETC PUBLICATIONS

1993 Statement: First printings are not designated as such. Subsequent printings are noted. All imprints and subsidiaries follow this practice, which was begun in 1972.

2000 Statement: *See* 1993 Statement

EUROPA PUBLICATIONS LIMITED (UNITED KINGDOM)

1988 Statement: "We designate the first printing of a first edition by putting 'First Edition 1988' or 'Second Edition 1989' on the copyright page."

1994, 2000 Statements: *See* 1988 Statement

EVANGEL PUBLISHING HOUSE

2001 Statement: "We state 'First edition' on the copyright page. We also identify the first printing of a first edition by a number line, the lowest number indicating the printing."

M. EVANS AND COMPANY, INC.

1976 Statement: "We usually do not designate first editions as separate from first printings. Our printing history is usually listed on the very last line of the copyright page. For example: '9 8 7 6 5 4 3 2 1' means that it is the first printing. If the right hand digit is deleted, the final digit is the printing. For example, if the final digit is 2, it is the second printing."

1981, 1988, 1993, 2000 Statements: *See* 1976 Statement

EVANS BROTHERS LIMITED (UNITED KINGDOM)

1976 Statement: "We . . . include the year of first publication, i.e.

First published 1976 by
Evans Brothers Limited,
Montague House,
Russell Square,
London WC1B 5BX.

"For a reprint we would add the words 'reprint' and the date for the reprint under the above."

1981 Statement: "An example of our current verso copy is [as shown]. For reprint we would add the words 'reprinted' and the date for the reprint under first published.

Published by
Evans Brothers Limited
Montague House
Russell Square, London WC1 5BX
Text © [holder] 1981
Illustrations © [holder] 1981
First published 1981"

1989 Statement: *See* 1981 Statement, but note that publisher's address will now read: 2a Portman Mansions, Chiltern Street, London W1M 1LE.

2000 Statement: *See* 1981 Statement, but note that publisher's address will now read: London W1U 6NR.

EVANSTON PUBLISHING, INC.

1993 Statement: "Evanston Publishing, Inc. designates the first printing of a book with printer's codes on the bottom of the copyright page. The numbers are listed in descending order, with ascending numbers deleted with each new printing.

"We do not identify a book as a first edition. Any edition after the first is indicated as such on the title page. This has always been Evanston Publishing's policy."

2000 Statement: *See* 1993 Statement

HUGH EVELYN LTD. (UNITED KINGDOM)

1976 Statement: "The imprint carries the words 'first published in 19...' Any subsequent printing or new edition would carry the same statement followed by the year of the new printing."

EVERGREEN

1988 Statement: *See* 1988 Statement of Grove Press, Inc.

EVERGREEN ENTERPRISES LLC

2001 Statement: "We do not identify a first printing; we do identify subsequent printings on the copyright page."

EVERGREEN PACIFIC PUBLISHING LTD

2001 Statement: "First printings are not identified, but we do identify all those after the first. This is shown on the copyright page."

EVERYMAN'S LIBRARY

2000 Statement: *See* 2000 Statement of Alfred A. Knopf

EX LIBRIS PRESS (UNITED KINGDOM)

2001 Statement: "We do not identify a first printing. Subsequent printings are identified on the copyright page."

EXCELSIOR CEE PUBLISHING

2001 Statement: "We designate the premier edition of our books with the words 'First Edition' and the printings are noted with a series of numbers '1 2 3 4 5 6.' This is printed on the copyright page of the text."

EXILE PRESS

1995 Statement: "Exile Press is the oldest independent small press in the United States . . . . Since 1949, when founded as Inferno Press, we published poetry and some prose in both hardback and paperback editions. Since 1982 all our books are in paperback, but we no longer publish poetry. Only one book went into a Second Printing, and we identified it by using a different colored cover. In our direct mailing we mentioned the volume as a Second Printing. Henceforth any Second Printing will be so listed under the copyright notice."

EXPERT BOOKS (UNITED KINGDOM)

2001 Statement: *See* 2001 Statement of Transworld Publishers Ltd (United Kingdom)

EXPRESSO EDITIONS

2000 Statement: "We do not do anything to denote a first edition . . . because they are handset, handprinted, handbound letterpress books and are only printed once."

See also Coffee House Press

EXTENDING HORIZONS BOOKS

2000 Statement: *See* 2000 Statement of Porter Sargent Publishers Inc.

EYRE & SPOTTISWOODE (PUBLISHERS) LIMITED (UNITED KINGDOM)

1937 Statement: "First Edition. Year of publication printed under our name at the foot of title page.

"Second and subsequent editions are shown as follows:
Upon the reverse side of the title page:

First published 19...
Reprinted   19...
Reprinted   19...

"Where two editions have been printed in the same year, the month is added, i.e.,

First published June 19...
Reprinted October 19..."

1947 Statement: "First Edition. Year of publication printed either under our name at the foot of the title page or included in the printer's imprint at the foot of the verso of the title page, in the form 'This book, first published 19.., is printed..'

"Second and subsequent editions are shown as follows:
Upon the reverse side of the title page:

First published 19...
Reprinted   19...
Reprinted   19...

"Where two editions have been printed in the same year, the month is added, i.e.,

First published June 19...
Reprinted October 19..."

EYRE METHUEN LTD. (UNITED KINGDOM)

1976 Statement: "Beyond the usual information about publisher and publication date, and the date of the copyright, we do not have any particular method of identifying first editions."

1981 Statement: *See* 1976 Statement

EZ NATURE BOOKS

1993 Statement: "We have not made any indication or differentiation of first or subsequent printings in our books."

2000 Statement: *See* 1993 Statement

F

FABER & FABER, LTD. (UNITED KINGDOM)
1937 Statement: "When, in 1929, the firm became Faber and Faber, we started our present method of wording the note on the back of the title page of all our books.
FIRST PUBLISHED MAY MCMXXXIV
BY FABER AND FABER LIMITED
24 RUSSELL SQUARE LONDON W. C. I.
SECOND IMPRESSION JULY MCMXXXIV
PRINTED IN GREAT BRITAIN BY
THE CURWEN PRESS, PLAISTOW
ALL RIGHTS RESERVED
"This is a typical example, and we now adhere rigidly to this form."
1947 Statement: "Our general practice is still the same as shown above.
"During the war, however, we have made one or two modifications as follows:—
"1. We generally omit the month, and content ourselves with naming the year. This is due to production delays.
"2. Any reprint in which substantial alterations appear is called a new edition. Otherwise we call the reprint a new impression.
"3. Sometimes, when the biblio is very extensive, we say 'reprinted 1938 and 1939' instead of 'second impression,' 'third impression,' etc."
Statement for 1960: "I don't really think that there is very much to add or subtract [from the 1976 statement]. I think that we have always treated this information in a similar fashion and the only thing which was obviously different in the year 1960 was the way in which we printed the date. Up to and including the year 1967 we indicated the publication dates in Roman numerals. Thus for the year 1960 the date would have read mcmlx. This policy became less common among London publishing houses after the World War II and some people seemed not to have learned how to read these dates! The practice was therefore changed and in 1968 we began to use Arabic numerals regularly."
1976 Statement: *See* 1976 Statement of Faber and Faber Ltd., Publishers (United Kingdom)

FABER AND FABER LTD., PUBLISHERS
(UNITED KINGDOM)
1976 Statement: "Our practice here is to print on the back of the title page 'First Published in 19.. by Faber and Faber Ltd.' That seems quite straightforward and is in fact so for all books originating here. But there is a slight difficulty that has to be watched. We sometimes use exactly the same formula for books that have already been published in the United States by an American publisher. This may seem a little odd at first, but you will see that

it is quite justifiable if you rearrange the words: that is to say, 'First Published by Faber and Faber Ltd, in 19...' Sometimes we do add 'First Published in the United States of America' which makes the situation clear.

"I have two new books in front of me at the moment which illustrate the situation. The first is *EZRA POUND: THE LAST ROWER* by C. David Heymann where you will find on the verso of the title page the following:
'First Published in Great Britain in 1976 by
Faber and Faber Ltd.'
and lower down
'First Published in United States of America 1976'

"I am not sure whether this does everything that is necessary, but at least it indicates that there is an American publication the date of which has to be checked. The second book is *NUREYEV: ASPECTS OF THE DANCER* by John Percival where we don't say that the book was first published in the United States, though in fact the first edition was published by Putnam's in 1975. There is a special reason for this because the book originated with us and we sold the rights to Putnam's, who published it very quickly. We published later and included some additional material, so the copyright notice reads: © 1975 and 1976 by John Percival.

"All I want to do in drawing attention to these points is to warn you that in cases where there is an American edition it is as well to check carefully when it was published.

"I might mention that for books by T.S. Eliot published after he became a director of this firm and published all his books through us, we always arranged that the English edition should be published at least a day before the American edition and thus the English edition becomes the real first edition.

"But as I said at the beginning of this letter, the collector must really be prepared to do a bit of work in order to make sure what he is getting hold of.

"In some ways the real question to be considered is, how are subsequent editions described? We always take care to indicate second, third impression or whatever it may be, or second, third, fourth edition if there has been an alteration in the text. I think you will find that this rule is carefully followed.

"In the case of translations, we give the title of the original and if possible the place of publication and the name of the publisher."

1981 Statement: *See* 1976 Statement

1988 Statement: "The only addition to the evolving story of Faber practice is that since the last statement on our behalf we have published very many more paperback editions simultaneously with the hard-cover edition, and this dual character is identified as such on the title page verso. Also, of course, the ISBNs for both editions are expressed in both versions. Limited editions, which we still occasionally do, usually have some extra feature which requires a different ISBN—the date of publication will usually be the same year, though it may well be that the limited edition will come out weeks or even months later than the trade edition. We regret to say that our practice is not perfect, and bibliographical niceties (on the Gallup scale) should ultimately be checked with the Faber archive."

1994 Statement: "Most of what we said in our previous statement still applies, with one or two extra complications. For titles which we expect to reprint regularly, especially fiction, we have adopted the practice of adding a row of arabic numerals from 1 to 10 or more at the foot of the verso of the title page. If the numerals include 1 it is the first edition; if the lowest number is 2 then the book is the second printing, and so on. Editions, as distinct from mere reprints, are usually described as such at the top of the verso bibliography. The system is not foolproof and where economic value is involved it is wise to get the book's status identified by Faber in London.

"One other factor to bear in mind is that Faber books are now often published directly in paperback, or simultaneously with a hardback from the same sheets. A pair of ISBNs is the obvious sign of this in the case of simultaneous publication: both versions are thus first editions, though inevitably fewer copies of the hardback will have been manufactured than the paperback. Textually they are identical."

2000 Statement: "There have been no changes in our general practice since the last statement. But there are always anomalies with such a large and variegated list, and in cases of ambiguity collectors should consult Faber. This especially applies in the case of limited editions and printed ephemera (memorial addresses, speeches, occasional poems etc) issued privately under the firm's imprint."

FABER & GWYER, LTD. (UNITED KINGDOM)
(Reorganized as Faber & Faber, Ltd. in 1929.)
1928 Statement: "Our practice—and I cannot say that we have adhered to it absolutely rigidly up to the present, has been to print on the back of the title page 'First published by Faber & Gwyer, Ltd. in so and so' and with subsequent editions, or impressions, 'Second Impression . . . ' etc. We do not as a rule print the date of publication on the title page itself."

FABIAN SOCIETY (UNITED KINGDOM)
1976 Statement: "We have no special method of identifying first editions. However, they can easily be identified as subsequent editions would contain the information that the particular pamphlet or book was reprinted."
1981, 2001 Statements: *See* 1976 Statement

FACTOR PRESS
2001 Statement: "We do not identify a first printing; we do identify subsequent printings on the copyright page."

FACTS ON DEMAND PRESS
2000 Statement: *See* 2000 Statement of BRB Publications, Inc

FADED BANNER PUBLICATIONS
2000 Statement: "First editions have no such notation—no number or indication. Subsequent printings state on the title page 'Second Printing,' 'Third Printing,' etc."

FAIRCHILD BOOKS

2000 Statement: *See* 2000 Statement of Fairchild Books & Visuals

FAIRCHILD BOOKS & VISUALS

1993 Statement: The first edition is indicated by the words "First Edition" and the copyright date. Subsequent printings and editions are so noted with their dates (e.g. "Second printing, 1984").

2000 Statement:*See* 1993 Statement of Fairchild Books

FAIRCHILD PUBLICATIONS

1947 Statement: "We are publishers of semi-technical or business books and have no particular way of designating first printings. Obviously second or revised printings are so noted and in this way at least we do have a key to first editions by the process of elimination."

FAIRLEIGH DICKINSON UNIVERSITY PRESS

1976, 1981, 1988, 1993, 2000 Statements: *See* 1976 Statement of Associated University Presses

FAIRVIEW PRESS

2001 Statement: "We state 'First printing' on the copyright page. We also identify the first printing by a number line. The lowest number indicates the printing."

FAIRVIEW PUBLICATIONS

2001 Statement: *See* 2001 Statement of Fairview Press

FALCON PRESS

See 2000 Statement of New Falcon Publications

THE FALCON PRESS (LONDON) LIMITED
(UNITED KINGDOM)

1947 Statement: "Our only method is to examine the biblio on the reverse of the title page.

"This always reads in this order:

First published in 1947 (or other date.)
by The Falcon Press (London) Ltd.
7, Crown Passage, Pall Mall
London, S. W. 1
Printed in Great Britain (or other country.)
by Tonbridge Printers Limited (or other printer.)
Tonbridge, Kent.
All rights reserved.

"In the event of a second or subsequent impression being published that fact and the date would also be given on the reverse of the title page as follows:

Second impression November 1947
Third impression   December 1947"

FALLEN LEAF PRESS

1995 Statement: "We do not identify first printings of first editions."

FALMOUTH PUBLISHING HOUSE, INC.
1947 Statement: "We would distinguish a first edition from subsequent editions by stating so, most always on the back of the title page. We would say either 2d edition, etc. or 2d printing, etc.

"However, of the 75 or so titles we have published all are first editions except *The Umbrella Bird*. The same would hold true of the Dirigo Editions and Triad Editions. Wherever they are found they are first editions.

"We do mostly small editions. In the future, however, we will be publishing on a larger scale."

FAMEDRAM PUBLISHERS LIMITED (UNITED KINGDOM)
1994 Statement: "We have no special method of identifying first editions. However, they can easily be identified as subsequent editions would contain the information that a particular title had been reprinted and the year of reprint."

FAMILY LAW (UNITED KINGDOM)
1994, 2000 Statements: *See* 1994 Statement of Jordan Publishing Limited (United Kingdom)

FANTAGRAPHICS BOOKS
1994 Statement: "All our books include, in the indicia, a statement as to which printing that book comes from."
2000 Statement: *See* 1994 Statement

FANTAIL
2000 Statement: "We identify the first printing of a first edition by the statement 'First Printing.' This is used consistently in all our books."

FAR CORNER BOOKS
1995 Statement: "Far Corner Books identifies first printings of first editions with the words 'First Edition' and '9 8 7 6 5 4 3 2 1' at the bottom of the copyright page. When a book is reprinted we delete figure 1, etc. and insert 'Second printing,' and the date. Far Corner also distributes the books published by Breitenbush Publications between 1978 and 1990. First editions of Breitenbush titles state either 'First edition' or 'First printing' and often use the date or '2 3 4 5 6 7 8 9.' Later printings are so noted and usually include the date."

FARMING PRESS (UNITED KINGDOM)
1994 Statement: "We designate first editions on the verso title page with the line 'First edition by . . . ' or 'First published in . . . ' "
2000 Statement: "We designate first editions on the verso title page with the line 'First published (year).' "

FARRAGUT PUBLISHING COMPANY
1993 Statement: "Farragut Publishing Company does not specifically designate the first printing of a first edition.

"We have not adopted a policy of identifying different printings or editions, but our rules of thumb are as follows: We generally designate the number and the year of printing on the reverse of the title page. Any printing subsequent to the first may include revisions or corrections. If a new printing does include revisions, we generally do not identify it as a 'revised edition,' although we have in one instance.

"The revised edition policy excludes our paperback reprints of previously published works, which include new material and are by definition revised editions.

"Our company has never had any other method of designation."

FARRAND PRESS (UNITED KINGDOM)
2001 Statement: "We do not identify first printings."

FARRAR AND RINEHART, INC.
(Became Rinehart and Co., Inc. on January 1, 1946.)
1937 Statement: "Farrar & Rinehart first editions can be identified by the small oval colophon, forming the letters F and R, which appears immediately above the copyright line in all first editions of our books."

FARRAR, STRAUS AND COMPANY, INC.
("On November 21, 1945, the firm of Farrar, Straus & Company was incorporated in New York. Roger W. Straus, Jr., and John Farrar [formerly of Farrar & Rinehart] were its founders.")
1947 Statement: "If our colophon appears on the copyright page it is a first edition. It will be dropped for subsequent editions; which in most cases can also be identified because the printings are indicated."

FARRAR, STRAUS & GIROUX, INC.
("On December 14, 1950, the name of Farrar, Straus & Company was changed to Farrar, Straus & Young, to include Stanley Young, a member of the Board of Directors who was appointed Managing Director in 1949. Mr. Young left the company in 1955, and the name again became Farrar, Straus & Company.
On March 18, 1955, the firm became Farrar, Straus & Cudahy. Sheila Cudahy had been on the Board of Directors since the acquisition of Pelligrini and Cudahy in 1953. [Creative Age Press was acquired in 1951.
Later acquisitions were: L. C. Page & Company in 1957; McMullen Books, Inc., in 1958; Noonday Press, Inc., in 1960; Octagon Books, Inc., in 1968; and Hill and Wang in 1971.] When Miss Cudahy left the company in 1962, the name was, once again, Farrar, Straus & Company.
It has been Farrar, Straus & Giroux, Inc., since September 21, 1964.")
1976 Statement: "In answer to your query, we designate first editions by saying just that, plus the year of publication, on the copyright page of our books. An earlier method was to use the words 'first printing.' "
1982 Statement: "I can amplify [the] previous statement by pointing out that we have never used an absolutely consistent method for designating first editions. I think it is safe to say, however, that virtually all of our first editions include the words 'First edition' or 'First printing,' followed by the year of publication, on the copyright page. (During the past ten years or so, 'First

edition' has been used almost exclusively.) Subsequent printings sometimes include information about the first edition, sometimes not."

1988 Statement: "The [1982] statement that you enclosed is by and large the policy Farrar, Straus & Giroux employs. On occasion an editor may use a different method. Again, our imprints and subsidiaries as a rule follow this procedure. There may be exceptions from time to time."

1993, 2000 Statements: *See* 1988 Statement

FARRAR, STRAUS & GIROUX BOOKS FOR YOUNG READERS

2000 Statement: *See* 2000 Statement of Farrar, Straus & Giroux, Inc.

FATHOM PUBLISHING COMPANY

2001 Statement: "We do not have a standard policy for identifying first printings or editions."

FAWCETT BOOKS

1981 Statement: "At Fawcett Books, we designate the first printing by number on the bottom of the copyright page. We list the numbers from left to right, with 1 being the first number in the case of a first printing.

"We do not designate a first edition in our books. This method of identification does not differ from past practice, and all the imprints of Fawcett follow the same method."

2001 Statement: *See* 2001 Statement of The Ballantine Publishing Group

FBA PUBLICATIONS (UNITED KINGDOM)

2001 Statement: "First printings are not identified; however, the date of publication is clearly noted on the copyright page. Subsequent printings identify the 'First Edition' and subsequent editions (i.e. 'Second Edition') along with their respective dates. Our books are published under the imprint of FBA Publications."

FC2/BLACK ICE BOOKS

2000 Statement: "We identify the first printing of a first edition by the statement
    'First Edition' on copyright page
    'First Printing xxxx' also on copyright page
"We have one imprint, Black Ice, and it follows the same practice."

FEDERAL STREET PRESS

2000 Statement: "Since its founding, Federal Street Press has followed this procedure:

"Our first editions are identified as first printings on the copyright page of each book. Later editions are also identified. This is the only identification we have ever used."

See also 2000 Statement of Merriam-Webster Inc.

PHILIPP FELDHEIM INC.

1994 Statement: The first printing of a first edition is indicated by the number line 10 9 8 7 6 5 4 3 2 1. The lowest number showing indicates the printing.

2000 Statement: *See* 1994 Statement

FELL
1993 Statement: *See* 1981 Statement of Frederick Fell Publishers, Inc.

FREDERICK FELL, INC.
1947 Statement: "We identify the first printings of our books by inserting on the copyright page the phrase 'First Printing, month, year.' Subsequent printings are differentiated by using the phrase 'Second Printing, month, year,' etc."

FREDERICK FELL PUBLISHERS, INC.
1976 Statement: "We use 1 2 3 4 5 6 7 8 9 0. When reprinted, we delete figure 1, etc., insert 2nd, 3rd, etc., printing on copyright page, change copyright year to Roman numerals."
1981 Statement: "We will merely revise our [1976 Statement] as follows: "We use 1 2 3 4 5 6 7 8 9 0. When reprinted, we delete figure 1, etc. and insert 2nd, 3rd, etc., printing on copyright page."
1988 Statement: *See* 1981 Statement
(Frederick Fell Publishers, Inc. changed its name to Lifetime Books, Inc. in 1990.)
1993 Statement: *See* 1981 Statement
2000 Statement: "We have dropped Lifetime and Compact. We are [now] publishing under Frederick Fell Publishers, Inc. Our new line of books is Fell's Official Know-It-All Guides." *See also* 1981 Statement.

THE FEMINIST PRESS
1976 Statement: "First printing of first edition just says first edition—subsequent printings say first edition, second printing, etc."
1981 Statement: "We say 'First edition, first printing,' 'First edition, second printing.' "
1988 Statement: "As of 1984, we have been listing in reverse sequence the years of printing and reprints; beside that sequence we list the number of the edition, in relative order to the year it is printed. For example:
89 88 87 86 5 4 3 2
"In this case, the second edition would have been printed in 1986."
1993 Statement: *See* 1993 Statement of The Feminist Press at the City University of New York

THE FEMINIST PRESS
AT THE CITY UNIVERSITY OF NEW YORK
1993 Statement: *See* 1988 Statement of The Feminist Press. The number line is still used, whereby the lowest number indicates the printing. The words "Published (date) by The Feminist Press at the City University of New York . . . " are also present.
2000 Statement: *See* 1993 Statement

FENLAND PRESS, LTD. (UNITED KINGDOM)
(Subsidiary of Williams and Norgate, Ltd.)
1937 Statement: "It is our practice to print the year of publication on the reverse of the title page, e.g.

FIRST PUBLISHED 1934

"When the book is reprinted we then insert the month and year when it was first published and the date of the 2nd impression, e.g.

FIRST PUBLISHED MARCH 1934
SECOND IMPRESSION APRIL 1934
THIRD IMPRESSION AUGUST 1934

and so on."

1947 Statement: *See* 1937 Statement

FERAL HOUSE

1994 Statement: "Our books, with the exception of *Cad: A Handbook for Heels*, delete numbers 1 or 2 or 3, etc., on all subsequent editions. *Cad* plainly reads First Printing on its copyright page; subsequent printings delete this notation."

FERNHURST BOOKS (UNITED KINGDOM)

1994 Statement: A first printing is noted on the copyright page by the line "First published in (date)." Subsequent impressions are noted.

2000 Statement: *See* 1994 Statement

HOWARD FERTIG INC PUBLISHER

2001 Statement: "We set a number string on the copyright page. The lowest number indicates the printing, for example: 1 2 3 4 5. This would indicate a first printing. Each of our titles carries the date of first publication on the copyright page. Later printings are indicated through the use of a number sequence as noted."

FESTIVAL

1988 Statement: *See* 1988 Statement of Abingdon Press

FICOA

2000 Statement: "We mark our subsequent (2nd, 3rd, 4th, etc.) editions, only."

FICTION COLLECTIVE

1988 Statement: "As we have from the onset, the Fiction Collective designates the first printing of the first edition with the following lines on the copyright page:

'First Edition
First Printing, 19—' "

1994 Statement: *See* 1988 Statement

FICTION COLLECTIVE TWO

1994 Statement: *See* 1988 Statement of Fiction Collective
2000 Statement: *See* 2000 Statement of FC2/Black Ice Books

FIDDLEHEAD POETRY BOOKS (CANADA)

See 1989 Statement of Goose Lane Editions (Canada)

FIDES/CLARETIAN

1981 Statement: "Fides/Claretian is now the imprint of Claretian Publications and is the successor of Fides Publishers.

"Our present practice is to indicate: First Printing, January 1981, on the copyright page.

"Since we are just initiating a new line, we have no policy regarding reprints."

See also Fides Publishers, Inc.

FIDES PUBLISHERS, INC.

1976 Statement: "We do not identify first editions in any particular way. Revised editions are usually noted on the back cover."

1981 Statement: *See* 1981 Statement of Fides/Claretian

FIELDING TRAVEL BOOKS

1988 Statement: *See* 1988 Statement of William Morrow & Co. Inc.

1994 Statement: *See* 1994 Statement of Tambourine Books

THE FIGURES

1988 Statement: "First printings are not in any consistently particular way indicated. Any The Figures book is a first edition if it lacks the words 'Second Printing' on the copyright page."

1995 Statement: "First editions are not marked in any way, other than to copyright them in the year of their publication. In the case of a signed edition, it will be the same book as the trade, except on the copyright page when the author's signature and a number are entered."

2000 Statement: *See* 1995 Statement

FILLMORE PUBLISHING COMPANY

2000 Statement: "Our first editions are marked by the fact that the copyright page bears *no* printing or edition notice; however, our subsequent editions note the printing date of each edition."

THE FILM INSTRUCTION CO. OF AMERICA

See FICOA

FILTER PRESS

1976 Statement: "Generally our first printings are 500 copies, and are so identified as 'First Printing, date, 1957,' etc. on the reverse of the title page. As succeeding printings are made they are not identified in most cases. The lateness of the printing can usually be determined by the fact that on the reverse of the title page we print a list of our Wild & Woolly West Series in chrono order, and the imprint date of latest on it shows it was ready at the time of that printing. For internal use we also use a digit such as 512 or 608, which indicates that particular printing was done on December of 1975 or August of 1976, etc. A single digit, such as 1 or 1/2 in lower right part of reverse of title page shows the size of the press run in thousands. We're pretty small, so rarely run more than 1500 or so at a time."

1981 Statement: *See* 1976 Statement

1988 Statement: "The information on our edition designations is still correct. All of our imprints follow the same system, though on a couple we may have failed to definitely state first printing. In that case, comparison of our 3 digit date with imprint date should be helpful."
2000 Statement: *See* 1988 Statement

FINANCIAL TIMES (UNITED KINGDOM)
1994 Statement: "As most of our reports are 'one-off' publications, the first printing is simply designated by copyright and trademark notice. E.g.:

Copyright © 1994 FT Business Enterprises Ltd.

'Financial Times' and 'FT' are among the Trade Marks and Service Marks of the Financial Times Group.

"Where a new edition (i.e., an update of an existing report under the same title) is published, we will put a line stating when the previous edition(s) was (were) published.

"With occasional, minor variations this has been standard practice since the 1970s, when Management Reports were first published."
2001: *See* 2001 Statement of Pitman Publishing (United Kingdom)

DONALD I. FINE, INC.
1994 Statement: The first printing of a first edition is indicated by the number line 10 9 8 7 6 5 4 3 2 1. The lowest number showing indicates the printing.

FINE ARTS MUSEUMS OF SAN FRANCISCO
2001 Statement: " 'The' was dropped from the name in 1995."
See 1976 Statement of The Fine Arts Museums of San Francisco

THE FINE ARTS MUSEUMS OF SAN FRANCISCO
1976 Statement: "We use no designation to indicate a first edition or a first printing. We note subsequent editions and printings as they occur."
1981, 1988 Statements: *See* 1976 Statement

FINE ARTS PRESS
1947 Statement: "So far I have not used any method except date on title page, as 'Fine Arts Press 1930' etc. I have published 23 books to date and never reprinted any. I am about to break over, however, as I am reprinting *Shadows of Old Saddleback*. So all of my books have been one printing only. The press was established in 1930."

FINE ARTS PRESS
(Tennessee)
2000 Statement: "We identify the first printing of a first edition by the words 'First Edition' on the copyright page."

FINE EDGE PRODUCTIONS, LLC
2001 Statement: "We state 'First edition' on the copyright page. Normally, we do not just reprint. We update with a new edition instead."

THE FIRE!! PRESS

2000 Statement: "We identify the first printing of a first edition by the statement 'First Edition' on the copyright page."

FIREBIRD BOOKS LTD. (UNITED KINGDOM)

1994 Statement: A first printing is designated by the phrase "First published . . . " on the copyright page.

2001 Statement: *See* 1994 Statement

FIREBIRD PRESS

2000 Statement: *See* 2000 Statement of Pelican Publishing Company

FIRESIDE BOOKS

An imprint of Warren H. Green, Inc.

2000 Statement: *See* 2000 Statement of Warren H. Green, Inc.

FIRESIDE PRESS, INC.

1947 Statement: "Fireside Press has a very limited list, and in the past we have done nothing to indicate first editions. In the future, however, I believe we will put a first edition line on the copyright page."

FIRST AMENDMENT PRESS INTERNATIONAL COMPANY

2000 Statement: "We print on the copyright page the words 'First Printing,' usually on the bottom left side of the page. Each subsequent printing will be printed as 'Second Printing,' 'Third Printing,' etc. usually on the bottom left side of the copyright page."

FIRST AVENUE EDITIONS

1993 Statement: *See* 1993 Statement of Lerner Publications Company

2000 Statement: *See* 2000 Statement of Lerner Publishing Group

FIRST CHOICE

2000 Statement: *See* 2000 Statement of Sunbelt Publications

L. B. FISCHER PUBLISHING CORPORATION

(Out of business prior to 1948.)

See A. A. Wyn, Inc.

FISHER BOOKS

2000 Statement: "The first printing of a first edition is identified by the following number line: 10 9 8 7 6 5 4 3 2 1."

FISHERMAN BIBLE STUDYGUIDES

2000 Statement: *See* 2000 Statement of Harold Shaw Publishers

FISHING NEWS

2000 Statement: *See* 2000 Statement of Blackwell Science Inc

FITHIAN PRESS

1995 Statement: "We do not specifically identify first editions or first printings. However, subsequent and/or revised editions are so noted on the copyright page. Therefore, any edition whose copyright page does not indicate otherwise is a first edition. This has always been our policy."

2001 Statement: *See* 1995 Statement. "Fithian Press is a division of Daniel & Daniel, Publishers, Inc. Other imprints are John Daniel & Co. and Perseverance Press. All three imprints use the same system."

FIVE STAR

2000 Statement: *See* 2000 Statement of Thorndike Press

FIVE STAR PUBLICATIONS, INC.
(Arizona)

2000 Statement: "First printings are designated by the following: 'Copyright © 2000 by Five Star Publications, Inc.' Subsequent printings are designated by First Edition 1990, Second Edition 1994, Third Edition 1996, etc."

FITZHENRY & WHITESIDE, PUBLISHERS (CANADA)

1993 Statement: *See* 1993 Statement of Clock House Publications (Canada)

FJORD PRESS

1988 Statement: "We designate the first printing of a first edition on the copyright page as follows:

First edition, 19XX

"A few years ago we included the month as part of the date, but we have stopped doing so. Second printings are designated as such immediately below the previous line:

Second printing, 19XX

"Sometimes we use the month here, sometimes we don't."

1993 Statement: "We designate the first printing of a first edition on the copyright page as follows:

First edition, 19XX

"Second printings are designated as such immediately below the previous line:

Second printing, 19XX."

2001 Statement: *See* 1993 Statement

FLARE

1981, 1993 Statements: *See* 1981, 1993 Statements of Avon Books

RONALD FLATTEAU & CO. (UNITED KINGDOM)

1947 Statement: "Typical of the rather uninspired and unimaginative British publisher, we have the usual method of differentiating between the first and subsequent printings. Namely, 'First Edition—May 1946,' 'Second Edition—June 1946.' "

FLEET PRESS CORPORATION

1988 Statement: "We do not designate a 'first printing' or 'first edition' on copyright page."

FLF PRESS

2000 Statement: *See* 2000 Statement of Starbooks Press

FLICKS BOOKS (UNITED KINGDOM)
2001 Statement: "We normally state on the first edition: 'First published in [date] by Flicks Books.' Any new editions (i.e. revised editions, NOT reprints) are stated as 'First published in [date] by Flicks Books; revised edition [date].' Any reprints (i.e. no change of text) are not always identified (we rarely do reprints), but in future I think we shall identify them with the line 'Reprinted [date].' "

FLOATING ISLAND PUBLICATIONS
1995 Statement: "All Floating Island Publications are first editions unless otherwise stated on the verso of the title page, in which case I'll state that it's a second printing."
2001 Statement: *See* 1995 Statement

J. FLORES PUBLICATIONS
1994 Statement: "We have no particular way to designate first printings."

FLORIDA A & M UNIVERSITY
(Tallahassee)
1976, 1981, 1988 Statements: *See* 1976, 1981, 1988 Statements of University Presses of Florida

FLORIDA ACADEMIC PRESS
2001 Statement: "We do not identify a first printing; we do identify subsequent printings on the copyright page."

FLORIDA ATLANTIC UNIVERSITY
(Boca Raton)
1976, 1981, 1988 Statements: *See* 1976, 1981, 1988 Statements of University Presses of Florida

FLORIDA INTERNATIONAL UNIVERSITY
(Miami)
1976, 1981, 1988 Statements: *See* 1976, 1981, 1988 Statements of University Presses of Florida

FLORIDA LITERARY FOUNDATION
1995 Statement: *See* 1995 Statement of Woldt Publishing Group

FLORIDA STATE UNIVERSITY
(Tallahassee)
1976, 1981, 1988 Statements: *See* 1976, 1981, 1988 Statements of University Presses of Florida

FLORIDA TECHNOLOGICAL UNIVERSITY
(Orlando)
1976 Statement: *See* 1976 Statement of University Presses of Florida

FLORIS BOOKS (UNITED KINGDOM)
2001 Statement: "First printings are not identified. Subsequent printings are identified on the copyright page."

FLYING FROG

2000 Statement: *See* 2000 Statement of Allied Publishing Group

FLYING PENCIL

2000 Statement: "Flying Pencil identifies first printings of all editions with the standard '1 2 3 4 5 6 7 8 9 10' on the verso. Though I confess to neglecting to direct the printer to opaque out '1' on a recent second printing of *Fishing in Oregon*. (Second printings will, however, be readily identifiable because we switched to a heavier cover stock.) Thus far, all subsequent editions of Flying Pencil titles have been identified as such in the title (e.g. *Fishing in Oregon, Ninth Edition*)."

FLYLEAF PRESS (REPUBLIC OF IRELAND)

1994 Statement: "Flyleaf Press does not specifically identify first editions as being such. However, second and subsequent editions are noted accordingly. First editions can therefore be identified, by default, as not being marked as later editions."

2001 Statement: *See* 1994 Statement

FOCAL PRESS

2000 Statement: *See* 2000 Statement of Butterworth-Heinemann

FOCAL PRESS (UNITED KINGDOM)

2000 Statement: *See* 2000 Statement of Butterworth-Heinemann

FOCAL PRESS, LTD. (UNITED KINGDOM)

1947 Statement: "Our method of indicating our first editions is as follows:— On the page following the title page—
First published in . . . by Focal Press.
"Subsequent reprints have their impression number or edition number quoted on the same page."

FOCUS PUBLISHING/R PULLINS CO INC

2001 Statement: "The printing is indicated by a reverse-order number string on the copyright page [10 9 8 7 6 5 4 3 2 1]. Revised or corrected editions are identified as such on the title page and the copyright page, and usually on the cover."

FODOR'S TRAVEL GUIDES (UNITED KINGDOM)

2000 Statement: *See* 2000 Statement of The Random House Group Limited (United Kingdom)

FODOR'S TRAVEL PUBLICATIONS,

(A Division of Random House, Inc.)
2000 Statement: *See* 1994 Statement of Fodor's Travel Publications, Inc.

FODOR'S TRAVEL PUBLICATIONS, INC.

1994 Statement: "We designate first editions with a first edition line immediately following the ISBN on the copyright page. Subsequent editions are not designated.

"Printings are identified with a 10 9 8 7 6 5 4 3 2 1 line at the bottom of the copyright page. When reprinting, we delete the last figure in the line."
2000 Statement: *See* 1994 Statement of Fodor's Travel Publications, A Division of Random House, Inc.

FOG PUBLICATIONS
2000 Statement: "We do not differentiate first editions."

FOLGER SHAKESPEARE LIBRARY
1988 Statement: *See* 1976 Statement of Associated University Presses

THE FOLIO SOCIETY LIMITED (UNITED KINGDOM)
1988 Statement: "The date of publication of the first edition is given on the title-page of all editions. The dates of subsequent editions are given as 'Second Impression 1988' (as applicable) on the title verso page."
2001 Statement: "The date of publication of the first edition is given on the title-page of all editions. The dates of subsequent editions are given as 'Second printing 1988' (as applicable) on the title verso page."

FOLLETT PUBLISHING COMPANY
1981 Statement: "Our policy regarding first printings of books varies. In the case of trade publications we print the words 'First Printing' on the copyright page. In our educational titles we use a printing key on the last page of the book. It reads '123456789/8584838281,' the first numbers indicating print-ing, the last numbers indicating year of printing. In either case the printing number changes with each subsequent printing.

"This has been our policy over the past several years."
1989 Statement: "Follett Publishing is out of business."

FONTANA PAPERBACKS (AUSTRALIA)
1981 Statement: "We designate the first printing of a first edition as follows:
Copyright: © A. B. & J. W. Smith 1975
First published in 1975 by William Collins
Publishers Pty Limited, Sydney
"This method does not differ from any previously used and all the imprints of our book follow the same practise."

FOODWAYS PUBLICATIONS
2000 Statement: *See* 2000 Statement of Mitchells

FOOLSCAP PRESS
2001 Statement: "Since we seldom intend to reprint an edition (like most very small presses), we don't identify our first editions as such."

FOOTPRINT PRESS
2000 Statement: "We do not differentiate first editions or subsequent print-ings of first editions. Second editions are identified on copyright page with: First edition: 'first edition year,' Second edition: 'second edition year.' "

FORDHAM UNIVERSITY PRESS

1976 Statement: "The first editions of books published by Fordham University Press carry the year of publication at the bottom of the imprint on the title page. This year will coincide with the year of (first) copyright. The publication and copyright information on the copyright page always carries enough information to enable the bibliographer to determine the edition or printing in his hands. A first edition is usually described as such, or no statement of edition is present; both carry equal weight. Our reprints or revisions are always designated as such: the year of first publication is either removed from the imprint on the title page or replaced by the new year of republication; the copyright information always carries a complete, if brief, printing history, specifying the years of editions, reprintings, and revisions."

1981 Statement: "Our 1976 statement is basically still accurate, and it may stand with, at most, a slight emendation. I suggest that the second sentence be rewritten to give the following version: 'This year will normally coincide with the year of first Fordham copyright.'

"The matter is a small point, but since you are concerned precisely with such questions of detail, you will probably find some background pertinent. I am speaking, of course, purely from the viewpoint of what constitutes a first-edition publication by us. On rare occasions, we bring out our first edition of a work by a member of our faculty, which was previously published elsewhere. Although the work which we publish is not necessarily the original edition of the book per se, it is the first edition which we have issued, and constitutes what some bibliographers and booksellers are wont to classify as 'first edition thus' or some similar designation."

1988 Statement: *See* 1981 Statement

2000 Statement: "Previous statements remain accurate. Since January 1999, the copyright page includes an edition statement (e.g., 'First Edition') and number series, the lowest numbers indicating the current printing and year."

FOREIGN POLICY RESEARCH INSTITUTE

1993 Statement: "The Foreign Policy Research Institute currently publishes all of its books and monographs through outside publishers and thus follows whatever system the publishers use in designating first editions."

THE FOREST PRESS (UNITED KINGDOM)

1937 Statement: "It is our practice to put the date of publication of any book on the title-page itself. If the book is reprinted, the date of the reprint appears on the title-page and a bibliographical description on the back of the title."

1947 Statement: *See* 1937 Statement

FORGE

1994 Statement: *See* 1994 Statement of TOR

FORIS PUBLICATIONS

2000 Statement: *See* 2000 Statement of Mouton de Gruyter

FORTH NATURALIST & HISTORIAN (UNITED KINGDOM)

2001 Statement: "We state 'First Edition' on the copyright page. We designate the first printing of a first edition by the published date; no printing designation is given as such. Subsequent printings are identified as such on the copyright page."

FORTRESS PRESS

2001 Statement: *See* 2001 Statement of Augsburg Fortress, Publishers

FORTUNE PRESS (UNITED KINGDOM)

2000 Statement: *See* 2000 Statement of The Albyn Press (United Kingdom)

FORUM
(California)

2000 Statement: *See* 2000 Statement of Prima Publishing

FORUM PUBLISHING COMPANY

1993 Statement: "When a book is updated or revised we do note this on the copyright page.

"This has been our policy since 1981."

2000 Statement: *See* 1993 Statement

FORWARD MOVEMENT PUBLICATIONS

1994 Statement: "We don't mark a first edition in any special way. However first editions are easily identified since subsequent editions (as well as printings after the first) are marked—usually on the back of the title page.

"While we are fairly consistent about this now, there is confusion in some earlier reprints. There is no specific date this policy went into effect."

2000 Statement: "Forward Movement does not mark first editions; however, all subsequent editions are clearly identified."

WALTER FOSTER (UNITED KINGDOM)

2001 Statement: *See* 2001 Statement of Apple Press (United Kingdom)

FOUL PLAY PRESS

1988, 1993 Statement: *See* 1988, 1993 Statements of The Countryman Press, Inc.

G. T. FOULIS & CO. LTD. (UNITED KINGDOM)

1988, 1994, 2000 Statements: *See* 1988, 1994, 2000 Statements of Haynes Publishing (United Kingdom)

T. N. FOULIS, LTD. (UNITED KINGDOM)
(Out of business prior to 1937.)

1928 Statement: "My usual plan with regard to title pages is to print the date of publication on the back thereof, e.g.

'First published January the fifteenth 1928.
Reprinted February 1928.
Reprinted March 1928.' "

FOUNDATION FOR "A COURSE IN MIRACLES"

1993 Statement: "We normally provide a 'printing history' on the copyright page, which is on the back of the title page. Readers could identify the date of the first edition from this history and/or the copyright dates."

FOUNDATION PUBLICATIONS, INC.

2000 Statement: "Other than the copyright year, we do not identify first edition printings."

FOUR COURTS PRESS (REPUBLIC OF IRELAND)

1994 Statement: *See* 1994 Statement of Irish Academic Press, Limited (Republic of Ireland)

FOUR O'S PUBLISHING CO. (UNITED KINGDOM)

1949 Statement: *See* 1947 Statement of The Oakwood Press (United Kingdom)

FOUR SEAS COMPANY
(Out of business before 1937.)
See 1937 Statement of Bruce Humphries, Inc.

FOUR SEASONS PUBLISHING LTD (UNITED KINGDOM)

2001 Statement: "The year of a first printing is indicated by the copyright date © year."

FOUR WALLS EIGHT WINDOWS

1988 Statement: "We identify first editions by printing 'First Edition' on the copyright page. We indicate which printing the book is in by printing 'First printing,' 'Second printing' etc., and the date, on the copyright page."
1993 Statement: *See* 1988 Statement
2000 Statement: "We indicate which printing the book is in by printing 'First printing,' 'Second printing' etc., and the date, on the copyright page."

FOUR WAY BOOKS

2000 Statement: "We do not identify a first edition. In the case of a subsequent printing we will designate the number of the printing and the year, as in second printing, 1999."

FOURMAT PUBLISHING (UNITED KINGDOM)

1994 Statement: *See* 1994 Statement of Tolley Publishing Co. Ltd. (United Kingdom)

L.N. FOWLER & CO LTD (UNITED KINGDOM)

2000 Statement: *See* 2000 Statement of The C.W. Daniel Co Ltd (United Kingdom)

FOX & WILKES

2001 Statement: "We do not identify a first printing or any printing after the first printing on the copyright page."

FOX CHAPEL PUBLISHING CO. INC.

1993 Statement: "We designate the first printing by number on the bottom of the copyright page. We list the numbers from left to right, with 1 being the first number in the case of a first printing.

"We do not designate a first edition in our books. This method of identification does not differ from past practice."

2000 Statement: "In a change from our 1993 Statement, we do not currently designate first printings in any way. We do not designate a first edition in our books."

FRAMEWORKS (UNITED KINGDOM)

2000 Statement: *See* 2000 Statement of Inter-Varsity Press (United Kingdom)

FRANCISCAN COMMUNICATIONS

2000 Statement: *See* 2000 Statement of St Anthony Messenger Press

FRANCISCAN PRESS

1994 Statement: "So far, our original titles simply specify 'first printing' . . . . In future . . . we will specify 'first edition' and date as well."

2000 Statement: *See* 1994 Statement

FRANCISCAN UNIVERSITY PRESS

1995 Statement: "We have no particular way of designating first printings. Any second printings since January 1995 are designated by inserting 'Second printing' and the date on the copyright page."

2000 Statement: *See* 1995 Statement

THE FRANKLIN LIBRARY

1981 Statement: "The Franklin Library is the exclusive publisher of a series of limited First Editions in deluxe bindings that are selected, printed, and bound for members of The First Edition Society.

"In each book, its First Edition status is designated in the front matter on the series identification page, on the title page, copyright page, and above the author's special introduction, as well as (since September 1976) on the spine. Wording on the copyright page may vary slightly from book to book dependent on arrangements made with the trade publisher who will handle subsequent editions. No essential changes in this identification method have been made since The First Edition Society's first selection in March 1976.

"Publishers use The First Edition Society copies for registration of the work with the Copyright office. Trade first printings cannot be coded simply as 'first edition' but must indicate that a privately printed First Edition has been published by The Franklin Library."

1988 Statement: "The Franklin Library is the exclusive publisher of a series of limited first editions in leather bindings that are selected, printed, and bound for members of the Signed First Edition Society.

"Each book is designated as a Signed First Edition in the front matter (on the series imprint page, the title page, copyright page, and above the author's special introduction, which is exclusive to this edition), on the colophon page, and on the spine. Each book is signed by the author. No essential changes in the identification method have been made since the Signed First Edition Society's first selection was published in July 1983.

"Trade first printings cannot be coded simply as 'first edition' but must indicate that a privately printed Signed First Edition has been published by The Franklin Library."

1993 Statement: *See* 1988 Statement

GORDON FRASER GALLERY LIMITED
(UNITED KINGDOM)

1976 Statement: "We designate first editions simply by having the words 'first published in 19..' on the copyright page. Any subsequent editions or reprints would include further information, e.g. 'reprinted 19..' or 'new edition 19..' "

1981, 1988 Statements: *See* 1976 Statement

THE FREE PRESS

1993 Statement: *See* 1993 Statement of Macmillan, Inc.

FREE SPIRIT PUBLISHING INC.

1994 Statement: "We do not make any special effort to designate first printings of first editions. However, we do indicate each print run with a print run number line on the copyright page of every book which reads '10 9 8 7 6 5 4 3 2 1' for the first printing. (We delete number '1' before the second printing, number '2' before the third, etc.)

"Also, on revised editions, we note the copyright date for both editions. This has [always] been our practice."

2000 Statement: "This [1994 Statement] is still accurate. For revised editions, we start the print run over."

FREEDEEDS BOOKS

1988 Statement: *See* 1988 Statement of Garber Communications Inc.

FREEDOM PRESS (UNITED KINGDOM)

1994 Statement: "Second and subsequent printings, and new editions, are always identified as such and the printing history given. Where this is not the case, the book may be assumed to be a first edition. Information is normally given on title page verso as 'First published' or simply 'Published' with the date."

2000 Statement: *See* 1994 Statement

W. H. FREEMAN (UNITED KINGDOM)

2000 Statement: *See* 2000 Statement of Palgrave Publishers Ltd (United Kingdom)

W. H. FREEMAN AND COMPANY, PUBLISHERS

1976 Statement: "All editions after the first are indicated. Printings are not designated. These methods do not differ from any previously used."

1981 Statement: "All editions after first are indicated. In the early 1970s, Freeman began the practice of indicating the *printing number* of each title by means of a keyline on the copyright page, whereby the printing was indicated by the lowest digit in the keyline."

1988 Statement: *See* 1981 Statement. "Our subsidiaries and joint-venture partners follow the same rule."

FREESTONE

2000 Statement: *See* 2000 Statement of Peachtree Publishers Ltd.

SAMUEL FRENCH, INC.

1976 Statement: "There is no way that I can answer you but to say that our reprints are not marked as such and our first printings are not marked as such. There is no difference between either, and we do not indicate a difference."

1981 Statement: "The only way you can determine if a play might have some author corrections since the first printing is to look at the copyright. If changes were made in the text it will be reflected in the copyright notice as (revised & rewritten) by such and such an author and the revised copyright date. By this, naturally, you can see it is not a first printing."

1988, 1993, 2001 Statements: *See* 1981 Statement

SAMUEL FRENCH LTD (UNITED KINGDOM)

1995 Statement: "We make no distinction between first editions, subsequent editions and reprints and print no identifying marks on our plays."

2000 Statement: *See* 1995 Statement

MAURICE FRIDBERG (REPUBLIC OF IRELAND)

1947 Statement: "We differentiate between our First and Second Editions by stating on the reverse of the title page if the edition concerned is not the First."

ELEANOR FRIEDE, INC.

1976 Statement: "I am an associate publisher with Delacorte Press, and we indicate First Printing on all books published first in America."

1981 Statement: *See* 1976 Statement

FRIENDS OF THE EARTH, INC.

1976 Statement: "Briefly, we publish two main lines of picture books, the Earth's Wild Places series (eight volumes now published) and the Celebrating the Earth series (three volumes in six editions now published). Each of the CTE books *(Only a little planet, Song of the Earth Spirit* and *Of all things most yielding)* have been published in hard and paperback; there is no way to tell from colophons or other marks between the various printings, so far as I know.

"On the Earth's Wild Places Series no attempt has been made to systematically distinguish between the editions, but it is possible, by comparing colophons and spines, and by the fact that second editions do not have spot varnished pages. By title, this is what I'd recommend a first edition seeker seek:

RETURN TO THE ALPS:

Colophon: (or publisher's note, as it is called in all FOE books) includes the phrase 'Color separations and lithography by Imprimeries Reunies SA, Lausanne,'

Spine: Friends of the Earth

Second and subsequent editions:

Colophon: says 'Lithographed and bound by Arnoldo Mondadori Editore, Verona'

Spine: Friends of the Earth, Seabury Press

Copyright page says 'This . . . printing contains corrections of minor errors but no substantive changes in text, photographs, or other illustrations.'

EARTH AND THE GREAT WEATHER:

Colophon: says 'printed by Imprimeries Reunies SA, Lausanne . . . color separations by Gravure De Schutter NV, Antwerp.'

Spine: Friends of the Earth, McCall

Second edition:

Colophon: says 'lithography and bound by Arnoldo Mondadori Editore, Verona.'

Spine: Friends of the Earth, Seabury Press

Copyright page includes the same statement as *RETURN TO THE ALPS.*

A SENSE OF PLACE:

Colophon: 'lithography and bound by Arnoldo Mondadori, color separations by Gravure De Schutter'

Spine: Friends of the Earth, Saturday Review Press

Second and subsequent editions:

Colophon: 'lithographed and bound by Arnoldo Mondadori'

Editore, Verona

Spine: Friends of the Earth, Seabury Press

Copyright page includes the same statement as *RETURN TO THE ALPS.*

MAUI: THE LAST HAWAIIAN PLACE:

Colophon: 'It was printed on Champion Kromekote by Barnes Press, Inc., New York City. It was double-spread collated and bound in Columbia Mills' Sampson linen by Sendor Bindery, New York City.'

Spine: Friends of the Earth, McCall

Second and Subsequent editions:

Colophon: 'lithographed and bound by Arnoldo Mondadori Editore, Verona.'

Spine: Friends of the Earth, Seabury Press

Copyright page includes the same statement as *RETURN TO THE ALPS.*

PRIMAL ALLIANCE: EARTH AND OCEAN:

(I don't have a copy at hand to check, but believe the colophon credits the color separations to H.S. Crocker Company in Burlingame, California, and the spine probably says Friends of the Earth, Saturday Review Press.)

Second and subsequent editions:

Colophon: 'lithographed and bound by Arnoldo Mondadori Editore, Verona'

Spine: Friends of the Earth, Seabury Press

Copyright page: same statement as *RETURN TO THE ALPS;* copyright page is the same page with 'Contents.'

"On the following three titles there have been no second editions:

ERYRI: THE MOUNTAINS OF LONGING:
Colophon: 'lithographed by Arnoldo Mondadori Editore, Verona . . . color separated by Gravure De Schutter NV, Antwerp'
Spine: FOE, McCall, George Allen & Unwin
  GUALE: THE GOLDEN COAST OF GEORGIA:
Colophon: 'lithographed and bound by Arnoldo Mondadori Editore, Verona'
Spine: Friends of the Earth, Seabury Press
  MICRONESIA: ISLAND WILDERNESS:
Colophon and spine are the same as on *GUALE: THE GOLDEN COAST OF GEORGIA*
  "I should point out that all books with Seabury Press on the spine also have 'A Continuum Book' on the title page.
  "We will be bringing out a limited-edition called *HEADLANDS* (signed and numbered, 700 for sale) in October, 1976."
1981 Statement: *See* 1976 Statement

FRIENDS UNITED PRESS
2001 Statement: "We do not identify a first printing; we do identify subsequent printings on the copyright page."

FRIENDSHIP PRESS
1994 Statement: "As of 1994, Friendship Press has adopted the following policy: We designate the first printing by using the last two digits of the present and future years (e.g. 98 97 96 95 94) followed by 5 4 3 2 1. When reprinted, we delete all years before the year of the reprinting, as well as the numeral 1 for the second printing, 2 for the third printing, etc."
2000 Statement: "We no longer indicate which printing."

FRITH PRESS
2000 Statement: "We identify the first printing of a first edition by the following statement: copyright © year by _____. We copyright the magazine *Ekphrasis* in the name of Frith Press and individual chapbooks in the name of the author."

FROG LTD
2001 Statement: *See* 2001 Statement of North Atlantic Books

FROMM INTERNATIONAL
1994 Statement: "From the very beginning, Fromm International designated the first printing of a first edition by printing either 'First US Edition' or 'First English Edition' on the copyright page."
2000 Statement: *See* 1994 Statement

FRONTIER PUBLISHING (UNITED KINGDOM)
2001 Statement: "We identify only editions, not printings; a first edition is so identified on the copyright page."

FUGUE STATE PRESS
1995 Statement: "Fugue State Press does not designate an edition or printing number in any of its books."

2001 Statement: *See* 1995 Statement. "It has also always been the case that all later editions always contain 'points' by which they can be distinguished from the first editions. These 'points' are different for each book."

FULCRUM PUBLISHING

1993 Statement: "Fulcrum Publishing designates the first printing of the first edition by listing the print history numbers, beginning with 0, 9, 8, etc., at left and moving down to 1 at right, on the copyright page. Subsequent printings are indicated by removal of the last number, going from right to left. This is the system we have used since we began publishing, and our North American Press division uses the same system."

2000 Statement: *See* 1993 Statement, but delete the last sentence following 'publishing, ...'

FULCRUM RESOURCES

2000 Statement: *See* 2000 Statement of Fulcrum Publishing

FULL COURT PRESS, INC.

1981 Statement: "Alas, our method varies. Our special signed limited first editions leave no doubt, including, as they do, a special colophon page."

WILFRED FUNK, INC.

1947 Statement: "First printings of books published by Wilfred Funk, Inc., carry the usual copyright line on the page following the title. When subsequent printings are issued we add the information to the copyright page, so—

First Printing, April 1945
Second Printing, May 1945

—the bottom line always designating the latest printing."

FUNK & WAGNALLS COMPANY

1937 Statement: "In February 1929 we published the first book in which we used the following line, under the copyright notice, to designate a first edition:

'First published—February, 1929.'

"A reprint of the same edition would be distinguished by a line beneath the above line such as:

'Reprinted—March, 1929.'

"A new edition would be designated by a line such as:

'Second Edition—April, 1930.'

"A book might then bear under the copyright notice,

'First published—February, 1929'
'Reprinted—March, 1929'
'Second Edition—April, 1930.' "

1947 Statement: *See* 1937 Statement

FUNK & WAGNALLS PUBLISHING COMPANY, INC.

1976 Statement: *See* 1976 Statement of Thomas Y. Crowell Company
1981 Statement: "The information you want updated was supplied in 1976 by the Funk & Wagnalls Publishing Company, an imprint at that time of the

Thomas Y. Crowell Company. Crowell has since been sold to Harper & Row, Publishers, along with all of the subsidiary imprints, including Funk & Wagnalls."

See 1981 Statement of Harper & Row, Publishers, Inc.

1988 Statement: "The trade imprint 'Funk & Wagnalls,' plus the entire backlist was sold to Harper & Row in 1977; it was an imprint owned by T. Y. Crowell.

"This firm, Funk & Wagnalls, is an encyclopedia publisher and owns the trademarks 'Funk & Wagnalls' and 'F & W.' At present we do no trade publishing."

FUNNY FARM BOOKS
2001 Statement: *See* 2001 Statement of Coda Publications

LEE FURMAN, INC.
(Out of business prior to 1949. Bought by Citadel Press.)
1937 Statement: "We make no particular attempt to distinguish first editions from subsequent printings."

FYFIELD BOOKS (UNITED KINGDOM)
2000 Statement: *See* 2000 Statement of Carcanet Press Limited (United Kingdom)

G

G W GRAPHICS & PUBLISHING
1994 Statement: "We do not put the words 'First Edition' on our first edition publishing. After the first edition, then we write second edition."

SAML. GABRIEL SONS & COMPANY
1947 Statement: "We make no differentiation, except for certain sheets that are kept in our files. We find no need in publications such as ours (some of which have little or no text) to identify first editions from subsequent editions."

GAFF PRESS
1995 Statement: "All First Edition volumes . . . say 'First Edition' at the bottom left of the copyright page. In addition, the standard, Library of Congress 'descending numeral' method of identifying editions of books will always be used. We do not identify 'printings'. . . . All Gaff Press books are hand-bound . . . . All are signed and dated by month and year by the author."
2001 Statement: *See* 1995 Statement

GALAXY 5000
1994 Statement: *See* 1994 Statement of Publishers Associates

GALAXY PRESS
1994 Statement: *See* 1994 Statement of Publishers Associates

GALEN PRESS, LTD.

2000 Statement: "First editions can usually be detected by only one year in copyright statement, and the number '1' in the following print run line: 10 9 8 7 6 5 4 3 2 1. The copyright notice provides information about revisions. If two or more years appear, the book is a revision of an earlier edition."

GALLERY WEST PRESS

2000 Statement: "We identify the first printing of a first edition by: copyright © year by author plus words 'First Edition' on same page."

GALLIARD (UNITED KINGDOM)

2001 Statement: *See* 2001 Statement of Stainer & Bell Ltd. (United Kingdom)

GALT PRESS

2001 Statement: "We state 'First edition' on the copyright page."

GAMBIT, INC.

1976 Statement: "We continue to identify first editions as we always have by carrying the words First Printing in a separate line above the copyright notice."

1981 Statement: "We haven't changed our policy vis-a-vis the identification of first editions.

"In your revision you will face a somewhat different problem. Here's how we solved it recently:

Sixth Printing

First Revised Edition."

1988 Statement: *See* 1981 Statement

GAMBIT BOOKS

2000 Statement: *See* 2000 Statement of Harvard Common Press

GAMBLING TIMES INCORPORATED

1994 Statement: "We do not generally identify a first edition as such. We have no designation for the first edition other than the fact that subsequent editions will either state, 'second printing,' etc. or the date of the first edition will be noted in subsequent printings, e.g., Copyright 198X, 'First Edition 1971.' These are the only methods we have used since starting our company in 1971."

2001 Statement: *See* 1994 Statement

GANLEY PUBLISHER

1995 Statement: The first printing of a first edition is indicated by the statement: "First Edition (or First Hardcover Edition or First American Edition, where appropriate) or: nothing at all."

GANNETT BOOKS

1988 Statement: "Every new book is identified as a First Edition on the copyright page. Future reprints are identified as Second, Third, etc. printing on the copyright page and on the cover, if appropriate for marketing purposes.

"For example, cookbooks may be so successful that they are in their Fourteenth Printing. That we feature on the cover and in all advertising.

"For some specific titles, we have and may again print and bind a limited number of Special First Editions in different color and quality cloth covers. Normally this would be no more than 1,000 copies. These are identified as Special Signed and Numbered First Editions. The author will then sign and number them and they will be featured as such in marketing and advertising. Regular hardcover cloth editions are sold through stores, but many key bookstores will order, stock and sell the signed, numbered First Editions."

GARAMOND PRESS (CANADA)

1988 Statement: "Our first editions simply indicate copyright and the year of publication.

"For second, third, or revised editions, again we indicate the copyright and year of publication, followed somewhere further down the page, by a numeric statement—e.g. '2nd. ed.' "
2000 Statement: *See* 1988 Statement

GARBER COMMUNICATIONS INC.

1988 Statement: "In all our books we indicate on the copyright page the year of publication as well as the edition whether it is first or whatever. This is true for reprints as well."

This method was adopted in 1959 and does not differ from any previously used. All imprints and subsidiaries follow this practice.

GARDEN ART PRESS (UNITED KINGDOM)

2001 Statement: *See* 2001 Statement of Antique Collector's Club Ltd (United Kingdom)

GARDEN WAY PUBLISHING CO.

1981 Statement: "We do very little to designate our editions as first or second (we've never had a third). What we prefer to do is to do a revision, which then gets a new cover, updated material, often a new design, and even a new title sometimes.

"We usually print the printing number on the copyright page starting with the second printing. If the book carries no printing notice, it presumably is a first printing of that edition. Otherwise it will state 'Second printing, March 1979' or something similar.

"Garden Way has no other imprints, and we have followed more or less these practices since our beginning in 1971."
1988 Statement: *See* 1988 Statement of Storey Communications, Inc.

WELLS GARDNER, DARTON & CO., LTD.
(UNITED KINGDOM)

1928 Statement: "We have followed no strict principle in designating our first editions or first impressions. The nature of our publications, which include fiction, children's books, Religious books, and some poetry as well as miscellaneous works, has been so varied and the Trade conditions in regard to format, price, re-prints, and other details have changed so frequently during the past quarter of a century, our methods have depended very much on circumstances of the particular time, and, of course, to a certain extent also on the personal discretion of the author and the member of the firm concerned with a particular book. We are, therefore, unable to give you any definite information in general. If there is any particular book which we publish, about which you wish to make enquiry, we can probably give you the accurate facts whether they are printed in the book or not."

1937 Statement: *See* 1928 Statement

GARRETT COUNTY PRESS

2000 Statement: "On the copyright page it will say 'first edition, year.' We do not use a number line. The first 150 copies of each new title are hand-numbered and signed by the author."

GARRIGUE BOOKS

2000 Statement: *See* 2000 Statement of Catbird Press

GASLIGHT PUBLICATIONS, INC.

1995 Statement: "The designation of editions and printings has been entirely consistent since the founding of Gaslight Publications in 1979. An edition statement will be found on the copyright page. In the event that the edition statement has been overlooked, the absence of such a statement invariably indicates a first edition. Second and subsequent printings are listed, with the date of printing, within each edition statement, without exception."

2000 Statement: *See* 2000 Statement of Empire Publishing Service

GASOGENE PRESS, LTD.

1989 Statement: "We do designate first editions but do not distinguish between printings. Our designation is by date only for first editions. A second edition is so designated. This has been our policy from the beginning."

1993 Statement: *See* 1989 Statement

GATEWAY BOOKS

1994 Statement: The first printing of a first edition is indicated by the number line 10 9 8 7 6 5 4 3 2 1. The lowest number showing indicates the printing.

GATEWAY EDITIONS

2000 Statement: *See* 2000 Statement of Regnery Publishing

GAY & HANCOCK, LTD. (UNITED KINGDOM)

(Purchased by A. & C. Black, Ltd., April, 1929, who continued to issue a few volumes under Gay & Hancock, Ltd. imprint at least as late as 1935.)

1928 Statement: "*First Editions* of our publications have the date on the title page; second and reprints are notified on the back of the title page."

1937 Statement: "*First Editions* of our publications have the date on the title-page only; Second and Reprints have the date of reprint on the title-page and particulars of all printings in a bibliography on the verso."

GAY SUNSHINE PRESS

1994 Statement: *See* 1994 Statement of Leyland Publications

GAYOT/GAULT MILLAU INC

2000 Statement: "We do not differentiate first printings. As all of our books are travel or restaurant guides, we use editions to designate completely revised and updated versions of a single title."

GAZELLE PUBLICATIONS

2000 Statement: "We do not now have a way to designate first editions, but will consider using an appropriate statement with the copyright information."

GEM GUIDES BOOK CO.

1988 Statement: "A book published by Gem Guides Book Company is a first edition unless stated otherwise. The copyright date is the date of the first edition and the first printing. Subsequent printings or revisions are indicated below the copyright line. In the case of revisions, the date of original printing and the last copyrighted revision are indicated. Thus:

First edition 1971

Second Revised Edition 1987."

1993, 2000 Statements: *See* 1988 Statement

GEM PUBLICATIONS

2001 Statement: "We do not identify a first printing or any printing after the first printing on the copyright page."

GEMSTONE PRESS

1994 Statement: "The first printing of a first edition is indicated by the following number line: etc. 5 4 3 2 1."

2000 Statement: *See* 1994 Statement

GENEALOGICAL PUBLISHING CO., INC.

1994 Statement: The first printing of a first edition is indicated by the statement "Copyright © 1994 by . . . Published by Genealogical Publishing Co., Inc . . . ."

"Second printings are designated 'Second Printing' and so forth."

2000 Statement: *See* 1994 Statement

GENESIS PUBLISHING CO. INC.

2001 Statement: "We do not identify a first printing; we do identify subsequent printings as such on the copyright page."

GENTRY PRESS
(Out of business.)

1947 Statement: "We never reprinted any of our books when our press was alive, so they are all first editions."

THE GEOGRAPHICAL ASSOCIATION
(UNITED KINGDOM)

1994 Statement: "In the event of a reprint, we add the information that the book was first published in, say, 1994, and reprinted, with a note of whether it was revised as well, and give the year of reprint. So a subsequent imprint page for the book in question might read:

© the Geographical Association, 1994
First published 1994
Reprinted 1994 (twice)
Revised and reprinted 1995

This is our practice now; I'm afraid I cannot say how long it has been so."

2000 Statement: "In 1997 we adopted a new system for indicating first and subsequent editions. The first edition of a new book gives the information thus:

Impression number 10 9 8 7 6 5 4 3 2 1
Year 2003 2002 2001 2000 1999 1998 1997

"For straight reprints, we ask the printer to scratch off the film for the imprint page the previous impression and year."

GEOGRAPHICAL PUBLICATIONS LIMITED (UNITED KINGDOM)

1976 Statement: No particular methods are used.
1981 Statement: *See* 1976 Statement

GEORGETOWN UNIVERSITY PRESS

2001 Statement: "We identify the first printing of a first edition by the number line '10 9 8 7 6 5 4 3 2 1.' Books published prior to 1990 do not indicate first edition."

GEORGIA STATE UNIVERSITY, COLLEGE OF BUSINESS ADMINISTRATION, BUSINESS PUBLISHING DIVISION

1981 Statement: "Our approach to designating a first edition, first printing is by the absence of a designation. Only the second and succeeding editions carry these notices. A second or third edition notice is carried on the cover and title page. We do not designate additional printings."
1988 Statement: *See* 1981 Statement
1993 Statement: "We designate [all printings after the first] by using a numerical system: 97 96 95 94 93 5 4 3 2 1."

GEORGIA STATE UNIVERSITY, SCHOOL OF BUSINESS ADMINISTRATION, PUBLISHING SERVICES DIVISION

1976 Statement: "Our approach to designating a first edition, first printing is by the absence of a designation. Only the second and succeeding editions and printings carry these notices—verso title page."
1981 Statement: *See* 1981 Statement of Georgia State University, College of Business Administration, Business Publishing Division.

GEORGIA STRAIGHT WRITING SERIES (CANADA)

See 1988 Statement of New Star Books (Canada)

GEOSCIENCE PRESS, INC.

2000 Statement: "We identify the first printings of first editions by the use of a number line as follows: 10 9 8 7 6 5 4 3 2 1. Some, but not all first editions contain a statement: First published in ___ by Geoscience Press, Inc.' In the case of an English language edition first published abroad, the words 'English edition' or 'English Language translation' appear near the copyright notice. Except in the case of translations, copyright notices are in the name of the author. Our first books were issued in 1988."

LAURA GERINGER BOOKS

1993 Statement: *See* 1993 Statement of HarperCollins Publishers
2001 Statement: *See* 2001 Statement of HarperCollinsPublishers

GESTALT JOURNAL PRESS

2000 Statement: The Press has no method of identification.

GHOST PONY PRESS

2000 Statement: "From 1980-1991 [we identified the first printing of a first edition by] © (year) (author).

"We now copyright Ghost Pony Press: © (year) (Ghost Pony Press). We indicate the copyright date, but do not use the term 'first printing.' Second editions . . . will indicate all dates/editions; signed editions give exact dates (month/day/year)."

STANLEY GIBBONS PUBLICATIONS (UNITED KINGDOM)

1994 Statement: "Annual editions are dated, but also carry an edition number on the title page. This has been the practice for many years, but in the early days the firm's founder, Edward Stanley Gibbons, merely provided a month and year date. The first edition of the Stanley Gibbons Catalogue is dated November 1865. Only two original copies are known to survive although facsimiles have been produced in the past.

"Modern non-annual catalogues carry the edition number and the date on the title page and will show a complete printing history from the first to the latest edition, including months of publication, on the reverse of title."

DOUGLAS GIBSON BOOKS (CANADA)

See McClelland & Stewart Ltd. (Canada)

GILL AND MACMILLAN LTD. (REPUBLIC OF IRELAND)

1976 Statement: "We do not in fact have a particular method of identifying first editions of our books. The relevant information is included on the reverse title, or imprint, page of each book we publish."
1981 Statement: *See* 1976 Statement
1988 Statement: "Date of first publication is always included on our books and is shown on reverse title or imprint page of each book."
1994 Statement: "Unless otherwise stated, the date of first publication is that indicated in the copyright notice."

GINGERBREAD PUBLISHING HOUSE, LLC.

2001 Statement: "We identify the first printing of a first edition by the words 'First Edition.' We distinguish printings by counting up: 1 2 3 4 5 6 7 etc. and deleting the numeral which represents the past printing."

THE K.S. GINIGER CO., INC.

1994 Statement: "All Giniger books are published under joint imprint arrangements with other publishers and therefore follow the practice of each co-publisher."

2000 Statement: *See* 1994 Statement

GINKO PRESS INC
(Corte Madera, California)

2001 Statement: "We do not identify a first printing or any printing after the first printing on the copyright page."

GINN (UNITED KINGDOM)

1989 Statement: *See* 1989 Statement of The Octopus Publishing Group PLC (United Kingdom)

GINN AND COMPANY

1988 Statement: *See* 1988 Statement of Silver Burdett & Ginn

GIRL SCOUTS OF THE UNITED STATES OF AMERICA

1993 Statement: "For first printings, we use the words 'First Impression 199-' below our copyright notice. We include a line of numbers in descending order; for example, 10 9 8 7 6 5 4 3 2 1.

"Previously to adopting the number system, we had been adding 'Second printing, November 199-.'"

2001 Statement: *See* 1993 Statement

GLADE HOUSE, PUBLISHERS

1947 Statement: "First editions are so marked on the copyright page, which follows or precedes the title page, depending on the design of the book. Subsequent printings are similarly identified."

GLASGOW CITY LIBRARIES AND ARCHIVES (UNITED KINGDOM)

2001 Statement: "We do not identify a first edition, but we do identify subsequent printings."

GLB PUBLISHERS

1995 Statement: "We have only one imprint, GLB, although for our nonfictions we add the nf Division imprint. We have not always been consistent in regard to identifying First Editions; the first few books carried the 'First Edition' phrase on the title page, but that practise was abandoned in 1992. From the start we have used the '9 8 7 6 5 4 3 2 1' system for identifying printings, deleting the '1' for second printings, etc. Above these numbers we usually also state 'First Printing (month, year)' or 'Second Printing (month, year).' The year of the first printing is given with the copyright statement, which is actually, then, a statement of First Editions. Thus a book copyrighted in 1994 which states it is the first printing, 1994, would be a First Edition.

"In the future we will include the statement 'First Edition' on the copyright page."

2000 Statement: "The edition statement e.g. 'First Edition' is the first line printed on the copyright page of all of our books."

GLENBRIDGE PUBLISHING LTD

2001 Statement: "We do not identify a first printing; we do identify subsequent printings. We also use a number line; the lowest number is the printing."

THE GLENCANNON PRESS

2000 Statement: "We identify the first printing of a first edition by the statement 'First Edition, First Printing.' "

GLENIFFER PRESS (UNITED KINGDOM)

1981 Statement: "The statement 'First Edition' has always been used. All imprints use the same method."

GLIDE PUBLICATIONS

1976 Statement: "No mention is made of *any* edition unless there is a Revised Edition, which is so indicated."

GLOBAL SPORTS PRODUCTIONS, LTD.

2000 Statement: "Global Sports indicates First Printing by the fact that the copyright bears no previous date of publication."

THE GLOBE PEQUOT PRESS

2000 Statement: *See* 1993 Statement of The Globe Pequot Press, Inc. Note that the Press changed its name to The Globe Pequot Press in 1997.

THE GLOBE PEQUOT PRESS, INC.
(The Pequot Press, Inc. changed its name to
The Globe Pequot Press, Inc. in 1978.)

1988 Statement: "Our normal procedure is to put on the verso of the title page the words FIRST EDITION. With minimum or no changes we will list again the words FIRST EDITION and add the words, 'Second Printing.' When revisions are more than minimal, we will list SECOND EDITION.' "
See also The Pequot Press, Inc.

1993 Statement: "We set the words 'First Edition/First Printing' near the base of the copyright page (the verso of the title page). For a new printing, which incorporates minimal change, we set the words 'First Edition/Second Printing.' For significant revisions, we set the words 'Second Edition/First Printing.' "

GLOBE PRESS BOOKS

1994 Statement: The first printing of a first edition is indicated by the number line 10 9 8 7 6 5 4 3 2 1. The lowest number showing indicates the printing. "First Edition" is also stated.

GNOMON PRESS

1988 Statement: "Re: first editions. None are labelled such and you'd have to know your stuff to detect one. But some have information on colophon as to limitation, etc."

1993 Statement: "Starting in 1991 we have indicated FIRST EDITION or FIRST GNOMON PRESS EDITION (for reprints) on copyright pages, which indicates first edition/first printings only. Later printings will have no such line on copyright pages."

2000 Statement: *See* 1993 Statement

GNOSTICOEURS, LTD.

See Religious Research Press

DAVID R. GODINE, PUBLISHER, INC.

1988 Statement: "When we are printing a book which we acquired and produced from the manuscript, we will print 'First Edition' at the bottom of our copyright page. For subsequent printings, we will write 'first published in 19xx by David R. Godine,' and then at the bottom of the page we will print 'second printing' or 'third printing' or whatever the case may be.

"As we often produce books which were originally published at other houses, we will in such cases write 'first published by David R. Godine in 19xx' and will also include a line about where it was originally published, and when.

"As for imprints and subsidiaries, we have only one of the former and none of the latter and yes we use the same practices for our imprints."

1994 Statement: *See* 1988 Statement

2000 Statement: *See* 1988 Statement. Note that of the earlier imprints (Godine Country Classics, Godine Double Detectives and Nonpareil), only Nonpareil books are still in production. To identify printings of current imprints—Imago Mundi, Pocket Paragon, and Verba Mundi—refer to the 1988 Statement.

GODINE COUNTRY CLASSICS

1988 Statement: *See* 1988 Statement of David R. Godine, Publisher, Inc.

GODINE DOUBLE DETECTIVES

1988 Statement: *See* 1988 Statement of David R. Godine, Publisher, Inc.

THE GODMANSTONE PRESS (UNITED KINGDOM)

1994 Statement: "First impressions are not identified."

2001 Statement: "First impressions are identified by a number on the lower-left corner of the last odd-numbered page in the book. The number indicates the impression."

WILLIAM GODWIN

See Hillman-Curl, Inc.

GOLD EAGLE BOOKS (CANADA)

1989, 1993, 2000 Statements: *See* 1989, 1993, 2000 Statements of World-wide Library (Canada)

GOLDEN BOOKS

1988 Statement: *See* 1988 Statement of Western Publishing Company, Inc.

THE GOLDEN COCKEREL PRESS (UNITED KINGDOM)

1937 Statement: "With a few exceptions all our books have been issued in a first edition only limited to between 150 and 750 copies, often signed by the author and the artist, for collectors of finely produced and illustrated books of literary worth.

"The exceptions are:

1921, *ADAM & EVE & PINCH ME* by A. E. Coppard

(of which there were three editions)

1921, *TERPSICHORE & OTHER POEMS* by H. T. Wade-Gery

(of which there were two editions)

1922, *THE PUPPET SHOW* by Martin Armstrong

(of which there were two editions)

1932, *RUNNING* by A. E. Coppard

(of which there were two editions)

1932, *CONSEQUENCES*

(of which there were two editions)

"The Press will be pleased to answer any questions which may arise about any of their books."

1948 Statement: "With a few exceptions all our books have been issued in a first edition only, limited to between 150 and 750 copies, often signed by the author and the artist, for collectors of finely produced and illustrated books of literary worth. The exceptions are:

April 1921. *ADAM & EVE & PINCH ME* by A. E. Coppard

550 copies.

July, 1921.

500 copies

Dec., 1921.

1000 copies.

April 1921. *TERPSICHORE & OTHER POEMS* by H. T. Wade-Gery

350 copies.

2nd. edition:

350 copies.

June 1922. *THE PUPPET SHOW*: Tales and Satires.

By Martin Armstrong.

25 signed copies: 1200 unsigned copies.

1923: 2nd. edition—1500 copies.

Oct. 1932. *RUMMY*: That Noble Game Expounded in Prose, Poetry, Diagram and 15 Engravings by A. E. Coppard and Robert Gibbings with an Account of Certain Diversions into the Mountain Fastnesses of Cork and Kerry.

250 numbered and signed copies: 1000 unsigned copies.

Oct. 1932. *CONSEQUENCES*. A Complete Story in the Manner of the Old Parlour Game in Nine Chapters, each by a different author.

200 numbered and signed copies: 1000 unsigned copies.

March 1935. *THE HANSOM CAB AND THE PIGEONS* by L. A. G. Strong.

200 numbered and signed copies: and unlimited unsigned edition.
Nov. 1936. *THE EPICURE'S ANTHOLOGY*. Collected by Nancy Quennell.
150 numbered copies: and an unlimited edition.
Nov. 1936. *THE TALE OF THE GOLDEN COCKEREL* by A. S. Pushkin.
Translated by Hannah Waller.
100 numbered copies: and unlimited unsigned edition.
Nov. 1936. *CHANTICLEER*. A Bibliography of the Golden Cockerel Press,
April 1921-August 1936.
300 numbered and signed copies: and unlimited unsigned edition.
July 1937. *ANA THE RUNNER*: A Treatise for Princes and Generals, attrib-
uted to Prince Mahmoud Abdul. By Patrick Miller.
150 numbered and signed copies: and unlimited unsigned edition.
Aug. 1937. *HERE'S FLOWERS*: An Anthology of Flower Poems, compiled
by Joan Rutter.
200 numbered copies: and unlimited unsigned edition.
Sept. 1937. *MR. CHAMBERS AND PERSEPHONE* by Christopher Whit-
field.
150 numbered and signed copies: and unlimited unsigned edition.
Aug. 1937. *ANIMAL ANTICS* by Elizabeth Geddes.
Unlimited edition only.
Oct. 1937. *GOAT GREEN* of the Better Gift by T. F. Powys.
150 numbered and signed copies: and unlimited unsigned edition.
Feb. 1938. *THE WHITE LLAMA*, being La Venganza del Condor of V. G.
Calderon. Translated by Richard Phibbs.
75 numbered copies: and an unlimited edition.
March 1938. *TOMORROW'S STAR* by L. Cranmer-Byng.
Unlimited edition only.
Aug. 1938. *TAPSTER'S TAPESTRY* by A. E. Coppard.
75 numbered and signed copies: and unlimited unsigned edition.
Aug. 1938. *BRIEF CANDLES* by Lawrence Binyon.
100 numbered and signed copies: and unlimited unsigned edition.
Sept. 1939. *LADY FROM YESTERDAY* by Christopher Whitfield.
50 numbered and signed copies: and unlimited unsigned edition.
Oct. 1939. *THE WISDOM OF THE CYMRY* translated from the Welsh Triads
by Winifred Faraday.
60 numbered copies: and unlimited edition.
   "The Press will be pleased to answer any questions which may arise about
any of their books."

GOLDEN DAWN PUBLICATIONS
See 2000 Statement of New Falcon Publications

GOLDEN DAWN PUBLISHING (UNITED KINGDOM)
1994 Statement: *See* 1994 Statement of Mandrake of Oxford (United Kingdom)
2000 Statement: *See* 2000 Statement of Mandrake of Oxford (United Kingdom)

GOLDEN GATE JUNIOR BOOKS
1976, 1981, 1988 Statements: *See* 1976 Statement of Childrens Press®

GOLDEN GRYPHON PRESS
2001 Statement: "1st edition follows author name in CIP data."

GOLDEN HORUS
1995, 2001 Statements: *See* 1995 Statement of Erespin Press

GOLDEN PRESS
1976, 1981, 1988 Statements: *See* 1976, 1981, 1988 Statements of Western Publishing Company, Inc.

GOLDEN PRESS PTY LTD. (AUSTRALIA)
1988 Statement: *See* 1988 Statement of Western Publishing Company, Inc.

GOLDEN WEST BOOKS
1976 Statement: "The first edition is the first printing of a book. It lacks any comment on the copyright page. As it receives a second printing it is noted here that this happens to be the second printing and the date. If it is revised it so states."
1988, 1993, 2000 Statements: *See* 1976 Statement

GOLDEN WEST HISTORICAL PUBLICATIONS
1995 Statement: "We designate our books with 'First Printing, (month), (year).' Subsequent printings follow the same format beneath the original. Example:
    1st Printing, July 1979
    2nd Printing, April, 1980
etc."
This method has been in use since 1977.

GOLDEN WEST PUBLISHERS
2001 Statement: "We do not identify a first printing, but we do identify printings after the first on the copyright page."

GOLDENCRAFT
1988 Statement: *See* 1988 Statement of Western Publishing Company, Inc.

GOLDENISLE PUBLISHERS, INC.
2000 Statement: "We identify the first printing of a first edition by the following statement: First Edition. [We also use] the following number line: 10 9 8 7 6 5 4 3 2 1. The 2nd Printing Number Line: 10 9 8 7 6 5 4 3 2."

VICTOR GOLLANCZ, LTD. (UNITED KINGDOM)
1928 Statement: "Our first editions are distinguished by the fact that they contain no information on them as to what edition they are. All editions other than first editions bear, at the back of the title-page, the words 'First Published—second impression (date)' and so on."
1937, 1947 Statements: *See* 1928 Statement

Statement for 1960: "The statement for identifying a Gollancz first edition between 1949 and 1976 is identical to the [1976 statement]."

1976 Statement: "The only way to identify a Gollancz first edition is the negative one of seeing that there is no reference to a second or subsequent impression or a revised edition or a reissue on the verso of the title page."

1981 Statement: *See* 1976 Statement

1988 Statement: "During 1984 Gollancz started to print 'First published in . . . .' on the verso of the title page."

1994 Statement: *See* 1988 Statement of Cassell plc (United Kingdom)

GOLLEHON BOOKS

1994, 2000 Statements: *See* 1994 Statement of Gollehon Press, Inc.

GOLLEHON PRESS, INC.

1994 Statement: "Gollehon Press, Inc., with the imprint of Gollehon Books, has published hard-cover, trade paperback, and mass-market books without any mention of 'first-printing,' or 'first edition,' on all copies published through 1994. However, that policy will change effective with new titles in 1995, whereby, on hard-cover titles only, we will use the term 'FIRST EDITION' to appear at the bottom of the copyright page."

2000 Statement: "Gollehon Press, Inc., with the imprint of Gollehon Books, has published hard-cover, trade paperback, and mass-market books without any mention of 'first-printing,' or 'first edition,' on all copies published through 2000. However, that policy will change effective with new titles in 2001, whereby, on hard-cover titles only, we will use the term 'FIRST EDITION' to appear at the bottom of the copyright page."

GOMER PRESS (WALES)

1988 Statement: "We do not adopt a standardised method of designating first editions other than to record the date of publication on the reverse of the Title Page."

1994 Statement: *See* 1988 Statement

GONDOLA (UNITED KINGDOM)

1989 Statement: *See* 1989 Statement of The Octopus Publishing Group PLC (United Kingdom)

GOOD BOOK PUBLISHING COMPANY

1995 Statement: "We do not designate first editions."

GOOSE LANE EDITIONS (CANADA)

1989 Statement: "Goose Lane Editions does not have any method of identifying first editions. Unless one of our books is clearly designated as either a second edition or a revised edition, the reader and bibliographer may assume that they are dealing with a first edition.

"This practise has remained unchanged since the founding of the house, under the original name of Fiddlehead Poetry Books, in 1957."

1993 Statement: "Since 1990, Goose Lane has begun to identify the first printing of each edition by printing the numbers 1 through 10, in reverse order, on the copyright page of each book. The number deleted from this sequence identifies the printing from which the copy has come. For example, copies from the first printing will have the number 1 deleted, copies from the second printing will have the number 2 deleted and so on."

2001 Statement: "Goose Lane Editions began using a new method of designating first printings of each edition in 1998.

"All books published by Goose Lane Editions in 1998 and subsequently, identify the state of each edition by printing the numbers 1 through 10, in reverse order, on the copyright page of each book. The lowest number identifies the printing from which the copy has come. For instance, if the lowest number is 1, the book is from the first printing of that edition; if the lowest number is 3, then the book is from the third printing. If a book is a second or subsequent edition, different enough from the first to have a different ISBN, this information is also included on the copyright page."

GORDIAN PRESS
2001 Statement: "We do not identify a first printing or any printing after the first printing on the copyright page."

GOVERNMENT SUPPLIES AGENCY (STATIONERY OFFICE) (REPUBLIC OF IRELAND)
1994 Statement: "We are publishers of Government material and have no particular way of designating first printings. First editions may possibly be traced through Print Orders, if not otherwise identifiable as such."

GOWER PUBLISHING LIMITED (UNITED KINGDOM)
1994 Statement: "We do not specifically identify first edition; subsequent editions will give dates of printing. Paperback editions will give the date of the first hardback edition, and the statement 'This paperback edition published . . . .' "
2000 Statement: *See* 1994 Statement

GP SUBSCRIPTION PUBLICATIONS
1995, 2000 Statements: *See* 1995 Statement of Greenwood Publishing Group Inc.

GPC BOOKS (WALES)
1988, 1994, 2000 Statements: *See* 1988 Statement of University of Wales Press (Wales)

GPC/GOLLEHON
2000 Statement: *See* 1994 Statement of Gollehon Press, Inc.

GRACELAND PRESS
2000 Statement: *See* 2000 Statement of Herald Publishing House

THE GRADUATE GROUP
2000 Statement: "We do not differentiate First Editions." This method was adopted in 1964.

GRAFTON BOOKS (UNITED KINGDOM)

1988 Statement: "On the copyright page we state:

'Published by Grafton Books 1988' (or other date)

"This indicates first publication in Great Britain. Reprints and subsequent editions are listed after the 'Published by' line.

"In the case of Grafton paperbacks, the first edition of a paperback original is indicated thus:

'A Grafton paperback original 1988'

"If the book has been previously published in the USA but has not been published in hardback in the UK the following statement appears:

'A Grafton UK paperback original 1988'

"As far as I know this has always been Grafton's (previously Granada Publishing's) practice."

See also Granada Publishing Limited (United Kingdom)

GRANADA MEDIA (UNITED KINGDOM)

2000 Statement: *See* 2000 Statement of Andre Deutsch (United Kingdom)

GRANADA PUBLISHING LIMITED (UNITED KINGDOM)

1976 Statement: "Our first editions are identified in the copyright notice appearing in the prelims of every book which of course incorporates the year of publication. Re-issues and reprints can easily be identified by a statement to this effect which would appear within the copyright notice which will also incorporate a statement as to the date the book was first published."

1981 Statement: "Granada Publishing Ltd is the parent company and the situation regarding first editions is as shown [in the 1976 statement].

"First editions of our hardcover imprints are identified on the title verso by the wording 'Published by Granada Publishing' plus the appropriate year. Reprints and new editions are listed below this statement, e.g.,

Published by Granada Publishing 1975

Reprinted 1976

Second edition 1981

"In the case of paperback first edition the words 'A Granada paperback original' appear."

1988 Statement: *See* 1988 Statement of Grafton Books (United Kingdom)

GRAND RIVER PRESS

2000 Statement: A number line is used on the copyright page whereby the lowest number indicates the printing.

GRANTA PUBLICATIONS LTD. (UNITED KINGDOM)

1994 Statement: "Our practice [when identifying first editions] is to print on the back of the title page 'First published in Great Britain by Granta Books 19—.' In the past, however, we have occasionally deviated if from this—cf. 'Published by Granta Books, First British Publication,' 'First published 19—.' "

2000 Statement: *See* 1994 Statement

GRAPEVINE (UNITED KINGDOM)

1988 Statement: *See* 1988 Statement of Thorsons Publishing Group Ltd. (United Kingdom)

GRAPHIC ARTS CENTER PUBLISHING COMPANY

1988 Statement: "First edition copies of all Graphic Arts Center Publishing Company (and/or Charles H. Belding) titles make no reference to edition or printing. All subsequent printings state the printing on the copyright page. From 1968 to 1977 all titles showed Charles H. Belding as publisher. From 1978 to 1981 titles showed either Charles H. Belding or Graphic Arts Center Publishing Company as publisher.

"Charles H. Belding founded the book division of Graphic Arts Center, Inc., in 1968. On November 13, 1974 Graphic Arts Center Publishing Company was incorporated in Oregon as a separate corporation."

1993 Statement: *See* 1988 Statement

GRAY'S PUBLISHING LTD. (CANADA)

1976 Statement: "It could be assumed that we designate only those printings and/or editions after the first. These methods of identification do not differ from any previously used."

1981 Statement: "Gray's still indicates only editions or printings after the first, on the copyright page."

GRAYSON & GRAYSON, LIMITED (UNITED KINGDOM)
(Formerly Eveleigh Nash & Grayson, Ltd.)

1937 Statement: "In all books published by us we insert bibliographical details on the back of the title page as follows:

For first editions

First published by
Grayson & Grayson Ltd.
1935

For reprints

First published by
Grayson & Grayson Ltd.
May 1935
Second Impression May 1935"

GRAYWOLF PRESS

1988 Statement: "Graywolf Press First Editions are specified by the following notation on the copyright page:

9 8 7 6 5 4 3 2

First Printing,___(year of publication)."

1993 Statement: *See* 1988 Statement

2000 Statement: "Graywolf Press First Editions are specified by the following notation on the copyright page:

2 4 6 8 9 7 5 3 1

First Graywolf Printing, (year of publication)."

THE GREAT EASTERN BOOK CO.
1981 Statement: *See* 1981 Statement of Shambhala Publications, Inc.
1988 Statement: This imprint no longer exists.

GREAT LAKES BOOKS
1988 Statement: *See* 1981 Statement of Wayne State University Press

GREAT OCEAN PUBLISHERS
1988 Statement: "Since our beginning (1975) we have indicated edition and printing on the copyright page."
1993 Statement: "We indicate edition and first printing. We usually do not number subsequent printings after the first."
2000 Statement: *See* 1993 Statement

THE GREAT RIFT PRESS
2000 Statement: "We do not make any special identification of first editions, but do identify reprints and new editions. Thus, any book not identified as a reprint or new edition is a first edition."

GREAT WESTERN PUBLISHING COMPANY
1994 Statement: "Great Western Publishing Company's policy has never been to specifically designate first editions. However, future editions are distinguished from first editions by being identified as revisions or reprintings."
2000 Statement: *See* 1994 Statement

GREBNER BOOKS PUBLISHING
1995 Statement: "We designate first printings with the phrase 'First Printing,' followed by the year, on the copyright page. Lack of printing designation also indicates first printing."

W. GREEN (UNITED KINGDOM)
2001 Statement: "We do not identify first printings; we do identify subsequent printings as such on the copyright page."

WARREN H. GREEN, INC.
1976 Statement: "First editions are not identified in any way. On the copyright page we simply put © (date), Warren H. Green, Inc.

"Then on the Title Page and on the Copyright Page, each straight reprinting is noted as 'second printing,' 'third printing' etc.

"If a printing is revised but not sufficiently to call it a new edition, on the Title Page and Copyright Page it is identified as 'Revised First Printing,' 'Revised Second Printing,' whatever applies.

"For new editions, on both the Title Page and the Copyright Page, we simply put new copyright information, i.e., © 'second edition.' "
1981, 1988, 1994, 2000 Statements: *See* 1976 Statement

GREEN BEAN PRESS
2000 Statement: "We identify a first edition, first printing in one of three ways: 'First Edition,' 'First Printing,' or no mention whatsoever of edition or

printing. Subsequently, second printings or editions are explicitly mentioned, i.e. 'First edition, second printing' etc."

GREEN BOOKS LTD (UNITED KINGDOM)

1994 Statement: "We don't have any particular formula for designating these, but the title verso of all our new titles states 'First published in 19XX by Green Books.' Unless this is qualified on the same page by a statement regarding reprinting or revision (e.g. 'reprinted 19XX'), the book must by default be a first edition."

2000 Statement: *See* 1994 Statement

GREEN EARTH BOOKS (UNITED KINGDOM)

2000 Statement: *See* 2000 Statement of Green Books Ltd (United Kingdom)

GREEN LIGHT READERS

2001 Statement: *See* 2001 Statement of Harcourt, Inc.

GREEN NATURE BOOKS

2000 Statement: "We identify the first printing of a first edition by no special designation other than 'This is the first edition' on copyright page."

GREEN RIVER WRITERS, INC./GREX PRESS

2000 Statement: "We use no printing or edition notice."

GREENART BOOKS

2000 Statement: *See* 2000 Statement of Warren H. Green, Inc.

GREENBERG BOOKS

2000 Statement: *See* 2000 Statement of Kalmbach Publishing Company

GREENBERG, PUBLISHER, INC.

1928 Statement: "We do not designate first editions in any special way. But all later editions bear a notice to that effect."

1937, 1947 Statements: *See* 1928 Statement

GREENE BARK PRESS INC

2000 Statement: "It is our practise to only designate an edition beyond the first. Said another way, first editions show no designation pertaining to edition."

THE STEPHEN GREENE PRESS

1976 Statement: "At the present time, we run a printing code line at the foot of the copyright page. Starting at the left, it shows printing numbers 1 through 9; and then, starting from the right it shows the current year and 5 or 6 succeeding years—as follows:

1 2 3 4 5 6 7 8 9 80 79 78 77 76

"The first printing carries the entire code line. The second printing carries the entire line minus the figure 1, and, if necessary, minus as many year figures at the end to make the line end with the current year.

"So that a third printing in 1979 would look like this:

3 4 5 6 7 8 9 80 79

"We do not now have any particular method of identifying first editions (as distinct from initial printings). We do identify subsequent editions— e.g., 'second edition,' 'first revised edition,' and the like. But for the most part our first editions are identified by the absence of any statement identifying them as anything but a first edition."

1981 Statement: "Since [1976] our practice has changed somewhat, and we are going to change it again.

"For the past year or two we have still not identified first editions in so many words, although we do identify subsequent editions. At the time of a reprint of whatever edition, we add or update a block spelling out the printing history of a title, stating when the book was first published and when its subsequent printings took place, such as:

Published October 1979

Second printing March 1980

Third printing July 1980

"We are now adding the words 'First edition' to our standard copyright page copy, and all first editions will carry these words."

1988 Statement: "Stephen Greene Press became a subsidiary of Viking Penguin in New York in 1984. Our books now follow whatever practices Viking uses."

See 1988 Statement of Viking Penguin Inc.

THE GREENFIELD REVIEW PRESS/ITHACA HOUSE

1994 Statement: "We print the words 'FIRST EDITION' on the acknowledgement page of each new title. When we do a reprint, those words are removed. We have done this since our first book was published in 1971."

2000 Statement: "No special designation other than 'First Edition.' "

GREENHAVEN PRESS INC

2000 Statement: "No designation."

GREENHILL BOOKS (UNITED KINGDOM)

1988 Statement: "Our imprint pages show the year of publication of our edition. Reprints following the first edition are not identified as such and they can only be dated by means of change of address, or change of advertisements for other books. In a short time in the evolution of this new imprint we have had three addresses and this is also one means of checking whether a book has been reprinted. Initially (1984-6) we were in Hampstead High St., London NW3, then briefly in 1987 at Barham Avenue, Elstree, Hertfordshire, and now, settled for some time we trust, at Russell Gardens, London NW11. This sequence of addresses would identify the sequence of reprints."

1994 Statement: *See* 1988 Statement. Note also the following: "Another key to dating our books would be when we undertook distribution arrangements for them in the United States, and showed on the title and imprint pages the US distributor's name. From the late 1980s it was Presidio Press of San Francisco, and this changed to Stackpole Books of Harrisburg, PA, in 1993 who then later in 1993 removed to Mechanicsburg, PA."

2000 Statement: *See* 1994 Statement

GREENHOUSE REVIEW PRESS
2000 Statement: "Greenhouse Review Press first editions are marked with the copyright date only. Subsequent editions bear the number of the edition and the date it was printed."

GREENLAWN PRESS
1993 Statement: "First edition [is] not stated. Subsequent printings and editions are described as such on © page."

GREENWICH PUBLISHING GROUP, INC.
2001 Statement: "We do not identify a first printing; we do identify subsequent printings. We use a number string (lowest number indicating the printing) only for those books that have a high likelihood of being reprinted."

GREENWILLOW BOOKS
1981 Statement: The copyright page will show the following information:
First Edition
1 2 3 4 5 6 7 8 9 10
"As we reprint, we drop the first number. For the second printing, cancel 1; for the third, cancel 2; etc. Also, on *reprints*, we delete 'First Edition.'"

"Before 1978, we did not print the words First Edition, only the number sequence showing printings."
1988 Statement: *See* 1981 Statement
1993 Statement: "The [1981] Greenwillow Books statement is still correct except that we do not now delete the words 'First Edition' on reprints. (Our position is that a reprint is not a new edition but simply a new printing of the original edition.) I did not know that Greenwillow ever made this deletion on reprints, and I regret that I cannot tell you when a change might have occurred. To the best of our knowledge, this deletion has not been done since at least 1987, possibly even before that."
2000 Statement: "The 1993 Statement is correct for Greenwillow Books. But please note that Greenwillow Books has never been a 'company.' Prior to the summer of 1999, Greenwillow was 'a division of William Morrow & Company, Inc.' We are now 'Greenwillow Books, An Imprint of HarperCollinsPublishers.' . . . This statement . . . applies only to Greenwillow Books."
See also HarperCollinsPublishers

GREENWOOD PRESS
1995, 2000 Statements: *See* 1995 Statement of Greenwood Publishing Group Inc.

GREENWOOD PRESS, INC.
1976 Statement: The first printing of a first edition is designated by: "First published in 19..." All printings thereafter are indicated. Revised editions and editions after the first are indicated on the copyright page.

GREENWOOD PUBLISHING GROUP INC.
1995 Statement: "The method used by the Greenwood Publishing Group, Inc. in noting first editions is as follows:

Copyright © 19.. by
All rights reserved. No portion of this book may be reproduced, by any process or technique, without the express written consent of the publisher.
Library of Congress Catalog Card Number:
ISBN:
ISSN:
First published in 19..
Greenwood Press, 88 Post Road West, Westport, CT 06881
An imprint of Greenwood Publishing Group, Inc.
Printed in the United States of America
The paper used in this book complies with the Permanent Paper Standard issued by the National Information Standards Organization.
10 9 8 7 6 5 4 3 2 1
"A second printing will follow the same procedure except the number 1 will be dropped from the printing line at the bottom of the page. For example, 10 9 8 7 6 5 4 3 2. The number 2 indicates that this is a second printing.
"To the best of my knowledge, this method has been used since the beginning of the company back in 1967."
2000 Statement: *See* 1995 Statement

THE GRESHAM PRESS, INC.
1947 Statement: "Second, third, etc. printings are so designated beneath copyright notice, the first not being identified."

THE GREVILLE PRESS (UNITED KINGDOM)
1988 Statement: "Our current (1988) practice is to print the following on the reverse of the title page: First published in this edition (date) / by (publisher's name / address / © (author/date).
"Previous (1982-87) practice contained a variable to the above on the reverse of the title page: © (date/author); in the same period, the number of copies per edition was printed on the back page.
"In the period 1979-81, the practice was to print (usually on the reverse of the title page): Published by (publisher's name/address) © (author/date); with, usually on the back page: This edition is limited to (number) numbered copies signed by the poet / copy number / poet's signature."

GREX PRESS
2000 Statement: *See* 2000 Statement of Green River Writers, Inc./Grex Press

GREY FOX PRESS
1988 Statement: "We do not specially designate first editions, but we do indicate second printings with years and revised editions on the copyright page. If one of our editions has no indication of that sort it is the first."

GREY SEAL BOOKS (UNITED KINGDOM)
1994 Statement: "When there is more than one edition, we would say 'First published in England by . . .' and 'First published in the US by . . . .' We note second and subsequent printings, as well as second and subsequent editions."

THE GREY WALLS PRESS, LIMITED (UNITED KINGDOM)

1947 Statement: "The biblio of all GREY WALLS books appears on the reverse of the title page; first printed, followed by date of year, in the case of succeeding printings second impression and date, etc. Our firm was founded in 1939 and we have since published books interesting to collectors and dealers."

GREYSTONE PRESS

(Established 1936. Ceased publishing 1942. Bought by Book Presentations in 1943; operated in the direct mail field until August, 1947 when the Greystone Press imprint was again used for trade books.)

1947 Statement (by one of the editors of the original Greystone Press): "First printings of all Greystone Press books published before 1942 have the words 'First Printing' on the back of the title page, or else they have no reference at all to printings, which means that they are first editions. In that case, subsequent printings would say 'first printing such and such a date, reprinted such and such a date.' In general, however, first printings actually say so."

1947 Statement (by one of the editors of the new Greystone Press): "As far as I can discover, there is no system used to identify printings on the current Greystone and Book Presentations titles."

THE GRIFFITH INSTITUTE, ASHMOLEAN MUSEUM (UNITED KINGDOM)

1994 Statement: *See* 1988 Statement of Ashmolean Museum (United Kingdom)

GRINDSTONE PRESS

1995 Statement: "We do small editions. All that we have done are first editions, first printings. Should we publish a second printing or edition we will say either 'second printing' or 'second edition' on the back of the title page."

GROLIER, INC.

1988 Statement: "As a general rule, we do not identify first editions or first printings of our publications. Subsequent reprintings are also not identified. Revised editions, those editions which have had significant changes made from the first editions are generally not identified by a special notice. They are, however, identifiable because they contain a copyright year for the revised edition in addition to the copyright year of the first editions. These are general practices and are not absolutely observed in all publications."

1993 Statement: *See* 1988 Statement

GROSSET (AUSTRALIA)

2000 Statement: *See* 2000 Statement of Penguin Books Australia Ltd (Australia)

GROSSET & DUNLAP

1988 Statement: *See* 1988 Statement of The Putnam & Grosset Group (Children's)

1994 Statement: *See* 1993 Statement of The Putnam & Grosset Group
2000 Statement: *See* 2000 Statement of Penguin Putnam Books for Young Readers

GROSSMAN PUBLISHERS

1976 Statement: "There is no designation for the first edition of Grossman Publishers' books. Other printings are so indicated on the copyright page."
1981 Statement: "As of 1977, all [Grossman Publishers] titles were incorporated into the Viking list. Grossman Publishers no longer exist—all titles have been absorbed by Viking Penguin, Inc."

GROVE / ATLANTIC INC.

2000 Statement: The edition (e.g., First Edition or First American Edition) is indicated on the copyright page. A number line is used as well, indicating the year of publication and the printing: 00 01 02 03   10 9 8 7 6 5 4 3 2 1.

GROVE PRESS, INC.

1976 Statement: "All our books carry a printing history on their copyright page.

"The legend says 'First Printing,' 'Second Printing,' etc. This means of identification has been in use at Grove at least since 1970."
1981 Statement: "The [1976 Statement] is still accurate. We now, however, include the exact same copy on the copyright page for the first editions of both paperback and hardcover. This way, we don't have to reset the page for the paperback edition. The way you can tell whether or not it is a first edition paperback or hardcover should be apparent from the binding. (We often issue first editions of books in paper and hardcover simultaneously.)

"Later editions say either 'First Edition 1979/Third Printing 1980' (or whatever). New editions will say something like 'First Revised Evergreen Edition 1981/First Printing 1981' (or whatever). Essentially, to tell whether or not a Grove book is a real 'first edition' is to see whether or not it says 'First Edition (Date)/First Printing (Date).' "
1988 Statement: "All our books carry a complete printing history on their copyright page. A Grove Press hardcover first edition and an Evergreen paperback first edition say 'First edition' and the year near the bottom of the page.

"When a second edition or a revised edition is published, this edition and date appear following an information line about the first edition and year. When Grove Press reprints a book from another publisher's edition, this history appears on the copyright page following the copyright holder information.

"Printings of an edition are shown by the serial numbers at the very bottom of the page. For example, 10 9 8 7 6 5 4 indicates that an edition is in its fourth printing."
2000 Statement: *See* 2000 Statement of Grove/Atlantic Inc.

THE JOHNNY GRUELLE COMPANY

1947 Statement: "There is no way of surely identifying the first printings of 'Raggedy Ann' books.

"The first title, *Raggedy Ann Stories*, was published by P. F. Volland and Co., Chicago in 1918 and the first printing was 5,000 copies with no mark designating them as the first printing. Public acceptance of this material was such that we simply put edition after edition on the press and continued to add titles to the series, each of which enjoyed unprecedented popularity. About five years after the start we began running such lines on the copyright page, as, Fifty-six Printing, etc. This, however, meant little because the size of the various printings ranged from five to fifty thousand copies.

"Under the circumstances, I think it can only be said that there is no way of being sure in this matter."

GRUNE & STRATTON, INC.

1976 Statement: "The last page of the index has a code, a lettered code. 'A' is a first printing; 2nd printing, the 'A' is deleted and the top letter is 'B', etc.

"Following editions become part of the title of the book."

1981 Statement: *See* 1976 Statement

GRYPHON BOOKS

2000 Statement: *See* 1993 Statement of Gryphon Publications

GRYPHON PUBLICATIONS

1993 Statement: "Gryphon Publications lists copyright data on title page reverse. An original (so stated) means the work has never before been in print. It will say so on the © page and usually on the back cover as 'A Gryphon Books original.' Printing info on the © page will list if it is a 'First Edition' (first time in book form, or as a separate edition) and reprints will be listed showing previous publication either by me or a previous publisher."

2000 Statement: *See* 2000 Statement of Gryphon Books

GSWS (CANADA)

See 1988 Statement of New Star Books (Canada)

GUANTLET PRESS

2001 Statement: "We state 'First edition' on the copyright page."

GUERNICA (CANADA)

2000 Statement: "Guernica always puts the year of the printing on its copyright page. It appears after the copyright © symbol. For example, Copyright © 2001, Daniel Sloate and Guernica Editions. Other copyrights are mentioned if the works appeared elsewhere. But there always is the year of publication of the present edition. We rarely simply reprint a book. We prefer to change its format and give the book a new life in our reprint series, Picas Series. But here again, the book has a new life as a first edition.

"When there is a second printing, or a second edition, we mention this on the copyright page. If there is no mention of a second edition or printing, then one can assume that it is a first edition. 99% of our books carry on the last page of the book the name of the printer and month and year that this book was printed."

GUINNESS PUBLISHING LTD (UNITED KINGDOM)
(Name changed to Guinness World Records Ltd.

1994 Statement: First printings are indicated by the line "First published (date)" on the copyright page.

2000 Statement: *See* 2000 Statement of Guinness World Records Ltd. (United Kingdom)

GUINNESS SUPERLATIVES LTD (UNITED KINGDOM)
(Name changed to Guinness Publishing Ltd in 1988.)

Statement for practices prior to 1988: First editions are unmarked on the copyright page or carry the line "First published in (date)."

GUINNESS WORLD RECORDS LTD. (UNITED KINGDOM)
2000 Statement: "Please note that Guinness Publishing Ltd is now known as Guinness World Records Ltd.

"Guinness World Records Ltd does not identify first printings as such, but subsequent printings are identified by 'Reprinted [year].'

"Since our book publishing activity is currently concentrated on the annual Guinness World Records and Guinness British Hit Singles books, we are unlikely to produce any genuine first editions (i.e. completely new titles) in the near future."

GULF PROFESSIONAL PUBLISHING
2000 Statement: *See* 2000 Statement of Butterworth-Heinemann

GULF PROFESSIONAL PUBLISHING (UNITED KINGDOM)
2000 Statement: *See* 2000 Statement of Butterworth-Heinemann

GULF PUBLISHING COMPANY
1988 Statement: "The first printing of the first edition of a book contains no specific designation beyond the copyright notice. Subsequent printings and subsequent editions show the printing history:
    First edition 1975
    2nd printing 1976
    3rd printing 1978
    Second edition 1980."

1993 Statement: *See* 1988 Statement
2001 Statement: "We no longer publish or sell books."

GULLIVER BOOKS
1995 Statement: *See* 1995 Statement of Harcourt Brace and Company
2001 Statement: *See* 2001 Statement of Harcourt, Inc.

GULLIVER GREEN BOOKS
1995 Statement: *See* 1995 Statement of Harcourt Brace and Company
2001 Statement: *See* 2001 Statement of Harcourt, Inc.

GUMBS & THOMAS PUBLISHERS INC.
1994 Statement: The first printing of a first edition is indicated by the statement "First Edition, 1st printing."

GEORGE GUND FOUNDATION IMPRINT
IN AFRICAN-AMERICAN STUDIES
2000 Statement: *See* 2000 Statement of University of California Press

GUT PUNCH PRESS
1995 Statement: "On all of our first printings the words 'first edition' appear above the copyright notice on the verso of the title page. These words are removed or updated for subsequent printings."

THE GUTENBERG PRESS
2000 Statement: "We identify the first printing of a first edition by 'First Printing, (Year).' "

GWASG GWENFFRWD CYMRU (WALES)
1994 Statement: "Each of our publications bears the year of printing at the foot of the title page and the copyright year on the verso. No explicit statement of first edition is made, nor of any reprint of that edition, until a new edition appears. New editions are so designated, on the verso, by an extra date in the copyright statement e.g. © H.G.A. Hughes: 1947, 1994. This indicates that the first edition was that of 1947; the second edition 1994. In addition, which edition is indicated on the verso of the title page:

First published 1947
Second edition 1994
Third edition 1994   (Months are not specified.)

"Occasionally only, a reprint may be mentioned but only in the case of a change of format or when extra matter such as a map is added—without change or addition to text. We have followed this style since 1947."
2000 Statement: *See* 1994 Statement

GWASG PRIFYSGOL CYMRU (WALES)
1988, 1994, 2000 Statements: *See* 1988 Statement of University of Wales Press (Wales)

GYNERGY BOOKS (CANADA)
1995, 2000 Statements: *See* 1995 Statement of Ragweed Press (Canada)

H

MICHAEL HAAG (UNITED KINGDOM)
1988 Statement: "Our first editions are identified on the reverse of the title page as 'First edition' and then the date, or possibly (when it is the same) the date of copyright. Second and subsequent editions are similarly identified, though the date of first edition might not then be mentioned.

"We have always done things thus. We have no other imprints and no subsidiaries."

HACKER ART BOOKS INC
2001 Statement: "We do not identify a first printing; we do identify subsequent printings as such on the copyright page."

THE HAKLUYT SOCIETY (UNITED KINGDOM)
2001 Statement: "The Hakluyt Society has a policy of never reprinting any of our titles and so by definition, all are first editions. Occasionally other publishers are given permission to do a reprint but under their own imprint."

PETER HALBAN PUBLISHERS LTD. (UNITED KINGDOM)
1988 Statement: "We do indeed designate the date of first publication and where a reissue or new edition of a work is brought out it is clearly marked on the copyright page. If it is a question of a translation we generally put the original title either in the English or the original language together with the copyright and date of first publication in the original language."
1994, 2000 Statements: *See* 1988 Statement

THE HALCYON PRESS (NEW ZEALAND)
1994 Statement: "The first edition of our books is identified with the words 'First Published' and the year. Subsequent printings of the edition are identified with the words 'Reprinted' and the year. Later editions are identified with the words 'This edition' and the year. We have followed this practice since 1984."
2000 Statement: *See* 1994 Statement

E. M. HALE & COMPANY
1976 Statement: "We do not identify a first edition, but we do identify subsequent printings: 'Second printing,' 'Third printing,' etc. Our books are published under the imprint of Harvey House, Publishers."
1981 Statement: *See* 1981 Statement of Harvey House, Publishers

RALPH T. HALE AND CO.
(Succeeded by Charles T. Branford Co.)

ROBERT HALE AND COMPANY (UNITED KINGDOM)
1937 Statement: "This Company was formed in February 1936, and we have not yet published any books—the first lot of titles will be issued next month (September).

"Our books may be divided into two categories—non-fiction and fiction. The title-pages of the former will bear the year of issue in roman numerals beneath our imprint at the foot; and where they are first editions the title-page itself will bear no date. When the book is reprinted the bibliography will be placed at back of title.

"In the case of fiction, the title-page will bear no date of issue, but at back of title-page will be given the month and the year when the book was first published. Any subsequent reprints will be added to that bibliography."

ROBERT HALE LIMITED (UNITED KINGDOM)
(Formerly Robert Hale and Company.)

1947 Statement: "This company was formed in February 1936.

"Our books may be divided into two categories—non-fiction and fiction. The title-pages of the former bear the year of issue on the reverse of title. When the book is reprinted the bibliography is placed at back of title.

"In the case of fiction, the title-page bears no date of issue, but on the reverse of title is given the year when the book was first published. Any subsequent reprints will be added to that bibliography."

Statement for 1960: "From 1941-56 many books have simply, for example, 'First published 1951,' though some early books have nothing at all on the imprint page. Others have copyright date and author, e.g. 'F. Bloggs copyright 1939.' Since 1958 the bibliographical line has been in the form as 'First published in Great Britain 1961.' "

1976 Statement: "There is not a great deal I can say about our method of identifying first editions. This is mainly by implication. The first bibliographical line that appears on our imprint page is, for example, 'first published in Great Britain 1976.' If there is no following bibliographical detail the book is our first edition. Publication or prior publication in another country would be noted if the book were a translation. In the case of publication in English (in America, for instance) there would not necessarily be a mention unless it originally appeared under another title.

"It is necessary to read the bibliographical details in conjunction with the copyright line which in the case of prior publication in America will have a different date from the British publication date.

"As a matter of interest a considerable number of books produced by us which appeared both in America and Britain have joint imprints on all copies."

1982, 1988 Statements: *See* 1976 Statement

1994 Statement: "Since the beginning of this year we have included an edition line of numerals e.g. 2 4 6 8 10 9 7 5 3 1 on the title verso of non-fiction books only.

"With titles of American origin we are now including a reference to the original publisher on the title verso page.

"The publications of our recently acquired subsidiary NAG Press Ltd will follow the practice adopted by that company until any of their titles are reprinted in which case Robert Hale's current procedure will apply."

2000 Statement: "The 1994 statement we provided is still relevant except that having acquired the publishing company J A Allen & Co Ltd we now have a new imprint but identification of first editions will follow the Hale pattern."

HALE, CUSHMAN & FLINT, INC.
(Bought in 1942 by Ralph T. Hale and Co. which was in turn succeeded by Charles T. Branford Co.)

1937 Statement: "In books published by us we give on the copyright page the information as to the edition or printing."

HALF HALT PRESS INC

2001 Statement: "We do not identify a first printing or any printing after the first printing on the copyright page."

G K HALL & CO

1993 Statement: *see* 1993 Statement of Macmillan Inc.

HALO BOOKS

2000 Statement: "We identify the first printing of a first edition by the number line 1, 2, 3, 4, 5, 6, 7, 8, 9, 0 on copyright page."

HAMBLEDON PRESS

1994 Statement: "I seldom get to second printings. Of recent publications are *Anglo-Indian Attitudes* can be told by its pinker elephant on the dust-wrapper; *Jane Austen and the Clergy* by the restoration of horse's feet on dust-wrapper; *English Medieval Indentures* by the cheaper dots."

2000 Statement: "The second edition/printing of *The White Death* by Thomas Dormandy has four ecstatic reviews on the back lower flap of the dustwrapper; the third printing has 130 spelling mistakes removed."

HAMBLETON-HILL PUBLISHING, INC.

2000 Statement: The first printing of a first edition is identified by printing the words "First Edition" on the copyright page. Second printings do not carry this designation. This method has always been followed.

HAMEWITH

2000 Statement: *See* 2000 Statement of Baker Book House

HAMISH HAMILTON (AUSTRALIA)

2000 Statement: *See* 2000 Statement of Penguin Books Australia Ltd (Australia)

HAMISH HAMILTON LTD. (UNITED KINGDOM)

1937 Statement: "When a book is first published, we print a notice at the top of the reverse of the title page reading 'First Published, 1934, 1935 or 1936,' as the case may be. When we come to a second impression, we alter this notice by inserting in the top line the month upon which the book was published, January, February, etc., and beneath it we insert a second line reading Second Impression . . . . (Month) 1934, 1935, 1936, as the case may be, and so on for subsequent reprints."

1947 Statement: *See* 1937 Statement

Statement for 1960: "We designated a first printing in 1960 in the same way as described in our 1976 statement."

1976 Statement: "The only method of identifying first impressions (I think this is safer nomenclature than 'editions') is to say 'first published in Great Britain 19.. by Hamish Hamilton Limited.' Any further impressions are simply along the lines of 'second impression July 1976,' etc."

1981 Statement: *See* 1976 Statement

1988 Statement: "This style was introduced during 1988 and is followed by the whole of the Penguin Group.

First published in Great Britain 1988
by Hamish Hamilton Ltd.
Copyright 1988 by Hugh Thomas
1 3 5 7 9 10 8 6 4 2"

See also 1988 Statement of Penguin Publishing Co Ltd. (United Kingdom)
1994 Statement: "In 1990 the style First published 1990 was introduced to indicate first publication anywhere. The style First published in Great Britain by Hamish Hamilton Ltd 1990 was retained to indicate first British publication. The style of copyright line was amended to Copyright © Hugh Thomas, 1990."
2001 Statement: *See* 2001 Statement of Penguin Publishing Co Ltd (United Kingdom)

HAMISH HAMILTON CHILDREN'S BOOKS (UNITED KINGDOM)

1988 Statement: *See* 1988 Statement of Hamish Hamilton Ltd. (United Kingdom)
2001 Statement: *See* 2001 Statement of Penguin Publishing Co Ltd (United Kingdom)

JOHN HAMILTON, LTD. (UNITED KINGDOM)
(Firm was in liquidation in 1941.)

1937 Statement: "It is our practice to have no date shown on our first edition. If the book is reprinted then the date of the first edition appears together with the reprint date underneath, e.g.:
    First Edition 1922.
    Reprinted 1923."

HAMILTON PRESS

2000 Statement: *See* 2000 Statement of Madison Books

HAMLYN (UNITED KINGDOM)

1994 Statement: *See* 1994 Statement of Reed Consumer Books (United Kingdom)

HAMLYN CHILDREN'S BOOKS (UNITED KINGDOM)

1994 Statement: *See* 1994 Statement of Reed Consumer Books (United Kingdom)

HAMLYN PUBLISHING GROUP LTD. (UNITED KINGDOM)

1989 Statement: *See* 1989 Statement of The Octopus Publishing Group PLC (United Kingdom)

HAMMOND, INC.

1981 Statement: "We do not designate the first printing of first editions."
1988 Statement: *See* 1981 Statement

HAMMOND, HAMMOND & COMPANY, LTD.
(UNITED KINGDOM)

1947 Statement: "Our first edition of any important book is usually indicated by having the month and year of production given in Arabic figures under the imprint of the printers. Any reprint is marked on the imprint page as a reprint, with the date in full."

THE HAMPSHIRE BOOKSHOP, INC.

1947 Statement: "In the last thirty years we have published about twenty books with printings not over one thousand copies. If the designation 'second edition' does not appear on the reverse of the title page, it is a first printing."

HAMPTON ROADS PUBLISHING COMPANY, INC.

1994 Statement: "We use the 10 9 8 7 6 5 4 3 2 1 method. We have always used this method."
2000 Statement: *See* 1994 Statement

HANCOCK HOUSE PUBLISHERS LTD.

1994 Statement: "First printings have no special designation. Second and subsequent printings [are indicated]."
2001 Statement: *See* 1994 Statement

HANCOCK HOUSE PUBLISHERS LTD. (CANADA)

1989 Statement: "We do not designate first editions as such. Further editions are labelled as 2nd, 3rd, etc., on the copyright page. Likewise for printings.

"This is simply the way it is at Hancock House. There are no current plans to alter the system. We do not have other imprints or subsidiaries."
1993 Statement: *See* 1989 Statement

HANDS & HEART BOOKS

2000 Statement: *See* 2000 Statement of Toad Hall, Inc.

HANDSHAKE EDITIONS (FRANCE)

2001 Statement: "We identify each printing."

HANGING LOOSE PRESS

1976 Statement: "We only started publishing books about a year ago and have yet to reprint a book. When we do, I suppose we will add 'Second Printing.' There is nothing in the original copies of the first 6 titles to indicate that they are first editions or first printings."
1981 Statement: "First Editions could be identified only by the copyright date. Second printings are clearly identified as such, with the year."
1988 Statement: "50 titles later, ditto."
1993 Statement: "For awhile (mostly as a result of your periodic inquiries) we were stating 'First Edition' on the copyright page. For the past couple of years, we have been using a printing code: 10 9 8 7 6 5 4 3 2 1 and deleting numbers if we reprint."
2000 Statement: *See* 1993 Statement

HANNIBAL BOOKS

1994 Statement: The first printing of a first edition is indicated by the statement "First Edition printed _____, (Month) (year)."

HANSOM BOOKS

1995 Statement: *See* 1995 Statement of Gaslight Publications

HAPPYTIME (UNITED KINGDOM)

1994 Statement: *See* 1994 Statement of Ladybird Books Ltd (United Kingdom)

HARBOR HILL BOOKS

1994 Statement: *See* 1994 Statement of Purple Mountain Press, Ltd.

2000 Statement: *See* 2000 Statement of Purple Mountain Press, Ltd.

HARBOR PRESS INC

2000 Statement: "We identify any first editions with a copyright page notice as follows:

© Copyright 2000, Harbor Press, Inc.

"Subsequent editions are identified with a copyright page notice as follows:

Second Edition

© Copyright 2005, Harbor Press, Inc.

"We identify the first printing of any edition with a copyright page notice as follows:

10 9 8 7 6 5 4 3 2 1

—or—

1 3 5 7 9 10 8 6 4 2

"Subsequent printings delete the lowest numeral in the series so that the remaining lowest numeral designates the number of the printing."

HARCOURT

2001 Statement: *See* 2001 Statement of Harcourt, Inc.

HARCOURT, INC.

2001 Statement: "I believe our method of designating first editions is fairly standard throughout the industry. On the first printing, the words 'First edition' appear on copyright page. On each subsequent printing, the phrase 'First edition' is dropped and the printing is identified by a letter: the second printing is identified by the letter B, the third printing is C (and the letter B is dropped). This goes up to the letter Z. If there are more than 26 printings, we start using double letters: AA, BB, and so on.

"If the material in the book is substantially changed, we will identify it as the second edition, apply for a new copyright, and begin the same numbering sequence as for a first edition.

"All Trade Books follow this method. The name was changed to Harcourt, Inc. in 1999."

HARCOURT/ACADEMIC PRESS

2001 Statement: *See* 2001 Statement of Academic Press, A Harcourt Science and Technology Company

HARCOURT BRACE AND COMPANY

1995 Statement: *See* 1981 Statement of Harcourt Brace Jovanovich, Inc. "All imprints and subsidiaries of the Trade Division follow the same procedures."

2001 Statement: *See* 2001 Statement of Harcourt, Inc.

HARCOURT, BRACE & CO., INC.

1928 Statement: "We have not been following any fast rule for indicating first editions. On all books for which we think there may be some demand, we indicate the first edition by placing a small figure 1 on the copyright page under our copyright notice, or by putting on a line 'Published' and then the date. Subsequent editions have either a number 2 on them or a line 'Second Printing,' and then the date."

1936 Statement: "In general it is the practice of Harcourt, Brace & Company to indicate the first impression of their general trade books by the words 'first edition' on the copyright page underneath the copyright notice. In cases where the book has been first published in another country, the words 'first American edition' or 'first printing' are substituted. Previous to about 1930, first editions were generally indicated by placing a small figure 1 underneath the copyright notice, or by putting on a line 'Published' and then the date."

1947 Statement: *See* 1936 Statement

See also 1948 Statement of Reynal and Hitchcock, Inc.

HARCOURT BRACE JOVANOVICH, INC.

(Name changed to Harcourt Brace and Company in 1993.)

1976 Statement: "I believe our method of designating first editions is fairly standard throughout the industry. On the first printing, the words 'First edition' appear on the copyright page. On each subsequent printing, the phrase 'First edition' is dropped and the printing is identified by a letter: the second printing is identified by the letter B, the third printing is C (but the letter B is also retained, so that on the copyright page this designation appears 'BC'). This goes up to the letter J. At the 11th printing, we begin using a number identification: 11th printing, 12th printing, etc. However, in the case of *juvenile* or paperback titles, we do *not* start using numbers at the 11th printing, but instead continue with letters right through Z. If there are more than 26 printings, we start using double letters: AA, BB, and so on.

"If the material in the book is substantially changed, we will identify it as the second edition, apply for a new copyright, and begin the same numbering sequence as for a first edition."

1981 Statement: "I believe our method of designating first editions is fairly standard throughout the industry. On the first printing, the words 'First edition' appear on copyright page. On each subsequent printing, the phrase 'First edition' is dropped and the printing is identified by a letter: the second printing is identified by the letter B, the third printing is C (and the letter B is dropped). This goes up to the letter J. At the 11th printing, we begin using a number identification: 11th printing, 12th printing, etc. However, in the case of *juvenile* or paperback titles, we do *not* start using numbers at the 11th printing, but instead continue with letters right through Z. If there are more than 26 printings, we start using double letters: AA, BB, and so on.

"If the material in the book is substantially changed, we will identify it as the second edition, apply for a new copyright, and begin the same numbering sequence as for a first edition."

1988 Statement: *See* 1981 Statement
2001 Statement: *See* 2001 Statement of Harcourt, Inc.

HARCOURT PAPERBACKS
2001 Statement: *See* 2001 Statement of Harcourt, Inc.

HARCOURT TRADE PUBLISHERS
2001 Statement: *See* 2001 Statement of Harcourt, Inc.

HARCOURT YOUNG CLASSICS
2001 Statement: *See* 2001 Statement of Harcourt, Inc.

PATRICK HARDY BOOKS (UNITED KINGDOM)
2000 Statement: *See* 2000 Statement of The Lutterworth Press (United Kingdom)

HARLEQUIN BOOKS (CANADA)
1994, 2000 Statements: *See* 1994 Statement of Harlequin Enterprises Limited (Canada)

HARLEQUIN ENTERPRISES LIMITED (CANADA)
1994 Statement: "We used to indicate first editions by writing 'First Silhouette Books printing' with the month and year. However, approximately two years ago we decided to discontinue this notice. It has recently been decided that we will include the notice 'First North American publication' followed by the year, on those of our books that were originally published overseas and thus have a copyright date that does not coincide with the North American publication date. For any other first editions in North America we will not carry any first edition notice."

2000 Statement: *See* 1994 Statement

HARLEQUIN MILLS & BOON LIMITED (UNITED KINGDOM)
2000 Statement: *See* 2000 Statement of Mills & Boon Limited (United Kingdom)

HARMONIE PARK PRESS
2001 Statement: "We don't identify printings, not the first printing or any printing after the first."

HARMONY
1981, 1988, 1994 Statements: *See* 1981, 1988 Statements of Crown Publishers

HARPER & BROTHERS

1928 Statement: "It is our custom to print on the copyright page, of all first editions the two words 'First Edition.' These are removed from the plate on all subsequent printings.

"In addition to these you will find on our copyright pages two key letters beneath the copyright.

"These give the month and year when the edition was printed. This key may be read by referring to the enclosed card."

1937 Statement: *See* 1928 Statement, plus the following statement.

"The use of the key letters on copyright pages began in 1912. The use of the words 'First Edition' began a number of years later, so that there are early copies of books by Harpers in the area between 1912 and perhaps 1920 or thereabouts (unfortunately the date is not a matter of record) which have the key letters but which do not have the words 'First Edition.' This is, of course, important."

1947 Statement: *See* 1937 Statement

Harper & Brothers Key to Editions on Copyright Page

Months

A	January	G	July
B	February	H	August
C	March	I	September
D	April	K	October
E	May	L	November
F	June	M	December

Years

M	1912	Z	1925	N	1938
N	1913	A	1926	O	1939
O	1914	B	1927	P	1940
P	1915	C	1928	Q	1941
Q	1916	D	1929	R	1942
R	1917	E	1930	S	1943
S	1918	F	1931	T	1944
T	1919	G	1932	U	1945
U	1920	H	1933	V	1946
V	1921	I	1934	W	1947
W	1922	K	1935	X	1948
X	1923	L	1936	Y	1949
Y	1924	M	1937		

HARPER & BROTHERS (UNITED KINGDOM)
(London house discontinued prior to 1937.)

1928 Statement: "Our first editions are designated by printing at the back of the title page the following words: First Edition."

HARPER & ROW, PUBLISHERS, INC.

1976 Statement: "The copyright page says 'First Edition.' Under that is a chain of numbers, 76 77 78 79 9 8 7 etc.

"As a book reprints, the First Edition line gets dropped and so do the outdated numbers.

"A book in its third printing in 1976 would have a line that looks like:
76 77 78 79 9 8 7 6 5 4 3."

1981 Statement: "According to our Production Department we are still using the same First Edition form on the Harper & Row books.

"Thomas Y. Crowell was merged into Harper & Row after its purchase in 1977. All imprints then owned by Crowell now follow the procedures of Harper & Row.

"In 1978 Harper purchased J. B. Lippincott Company which, in 1979, they combined with Thomas Y. Crowell to form a new imprint of Lippincott & Crowell. In 1980 Harper abolished this new imprint and reabsorbed Lippincott & Crowell into the Harper & Row imprint."

1988 Statement: "The [1981] Statement is still correct. There should be no change to that statement."

1993 Statement: *See* 1993 Statement of HarperCollins Publishers

HARPER BUSINESS
1993 Statement: *See* 1993 Statement of HarperCollins Publishers
2001 Statement: *See* 2001 Statement of HarperBusiness

HARPER FESTIVAL
1993 Statement: *See* 1993 Statement of HarperCollins Publishers
2001 Statement: *See* 2001 Statement of HarperFestival

HARPER LARGE PRINT EDITIONS
2001 Statement: *See* 2001 Statement of HarperCollinsPublishers

HARPER MONOGRAM
1993 Statement: *See* 1993 Statement of HarperCollins Publishers

HARPER PAPERBACKS
1993 Statement: *See* 1993 Statement of HarperCollins Publishers
2001 Statement: *See* 2001 Statement of HarperTorch

HARPER PERENNIAL
1993 Statement: *See* 1993 Statement of HarperCollins Publishers

HARPER PRISM
1993 Statement: *See* 1993 Statement of HarperCollins Publishers

HARPER REFERENCE
1993 Statement: *See* 1993 Statement of Basic Books

HARPER SAN FRANCISCO
1993 Statement: *See* 1993 Statement of HarperCollins Publishers
2001 Statement: *See* 2001 Statement of HarperSanFrancisco

HARPER STYLE
1993 Statement: *See* 1993 Statement of HarperCollins Publishers

HARPER TROPHY

1993 Statement: *See* 1993 Statement of HarperCollins Publishers
2001 Statement: *See* 2001 Statement of HarperTrophy

HARPERBUSINESS

2001 Statement: *See* 2001 Statement of HarperCollinsPublishers

HARPERCOLLINS

2001 Statement: *See* 2001 Statement of HarperCollinsPublishers

HARPERCOLLINS CHILDREN'S BOOKS

1993, 2001 Statements: *See* 1993 Statement of HarperCollins Publishers

HARPERCOLLINS PUBLISHERS

1993 Statement: "According to our production department, HarperCollins still follows the same practice outlined in the 1976 statement [of Harper & Row, Publishers, Inc].

"The above applies also to designating first printings. Harper & Row changed its name to HarperCollins Publishers in 1990.

"J.B. Lippincott and T.Y. Crowell are no longer being used as imprints of new HarperCollins Children's Books. All children's books are being published under the HarperCollins Children's Books imprint."

2001 Statement: *See* 2001 Statement of HarperCollinsPublishers

HARPERCOLLINS PUBLISHERS (AUSTRALIA) PTY LIMITED (AUSTRALIA)

1994 Statement: "In 1989 Angus & Robertson Publishers merged with William Collins Pty Limited, Australia. The company name subsequently became HarperCollins Publishers (Australia) Pty Limited.

"Angus & Robertson is now an imprint of HarperCollins Publishers (Australia) Pty Limited.

"In Australia both Angus & Robertson Publications and HarperCollins Publishers designate first editions on the imprint page with the words—

(Imprint)

First published in Australia in... (year of publication)

"If these words are *not* followed by a list of reprint dates, then the reader can assume that the copy he or she holds is the first edition. However, the wording above, which is used to denote the first-ever edition, anywhere in the world, of a particular title, is also used to denote the first *Australian* edition. Because of this ambiguity, the reader can only be absolutely certain that he or she is looking at the first Australian edition, though in the majority of cases it would also be the first edition world-wide."

HARPERCOLLINS PUBLISHERS (NEW ZEALAND) LIMITED (NEW ZEALAND)

1994 Statement: "First Editions are indicated by a line on the title verso which reads: First published 19xx (year), which is usually the same date as the copyright line. All reprints are also indicated by the year of each publication."

2000 Statement: *See* 1994 Statement

HARPERCOLLINS TRADE
1993 Statement: *See* 1993 Statement of Basic Books

HARPERCOLLINS WEST
1993 Statement: *See* 1993 Statement of HarperCollins Publishers

HARPERCOLLINSPUBLISHERS
2001 Statement: "According to our production and managing editorial departments, HarperCollinsPublishers follows the following procedure:

"The copyright page says 'First Edition.' Under that is a chain of numbers, 76 77 78 79 9 8 7 etc.

"As a book reprints, the outdated numbers get dropped; however the 'First Edition' Statement may remain until the book is revised. A book in its third printing in 1976 would have a line that looks like: 76 77 78 79 9 8 7 6 5 4 3.

"A First Edition book in its first printing in 2001 would have a line that looks like: 01 02 03 04 5 4 3 2 1.

"With minor variation, this procedure is consistent among all of Harper-CollinsPublishers imprints. We will not vouch for book club handling of our titles. We have not changed our corporate name since 1990. We have acquired several imprints."

HARPERENTERTAINMENT
2001 Statement: *See* 2001 Statement of HarperCollinsPublishers

HARPERFESTIVAL
2001 Statement: *See* 2001 Statement of HarperCollinsPublishers

HARPERRESOURCE
2001 Statement: *See* 2001 Statement of HarperCollinsPublishers

HARPERSANFRANCISCO
2001 Statement: *See* 2001 Statement of HarperCollinsPublishers

HARPERTORCH
2001 Statement: *See* 2001 Statement of HarperCollinsPublishers

HARPERTROPHY
2001 Statement: *See* 2001 Statement of HarperCollinsPublishers

HARPSWELL PRESS
1988 Statement: "Harpswell Press titles are all identified for editions on the copyright page. First editions are marked as such; subsequent printings, revised editions, etc., are noted."
2001 Statement: *See* 2001 Statement of Tilbury House, Publishers

GEORGE G. HARRAP & COMPANY LIMITED
(UNITED KINGDOM)

1928 Statement: "Our first editions are distinguishable by the date of publication appearing on the reverse of the title-page. We print a notice in that place, running for example:

First published 1928
By . . . .

followed by the name of the firm and the address. Should the book reprint the notice is added as follows:

Reprinted March 1928

and the month of publication is added to the original notice (the month is not put in at first because when a book goes to press the date of publication cannot conveniently be determined to a nicety). The notice in the case of a reprint, therefore, would be, for example:

First published June 1916
By . . . .
Reprinted March 1928

"Succeeding reprints are entered thus:

Reprinted: July, 1925; January 1927
February 1928

"When a book has previously been printed in America or elsewhere abroad we omit 'First' from the notice reading:

Published 1928
By . . . .

"But a translation first issued by ourselves would be marked 'First published.' "

1937 Statement: *See* 1928 Statement, plus the following statement.

"When a book has been previously printed in America or elsewhere abroad we nevertheless include 'First' in the notice, implying that publication under our imprint was first made at the time referred to.

"We began using our present method at some time prior to 1924."

1947 Statement: "Our practice in regard to the bibliographical notice on the reverse of the title page follows, with temporary modifications what is laid down in your 1937 edition [1928 and 1937 Statements]. The parenthetical remark that 'when a book goes to press the date of publication cannot conveniently be determined to a nicety' has been greatly emphasized in these difficult days of production, and it applies now to reprints as well as to new books. For this reason we do not at present attempt to give the month of publication. For books that were issued during or after 1945 therefore, the bibliographical notice would read on these lines.

First published 1945
By . . . .
Reprinted: 1946; 1947"

Statement for 1960: "The method this company uses to identify first editions is to print the publication date; any reprint dates follow this date in subsequent impressions as do the dates of any new or revised editions. This system has always been followed including for the years 1949 through to 1976."

1976 Statement: "The method which we . . . use to identify first editions, is to print the publication date; any reprint dates follow this date in subsequent impressions, as do the dates of new or revised editions."

1981 Statement: *See* 1981 Statement of Harrap Limited (United Kingdom)

HARRAP LIMITED (UNITED KINGDOM)

1981 Statement: *See* 1976 Statement of George G. Harrap & Company Limited (United Kingdom)

1988 Statement: *See* 1988 Statement of Harrap Publishing Group Ltd (United Kingdom)

HARRAP PUBLISHING GROUP LTD (UNITED KINGDOM)

1988 Statement: "The method this Company uses to identify first editions is to print the publication date on the title-page verso; any reprint follows this date in subsequent impressions, as do the dates of any new or revised editions. Example:

> First published 1987 by Harrap Books Ltd.,
> 19-23 Ludgate Hill, London EC4M 7PD
> Reprinted 1988

(We do *not* include the month of publication in the reprint line.)"

The company is moving to new premises in the spring of 1989. Thus, the address on the copyright page will be different from that given in the example above.

HARRISON-HILTON BOOKS, INC.

(In 1940 changed name to Smith and Durrell, which in 1947 became Oliver Durrell, Inc.)

RUPERT HART-DAVIS, LIMITED (UNITED KINGDOM)

1948 Statement: "The principles we use to identify the various printings of our books are as follows:

"The first printing is distinguished by either (a) the date (year) on the title page, or (b) by the words 'First published 194-' on the reverse of the title page. Sometimes we use both (a) and (b).

"The second printing has the words 'Second Impression 194-' added on the reverse of the title page, leaving the original date on the title page itself. If the second printing, or any subsequent printing, contains enough alterations to merit the distinction, we should use the words 'Revised Edition 194—.' "

HART-DAVIS, MACGIBBON LIMITED (UNITED KINGDOM)

1976, 1981, 1988 Statements: *See* 1976, 1981, 1988 Statements of Granada Publishing Limited (United Kingdom)

HARTSDALE HOUSE, INC.

1947 Statement: "We have made no attempt to distinguish first printings from later printings of any books which we publish."

HARVARD BUSINESS SCHOOL DIVISION OF RESEARCH

1976 Statement: "We use no unusual identification for First Editions: the date of publication on the title page. Second, Third, etc., Printings are noted on the Copyright Page.

"Date of publication is on title page of *all* printings. The absence of a 2nd printing, etc., on copyright page does not necessarily assure the reader of 1st ptg. of 1st edition."

1981 Statement: *See* 1976 Statement

HARVARD BUSINESS SCHOOL PRESS

(Formerly known as the Harvard Business School Division of Research.)
1988 Statement: "We use no unusual identification for First Editions. All printings are noted on the copyright page."
1993 Statement: *See* 1988 Statement

THE HARVARD COMMON PRESS

1981 Statement: "We identify the various printings of each of our books on the copyright page, by using the series of numbers '10 9 8 7 6 5 4 3 2 1.' At each subsequent printing of the book, we delete the last number on the list, so that the last number appearing indicates what printing the book is in."
1988 Statement: *See* 1981 Statement. All imprints and subsidiaries follow this practice.
1993, 2000 Statements: *See* 1988 Statement

HARVARD UKRAINIAN RESEARCH INSTITUTE

2000 Statement: "We only indicate subsequent editions on the copyright page."

HARVARD UNIVERSITY PRESS

1928 Statement: "We have no distinguishing mark which signifies that a book is a first edition. As a general thing, we put second, third, fourth impression, etc. on the reverse of the title-page whenever we make new printings."
1937 Statement: *See* 1928 Statement
1947 Statement: "May we say that a statement made some years ago still applies. Our books are not labeled 'first edition,' but if a second or later edition has been published this is stated below the copyright notice on the reverse of the title page."
Statement for 1960: "To answer your question about how we designated a first printing in 1960, we did not then have any special way of indicating a first edition—that is, if the edition was not identified as second or revised, it was a first edition."
1976 Statement: "We do not have a special way of identifying first editions. In other words, if the edition is not identified as second or revised, it is a first edition. The first printing of the first edition carries the same date on the title page as on the copyright notice. When the edition is reprinted, the printing is identified on the copyright page, as, for example, Second printing, 1976, and the date on the title page is deleted. A second edition is called that on the title

page and dated. If a second edition is reprinted, the words 'second printing' refer to a reprint of the second edition."

1981 Statement: "We do not have a special way of identifying first editions. In other words, if the edition is not identified as second or revised, it is a first edition. The first printing of the first edition carries the same date on the title page as on the copyright notice. When the edition is reprinted, the printing is identified on the copyright page, as, for example, Second printing, 1976, and no date appears on the title page."

1982 Statement: "Beginning some time in 1983, we will change our way of designating second and successive *printings*. We will still delete the date on the title page, but instead of inserting on the copyright page 'Second printing, 1983' (for example), we will simply remove the '1' from a row of numbers running from 10 to 1; we will not add the date of the second printing."

1988 Statement: "The statement we made in 1982 still stands, and it applies to all books published under our imprint and that of The Belknap Press of Harvard University Press. We have no subsidiaries."

1993 Statement: "The first printing of the first edition carries the date of publication on the title page. When the edition is reprinted, the printing is identified on the copyright page with, for example, 'Second printing, 1994,' and the date is removed from the title page. This applies to all hardcover books published under our imprint and that of The Belknap Press of Harvard University Press. First editions of paperback books are identified on the copyright page with, for example, 'First Harvard University Press paperback edition, 1994,' unless a portion of the printing was bound in hardcover."

2001 Statement: *See* 1993 Statement

HARVEST BOOKS
1995 Statement: *See* 1995 Statement of Harcourt Brace and Company
2001 Statement: *See* 2001 Statement of Harcourt, Inc.

HARVEST HILL PRESS
2000 Statement: "We do not designate first printings, (except by process of elimination). We designate second and subsequent printings by including the statement on the verso page that reads 'second printing (year)'. 'First edition' is always stated on the first printing and remains on subsequent printings."

HARVEST HOUSE PUBLISHERS
1988 Statement: "We do not indicate at the present time. However, beginning in 1989 we will use the listing of numbers 1-10 on bottom of copyright page and delete a number with each printing."

1993 Statement: "We currently use the listing of numbers 1-10 on the bottom of the copyright page which indicates the current print number and date."

THE HARVESTER PRESS LTD. (UNITED KINGDOM)
1988 Statement: "For your information, this Company, and also Wheatsheaf Books Limited, has recently been sold and is now a division of Simon & Schuster International Group.

"Our current copyright page states 'First published 1988' and below we print a series of numbers '1 2 3 4 5 92 91 90 89 88.' The first number and the last eighty-eight indicate the printing and date of the current publication. Therefore a second edition would carry the line '2 3 4 5 92 91 90 89.'

"The system of the line of numbers has been adopted since the sale of the Company. Previously, we simply added a reprint line: 'Reprinted 1988,' for instance.

"All of this also applies to Wheatsheaf Books Limited, which is another imprint of this Company."

HARVEY HOUSE, PUBLISHERS
1981 Statement: "Harvey House, Publishers does not identify a first edition or subsequent printings. At one time we identified each new printing but we have not been doing that lately. A new edition (where there are substantive changes in text) is identified as a 'second edition' etc., but we seldom do second editions. If there is a considerable change and updating of a title we are more inclined to redo the entire book with a new title."

ROLAND HARVEY STUDIOS (AUSTRALIA)
1994 Statement: "We indicate first editions simply by printing the line 'First published 199*' on the imprint page. Reprints are indicated by adding a line 'Reprinted 199*.' "

HASTINGS HOUSE
1947 Statement: "Our books are printed by three different processes, letter-press, gravure and offset. First editions of letterpress books can be identified by the lack of any other printing notices. On both the gravure and offset books this method of marking subsequent printings is quite difficult and therefore is not done. The printing notice is frequently carried on the dust jacket of the book. This, however, is done more for the convenience of the bookseller than for the aid of the book collector."

HASTINGS HOUSE, BOOK PUBLISHERS
(A Division of Eagle Publishing, Corp.)
1993 Statement: "Our first editions are identified in two ways: (a) copyright notice for the year, and (b) 10 9 8 7 6 5 4 3 2 1 to identify the first printing."
2000 Statement: *See* 2000 Statement of Hastings House Books, Inc.

HASTINGS HOUSE BOOKS, INC.
2000 Statement: *See* 1993 Statement of Hastings House, Book Publishers

HASTINGS HOUSE, PUBLISHERS, INC.
1976 Statement: "First printings are identified only by the copyright notice. Subsequent *printings* give date. Subsequent editions so state and give date."
1981, 1988 Statements: *See* 1976 Statement
See also Hastings House, Book Publishers

HAWK PUBLISHING GROUP
2000 Statement: No identifying statement is used. The first printing of a first edition is identified by the following number line: H 9 8 7 6 5 4 3 2 1.

HAWTHORN BOOKS, INC.

1976 Statement: "Although Hawthorn does not use the phrase 'First Edition' on its copyright page, we do have a method of identifying various printings of a book. At the foot of the copyright page we set Arabic numerals from one to ten. For the second printing we delete the one, etc., so that the first number indicates the number of the printing.

"According to copyright law, a specified amount of material in a book must be completely new if a book is to be considered a second edition. On any title for which these requirements are fulfilled, we print the words 'Second Edition' on the jacket, title page, and copyright page. This second edition is not, however, indicated in the Arabic numbering codes. The first printing of the second edition would simply list all the numbers from one to ten again, indicating that it was the first printing of the second edition.

"A revised or updated edition of a book will be so listed on the jacket, title page, and copyright page—just as with a second edition. But in this instance, since the work cannot legally be called a second edition, we delete another number in the code and call it a third, fourth, or whatever, printing."

HAWTHORN HOUSE
(No longer in operation in 1949.)

1947 Statement: "Perhaps to the despair of the bibliographer, Hawthorn House had no orderly plan for identifying First Editions. Publishing activities of the press were always on a small scale, and often in limited editions. The problem of what to do about repeated printings was not a very live one!

"In one instance a practice was used that might confuse bibliographers. When we published '*Notes on the Care & Cataloguing of Old Maps*' by Lloyd A. Brown, in 1940, it was apparent that production could not be completed until nearly the turn of the year. Accordingly, when the sheet that included the title page was run through the press, only 100 copies were run off with the date *1940* on the title page, and the press then stopped and the date for the remaining sheets changed to 1941—the humdrum effort of a publisher to make his wares appear as fresh as possible."

HAY HOUSE INC

2000 Statement: "We identify the first printing of a first edition by the following statement: 1st printing, month, year. Subsequent printings would be identified by: 4th printing, month, year.

"We identify the first printing of a first edition by the following number line:

$$03\ 02\ 01\ 00 \quad 4\ 3\ 2\ 1$$

Subsequent printings would show:

$$03\ 02\ 01\ 00 \quad 7\ 6\ 5\ 4$$

"We only list the 1st printing and then the latest printing, not all the ones in-between; except when a book is first published as a hardcover, and then becomes a tradepaper, we point that out, but continue the number sequence. For example: 1st printing, May 1999, 2nd printing (1st tradepaper edition) July 2000, 6th printing, May 2001. We have always used this method."

HAY HOUSE LIFESTYLES

2000 Statement: *See* 2000 Statement of Hay House Inc

HAYNES PUBLISHING (UNITED KINGDOM)

1988 Statement: "First Editions are indicated on the copyright page for all Haynes Publishing publications bearing the Haynes Publishing imprint as follows:

1) By the absence of any acknowledgement of previous publication of the book in its entirety; or

2) By the words 'First Edition' printed on the title verso.

"Revised editions are designated on the copyright page.

"Printings are indicated by a line of code letters (A-Z) on the outside back cover, the highest remaining letter being deleted at each reprinting."

1994 Statement: "Haynes Publishing owns the following imprints under which books are currently being published: Patrick Stephens Limited, Oxford Publishing Company, G T Foulis & Co. and Oxford Illustrated Press. All these imprints follow the [1988 Statement] to designate the first printing."

2000 Statement: "The 1994 and 1988 statements still apply, except that Oxford Publishing Company is no longer an imprint, and most titles are published under the Haynes imprint."

J. H. HAYNES & CO. LTD (UNITED KINGDOM)

1988 Statement: *See* 1988 Statement of Haynes Publishing (United Kingdom)

J. H. HAYNES (OVERSEAS) LTD. (UNITED KINGDOM)

1988 Statement: *See* 1988 Statement of Haynes Publishing (United Kingdom)

HBJ MODERN CLASSICS

1995 Statement: *See* 1995 Statement of Harcourt Brace and Company

HEADLINE BOOK PUBLISHING (UNITED KINGDOM)

2001 Statement: *See* 2001 Statement of Hodder Headline (United Kingdom)

HEALING ARTS PRESS

1988, 2000 Statements: *See* 1988 Statement of Inner Traditions International Ltd.

HEALTH PROFESSIONS PRESS

2000 Statement: *See* 2000 Statement of Paul H Brookes Publishing Co

HEALTH SCIENCE PRESS (UNITED KINGDOM)

1994, 2000 Statements: *See* 1994 Statement of The C.W. Daniel Company Ltd (United Kingdom)

HEALTHWATCH

2000 Statement: *See* 2000 Statement of Players Press Inc.

HEARST BOOKS

1994 Statement: *See* 1994 Statement of Tambourine Books

268

HEARST MARINE BOOKS
1994 Statement: *See* 1994 Statement of Tambourine Books

HEART OF THE LAKES PUBLISHING
1988 Statement: "We have no system to indicate first printings. Most of our titles see only one printing due to the limited demand for our type of historical research materials. On some of our trade titles we have gone into multiple printings. Some are so indicated on the copyright page while others are not. Some changes may be made (typos etc corrected) between printings. Our reprints of ōlder/antique/out-of-print type books are clearly indicated by a new title page inserted in front of the old title page. When possible CIP information is added to a title on the copyright page.

"This applies to our publications under all of our imprints at present, i.e., Heart of the Lakes Publishing, Empire State Books and Windswept Press."
1995 Statement: "A limited number of our books carry printing information (edition and/or printing). There really is no need of such since 95% of our books only ever have one printing."

HEAT PRESS
1995 Statement: "First Editions are designated as such on the copyright page according to *The Chicago Manual of Style*. Subsequent editions will be designated as such, as well as 2nd, 3rd, etc., printings for each edition."
2001 Statement: *See* 1995 Statement

HEATH CRANTON, LTD. (UNITED KINGDOM)
1937 Statement: "In the first edition of books published by us, the year of publication will be found on the Title page or on the back thereof. In the case of a reissue or further edition, we insert on the back of the Title page the year of the original publication with a note of the year when the reissue or further edition first appears."
1947 Statement: *See* 1937 Statement

HEBREW PUBLISHING COMPANY
1976 Statement: "We really have no system for indicating first editions."
1988, 1994 Statements: *See* 1976 Statement

HEBREW UNION COLLEGE PRESS
1994 Statement: "We do not specifically designate first editions."
2000 Statement: *See* 1994 Statement

CHESTER R. HECK, INC.
1947 Statement: "Generally we don't have any identifying marks of first printings unless we definitely indicate on the copyright page 'Second,' 'Third' and the like. On books that have a collector's appeal we would use a symbol of some sort."

W. HEFFER & SONS, LTD. (UNITED KINGDOM)
1928 Statement: "It is our custom to put the date on the title page as part of our imprint. Only in the case of later impressions or editions do we put bibliographical data on the verso of the title page. May we say that although

this is our invariable practice now, we have not been strictly consistent in the past."

1936 Statement: "Our present custom is to put the date of the book and other bibliographical details on the verso of the title page. This is our invariable practice now, although we were not consistent in books published by us before 1930."

1947 Statement: *See* 1936 Statement

HEIDELBERG GRAPHICS

2000 Statement: "Heidelberg Graphics identifies a first edition by stating 'First Edition' on the copyright page. First Edition is meant to indicate the version of the title, namely with a few exceptions, whether it is the original version or has been changed by new or corrected content."

HEIMBURGER HOUSE PUBLISHING CO.

1994 Statement: "First editions will be designated on the copyright page by reading 'First Edition.' "

2000 Statement: *See* 1994 Statement

JAMES H. HEINEMAN INC. PUBLISHER

1994 Statement: "We make no special designation for first printing or first edition. If we go into a second printing we designate on the verso page the number and date of that particular printing."

THE HEINEMANN GROUP (UNITED KINGDOM)

1989 Statement: *See* 1989 Statement of The Octopus Publishing Group PLC (United Kingdom)

W. HEINEMANN, LTD. (UNITED KINGDOM)

(For statement of practice from 1890 through 1989, please see 1989 Statement of The Octopus Publishing Group PLC [United Kingdom])

1928 Statement: *See* 1937 Statement of William Heinemann, Ltd. (United Kingdom)

WILLIAM HEINEMANN (UNITED KINGDOM)

1994 Statement: *See* 1994 Statement of Reed Consumer Books (United Kingdom)

2000 Statement: *See* 2000 Statement of The Random House Group Limited (United Kingdom)

WILLIAM HEINEMANN, LTD. (UNITED KINGDOM)

1937 Statement: "During the early years of the history of this firm there was, I believe, no attempt made specially to designate first editions. The date of publication of a book was usually placed underneath the imprint on the title page. In some cases when further editions or further impressions were issued, the words 'second edition,' 'third edition,' etc., appeared either on the title page or on the fly overleaf, and the absence of such a notice was the only indication of the fact that the book was a first edition. In recent years, however, we have instituted the practice of printing on the back of the title page, or on a fly, a bibliographical note in all the books we publish. That is to say, on the first edition we print 'First published such and such a date' and as each new impression or new edition is called for we add the note 'second impression such and such a date' and so on. We take great pains to get these bibliographical notes accurate and to discriminate carefully between new impressions and new editions. In the event of a book being reprinted without any alterations in the text as it originally appeared, we call the re-issue a new impression. If the text is changed in any way we call it a New Edition.

"We do not follow the American practice of printing the words 'First Edition' anywhere in our books. This I believe is quite a recent idea inspired by the interest taken by the modern American in first editions of modern books.

"I am afraid I cannot tell you the date at which we first began using this present method, but it was certainly soon after 1920."

1947 Statement: *See* 1937 Statement

Statement for 1960: "Our 1976 statement would equally have applied to the situation in 1960 and continues to reflect our current practice. If a book is a first edition it will carry the notice 'First published/First published in Great Britain 19..'

"If it is a reprint or a second or subsequent edition the original notice will be followed by 'Reprinted 19..' or 'Second edition 19..' as appropriate."

1976 Statement: "All our new books carry the line 'First published in 19..' When we reprint the date of the reprint is shown and in this way one can always tell first editions."

1981, 1988 Statements: *See* 1976 Statement

See also 1989 Statement of The Octopus Publishing Croup PLC (United Kingdom)

HEINEMANN NEW ZEALAND (NEW ZEALAND)
1994, 2000 Statements: *See* 1994 Statement of Reed Publishing (NZ) Ltd (New Zealand)

HEINEMANN YOUNG BOOKS (UNITED KINGDOM)
1994 Statement: *See* 1994 Statement of Reed Consumer Books (United Kingdom)

HELICON (UNITED KINGDOM)
2001 Statement: *See* 2001 Statement of Hodder Headline (United Kingdom)

HELLENIC COLLEGE PRESS
2000 Statement: *See* 2000 Statement of Holy Cross Orthodox Press

HELLMAN, WILLIAMS AND COMPANY
1947 Statement: "Herewith, our method of distinguishing between first editions and subsequent printings:

"1. Identification, if any, is on the copyright page.

"2. Actually, we have two 'first' editions. The first edition proper is marked 'First Pre-publication Printing.' This edition may be followed by a second or third pre-publication printing. The 'first' edition after pre-publication printings is unmarked unless the book was originally published in a foreign country, in which case the words 'American Edition' will be found on the copyright page.

"3. Subsequent printings are known as 'Second Edition,' 'Third Edition,' etc."

CHRISTOPHER HELM (UNITED KINGDOM)

1994 Statement: *See* 1994 Statement of A & C Black (Publishers) Limited (United Kingdom)

2000 Statement: *See* 2000 Statement of A & C Black (Publishers) Limited (United Kingdom)

CHRISTOPHER HELM PUBLISHERS LIMITED (UNITED KINGDOM)

1988 Statement: "In answer to your enquiry: we do not have any special way of identifying first editions as such, but subsequent printings are marked thus:

Reprinted, date

Revised edition, date

Second edition, date

and so on.

"We have always adopted this form of designation as far as I can remember."

2000 Statement: *See* 2000 Statement of A & C Black (Publishers) Limited (United Kingdom)

HELM PUBLISHING

1988, 1994 Statements: *See* 1988, 1994 Statements of Padre Productions

HENDRICK-LONG PUBLISHING CO.

1994 Statement: "We do not designate first printings. On second printings, the words 'Second Printing' appear beneath the copyright information. Third printings say 'Third Printing' and so on.

"We have followed this method of designation since our company's inception in 1969.

"We do not have any other imprints or subsidiaries."

2001 Statement: "The [1994 Statement] is still our most common designation. However, some may show the number of printings '5 4 3 2 . . . ' under the copyright."

RAE D. HENKLE CO., INC.

(Established 1927. Became The Henkle-Yewdale House in early 1936.)

1928 Statement: "As to our method of marking first editions, we omit any edition reference on the first printing and on the reverse of the title page note the first, second and other printings in subsequent editions."

THE HENKLE-YEWDALE HOUSE, INC.

(Succeeded Rae D. Henkle Co., Inc, in 1936.
Out of business prior to 1949.)

1937 Statement: "As to our method of marking first editions, we omit any edition reference on the first printing and on the reverse of the title page note the first, second and other printings in subsequent editions. It has been in continuous use since 1928."

IAN HENRY PUBLICATIONS LIMITED
(UNITED KINGDOM)

1994 Statement: "When we do an original we do not even mention that it is a 'first edition,' but merely give the author's copyright declaration, which simply designates a year. When reprinting, the formula is: First published by Mayflower Books, 1970/Library edition published by Ian Henry Publications, 1975/Reprinted 1993."

2000 Statement: *See* 1994 Statement

JOSEPH HENRY PRESS

2001 Statement: *See* 2001 Statement of National Academy Press

HER MAJESTY'S STATIONERY OFFICE
(UNITED KINGDOM)

1988 Statement: "Our first editions are distinguishable by the date of publication appearing with the Crown copyright legend, normally on the reverse of the title page. Typical examples are:

i.

© Crown copyright 1984

First published 1984

Second Impressions:

ii.

© Crown copyright 1983

First published 1983

Second impression 1984

iii.

© Crown copyright 1976

First published 1976

Third impression (with amendments) 1981

"Non Crown copyright material published by HMSO may carry a legend similar to the following:

iv.

© Royal Botanic Gardens Kew

First published by HMSO 1984

"Publications in the Parliamentary series do not carry a Crown copyright legend, and publishing history details are usually shown as part of the publisher's imprint, normally at the foot of the title page or, in the case of an Act of Parliament, at the end of the text."

1994 Statement: "Our first editions are distinguishable by the date of publication appearing with the Crown copyright legend, normally on the reverse of the title page. Typical examples are:

i.

© Crown copyright 1992

Applications for reproduction should be made to HMSO

New Impressions:
ii.

© Crown copyright 1993
Applications for reproduction should be made to HMSO
Second impression 1994

iii.

© Crown copyright 1992
Application for reproductions should be made to HMSO
Third impression (with amendments) 1994

"Non Crown copyright material published by HMSO may carry a legend similar to the following:

iv.

© the Board of Trustees of the Royal Botanic Gardens Kew 1992
Applications for reproduction should be made to HMSO

"Publications in the Parliamentary series do not carry a Crown copyright legend, and publishing history details are usually shown as part of the publisher's imprint, normally at the foot of the title page or, in the case of an Act of Parliament, at the end of the text.

"These revisions to practice came into effect in December 1992."

HERA
2000 Statement: *See* 2000 Statement of Soho Press Inc.

HERALD PRESS
1976 Statement: "The first edition of a Herald Press book carries only the standard copyright notice.

"Herald Press reprints always carry an additional line indicating the current printing and the date of the reprint.

"I believe we have followed this pattern consistently over the years."

1981 Statement: "The first edition of Herald Press books includes the year beneath the publisher's imprint on the title page:

HERALD PRESS
Scottdale, Pennsylvania
Kitchener, Ontario
1981

The date is deleted on subsequent printings.

"Information on reprints always appears under the copyright notice. Until about 1978 this was written out (Third Printing, 1977). Then for several years we often used a code 10 9 8 7 6 5 4, with the last number to the right indicating the printing involved (in the example, Fourth Printing). However, this code did not include information on the year of the reprint.

"Beginning in 1980 we refined the code so that the number at the left indicates the year of the reprint and the one at the right which reprint is involved. For example, 81, 82, 83, 84, 85, 10, 9, 8, 7, 6, 5 indicates Fifth Printing, 1981. Numbers can be deleted from either end of the code in the above example to identify any combination of years and printings through Tenth Printing, 1985, without needing to set new type."

1993 Statement: *See* 1981 Statement, but note that the first printing of a Herald Press book no longer carries the year beneath the publisher's imprint on the title page.
2000 Statement: *See* 1993 Statement

HERALD PUBLISHING HOUSE
1988 Statement: "We use a code on the copyright page which shows the year each edition was printed."
1994, 2000 Statements: *See* 1988 Statement

THE HERBERT PRESS (UNITED KINGDOM)
2000 Statement: "The entry statement [the 1988 Statement of The Herbert Press Limited (United Kingdom)] is fine except 'Limited' must be removed from the Herbert Press name. The Herbert Press is now an imprint of A&C Black (Publishers). Our address remains the same."
See A&C Black (Publishers) Limited (United Kingdom)

THE HERBERT PRESS LIMITED (UNITED KINGDOM)
1988 Statement: "The first printing of the first edition of one of our books is indicated on the title-verso page with the words 'First published in Great Britain [date] by The Herbert Press Ltd.' Subsequent reprintings are shown by the word 'Reprinted' and the date. The company has followed this style since its first book was published in 1975.
"We have no imprints or subsidiaries."
1994 Statement: *See* 1988 Statement
2000 Statement: *See* 2000 Statement of The Herbert Press (United Kingdom)

HERCULES PUBLISHERS
1994 Statement: *See* 1994 Statement of Publishers Associates

HERDER AND HERDER
1988 Statement: *See* 1988 Statement of Crossroad/Continuum

HERITAGE BOOKS, INC.
(Maryland)
2001 Statement: "We do not identify a first printing or any printing after the first printing on the copyright page. Heritage Books, Inc. has never identified the order of printings, but we do identify revised editions."

HERITAGE FOUNDATION
2001 Statement: "We do not identify a first printing; we do identify subsequent printings as such on the copyright page."

HERITAGE HOUSE
2000 Statement: "Sorry, we do not identify first editions or first printings in any special manner."

HERITAGE PRESS (UNITED KINGDOM)

2001 Statement: "First editions and first printings are not identified. Later printings are usually revised and so have more than one copyright date, usually on the last page, but no other identification."

HERITAGE PRESS/WISCONSIN

1995 Statement: "Edition numbers in all our books are noted on the copyright page as first, third, etc."

JOHN HERITAGE, PUBLISHER (UNITED KINGDOM)
(Incorporated with Unicorn Press, Ltd.)

1937 Statement: *See* Unicorn Press (United Kingdom)

HERMAN PUBLISHING, INC.

1976 Statement: "We're too new to have any single established method of identification. However, a second printing is *usually* identified as such on the copyright page."

1981 Statement: "*Newer* titles use this method to identify printings of an edition: for instance, '10 9 8 7 6 5 4' would indicate 4th printing."

HERMITAGE

1988 Statement: "When we reprint a book we indicate that it is the second or whatever printing. On the first edition we say nothing. In other words, if a book does not refer to any particular printing, you might rightly assume that it is in the first printing of the first edition."

1993, 2000 Statements: *See* 1988 Statement

THE HERMITAGE BOOKSHOP

1995 Statement: "At this time we do not plan later printings of our publications. Should we ever do new editions or printings, they will be so stated on the copyright page."

2001 Statement: *See* 1995 Statement

HERON PRESS

2000 Statement: "Heron Press makes no special statement to indicate a first printing; however subsequent printings or editions are so noted."

HEYDAY BOOKS

1994 Statement: "In truth, we have not been as careful as we should be about differentiating our various printings and impressions. Since about 1980 we have tended to use a count-down line, 10, 9, 8, 7, 6, 5, 4, 3, 2, 1, doing the obvious—dropping a number each time we reprint. Before that we tended simply to print onto the copyright page things like 'second edition,' or some other designation. But in truth I'm not sure that we have been conscientious about this."

2000 Statement: *See* 1994 Statement

HIGGINSON BOOK CO

2001 Statement: "We do not identify a first printing or any printing after the first printing on the copyright page. We print on demand."

HIGH-LONESOME BOOKS
1994 Statement: "Edition number stated on copyright page."

HIGH MOUNTAIN PRESS
1994 Statement: "At present, High Mountain Press, Inc. has two book publishing imprints: OnWord Press and InWord Press. Both imprints follow the same practice which is as follows:

"High Mountain Press does not cite a first edition on the cover, in the front matter, or in body.

"In 1990 High Mountain Press adopted the commonly used printing impression numbering system, i.e., a sequence of numbers beginning with 9 or 10 on the left and descending to 1 on the right. The number furthest to the right in this sequence identifies the printing impression of the copy in question."

HIGH PLAINS PRESS
1994 Statement: "At High Plains Press, we have not been officially designating printings. Often times small changes are made by which print runs could be distinguished, and we'd be glad to help collectors identify those."
2000 Statement: "Since 1995, we have designated printings with a numbered print code on the copyright page. Usually the first printing also has the words 'first printing'. We also print limited editions which are signed & numbered."

HIGH PLAINS PUBLISHING CO, INC.
1994 Statement: First editions and first printings are not identified.

HIGH TIDE PRESS
2000 Statement: "Our first editions are identified as first printings on the copyright page of each book. Later editions are also identified in that manner."

HIGHWAY BOOK SHOP (CANADA)
1976 Statement: "We have very short press runs & no exciting system for designating first editions. Most of our books are of regional and local interest."

ADAM HILGER LTD. (UNITED KINGDOM)
1976 Statement: "The first edition of an Adam Hilger book is identified as such by its very omission of all identifying statements. The second edition is marked 'Second Edition' and so on for all later editions."
1981, 1988 Statements: *See* 1976 Statement
1994, 2000 Statements: *See* IOP Publishing Ltd. (United Kingdom)

LAWRENCE HILL & CO. PUBLISHERS, INC.
1976 Statement: "Lawrence Hill & Company books contain on the copyright page of each title the phrase 'first edition.' It is followed by the month and year of publication."
1981 Statement: "Subsequent editions are indicated by a number system." The system employed is a line of numbers from 1 through 10, with deletion beginning at the lowest number.

1988 Statement: *See* 1981 Statement

LAWRENCE HILL BOOKS
1993 Statement: *See* 1988 Statement of Lawrence Hill & Co. Publishers, Inc.
2000 Statement: *See* 2000 Statement of Chicago Review Press

HILL & WANG
1981 Statement: "At Hill and Wang, which is a division of Farrar, Straus, and Giroux, we try to identify our first editions by stating on the copyright page 'first edition.' We also include a line that stipulates First printing (with date). For the purposes of the collector, the first printing of the first edition is the book to be sought after.

"In subsequent printings of the first edition, we usually, but not always, include a line that indicates it is the second printing, with the date. But unless the text has been changed, the second printing is identical with the first printing.

"When an author revises a book and we reissue it, we of course stipulate that the book is a revised edition, and this revised edition notice is followed by a printing notice (first, second, third, etc.). For the bibliographer or scholar, the second edition may represent important changes he will want to know about. During the years Hill and Wang has published, we may indeed have varied from this pattern, but what I've described is the general rule."
1988 Statement: "Our 1981 statement regarding first editions still applies."
1993 Statement: *See* 1988 Statement
2000 Statement: "At Hill and Wang, which is a division of Farrar, Straus, and Giroux, we try to identify our first editions by stating on the copyright page 'first edition.' For the purposes of the collector, the first edition with no printing history is the book to be sought after.

"In subsequent printings of the first edition, we include a line that indicates it is the second printing, with the date. But unless the text has been changed, the second printing is identical with the first printing.

"When an author revises a book and we reissue it, we of course stipulate that the book is a revised edition, and this revised edition notice is followed by a printing notice (first, second, third, etc.). For the bibliographer or scholar, the second edition may represent important changes he will want to know about. During the years Hill and Wang has published, we may indeed have varied from this pattern, but what I've described is the general rule."

HILL COUNTRY BOOKS
2000 Statement: "First printing is designated by the following: 'Copyright © 2000 by Hill Country Books.' "

HILL OF CONTENT PUBLISHING (AUSTRALIA)
1994 Statement: "Our imprint page states:
'First published in Australia 1994
by Hill of Content Publishing Co Pty Ltd
86 Bourke Street Melbourne'
and in the case of continuing editions we have

'Reprinted . . . .' "
2000 Statement: *See* 1994 Statement

HILLMAN-CURL, INC.
(Including Arcadia House and William Godwin as additional imprints.
Hillman-Curl was succeeded by Samuel Curl, Inc.)
1937 Statement: "First editions of our publications are distinguished by the lack of any printing notice on the copyright page. Following editions bear the date of the first printing, together with the date of new printing, and which printing it is."

HILLSDALE COLLEGE PRESS
2001 Statement: "We state 'First printing' on the copyright page."

HIMALAYAN INSTITUTE PRESS
2001 Statement: "We state 'First printing' on the copyright page. Until this year, we set a number string on the copyright page. Now, we state 'First printing.' "

THE HISTORIC NEW ORLEANS COLLECTION
1994 Statement: "We identify our books in the following way: First edition, and the number of copies printed."
2000 Statement: *See* 1994 Statement

HISTORICAL COMMEMORATIONS
1994 Statement: *See* 1994 Statement of White Mane Publishing Co., Inc.

HISTORICAL IMAGES
2000 Statement: *See* 2000 Statement of Bright Mountain Books, Inc.

HMSO (UNITED KINGDOM)
See Her Majesty's Stationery Office (United Kingdom)

W.D. HOARD & SONS CO.
1994 Statement: "We have no special method. To distinguish [a first edition] from a previous edition, some titles have 'Second edition' above the copyright notice, on the page following the title page. Others have 'Second edition' directly after the title on the title page."

HOBBY HOUSE PRESS INC.
1995 Statement: "We identify the first printing of a first edition by the following statement: © 1994 'author name.'

"If there are no changes to the second printing it is denoted in this manner below the original copyright: Second Printing 1995.

"If there are changes to the second printing it is denoted in this manner under the original copyright: Revised Edition © 1995."
2000 Statement: *See* 1995 Statement

HODDER & STOUGHTON LIMITED (UNITED KINGDOM)
1928 Statement: "We are unable to help you with regard to our First Editions, as our methods vary with every book."

1937 Statement: *See* 1928 Statement

1947 Statement: "The date of every edition of every book is printed on the reverse of the title-page, where the number of the edition is usually recorded. The words 'First Printed' are usually included on all first editions."

1976 Statement: "Brockhampton Press has now changed its name to Hodder & Stoughton. The information given below was standard for Brockhampton Press and is now used by Hodder & Stoughton.

"With a Hodder & Stoughton original we state: First published in 19... The absence of any second edition information identifies this as a first edition. For subsequent editions we state: First published in 19... Second edition 19...

"For a title that has previously been published elsewhere we always state: Date, Name of original publisher, and original title. Then: This edition first published by Hodder & Stoughton 19.., and subsequently: This edition first published by Hodder & Stoughton 19.., second impression 19..."

1981 Statement: "Our methods of designating First Editions are exactly the same as were printed [in the 1976 Statement] and this is relevant for all our Publishing Divisions."

1988 Statement: "I can confirm that the statement of 1976, confirmed in 1981, is still our current policy."

2001 Statement: *See* 2001 Statement of Hodder Headline (United Kingdom)

HODDER AND STOUGHTON EDUCATION (UNITED KINGDOM)

2001 Statement: *See* 2001 Statement of Hodder Headline (United Kingdom)

HODDER CHILDREN'S BOOKS (UNITED KINGDOM)

2001 Statement: *See* 2001 Statement of Hodder Headline (United Kingdom)

HODDER HEADLINE (UNITED KINGDOM)

2001 Statement: "[This statement incorporates] Hodder and Stoughton, Headline Book Publishing, Hodder Children's Books, Arnold, Hodder and Stoughton Education [and] Helicon. Hodder and Stoughton are now part of the Hodder Headline Group. With any original publication we state: 'First published in 20...' Below this appears a line of numbers '10 9 8 7 6 5 4 3 2 1'; if this list is complete then the book is a first edition. One number is deleted (starting with '1') for each subsequent printing.

"For a title that has previously been published elsewhere we always state: 'Date, Name of original publisher, and original title.' Then: 'This edition first published by H . . . . in 20...' Below which will appear the line of impression numbers as described above."

THE HOFFMAN PRESS

1995 Statement: "We designate first editions with the Copyright date. Subsequent editions are designated 'Second Printing, and the date' but the Copyright date is always the date of the first printing. When subsequent printings have changes requiring a new ISBN number we use the original Copyright date and add the date of the reprint."

2001 Statement: *See* 1995 Statement

THE HOGARTH PRESS (UNITED KINGDOM)

1928 Statement: *See* 1937 Statement

1937 Statement: "In first editions our custom is to have the year of publication on the title page and no other indication. In case of a second impression or edition we print 'Second Impression (or edition)' on the title page with the year of publication and on the back the dates of first and second editions.

"The method as set out has been our method since the beginning of the Press."

1947 Statement: *See* 1937 Statement

1988 Statement: *See* 1988 Statement of Chatto & Windus Ltd (United Kingdom)

HOHM PRESS

2000 Statement: "We do not identify first editions."

HOLIDAY HOUSE, INC.

1947 Statement: "We have had no particular system, consistently followed in the past. We now plan to use the words 'second printing' on the copyright pages, above or below the copyright line, for the next printings (second printings), and to number each subsequent printing."

1976 Statement: "Currently, most of the time, only the first printing has a price on the jacket."

1981 Statement: *See* 1976 Statement

1988 Statement: "Usually 'First Edition' appears on the copyright page of the first printing only of the first edition."

1995, 2000 Statements: *See* 1988 Statement

HOLLIS AND CARTER, LTD. (UNITED KINGDOM)

1947 Statement: "We always put on the verso of the title page, '1st published, 1947. Second Impression,' etc. The last date on this list therefore will tell the book collector which edition or printing he is buying."

HOLLYWOOD FILM ARCHIVE

2001 Statement: "We identify the first printing of a first edition on the copyright page by a number line, the lowest number indicating the printing."

HOLMAN BIBLE PUBLISHERS

1994 Statement: "We do not identify printings."

HOLMES AND MEIER PUBLISHERS, INC.

1976 Statement: "Many of our books are scholarly monographs which, as yet at least, have not been issued in revised second editions. If we were to do so, however, we would identify only editions after the first.

"The first printing of a first edition is distinguished by: carrying no printing or edition number. Subsequent printings would be identified by number—Second Printing, Third Printing, etc."

1993 Statement: *See* 1976 Statement

2000 Statement: *See* 1976 Statement, but note that the practice described in the second paragraph is "not necessarily" always followed.

HOLMES PUBLISHING CO.
1995 Statement: "All our publications are first editions. They are limited to 650 copies or less, and are described as first editions on the limitation leaf in each book."

HENRY HOLT
2000 Statement: *See* 2000 Statement of Henry Holt and Company, LLC.

HENRY HOLT AND COMPANY, INC.
1928 Statement: "We have never had a definite method of indicating a first edition in our books. Ordinarily, under the copyright line, we insert the dates of the printings so that any book which bears a single date is probably a first edition. In some cases, however, where we know there is to be only one printing, no date is inserted. Also, when sheets are imported from Europe, no special notation is made."

1937 Statement: *See* 1928 Statement

1947 Statement: "Prior to 1945 we never used a definite method of indicating a first edition in our books. Up to that time it was our general practice to insert the date of printing under the copyright notice and a book bearing but one date line of printing was usually a first edition. In some cases, however, when we knew that only one printing was to be made, the date line was omitted. Also, no date line appeared in books bound from sheets that had been printed abroad. Since 1945 it has been our custom to insert the words 'first printing,' or similar language, and first editions may be so recognized—with the exception of foreign sheets as mentioned above."

1988 Statement: "Please be advised that we are no longer part of Holt, Rinehart & Winston, but are now an independent trade book publishing company called Henry Holt and Company, Inc. Holt, Rinehart & Winston still does exist, but it is a *different* company that produces textbooks rather than trade books.

"We signify our first editions with a line stating 'First Edition' on the copyright page and a reprint code that shows numbers 10 to 1. If it is the first printing of the first edition, all 10 numbers appear. If the book is the second printing of a first edition the line 'First Edition' is deleted and so is the number 1, leaving the last in the number code as 2, or second printing. The same is done for subsequent printings.

"There was a time when we left on the words 'First Edition' but also ran a line stating 'Second printing' with the month and year, but found the above to be more efficient."

2000 Statement: *See* 2000 Statement of Henry Holt and Company, LLC

HENRY HOLT AND COMPANY, LLC
2000 Statement: "We are now called Henry Holt and Company, LLC.

"We signify our first editions with a line on the copyright page stating 'First Edition' followed by the year of publication (e.g., 'First Edition 2000') and a printing line showing the numbers 1 to 10. The lowest number in the line indicates the printing of the book. If it is the first printing of the first edition, all ten numbers appear; in the second printing, the number 2 will be the lowest in the printing line. For printings beyond the tenth, numbers are added, dependent upon the anticipated number of future printings (e.g., '11, 12, 13, 14'). They, too, are deleted with each additional printing.

"The words 'First Edition' continue to appear throughout subsequent printings, until such time (if ever) as a second or revised edition is produced (usually with updated or additional material)."

HOLT, RINEHART AND WINSTON

1976 Statement: "We signify our first editions with a line stating 'First Edition' on the copyright page and a reprint code that shows numbers 10 to 1. If it is the first printing of the first edition, all 10 numbers appear. If the book is the second printing of a first edition the line 'First Edition' is deleted and so is the number 1, leaving the last in the number code as 2, or second printing. The same is done for subsequent printings.

"There was a time when we left on the words 'First Edition' but also ran a line stating 'Second printing' with the month and year, but found the above to be more efficient."

1993 Statement: "First editions are not identified as such except in the print code that appears on the copyright page. The print code is divided into three parts, and the first seven numbers to the left identify the printing. On the first printing, the print code starts with 1. On the second printing, the 1 is deleted, and the print code begins with the number 2. The same is done for subsequent printings."

2000 Statement: *See* 1993 Statement

HOLY CROSS ORTHODOX PRESS

2000 Statement: "We have no specific method of identifying the first printing."

HOLYOAKE BOOKS (UNITED KINGDOM)

1994 Statement: *See* 1994 Statement of Co-Operative Union Ltd (United Kingdom)

2001 Statement: *See* 2001 Statement of Co-Operative Union (United Kingdom)

HOME & VAN THAL, LTD.

1947 Statement: "As far as we are concerned we strictly adhere to what I have always understood to be the correct bibliographical details, viz. that an impression is simply a reprint of the first edition without any textual alterations. A second edition would be a revision of the text of the first edition."

HOMESTEAD PUBLISHING

1995 Statement: "At Homestead Publishing we designate guide book first editions with no special designation. Subsequent editions are indicated as revised editions with a list of all previous copyright dates. The first date reflecting its first appearance.

"Most fiction and art books are designated on the copyright page as 'First Edition.'

"Other publications, including nonfiction, are either designated as 'First Edition' or we designate the first printing by number on the copyright page. We list the numbers from left to right, with 1 being the first printing or first edition."

2000 Statement: "Our first editions are still marked as previously noted. However, we have added an new logo. In addition to a walking moose, in 1999 we introduced a moose splashing through water. This appears on the title page or spine of some editions."

ALAN C. HOOD & COMPANY, INC.

2000 Statement: "We identify the first printing of a first edition by the following number line: 10 9 8 7 6 5 4 3 2 1."

HOOVER INSTITUTION PRESS

1976 Statement: "Our Press does not have a particular method of identifying first editions. Subsequent editions of a book are identified by the entry on the copyright page as second edition, third edition, etc."

1981 Statement: "First editions are not identified as such. Subsequent editions are identified by entries on the title and copyright pages.

"First printings carry only our standard copyright notice.

"Second printings would be marked 'Second Printing, (date).' "

1988 Statement: "The Hoover Institution Press has not changed its designation of first editions since your guide was published in 1984. We have no subsidiaries or special imprints."

1993 Statement: "Editions other than the first would be specifically indicated on the title and copyright pages.

"To discern the first printing of the first edition, refer to the printing indicator line on the copyright page, which contains successive years grouped on the left and a range of possible printings grouped on the right. The date of the first printing is shown just above the printing indicator line.

"A first printing of the first edition would be as follows:

First printing, 1993

97 96 95 94 93 5 4 3 2 1"

2000 Statement: *See* 1993 Statement

HOPE PUBLISHING COMPANY

1995 Statement: "We are publishers of music and books about music and to date have had no particular way of designating first printings. Our book *Church Music and the Christian Faith* is our only publication that indicates which printing it is on the back of the title page. This year we are adopting the policy of indicating First Printing, with the month and year, on the back of the title page."

HOPE PUBLISHING HOUSE

1994 Statement: "Although we have not always been consistent in the past, we are currently implementing a system that adds a line to the copyright page that states: 'Second printing (year), (revised, updated, etc. [when applicable]).'

"We are also considering using the numbering system that is becoming the vernacular, i.e. 1 2 3 4 5 6 7 8 9 0 and deleting the appropriate number for the various reprints. This system will probably be used for our late fall books, since our early fall books are already being printed."

2000 Statement: "First editions bear no printing or editing notices. Subsequent editions state, 'second printing . . . ' or 'second edition.' "

MARTIN HOPKINSON, LTD. (UNITED KINGDOM)
(Out of business prior to 1949; publications taken over by John Lane [United Kingdom].)

1928 Statement: *See* 1937 Statement

1937 Statement: "Our practice is to put the date of publication on the title page. When a reprint takes place we place on the back of the title page the usual bibliographical information 'First Printed' with date—and date of reprint.

"If material alterations are made in the text or format we should call the reprint a new edition.

"We have followed our present practice since 1928."

HORIZON
2000 Statement: *See* 2000 Statement of Horizon Books

HORIZON BOOKS
2000 Statement: "We identify the first printing of a first edition by 00 01 02 03 04   5 4 3 2 1. Where the last number on the left (in this case '00') indicates the year of printing (in this case, 2000) and the last number on the right indicates the printing, ('1') would be a First Edition." Horizon Books is located in Camp Hill, PA, but previously (over 10 years ago) in Beaverlodge, Alberta, Canada. It is a division of Christian Publications, Inc.

HORIZON PRESS PUBLISHERS
1976 Statement: "We do not designate first editions."
1981 Statement: *See* 1976 Statement

HORIZON SCIENTIFIC PRESS (UNITED KINGDOM)
2001 Statement: "We do not identify a first printing; we do identify subsequent printings on the copyright page."

THE HORN BOOK, INC.
("The Horn Book Magazine was founded in 1924 by Bertha Mahony who ran The Bookshop for Boys and Girls for The Women's Educational and Industrial Union in Boston. The Union published the magazine until 1936 when the Bookshop was closed and Bertha Mahony founded The Horn Book, Inc. which published The Horn Book Magazine from then on and still does.")

1947 Statement: "We follow the plan of making a statement on one of the back fly leaves of our books, such as that given here, to note our first editions:
ILLUSTRATORS OF CHILDREN'S BOOKS
This book issued in a first edition of 5,000 copies, etc.

"Such a note together with the year of publication on the title page gives the necessary data.

"On the third edition of *Books, Children and Men* we have given on the back fly leaf publication dates, size of editions for each printing.

"On our books, too, we always give all typographical information and wish all other publishers would do so."

Statement for 1960: All printings and editions after the first are so designated. A first printing, first edition will have no identifying notice. There are no imprints.

1976, 1982, 1988 Statements: *See* Statement for 1960

HORWITZ GRAHAME BOOKS PTY LTD. (AUSTRALIA)

1981 Statement: "In response to your inquiry, we do not usually indicate the first edition of trade books and paperback novels as 'First Edition.' However, when we reprint the books we always give the publishing history, e.g., 'First published . . . .This edition . . . .'

"In our Educational books, since these are likely to be reprinted over a number of years, we usually do have symbols at the foot of the imprint page giving the year of first publication. As each edition is reprinted the early symbols are dropped so that at any time we can always see at a glance which edition it is."

1989 Statement: *See* 1981 Statement

HOT PEPPER PRESS

1994 Statement: "We do not consider subsequent printings as anything but a delayed press run unless the copy is revised, corrected, or there is some other substantial change. Subsequent editions will be identified."

HOUGHTON MIFFLIN AUSTRALIA PTY LTD (AUSTRALIA)

1989 Statement: "J. M. Dent Pty Ltd (commonly known as Dent Australia) was purchased by Houghton Mifflin Company of Boston in October 1988 and is a subsidiary of that company, under the name of Houghton Mifflin Australia. J. M. Dent & Sons is now an imprint of Weidenfeld and Nicolson in the UK and no longer exists as an independent company.

"Practice at Dent Australia was to indicate first editions and first printings by noting 'First Published . . . .' Houghton Mifflin Australia will continue this practice. Subsequent printings are indicated by the words 'Reprinted . . '

"New or revised editions will be shown as such on the imprint page, and there may be a banner or notice on the title page and/or cover also. New editions of our own titles will normally be numbered (e.g. second edition). Titles originally published by another publisher and reissued in the same or a new edition by Houghton Mifflin Australia will have the publishing history set out on the imprint page."

HOUGHTON MIFFLIN COMPANY

1928 Statement: "It is our general custom to place the date on the title page of the first edition of all of our books and to drop this date on all subsequent editions. Perhaps we have not invariably followed this custom, but it is our intention to do so.

"The copyright page after the first printing sometimes bears the legend 'second impression,' 'third impression,' 'fourth impression' etc. This, however, is not the general practice.

"There are very likely instances where the date has not been removed from the title, after the printing of the first edition and therefore it would not be an infallible rule to look for a date on the title page, but you may be sure that if the date is omitted it is not a first edition."

1937 Statement: "We endeavor to make a clear distinction between 'edition' and 'printing.'

"It is our general custom to place the date on the title page of the first printing of all of our books and to drop this date on all subsequent printings. There have been cases when for special reasons this rule has not been followed, but the custom so far as this House is concerned is almost invariable.

"When a new edition—meaning a revision on which new copyright is taken—is printed, the same procedure is followed: that is, the date appears on the first printing of the new edition and is omitted from the second and subsequent printings.

"The copyright page after the first printing sometimes bears the legend 'second impression,' 'third impression,' 'fourth impression,' etc. This, however, is not the general practice.

"There are very likely instances where the date has not been removed from the title, after the first printing, and therefore it would not be an infallible rule to look for a date on the title page, but you may be sure that if the date is omitted, it is not a first edition.

"We are sorry that we can't tell you just when the custom of omitting the date from the title page of later impressions of the book was instituted. It was a good many years ago. Our best impression is that it was about 1891."

1947 Statement: *See* 1937 Statement

1976 Statement: "Please let me define two words first: 'edition' and 'printing' In times past a book was set in type every time it was printed and the type was redistributed after the printing was complete. This meant that each printing was a new edition and there could be variations caused by error from the typesetter or alterations made in the text by the author or publisher. Therefore, a first edition could often be different from subsequent editions. Most modern publishers now print from permanent plates which are photographed or cast in plastic or metal, or from electronic files, so the content of the book should be identical from printing to printing without change. A new edition of a book in present day terminology, must contain at least 6% new material if it is to be registered with the copyright office and have the words 'revised edition' or 'second edition' printed on the title page. Of course there can be limited editions or paperbound editions in which the only difference is the style of binding and possibly an author's signature or some other added item like special illustrations.

"On our fiction, all of our title pages have the year of publication in Arabic numerals on the first printing only. This is removed for all subsequent printings. Occasionally a printer fails to remove this number in spite of our instructions so that it does appear in about one title out of two years' publications on the second printing.

"On the copyright page we place a line on every book which has the digits 10 9 8 7 6 5 4 3 2 1 and the last number is removed for every subsequent printing. There is a code letter after these words which indicates which of our manufacturers (we have several) has produced the book, as we return faulty books to the manufacturer for credit. From time to time we change manufacturers so we need to know where a particular book is made.

"If we are publishing the novels of an author who has published other books earlier with another publisher and we release the earlier work, our title page and copyright page would indicate that this was a reissue but we would start out with first printing for our publication."

1981 Statement: *See* 1976 Statement
1988 Statement: *See* 1988 Statement of Ticknor & Fields
1993 Statement: *See* 1993 Statement of Clarion Books
2000 Statement: *See* 2000 Statement of Clarion Books

HOURGLASS
2000 Statement: *See* 2000 Statement of Baker Book House

HOUSE OF ANANSI PRESS LIMITED (CANADA)
1976 Statement: "I'm sorry to say that we never specifically identify first editions or first printings of books. So it's only when the book goes into a second printing that you can tell for sure.

"We usually include a line on the back of the title page, toward the bottom, which is changed with succeeding printings. The line usually takes the form:
2 3 4 5 6 78 77 76 75 74
"If our third printing was in 1976, then the line would read:
3 4 5 6 78 77 76
for example. Unfortunately, once or twice we've forgotten to erase the numbers on the plate for a particular printing, so that we will have two printings showing the same numbers.

"We know that this sort of slip is the bane of bibliographers and collectors, but it occasionally happens to us, and, I'm sure, to many other publishers too. With a staff as small as ours, it's all too easy for one small detail to be forgotten.

"Rarely, we have made the indication:
First printing *date*
Second printing *date* etc.
But we try not to do this, as it necessitates a plate change for each printing, and since plates are good for about five printings, this is unnecessary expense."

1981 Statement: "The above is still generally correct, except that our printing line now normally includes the '1' in the sequence 1 2 3 etc. and the year of first printing at the end of the year sequence. I'm not sure when we started doing that. Unfortunately, we still slip occasionally on reprints."

1988 Statement: *See* 1981 Statement

2000 Statement: "Our 1981 statement still applies generally—we use the number sequence but still do mess up now and again."

HOUSE TO HOUSE PUBLICATIONS

2001 Statement: "We do not identify a first printing; we do identify subsequent printings on the copyright page."

HOWARD UNIVERSITY PRESS

1976 Statement: "Our books carry the usual data on the copyright page indicating the date of publication. If we were to reprint a title this would be added to the information already appearing."

1988 Statement: "We do not designate the first printing of a first edition. Therefore, please use our [1976] statement.

"Our books carry the usual data on the copyright page indicating the date of publication. If we were to reprint a title this would be added to the information already appearing."

1993 Statement: "Since 1991 Howard University Press has used a line of figures on the copyright page to designate reprintings. The final number, reading from right to left, designates the printing. For example, when a book is reprinted for the first time, the number '1' from the end of the line is deleted. The final number is '2' which designates the second printing of a book."

HOWE BROTHERS

1988 Statement: "We do not designate a first printing or first edition by any special wording on the copyright page. However, subsequent printings and editions are identified: for example, Second printing 1988.

"The first printing of the first edition, therefore, can be identified by the absence of such a statement. This is the method that we have always used on our Howe Brothers and Westwater Press imprints."

GERALD HOWE, LTD. (UNITED KINGDOM)

(Out of business prior to 1949; publications taken over by John Lane.)

1937 Statement: "In our first editions the top of the title-page verso either contains the statement 'first published' with the date or is left blank, and in subsequent printings the dates of the first edition and of reprints and new editions are given in this place. This has been our practice since 1926 when we began business."

HOWELL BOOK HOUSE

1993 Statement: *See* 1993 Statement of Macmillan, Inc.

HOWELL-NORTH BOOKS

1976 Statement: "We have no special designation, except that subsequent editions (usually subsequent printings) are so stated on reverse of title page—our limited editions (now all O.P.) are so stated."

1988 Statement: *See* 1976 Statement

HOWELL PRESS INC.

1994 Statement: The first printing of a first edition is indicated by the statement "First printing."

2000 Statement: "[From] late 1998 . . . : First edition unless otherwise stated on title/copyright page; first printing if numeral 1 is showing in the sequence 10 9 8 7 6 5 4 3 2 1 on the copyright page."

HOWELL, SOSKIN, PUBLISHERS, INC.

1947 Statement: "Unless books are specifically designated as second or third printings, our editions may be regarded as first editions."

HOWELLS HOUSE

1994 Statement: "All the titles of both our imprints—The Compass Press and Whalesback Books—are first editions and first printings with no special designation as such, but will indicate 'Second (or Revised) edition' or 'Second Printing' and date on the copyright page when appropriate. Our one reprint to date, *The Architectural Heritage of the Piscataqua*, includes a brief history of the book's previous editions and printings in a 'Publisher's Note' at the top of the copyright page, and this format will be continued in any future reprints of titles not originating with us."

2000 Statement: *See* 1994 Statement

HPBOOKS

1995 Statement: *See* 1995 Statement of The Berkley Publishing Group
2000 Statement: *See* 2000 Statement of The Berkley Publishing Group

HUDSON HILLS PRESS, INC.

1988 Statement: "The words 'First Edition' appear as the first line on the copyright page of the first edition/first printing of each of our books. These words are removed from any subsequent printings of the first editions, but no further identification is added specifying which printing it is. Any further editions which incorporate modest corrections are not specifically identified, but any further edition that involves substantial revision is usually identified as a revised edition."

1993, 2000 Statements: *See* 1988 Statement

HUDSON INSTITUTE

2000 Statement: "Hudson Institute does not have a special method for designating a first edition. Mention of 'second edition' or 'second printing' is provided on the copyright page."

B. W. HUEBSCH, INC.
*(Merged in August, 1925 with The Viking Press, to become
The Viking Press Inc.)*
See 1937 Statement of The Viking Press Inc.

HULL UNIVERSITY PRESS (UNITED KINGDOM)

1989 Statement: First editions are not identified in any way. On the title page and on the copyright page, straight reprints are noted as "second printing," "third printing," etc.

If a printing has been revised—but not sufficiently to call it a new edition—it is identified on the title page and copyright page as "Revised First Printing," or whatever applies.

New editions are identified on the title page and copyright page. For example, the copyright page would note new copyright information, i.e., © second edition.

("The name of the Press was changed in 1993 to The University of Hull Press.")

HUMAN KINETICS

1994 Statement: "We use a row of numbers on the copyright page to indicate which printing that copy of the book is from. The first printing will show a row of numbers like this: 10 9 8 7 6 5 4 3 2 1.

"Each time the book is reprinted a number is removed (e.g., 1 is removed for the second printing; a book from the third printing would have numbers 10 through 3 in place; etc).

"It appears we started using this designation at least as early as 1982, but did not do so consistently until about 1985. So books published between 1974 (our first book) and 1985 would show inconsistent use of the reprint numbers. We've used no other system for indicating reprint numbers.

"All of our imprints and subsidiaries follow this practice.

"When we release a book in paperback after a hardcover version has been in print for some time, we will consider the first paper printing a first printing and start over with the removal of numbers for each subsequent printing."
2000 Statement: *See* 1994 Statement

HUMAN RIGHTS WATCH

2001 Statement: "We do not identify a first printing or any printing after the first printing on the copyright page."

HUMANA PRESS INC.

1994 Statement: "Humana Press has started to use the '10 9 8 7 6 5 4 3 2 1' designation on the copyright page. After the first printing, the 1 is dropped, etc. This method was put into effect in 1992; previous to that year, we used no other designation of a first printing other than with the © with the date."

HUMANICS CHILDREN'S HOUSE

1994, 2000 Statements: *See* 1994 Statement of Humanics Publishing Group

HUMANICS LEARNING

1994, 2000 Statements: *See* 1994 Statement of Humanics Publishing Group

HUMANICS PSYCHOLOGICAL TEST CORPS

2000 Statement: *See* 2000 Statement of Humanics Publishing Group

HUMANICS PUBLISHING GROUP

1994 Statement: "A first edition Humanics book is identified simply with the notation 'first printing' along with the year of publication. All imprints of Humanics Publishing Group follow this system."
2000 Statement: *See* 1994 Statement

HUMANICS SYSTEMS

1994 Statement: *See* 1994 Statement of Humanics Publishing Group

HUMANICS TRADE PAPERBACKS
1994 Statement: *See* 1994 Statement of Humanics Publishing Group

HUMANITIES PRESS, INC.
1976 Statement: "We do not stipulate any special designation to indicate that our books are first editions. All subsequent editions carry the notation 'second edition' or any other numbered edition which may be the case."

1981 Statement: "A first printing carries the message 'First published in the USA by Humanities Press Inc.' Subsequent editions would simply read 'Reprinted (year),' and if additional reprints were made they would also read 'Reprinted (year).' "

1988 Statement: *See* 1988 Statement of Humanities Press International, Inc.

HUMANITIES PRESS INTERNATIONAL, INC.
1988 Statement: "First printings read 'First published in the USA by Humanities Press International, Inc.' Subsequent printings read 'Reprinted (year).' New editions and subsequent editions would carry the legend 'Second edition (year).' Subsequent printings of subsequent editions would read 'Reprinted (year)' starting with new numbering for each edition.

"You should also note that this Company changed its name in 1985 [to Humanities Press International, Inc.]."

1993 Statement: *See* 1988 Statement

BRUCE HUMPHRIES, INC.
1937 Statement: "Books published by Bruce Humphries, Inc., if limited editions, contain a colophon giving the details of the edition, and when these books are reissued the colophon is dropped. Other books generally contain no special marking in the first edition, but second printings are almost invariably so marked on the copyright page.

"Bruce Humphries, Inc., took over many, but not all, of the publications of the Four Seas Company in 1930. In books published by the Four Seas Company there was apparently no uniform system for indicating first editions, but generally first editions were not marked, but second printings were so marked on the copyright page."

1947 Statement: *See* 1937 Statement

HUNT & THORPE (UNITED KINGDOM)
2000 Statement: *See* 2000 Statement of The Paternoster Press Ltd. (United Kingdom)

HUNT INSTITUTE FOR BOTANICAL DOCUMENTATION
1995 Statement: A first printing is not identified.

2001 Statement: *See* 1995 Statement

SUSAN HUNTER PUBLISHING
2000 Statement: *See* 2000 Statement of Cherokee Publishing Co

HUNTER HOUSE INC., PUBLISHERS
2001 Statement: "We identify the first printing of a first edition by stating the edition and by setting a number string to indicate what number reprint."

HUNTER PUBLISHING INC

2001 Statement: "We do not identify a first printing; we do identify subsequent printings on the copyright page."

HENRY E. HUNTINGTON LIBRARY AND ART GALLERY

1947 Statement: "We do not identify the first printings of our books. A second printing is called either 'second printing' or 'second impression.' If there are revisions it is called 'second edition,' 'third edition,' etc.

"The books published by the Friends of the Huntington Library as souvenirs for the members, and some of which we have for sale, have a note to the effect that 'This edition consists of 1000 copies specially printed for the Friends of the Huntington Library. This copy is No....' and the copies which go to Friends are numbered by hand; those for sale are not numbered.

"The Library published books beginning in 1929 in cooperation with the Harvard University Press; since 1936 it has published its own books."

Statement for 1960: *See* 1976 Statement of Huntington Library Publications

HUNTINGTON LIBRARY PRESS

1993, 2000 Statements: *See* 1981 Statement of Huntington Library Publications

HUNTINGTON LIBRARY PUBLICATIONS

1976 Statement: "We do not have any specific way of indicating first editions, except on the copyright page. Actually, although a number of our titles have gone through several printings, it is seldom that we bring out a book in a new edition.

"We do not indicate the number of a printing until it is second or more, at which time we give the date of the first printing, and that of, say, the fourth printing."

1981 Statement: "First editions are not indicated as such. Subsequent editions are identified by printing the number and date on the copyright page. Additional printings of an edition are so labelled."

1988, 2000 Statements: *See* 1981 Statement

HUNTINGTON PRESS PUBLISHING

2001 Statement: "We do not identify a first printing; we do identify subsequent printings as such on the copyright page."

HURST & BLACKETT (UNITED KINGDOM)

1928, 1937 Statements: *See* 1928, 1937 Statements of Hutchinson & Co., Ltd. (Publishers) (United Kingdom)

HURTIG PUBLISHERS (CANADA)

1976 Statement: We have no method of designating a first edition. Only those printings and/or editions after the first are designated. These methods of designation do not differ from any previously used.

2000 Statement: *See* 2000 Statement of McClelland & Stewart Ltd. (Canada)

HUTCHINSON (UNITED KINGDOM)

1988 Statement: *See* 1988 Statement of Century Hutchinson Publishing Group Limited (United Kingdom)
1994 Statement: *See* 1994 Statement of Random House UK Limited (United Kingdom)
2000 Statement: *See* 2000 Statement of The Random House Group Limited (United Kingdom)

HUTCHINSON & CO., LTD. (PUBLISHERS) (UNITED KINGDOM)

1928 Statement: "We do not mark First Editions in any way. This may be taken to apply also to those firms which have amalgamated with Messrs. Hutchinson."
1937 Statement: *See* 1928 Statement

HUTCHINSON CHILDREN'S BOOKS (UNITED KINGDOM)

1988 Statement: *See* 1988 Statement of Century Hutchinson Publishing Group Limited (United Kingdom)
1994 Statement: *See* 1944 Statement of Random House UK Limited (United Kingdom)
2000 Statement: *See* 2000 Statement of The Random House Group Limited (United Kingdom)

HUTCHINSON PUBLISHING GROUP LTD. (UNITED KINGDOM)

1976 Statement: "We indicate the time of first publication on the fourth page of the prelims of a book with the statement: First published month year (i.e. December 1976)."
1981 Statement: "On checking through books published before 1976 it seems that Hutchinson has never included the month in the relevant statement.

"The normal form is: 'First published year (i.e. 1976)'

"However, we sometimes include 'in Great Britain' in the statement, thus: 'First published in Great Britain year (i.e. 1976)'

"This implies that the book has been published somewhere other than in Great Britain in a different year. However, if the overseas edition and our edition are published in the same year, then we use the first version. The edition in question could either be an entirely reset version, or offset from (usually) the US or sometimes the Australian edition with new prelims prepared here, or it could be bought in from the overseas publisher with our prelims substituted in the country of origin. Unfortunately, it is not obvious from the prelims how the book has been produced, although one could probably distinguish an offset or bought-in edition by looking at the text (points of house style, etc.).

"So far as I know all our imprints use this form, certainly those of the General Books division."
1988 Statement: *See* 1988 Statement of Century Hutchinson Publishing Group Limited (United Kingdom)

HYDRA BOOKS/NORTHWESTERN UNIVERSITY PRESS
1995, 2000 Statements: *See* 1995 Statement of Northwestern University Press

HYPERION BOOKS FOR CHILDREN
1993, 2000 Statements: *See* 1993 Statement of Disney Publishing

HYPERION PAPERBACKS FOR CHILDREN
1993, 2000 Statements: *See* 1993 Statement of Disney Publishing

THE HYPERION PRESS, INC.
1947 Statement: "In all our books we indicate on the colophon page the date of our first publication. In case of re-prints, we indicate also the date of the re-prints."
1988, 1994 Statements: *See* 1947 Statement

I

IBBETSON ST. PRESS
2000 Statement: "First printing is indicated on the copyright page. If nothing is written, then assume it is a first edition."

IBEX PUBLISHERS
2000 Statement: "Unless indicated on the copyright page, it is a first edition. The printing is indicated by the 1 2 3 4 5 6 7 8 9 numbers on the copyright page."
This method has been used since 1979.

ICA PUBLISHING
2000 Statement: "We do not specifically identify printings."

ICARUS PRESS, INC.
1981 Statement: "Quite frankly, we have a rather mixed-up way of so designating them. We state nothing at all on the first edition, but we always designate a second printing or second edition on the copyright page.

"I am thinking of using a system of markings on the bottom of the page—below our CIP Date—which would designate printing number and year— i.e.
84 83 82 81 9 8 7 6 5 4 3 2
"Then we could merely opaque out the indicated year and number upon a new printing. But we haven't yet instituted this."
1988 Statement: Icarus Press is now out of business.

ICARUS PRESS
(Baltimore, Maryland. Formerly Icarus Books.)
2000 Statement: "Our first editions are marked by the fact that the copyright page bears no printing or editions notice."

ICON EDITIONS
1993 Statement: *See* 1993 Statement of HarperCollins Publishers

ICONOGRAFIX INC

2000 Statement: "We identify the first printing of a first edition by the use of the copyright line, e.g., © 2000 name of author, and 00 01 02 03 04 05 06 5 4 3 2 1, then we would delete numbers for 2nd printing."

IDE HOUSE INC.

1994 Statement: The first printing of a first edition is indicated by the statement "This is the First Edition of this book."

IDE HOUSE PUBLISHERS

1994 Statement: *See* 1994 Statement of Publishers Associates

IDEALS CHILDRENS BOOKS

2000 Statement: *See* 2000 Statement of Hambleton-Hill Publishing, Inc.

IDOL (UNITED KINGDOM)

2000 Statement: *See* 2000 Statement of Virgin Publishing Ltd (United Kingdom)

IEEE COMPUTER SOCIETY PRESS

1995 Statement: "First printings of first editions carry no special identifier; subsequent editions, revisions are noted as such."
2000 Statement: *See* 1995 Statement

IEEE PRESS

1994 Statement: "We do not designate a first edition of the book in any specific way. Reprintings are identified using the 10 9 8 . . . line, where '1' is deleted for the first reprinting, '2' is deleted for the second reprinting, etc. This practice has always remained the same."
2000 Statement: *See* 1994 Statement

IGI PUBLICATIONS

1994 Statement: "Our first printings are identified by a small number one next to the last page number of the book. This number does not appear in subsequent printings."

IGNATIUS PRESS

1994 Statement: "We do not have a special method of identifying first editions. Exact reprints are not indicated in any way, but a changed edition would be indicated: Second edition 1995.

"If the book was previously published, for example in England, we give that information as the 'original edition' and may then say: 'Published in 1992 by Ignatius Press.' "
2000 Statement: *See* 1994 Statement, but note: "Exact reprints of our books are not indicated in any way, but a changed edition would be indicated: e.g., 'Second edition 1995, or Revised edition 2000."

IGNITE! ENTERTAINMENT

2000 Statement: " 'First Edition' appears on the copyright page."

ILLINI BOOKS
2000 Statement: *See* 2000 Statement of The University of Illinois Press

ILLINOIS STATE MUSEUM
2001 Statement: "We do not identify a first printing or any printing after the first printing on the copyright page."

ILLINOIS STATE MUSEUM SOCIETY
2001 Statement: *See* 2001 Statement of Illinois State Museum

ILLUMINA BOOKS
2001 Statement: *See* 2001 Statement of Avalon Publishing Group Incorporated

ILLUMINATED WAY PUBLISHING, INC.
1994 Statement: "First printings are not specifically marked; date of printing is determined by the copyright date. The second printing will have 'Second printing—1994' on the copyright page. Subsequent printings will replace 'Second printing—1994' with the next ordinal and current year (Third printing—1995).

"The first printing of a second edition will have 'Second edition—1994'; the second printing of the second edition will have 'Second edition—1994' and 'Second printing—1995.' Subsequent printings of the second edition keep the 'Second edition—1994' and the ordinal and date of the printing is updated as with first edition printings."

ILO (SWITZERLAND)
See International Labour Office (Switzerland)

ILR PRESS
1994 Statement: The first printing of a first edition is indicated by the number line 5 4 3 2 1. The lowest number showing indicates the printing.
2000 Statement: *See* 2000 Statement of Cornell University Press

IMAGES AUSTRALIA PTY LTD. (AUSTRALIA)
1995 Statement: "We have no particular way of designating first printings. Obviously second or revised printings will be so noted (all of our books are first editions at present)."

THE IMAGES PUBLISHING GROUP PTY LTD (AUSTRALIA)
1995, 2000 Statements: *See* 1995 Statement of Images Australia Pty Ltd. (Australia)

THE IMAGINARY PRESS
2000 Statement: "The words 'First Edition' followed by the year appear on the bottom line of the copyright page."

IMAGO MUNDI
2000 Statement: *See* 2000 Statement of David R. Godine, Publisher, Inc.

IMMEL PUBLISHING LTD (UNITED KINGDOM)
2001 Statement: "We do not identify first printings; we do identify subsequent printings as such on the copyright page."

IMPACT PUBLISHERS
1994 Statement: "We do not make any distinction for a first printing. For second and subsequent printings, a line is inserted under the copyright line, replaced with each printing. If a second edition is done the date of the first edition is listed, along with the date of the second edition, and the number of printing for the second edition.

"I believe this method has been in effect since the inception of our company in 1970."

2000 Statement: *See* 1994 Statement

IMPRINT (AUSTRALIA)
1988 Statement: *See* 1988 Statement of William Collins Pty Ltd (Australia)

IN BETWEEN BOOKS
2000 Statement: "At this time all our books are first printing, with the exception of 'The Doorway' by Karla Andersdatter. The second edition says: 'Second Printing: January, 1991' on the copyright page."

IN PRINT PUBLISHING LTD (UNITED KINGDOM)
1994 Statement: "The imprint pages of all our books say 'First published in 19__ by In Print Publishing Ltd, 9 Beaufort Terrace, Brighton BN2 2SU, UK. Tel: (0273) 682836. Fax: (0273) 620958.' "

INDEPENDENCE PRESS
1976 Statement: "Any books that we think will be in production through more than one printing we identify on the copyright page with the system used by many publishers. It is made up of two lines of numbers. One line is numbered one through six or seven. The second line is a listing of the next seven or eight years (the last two numbers of each year). With each new printing we erase from our offset press the appropriate number so that the first number in the first row represents the present edition and the first number in the second row represents the year of its printing.

"Sometimes this varies a bit. All numbers may be placed in one row, the edition identification on the left hand side and the year on the right hand side, numbering from gutter toward the center of the page. Then numbers are erased from each end to secure the proper identification of edition and year of printing."

1981, 1988 Statements: *See* 1976 Statement

INDEPENDENCE PRESS
(Missouri)
2000 Statement: *See* 2000 Statement of Herald Publishing House

INDIANA HISTORICAL SOCIETY
1994 Statement: "The Indiana Historical Society does not designate a first edition in its books. We distinguish a first edition from subsequent editions

or reprintings by stating so on the back of the title page. We would say either 2d edition, or Reprinted 1977 for example. This method of identification does not differ from past practice."

2000 Statement: *See* 1994 Statement

INDIANA UNIVERSITY PRESS

1976 Statement: "Our only definition of editions is essentially a negative one: there is no marking on the copyright or title page indicating whether it is a first or second edition. However, if we ever issue second editions of any book, we announce that fact in the book."

A first printing of a first edition may be distinguished from later printings of the same edition by the fact that later printings are indicated on the copyright page as second printing, etc.

1981, 1988, 1995, 2000 Statements: *See* 1976 Statement

INDUSTRIAL PRESS INC.

1994 Statement: The first printing of a first edition is indicated by the number line 10 9 8 7 6 5 4 3 2 1 and the statement "First Edition." Or, the statement "First Edition, First Printing" is used.

2000 Statement: *See* 1994 Statement

INFERNO PRESS

See Exile Press

THE INFO DEVEL PRESS

1994 Statement: "The first printing of a first edition is indicated by First edition: [month, year].

"Thereafter, we print the printing history and a numbered 'countdown.' This has been our standard method since founding in 1988."

2000 Statement: *See* 1994 Statement

INFORM, INC.

1994 Statement: "We have no identification for a first printing; however, subsequent printings contain the line 'second printing,' 'third printing,' etc."

2000 Statement: *See* 1994 Statement

INKATA PRESS

2000 Statement: *See* 2000 Statement of Butterworth-Heinemann

INKATA PRESS (UNITED KINGDOM)

2000 Statement: *See* 2000 Statement of Butterworth-Heinemann

INNER TRADITIONS INTERNATIONAL, LTD.

1988 Statement: "We began using a rub-out line in 1978, or earlier, and now use this device consistently to indicate the edition of a book. Earlier books may say 'First edition,' or nothing except the copyright date, for first edition.

"However, subsequent editions will always say '2nd edition,' '3rd printing,' or have rub-out."

1993, 2000 Statements: *See* 1988 Statement

INNERCHOICE PUBLISHING
2000 Statement: *See* 2000 Statement of Jalmar Press

INNERER KLANG PRESS
2001 Statement: "We state 'First edition' on the copyright page. We seldom reprint editions . . . but generally print the words 'first edition' on the copyright page."

INSIGHT BOOKS (UNITED KINGDOM)
See 2001 Statement of Kluwer Academic/Plenum Publishing (United Kingdom) *and* 1994 Statement of Plenum Publishing Corporation

INSTITUTE FOR HISTORICAL REVIEW
2000 Statement: *See* 2000 Statement of The Noontide Press

INSTITUTE FOR PALESTINE STUDIES
1994 Statement: "Nothing distinguishes a first edition. Subsequent editions state 'second edition' or 'third edition' on the copyright page."
2001 Statement: "Nothing distinguishes a first edition. Subsequent editions state 'reprint edition' or 'third edition' on the copyright page."

INSTITUTE FOR THE STUDY OF MAN, INC.
2000 Statement: "We do not specifically identify first printings—only subsequent editions."

INSTITUTE OF ECONOMIC AFFAIRS (UNITED KINGDOM)
2001 Statement: "We do not identify a first printing; we do identify subsequent printings as such on the copyright page."

INSTITUTE OF EDUCATION (UNITED KINGDOM)
1994 Statement: "Our system for designating a first edition when I was Publication Officer at the Institute was as follows.
  "On the Imprint Page we printed the following statement:
    First published in (year of publication) by the Institute of Education, University of London, 20 Bedford Way, London WC1H 0AL.
    Reprinted (year/s of reprinting)
    Revised edition (year)
  "We adopted this practice in 1980.
  "We did not print the date of publication on the title page, just the name of the publisher, after the title and the author's or editor's name."

THE INSTITUTE OF IRISH STUDIES, QUEEN'S UNIVERSITY BELFAST (UNITED KINGDOM)
2001 Statement: "Our policy is to use the words 'First published' followed by the year, on the copyright page but I am afraid that we have not always been consistent in the past and some books merely say 'Published in' followed by the year. A further edition would always state 'First published . . . ' and then 'Reprinted . . . .' We have no subsidiaries."

THE INSTITUTE OF JESUIT SOURCES

1994 Statement: "Only recently have we begun to put the designation, 'first edition,' into our books. We have, however, regularly noted what 'printing' a particular book might have along with the year of that printing, e.g. 'third printing, 1986.'

"Both the recently begun notation, 'first edition,' and the designation we have used for a long time, such as 'second printing' etc. are both placed on the page on the back of the title page. It also contains copyright and Library of Congress information."

2000 Statement: *See* 1994 Statement

INSTITUTE OF MEDIAEVAL MUSIC RESEARCH

2000 Statement: "Our designations are always given in the German language. From among our approximately 200 titles, it is rare for us to bring out a new edition or even reprint an out-of-print book. In only four cases have we ever reprinted an out-of-print book. In three cases it was not designated at all; in one case we gave the designation of 'second expanded edition.' "
(Statement translated from the German)

THE INSTITUTE OF MIND AND BEHAVIOUR

2000 Statement: "We do not identify first printing, but only subsequent printings, and when this is the case, such appears underneath ISBN."

INSTITUTE OF PHYSICS PUBLISHING
(UNITED KINGDOM)

1994 Statement: *See* IOP Publishing Ltd. (United Kingdom)

INSTITUTE OF PSYCHOLOGICAL RESEARCH, INC.
(CANADA)

1995 Statement: "We have no particular way to designate first editions. However, revised editions are indicated so."

2000 Statement: *See* 1995 Statement

INSTITUTION OF CHEMICAL ENGINEERS
(UNITED KINGDOM)

1994 Statement: "We do not use a special designation for first printings of first editions, but subsequent printings record on the back of the title page that the book has been reprinted."

2000 Statement: *See* 1994 Statement

INSTITUTION OF CIVIL ENGINEERS
(UNITED KINGDOM)

1994, 2001 Statements: *See* 1994 Statement of Thomas Telford Publications (United Kingdom)

THE INSTITUTION OF ELECTRICAL ENGINEERS
(UNITED KINGDOM)

1994 Statement: "Our current publishing practice does not employ any special method of identifying first editions. However, first editions can be identified as all subsequent editions, reprints or new impressions carry additional wording. First editions simply carry the standard words 'Published by the Institution of Electrical Engineers . . . ' preceding the (dated) copyright statement on the reverse of the title page. Any subsequent printing, impression or new edition will be designated as such by additional wording together with a date (e.g. Reprinted 1994).

"This practice appears to have been standard within the Institution since 1978, and applies equally to our imprint Peter Peregrinus Ltd. Prior to that time, when in fact the majority of books were published under the Peter Peregrinus Ltd imprint, the additional words 'First published in XXXX' also appear, immediately preceding the copyright statement, on first printings. The most recent example of this style that I can find is a 1977 publication."

2000 Statement: *See* 1994 Statement

INTELLECT (UNITED KINGDOM)
1994 Statement: "First editions of Intellect books are always marked on the copyright page as:

First published in 19XX by

Intellect Books

Suite 2, 108/110 London Road, Oxford OX3 9AW

"Since beginning to publish in 1985 Intellect has always marked their books and journals in the same way. The only instances where it has been varied has been when a co-publication agreement has been entered into with another publisher for foreign or hard cover editions. In these cases the statement would read 'First published in Great Britain by . . . ' or 'First published in paperback by . . . .' "

2000 Statement: "First editions always identify place of publication, binding, year of publication and publisher address in the following way: First published in (Great Britain) in (Hardback/Paperback) in (2000) by Intellect Books, PO Box 862, Bristol BS99 1DE, UK."

INTER-AMERICAN DEVELOPMENT BANK
2001 Statement: "We do not identify a first printing; we do identify subsequent printings on the copyright page."

INTERALIA/DESIGN BOOKS
2000 Statement: "We designate the first edition as follows:

Benson, Robert A.: Essays on Architecture in the Midwest (1992):

'First Edition published 1992' and '95 94 93 92 5 4 3 2 1' (on copyright page)

Brown-Manrique, Gerardo (editor): O.M. Ungers A Comprehensive Bibliography 1953 to 1995 (1996):

'©1996 by INTERALIA/Design Books'

Bess, Philip: Inland Architecture: Subterranean Essays on Moral Order and Formal Order in Chicago (2000):

'©2000 by Philip Bess and Interalia/Design Books'

"We are not yet in the situation where we reissue titles or issue revisions to titles."

INTERCULTURE ASSOCIATES
1976 Statement: "We do nothing to identify first editions."

INTERLINK BOOKS
2001 Statement: *See* 2001 Statement of Interlink Publishing Group Inc

INTERLINK PUBLISHING GROUP INC
2001 Statement: "We identify the first printing of a first edition by a number line, the lowest number indicating the printing."

INTERMEDIA PRESS (CANADA)
1976 Statement: "Our current process is to include on the back of the title page the number of the edition, i.e.

'Printed in a limited edition of 1000 copies
of which 950 are paperbound and 50 are
hardbound and signed by the author.'

"If we do a second edition we print on the back of the title page i.e.

First edition, 1975
Second edition, 1978.

1981 Statement: "Our policy is still essentially the same."

INTERNATIONAL ARTS AND SCIENCES PRESS, INC.
1976 Statement: "In response to your query about identifying first editions, it is not the practice of this house to do so. We have recently begun, however, to identify second printings with that phrase appearing on the copyright page.

"If the bibliographic history of the work is complicated, a revision for republication, it is usually made clear either in the author's introduction or on the copyright page."

INTERNATIONAL BEE RESEARCH ASSOCIATION (UNITED KINGDOM)
1994 Statement: "IBRA has no special format for indicating first editions. The last book we published has 'First edition' on the title-verso page, but this is not usual. The title-verso is where we usually put the cataloguing information and we would normally say something like 'First published 1962. Reprinted 1994' in any *subsequent* editions."
2000 Statement: *See* 1994 Statement

INTERNATIONAL CHESS ENTERPRISES
2000 Statement: "We identify the first printing of a first edition by 'First Printing; (then a date).' "

INTERNATIONAL DESIGN LIBRARY
2000 Statement: *See* 2000 Statement of Stemmer House Publishers Inc.

INTERNATIONAL INFORMATION ASSOCIATES, INC.
1994 Statement: "First printings are designated using the words Current Printing (last digit): 10 9 8 7 6 5 4 3 2 1 on the bottom of the copyright page. We delete the right hand number for each subsequent printing.

"This method was adopted in 1988, the year of publication of our first book, and has not changed."

INTERNATIONAL JEWELRY PUBLICATIONS

2000 Statement: "The first editions of International Jewelry Publications are marked by the fact that the copyright page bears no printing or edition notices, whereas in subsequent printings the new printings and editions are indicated below the copyright notice."

INTERNATIONAL LABOUR OFFICE (SWITZERLAND)

1994 Statement: "The ILO practice is to print the publishing history on the back of the title page (copyright page) e.g. 'First published 1994' (or whatever year is applicable). In case of a reprint, is added e.g. 'Second impression 1994' (or whatever impression and year is applicable). For new editions, we give the year of the first edition and add e.g. 'Second edition 1994' and, if a reprint of the second edition, we add 'Second impression 1994' (or whatever impression and year is applicable)."

2001 Statement: *See* 1994 Statement

INTERNATIONAL PUBLISHERS CO., INC.

1988 Statement: "We designate all new titles (on the verso of the title page) as

> '1st printing, 19—'

and continue to number each printing (we number the printings up to 12 or 13, after which sometimes we simply enter 'this printing, 19—').

"A new edition (content of a book has been added to or altered in some way) [is designated] as

> '2nd edition, 1st printing, 19—'

and thereafter as '2nd edition, 2nd printing,' etc., unless there is a 3rd edition."

1993, 2000 Statements: *See* 1988 Statement

INTERNATIONAL RESOURCES

1988, 1994 Statements: *See* 1988, 1994 Statements of Padre Productions

INTERNATIONAL SELF-COUNSEL PRESS LTD

1994 Statement: *See* 1994 Statement of Self Counsel Press Inc.

INTERNATIONAL UNIVERSITIES PRESS, INC.

1976 Statement: "Unless otherwise stated on the copyright page, the first date of copyright is the date of the first edition.

"A first printing of a first edition may be distinguished from later printings of the same edition by the fact that it either says 'first printing' or nothing at all. Subsequent printings are marked 'second printing,' etc."

1981, 1988, 1993, 2000 Statements: *See* 1976 Statement

INTERNATIONAL UNIVERSITY LINE (IUL)

2000 Statement: "We identify the first printing of a first edition by the number line 10 9 8 7 6 5 4 3 2 1. If you look at the first number on the right you will know which printing you have in hand."

INTERURBAN PRESS

1994 Statement: "Interurban Press has not used a consistent method for identifying the first printings of first editions over the years. Often, these books contain no specific information relating to edition or printing, whereas later editions or printings will have these specifically stated on the masthead page.

"In some cases, the wording 'First Printing (date)' is used to identify the first printing of the first edition. Later printings of books so designated include their printing number, date, and, if applicable, their edition number as well."

INTER-VARSITY PRESS (UNITED KINGDOM)

1976 Statement: "Our usual practice is simply to state 'First Edition October 1976.' On reprints we usually omit the month, giving just the year date, 'Reprinted 1977, 1979.' "

1981 Statement: "We have indeed changed our method of designating the first printing of a first edition since we corresponded with you in 1976. The change took effect from May 1978, when we dropped the inclusion of the month of publication.

"Our current practice is simply to state: First published 1980 with reprints also giving just the year date: Reprinted 1981."

1994 Statement: *See* 1981 Statement

2000 Statement: "Our current imprints are Inter-Varsity Press, Apollos, and Crossway, though we have a few titles still in print under our (discontinued) Frameworks imprint; all these follow our practice as stated in [the 1981 statement].

"I should perhaps add that there are some exceptions to normal practice: books imported from US publishers, where we follow their style, and joint imprints, where some adjustments may be needed on an ad hoc basis."

INTERWEAVE PRESS

2001 Statement: "We state 'First edition' and 'First printing' on the copyright page."

THE INTREPID TRAVELER

2000 Statement: "The words 'First Edition' are printed on the copyright page. To the best of my knowledge, [this method] was adopted in 1990, with our first title."

INWORD PRESS

1994 Statement: *See* 1994 Statement of High Mountain Press

IONE PRESS

2000 Statement: "We identify the first printing of a first edition with the words 'First Edition' [and] the following number line: 5 4 3 2 1."

IOP PUBLISHING LTD. (UNITED KINGDOM)

1994 Statement: "The copyright line given on the title verso pages of our books denotes the year of publication. Details of subsequent impressions, editions, etc, are given in the printing history of each title, which is again contained on the title verso page of the book. If no printing history is listed then this signifies that the edition in question is the first edition/first impression.

"The printing history will also give details of editions previously published by a company other than ours."

2000 Statement: *See* 1994 Statement

(Adam Hilger and Institute of Physics were former imprints of IOP Publishing, Ltd.)

THE IOWA STATE COLLEGE PRESS
(Formerly Collegiate Press Inc.)

1947 Statement: "When we publish a first edition, we merely list the date of publication and date of copyright in the copyright notice.

"When the book is reprinted with little or no revision, we may or may not specify that it is a 'second printing.'

"When the book is revised sufficiently that it can be called a new edition, we label it 'Second edition,' or 'Third edition,' etc."

IOWA STATE UNIVERSITY PRESS

1976 Statement: "The only identification of first edition that we make for our books is the identification 'First edition, date' that appears on the verso (copyright page) of the title page. I believe this method of identification does not differ from that always previously used by this press."

The first printing of a first edition is indicated by the fact that it does not carry the designation "Second printing, date."

1981, 1988, 1995 Statement: *See* 1976 Statement

2000 Statement: *See* 1976 Statement. *See also* 2000 Statement of Blackwell Science Ltd (United Kingdom)

I.P.A.C.S. LTD. (CANADA)

1995 Statement: "Example (A) indicates the number published in a particular month and year. In this case it is the first and only edition to date:

2M — January 1983

"Example (B) shows four printing dates and the numbers issued with each; the top line is the first edition, the fourth line is the fourth edition. It should be noted that subsequent editions of some titles are expanded from the originals run:

5C — June 1967
5C — July 1970
2M — December 1984
4M — December 1991."

IPD ENTERPRISES LTD (UNITED KINGDOM)

1994 Statement: "It has been our habit for the last ten years to designate the first printing of a title as follows:

First published in 1994
© (Author or the Institute) 1994

"For reprints the lines read:

First published in 1994
Reprinted 1994
© (Author or Institute) 1994."
2001 Statement: *See* 2001 Statement of Chartered Institute of Personnel and Development (United Kingdom). The name was changed to Chartered Institute of Personnel and Development, or CIPD, in July 2000.

IRANBOOKS INC.
1994 Statement: "First or subsequent editions are designated as such. First printings are not indicated, but subsequent ones are."
This method does not differ from any previously used.
2001 Statement: *See* 1994 Statement

IRANBOOKS PRESS
2000 Statement: *See* 2000 Statement of Ibex Publishers

IRIS I O PUBLISHING
1988 Statement: *See* 1988 Statement of Strawberry Hill Press

IRISH ACADEMIC PRESS, LIMITED
(REPUBLIC OF IRELAND)
1981 Statement: "We don't formally designate the first printing of a first edition. We usually just say on the title verso:
This book was printed in the
Republic of Ireland by [name of printer]
for Irish Academic Press Limited,
Kill Lane, Blackrock, County Dublin
© [author] 1981 (This is the only indication of date).
"It is only later printings that carry any sort of printing history e.g.
First edition May 1981
Second impression July 1981
Second edition January 1982."
1988 Statement: *See* 1981 Statement
1994 Statement: "The following applies: 'This book was typeset in . . . by . . . and first published in 19... by Irish Academic Press, Kill Lane, Blackrock, County Dublin, Ireland, and in the US of A by Irish Academic Press at International Specialized Book Services, Portland, Oregon.'

"If rights of an edition have been sold, this will be acknowledged: 'Published in America by . . . ' etc., but the Irish edition will always be the first. We always publish ahead of foreign editions to reinforce this practice.

"As a rule, we do not print the date of publication on the title page. Copyright is acknowledged (© author's name 19...) while subsequent editions are acknowledged by their relevant impression.

"Translations: we give the title of the original and if possible, the place of publication and name of publisher."

IRON GATE PUBLISHING
2001 Statement: "We identify the first printing of a first edition by a number line on the copyright page, the lowest number indicates the printing."

IRONBARK (AUSTRALIA)

1994 Statement: *See* 1994 Statement of Pan Macmillan Australia (Australia)

IRONWEED PRESS

2000 Statement: "Our first editions are distinguished by the absence of printing or edition notices on the copyright page."

THE ISLAMIC FOUNDATION (UNITED KINGDOM)

1994 Statement: "We do not designate any method of identifying a first edition. On page two at the top of the page we list © which stands for copyright: The Islamic Foundation 1992/1412 A.H. This has been used since 1978.

"When we reprint a book, we repeat the above line added to this 'Reprinted 1993' for example."

2000 Statement: *See* 1994 Statement

ISLAND PRESS

1994 Statement: "The way we've designated first printings of first editions since 1984 is as follows:

Manufactured in the United States of America

10 9 8 7 6 5 4 3 2 1

"The numbers 1-10 represent the number of printings. The last number in the list is the number of the printing. Because there is a '1' in this list, the book is in its first printing. Each time the book is reprinted, the last number is dropped from the list.

"Yes, our imprints and subsidiaries follow our practices."

2000 Statement: *See* 1994 Statement

ISLAND PRESS (AUSTRALIA)

1988 Statement: "All bibliographical information is given on the back of the title page. [This method was] adopted in 1970 [and there has been] no change. The imprints and subsidiaries follow this practice."

1994 Statement: *See* 1988 Statement

ISLAND PRESS COOPERATIVE, INC.

1947 Statement: "Island Press Cooperative, Inc., is the same as Island Workshop Press. We merely dropped the Workshop from our name because the name was too long and unwieldy, and we had long ago outgrown the Workshop aspect, and were concentrating primarily on book publishing.

"In regard to first printings, we have no special way of indicating them other than the fact that they carry no printing notice whatsoever. In other words, when we print a second or third edition, this fact is noted on the copyright page, but when we print a first edition, no mention is made to single it out as a first edition. This sounds pretty involved but in practice it is very simple."

ISLAND WORKSHOP PRESS

1947 Statement: *See* 1947 Statement of Island Press Cooperative, Inc.

IT PUBLICATIONS (UNITED KINGDOM)

1994 Statement: "From approximately 1982 . . . we adopted the policy of including the date of publication as part of the imprint on the first printing i.e., 'IT Publications 1994' or 'Intermediate Technology Publication 1994,' and removing the date for subsequent printings. For the first printing the verso of the title page would record the date against the copyright, but there would be no other reference to the date of the first printing. Subsequent impressions would record, on the verso of the title page: 'First printed: 1994' and beneath, for example, 'Reprinted 1995.' Sometimes, now that I notice it, we record the printing history in a single line, thus: 'Reprinted 1990, 1993.' "

2001 Statement: *See* 2001 Statement of ITDG Publishing (United Kingdom)

ITALICA PRESS

1995 Statement: "Italica Press designates first editions by the use of the '5 4 3 2 1' system under the CIP notice. For subsequent editions we state 'Second edition' etc. on the second line of the copyright notice. Some of *our* first editions were actually *second* editions of out-of-copyright works. These we indicated on the copyright page with a 'First published Date/Name of Original Copyright Holder' above our copyright notice.

"Of additional interest to those looking into first editions is the first appearance of our printer's mark, a variant of the Jenson orb-and-cross type, with the orb open at the bottom and 'Italica Press' appearing across the top third inside the orb. This mark appears on the title page, below title and author and above city and publication date. This is lacking on our books published from 1986 into 1987 (appearing first in *Florilegium Columbianum*, now OP). Our printer's mark has been applied consistently since, and has gone through several refinements. It has also begun to appear on second and subsequent printings of our 1986 and 1987 editions.

"We also have consistently used a colophon page, indicating date page composition was completed, typeface, paper stock and printer. This is retained through subsequent printings, changed only for new printers or paper stock."

2000 Statement: *See* 1995 Statement, but note that the first sentence should read: "Italica Press designates the various first printings of first editions by the use of the '5 4 3 2 1' system under the CIP notice."

ITASCA PRESS

1947 Statement: *See* 1947 Statement of The Webb Publishing Company

ITDG PUBLISHING (UNITED KINGDOM)

2001 Statement: "The company [IT Publications] is now trading under the name ITDG Publishing. Our practice has changed slightly since mid-2000. We include the wording 'First printed xxxx' on the first and all subsequent impressions. On a reprint 'Reprinted xxxx' would be inserted beneath this line, with subsequent reprint years added, separated by commas, thus: 'reprinted xxxx, xxxy.' "

ITHACA HOUSE

1976 Statement: "First printings of first editions carry only the copyright notice."

1981 Statement: *See* 1976 Statement

1988 Statement: "Our imprints and subsidiaries follow the practice as outlined in the 1976 Statement for Ithaca House."

IVORY TOWER PUBLISHING CO., INC.

1994 Statement: "We identify first printings by using 0 9 8 7 6 5 4 3 2 1 on the copyright page, deleting each figure upon reprinting."

IVY

2001 Statement: *See* 2001 Statement of The Ballantine Publishing Group

IVY HOUSE PUBLISHING GROUP

2000 Statement: *See* 2000 Statement of Pentland Press, Inc.

J

J & S PUBLISHING CO., INC.

2000 Statement: "We do not have a special method for designating a first edition. The copyright © [date] J & S Publishing Co., Inc. designates both a first edition and a first printing. If subsequent editions or printings are needed, these are identified by the addition of 'Second edition' or 'Second printing' to the copyright notice. A hardback reissued in paper carries in addition to the copyright line the notice: 'Paperback edition, 19...'

"Below is an example of a first edition, first printing copyright notice:

© copyright J & S Publishing Co., Inc.

10 9 8 7 6 5 4 3 2 1

Printed in the United States of America

J & S Publishing Co., Inc."

THE JACARANDA PRESS (AUSTRALIA)

1976 Statement: "It is the policy of the Jacaranda Press to list on the imprint page the date of first publication (which also indicates first edition). Each reprinting is also listed and subsequent editions are noted accordingly. This particular method of identification has been used throughout the history of the Jacaranda Press."

1981 Statement: *See* 1976 Statement

1994 Statement: *See* 1994 Statement of Jacaranda Wiley (Australia)

2000 Statement: *See* 2000 Statement of John Wiley & Sons Australia, Ltd (Australia)

JACARANDA WILEY (AUSTRALIA)

1994 Statement: "Since 1992 Jacaranda Wiley has designated the first edition of a book at the top of the imprint page by the words 'First printed in XXXX by . . . (followed by the appropriate imprint—*John Wiley & Sons* for tertiary titles; *The Jacaranda Press* for school titles).' The numbers 10 9 8 7

6 5 4 3 2 1 at the foot of the imprint page show that the book is a first printing. We delete the last number each time we reprint the book. We indicate second and subsequent editions by the words 'Second Edition published XXXX by . . . ' at the top of the imprint page.''

2000 Statement: *See* 2000 Statement of John Wiley & Sons Australia, Ltd (Australia)

JACKSON HARBOR PRESS

2000 Statement: "Our first editions contain only the copyright date. We identify [printings] either by: 'First printing 1994, Second printing 2000' or 'First printing 1994, Revised Edition 2001.' ''

JACKSON SQUARE PRESS

2000 Statement: *See* 2000 Statement of Pelican Publishing Company

JAHBONE PRESS

2000 Statement: "All Jahbone Press books use 1 2 3 4 5 6 7 8 9 0 on the copyright page to mark the number of the edition. The first number to appear on the left indicates the edition."

JALMAR PRESS

1994 Statement: "10 9 8 7 6 5 4 3 2 1. We delete [the number] 1 for second printing etc."

2000 Statement: *See* 1994 Statement

JAMES & JAMES (PUBLISHERS) LTD. (UNITED KINGDOM)

1994 Statement: "The first printing is designated by the line:

© [copyright owner] [date]

First published [date].

"This method was adopted in 1981."

2000 Statement: *See* 1994 Statement

JAMESON BOOKS, INC.

1988 Statement: To designate a first edition the words First Edition are used on the copyright page. The first printing of an edition is indicated as follows on the copyright page:

76 77 78   10 9 8 7 6 5 4 3 2 1

The second printing is indicated like this:

76 77 78   10 9 8 7 6 5 4 3 2

The numbers before 10 indicate years.

1993 Statement: The first printing of an edition is indicated as follows on the copyright page:

76 77 78   10 9 8 7 6 5 4 3 2 1

The second printing is indicated like this:

76 77 78   10 9 8 7 6 5 4 3 2

The numbers before 10 indicate years.

JANE'S INFORMATION GROUP
1995 Statement: " 'First Edition' is noted on the title page. No other designation is used."
2000 Statement: *See* 1995 Statement

JANUS LIBRARY
2000 Statement: *See* 2000 Statement of Abaris Books, Inc.

JANUS PRESS
(West Burke, Vermont)
1981 Statement: "Copyright is same year as publication year." This system of designation does not differ from any previously used.

JAPAN LIBRARY (UNITED KINGDOM)
2001 Statement: *See* 2001 Statement of Curzon Press Ltd (United Kingdom)

THE JARGON SOCIETY, INC.
1981 Statement: "The books of the *Jargon Society* do not designate first printing or first edition, simply because the books are all first editions and we do not re-print. The only exception has been The *Appalachian Photographs of Doris Ulmann* (#50 in the series) which had nary a poem in it to scare away the post-literate."
1988 Statement: "The books of The *Jargon Society* do not designate first printing or first edition, simply because the books are all first editions and we do not reprint. Two exceptions to this rule are *The Appalachian Photographs of Doris Ulmann* which was reprinted once and *White Trash Cooking*. The latter, with 400,000 copies now in print, was printed in a First Printing of 5,000 copies, but the First Printing is not so marked because a second printing seemed unimaginable. After 100 titles of 2,500 or less copies, we are glad to have been wrong once."

JARROLDS PUBLISHERS (LONDON), LTD.
(UNITED KINGDOM)
1937 Statement: "In the case of first editions of all our non-fiction books, the year of issue is placed in roman numerals below our imprint on the title page. There is no reference anywhere else in the book to the fact that it is the first edition. In the event of further reprint(s) being called for, the bibliography is set up on back of title, thus, for example:
> First Published   May 1934
> Second Impression   June 1934
> Third Impression   August 1934

"In the case of fiction, the month and year of first publication in this country are set up at back of title page, thus, for example:
> First Published in Great Britain May 1934

"In the event of subsequent reprint(s) the dates are set forth as in the example for non-fiction given above."
1948 Statement: "It is not our present practice to include dates in our publications. In cases where books are reprinted, we state 'Second impression,' and so on, as appropriate."

JAVELIN BOOKS (UNITED KINGDOM)
1988 Statement: *See* 1988 Statement of Cassell plc (United Kingdom)

JEFFERSON HOUSE
1947 Statement: "First printings of our books carry only the copyright notice, except in a few instances the line 'FIRST PRINTING (month, year)' below the copyright notice.

"All subsequent printings are marked 'SECOND PRINTING, THIRD PRINTING, FOURTH PRINTING,' as the case may be, and any new editions of the book are clearly marked. A distinction should be made between an edition and a printing, an edition always having some material change in either the text or format of the publication."

THOMAS JEFFERSON UNIVERSITY PRESS
1994 Statement: "We have always stated on the copyright page the date of first publication. If there is a second printing or a subsequent edition, it is so stated on that page."
2001 Statement: *See* 2001 Statement of Truman State University Press

JELMAR PUBLISHING CO INC
2000 Statement: "We do not designate first printings or first editions except by the process of elimination. We designate second and subsequent printings by including the statement on the verso page that reads 'second printing.' Second and subsequent editions are designated either as 'revised,' for the first revision, or 'third edition,' for third and similarly for subsequent revisions."

HERBERT JENKINS, LTD. (UNITED KINGDOM)
1928 Statement: *See* 1937 Statement
1937 Statement: "It is now our custom to put the date of our publications on the back of the title page, and if a reprint is called for we show the date of the reprint also on the back of the title page. If, however, we produce a cheap edition of the work we omit the date therefrom.

"We began using our present method about 1924."
1948 Statement: "At present and during the war, owing to existing conditions and the very considerable delays in production, we are omitting the dates of publication from our books and are using the term 'First Printing.' This is a temporary measure only and we hope later to be able to revert to our normal practice which is mentioned in our previous statement."

JEWISH CHRONICLE PUBLICATIONS
(UNITED KINGDOM)
1976 Statement: "We have no particular method of identifying first editions of our books."
1994 Statement: *See* 1976 Statement
2000 Statement: "The Jewish Chronicle is no longer directly involved in book publishing and all former JCP titles are now published and distributed under licence by Vallentine Mitchell."

JEWISH LIGHTS PUBLISHING

1994 Statement: "The first printing of a first edition is identified by the following number line: etc. 5 4 3 2 1."
2000 Statement: *See* 1994 Statement

THE JEWISH PUBLICATION SOCIETY OF AMERICA

1947 Statement: "The first printings of our books contain the year in which the book was published on the title page, and on the copyright page the same information. Subsequent editions carry the year in which the book was reprinted on the copyright page; we state whatever printing it is plus the date."
1976 Statement: A first edition will carry the designation "First Edition" on the copyright page. This method of designation does not differ from any previously used.
1981, 1988, 1994 Statements: *See* 1976 Statement
2000 Statement: "Both the 1947 & 1976 Statements hold true for us today."

JIST WORKS INC

2001 Statement: "We identify the first printing of a first edition on the copyright page by a number line, the lowest number indicating the printing."

JLA PUBLICATIONS

2000 Statement: "We identify all editions and printings at the beginning of each book. A First Edition would be identified as: First Edition, January, 2001. 2nd Printing, March, 2001. Second Edition, January, 2002, etc."

JM PUBLISHERS, INC.

2001 Statement: "We don't identify the first printing of a first edition with any particular statement or line. We identify subsequent printings with the proper designations 'second printing' or 'third printing,' etc."

THE JOHNS HOPKINS PRESS

1937 Statement: "We seldom publish but one edition of the work, endeavoring to estimate the number of copies that will be required for some time in the future. There have been, however, several instances in which another edition was published and these are indicated as a second edition or a second impression. The latter reference is used if no change is made from the original edition."
1947 Statement: "When it is not so stated in the description of the book, it is considered as the first edition or printing. We mention it if a second printing is made."

THE JOHNS HOPKINS UNIVERSITY PRESS

1976 Statement: "First editions are only designated by their copyright date. Subsequent editions are noted accordingly."

"The first printing of the first edition is designated only by the copyright date. Later printings are designated as follows.

      Originally published, date
      Second Printing, date

Third Printing, date
Paperback edition, date."

1982 Statement: "First editions are designated only by copyright date. First printings are not designated separately. Second, third, and subsequent printings are designated by date of manufacture. Revised editions are also designated by copyright date, and subsequent printings of revised editions are designated by date of manufacture. Thus, the printing history of a long-lived book might typically show the following sequence on the copyright page:

Originally published, date
Second printing, date
Third printing, date
Second edition, date
Second printing, date
Paperback edition, date."

1988 Statement: "We have not changed our practice in designating editions for some years. My only question is whether the item 'Second edition, date' is accurate. We would normally indicate a second edition by a new copyright line and make mention of the date of the original edition, but we would not specifically note 'Second edition, date.'"

1993 Statement: "First editions are only designated by their copyright date. Subsequent editions are noted accordingly."

"The first printing of the first edition is designated only by the copyright date. Later printings are designated as follows.

Originally published, date
Second impression, date
Third impression, date
Paperback edition, date."

2000 Statement: "First editions are designated only by new copyright date. They are called First Editions (dated) only at the time a 2nd or revised edition is published. The statement about reprintings remains the same."

JOHNSON BOOKS

1995 Statement: "Designations of printings: numbers 1 through 9. The first number indicates the printing, e.g. for the second printing the 1 is dropped; for the third printing, the 2 is dropped, etc. We began using this method in 1987. Our Spring Creek Press and Cordillera Press imprints use the same method."

2000 Statement: *See* 1995 Statement. Note, however, that the Cordillera Press is no longer in operation.

JOHNSON INSTITUTE

1994 Statement: "We use 6 5 4 3 2 1 on the bottom of the copyright page. With each reprint, we delete the number and, in some cases, the year in which the reprint is done. We do not designate 'first edition' on any of our materials."

CHRISTOPHER JOHNSON PUBLISHERS LIMITED
(UNITED KINGDOM)

1947 Statement: "All bibliographical information is printed on the reverse of the title page. The formula used is: 'First published in 19..' for the first edition, and subsequent impressions and editions are printed below this."

JOHNSON PUBLISHING COMPANY, INC.

1976 Statement: "We have no particular method of identifying first editions other than copyright data for first editions."

1981 Statement: *See* 1976 Statement

1988 Statement: "Designation of printings: numbers 1 through 9. The first number indicates the printing, e.g.. for the second printing, the 1 is dropped; for the third, the 2 is dropped, etc. We began using this method in 1987. Our Spring Creek Press imprint uses the same method."

JONES & BARTLETT PUBLISHERS INC.

1995 Statement: The first printing of a first edition is indicated by the number line 97 96 95 94   10 9 8 7 6 5 4 3 2 1. The lowest number showing indicates the printing.

2000 Statement: *See* 1995 Statement

MARSHALL JONES COMPANY

1928 Statement: "It is our custom to print on the copyright page the date of printing, i.e., Printed April 1927, but we do not always do this. When we reprint we usually put on the date just below the other."

1936 Statement: "Since our practice has changed somewhat since the first edition of your book appeared, I think it would be best to substitute the following:

"We make a practice of giving the date of the second and subsequent printings or editions on the copyright page. In nearly all cases, if the copyright date alone appears, the book is of the first printing. The words FIRST EDITION on the copyright page, although we do not always use them, invariably designate the first printing."

1947 Statement: *See* 1936 Statement

JORDAN PUBLISHING

2001 Statement: *See* 2001 Statement of Evangel Publishing House

JORDAN PUBLISHING LIMITED (UNITED KINGDOM)

1994 Statement: "Subsequent editions are identified as appropriate on the cover and title page. Therefore, if a book is not so identified, it can safely be assumed that it is a first edition."

2000 Statement: *See* 1994 Statement

JORDANS (UNITED KINGDOM)

1994, 2000 Statements: *See* 1994 Statement of Jordan Publishing Limited (United Kingdom)

MICHAEL JOSEPH (AUSTRALIA)

2000 Statement: *See* 2000 Statement of Penguin Books Australia Ltd (Australia)

MICHAEL JOSEPH LTD. (UNITED KINGDOM)

1937 Statement: "It is our custom to print the year of publication of our books on the reverse of the title page.

"If the book is reprinted the arrangement indicated below is followed:

First published May, 1936

Second Impression June, 1936

"The word 'edition' is only used in the event of a cheaper reprint or when textual alterations have been effected."

1947 Statement: *See* 1937 Statement

1976 Statement: "Attached is a form of bibliography which appears in all our first editions. We have no other method of identification. If a title is re-printed, the date of the impression is inserted beneath the date of the first edition."

First printings carry the designation "First published in Great Britain by Michael Joseph Ltd. date."

1981, 1988 Statements: *See* 1976 Statement

(In late 1988, the Penguin Group changed its method of designating a first edition. For a book published in the latter part of 1988, see 1988 Statement of Penguin Publishing Co Ltd [United Kingdom].)

1994 Statement: "I am delighted to say that Michael Joseph Ltd, and our subsidiary Pelham Books, as well as the Mermaid Books imprint, continue to follow the designation 'First published in Great Britain by Michael Joseph Ltd date.' We do not follow the system used by the rest of the Penguin Group."

2001 Statement: *See* 2001 Statement of Penguin Publishing Co Ltd (United Kingdom)

JOSSEY-BASS INC, PUBLISHERS

1993 Statement: *See* 1993 Statement of Macmillan, Inc.

JOURNAL.CA

2000 Statement: *See* 2000 Statement of Townson Publishing Co. Ltd. (Canada)

JOURNEY EDITIONS

2000 Statement: "We identify books as first editions on the copyright page. This is true for Journey Editions, Periplus Editions, and Tuttle Publishing."

THE JOURNEYMAN PRESS, LTD. (UNITED KINGDOM)

1988 Statement: "We designate first editions by printing on the reverse of the title page the following:

'First published by the Journeyman Press Ltd, 19..'

and further down the page

'First edition 19...'

"New impressions are designated by eliminating the last number from the sequence:

    '10 9 8 7 6 5 4 3 2 1 printing'

"Reprints with corrections, or revised editions are specified as they occur, together with the relevant year of printing.

"This method was adopted in 1986, but prior to that we did not identify the first edition separately, and we always noted new impressions as reprints followed by the year of printing (unless of course there were corrections, etc.)."

JOVE

1995 Statement: *See* 1995 Statement of The Berkley Publishing Group
2000 Statement: *See* 2000 Statement of The Berkley Publishing Group

JSA PUBLICATIONS INC.

1994 Statement: "We identify the first printing of a first edition by the following number line: 2 3 4 5 6 7 8 9 0 and by the following statement: 'First Printing' followed by month and year."
2000 Statement: *See* 1994 Statement

JSOT PRESS (UNITED KINGDOM)

2001 Statement: *See* 2001 Statement of Sheffield Academic Press (United Kingdom)

JUDAIC INSIGHTS

2001 Statement: *See* 2001 Statement of JM Publishers, Inc.

JUDAICA PRESS INC

2001 Statement: "We do not identify first editions; however, we do identify second editions."

JUDSON PRESS

1976 Statement: "Our first edition is that which bears the original copyright date and no further information about its being a subsequent printing. When we reprint a book, we add the number of the reprinting and the date of the reprinting. If there is any substantial editorial revision, there will be some note made of that as well on the copyright page."
1981, 1988, 1993, 2000 Statements: *See* 1976 Statement

JUGGERNAUT

2000 Statement: "First editions are indicated by the phrase 'First published in (month) (year)' with no other publishing history. We do not employ number lines in our books."

JULY BLUE PRESS

2000 Statement: "We print the words 'First Printing' on the copyright page. Subsequent printings are designated 'Second Printing,' 'Third Printing,' etc. We do not use a number line."

JUNCTION PRESS

2001 Statement: "No indication of first printing. Subsequent printings indicated as '2nd printing,' etc."

JUNIOR ELF

See 1993 Statement of Checkerboard Press, Inc.

JUNIPER PRESS
(LaCrosse, Wisconsin)

1976 Statement: "Juniper Books have the number of the printing indicated on the reverse of each title page. As of this date some are in as many as their 6th printing.

"The William N. Judson series of fine printed books by contemporary American poets are all in first edition, except the first, *Ash is the Candle's Wick*, which is in its second printing. We do all printings after the first by offset from the original letter press books. All first editions are hand set and by letter press. This information may be found on the last page of any book of a later than first edition."

1981 Statement: "There are some changes to be made. The paragraph should read:

"Juniper Books have the number of the printing indicated on the reverse of each title page. As of this date some are in as many as their 6th printing.

"Many of the William N. Judson series of fine printed books by contemporary American poets have gone into the 4th printing. It is best to contact the printer for more information.

"We do all printings after the first by offset from the original letter press books. All first editions are hand set and by letter press. This information may be found on the last page of any book of a later than first edition."

1989 Statement: "Juniper Press of LaCrosse, Wisconsin has four series of books to offer, plus the literary magazine *NORTHEAST*. The *Juniper Books Series* are all first editions, but some have gone through as many as 6 printings. Juniper Books are in offset printing. The *William N. Judson Series* of fine printed books by contemporary American poets are all first editions, and some have gone into 4th printings. These are letterpress printing in the first printing. The *Voyages to the Inland Seas Series* began in 1981 with Juniper Press and publishes larger works of poetry, prose or anthologies. All are first editions and several have gone into 3rd printings and all are offset press printed. The *Haiku-short poem Series* are all first editions and no other printings are made, and most of these are letterpress printed. We have recently begun to use the laser printing techniques and many of our newer books will reflect this in order to bring more quality work to our readers. Please contact the publisher for more information as we begin our 26th year of publication."

1993, 2001 Statements: *See* 1989 Statement

JUNIUS-VAUGHN PRESS

1994 Statement: "Statement adopted in 1975 and remains unchanged. 'First edition. Published in the United States of America.' No further note is made in later impressions. Second and later editions are so noted on copyright page."

K

KABEL PUBLISHERS
1994 Statement: The first printing is not identified.

KALIMAT PRESS
1988 Statement: "Our first editions are identified by the words 'First Edition' printed on the copyright page. This designation is removed from subsequent printings. Sometimes, we have added the designation 'Second Printing,' 'Third Printing,' etc., to subsequent printings.

"Occasionally, we have left off the 'First Edition' designation by accident. Occasionally, a book has been reprinted with 'First Edition' left on the copyright page by accident. In such cases one can only identify the first edition by careful comparison with other books. Typos are always corrected in second printings."

KALMBACH BOOKS
2000 Statement: *See* 2000 Statement of Kalmbach Publishing Company

KALMBACH PUBLISHING COMPANY
1947 Statement: "Most of our books are marked with 'second edition,' 'third edition,' etc. These are on the title page or the page following it when the book is not a first edition. Some books have gone into a second printing without making any such mark; however, the only changes between the first and second printing, if any, would have been minor typographical errors. We would have no way ourselves of knowing which of these were from the first printing without having to go over the book word by word to find where such errors might have been. Most of our books have gone into printings of about 3,000 on the first edition with no additional printing until the second edition of another 3,000 is made."

1976 Statement: "Our firm publishes a line of hardcover books devoted to railroading and a line of softcover how-to-do-it books devoted to hobbies, especially model railroading. We have retained all of our hardcover books in print as they were originally published and have not labeled them 'first edition.' We have never updated them or otherwise done anything to create a 'second edition.' We have done this out of consideration for buyers of an original edition, who would later either find the book they own made obsolete or face a large expenditure for material they already own to gain the small percentage of new material. We do, of course, list the various printings in the book and enter necessary corrections.

"Out of some 23 softcover titles, about 5 or 6 are in a second edition. On the title pages of these books, our usual procedure is to list the various printings by year (sometimes by month if two printings occur within the same year). If a book is in a second edition, we'll then preface the printings by placing FIRST EDITION: before the list or corresponding years and SEC-OND EDITION: before the list of corresponding years.

"In summary, then, note that first editions are never identified as such within the first edition book. Only second editions are identified within the book, at which time the original book 'retroactively' becomes a first edition."

1981 Statement: "In summary, first editions are never identified; only second editions are identified within the book."

1988 Statement: *See* 1981 Statement

2000 Statement: "Only second and subsequent editions are identified within the book."

KANCHENJUNGA PRESS

1976 Statement: "All Kanchenjunga first editions are identified as such on the copyright page. The usual form is an announcement such as, 'This first edition is limited to X copies,' or simply the statement, 'First Edition.' Second or later printings are identified as such and do not carry the 'first edition' designation. Therefore any Kanchenjunga book marked 'first edition' is from the first printing of the first edition. (This information applies to all titles published 1972 through 1976. The fact that we've done it this way in the past doesn't prevent our adopting some other method in the future.)"

1981 Statement: *See* 1976 Statement

KANE/MILLER BOOK PUBLISHERS

1994 Statement: "We use 1 2 3 4 5 6 7 8 9 10. That designation, including the '1' indicates first edition. On subsequent reprintings, we simply eliminate a number, so that, for example, the second printing would be designated by 2 3 4 5 6 7 8 9 10."

2000 Statement: *See* 1994 Statement

KAR-BEN COPIES INC.

1994 Statement: First printings are not identified.

2000 Statement: *See* 1994 Statement

H. KARNAC (BOOKS) LTD (UNITED KINGDOM)

1994 Statement: "We have no particular set method of identifying our first editions. All our books would show on the copyright page the first edition by indicating 'first published by H Karnac (Books) Ltd in 19....' We would then obviously identify subsequent editions or reprints clearly."

KATYDID BOOKS

2000 Statement: "We identify the first printing of a first edition by 'First Edition'; 'Second Printing,' etc. is added from then on."

WILLIAM KAUFMANN, INC.

1981 Statement: "I'm sorry to say we've been somewhat inconsistent in designating first editions. Sometimes we have put the 11 10 9 8 7 6 5 4 3 2 1 sequence of numbers on our copyright pages, removing the digits in ascending order as new printings are done. On the other hand, we have designated some of our 'firsts' as 'Experimental' editions."

1988 Statement: *See* 1981 Statement

KAYAK BOOKS

1976 Statement: "I use no particular sign to designate either a first edition or a first printing. I know this makes it hard on bibliographers but it also encourages them in their detective talents."

1981 Statement: *See* 1976 Statement

KAZI PUBLICATIONS INC

2000 Statement: "We do not differentiate first editions."

KC PUBLICATIONS

1994 Statement: "The first edition designations for books in *The Story Behind the Scenery* series is the fact that there is nothing indicated on the title page. We would designate second and subsequent printings as such.

"On other series that we have developed, principally *in pictures . . . The Continuing Story*, we have marked the first printing from its inception—which is opposite the title page—page 4."

KEATS PUBLISHING, INC.

1994 Statement: "We have no policy of designating first or later printings of our books, though this has sometimes, rarely, been done. New editions may be identified or not, depending on the amount and nature of revisions, sometimes on the cover and title page, sometimes on the copyright page. We have followed this informal practice since the firm's beginning."

AUGUSTUS M. KELLEY, PUBLISHERS

2000 Statement: "We identify the first printing of a first edition by the statement: 'First published XXXX (Year).' "

KELSEY ST. PRESS

1995 Statement: "Kelsey St. Press designates a first edition in one of two ways. In most instances we have a separate colophon page. On this page the copy reads, this book is a limited edition of 'x' number of copies. Or we simply indicate on the copyright page the Copyright date without stipulating first printing. All subsequent printings clearly state second printing, third printing, etc."

2001 Statement: *See* 1995 Statement

CLAUDE KENDALL, INC.
(Out of business prior to 1949.)

1937 Statement: "It is our custom to identify first editions by printing the legend 'First Printing' on the copyright page."

CLAUDE KENDALL & WILLOUGHBY SHARP, INC.
See Claude Kendall, Inc.

KENNEDY BROTHERS
See Yachting

KENNIKAT PRESS CORPORATION

1976 Statement: "Kennikat Press does not designate a First Edition. Subsequent printings may or may not be designated 2nd, 3rd, etc.

"A bonafide second *edition* will no doubt have some sort of designation as such on the title page and will carry a copyright date differing from that of the first edition."

1981 Statement: *See* 1976 Statement

KENSINGTON

1995 Statement: *See* 1995 Statement of Kensington Publishing Corp.

KENSINGTON BOOKS

2000 Statement: *See* 1995 Statement of Kensington Publishing Corp.

KENSINGTON PUBLISHING CORP.

1995 Statement: "We identify the various printings of our books with a notice on the copyright page. For the first printing, the notice reads 'First Printing, month, year.' Subsequent printings state 'Second Printing, month year,' etc.

"When we publish a book first in hardcover and then in paperback, the hardcover edition will state 'First Printing, month, year' and the subsequent paperback edition will state 'First Hardcover Printing, month, year' and 'First Paperback Printing, month, year.' "

2000 Statement:*See* 1995 Statement, but note that "Subsequent printings [are] indicated by last digit on printing line. This method was begun in 1995."

THE KENT STATE UNIVERSITY PRESS

1976 Statement: "The absence of the words 'First Edition,' would indicate a first edition."

1981 Statement: "Second and additional printings are identified. Otherwise, no change."

1988, 1993 Statements: *See* 1981 Statement

2000 Statement: "1976 & 1981 Statements apply for books before 1995. For books published after 1995, printing number is identified by far-right number on line above CIP data, e.g.

02 01 00 99   4 3 2 1

indicates a first edition published in 1999."

KENYON-DEANE LTD. (UNITED KINGDOM)

1994 Statement: *See* 1994 Statement of Cressrelles Publishing Company Ltd. (United Kingdom)

KEOKEE CO. PUBLISHING, INC.

2000 Statement: "We have discontinued publishing proprietary books; however, we may on occasion help authors self-publish. In the past, we have indicated first editions by having a line on the copyright page like this:

10 9 8 7 6 5 4 3 2 1

"If the one is showing, it is the first edition of that book."

MICHAEL KESEND PUBLISHING LTD.
1994 Statement: The first printing of a first edition is indicated by the statement "First Printing (date)."
2000 Statement: *See* 1994 Statement

KEYSTONE BOOKS
1988 Statement: *See* 1988 Statement of The Pennsylvania State University Press

KIDS CAN PRESS (CANADA)
1995 Statement: "We use a reprint line on our copyright page to indicate which printing a specific book is from. A number '1' at the end of the reprint line indicates a first printing.

"For casebound books, the reprint line begins with the last two digits of the year in which the book was produced followed by the numbers: 0 9 8 7 6 5 4 3 2 1. We delete the last number in the reprint line each time a book is reprinted.

"Our casebound titles are often converted to paperback editions and we generate a new print line for these paperback conversions. These reprint lines begin with the notation 'PA,' followed by the last two digits of the year the book was produced followed by 0 9 8 7 . . . as indicated above. (So our paperback conversions would have a different first printing designation and date than our casebound books.) Our books which appear in paperback from the time they are first issued bear our standard reprint line with a year/number notation (no PA is used on these reprint lines).

"This method of designating first and subsequent print runs was begun in 1987. Prior to 1987 there was no method used to designate first printings. This method of indicating which printing our titles have reached is the only method used by Kids Can Press."
2000 Statement: "The information you have indicated [in the 1995 Statement] is still correct with one revision. All of our paperback reprint lines include the PA designation even if we are only printing a paperback edition of that particular title."

KIDSRIGHTS
2001 Statement: *See* 2001 Statement of JIST Works Inc

KILLALY PRESS (CANADA)
1976 Statement: "As my publications are published to further the writing careers of the authors and not to make a profit, there is no thought of a second printing, edition, etc., and consequently the edition is not designated. There never has been any change in policy since we began publishing in 1972.

"All publications contain the following statement:
Publication is limited to 100 copies of which the 1st 15 are signed.
This is copy number...."
1981 Statement: *See* 1976 Statement

KILLICK PRESS (CANADA)
2001 Statement: *See* 2001 Statement of Creative Book Publishing (Canada)

WILLIAM KIMBER & CO. LIMITED (UNITED KINGDOM)
1976 Statement: "Set out below is an actual example of our method of identifying first editions and the same method we have always used. (The book in question is *British Political Crises*.)

First published in 1976 by
WILLIAM KIMBER & CO LIMITED
Godolphin House, 22a Queen Anne's Gate,
London SW1H 9AE
© Sir Dingle Foot, 1976
ISBN 0 7183 0194 3."

1981 Statement: *See* 1976 Statement
1988 Statement: *See* 1976 Statement. Note, however, that the publisher's address will now read 100 Jermyn Street, London, SW1Y 6EE.

KIMMEL PUBLICATIONS
2000 Statement: "To date (2000), the first edition has been the only edition. If and when additional editions are published, it will be so noted on the copyright page."

KINDRED PRODUCTIONS
1995 Statement: "We have no particular way of designating first printings. Subsequent printings are listed at which time the date of the first printing is added."

ALFRED H. KING, INC.
(Acquired by Julian Messner, Inc., prior to 1949.)

THE KING LIBRARY PRESS
2001 Statement: "We designate a first printing by a note on the colophon page. We usually identify a 'first edition' by a note to that effect in the text of the colophon."

KING'S CROWN PRESS
(A Division of Columbia University Press.)
1947 Statement: "The King's Crown Press identifies its first printing by the date at the foot of the title page; on subsequent printings that date is removed and on the title page verso the dates of the various printings are given in chronological order."

KINGSWOOD BOOKS
1988 Statement: *See* 1988 Statement of Abingdon Press

H. C. KINSEY & COMPANY, INC.
(Bought by G. P. Putnam's Sons in 1943.)
1937 Statement: "Our system is very simple—if there is no printing date under the copyright notice then that is the first edition. The second printing is always indicated by a line giving the date and all subsequent editions in the same way:

First Editions—November 1949
Second Edition—December, etc.

"The Mary Pickford books were the only exception to this rule and we included 'First Edition' on the copyright page of the small first order for *Why Not Try God*."

KIPLINGER BOOKS & TAPES
2000 Statement: "We identify the first printing of a first edition by the following statement: 'First edition. Printed in the United States of America' [and by] the number line: 9 8 7 6 5 4 3 2 1."

KITCHEN SINK PRESS INC.
1994 Statement: "All printings, where applicable, in Kitchen Sink Press titles are listed as follows: 'First Printing: Month Year.' We list printing numbers from right to left, with 1 being the first number in the case of a first printing."

KIVAKÍ PRESS
1995 Statement: "Kivakí Press designates a first edition directly on the verso page by stating that the book is a First Edition. We also use the standard numerical designator system to indicate the print run and print year (e.g., 2 3 4 5 6 7 8 9 99 98 97 96) with the appropriate print run and print year deleted from the list."
2001 Statement: *See* 1995 Statement

NEIL A. KJOS MUSIC COMPANY
1994 Statement: "We do not identify first editions and we expect to reprint every publication which we issue. Reprintings are numerous."

KLUWER ACADEMIC/PLENUM PUBLISHERS (UNITED KINGDOM)
2001 Statement: " Since Plenum's takeover by Kluwer Academic Publishers in 1998, we are now known as Kluwer Academic/Plenum Publishers.

"We give no printing designation, and do not identify first editions, only subsequent editions. Books published prior to January 1998 were published under the imprint of Plenum Press, a subsidiary of Plenum Publishing Corporation. Insight Books and Plenum Trade were imprints also used although these imprints were sold to Perseus Books in 1999. We now publish under Kluwer Academic/Plenum Publishers (KA/PP)."
See also 1994 Statement of Plenum Publishing Corporation

ROBERT R. KNAPP, PUBLISHER
1976 Statement: "We label edition on the verso and include printing information for each successive printing."

CHARLES KNIGHT & COMPANY (UNITED KINGDOM)
1976 Statement: "In new books we use the phrase 'First published (date)', and this is how our first editions may be identified. Information about subsequent impressions or editions is listed underneath the original statement and this information is generally to be found on the reverse of the title page of a book . . . . Charles Knight and Company have been publishing books since 1833, and I am fairly certain that it is not possible to generalize about

previous methods. I know from reference to our library shelves that many books are undated. The method I have described dates from 1974. From about 1969 onwards, any editions subsequent to first editions are described as such on our title pages."

1981 Statement: *See* 1976 Statement

CHARLES KNIGHT PUBLISHING (UNITED KINGDOM)

1994 Statement: *See* 1994 Statement of Tolley Publishing Co. Ltd. (United Kingdom)

KNIGHTS PRESS

1988 Statement: "Sorry, but we do not differentiate First Editions."

ALLEN A. KNOLL, PUBLISHERS

1994 Statement: "We do not designate first printings, (except by process of elimination) only first editions. We designate second and subsequent printings by including the statement on the verso page that reads 'second printing, (year).' We adopted this policy in 1992. 'First edition' is always stated on the first printing and remains on subsequent printings. This is the only method we have used to date."

2000 Statement: "We continue to specify first editions with the words 'first edition' on the verso page. Regarding second and subsequent printings, we take off the words 'first edition' and use the *Chicago Manual of Style*'s subsequent printings version. A line of numerals run on the verso page. The first group, reading from right to left, represents the last two digits of succeeding years starting with the date of original publication. The second set of numerals, following a space and also reading from right to left, represents the numbers of possible new impressions. The lowest number in each group indicates the present impression and date. Our printer simply paints out the obsolete numerals in the impression line on the copyright page negative, and what remains shows the correct impression number and date."

ALFRED A. KNOPF

2000 Statement: "We still follow the same practice as stipulated in the 1936 statement [of Alfred A. Knopf, Inc.]. Note, however, that Knopf is no longer 'Inc.,' we are a division of Random House, Inc."

ALFRED A. KNOPF, INC.

1928 Statement: "It is our practice to indicate on the copyright page with a line thus: 'Second Printing, Third Printing,' etc. This note does not appear on the first edition."

1936 Statement: "Up until 2 1/2 or 3 years ago, the first editions of our books bore no note on the copyright page. When a book was reprinted, however, a notice of the printing was added to the copyright page. If a book was reprinted before publication date a note reading 'First and second printings before publication' was added to the copyright page and this indicated that the particular book belonged to the second printing.

"About 2 1/2 or 3 years ago, however, we changed our practice only in the matter of first printings. On the copyright page of any one of our books issued since then we carry the note 'First Edition' or 'First American Edition.' The latter term is used only where the English edition precedes or is simultaneously published with ours."

1947 Statement: "Our present practice is to print on the copyright page of the first printing of any book we publish either the words 'first American edition' or 'first edition.' We use 'first American edition' in the case of a book which has already been published abroad, whether in English or another language."

1976 Statement: "Knopf identifies a book's edition on the copyright page. We do not indicate that a particular work is part of a first printing, but for second or subsequent printings, the information is also carried on the copyright page.

"We have been using these methods of identification for a great many years."

1981 Statement: "We have made no changes in our method of identifying editions and printings on the copyright pages of our books."

1988, 1993 Statements: *See* 1981 Statement
See also 1976 Statement of Random House, Inc.

ALFRED A. KNOPF, INC. (UNITED KINGDOM)
(English house discontinued December 1930.)

1928 Statement: "Our practice of designating our first editions is to place on the verso of the title page the legend 'first published' followed by the month and year. The further impressions are designated by the number of the impression, and further editions by the number of the edition. In both cases the dates are shown."

KNOW, INC.

1976 Statement: "Our first editions are identified as first printings on the copyright page of each book. Later editions are also identified. This is the only identification we have ever used."

1981 Statement: *See* 1976 Statement

JOHN KNOX PRESS

1976 Statement: "We do not have a special method for designating a first edition. The copyright © 1976 John Knox Press designates both a first edition and a first printing. If subsequent editions or printings are needed, these are identified by the addition of 'Second edition' or 'Second printing' to the copyright notice. A hardback reissued in paper carries in addition to the copyright line the notice: 'Paperback edition, 19...' "

1981 Statement: "Below is an example of a first edition, first printing copyright notice:

© copyright John Knox Press 1981
10 9 8 7 6 5 4 3 2 1
Printed in the United States of America
John Knox Press
Atlanta, Georgia 30365

"Any subsequent printings would be acknowledged by the dropping of a number. For example, the second printing would drop the 1, the third, the 2, etc.

"A second edition would be acknowledged on the cover and title page as 'new, revised edition' and on copyright page as 'second edition' under the copyright notice; the numbering would return to original: 10 9 8 7 6 5 4 3 2 1.

"The first paperback of a hardback edition, somewhere, probably after copyright notice, will have a notice to that effect: 'First paperback edition (date).' If the original edition had a different title, there will be a notice to that effect: 'Originally published as (original title).' This will be placed under copyright notice.

"John Knox Press began using the 'drop number' system for reprints in late 1979. The imprints follow the same procedure."

1988 Statement: *See* 1988 Statement of Westminster/John Knox Press

KODAK BOOKS
2000 Statement: *See* 2000 Statement of Silver Pixel Press

KODANSHA INTERNATIONAL/USA, LTD.
1976 Statement: First editions are indicated by the words "First Edition" and the date of publication. The number and date of subsequent printings and editions are indicated.
1988 Statement: *See* 1976 Statement

KODIAK MEDIA GROUP
2000 Statement: "We print each printing on the copyright page. Thus a book that is indicated 'First printing' but not followed by 'second printing' is the first edition."

KONOCTI BOOKS
2001 Statement: "Since our print runs are very small we never have more than one printing."

KOSMIC KURRENTS
1995 Statement: *See* 1995 Statement of Anti-Aging Press

H J KRAMER INC
1994 Statement: "H J Kramer, Inc. indicates printings by numbers on the copyright page as follows:

10 9 8 7 6 5 4 3 2 1

"When we reprint, we delete the 1, 2 or appropriate number. Unless otherwise indicated as a revised edition, all printings are the first edition. We have always used this method."
2000 Statement: *See* 2000 Statement of New World Library

KREGEL CLASSICS
2000 Statement: *See* 2000 Statement of Kregel Publications

KREGEL PUBLICATIONS

1994 Statement: "First editions [are indicated] by the printing/year line on the copyright page as follows:

1 2 3 4 5 printing/year 98 97 96 95 94

"Each subsequent printing will be indicated by the removal of the previous printing number (e.g., '1') and the next printing year being indicated ('97). Therefore, a third printing in the year 1996 would be indicated as such:

3 4 5 6 7 printing/year 00 99 98 97 96."

2000 Statement: *See* 1994 Statement

KRIEGER PUBLISHING CO.

1995 Statement: "We identify the first printing of a first edition by the following number line: 10 9 8 7 6 5 4 3 2. With each print run the lower number is dropped."

A. KROCH AND SON, PUBLISHERS

1947 Statement: "We usually indicate the second edition of our publications under the copyright notice."

KROSHKA BOOKS

2000 Statement: *See* 2000 Statement of Nova Science Publishers, Inc.

KUMARIAN PRESS INC

2001 Statement: "We identify the first printing of a first edition by a number line; the lowest number reflects the printing."

L

LA CASA PRESS

2000 Statement: "We identify the first printing of a first edition by 'First printing, (date)' on copyright page."

LABYRINTH PRESS

2000 Statement: *See* 2000 Statement of Baker Book House

LABYRINTHOS

2000 Statement: "First printings of a first edition are not so identified."

LACIS PUBLICATIONS

1994 Statement: "No special notation on first printing. Subsequent printings would have notation on copyright page such as: Second Printing 1994 or Second Edition (if text changes have been made)."

LADAN RESERVE PRESS

1995 Statement: "Status of edition stated on verso of title page.

1st Edition. Original printing
1st Edition. 2nd printing
1st Edition. 3rd printing, etc.
2nd Edition, ditto."

2001 Statement: *See* 1995 Statement

LADYBIRD (AUSTRALIA)

2000 Statement: *See* 2000 Statement of Penguin Books Australia Ltd (Australia)

LADYBIRD BOOKS LTD. (UNITED KINGDOM)

1976 Statement: There is no method whatsoever of identifying a first edition of a Ladybird book. The year of publication is printed by the side of their name on the title page, but then this same date is repeated in subsequent printings in following years. It serves more to indicate copyright protection than a method to designate a first edition.

1981, 1988 Statements: *See* 1976 Statement

1994 Statement: "We do not designate the first printing of a book at all. The usual practice is to give the copyright date on the facing title page—which gives the year of first publication. If the title is subsequently amended or updated the new edition will state that it is a 'revised edition' or 'this edition (date).' This practice is common throughout our imprints and subsidiaries."

2000 Statement: "We do designate the first printing of a book. The standard practice is to give the copyright date on the facing title page, which gives the year of first publication. In addition we include a reprint number line (usually numbered 1 to 10) and strike off consecutive numbers as we reprint. The lowest number in the line will tell the reader which printing the copy belongs to. Therefore if the line contains the number 1, the copy will be the first edition."

See also 2001 Statement of Puffin Books (United Kingdom)

LADYBUG PRESS

2000 Statement: "LadyBug Press does not have a special method for designating a first edition. If subsequent editions or printings are printed, they are identified by the addition of 'Second edition' or 'Second printing' to the copyright notice."

LAHONTIAN IMAGES

1995 Statement: "The verso/copyright page simply states 'First Edition' and subsequent printings state, Second, Third and so forth. This has been our practice since we published our first book in 1983."

THE LAMPADA PRESS (UNITED KINGDOM)

1994 Statement: *See* 1994 Statement of The University of Hull Press (United Kingdom)

2000 Statement: The Lampada Press closed in 1999.

LAMPLIGHT EDITIONS

2000 Statement: *See* 2000 Statement of Blind Beggar Press, Inc.

LANDMARK EDITIONS

1988 Statement: *See* 1988 Statement of University of Nebraska Press

LANDWASTER BOOKS

2000 Statement: "We identify first printing of a first edition by the following statement: Copyright © 2000 Landwaster Books, Inc.

"Subsequent revised editions have more copyrights on them. Such as: Copyright © 2000, 2001 Landwaster Books, Inc. And if the edition is not revised, then it will say nothing for first edition, then: 'second edition' on the copyright information page and so on."

LANDY PUBLISHING (UNITED KINGDOM)

2001 Statement: "We do not identify a first printing; we do identify subsequent printings; [however,] none of our books have gone to a second printing."

ALLEN LANE (AUSTRALIA)

2000 Statement: *See* 2000 Statement of Penguin Books Australia Ltd (Australia)

ALLEN LANE (UNITED KINGDOM)

2001 Statement: See 2001 Statement of Penguin Publishing Co Ltd (United Kingdom)

LANE PUBLISHING CO.

1947 Statement: "If first printing, this fact and date of same is stated on back of title page, i.e.,

FIRST PRINTING, JULY, 1947

"The same is true for subsequent printings, i.e.,

TENTH PRINTING OCTOBER, 1947

"If a revised and/or enlarged edition, this fact is so stated, i.e.,

FIRST EDITION, 14 printings

REVISED (and/or enlarged) EDITION,

FIRST PRINTING, JANUARY, 1947

Statement for 1960: The printing information is given on the copyright page. Occasionally the words "First Edition" will be omitted, but this is not the usual policy. The first printing will always be identified as such, however. Subsequent printings are also noted.

1981 Statement: "Sunset does not have any specific means of identifying first printings—all printings are handled in the same manner. For instance, our current *Casseroles* book states 'First Printing September 1980'; our *Favorite Recipes* book says 'Seventeenth Printing December 1979.' "

1988 Statement: "If first printing, this fact and date of same is stated on back of title page, i.e.,

FIRST PRINTING, JULY, 1988

"The same is true for subsequent printings. Sunset does not have any specific means of identifying first printings—all printings are handled in the same manner."

1993 Statement: *See* 1993 Statement of Sunset Publishing Corporation

("The name was changed to Sunset Publishing Corporation in 1990.")

JOHN LANE THE BODLEY HEAD, LTD.
(UNITED KINGDOM)

1928 Statement: "With regard to first editions, the practice here has varied in the course of time. Originally first editions had simply the date on the title page; further printings had the words 'Second' or 'Third Edition' as the case might be, and also the date, though there may have been cases in which the practice was varied slightly. Nowadays we print on the back of the title page the words 'First Published in' followed by either the date of the year or the month and the year. In event of reprints the words are added 'Second Impression' with the month and the year. In no case have we ever printed the words 'First edition' on a book."

1937, 1949 Statements: *See* 1928 Statement

1976, 1981 Statements: *See* The Bodley Head Limited (United Kingdom)

MITCHELL LANE PUBLISHERS INC

2000 Statement: "We identify the first printing of a first edition by the following statement: 'First printing' which is located on the copyright page of each book."

LANGHAM PRESS (UNITED KINGDOM)

1989 Statement: *See* 1989 Statement of The Octopus Publishing Group PLC (United Kingdom)

LANGMARC PUBLISHING

2001 Statement: "We state 'First Printing.' "

LANSDOWNE PRESS (AUSTRALIA)

1976 Statement: "Our imprint page identifies editions in the following format:

Lansdowne Editions
(a division of Paul Hamlyn Pty Ltd)
37 Little Bourke Street, Melbourne 3000
© (Author)
First published 1974

"If there are reprints on subsequent editions we would run under:

First published 1974
· Reprinted 1975 (twice)
Reprinted 1976
Reprinted 1976

"With limited editions we state this on the imprint page and on a recto page of the prelims, usually after the title page.

"We will probably move any certificate of limitations to the final verso page in the future."

1981 Statement: "We no longer use the Ure Smith imprint publishing now under the imprints—Lansdowne Press, Landsdowne Editions and Summit Books.

"We indicate that a book is a first edition by the words 'First published 19..' or occasionally 'First Edition.' Sample imprint data follows:

Published by Lansdowne Press, Sydney,
176 South Creek Road, Dee Why West, N.S.W.
Australia, 2099.
First published 1981
© Author

"The same format is used for Summit Books, which are also published in Sydney, and for Lansdowne Editions. However, these are published in Melbourne."

1988 Statement: *See* 1988 Statement of Kevin Weldon & Associates Pty Ltd (Australia)

LANTERN PRESS, INC.

1947 Statement: "First printings are not identified in any way, but subsequent printings are identified with the month and year of printing.

"Thus if no notation appears on the copyright page of our books, the reader will know that it is a First Printing."

THE LAPIS PRESS

1994 Statement: "First printing and first edition are synonymous with us. Some books published by us do not include this designation on the colophon, others carry the mark 'first edition.'

"A subsequent reprint is noted as such on the colophon. A reprint is a duplication of the original edition without any changes. The designation would be: 'first edition, second printing.'

"A designation 'second edition' would mean that this volume carries changes from the previous printing.

"A subsequent reprint would be noted as 'Second edition, second printing,' and so forth.

"The above applies only to our tradebooks. Our limited edition artist books exist only in first editions, first printings only."

LARK BOOKS

1994 Statement: *See* 1994 Statement of Altamont Press, Inc.

LARLIN CORPORATION

1988 Statement: "We have not been consistent with our identifications of first editions, but we normally use the term 'First Edition' and the coding device as shown on the enclosed sample.

"First Edition
ISBN 0-87797-1144-7
91 90 89 88 10 9 8 7 6 5 4 3 2 1"

1994 Statement: *See* 1988 Statement
2000 Statement: *See* 2000 Statement of Cherokee Publishing Co

LARSEN'S OUTDOOR PUBLISHING

1994 Statement: "We designate the first printing by number on the bottom of the copyright page. We list the numbers from left to right, with 1 being the first number in the case of a first printing.

"We do not designate a first edition in our books."

2000 Statement: *See* 1994 Statement

LARSON PUBLICATIONS

1994 Statement: The first printing of a first edition is indicated by the number line 10 9 8 7 6 5 4 3 2 1. The lowest number showing indicates the printing.
2000 Statement: *See* 1994 Statement

LATIMER HOUSE, LTD. (UNITED KINGDOM)

1947 Statement: "In the case of a first edition of a book the words 'First Published 1947' appear on the verso of the title page. Subsequent printings bear the words 'Second Impression October 1948,' 'Third Impression January 1949' and so on."

THE LATONA PRESS

2000 Statement: "We identify the first printing of a first edition by the words 'First Printing.' "

OWEN LAUGHLIN PUBLISHERS

2000 Statement: "We do not differentiate First Editions."

LAUGHTER LIBRARY

1989 Statement: *See* 1989 Statement of Price/Stern/Sloan Publishers, Inc.

LAUREATE PRESS

2000 Statement: "First editions are identified on the copyright page with the words 'First Edition.' "

LAUREL CREEK PRESS

2000 Statement: *See* 2000 Statement of Blue Dove Press

T. WERNER LAURIE, LTD. (UNITED KINGDOM)

1928 Statement: *See* 1937 Statement
1937 Statement: "We follow the custom laid down by the Publishers' Association; namely, we print on the *back of the title*, the words:
    First Published in 1926
    Second Impression—1926
    Third Edition—1928
  "An impression is an exact reprint of a former edition. An edition is where some alterations have been made.
  "We cannot tell you the exact date we first issued the form but we believe it was sometime in 1925."
1947 Statement: *See* 1937 Statement

SEYMOUR LAWRENCE INCORPORATED

1976 Statement: "First editions of Delacorte Press/Seymour Lawrence titles are identified by the words 'first printing' on the copyright page. In the case of translations, we use the designation 'first American edition' or 'first American printing.' "
1981 Statement: *See* 1976 Statement

1994 Statement: "First editions of Houghton Mifflin/Seymour Lawrence titles are identified by the words 'first edition' on the copyright page (effective January 1994)."

LAWRENCE AND WISHART, LTD. (UNITED KINGDOM)

1948 Statement: "In recent years we simply put the year of publication at the bottom of the title page—usually in this style:

London
Lawrence and Wishart
1948

"It is quite impractical to put the month of publication in the verso title page because production is still so difficult here that we never know when a book will arrive."

1976 Statement: "We have no special way of designating first editions, except that on any subsequent printing, or new editions, the previous history is always given on the verso of the title page. Therefore it is, in fact, possible to identify if a particular copy is of the first edition."

1981, 2000 Statements: *See* 1976 Statement

LAXTONS

2000 Statement: *See* 2000 Statement of Butterworth-Heinemann

LAXTONS (UNITED KINGDOM)

2000 Statement: *See* 2000 Statement of Butterworth-Heinemann

LEA (UNITED KINGDOM)

1994 Statement: "We have no special method of identifying first editions. However, they can easily be identified as subsequent editions would contain the information that the particular book was reprinted."

2001 Statement: *See* 2001 Statement of Psychology Press Ltd. (United Kingdom)

LEA & FEBIGER

1988 Statement: "We have been publishers since 1785 and as far as I know, we have never indicated on the title page or copyright page that a book is a 'First Edition.' Subsequent editions of the same book are indicated as 'Second, Third, etc. Editions.' Reprints are indicated by numerical symbols 1, 2, 3, 4, etc. Deleting whatever print number the reprint might be indicates the number of prints.

"We usually list editions after the first on the copyright page.

"We have no imprints or subsidiaries."

1993 Statement: *See* 1988 Statement

LEARNING & COLORING BOOKS

2000 Statement: *See* 2000 Statement of Quincannon Publishing Group

LEFT HAND BOOKS

1994 Statement: *See* 1994 Statement of Woodbine Press

LEGACY BOOKS
1994 Statement: "We do not make any note of [the first edition]. If it's a reprint of an earlier edition, we give this information and indicate if there are any additions or changes."

LEGEND (UNITED KINGDOM)
1994 Statement: *See* 1994 Statement of Random House UK Limited (United Kingdom)
2000 Statement: *See* 2000 Statement of The Random House Group Limited (United Kingdom)

LEHIGH UNIVERSITY PRESS
1988, 2000 Statements: *See* 1976 Statement of Associated University Presses

LEICESTER UNIVERSITY PRESS (UNITED KINGDOM)
1976 Statement: "We print 'First published in 1976 by Leicester University Press' on the reverse of the title page of the first edition of our books, with the appropriate date, of course. This is the procedure we have followed for many years."
1981, 1988 Statements: *See* 1976 Statement

LEISURE BOOKS
2001 Statement: *See* 2001 Statement of Dorchester Publishing Co., Inc.

LEMIEUX INTERNATIONAL LTD.
2000 Statement: "Our first editions are marked by the fact that the copyright page bears NO printing or edition notice, whereas in subsequent editions the dates appear as:

1st Printing March 1998
2nd Printing June 1999 etc."

LENNARD ASSOCIATES (UNITED KINGDOM)
1994 Statement: "We started publishing under the Lennard Publishing imprint in 1987 and purchased the Queen Anne Press imprint from Macdonald in 1991. In the case of both imprints we make no specific reference to the first edition. Our books carry the wording 'First published in Great Britain' and give the date of publication. Any subsequent printings would normally have an additional reference to a second, third etc. impression plus date or revised edition plus date. In certain cases where reprints are required in great haste, usually for the Christmas market, the wording on the title verso may not be changed."
2000 Statement: *See* 1994 Statement

LENNARD PUBLISHING (UNITED KINGDOM)
1994, 2000 Statements: *See* 1994 Statement of Lennard Associates (United Kingdom)

LERNER PUBLICATIONS COMPANY

1976 Statement: "In our publications, 'first edition' and 'first printing' are usually synonymous. A first printing is identified by either the words 'First Printing, 1977' on the copyright page or by the following code:

1 2 3 4 5 6 7 8 9 10 85 84 83 82 81 80 79 78 77

"When the book is reprinted, the appropriate printing number and year of reprint are removed. (That is, a second printing done in 1978 will have the '1' and the '77' omitted.)"

1981, 1988 Statements: *See* 1976 Statement

1993 Statement: "We are still using the printing identification information as shown in the [1976 statement], with one alteration: currently, we are using a maximum of six numbers (one through six), and six years including the copyright year.

"So, for example, if this book had been copyrighted in 1980, the printing code might read:

1 2 3 4 5 6 85 84 83 82 81 80

All other information would stay the same."

2000 Statement: *See* 2000 Statement of Lerner Publishing Group

LERNER PUBLISHING GROUP

2000 Statement: "First editions are identified by print code. When we print the book a second time, we remove the "1" from the print code leaving 2 3 4 etc. and the date changes as well to reflect the year of the current printing. All divisions/imprints follow this method. Our company name has changed and we are now known as Lerner Publishing Group. This has been in effect since 1999. Carolrhoda Books, Inc. and Lerner Publications Company are divisions of Lerner Publishing Group. Runestone Press, First Avenue Editions, LernerSports, and LernerClassroom are imprints of Lerner Publishing Group."

LERNERCLASSROOM

2000 Statement: *See* 2000 Statement of Lerner Publishing Group

LERNERSPORTS

2000 Statement: *See* 2000 Statement of Lerner Publishing Group

LES FEMMES PUBLISHING

See Celestial Arts

HUGH LAUTER LEVIN ASSOCIATES INC.

1994 Statement: "We don't designate the first edition from reprints."

LEVITE OF APACHE

1994 Statement: "We do a limited edition of the first 50 books in each press run of the first printing of each new title in our nonfiction line. These fifty books have a special page 'tipped' in which reads: 'This is book number____ (hand lettered in calligraphy) of a limited edition of 50 books.' We also have the words 'First Edition' on the back of the title page. For our fiction titles, we use the same wording but do 100 limited edition copies."

2001 Statement: "We are no longer in the publishing business."

LEXINGTON BOOKS
1993 Statement: *See* 1993 Statement of Macmillan, Inc.
2000 Statement: "We are no longer owned by MacMillan. After having first been sold to Jossey-Bass, we currently reside within the Rowman & Littlefield Publishing Group. RLPG includes nothing on the copyright page to indicate first or subsequent editions."

LEYERLE PUBLICATIONS
2001 Statement: "We do not identify a first printing; we do identify subsequent printings on the copyright page."

LEYLAND PUBLICATIONS
(San Francisco)
1994 Statement: "We designate the first printing of a first edition as follows on copyright page:
    First edition 1975
    "We have been following this policy since 1975. However, not every single title published by us necessarily has this information, although it's true for the great majority of the 100+ books we've published.
    "Second printings are noted as: e.g. Second Printing 1994
    "Second editions are noted as: e.g. Second Edition 1994."

JOHN LIBBEY
2000 Statement: *See* 2000 Statement of Butterworth-Heinemann

LIBERAL ARTS PRESS
1994 Statement: *See* 1994 Statement of Publishers Associates

THE LIBERAL PRESS
1994 Statement: *See* 1994 Statement of Publishers Associates

LIBERTY BELL PRESS AND PUBLISHING CO.
1994 Statement: "We identify our first edition by so stating on the title page. We make no identification of additional print runs. This method has been used since 1990."

LIBERTY FUND, INC.
1988 Statement: "Our publishing imprints are Liberty*Press* and Liberty-*Classics* and we bring back into print works which are not available from any commercial publisher. We sometimes do collections of previously published or new material but do not identify our books as first editions. We do use a printing line to identify subsequent printings."
1993 Statement: *See* 1988 Statement
2000 Statement: *See* 1988 Statement, but note that "Liberty*Press* and Liberty*Classics* imprints are no longer used."

LIBERTY*CLASSICS*
1988, 1993 Statements: *See* 1988 Statement of Liberty Fund, Inc.

2000 Statement: Liberty*Classics* imprint is no longer used.

LIBERTY*PRESS*
1988, 1993 Statements: *See* 1988 Statement of Liberty Fund, Inc.
2000 Statement: Liberty*Press* imprint in no longer used.

LIBEY PUBLISHING, INCORPORATED
1993 Statement: *See* 1993 Statement of Regnery Gateway, Inc.

LIBRA PRESS
1994 Statement: A first printing would carry the following information: First printing [year].

LIBRA PUBLISHERS, INC.
1995 Statement: A first edition is noted on the copyright page. This method was adopted in 1960 and does not differ from any method previously used.
2000 Statement: *See* 1995 Statement

LIBRA PUBLISHERS, INC.
(Chicago)
1976 Statement: "We use no identifying method."
1981 Statement: *See* 1976 Statement
1988 Statement: "We print 'First Edition' on the copyright page of our books. We have been doing this for several years."
1993 Statement: *See* 1988 Statement

THE LIBRARY OF AMERICA
1988 Statement: "Since 1983, all titles published by The Library of America have stated the printing on the copyright page (p. iv), as follows: 'First Printing,' 'Second Printing,' etc. If a second edition is published, it will be indicated on the copyright page as 'Second Edition.'

"In 1982, our first year of publications, we did not indicate the printings, but the following titles that appear with no indication on the copyright page are first printings: Herman Melville, *Typee, Omoo, Mardi*, Nathaniel Hawthorne, *Tales and Sketches*, Mark Twain, *Mississippi Writings*, Jack London, *Novels and Stories*, Jack London, *Novels and Social Writings*, and William Dean Howells, *Novels 1875-1886*.

"Two titles from 1982 had multiple printings in that year, and they may be distinguished as follows:
Walt Whitman, *Poetry and Prose*
> First Printing: no indication on copyright page.
> Second Printing: no indication on copyright page *and* the second line of the Contents page (p. ix) reads: 'Each section has its own table of contents.'

All subsequent printings are indicated on copyright page.
Harriet Beecher Stowe, *Three Novels*
> First Printing: no indication on copyright page *and* 'Three Novels' *does not* appear on the title page (p. iii).

Second Printing: the copyright page reads 'June 1982.'
All subsequent printings are indicated on copyright page."
1993 Statement: *See* 1988 Statement

LIBRARY OF CONTEMPORARY THOUGHT
2001 Statement: *See* 2001 Statement of The Ballantine Publishing Group

LIBRARY OF VIRGINIA
2000 Statement: "The Library of Virginia has not followed any consistent pattern in indicating first editions. Rarely, until now, has the designation 'first edition' appeared in a Library publication, although second and subsequent editions are always marked as such. Revised editions are often, although not always, so indicated."

LIBRARY PROFESSIONAL PUBLICATIONS
2000 Statement: *See* 2000 Statement of The Shoe String Press, Inc.

LIBROS LIGUORI
2000 Statement: *See* 2000 Statement of Liguori Publications

LIFE LESSONS
2000 Statement: "We identify the first printing of a first edition by '10 9 8 7 6 5 4 3 2 1.' "

LIFE JOURNEY
1993 Statement: *See* 1993 Statement of Chariot Family Publishing

LIFELINE PRESS
2000 Statement: See 2000 Statement of Regnery Publishing

LIFETIME BOOKS, INC.
1993 Statement: *See* 1981 Statement of Frederick Fell Publishers, Inc.

LIFEQUEST
2000 Statement: "We do not have a special method for identifying a first edition. Subsequent editions and printings, however, are identified: Second edition; third printing; etc."

THE LIGHTNING TREE
1976 Statement: "It took me some time to decide how to indicate first editions of TLT books. I have started including a First Printing line on the copyright page to satisfy that need. Subsequent printings are appropriately marked by the number of the printing.

"For the books published with no indication, one can be sure they are first editions. We drop in the second printing, etc., line if they are reprinted.

"But I must add the caveat that there is no way of telling which binding of which edition one might have. As do many small publishers, we frequently print larger quantities of books than we may bind. Since we print most of our own books in house, but have all binding jobbed out, it is to our economic advantage to print larger editions, and have them bound depending on sales."
1981, 1988 Statements: *See* 1976 Statement

LIGHTNING TREE PRESS
1993 Statement: *See* 1976 Statement of The Lightning Tree

LIGUORI LIFESPAN
2000 Statement: *See* 2000 Statement of Liguori Publications

LIGUORI PUBLICATIONS
1994 Statement: "In the past, Liguori Publications had no way of identifying first edition books. However, Triumph Books, an imprint of Liguori Publications, has always listed the first edition on the title page verso. In the future, this will also be listed on all Liguori Publications titles."
2000 Statement: "Imprint change: Triumph Books to Liguori/Triumph in 1997. Practice remains the same as in 1994 Statement."

LIGUORI/TRIUMPH
2000 Statement: *See* 2000 Statement of Liguori Publications

PHILIP E. LILIENTHAL ASIAN STUDIES
2000 Statement: *See* 2000 Statement of University of California Press

LIMELIGHT EDITIONS
1994 Statement: "Since we are primarily a publisher of paperback reprints, rarely do we have a true first edition. However, every book we publish has a line on the copyright page identifying it specifically as First Limelight Edition, Second Limelight Edition, etc., followed by a month and year."
2000 Statement: "Since we are to a large extent a publisher of paperback reprints, a majority of our books are not true first editions. However, every book we publish has a line on the copyright page identifying it specifically as First Limelight Edition, Second Limelight Edition, etc., followed by a month and year. Those books of ours that are reprints invariably give the name of the original publisher on the copyright page."

LIMES REVIEW EDITION (UNITED KINGDOM)
1994 Statement: *See* 1994 Statement of The Saltire Society (United Kingdom)

THE LIMESTONE PRESS (CANADA)
1994 Statement: "The Limestone Press publishes reprints, translations and original works concerning Alaska. All put out so far have been first editions, but some reprints are planned for volumes now out of print. Indication of status as first printing or reprint will henceforth be placed on back of title page."

FRANCES LINCOLN LTD. (UNITED KINGDOM)
1994 Statement: "Until 1988, there was little consistency in our statements although it is common for the dates of reprints to be listed and a first edition can therefore be identified as only one year would be mentioned, as in 'VIKING WORLD printed 1980.' A reprinted edition would state 'VIKING WORLD printed 1980, 1989.'

"Since 1988 we have used a fairly standard format, stating that the work was 'First published in 19** by Frances Lincoln Ltd,' followed by our address and using as a reprint indicator a line of figures from '1' to '9', the lowest of which indicates the number of the reprint. On any first printing therefore the figure '1' would appear in the line whilst on any subsequent reprints it would not.

"Concerning the US edition, most of our US co-publishers print either reprint indicator lines as described above or the words 'First US edition.' There is, however, no way of telling (when both US and UK publications happen in the same year) which was published first without checking actual publication dates."

THE LINCOLN RECORD SOCIETY (UNITED KINGDOM)
1988 Statement: *See* 1988 Statement of Boydell & Brewer, Ltd. (United Kingdom)

LINCOLN SPRINGS PRESS
2000 Statement: "Our first editions are marked, copyright 1995 by author's name and Lincoln Springs Press. Subsequent editions say 'second printing, and date.' "

LINDEN PUBLISHERS
2000 Statement: "We identify the first printing of a first edition by the statement 'first published month year."

LINDISFARNE BOOKS
2000 Statement: *See* 2000 Statement of Anthroposophic Press, Inc.

LINDISFARNE PRESS
1994 Statement: The first printing of a first edition is indicated by the number line 10 9 8 7 6 5 4 3 2 1. The lowest number showing indicates the printing.
2000 Statement: *See* 2000 Statement of Lindisfarne Books

THE LINEN HALL LIBRARY (NORTHERN IRELAND)
1994 Statement: "The Linen Hall Library publishes a very small number of books on an intermittent basis. Our accepted method of wording is, e.g.:

> Published 1990 by
> The Linen Hall Library
> 17 Donegall Square North
> Belfast BT1 5DG
> © John Killen 1990
> ISBN 0 9508985-4-6
> Printed by W&G. Baird Ltd, at the Greystone Press, Antrim.
> The Linen Hall acknowledges the financial assistance of the
> following........... in printing this edition.

"We have also published one limited edition—*The Tree Clock* by Seamus Heaney—in a situation where copyright did not reside with us; the designation in this case would have been treated differently."

LINNET BOOKS
2000 Statement: *See* 2000 Statement of The Shoe String Press, Inc.

LINNET PROFESSIONAL PUBLICATIONS
2000 Statement: *See* 2000 Statement of The Shoe String Press, Inc.

LINUX JOURNAL PRESS
2000 Statement: *See* 2000 Statement of No Starch Press

LION
1993 Statement: *See* 1993 Statement of Chariot Family Publishing

LION POEM PUBLISHING
1995 Statement: *See* 1995 Statement of Ranger International Productions

J. B. LIPPINCOTT CO.
1928 Statement: "For the last two or three years only we have been putting First Edition on the copyright page of our important books only, such as *Hawkers and Walkers, The Practical Series*, etc. Before that, and at present on general works including fiction, we have not indicated the first edition, but we indicate all subsequent printings by placing on the bastard title the words 'Second Impression' and so on.

"Twenty years or so ago it used to be the habit, we think, of most publishers to date the first edition of Fall books the following year so that for instance a book might bear the date 1901 when it was copyrighted and first published in the Fall of 1900."

1937 Statement: *See* 1928 Statement

1947 Statement: "We now put the words First Edition on the copyright page of all of our trade publications and we still indicate all subsequent printings by using the words Second Impression, etc."

1976 Statement: "For trade books, first editions are designated by 'First Edition' printed on copyright page, with or without the number sequence '9 8 7 6 5 4 3 2 1.' Second printings of first editions are designated in one of two ways: Either 'Second Printing' is substituted for 'First Edition' or 'First Edition' is retained with the number sequence '9 8 7 6 5 4 3 2' (the 1 being omitted)."

1981 Statement: *See* 1981 Statement of Harper & Row, Publishers, Inc.

1988 Statement: *See* 1988 Statement of J. B. Lippincott Company

J. B. LIPPINCOTT COMPANY
1988 Statement: "We do not use 'First Edition' in our books. If, however, a book has been successful and warrants subsequent editions, they will be marked with edition numbers.

"The printing number sequence is shown as '9 8 7 6 5 4 3 2 1' for a flush left layout and '1 3 5 7 9 8 6 4 2' for a centered layout. The copyright notice will include references to the copyright dates of previous editions, if there are any.

"J. B. Lippincott Company is today a publisher of books in the health sciences and all titles previously published in other areas are now incorporated with the Harper & Row publishing programs."

See also 1981 Statement of Harper & Row, Publishers, Inc.

1994 Statement: "We do not use 'First Edition' in our books. If, however, a book has been successful and warrants subsequent editions, they will be marked with edition numbers.

"The printing number sequence is shown as '9 8 7 6 5 4 3 2 1' for a flush left layout and '1 3 5 7 9 8 6 4 2' for a centered layout. The copyright notice will include references to the copyright dates of previous editions, if there are any.

"J.B. Lippincott, a Wolters Kluwer U.S. company since 1990, is today a publisher of books in the health sciences. All titles previously published in other areas were incorporated with the Harper & Row publishing programs."

J. B. LIPPINCOTT COMPANY (UNITED KINGDOM)

1928 Statement: *See* 1937 Statement

1937 Statement: "Our books are usually designated as follows: Copyright notice followed by the date and the name of author or this Company on the back of the title, followed by the words 'First Edition' on important books. The date also sometimes appears on the front. In any case subsequent impressions are so noted on the copyright page or the bastard.

"With regard to limited editions, we usually state the words 'Limited edition printed from type and type distributed.' This information appears as a rule on the half title; copyright notice, name of author, date, or our name also appearing on the back of the title.

"We began using our present method many years ago."

1947 Statement: "So far as we are aware this Company has not changed in any way its method of identifying first editions of our publications, and first printings are still based on the information which we supplied in 1937.

"However, all our publications are printed in America and we do not make special printings of them for sale in this country. Therefore the information given [for American printings] should be exactly similar to that [supplied for English printings]."

LIPPINCOTT & CROWELL

1981 Statement: *See* 1981 Statement of Harper & Row, Publishers, Inc.

ALAN R. LISS

1988 Statement: "We do not identify first editions as such. We do identify second and subsequent printings."

LITERARY FRAGMENTS

1995 Statement: *See* 1995 Statement of Cedar Bay Press

LITTLE, BROWN & COMPANY

1928 Statement: "With few exceptions we make no attempt to designate first editions.

"Where we have brought out limited editions as well as trade editions of the same book we have sometimes indicated the first trade edition."

1936 Statement: "A Little, Brown or Atlantic Monthly Press first edition can for the most part be identified by a single line on the copyright page giving the month and year of first publication. Each new printing of a book carries an additional line on the title page also giving the month and year."

1947 Statement: *See* 1936 Statement

See also The Atlantic Monthly Press, Inc.

1988 Statement: "The edition (e.g., First Edition or First American Edition) is shown on the copyright page. Also, the first printing of a first edition is indicated by our printing line (10 9 8 . . . 3 2 1); the '1' indicates this is the first printing.

"Also . . . we have deleted the cross reference to Atlantic Monthly Press, Inc. because Atlantic Monthly Press books are published under the Atlantic Monthly Press imprint and are no longer published under the Atlantic Monthly Press/Little, Brown joint imprint."

1995 Statement: *See* 1988 Statement

2000 Statement: "The first-edition statement for Little, Brown and Company's adult trade and children's divisions remains as it has in previous editions of your handbook.

"For Bulfinch Press, the edition (e.g., First Edition, First North American Edition) appears on the copyright page, as it does for the other divisions. Second and subsequent printings are spelled out, along with the year of the printing (e.g., Second Printing, 2000).

"Arcade is an active imprint. New York Graphic Society (NYGS) was renamed Bulfinch Press."

LITTLE, BROWN AND COMPANY (UNITED KINGDOM)
2001 Statement: "The first edition of our books is identified on the copyright page with the words 'First published' and the year. Subsequent printings of the edition are identified with the words 'Reprinted' and the year. Later editions are identified with the words 'This edition' and the year or 'Second/Third/Fourth edition' and the year.

"All our imprints: Little, Brown; Abacus; Orbit; Virago; and Warner follow this practice."

LITTLE AMERICA PUBLISHING COMPANY
1995 Statement: *See* 1995 Statement of Beautiful America Publishing Company

LITTLE BAREFOOT BOOKS
1993 Statement: *See* 1993 Statement of Shambhala Publications, Inc.

LITTLE HILLS PRESS PTY LTD (UNITED KINGDOM)
1988 Statement: "Although no strict rule is followed, in general it will be found that unless books are marked 'Reprinted, date' they are first editions."

LITTLE IMP™ BOOKS
1994, 2000 Statements: *See* 1994 Statement of Impact Publishers

LITTLE LADYBIRD (UNITED KINGDOM)
1994 Statement: *See* 1994 Statement of Ladybird Books Ltd. (United Kingdom)

LITTLEBURY & COMPANY, LTD. (UNITED KINGDOM)
1947 Statement: "Post-war production has been so erratic that to insert the actual date of publication of a book has been impractical. Publications issued on any one date in the year have been as late as eighteen months in production, owing to shortage of materials and labour in the Binding and other Departments.

"For this reason alone publication dates have been omitted and they will not be inserted until a more settled state in the Industry can be assured."

LITTMAN FOUNDATION
1981 Statement: *See* 1981 Statement of Associated University Presses

THE LIVE OAK PRESS
2000 Statement: "We identify the first printing of a first edition by the number line '10 9 8 7 6 5 4 3 2 1.' "

HORACE LIVERIGHT, INC.
(Became Liveright Publishing Corporation.)
See Liveright Publishing Corporation

LIVERIGHT PUBLISHING CORPORATION
1937 Statement: "As a general rule we have no marking on the copyright page of our publications to show our first edition although on subsequent editions we print Second, Third, Fourth, Fifth, Sixth edition, etc. We have had one or two books with first edition marked on the copyright page but this is not our general practice."

1947 Statement: *See* 1937 Statement

1976 Statement: "Liveright Publishing Corporation is now a wholly owned subsidiary of W. W. Norton & Company, Inc. For both Liveright and Norton books we currently indicate first editions with a series of numbers 1 through 9 on the copyright page. A first edition has all of the numbers. The second printing is indicated by the deletion of the number 1. The third by the deletion of number 2, and so on. An actual new edition is indicated either by the words 'revised edition,' or 'second edition.' . . . From house to house the practice varies and we ourselves in years past have indicated first editions with the words 'first edition.' "

1981 Statement: "Liveright Publishing Corporation is now a wholly owned subsidiary of W. W. Norton & Company, Inc. For both Liveright and Norton books we currently indicate first editions with a series of numbers 1 through 9 on the copyright page. A first edition has all of the numbers plus the words 'First Edition.' The second printing is indicated by the deletion of the number 1 and the words 'First Edition.' The third by the deletion of number 2, and so on. An actual new edition is indicated either by the words 'revised edition,' or 'second edition.' . . . From house to house the practice varies and we

ourselves in years past have indicated first editions with the words 'first edition.' "
1988 Statement: *See* 1981 Statement

LIVERPOOL UNIVERSITY PRESS (UNITED KINGDOM)
1976 Statement: "We do not have any particular method of identification for first editions. We publish books for use in University teaching and research and normally we are not concerned with identifying first publication, other than by mentioning this and listing subsequent printings or editions in the usual way on the copyright page, which is the verso of the title page."
1981 Statement: *See* 1976 Statement
1988 Statement: "The current practice of Liverpool University Press is to identify, on the title verso page, the original publisher of a book if other than ourselves. Where a book is first published by ourselves, this is also stated; in this case the book is a first edition unless otherwise stated. Reprints and new editions are always identified and the year in which they were issued is given."
1994 Statement: *See* 1988 Statement

LIVING BOOKS
2000 Statement: *See* 2000 Statement of Tyndale House Publishers Inc.

LIVINGSTON PRESS
1995 Statement: "Any publication of either Livingston Press (formerly Livingston University Press) or its division Swallow's Tale Press that is not a first edition will have 'Second Printing' on the copyright page—sometimes with a publication date, sometimes not. All other books by these two presses should be considered first editions—most of them, though not all, will have 'first edition' printed on the copyright page."
2000 Statement: "Our first editions are marked with 'First Edition.' The first printing is indicated by the sequence 5 4 3 2 1. Both are placed on the copyright page."

LIVINGSTON UNIVERSITY PRESS
See Livingston Press

LLEWELLYN PUBLICATIONS
1976 Statement: "On the copyright page we put 'First Edition, date.' If it is a second printing of a first edition, we add under 'First Edition' 'Second Printing, date.' We also change the date on the title page of successive printings of a book, so that discrepancy between the date on the title page and that on the copyright page would be a clue that the book is a subsequent printing of an edition. In the past, we have not been careful to distinguish between new printings and new editions, and so the copyright page might list first, second, third, etc, editions, when what is meant is first edition, second printing, third printing.
1981, 1988, 1994 Statements: *See* 1976 Statement

THE LOCKHART PRESS

2000 Statement: "We do not identify first editions, only subsequent editions or reprints or if the edition is in a new form, e.g., paper editions, electronic editions, etc."

LOCUST HILL PRESS

1994 Statement: "We are a specialized, very short-run press, and rarely do more than one printing. On these rare occasions, we do not differentiate between printings."
2000 Statement: *See* 1994 Statement

LOG HOUSE PUBLISHING CO LTD (CANADA)

1995 Statement: "Our practice has been to remain silent on first printing, identifying only subsequent editions or printings."

LOIZEAUX

1994 Statement: "Most of our older books contain nothing to indicate whether they are first editions. More recent books have a line of numbers on the bottom of the copyright page; if the smallest number is a '1,' the book is a first edition. For a second printing, the '1' would be deleted and the smallest number would be '2,' etc."
2000 Statement: *See* 1994 Statement

LONDON LIMITED EDITIONS (UNITED KINGDOM)

1988, 1995, 2001 Statements: *See* 1989 Statement of Bertram Rota (Publishing) Ltd (United Kingdom)

THE LONDON OFFICE (UNITED KINGDOM)

1994 Statement: *See* 1988 Statement of Trigon Press (United Kingdom)

LONE EAGLE PUBLISHING COMPANY

1994 Statement: The first printing of a first edition is indicated by the statement "First Printing, (Month) (Year)."
2000 Statement: *See* 1994 Statement

LONE OAK PRESS LTD

2000 Statement: "Our first editions, first printing say First Edition on the copyright page. Second and subsequent printings say First Edition: Second Printing, Date of Printing and so on."

LONE WILLOW PRESS

2000 Statement: "We identify the first printing of a first edition by the words 'First Edition' (date)."

LONELY PLANET PUBLICATIONS (AUSTRALIA)

1988 Statement: "We do not designate print runs on any edition. Nearly every one of our books manages to go through more than one print run in an edition and we'd find it tedious indicating each print run.

"On the imprint page we specify the edition of the title, the first publication date of the title, and the publication date of the current edition, i.e:

India—a travel survival kit
3rd edition
First published
October 1981
This edition
June 1987

"In addition the edition number is specified on the back cover below the prices, i.e.

Australia $9.95	USA $7.95
UK £4.95	New Zealand $11.95
Canada $9.95	India Rs 80
4th edition."	

1994 Statement: *See* 1988 Statement

LONELY PLANET PUBLICATIONS LTD (UNITED KINGDOM)
2001 Statement: "We identify only editions, not printings; a first edition is so identified on the copyright page."

JOHN LONG, LIMITED (UNITED KINGDOM)
1928 Statement: "New books published by us are printed with year date of Copyright on back of Title Page in the first edition and subsequent editions are marked 2nd Edition, etc., on title page. This applies to novels published at 7s.6d., the cheaper editions being issued later."

1935 Statement: "Actually, though we put the date in our General Books, this practice does not apply to novels. In cases, however, where 7/6 novels are reprinted at the same price, we put Second or Third Impression, as the case may be.

"We would also mention that the same procedure also applies to our affiliated company, Messrs. Andrew Melrose, Ltd."

1948 Statement: "It is not our present practice to include dates in our publications. In cases where books are reprinted, we state 2nd impression, and so on, as required."

LONGHOUSE
1995 Statement: "All Longhouse publications . . . are first editions with no reprints. Longhouse has published various tributary streams under the imprints: Our Poets Workshop, Workshop, Poets Who Sleep, and Scout, all within a first printing and very limited. Since 1988 Longhouse subsidiary Origin Press . . . has published four books of poetry and prose, each book identified by a First Edition heading on the copyright page."

2001 Statement: *See* 1995 Statement

LONGLEAF PRESS
2000 Statement: "First editions have no special printing or editorial statement. Second printings are marked as such i.e. (second printing 1999) on the copyright page."

LONGMAN INC.

1976 Statement: "Normally we make it a practice to include the legend 'First Published In . . . ' on the verso of the title page of all first editions. This is definitely true of all books published under the Longman imprint. It is true for most books published under our Churchill Livingstone imprint (medical), but it is not the case with Oliver & Boyd publications.

"However, with all three imprints all subsequent printings or editions are clearly identified."

1981 Statement: *See* 1976 Statement

LONGMAN AUSTRALIA PTY LIMITED (AUSTRALIA)

1994 Statement: *See* 1988 Statement of Longman Cheshire Pty Limited (Australia)

LONGMAN CHESHIRE PTY LIMITED (AUSTRALIA)

1988 Statement: "The way we normally identify the First Edition is by printing on the verso of the title page 'first published 1981.' When the same edition is reprinted we add underneath first published 1981 'reprinted 1982.' After a further Edition is subsequently published we would again add 'second edition published 1984' and we would continue to identify additional reprints in the same way as they were identified for the first edition."

("Note that the company name was changed to Longman Australia Pty Limited in July, 1994.")

LONGMANS, GREEN & CO.

1928 Statement: "With regard to the identification of our first editions, we would say that at the present time we are printing 'First Edition' on the reverse of the title page of our general literary works.

"To distinguish between first editions and others of those books printed previous to the adoption of the present method, one may compare the date used on the title page with that of the copyright date to appear. If the date appearing at the foot of the title page and that of the copyright are the same, the volume is a first edition."

1936 Statement: "We are identifying 'First Editions' by printing the words 'First Edition' on the reverse of the title page of all works printed in the U.S.A.

"In the case of a reprint, we give a notation of the month and year in which the first edition was published and the month and year of each reprint.

"In case of a 'Revised Edition' (where there have been major changes made in the text of a new printing) we indicate that it is a new edition and not merely a reprint."

1947 Statement: *See* 1936 Statement

LONGMANS, GREEN & CO., LTD. (UNITED KINGDOM)

1928 Statement: "We always date the title page of our books, and unless the book is marked ' . . . . Impression' or ' . . . . Edition' it is a first edition."

1936 Statement: "Since 1928 we have modified our practice, in that we do not now put the bibliographical information regarding edition, impression or date on the title page. It is all, however, given on the back of the title."

1948 Statement: "We still follow the same arrangement as in our statement of 1936, i.e.: all bibliographical information is given on back of title page."

LONGSTREET HOUSE
1994 Statement: "All our books are first printing unless marked otherwise ('Reprinted 1992,' 'Second Edition 1992')."

LONGSTREET PRESS
1994 Statement: A first printing is indicated by the statement "1st printing [year]" on the copyright page.
2000 Statement: *See* 1994 Statement

LORD JOHN PRESS
1988 Statement: "We print 'first edition' on the verso of the title page. On our limited editions we also state that the book is a first edition on the colophon page.
"We have used this practice from the first publication."
1993, 2000 Statements: *See* 1988 Statement

LORING & MUSSEY, INC.
(Became Barrows Mussey, Inc, and is now out of business.)
1937 Statement: "We have not followed a consistent practice in regard to first printings. One or two of our books contain the words 'First Edition' with the printer's colophon. In general we would probably print 'Second printing' on the copyright page when reprinting a book.
"The name of this firm will very shortly be changed to Barrows Mussey, Inc."

LOS HOMBRES PRESS
1994 Statement: The first printing of a first edition is indicated by the number line 1 2 3 4 5 6 7 8 9 10. The lowest number showing indicates the printing.

LOST HORSE PRESS
2000 Statement: "First printing is designated by the term 'First Edition.' "

LOTHROP, LEE & SHEPARD BOOKS
1981 Statement: "The only change is that Lothrop has changed its name to Lothrop, Lee & Shepard Books, which is an imprint of William Morrow & Company, Inc. All imprints in William Morrow would follow the same practice.
"I have checked with our production department about our designation of printings, and they tell me that we continue to use the same method, except we no longer substitute the years.
"We print a strip of code numbers on the copyright page to designate the printing. For a first printing it reads:
1 2 3 4 5 6 7 8 9 10
"For the second printing, the number '1' is knocked off, and so on.
"There is only one printing of each edition; there rarely are any changes, such as corrections, to be made, so except for the code strip each edition is exactly like the previous ones."

1988 Statement: "We print a strip of code numbers on the copyright page to designate the printing. For a first printing it reads:

1 2 3 4 5 6 7 8 9 10

"For the second printing, the number '1' is knocked off, and so on. Prior to 1976, we included the years, as:

1 2 3 4 5 80 79 78 77 76

"In this case, the two end numbers (indicating the printing and the year) were knocked off each time.

"There is only one printing of each edition; there rarely are any changes, such as corrections, to be made, so except for the code strip each edition is exactly like the previous ones."

1993 Statement: *See* 1988 Statement

LOTHROP, LEE & SHEPARD CO., INC.

1948 Statement: "First editions published by our company have no markings. Subsequent editions are marked with the proper edition number on the copyright page.

1976 Statement: "We print a strip of code numbers on the copyright page to designate the printing. For a first printing it reads:

1 2 3 4 5 6 7 8 9 10

"For the second printing, the number '1' is knocked off, and so on. Heretofore we have had a different designation including the year, as:

1 2 3 4 5 80 79 78 77 76

"In this case, the two end numbers (indicating the printing and the year) are knocked off each time.

"There is only one printing of each edition; there rarely are any changes, such as corrections, to be made, so except for the code strip each edition is exactly like the previous ones."

1981 Statement: *See* 1981 Statement of Lothrop, Lee & Shepard Books

LOTUS LIGHT/SHANGRI-LA

2001 Statement: *See* 2001 Statement of Lotus Press (Twin Lakes, Wisconsin)

LOTUS LIGHT PUBLICATIONS

2001 Statement: *See* 2001 Statement of Lotus Press (Twin Lakes, Wisconsin)

LOTUS PRESS
(Twin Lakes, Wisconsin)

2001 Statement: "We state 'First edition' on the copyright page."

LOTUS PRESS/SHANGRI-LA

2001 Statement: *See* 2001 Statement of Lotus Press (Twin Lakes, Wisconsin)

LOTUS PRESS, INC.
(Michigan)

1976 Statement: "We are still a very small company and so far have published only first editions, with the exception of *Star by Star* which originally came out as a hard cover first edition with another company. We have no immediate plans for issuing other than first editions at this time."

1981 Statement: "We have not changed our policy regarding first editions. In addition to *Star by Star*, which we mentioned in our first report, we have made another exception in the publication of a second edition (first U.S. edition) of *Rufus*, by Ronald Fair. The first edition was published in West Germany in 1977 by Peter Schlack Verlag, Stuttgart, West Germany and was not available to American audiences. We agreed to handle individual orders for that first edition ($12.00), but at the same time made an agreement with the original publisher whereby a cheaper edition could be made available in this country ($4.00).

"We do not plan to publish any further reprints or publications of anything other than first editions except perhaps a limited edition (about 250 copies) of the first two out-of-print books of Naomi Long Madgett in one volume which will include a number of unpublished juvenile poems. We are not yet certain about this possibility, but we are considering it.

"All of which is to say that our policy has not changed, but we are willing to consider exceptions once in a while."

1988 Statement: "1976 Statement: Essentially correct except that we have recently reprinted *Halfway to the Sun* by May Miller, originally published by another company.

"1981 Statement: OK as is. We decided not to reprint the early volumes of Naomi Long Madgett.

"The company's policy has not changed."

1995 Statement: *See* 1995 Statement of Michigan State University Press

2000 Statement: *See* 2000 Statement of Michigan State University Press

LOUISIANA STATE UNIVERSITY PRESS

1976 Statement: "We do not use any method of identifying our books as first editions. The only thing we do is indicate subsequent printings or editions by date or the words 'Revised edition,' if such is the case, or 'Second edition,' if there has been no substantial revision of the first edition. The assumption regarding our books, thus, would be that they are first editions, unless otherwise described."

1981 Statement: *See* 1976 Statement

1988 Statement: "We do not use any method of identifying our books as first editions. On the copyright page, we indicate subsequent printings by date and number, and we spell out 'Revised edition' and, in the case of a new edition with no substantial changes, 'Second edition.' Thus the assumption regarding our books would be that they are first editions unless otherwise described.

"We began using this system in 1986. We have no subsidiaries."

1994 Statement: "Since January, 1988, our company has had the following policy concerning first editions:

"A first printing of a first edition is identified on the copyright page by the words 'First printing.' Below that is a string of numbers that designate the number of printings as well as the year of a printing. Revised editions are so identified on the copyright page."

2000 Statement: *See* 1994 Statement

SAMPSON LOW, MARSTON & CO., LTD.
(UNITED KINGDOM)

1937 Statement: "We beg to say we have no settled rule with regard to stating on the title page or elsewhere, the date of first publication or reprints."

1949 Statement: *See* 1937 Statement

LOYOLA UNIVERSITY PRESS

1976 Statement: "The absence of any identifying statement does indicate a first edition. However, reprinting without revision is not indicated. So a 'first edition' may go through a number of reprintings. When a book is revised or substantially changed, the fact is noted, and a new copyright year is printed."

1981, 1988, 1993 Statements: *See* 1976 Statement

LP PUBLICATIONS

2000 Statement: "We identify the first printing of a first edition by the following statement: 'First printing: mo, year.' "

LPD PRESS

2000 Statement: "We identify the first printing of a first edition by the number line 10 9 8 7 6 5 4 3 2 1 on the copyright page."

LUATH PRESS LTD (UNITED KINGDOM)

2001 Statement: "We state 'First edition' on the copyright page."

JOHN W. LUCE & COMPANY
(Merged with Manthorne and Burak prior to 1949.)

1937 Statement: "We have never made a practice of specifically designating the different editions of the works of our authors. Had we done so with the books of Mencken, Lord Dunsany Synge and certain of Wilde's work which we published for the first time it would have been a distinct convenience. In the case of *George Bernard Shaw; his Plays* by Mencken, which was his first published book, we made but one printing. His other books ran into a number of editions which we can identify but which would not be easily recognized by a casual collector. The same holds true of other authors, though there was but one printing in separate form of the complete *A Florentine Tragedy* by Wilde and one printing of *Pan and Desespoir*, previously unpublished poems by the same author."

1949 Statement: *See* 1937 Statement

LUCENT BOOKS INC.

1993 Statement: "We don't designate."

LUMEN CHRISTI PRESS

1994 Statement: The first printing of a first edition is indicated by the statement "First Printing: (Month), (Year)."

LUNA BISONTE PRODS

2000 Statement: "Subsequent editions or printings are indicated by a statement: '2nd printing' or '2nd edition,' etc."

LUND HUMPHRIES PUBLISHERS LTD.
(UNITED KINGDOM)

1994 Statement: "We designate the first printing of a first edition with the wording 'First published in Great Britain in 19... by Lund Humphries Publishers, Park House, 1 Russell Gardens, London NW11 9NN.' Reprints or revised editions then have the wording 'Reprinted . . . ' or 'Revised edition . . . ' with the date.

"In cases where we have reissued a book first published by another publisher, we state 'This edition of . . . published 19.. by Lund Humphries Publishers . . . .' Under the heading 'Publishing History' we will add that the book 'was first published in 19... by (company).'

"This is the wording that has become standard over the last two to three years. It is unlikely that it has been completely consistent in previous years."
2000 Statement: *See* 2000 Statement of Gower Publishing Limited (United Kingdom)

LUTHERS

2000 Statement: "Since its founding in 1988, Luthers has identified all first editions: FIRST EDITION, above the copyright notice on the copyright page.

"Subsequent printing history is noted on the copyright page, for example: First Edition, August 1999; Second Edition, October 1999; etc."

LUTTERWORTH PRESS (UNITED KINGDOM)

1976 Statement: "Our only method of identifying first editions is by stating the fact, though the wording does vary depending on the circumstances. For instance the bibliography might read:

First published 19..
First paperback edition 19..
First published in Great Britain 19..
First published in this collected form 19.. etc."
1981 Statement: "I see no reason for changing the entry which you have provided from the previous edition of your publication, but I could add the following examples:

Second impression 19..
New Revised Edition 19..."
1988, 1994 Statements: *See* 1981 Statement
2000 Statement: "In connection with the listing for The Lutterworth Press . . . I take it that this also relates to the publishing carried out from the 1790s onwards by the Religious Tract Society before the Lutterworth name was introduced in the 1930s.

"The previous statements remain correct. We do, however, have additional internal editorial and production information for some but not all titles, and can research particular problems for £30 (approximately $50) per hour. In addition, our archives (on deposit elsewhere) can be made available for research."

LUXOR PRESS LTD. (UNITED KINGDOM)
1994, 2000 Statements: *See* 1947 Statement of The Albyn Press (United Kingdom)

LYCANTHROPE PRESS
2000 Statement: "Our first editions are signed by the author and bear a hand-written note by the author stating 'First edition.' Each book may be personalized with the purchaser's name. Since we are relatively small we can offer this unique service."

LYFORD BOOKS
1993, 2000 Statements: *See* 1981 Statement of Presidio Press

LYNX IMAGES (CANADA)
2001 Statement: "We identify the first printing of a first edition as follows: 1st Edition: September 2000."

NICK LYONS BOOKS, INC.
1988 Statement: "On all our books a first edition can be identified by the printing code on the copyright page. This is a series of numbers which, for the first printing, proceeds in descending order from 10 to 1. On subsequent printings the 1 is deleted, then the 2, and so on. Thus the printing number is represented by the lowest number in that sequence.

"Our books have used this system since we started business in 1978."
1993 Statement: *See* 1993 Statement of Lyons & Burford, Publishers

LYONS & BURFORD, PUBLISHERS
1993 Statement: *See* 1988 Statement of Nick Lyons Books, Inc.
2001 Statement: *See* 2001 Statement of The Lyons Press

THE LYONS PRESS
2001 Statement: "This [1988 Statement of Nick Lyons Books, Inc.] has not changed. But . . . our company name . . . is now 'The Lyons Press, an imprint of Globe Pequot Press.' "
See 1988 Statement of Nick Lyons Books, Inc.

M

M & E (UNITED KINGDOM)
1994 Statement: *See* 1994 Statement of Pitman Publishing (United Kingdom)

2001 Statement: *See* 2001 Statement of Pitman Publishing (United Kingdom)

MACADAM/CAGE PUBLISHING INC.
2000 Statement: "MacAdam/Cage and MacMurry & Beck use numerical cascade, 10 9 8 7 6 5 4 3 2 1. If #1 is present, it's a first."

THE MACAULAY COMPANY
(Out of business. Publications issued through 1939
bought by Citadel Press.)
1928 Statement: "We have not been marking our first editions in any particular way. Usually, when second and further editions are issued of the same title, they are so marked."
1937 Statement: *See* 1928 Statement

MACDONALD & CO., (PUBLISHERS) LTD.
(UNITED KINGDOM)
1947 Statement: *Furnished sample title page showing method. This bears on verso:*

First published 1947
Second Impression December 1947

MACFARLANE WALTER & ROSS (CANADA)
1995 Statement: "We designate second and subsequent printings on the copyright page."
2000 Statement: *See* 1995 Statement

MACLAY & ASSOCIATES
1988 Statement: "On our local-interest titles, we do not designate a first edition, since there is only one printing. On our nationally-distributed fiction titles, the words FIRST EDITION appear on the copyright page of such, and are dropped on any succeeding printings.

"We have no other imprints or subsidiaries.

"This has been our only method since we began in 1981."

ALEXANDER MACLEHOSE & CO. (UNITED KINGDOM)
(Out of business prior to 1947.)
1937 Statement: "It is our general practice to put the date of the publication of any book on the title page itself. If the book is reprinted, the date of the reprint appears on the title page and a bibliographical description on the back of the title."

MACMILLAN (AUSTRALIA)
1994, 2001 Statements: *See* 1994 Statement of Pan Macmillan Australia (Australia)

MACMILLAN, INC.
1993 Statement: *See* 1981 Statement of Macmillan Publishing Co., Inc.

358

MACMILLAN & CO., LTD. (UNITED KINGDOM)
1928 Statement: *See* 1937 Statement
1937 Statement: "Our first editions carry the date of publication on the title page. If the book is reprinted a statement is put on the back of the title page, saying: 'First edition (say) 1900 Reprinted 1902.' Any subsequent reprints are indicated in the same way. We do not call a book 'second edition' unless (1) the type has been reset, or (2) very substantial alterations have been made, In that case instead of 'Reprinted,' 'Second Edition' would be printed on the back of the title page and occasionally on the title page itself, though there is no special rule about this. The date appearing on the title page itself is the date of printing in every case.

"To give a concrete example, a book that was first published in 1900 and then reprinted without much alteration in 1902, and of which a second edition appeared in 1908, would be designated as follows: On the title page the date 1908 would appear, and on the back of the title page the words

First Edition 1900
Reprinted 1902
Second Edition 1908

"We are sorry to say that it is impossible for us to give the date when we first adopted this practice."
1947 Statement: *See* 1937 Statement
See also Macmillan Publishers Limited (United Kingdom)

MACMILLAN CHILDREN'S BOOKS (UNITED KINGDOM)
2000 Statement: *See* 2000 Statement of Macmillan Publishers Limited (United Kingdom)

THE MACMILLAN COMPANY
1928 Statement: "On the reverse of the title page of our books, just below the copyright notice always appears a notice to the following effect: 'Set up and electrotyped. Published . . . .' or 'Set up and printed. Published . . . .' Usually any reprintings or new editions are listed below. If there are no such reprintings or new editions listed and if the date above our imprint on the title page and the publishing date as given above coincide, the book is a first edition. In cases where the reprintings are listed on the back of the title page, a comparison of this imprint date and the publishing date is usually sufficient to identify the book."
1937 Statement: "On the reverse of the title page of our books, just below the copyright notice, always appears a notice to the following effect: 'Set up and electrotyped. Published . . . .' or 'Set up and printed. Published . . . .' Usually any reprintings or new editions are listed below. If there are no such reprintings or new editions listed and if the date above our imprint on the title page and the publishing date as given above coincide, the book is a first edition. In cases where the reprintings are listed on the back of the title page, a comparison of this imprint date and the publishing date is usually sufficient to identify the book.

"From now on (April 24, 1936), however, we propose to place the words 'First Printing' under the copyright of all trade books which we print here in America, these words to be deleted with the second printing.

"We are unable to tell you just when we used our present method of identifying first printings. In checking up renewal of copyright notices, we find that books reprinted since 1894 as a rule have had their imprint date corrected with each printing, but the words 'Reprinted,' etc., do not always appear."

1947 Statement: "The Macmillan practice concerning the edition notice has now changed and we no longer include a statement to the following effect: 'Set up and electrotyped. Published . .' or 'Set up and printed. Published . . .'

"The words *first printing* always appear on the back of the title page of a first edition. Should the book go into a second edition either the word *second* is substituted for *first* or the statement *second* printing listed below *first printing*."

See also Macmillan Publishing Co., Inc.

MACMILLAN EDUCATION AUSTRALIA (AUSTRALIA)

1994 Statement: "When we did publish general books, and our current style with educational texts, has always been the same:

'First published (year) by'

followed by our company name and address.

If a book is reprinted, a line was added after the address as:

'Reprinted (year/s).' "

MACMILLAN GENERAL BOOKS (UNITED KINGDOM)

1994, 2000 Statements: *See* 1994 Statement of Macmillan Publishers Limited (United Kingdom)

MACMILLAN OF CANADA (CANADA)

1989 Statement: "Macmillan of Canada does not designate first editions."

1993 Statement: *See* 1989 Statement

MACMILLAN PRESS LTD (UNITED KINGDOM)

1994 Statement: *See* 1994 Statement of Macmillan Publishers Limited (United Kingdom)

2000 Statement: *See* 2000 Statement of Palgrave Publishers Ltd (United Kingdom). "Macmillan Press Ltd (United Kingdom) from 1 September, 2000 [was] rebranded as Palgrave Publishers Ltd (United Kingdom)."

MACMILLAN PUBLISHERS LIMITED
(UNITED KINGDOM)

Statement for 1960: *See* 1982 Statement

1976 Statement: *See* 1982 Statement

1982 Statement: "Until 1968/9 our first editions carried the date of publication on the title page. If the book was reprinted or a new edition was produced, a statement was added to the back of the title page saying 'First edition (say) 1900/Reprinted 1902/Second edition 1908/Reprinted 1910'; the date of the latest printing then appeared on the title page.

"Since 1968/9 our practice has been to omit the date from the title page. Instead, the words 'First published (say) 1972 by . . . ' now appear on the back of the title page of all first editions. Subsequent reprints and new editions replace this with the wording 'Published by . . . .' and a statement similar to that used before 1968/9 to show the bibliographical history of the book.

"During 1968 and 1969 either practice may have been used."

1994 Statement: "Since its foundation in 1843, Macmillan has always dated books, and listed new editions and reprints on the biblio page.

"Up to about 1970, the date was printed at the foot of the title page. This is the date of printing, and was altered on reprint. By about 1970, the use of the copyright line with the UCC symbol and date had become general, and the date on the title page was considered redundant.

"Where a book has either no bibliographical history on the biblio page (usually, but not always the title verso), or only 'First published [date] by...,' it is almost certainly a first edition. Where the wording is 'First published in the United Kingdom . . . ' or similar, it is probable that earlier or simultaneous publication took place elsewhere. Where a book was translated from another language, it is usually evident. Where a joint imprint appears, often with an associated publisher in another country, simultaneous publication can be assumed, though synchronisation to the day was not normally attempted. Where copies of the same edition are bound in both hard covers and paper, they were often, but not invariably, published simultaneously; where the paperback appeared later, its date is not always recorded on the biblio page.

"Over the years, Macmillan has taken over many publications from elsewhere. The most notable instances are the works of Julius Charles Hare (1856), Lord Tennyson (1884), the publications of the house of Richard Bentley (1898), Thomas Hardy (1902) and W.B. Yeats (1916). (But note that we had published some of the works of Hare and Hardy before those dates.) The implications of these acquisitions have been well documented by bibliographical scholars, as have the pre-Macmillan and US (both legitimate and pirated) editions of the works of Rudyard Kipling.

"The date of publication of *Through the Looking-Glass* by Lewis Carroll is often given as 1871, though the edition is dated 1872. The actual date of publication is 11 December 1871.

"The practice of Macmillan and associated companies in other countries has been generally similar to that described here. It should, however, be remembered that the Macmillan Co, New York and the Macmillan Company of Canada ceased to be subsidiaries of the British parent in 1951 and 1973 respectively.

"Pan Macmillan is an imprint used until recently by our general books division. This information also applies to Pan Macmillan."

2000 Statement: "We wish to add the following paragraph [which] should follow ' . . . UCC symbol . . . title page was considered redundant.' in our last [1994] statement:

"From 1996 Macmillan began the practice of marking printings and reprints with a string of numbers, 1 to 10. To establish the first printing of the first edition, number 1 has to be present in the string.

"The following should be added to our list of companies: Macmillan Press Ltd (UK) from 1st September, 2000 rebranded as Palgrave Publishers Ltd (UK), Macmillan Children's Books (UK), Pan Macmillan (UK), Pan Macmillan (UK) imprints: Picador, Boxtree, Sidgwick and Jackson."

MACMILLAN PUBLISHING CO., INC.

1976 Statement: "If I understand your use of the term 'first impressions' as meaning what we would call the first 'printing' of a new title, the answer to your question is simple.

"On the reverse side of the title page where all the copyright information is recorded you will find, in all Macmillan titles (for books published in 1976 for example) the statement 'First Printing 1976.' This has been and will continue to be our method of identification of first printings on new titles."

1981 Statement: "We have noted the reply sent you in 1976 in answer to your question concerning the designation of a 'first edition' published by Macmillan Publishing Co., Inc., or its divisions.

"In December 1979 it was decided that the policy of placing the printing line on the copyright page would be changed. Instead of printing a line, e.g. 'First Printing 1979' or 'Tenth Printing 1978' etc., [it was decided] that a numbering system would be used. When a new title (manuscript) is published the following is added to the copyright page:

10 9 8 7 6 5 4 3 2 1

and whenever the title is reprinted, the previous number is removed before it is sent to the press. Thus, the second printing would begin the print line at the right with '2,' the '1' having been removed. (For back list titles the numbers will start with the current printing number and ascend as high as the space will allow.) This procedure had been used by the Children's Books Department at Macmillan since 1971-72, being an informal adaption of some other publisher's method.

"It was decided that the indications of First Collier Books Edition (date) would be retained, but other divisions and imprints adopted the new system in 1979."

1989, 1993 Statements: *See* 1981 Statement

MACMURRY & BECK

2000 Statement: *See* 2000 Statement of MacAdam/Cage

JOHN MACRAE BOOKS

2000 Statement: *See* 2000 Statement of Henry Holt and Company, LLC

JULIA MACRAE (UNITED KINGDOM)

1994 Statement: *See* 1994 Statement of Random House UK Limited (United Kingdom)

2000 Statement: *See* 2000 Statement of The Random House Group Limited (United Kingdom)

MACRAE SMITH & CO.

1928 Statement: "On the copyright page, which is the back of the title page on our books the first edition contains only the copyright notice. Following editions give a record of the number of printings and the dates."

1937 Statement: "Prior to 1930, the copyright page of our books contained only the copyright notice. Subsequent printings were identified with the number of the printing and occasionally the date. Since 1930 the copyright page has contained either of the following to indicate a first edition: 'First Edition' or 'First Printing.' "

1947 Statement: *See* 1937 Statement

LINCOLN MACVEAGH, THE DIAL PRESS

1928 Statement: "We wish to state that our system is to carry on the title page the year in which the edition is published and on the back of this page, merely a note as to when it was reprinted, such as is done by most publishers." *See also* Dial Press, Inc.

MACY-MASIUS
(Combined with Vanguard Press.)

1928 Statement: "On the page backing the title page, we place invariably this legend on the first editions of our books:

Published (with the date of publication).

"We don't refer to further printings as editions, since they obviously aren't in the true sense of the word. But we list the date of each further printing within the first edition. We call a printing a second edition only if there is something different in it from the first."

MAD BOOKS

2000 Statement: *See* 2000 Statement of DC Comics

MAD MAGAZINE

2000 Statement: *See* 2000 Statement of DC Comics

MADISON BOOKS

1988 Statement: "Our first editions have no designation on the copyright page. However, near the bottom of the page, we indicate subsequent printings:

Second Printing

Third Printing, etc."

1994, 2000 Statements: *See* 1988 Statement

MADISON HOUSE PUBLISHERS, INC.

1994 Statement: "Since its founding in 1988, Madison House has designated its initial printing of the first edition with the words 'FIRST EDITION' inscribed at the bottom of the copyright page. This line is struck from all subsequent printings of that title.

"At this time we have no imprints or subsidiaries."

2000 Statement: *See* 1994 Statement

MADISON PRESS BOOKS (CANADA)

1995 Statement: "On the copyright page of a first edition, we simply indicate Copyright © and the year of printing. On subsequent reprints, we indicate

First edition 19___

Reprinted 19___ (and list year of each reprint, with most recent reprint date first.)

"Madison Press Books has used this method of designating first editions throughout its 16-year history."

2000 Statement: "Madison Press Books now follows a slightly different practice than outlined in [the 1995 Statement].

"On a first edition, we now indicate First edition and the year, and add an edition line of either 1 2 3 4 5 6 7 8 9 10 (if type is left justified) or 1 3 5 7 9 10 8 6 4 2 (if type is centered). For reprints of a first edition, we then knock off the appropriate number (e.g. 1 on the first reprint).

"Only if there is a substantial change to the pages of the book do we indicate a new edition, usually by the words 'Revised edition' and the year."

MADRONA PRESS, INC.

1976 Statement: "Our first editions carry the notation 'First Edition' on the copyright page. Any subsequent printings carry the notation 'Second Printing 1975' or 'Third Printing 1976' etc. also on the copyright page. We have only done second and third printings, and no further editions on any of our books."

1981 Statement: *See* 1976 Statement

MAGE PUBLISHERS INC.

1994 Statement: "On the ISBN/copyright page there is a line which will indicate the edition."

2000 Statement: *See* 1994 Statement

MAGNUS PRESS

2000 Statement: "We identify the first printing of a first edition by the following statement: 'First Edition, 2000' [and by] the following number line: '10 9 8 7 6 5 4 3 2 1.' All books published by Magnus Press and its imprint Canticle Books follow the same format."

MAHARISHI INTERNATIONAL UNIVERSITY PRESS

1994 Statement: "We have no way of designating first printing. Subsequent printings are stated so on the inside cover page as '2nd printing 1994' etc."

2001 Statement: "The name of the University changed in June 1995."

See 2001 Statement of Maharishi University of Management Press

MAHARISHI UNIVERSITY OF MANAGEMENT PRESS

2001 Statement: *See* 1994 Statement of Maharishi International University Press.

THE MAIN STREET PRESS

1976 Statement: "No, we have no particular manner in which to indicate first editions, other than the usual 'FIRST PRINTING' on the copyright page."

1981 Statement: "No, we have no particular manner in which to indicate first editions, other than the usual 'FIRST EDITION' on the copyright page."
1988 Statement: "Our general copyright notice carries the year of first publication. Subsequent printings or editions are indicated as such on the copyright page."

MAISONNEUVE PRESS
1995 Statement: "In the past, we have never identified the first printing of first editions . . . . We print cloth and paper books simultaneously and release them at the same time. We do identify second editions (i.e., with changes in the content) on the copyright page."

MALEDICTA PRESS
2000 Statement: "We identify the first printing of a first edition by printing 'First Edition' on the copyright page."

MALLINSON RENDEL PUBLISHERS (NEW ZEALAND)
1994 Statement: "We identify first printings of first editions by stating on the imprint page:
　　First published in 1994 by
　　Mallinson Rendel Publishers
"Reprints are listed on the imprint page."
2000 Statement: *See* 1994 Statement

MANCHESTER UNITED (UNITED KINGDOM)
2000 Statement: *See* 2000 Statement of Andre Deutsch (United Kingdom)

MANCHESTER UNIVERSITY PRESS (UNITED KINGDOM)
1976 Statement: "As a matter of fact we don't really have anything to identify our first editions: it is only reprints or subsequent editions that are identified by some such statement as 'reprinted 1976' or 'Second edition 1976', or 'Second, revised, edition 1976.' "
1981 Statement: "The Press goes on the assumption that a book is a first edition unless otherwise indicated: a new MUP book will include no specific statement that it is a first edition, but a new impression or edition will always be designated as such on the back of the title page."
1988 Statement: "The absence of any indication on the reverse of the title page that the book is a new impression or a new edition indicates that the book is published for the first time. A new impression or new edition will always be designated as such."

MANDARIN NZ (NEW ZEALAND)
1994 Statement: *See* 1994 Statement of Reed Publishing (NZ) Ltd (New Zealand)

MANDRAKE OF OXFORD (UNITED KINGDOM)
1994 Statement: "I have to admit that we have not been very consistent in identifying first editions of our books. It used to be easier when the British Library was issuing CIP data and we simply copied this information onto the reverse title page of our books.

"Mandrake of Oxford started publishing in 1988. Up until 1994 we have only reprinted one or two pamphlets, so anything of ours dated before then is a first edition. The exceptions are: Jean Overton Fuller, *The Magical Dilemma of Victor Neuburg* and Jan Fries, *Visual Magick.*

"I will try to ensure that from now on all first editions are clearly marked as such on the reverse titles page, or other convenient spot. The form of words will be '© Mandrake of Oxford and respective author, first edition date.' "

2000 Statement: "No real change although I've been using 'year zero' as designation for YTK. The first edition of Snoo Wilson's black comedy *I Crowley* can be identified by the numberous typos and the goatskin 'tail' pasted on the spine."

MANIC D. PRESS

1995 Statement: "We designate the first printing by number on the bottom of the copyright page. We list the numbers from left to right, with 1 being the first number in the case of a first printing. We do not designate a first edition in our books."

MANIFEST PUBLICATIONS

2000 Statement: "Subsequent printings of our titles are identified by Second Printing, Ninth Printing, etc. If the volume has no indication of subsequent printings it is a first edition."

GEORGE MANN BOOKS (UNITED KINGDOM)

2001 Statement: "We identify only editions, not printings; a first edition is so identified on the copyright page."

MANSELL PUBLISHING (UNITED KINGDOM)

1994 Statement: *See* 1988 Statement of Mansell Publishing Limited (United Kingdom)

MANSELL PUBLISHING LIMITED (UNITED KINGDOM)

1988 Statement: "Mansell use the following legend on the reverse title page of all books:

First published 1988 (or whatever year)
by Mansell Publishing Limited (followed by address).

"If there is a second printing, the above would be followed by the following:
Reprinted 1989.

"And:
Second reprinting 1990.

"If we have limited territories, the first line might read:
First published in the United Kingdom 1988
by Mansell Publishing Limited"

MANUSCRIPT MEMORIES

1994, 2001 Statements: *See* 1994 Statement of Pocahontas Press

MANUSCRIPT PRESS

2000 Statement: "We identify the first printing of a first edition by the statement 'FIRST EDITION' on reverse title page."

PETER MARCAN PUBLICATIONS (UNITED KINGDOM)
1994 Statement: "My first editions are not normally designated as such on the title page, but the first edition of a new directory can be clearly deduced from introductory comments; second or third impressions are not normally designated as such. Any edition subsequent to the first will be designated as such on the title page, and on the reverse of the title page, with details of previous editions."

2000 Statement: *See* 1994 Statement. Note that, "In addition to directories, there are catalogues, reprints and pictorial publications on various London localities."

MARCH STREET PRESS
1995 Statement: "Unless a book is a special numbered printing, there is nothing to distinguish the first edition from the last, except the actual edits, of course."

2000 Statement: *See* 1995 Statement

MARCHAM BOOKS (UNITED KINGDOM)
1994, 2000 Statements: *See* 1994 Statement of Appleford Publishing Group (United Kingdom)

MARCHAM MANOR PRESS (UNITED KINGDOM)
1994, 2000 Statements: *See* 1994 Statement of Appleford Publishing Group (United Kingdom)

RICHARD MAREK PUBLISHERS, INC.
1981 Statement: "Our first printing, as it always has, goes unmarked; however subsequent printings are identified by '(*the number*) impression,' i.e., first impression, second impression, etc., on the copyright page."

MARGENT PRESS
1947 Statement: *See* 1947 Statement of Richard R. Smith

CC. MARIMBO COMMUNICATIONS
2000 Statement: "CC. Marimbo minichaps are issued in editions of 26 copies, lettered A-Z. Larger collections will say on the copyright page, printing & date, i.e., 1st printing, Oct., 2000."

MARINO BOOKS (REPUBLIC OF IRELAND)
2001 Statement: *See* 2001 Statement of The Mercier Press Ltd (Republic of Ireland)

MARKOWSKI INTERNATIONAL PUBLISHERS
2001 Statement: "We do not identify first editions."

MARLBORO PRESS/NORTHWESTERN UNIVERSITY PRESS
1995, 2000 Statements: *See* 1995 Statement of Northwestern University Press

MARLOR PRESS INC
2001 Statement: "We do not identify a first printing; we do identify subsequent printings. Second and following editions are designated on the copyright page. We also add 'revised' if the text is substantially updated."

MARLOWE & COMPANY
2000 Statement: "We identify the first printing of a first edition by the number line 9 8 7 6 5 4 3 2 1. Any subsequent printings are acknowledged by the dropping of a number."
See also Avalon Publishing Group Incorporated

MARQUETTE UNIVERSITY PRESS
2001 Statement: "We do not identify first printings. We do identify subsequent editions on the copyright page and front jacket. Interested individuals may contact the Press for the Book Title's history."

MARTELLO BOOKS (REPUBLIC OF IRELAND)
1994 Statement: *See* 1994 Statement of The Mercier Press Ltd (Republic of Ireland)
(Martello Books was renamed Marino Books several years ago.)

PETER MARTIN ASSOCIATES LIMITED (CANADA)
1976 Statement: "Our practice here is to designate only editions after the first (*second edition*, etc.); we do not designate printings."
1981 Statement: Since 1976, a new system was initiated. Besides the copyright date, the numbers 1 through 10 are printed in a line at the right side of the page. A first printing would show all of the numbers.
"In subsequent printings one of the numbers for the string of numbers (1-10) at the right side of the page would be dropped; e.g. for a second printing the '1' would be dropped so that the first number appearing would be '2.' A second edition would be designated as such with a string of numbers 1-10 for that edition."

MARTIN BRIAN & O'KEEFFE LTD. (UNITED KINGDOM)
1976 Statement: "Our first editions are identified quite simply, by the words 'First published in (year) by Martin Brian & O'Keeffe Ltd. 37 Museum Street London WC1,' followed by 'Copyright (©) (author's name) (year).' "

MARYLAND HISTORICAL SOCIETY
2001 Statement: "The Press at the Maryland Historical Society does not normally signify a first edition or a first printing, but subsequent editions and printings are so noted on the copyright page."

MARYLAND STATE ARCHIVES
1994 Statement: "The Maryland State Archives has not adopted a method of designating first editions. We publish little, most of what we do publish never goes beyond a first edition, and were this to happen, a statement such as 'second edition,' along with the year of publication, would be all that would appear."

MASQUERADE BOOKS

1994 Statement: "We identify the first printing of our books by inserting on the copyright page the phrase 'First printing, month, year.' Subsequent printings are differentiated by using the phrase 'Second printing, month, year,' etc.

"This is Masquerade Books' method for all publications and imprints."

MASTER KEY PRODUCTIONS

2000 Statement: *See* 2000 Statement of Blue Dolphin Publishing Inc.

ELKIN MATHEWS & MARROT, LTD.
(UNITED KINGDOM)
(Succeeded prior to 1937 by Ivor Nicholson & Watson, Ltd.)

1928 Statement: "In the case of a first impression we make no special mention; subsequent printings are noted on verso of title-page. In the case of Limited Editions we insert an explanatory note. All our books without exception we date on the title page. Such has in former years been the usual practice it is now invariable."

1937 Statement: "In the case of a first impression we make no special mention, subsequent printings are noted on verso of title-page. In the case of Limited Editions we insert an explanatory note. All our books without exception we date on the title page. Such has in former years been the usual practice: it is now invariable.

"Since 1933, when the policy of the firm changed and only educational text books have been issued, no indication whatsoever of a first edition or subsequent edition is given."

MATSON'S PUBLICATIONS (UNITED KINGDOM)

1947 Statement: "All our editions bear the date of publication. Thus the first edition might be—
'First published November 1947'
"The next edition would carry the lines—
'First published November 1947
Reprinted December 1947,' and so on."

MAUPIN HOUSE

1994 Statement: The first printing of a first edition is indicated by the words "First Edition" on the copyright page. This method has been in use since 1988.

MAXIMA NEW MEDIA

2000 Statement: "Our books are first editions unless copyright page explicitly states otherwise."

MAYHAVEN PUBLISHING

1994 Statement: The printing is identified by a numerical string (10 9 8 7 6 5 4 3 2 1). The lowest number indicates the printing. This method of designation does not differ from any previously used.
2001 Statement: *See* 1994 Statement

MBI PUBLISHING COMPANY

2001 Statement: *See* 2001 Statement of Motorbooks International

McBOOKS PRESS

1995 Statement: "McBooks Press generally indicates the number of printings of a title by printing a descending sequence of numerals at the bottom of the copyright page: '9 8 7 6 5 4 3 2 1.' All the numbers including the '1' appear on the first printing. In each subsequent printing, the last numeral is deleted. Therefore, the lowest numeral present indicates the number of the printing."

2000 Statement: *See* 1995 Statement

ROBERT M. McBRIDE & CO.

1928 Statement: "Our designation of the first edition is usually the line reading either First Published April 1927 or Published April 1927. This line is retained in all subsequent editions but the number of the printing is added below it in the second line such as Second Printing, June, 1927, changed on the next printing to Third Printing, etc.

"Our practice, of course, in the past has not been uniformly thus, but we are among the few houses which has consistently printed the number of the edition on the back of the title page."

1937 Statement: *See* 1928 Statement

1947 Statement: "Our designation of the first edition is the line stating First Edition. The date of the first edition, of course, appears above this designation in the copyright notice. In the case of second and subsequent printings, we use the line Second Printing, March 1948. You can see from this that only those volumes that are actually first editions carry the designation of first editions. All following editions are marked with the number of the printing."

McCLELLAND & STEWART LTD. (CANADA)

2000 Statement: "Our practice has not changed since our last [1993 Statement of McClelland and Stewart Inc. (Canada)] statement. All of our imprints follow this practice. Macfarlane Walter & Ross and Tundra Books are *not* imprints of McClelland & Stewart, rather they are separate companies that are owned by McClelland & Stewart . . . Stewart House Publishing is no longer an imprint of M&S, they are now a separate company. Douglas Gibson Books are a series produced by McClelland & Stewart, sharing the same ISBN prefix as we do, and not a separate imprint. Hurtig is still an M&S imprint. Our company name changed July 1, 2000."

McCLELLAND AND STEWART INC. (CANADA)

1993 Statement: "As previously [under the 1976 Statement of McClelland and Stewart Limited (Canada)], we give no explicit designation to a first edition. As of Fall 1993, the number and year of printing and reprintings are indicated by number lines at the bottom of the copyright page [e.g. 1 2 3 4 5 97 96 95 94 93. The lowest number designates the printing]. New format editions are specifically designated on the copyright page. There are occasional exceptions."

2000 Statement: *See* 2000 Statement of McClelland & Stewart Ltd. (Canada)

McCLELLAND AND STEWART LIMITED (CANADA)

1976 Statement: McClelland and Stewart has no specific designation for a first edition. All reprintings or editions are indicated on the copyright page. While this practice is usually consistent, there are exceptions.

1981 Statement: *See* 1976 Statement

1993 Statement: *See* 1993 Statement of McClelland and Stewart Inc. (Canada)

McFARLAND & COMPANY, INC., PUBLISHERS

1988 Statement: "We do not designate first *editions* or first *printings*; we rarely designate *reprintings* except that if corrections are made we say so near the C.I.P./copyright page (e.g., 'second printing with corrections and revisions').

"All subsequent *editions* are clearly marked."

1993 Statement: *See* 1988 Statement

2000 Statement: "We do not designate first *editions* or first *printings*; we rarely designate *reprintings* except that if a substantial number of corrections are made we say so near the C.I.P./copyright page (e.g., 'second printing with corrections and revisions').

"All subsequent *editions* are clearly marked."

"[Our] practices have not changed [from 1988] except that we now do 'First Edition, first printing' on about 1% of our titles each year.

"We very seldom designate 'First edition, first printing.' When we do it is because we believe (e.g., with two Edgar Rice Burroughs reference books) there is a potential antiquarian or bibliophile interest beyond the ordinary; in such cases we scrupulously scrap the statement in any print run after the first. Our books are frequently 'reprinted' because, as a nontrade publisher . . . our initial print runs are frequently 1000 or even fewer. So the terms don't apply to us as they do to many (i.e., our average title is *intended* to have more than one print run).

"Any true second or succeeding editions are very clearly designated as such.

"Occasionally (seldom) a second or later printing has had a sufficient number of corrections that we say so—e.g., 'second printing with corrections.' "

McGRAW-HILL PUBLISHING COMPANY

1988 Statement: *See* 1988 Statement of McGraw-Hill Ryerson Limited (Canada)

McGRAW-HILL RYERSON LIMITED (CANADA)

1988 Statement: "First and subsequent editions of our books are designated in the copyright notice, indicating the copyright year of the first edition and each subsequent edition. This method has been used since we started publishing in Canada around 1954.

"Printings are indicated in a reprint line on the copyright page showing the number of the printing and the year in which the reprint was made. This style has been used since 1965. We had previously listed the number of printings made.

"We follow the style used by our parent company, McGraw-Hill Publishing Company."

1993 Statement: *See* 1988 Statement

McGUFFIN BOOKS

1995 Statement: *See* 1995 Statement of Gaslight Publications, Inc.

DAVID McKAY CO.

1928 Statement: "There isn't any way you could identify the first editions of our books."

1937, 1947 Statements: *See* 1928 Statement

1988 Statement: " 'First Printing' will appear on copyright page of a first edition book."

See also 1976 Statement of Random House, Inc.

THE DECLAN X. McMULLEN COMPANY, INC.

1947 Statement: "Only two of our books have gone into second printings. As a temporary measure we have indicated this fact on the jacket.

"Should our later publications go into additional printings, and we expect that they will, we shall probably include the fact on the copyright page. No decision has been made as yet, however, on this point.

"Several books published in England, to which we have the American rights and which have been issued under our imprint, announce this fact also only on the jacket."

McNALLY & LOFTIN, PUBLISHERS

1976 Statement: "We've never paid any heed to this aspect of our work. Some of our books are now in their 17th or 18th printing. I'd have to spend a week in trying to figure out my own first editions."

1981 Statement: *See* McNally & Loftin, West

1989 Statement: "Our first printings are now noted as 'First Edition' on the © page. It is removed on subsequent printings."

1994 Statement: *See* 1989 Statement

McNALLY & LOFTIN, WEST

1981 Statement: "We still reprint books with little regard for exactly which edition is involved. I myself have found that the first edition is likely to have typos that are corrected in subsequent reprints."

See also McNally & Loftin, Publishers

WAYNE L. McNAUGHTON, PUBLISHER

1947 Statement: "We use three figures separated by periods, thus: 1.1.1. The first designates the stock number of the title, the second the edition, and the third, the printing. 10.2.4, for instance, would mean title #10, second edition, and 4th. printing of the 2d. edition."

McPHEE GRIBBLE (AUSTRALIA)
1994 Statement: *See* 1994 Statement of Penguin Books Australia Ltd (Australia)

McPHEE GRIBBLE PUBLISHERS PTY LTD (AUSTRALIA)
1988 Statement: "McPhee Gribble began publishing in 1975.

"Our company indicates first printings on all our publications.

"Since 1983 marketing and distribution has been handled by Penguin Books and all our paperback publications carry a joint imprint to maximize sales. We are, however, the initiating publisher."

Sample imprint pages supplied show hardback first printings identified on copyright page by:

"First published 19—."

Paperback first printings are identified by:

"First published by McPhee Gribble Publishers
in association with Penguin Books Australia 1986"

McPHERSON & COMPANY
1988 Statement: "McPherson & Company was developed in 1983 from Treacle Press (founded in 1973) and Documentext (an imprint added in 1979). No Treacle Press books were reprinted, aside from a second edition of *Shamp of the City-Solo* in 1980.

"In most cases for all books of our imprints the copyright page will state 'first edition,' which is removed in subsequent printings. Often a series of numbers also appears on the copyright page, the lowest number being the printing.

"Special edition notices are dropped from second and subsequent printings, and often we provide a publishing history if we are presenting a new edition of a book originated elsewhere. It should be noted that simultaneous hardcover, paperback, and/or deluxe signed hardcover versions are often released together as the first edition of a book."

1993, 2000 Statements: *See* 1988 Statement

WALTER McVITTY BOOKS (AUSTRALIA)
1994 Statement: "On our reprint page we state 'First published 1994' (or other date). If no other date appears, this is our first edition. This statement remains on all editions. For subsequent reprints we add 'Reprinted 1994 (twice), 1995' etc. For paperback editions of former hardbacks we add 'First published in this edition 1995.' We have used this method of designation from our first publication in 1985."

MD BOOKS
2000 Statement: *See* 2000 Statement of May Davenport Publishers

P D MEANY CO INC (CANADA)
2001 Statement: "We do not do anything to identify a first printing of a first edition."

MEDFORD PRESS
2000 Statement: *See* 2000 Statement of Plexus Publishing, Inc.

THE MEDIA INSTITUTE
2000 Statement: "We do not specifically identify first editions since we have never issued a second edition of a book. We treat an annual edition of an ongoing title as a first edition . . . . However, we do identify printings on the copyright page of every book with the following statement: 'First printing (month, year).' "

MEDICAL EXAMINATION PUBLISHING COMPANY
1988 Statement: *See* 1988 Statement of Elsevier Science Publishing Company, Inc.

MEDICAL PHYSICS PUBLISHING CORP
2000 Statement: "We do not use a statement to designate the first edition of one of our books. We do use the impression line 06 05 04 03 02 01 5 4 3 2 1 [which] would indicate the first edition published in 2001. The line would be modified to indicate subsequent printings in different years or a new edition. Cogito Books is an imprint of Medical Physics Publishing but is not in use at present . . . If we were to resurrect Cogito Books, we would use the same methods used for MPP books."

MEDICI SOCIETY, LTD. (UNITED KINGDOM)
1937 Statement: "As you are probably aware, we are publishers of both the Riccardi Press books, which are set by hand, and also books produced in the normal manner from machine set type. All the Riccardi Press books are published in limited editions and not reprinted, the editions being limited to the number stated on the certificate which faces the half-title. Date on title page. With our ordinary books it is usual to put the publication date:
1. On the foot of the title page, or
2. On the reverse of the title page below the line 'Printed in Great Britain.'
   "On reprints we do not usually put the date on the title page, but on the reverse, printing a bibliographical note as—
   FIRST PUBLISHED (or FIRST PRINTED) 1930
   REPRINTED (or 2d. EDITION) 1931
the difference being that if the book is printed from standing type we state REPRINTED or if the book is revised to any extent then we use the words, 2d. EDITION."
1947 Statement: *See* 1937 Statement

THE MEDICI SOCIETY LIMITED (UNITED KINGDOM)
1976 Statement: "In answer to your query: no, we do not identify first editions of our children's books and art books. The Publisher's copyright line carries the year of first publication and is repeated unchanged in subsequent impressions. If we make any revisions in a particular title, we would print, for instance, *Revised, 1976*."
1981, 1988, 1994 Statements: *See* 1976 Statement

MEL BAY PUBLICATIONS INC

2001 Statement: "We do not identify a first printing or any printing after the first printing on the copyright page."

MELBOURNE UNIVERSITY PRESS (AUSTRALIA)

1976 Statement: "Our method of identifying first editions is quite simply to place upon the imprint page (the title page verso) the words 'First published 1976' (or whatever year the publication first appeared)."

1981, 1988, 1994 Statements: *See* 1976 Statement

MELLEN BIBLICAL PRESS

2000 Statement: *See* 2000 Statement of The Edwin Mellen Press

MELLEN POETRY PRESS

2000 Statement: *See* 2000 Statement of The Edwin Mellen Press

THE EDWIN MELLEN PRESS

2000 Statement: "We do not designate first editions as Mellen books remain in print indefinitely. We reprint and rebind our books continuously 'on demand', making the scholarship available for many years. If the book is substantially revised, we indicate 'Revised Edition' on the copyright page with date of revision."

ANDREW MELROSE, LTD. (UNITED KINGDOM)

1935 Statement: *See* 1935 Statement of John Long, Limited (United Kingdom)

MEMPHIS STATE UNIVERSITY PRESS

1976 Statement: "We do not indicate 'first editions' as such but do indicate subsequent 'printings' and editions and revisions as they occur."

1981 Statement: "Our policy on the designation of first printing has not changed. Therefore, 1976 statement is accurate for all our publications including imprints."

1988 Statement: *See* 1981 Statement

MENASHA RIDGE PRESS

1994 Statement: "Before 1990, books published by us were sporadically indicated as first editions, though more often than not. After 1990, notice of first edition appears on the copyright page, sometimes followed by 'first printing' and the year. One exception is our 'cartoon' books which simply list the current printing with (sometimes) the year."

MENTOR

1988 Statement: *See* 1988 Statement of New American Library

1993, 2000 Statements: *See* 1993 Statement of Dutton Signet

MERCAT PRESS (UNITED KINGDOM)

1993 Statement: "To designate a first edition we print, on the title page verso, the following:

First published in 19... by Mercat Press
James Thin, 53 South Bridge, Edinburgh EH1 1YS
© [the author] 19...

"If the book is a reprint or new edition we add this information under the second line, e.g.

Reprinted 1991, 1994

"We have used the same or very similar designation since we started publishing in 1970."

2000 Statement: *See* 1993 Statement

MERCER UNIVERSITY PRESS

1988 Statement: "First editions are not designated as such on our copyrights page; however, any succeeding edition—revised, second, and so forth—is so designated."

1993, 2000 Statements: *See* 1988 Statement

THE MERCIER PRESS, LIMITED
(CORK, REPUBLIC OF IRELAND)

1947 Statement: "There is an announcement, usually on the back of the title page of all our publications, indicating the year of issue, and all subsequent printings carry similar announcements giving full particulars of all previous printings. Where two or more reprints are issued in any one year it is usual to give the month of issue."

1988 Statement: *See* 1988 Statement of The Mercier Press Ltd (Republic of Ireland)

THE MERCIER PRESS LTD (REPUBLIC OF IRELAND)

1988 Statement: "The statement regarding Mercier Press published in your first edition still holds good."

1994 Statement: "There is an announcement, usually on the back of the title page, indicating year of issue. The figures 1 to 10 are also printed on this page and are deleted in ascending order to indicate the number of subsequent reprints."

2001 Statement: *See* 1994 Statement

MERCURY HOUSE

1994 Statement: "At Mercury House we print '5 4 3 2 1' at the bottom of the copyright page and for each subsequent reprint delete the lowest number, leaving the lowest number remaining to indicate the printing number. On a few occasions we will put 'FIRST EDITION' on the title page beneath our name."

2000 Statement: *See* 1994 Statement

MEREDITH BOOKS

1994 Statement: "We use 'First Edition. Printing Number and Year 5 4 3 2 1 97 96 95 94 93.' When reprinted we delete last digit of printing number, and past year(s) if appropriate. This information appears on the copyright page.

"We began this new practice in the Fall of 1991.

"In the past we used 'First edition, first printing,' and updated as we reprinted."

MERIDIAN
1988 Statement: *See* 1988 Statement of New American Library
1993, 2000 Statements: *See* 1993 Statement of Dutton Signet

MERIDIAN BOOKS, LTD. (UNITED KINGDOM)
1947 Statement: "It is not the policy of this firm to identify first printings of our books by any particular system. In the event of a second edition of a book it is our practice to insert:—
FIRST PUBLISHED (followed by month and year)
SECOND EDITION (date)."

MERIDIAN BOOKS (UNITED KINGDOM)
2001 Statement: "On the title verso we state: 'Published (year) by Meridian Books (Copyright symbol) (author) (year).'
"On subsequent editions we state:
First published (year) by Meridian Books
Second edition (etc) (year) (copyright symbol) (author) (year)
or:
Published by Meridian Books
First edition (year)
Second edition (etc) (year)
(copyright symbol) (author) (year)."

MERIDIONAL PUBLICATIONS
1995 Statement: "No indication is made on a first printing/first edition. In the few cases when we get into a second printing we add the line 'Second printing 19XX' to the copyright page. A similar indication is made for second editions."

MERIWETHER PUBLISHING LTD.
1988 Statement: "Since 1983, when we began publishing books in addition to plays, we put 'First Edition' under our copyright notice. When we do a second printing we indicate this under the edition designation. If we do a second edition revision we so indicate. We have no subsidiaries."
1993, 2000 Statements: *See* 1988 Statement

MEISHA MERLIN PUBLISHING, INC.
2000 Statement: "Meisha Merlin gives both the print date(s) and uses a number bar to show the print history of our titles on the bottom of the copyright page.
Example for the first edition:
First MM Publishing Edition February 1999
Printed in the United States
0 9 8 7 6 5 4 3 2 1
Example for later editions:
First MM Publishing edition February 1999

Second edition July 2000
Printed in the United States
0 9 8 7 6 5 4 3 2."

MERLIN BOOKS LTD PUBLISHERS (UNITED KINGDOM)

1988 Statement: "Our first editions are identified by the words:
First published in Great Britain—followed by the date.
"Reprints are identified by:
Reprinted—followed by the date.
"Subsequent impressions are not identified."
1994 Statement: *See* 1988 Statement

THE MERLIN PRESS LTD. (UNITED KINGDOM)

1988 Statement: "We endeavour to follow best British bibliographical practice, but Homer (and Merlin) frequently nods."

MERMAID BOOKS (UNITED KINGDOM)

1994 Statement: *See* 1994 Statement of Michael Joseph Ltd. (United Kingdom)

MERRIAM-WEBSTER INC.

1989 Statement: "Since the mid-1970s, the copyright pages of all of our books have included a printing key near the bottom of the page. The number that is farthest to the left is the printing number. Hence, the first printing can be identified by a '1' in the first position. (Note, of course, that the sequence of numbers would have to be '1234'; '121314' would indicate the twelfth printing.)

"Before the mid-1970s, the title pages of many of our books (but probably not all) included a boxed number that indicated the printing number. The first printing of *Webster's Third* includes no number on its copyright page, but I believe all subsequent printings do.

"First printings of the eighth edition of *Webster's New Collegiate Dictionary* and of *Webster's Ninth New Collegiate Dictionary* include the note 'First printing' on the copyright page."
See also 1988 Statement of Encyclopaedia Britannica, Inc.
1993 Statement: "First printings of the eighth edition of *Webster's New Collegiate Dictionary* and of *Webster's Ninth New Collegiate Dictionary* and of *Merriam-Webster's Collegiate Dictionary, Tenth Edition* include the note 'First Printing' on the copyright page."
2000 Statement: "Our 1989 and 1993 statements are still current. In addition, our Federal Street Press imprint began publishing in 1999. The printing key at the bottom of the copyright page of Federal Street Press books consists of spaced numbers ordered '1 3 5 ... 6 4 2' or ' ... 4 3 2 1'; as with our other book, the number of the previous printing is removed from the key when the book goes back to press, so the presence of '1' at the far left or far right of the key indicates a first printing."

MERRILL PUBLISHING CO/COLLEGE DIVISION

1993 Statement: *See* 1993 Statement of Macmillan, Inc.

MESORAH PUBLICATIONS LTD

2001 Statement: "We identify first editions as well as succeeding editions and printings on the copyright page."

JULIAN MESSNER, INC.

1937 Statement: "We have, up to now, made no differentiation between our first and subsequent editions of books other than the conventional copyright page revision."

1947 Statement: "Our first editions bear only the copyright date; subsequent editions bear the further legend of second printing, third printing, etc. as the case may be. This appears on the copyright page."

1976 Statement: "We do not identify a first edition. Subsequent reprintings bear the notation Second printing, 1977 or whatever, etc."

1981 Statement: *See* 1976 Statement

METACOM PRESS

1995 Statement: "We are a small press that specializes in limited first editions. To date (i.e., in the period 1980-95), we have published twelve titles, all of which are designated first editions in the colophon which follows the text, and sometimes also on the copyright page (verso of title page).

"Since we publish only limited, numbered editions, none of our publications ever goes into a second printing or second edition. However, since our standard contract gives us rights only to the first edition, works originally published by Metacom Press have regularly appeared later in some other publisher's commercial format.

"It should be pointed out that for whatever reason, we are rarely given credit for our first printings or first editions in these commercial volumes. The commercial publishers' tendency is to proceed as if our publication had never occurred, and their negligence occasionally causes confusion among collectors and scholars.

"Because of the similarity in our names, we are often confused with Metacom Inc., a Minnesota publisher of audio tapes. Our Metacom Press is not connected with Metacom Inc. in any way."

METHUEN (UNITED KINGDOM)

1994 Statement: *See* 1994 Statement of Reed Consumer Books (United Kingdom)

2000 Statement: *See* 2000 Statement of The Random House Group Limited (United Kingdom)

METHUEN, INC.

1988 Statement: *See* 1988 Statement of Routledge, Chapman and Hall, Inc.

METHUEN & CO. LTD. (UNITED KINGDOM)

(For statement of practice from 1889 through 1989 see 1989 Statement of The Octopus Publishing Group PLC [United Kingdom])

1928 Statement: "For some years past all first editions of books we have published have had on the back of the title page 'First Published in . . . .' As and when the book is reprinted so a further note is added.

"This does not apply to Limited Editions, which bear on the back of the title page a note to the effect that 'This Edition is Limited to . . . . copies of which this is No.. ...' "

1937 Statement: "Since 1905 all first editions of books we have published have had on the back of the title page 'First Published in . . . .' As and when the book is reprinted so a further note is added.

"In the case of books first published in the U.S.A. the words 'First published in Great Britain in . . . .' are used.

"Limited Editions bear on the back of the title page a note to the effect that 'This Edition is Limited to . . . copies of which this is No . . . .'

"Translations of foreign books published by us bear on the back of the title page 'First published in (French) under the title of . . . . This translation first published in Great Britain in . . . .' "

1947 Statement: *See* 1937 Statement

Statement for 1960: The copyright page of a book in its first printing would carry the statement "First published in 1960."

1976, 1982 Statements: *See* Statement for 1960

1988 Statement: *See* 1988 Statement of Routledge, Chapman and Hall (United Kingdom)

See also 1989 Statement of The Octopus Publishing Group PLC (United Kingdom)

METHUEN CHILDREN'S (UNITED KINGDOM)
1989 Statement: *See* the Methuen entry in the 1989 Statement of The Octopus Publishing Group PLC (United Kingdom)

METHUEN CHILDREN'S BOOKS (UNITED KINGDOM)
1994 Statement: *See* 1994 Statement of Reed Consumer Books (United Kingdom)

METHUEN LONDON (UNITED KINGDOM)
1989 Statement: *See* the Methuen entry in the 1989 Statement of The Octopus Publishing Group PLC (United Kingdom)

METIER EDITIONS
See Rising Tide Press

METROPOLITAN BOOKS
2000 Statement: *See* 2000 Statement of Henry Holt and Company, LLC

THE METROPOLITAN MUSEUM OF ART
1976 Statement: "This institution rarely produces a second edition, but often produces second and third printings of a first edition. In a second printing . . . we ordinarily make corrections in text or illustrations, whether minor or major, without calling attention to same. It would be routine, therefore, to expect some differences between first and second printings. In a current instance, our second printing of a book involves issuing copies in dust jackets, whereas the same book when first published, was put jacketless into a slipcase. In another instance, illustrations printed originally in one black (one

pass through the press), are printed in two blacks (a second press pass) in the second printing to improve the quality of the reproduction. In any of these cases, the original copyright date (or printing date, if the book was produced for us abroad) will tell the scholar that he is holding the first edition in hand. We routinely print the year and 'second printing,' etc., on the copyright page or in the colophon notice when we reprint."

This method of identification does not differ from any previously used.

1981 Statement: *See* 1976 Statement

1988 Statement: "This institution rarely produces a second edition, but often produces second and third printings of a first edition. In a second printing . . . we ordinarily make corrections in text or illustrations, whether minor or major, without calling attention to same. It would be routine, therefore, to expect some differences between first and second printings. In any case, the original copyright date will tell the scholar that he is holding the first edition in hand. We routinely print the year and 'second printing,' etc., on the copyright page when we reprint."

This method of identification does not differ from any previously used.

1994 Statement: "Nothing has changed since our last statement; we still rarely produce a second edition, instead print second and third printings. Our *Guide* has just appeared in the second edition: its copyright page reads 'Second Edition, 1994.' "

METROPOLITAN PRESS

1976 Statement: *See* 1976 Statement of Binford & Mort

DAVID MEYER MAGIC BOOKS

1994, 2000 Statements: *See* 1994 Statement of Meyerbooks Publisher

MEYERBOOKS PUBLISHER

1988 Statement: "First editions are *not* designated.

"Second, third and later printings are usually, but not always, designated by simple statement: 'Second printing.' No date of later printing is given.

"Revised editions are noted: 'This edition, with additions and modifications, copyright [year].'

"Price changes and new ad copy on back covers appears on later printings of every work."

1994 Statement: "Meyerbooks does not designate first printings on its books. However, later printings usually carry appropriate information on the copyright page, such as: 'Second printing, [month and year].'

"On titles which we issue under the imprint David Meyer Magic Books, first editions carry the year of publication on the title page. Later printings do not have a date on the title page. On the copyright page the later printing is noted as 'Second printing,' 'Third printing,' etc.

"The above designations have been employed since the founding of the business in 1976."

2000 Statement: *See* 1994 Statement

MFA PUBLICATIONS
(A Division of the Museum of Fine Arts, Boston.)
2000 Statement: *See* 2000 Statement of the Museum of Fine Arts, Boston

MIAMI UNIVERSITY PRESS
2000 Statement: "We identify the first printing of a first edition by the following number line: 9 8 7 6 5 4 3 2 1."

MICHI: JAPANESE ARTS AND WAYS
2000 Statement: *See* 2000 Statement of Stone Bridge Press

MICHIGAN STATE UNIVERSITY PRESS
1988 Statement: "Unless designated otherwise, assume that it is first printing."
1995 Statement: "I am writing to address your inquiry on how we and the Lotus Press identify first printings of books. This information is located on the copyright page, and is expressed in a series of numbers. This list numbers inward, years on the left, and editions on the right. If it is a first edition, the one is the central number, and the year of the first edition is to the one's left. For example, here is a sequence from one of our books: 01 99 98 97 96 95 1 2 3 4 5 6 7. From this list, the first edition was printed in 1995."
2000 Statement: "First edition information is located on the copyright page and is expressed as a series of numbers. The first portion of the series (the numbers to the left) represents a sequence of possible years of publication (in reverse order); the possible list of printing numbers appears to the right in (numerical order). If a book is, in fact, a first edition, then the lowest possible publication year (on the left) will be the actual year of publication; the number '1' (the first printing and the first year of publication) will appear as the first digit in the grouping of numbers to the right. For example, a first printing (edition) of a book published in the year 2000 would be indicated as follows: 05 04 03 02 01 00 1 2 3 4 5 6. A second printing of that same book in the year 2000 would be indicated as follows: 05 04 03 02 01 00 2 3 4 5 6."
"Lotus Press follows the same practice."

MICROSOFT PRESS
1988 Statement: "We do not designate a first edition, but we do indicate editions 2, 3, 4, etc. Printings are designated by a print line on the copyright page (1 2 3 4 5 6 7 8 9), with each number being omitted as the book is reprinted. We also use the print line to show when a title is printed or reprinted, using the same number method:
1 2 3 4 5 6 7 8 9 FGFG 3 2 1 0 9 8
(printing) (printer) (year completed)."
1993 Statement: *See* 1988 Statement
2000 Statement: "We do not designate a first edition, but we do indicate subsequent editions as part of the book's title. The print line on the copyright page shows the printing, the printer, and the year printed. The first digit in the print line reflects the printing. The last digit in the print line reflects the year

in which the title was printed or reprinted. For example, the following print line indicates a second printing, completed in 2000:

2 3 4 5 6 7 8 9 MLML 5 4 3 2 1 0."

THE MIDDLE ATLANTIC PRESS, INC.

1988 Statement: "We designate first printings on the copyright page by the notation, 'First Middle Atlantic Press printing, (month, year).'

"Subsequent printings are sometimes (but not always) indicated by the notation, 'Second printing, (date).'

"This method of designation is the one we are currently using. Previously, we did not always indicate the month of publication."

MIDDLETON PRESS (UNITED KINGDOM)

1994 Statement: "All our publications show the year first published on page 2, and also the month since 1985."
2000 Statement: *See* 1994 Statement

MIDLAND BOOKS

2000 Statement: *See* 2000 Statement of Indiana University Press

MIDLAND HOUSE

1947 Statement: *See* 1947 Statement of The Webb Publishing Company

MIDLAND PUBLISHING (UNITED KINGDOM)

2001 Statement: "Since April 1999, Midland Publishing and Aerofax have been imprints of Ian Allan Publishing Ltd. We identify only editions, not printings; a first edition is so identified on the copyright page."
See also 2000 Statement of Ian Allan Publishing (United Kingdom)

MIDMARCH ARTS PRESS

1994 Statement: "Other than including the year of original publication on the copyright page, there is no specific mention of first printing or first edition. There have been two exceptions: 'Guide to Arts Organizations,' which was so expanded in its 'reprint' that we regarded it as a new book and did not identify it as a revised edition, except by reference in the introduction. The other 'Voices of Women' was reprinted with a new cover, additional material, and acknowledged as both Second Printing on copyright page and Reissue on Credits page."
2000 Statement: "We do not identify a first printing but, when we add second and subsequent printings, we then use the following:

First Printing date (season/or month and year)
Second Printing date etc."

MIDWIFERY TODAY, INC.

2000 Statement: "First edition will not have a special statement, simply a copyright date. All subsequent editions will be noted as such, i.e. second edition, third edition, and so on."

MILESTONE PUBLICATIONS (UNITED KINGDOM)
1994 Statement: "Milestone Publications designates first editions in the manner 'First Printed 1978.' Where revised editions are in existence, we normally add on the line underneath 'Revised 1981, 1984, 1986, 1992.' All our imprints follow the same form."
2001 Statement: *See* 1994 Statement

THE MILITARY SERVICE PUBLISHING CO.
1947 Statement: "All of the books which we print are marked either with the edition number in the case of texts, or with the number of printings."

MILKWEED EDITIONS
2001 Statement: "We state 'First edition' on the copyright page. We identify the first printing of a first edition by a number line, the lowest number indicating the printing."

M. S. MILL CO., INC.
1947 Statement: "The method the M. S. Mill Company uses to identify first printings of its books is actually by omission of any reference to the edition on the copyright page. Subsequent editions will indicate the number of the edition and date of publication, so therefore a book not having this information on the copyright page can be assumed to be one of the first printing."

THE MILLBROOK PRESS INC.
1994 Statement: "At the Millbrook Press we designate the first printing of a first edition by a series of numbers under the copyright notice on the copyright page. The lowest number left in the series is the number of the current printing."
2000 Statement: *See* 1994 Statement

MILLE GRAZIE PRESS
2000 Statement: "The words 'First Edition' appear on the copyright page. For subsequent printings, this is replaced by the words 'Second Printing,' 'Third Printing,' and so on, designating the appropriate iteration of the reprint. This is and has been the method employed throughout our publishing history."

MILLENIUM (UNITED KINGDOM)
1994 Statement: *See* 1994 Statement of The Orion Publishing Group Ltd (United Kingdom)

HARVEY MILLER PUBLISHERS (UNITED KINGDOM)
1976 Statement: "We do not identify the first printing in any special way. The imprint page bears the copyright notice and date.

"Subsequent printings would bear the date of the first publication and the date of the reprint or new edition. So that, unless otherwise stated, the book would be a first edition."
1981, 1988 Statements: *See* 1976 Statement

J. GARNET MILLER LTD. (UNITED KINGDOM)

1976 Statement: "What we put in first editions is 'First published by J. Garnet Miller Ltd. in 19..'

"A subsequent printing would retain this and have '2nd Impression', or '2nd Edition' added. This material appears on the back of the title page.

"We have another firm at this address called The Actinic Press, Ltd., which is a medical publisher, and has done books since 1955 in this way. But it is possible that some titles published earlier had a different wording."

1981 Statement: "There is no change in our method of designating first editions in this firm or in The Actinic Press Ltd. The information on your print out is correct for your new edition."

1994, 2000 Statements: *See* 1994 Statement of Cressrelles Publishing Company Ltd. (United Kingdom)

ROBERT MILLER

1994 Statement: "All of our publications are first editions. We have only reprinted one title to date and that was when we licensed a softcover edition to an outside publisher for one of our hardcover titles. We publish in limited editions which have never exceeded 5000 copies."

MILLER FREEMAN BOOKS

2001 Statement: *See* 2001 Statement of Miller Freeman Inc

MILLER FREEMAN INC

2001 Statement: "We identify the first printing of a first edition by a number line, the lowest number indicates the printing."

MILLS & BOON, LTD. (UNITED KINGDOM)

1928 Statement: *See* 1936 Statement

1936 Statement: "We place on the back of the title page the month and the year that we publish our books; as for instance one published in January of this year would be as follows:

Published January 1936

"We have used this method since we first started publishing in 1909."

1947 Statement: "We have been compelled to revise that statement on the back of our title pages, owing to the difficulties of production. Our present method is that we omit the month of publication, and merely state:

First Published 1947 etc."

1976 Statement: First impressions are designated by the words "First published 19.." on the copyright page.

1981 Statement: *See* 1976 Statement

1994 Statement: "First impressions are designated by the words 'First published in Great Britain 19..' on the copyright page."

2000 Statement: "Designation of first printing is as per 1994 statement for all books published under various series. Please note we should be listed as Harlequin Mills & Boon Limited. Our series are Mills & Boon. We also publish under the series names MIRA Books and Silhouette; designation of first printing is as [in the 1994 Statement].

See also Harlequin Mills & Boon Limited (United Kingdom)

MINERVA NZ (NEW ZEALAND)

1994 Statement: *See* 1994 Statement of Reed Publishing (NZ) Ltd (New Zealand)

MINNESOTA HISTORICAL SOCIETY PRESS

1976 Statement: "First editions carry only the copyright date. Revised editions are clearly identified on the title page and in the copyright statement. Subsequent printings of each edition are specified, by date, following the copyright statement."

1981 Statement: *See* 1976 Statement

1988 Statement: "First editions carry the copyright date and the digits 1 through 10, in descending order. Subsequent printings of each edition are indicated by the last number shown; no date is specified. Revised editions are clearly identified on the title page and in the copyright statement.

"We have no separate imprints or subsidiaries."

1993, 2000 Statements: *See* 1988 Statement

MINREF PRESS

2000 Statement: "No indication for first editions; subsequent editions [are] indicated by 'Second Printing' etc."

MINTON BALCH & CO.

1928 Statement: "All first editions of our books contain the date on the title page and the copyright date following. Subsequent printings are indicated by the words (under the copyright notice) 'second printing' with the month and year in which this printing is made."

1937, 1947 Statements: *See* 1928 Statement

MINUTEMAN PRESS

1994 Statement: *See* 1994 Statement of Publishers Associates

MIP COMPANY

2000 Statement: "First printing is designated by copyright © 1984 by M.I.P. Co."

MIRA BOOKS (UNITED KINGDOM)

2000 Statement: *See* 2000 Statement of Harlequin Mills & Boon Limited (United Kingdom)

MISSISSIPPI VALLEY PRESS

1947 Statement: "We only publish one edition."

MISSOURI ARCHAEOLOGICAL SOCIETY

1994 Statement: "When we publish a new title we do not designate that it is a first edition. However, when we reprint an existing title, we do note that it is a second or third printing. This has been the method since 1934 when the Society began."

2001 Statement: *See* 1994 Statement

THE MIT PRESS

1976 Statement: "All first editions at the MIT Press include a copyright page (generally page iv of the front matter) to indicate that the material in the book has not been published before. Revised or subsequent editions of a book also have their own copyright date (through the Library of Congress). Any time material is added or changed in a book, it must receive a new copyright. Later editions of a book will often list the publication year of first, second, third printings, etc."

1981 Statement: "All first editions at The MIT Press include a copyright page (generally page iv of the front matter) to supply proper copyright notice, which includes copyright symbol, date and copyright owner. If the material has been previously published by a different press, then 'First MIT Press edition' is specified above the copyright notice. A revised edition of a book requires an additional copyrights notice for new material. Later editions of a book will often list the year of first, second, third printings, etc."

1994, 2000 Statements: *See* 1981 Statement

MIT PRESS LTD. (UNITED KINGDOM)

1994, 2000 Statements: *See* 1981 Statement of The MIT Press

MITCHELL BEAZLEY (UNITED KINGDOM)

1989 Statement: *See* 1989 Statement of The Octopus Publishing Group PLC (United Kingdom)

1994 Statement: *See* 1994 Statement of Reed Consumer Books (United Kingdom)

MITCHELLS
(Chatham, Virginia)

2000 Statement: "First printings and first editions are not designated except with copyright date. Subsequent printings and editions are specifically designated (printings by month and year, editions by year of copyright)."

MMB MUSIC INC.

1994 Statement: "Only second and later editions are actually so noted on the cover, title page and copyright page. Any MMB title should be considered a first edition that is not designated otherwise.

"Printing information usually appears on the copyright page using a phrase such as: 'First printing: Month, year.' "

2000 Statement: *See* 1994 Statement

MOCKINGBIRD BOOKS

1976 Statement: "We identify the first and each subsequent printing by date on the copyright page, e.g.

First Printing: January, 1976
Second Printing: June, 1976

and so on."

1981, 1988, 1994 Statements: *See* 1976 Statement

MODEL CRAFTSMAN PUBLISHING CORPORATION
1994 Statement: *See* 1994 Statement of Carstens Publications Inc.

MODERN LANGUAGE ASSOCIATION OF AMERICA
1981 Statement: "The Modern Language Association of America does not employ any uniform codes or other designations of first editions or first printings. In the absence of any statement or indication to the contrary, any book may be assumed to be the first printing of the first edition, as the Association publishes most of its books in only one edition with only one printing. With but few exceptions (and those only in small pamphlets), any edition or printing other than the first is clearly indicated on the verso of the title page."
1988 Statement: *See* 1981 Statement
1994 Statement: "The Modern Language Association of America does not employ any uniform codes or other designations of first editions or first printings. In the absence of any statement or indication to the contrary, any book may be assumed to be the first printing of the first edition. Subsequent editions are indicated on the verso of the title page; subsequent printings are usually indicated there as well."
2000 Statement: *See* 1994 Statement

THE MODERN LIBRARY
1988, 1995, 2001 Statements: *See* 1976 Statement of Random House, Inc.

MODERN LOGIC PUBLISHING
1995 Statement: "We do not designate first printings of first editions of our books. Subsequent printings of first editions would be designated by number, month and year on the copyright page, along with a printing history. Likewise, subsequent editions or revised editions would be designated by number and year on the copyright page, with a history of any previous editions."
2001 Statement: *See* 1995 Statement

MODERN MASTERS
2000 Statement: *See* 2000 Statement of Abbeville Press, Inc.

THE MODERN PILGRIM PRESS
1947 Statement: "The Modern Pilgrim Press publishes primarily pamphlet guides to Cape Cod, and probably has very little material that would be of interest to first edition collectors. Our *Modern Pilgrim's Guide to Provincetown*, *Modern Pilgrim's Bayshore Guide*, and *Modern Pilgrim's Oceanside Guide*, did not differentiate between first and subsequent editions. However, first editions of these guides could be spotted by the fact that they carried no illustrations other than linoleum initial pieces by Saul Yalkert. Subsequent editions carried photographic illustrations, or yellow overprinting on the initial spots. Our *Cape Cod Pilot*, by Jeremiah Digges (American Guide Series), carries only our own imprint on the first edition, whereas subsequent editions were brought out under the joint imprint of the Modern Pilgrim press and the Viking Press. Our *Vittles for the Captain*, a pamphlet cook book, does not differentiate between the first and subsequent editions. However, the

paper covers on the first edition were varnished, while the second edition has unvarnished covers."

MOGO BOOKS (UNITED KINGDOM)

2001 Statement: *See* 2001 Statement of Canongate Books Ltd (United Kingdom)

MOJAVE BOOKS

1976 Statement: "All information as to the printing history of our books is contained on the copyright pages of our books. The distinguishing characteristics are as follows

a. All first editions bear only the copyright date.

b. All subsequent printings and impressions of that edition are described in the printing history which follows the copyright date.

c. Editions subsequent to the first are explicitly stated on the title page and are followed by the history of previous editions."

1981, 1989 Statements: *See* 1976 Statement

MOMENTUM BOOKS LTD.

1995 Statement: "We insert 5 4 3 2 1 on the copyright page. The presence of the numeral 1 designates a first edition. Subsequent editions are designated by deletion of the previous numeral. This is the only method we have used."

2000 Statement: *See* 1995 Statement

MONAD PRESS OF THE ANCHOR FOUNDATION, INC.

1976 Statement: "First editions of Monad Press books generally say: 'First edition, (year).' In some cases a book will be labeled 'First U.S. edition, (year)' or 'Monad Press edition, (year),' and the year of previous publication will be given: 'First French edition, 1939' or 'copyright 1936 by—.' If no printing number is given, the printing is the first."

1981 Statement: *See* 1976 Statement

MONARCH LINE (REPUBLIC OF IRELAND)

1988, 1994 Statements: *See* 1981 Statement of Wolfhound Press (Republic of Ireland)

MONTANA HISTORICAL SOCIETY PRESS

1994 Statement: "The Montana Historical Society Press now uses (and has since 1990) the copyright symbol —©— and year along with an impression line (years and numbers) to indicate subsequent printings. When a new edition is published, the additional year is added behind the copyright symbol.

"Books published from the early 1980s through 1990 used © and year, but did not include the impression line. As these are reprinted, the impression line is being added to indicate subsequent printings."

2001 Statement: *See* 1994 Statement

MONUMENT (UNITED KINGDOM)

2000 Statement: *See* 2000 Statement of Witherby & Company Limited (United Kingdom)

MONUMENT PRESS

1994 Statement: *See* 1994 Statement of Publishers Associates

MOODY PRESS

1947 Statement: "We do not follow a definite plan of marking the various editions of the books we publish. Only on a few of our books are we indicating whether it is first, second or a subsequent edition. This is a matter which we are studying."

Statement for 1960: "Our hardbacks normally indicate 2nd, 3rd printings etc. Thus one without that identification in cloth (hardback) could be assumed to be a first printing.

"The same appears to be true on trade (quality) paperbacks.

"However, on mass paperbacks we give the number of printings only on a select number of fast-selling titles—and this is only a recent policy, so earlier editions probably do not have the printing indicated."

This practice was followed for books published from 1949 through 1981.

1976 Statement: *See* Statement for 1960

1982 Statement: "Beginning in 1982, *all* books published will indicate printing and year printed, regardless of type of book."

1989, 1993 Statements: *See* 1982 Statement

2000 Statement: "We no longer indicate the printing or edition in the books we publish. For internal purposes, we use a printing code on the copyright page to indicate the printing."

MOON PUBLICATIONS, INC.

1994 Statement: "Since the late '80s Moon Publications, Inc. has listed the printing history of the book near the top of the copyright page. The first printing of a first edition will say '1st edition—date' in its printing history. Subsequent editions are identified in the printing history and on the title pages as well."

MOON TRAVEL HANDBOOKS

2001 Statement: "We state 'First edition' and 'First printing' on the copyright page. We also use a number string, where the lowest number indicates the printing."

MOONSTAR BOOKS

1995 Statement: *See* 1995 Statement of Cedar Bay Press

MOORLEYS PRINT & PUBLISHING (UNITED KINGDOM)

1994 Statement: "We do not have a company policy of distinguishing first editions. In fact some of our publications are limited editions and so not reprinted as a matter of policy. Some local history or reference books do have their reprint date added to the reverse of the title page upon reprint."

2000 Statement: *See* 1994 Statement

MORAVIAN MUSIC FOUNDATION

1988 Statement: *See* 1988 Statement of Associated University Presses

THE THOMAS MORE ASSOCIATION (PRESS)
1976 Statement: "No designation is used."
1981 Statement: "[Any of our books] can be presumed to be a first printing unless otherwise indicated on the copyright page."
1988, 1993, 2000 Statements: *See* 1981 Statement

MOREHOUSE
See 1976 Statement of Morehouse-Barlow Co., Inc.

MOREHOUSE PUBLISHING
1993, 2000 Statements: *See* 1976 Statement of Morehouse-Barlow Co., Inc.

MOREHOUSE-BARLOW CO., INC.
1976 Statement: "Most Morehouse-Barlow volumes are first editions and are not identified as such. However, subsequent printings and editions are usually denoted as 'Revised Edition' or 'Second Printing' or 'nth printing' on the cover, title page or copyright page. It is safe to assume that in most, though not quite all, cases, books bearing the Morehouse (pre-1935), Morehouse-Gorham (1935-1958) or Morehouse-Barlow (1958-present) imprint are first editions unless otherwise noted."
1981, 1988, 2000 Statements: *See* 1976 Statement

MOREHOUSE-GORHAM
See 1976 Statement of Morehouse-Barlow Co., Inc.

WALT MOREY ADVENTURE LIBRARY
2000 Statement: *See* 2000 Statement of Blue Heron Publishing

MORGAN & LESTER
1988 Statement: *See* 1988 Statement of Morgan & Morgan Inc.

MORGAN & MORGAN INC.
1988 Statement: "Relevant information is given on copyright page, 'First Edition' is rarely used but '2nd (3rd, 4th etc.) printing' and/or 'Revised Edition' is used.

"[First Edition] was used in earlier publications, 1930s through early 60s, first [as] Morgan & Lester, then [as] Morgan & Morgan."

MORGAN KAUFMANN PUBLISHERS
2001 Statement: *See* 2001 Statement of Academic Press, A Harcourt Science and Technology Company

MORNINGSIDE
2000 Statement: *See* 2000 Statement of Morningside Bookshop

MORNINGSIDE BOOKSHOP
2000 Statement: "We do not designate a First Edition or First printing in our books. Second, subsequent and revised editions will be so identified on the copyright page. We make no distinctions between printings if there are no revisions."

MORNINGSIDE HOUSE, INC.
2000 Statement: *See* 2000 Statement of Morningside Bookshop

MORNINGSIDE PRESS
2000 Statement: *See* 2000 Statement of Morningside Bookshop

MORRISS PUBLISHING
2000 Statement: *See* 2000 Statement of Sono Nis Press

WILLIAM MORROW AND CO. INC.
1928 Statement: "The first printing of our books either carry on the page following the title page the line

First Printing . . . .

or in some cases merely the copyright notice without anything further.

"Subsequent printings are always designated as 'Second Printing' or 'Third Printing,' as the case may be.

"A new edition of the book is also clearly marked.

"You will note that we distinguish between editions and printing. An edition with us is where some material change has been made in the copy or the make up of the book."

1937 Statement: *See* 1928 Statement

1947 Statement: "First printings of Morrow books carry only the copyright notice, except in a few instances the line 'FIRST PRINTING (month—year)' below the copyright notice. All subsequent printings are marked 'SECOND PRINTING, THIRD PRINTING, FOURTH PRINTING,' as the case may be, and any new editions of the book are clearly marked. A distinction should be made between an edition and a printing, edition having some material change in the text or format of the publication."

1976 Statement: First editions are designated by the lack of any reference to the edition on the copyright page. Revised editions are designated on the copyright page.

Printings are indicated by a line of code numbers on the copyright page. The following line indicates a first printing, 1976:

1 2 3 4 5 80 79 78 77 76

The "1" would be deleted for a second printing.

1981 Statement: "First Editions are indicated on the copyright page for all William Morrow and Company, Inc. publications bearing the William Morrow and Company, Inc. imprint as follows:

1) By the absence of any acknowledgment of previous publication of the book in its entirety;

2) By the words 'First Edition' printed on the line directly above the line of code numbers indicating the printing, and

3) By the fact that the line of code numbers indicating the printing begins with the numeral '1.'

The line of code numbers and the 'First Edition' line appear on the copyright page of a first printing as follows:

First Edition

1 2 3 4 5 6 7 8 9 10

"A William Morrow and Company, Inc. publication that is a first edition published in the U.S.A. but which has been previously published in some other country is indicated on the copyright page as follows:

1) By the words 'First U.S. Edition' printed on the line directly above the line of code numbers indicating the printing and

2) By the fact that the line of code numbers indicating the printing begins with the numeral '1' (see above).

"A William Morrow and Company, Inc. publication that is published under the Morrow Quill Paperbacks imprint as a first edition under that imprint (but which has previously been published in a William Morrow and Company, Inc. hardcover edition or is being simultaneously published in a William Morrow and Company, Inc. hardcover edition) is indicated on the copyright page as follows:

1) By the absence of any acknowledgment of previous publication of the book in its entirety;

2) By the words 'First Morrow Quill Paperback Edition' printed on the line directly above the line of code numbers indicating the printing; and

3) By the fact that the line of code numbers indicating the printing begins with the numeral '1.'

The line of code numbers and the 'First Morrow Quill Paperback Edition' line are indicated on the copyright page as follows:

First Morrow Quill Paperback Edition
1 2 3 4 5 6 7 8 9 10

"If, however, a First Morrow Quill Paperback Edition has been previously published in a Morrow paperback imprint no longer in existence, then the line 'First Morrow Quill Paperback Edition' will not be printed- the fact that it is a First Morrow Quill Paperback Edition will be indicated by the fact that the line of code numbers indicating the printing begins with the numeral '1' (see above)."

1988 Statement: "William Morrow and Company, and all of its imprints and divisions, place the following information on the copyright page of first editions:

First Edition
1 2 3 4 5 6 7 8 9 10

"On subsequent printings, the number corresponding to the previous edition is deleted as is the edition statement, so that the second printing of the above books would read:

2 3 4 5 6 7 8 9 10

"We designate the first printing as the actual number of copies that have been ordered from the printer when the book is first produced. Should we ask for more copies, those copies become the second printing."

2001 Statement: *See* 2001 Statement of HarperCollinsPublishers

MORROW JUNIOR BOOKS

1988 Statement: *See* 1988 Statement of William Morrow and Co. Inc.

1994 Statement: "We use a number string on the copyright page. When reprinted, we delete figure 1, etc."

MORROW QUILL PAPERBACKS

1981, 1988 Statements: *See* 1981, 1988 Statements of William Morrow and Co. Inc.

MORTON PUBLISHING COMPANY

1994 Statement: "The only statement is the word First Edition on the cover and title page since 1977."
2000 Statement: *See* 1994 Statement

MOSAIC PRESS (CANADA)

1988 Statement: "First printings are always noted as Copyright . . . and year. Second and subsequent printings are noted as 'x printing, year.' "
1993 Statement: *See* 1988 Statement

MOSAIC PRESS MINIATURE BOOKS

1994 Statement: "In publishing 85 miniature books to date, we have never gone to a second printing."
2000 Statement: *See* 1994 Statement, but note that they have now published 95 miniature books.

MOSBY

2000 Statement: "We do not identify first editions. Subsequent editions are marked on the copyright page along with the copyright year(s) of previous edition(s). We identify the first printing of a first edition by the number line '9 8 7 6 5 4 3 2 1.' "

THE C. V. MOSBY COMPANY

1976 Statement: "No designation is used for the first edition. All editions after the first are indicated by stating '2nd edition', '3rd edition', etc., after the title."
1981 Statement: *See* 1976 Statement
1988 Statement: "Mosby still follows the practice outlined in our 1976 Statement. All Mosby subsidiaries follow this practice."
1993 Statement: *See* 1993 Statement of Mosby-Year Book, Inc.

MOSBY-YEAR BOOK, INC.

1993 Statement: "No designation is used for the first edition. All subsequent editions are indicated by stating 'Second Edition,' 'Third Edition,' etc., after the title on the title page. A series of dates and numbers appearing at the bottom of the copyright page indicates the year of the printing at the far left and the printing at the far right.

"In 1989 the company changed its name from 'The C.V. Mosby Company' to 'Mosby-Year Book, Inc.' "

MOTORBOOKS INTERNATIONAL

1994 Statement: "All our own published titles feature the phrase 'First published in 1994 . . . ' whether they are first or subsequent editions. New printings are not defined. Second and subsequent editions are marked as such elsewhere; not on the title verso page."
2001 Statement: *See* 1994 Statement

MOUNTAIN MEADOW PRESS

2000 Statement: "We identify the first printing of a first edition by the words 'First Edition' on the verso side of the title page."

MOUNTAIN MOVERS PRESS

2000 Statement: *See* 2000 Statement of Hay House Inc

MOUNTAIN N' AIR BOOKS

2001 Statement: "We do not identify a first printing or any printing after the first printing on the copyright page."

MOUNTAIN PRESS PUBLISHING CO.

1976 Statement: "First editions are not designated as such; it can be assumed that we indicate only those printings or editions after the first."
1981, 1988 Statements: *See* 1976 Statement
1994 Statement: "In all newer titles, if there is not a statement to the contrary identifying it as a second printing or later, then it should be construed as a first edition. We have been using that method of designation since 1988."
2000 Statement: *See* 1994 Statement

MOUNTAIN STATE PRESS

2000 Statement: "We do not identify 1st editions; each reprinting we do identify with 2nd, 3rd, etc."

THE MOUNTAINEERS BOOKS

1988 Statement: "Since we started publishing books in 1961, first editions of our titles have sometimes been identifiable by the words 'First Edition,' and sometimes by the *absence* of printing histories on the copyright pages. Subsequent printings, however, will usually be marked, for example:

First printing September 1984, second printing November 1986.

"An illustration of copyright-page printing information for second and succeeding editions is the following:

First edition May 1980, second printing January 1981
Second edition September 1982, second printing November 1983, third printing January 1985
Third edition May 1986

"Since 1986 or 7, we have been using for many (but not all) titles the following alternative numerical symbols:

0 9 8 7   the last number on the right on this line represents the year of printing (e.g. 1987)
5 4 3 2 1   the last number on the right on this line represents the number of the printing; the first, in this example."
1993 Statement: "Since we started publishing books in 1961, first editions of our titles have sometimes been identifiable by the words 'First Edition,' and sometimes by the absence of printing histories on the copyright pages. At the present time, the date of the edition is identifiable by the date of copyright; for example: '© 1993 by Mary Jones' would indicate a first edition

in 1993, while '© 1984, 1988, 1992 by Harvey Smith' would indicate a first edition in 1984, a second edition in 1988, and a third edition in 1992.

"We also include a printing history, for example:

76543
54321

"The last digit of the top line represents the last digit of the year of the printing; the last digit of the bottom line represents the number of the printing of the most recent edition."

2000 Statement: "We are no longer using the numbering system outlined in our 1993 statement. We have reverted to a system more like that described in our 1988 statement.

"Since we started publishing books in 1961, first editions of our titles have sometimes been identifiable by the words 'First Edition,' and sometimes by the absence of printing histories on the copyright pages. Subsequent printings were identified, however.

"Between about 1987 and 1997, we used alternative identification, two-line numerical symbols. The last digit of the top line represented the last digit of the year of the printing; the last digit of the bottom line represented the number of the printing of the most recent edition.

"At the present time, our copyright page would indicate the printing history by stating (for example):

First edition 1998

or in the case of subsequent printings:

First printing 1998, second printing 1999, third printing 2000.

"In the case of multiple editions, our copyright page would state:

First edition 1988. Second edition: first printing 1996, second printing 1999."

MOUNTAINTOP BOOKS

2000 Statement: "The first printing of a first edition is not identified except that subsequent printings and editions will be identified as 'Second Printing' or 'Second Edition.' "

MOVING PARTS PRESS

2001 Statement: "We do not identify a first printing; we do identify subsequent printings on the copyright page or the colophon page."

A. R. MOWBRAY & CO. LTD. (UNITED KINGDOM)

1976 Statement: "A book is a first edition (first printing) unless otherwise stated."

1981 Statement: *See* 1976 Statement

MOYER BELL

2000 Statement: "All our books are identified by the words 'First Edition' on the copyright page."

MR. COGITO PRESS

2000 Statement: "To date, all Mr. Cogito Press books are 1st editions."

JOHN MUIR PUBLICATIONS

1976 Statement: "We designate a first edition by printing 'First Edition, 19...' Then we say 'Second Printing' if the book has not been changed. If the book is substantially revised, we say 'Second Edition & date.' "

1981, 1988, 1993 Statements: *See* 1976 Statement

MULBERRY BOOKS

1994 Statement: *See* 1994 Statement of Tambourine Books

MULLER (UNITED KINGDOM)

1988 Statement: *See* 1988 Statement of Century Hutchinson Publishing Group Limited (United Kingdom)

FREDERICK MULLER, LTD. (UNITED KINGDOM)

1937 Statement: "On the back of the title pages of our books is a bibliographical note which reads: 'First published by Frederick Muller Ltd. (here follows the year in which the book was published).'

"When a second edition is published we add the words: 'Second Edition,' and the year. We then also add the month when the first edition was published."

1947 Statement: *See* 1937 Statement

1988 Statement: *See* 1988 Statement of Muller (United Kingdom)

MULTI-MEDIA PUBLISHING, INC.

1988 Statement: *See* 1988 Statement of The C. V. Mosby Company

MULTIMEDIA PUBLISHING CORPORATION

1976 Statement: "1. We put in a new book—First Edition.

2. If we print more we put—Second printing, Third Printing, etc.

3. Only if we change content, introduction etc. do we note—2nd Revised Edition, etc.—and this we put on copyright page."

1981 Statement: *See* 1976 Statement

MULTNOMAH PUBLISHERS INC

2001 Statement: "We identify the first printing of a first edition by a number line, for example: '0 1 2 3 4 5,' where '0' would represent the original and '1' the reprint."

JOHN MURRAY (UNITED KINGDOM)

1928 Statement: *See* 1937 Statement

1937 Statement: "The practice we have followed for many years is to omit the date from the title page and to insert at the back of the title page the words 'First Edition' together with the year of issue.

"In the case of certain books, chiefly those printed for private circulation, the date appears at the foot of the title page with no biblio on the reverse."

1947 Statement: *See* 1937 Statement

1982 Statement: "We now very rarely print the date of publication on the title page. Even in those rare cases we always print 'First published' or 'First Edition' with the date, as well as the copyright notice on the reverse of the title page."

1988, 1994, 2000 Statements: *See* 1982 Statement

MURRAY & GEE, INC.
1947 Statement: "We have no set rule in this respect. In general, however, the first editions carry only the copyright line and subsequent editions list the printing: second, third, etc."

MUSCADINE BOOKS
2000 Statement: *See* 2000 Statement of University Press of Mississippi

THE MUSE
1995 Statement: *See* 1995 Statement of Cedar Bay Press

MUSEUM OF FINE ARTS, BOSTON
2000 Statement: "We identify the first printings of our books with the words 'First Edition' on the copyright page. All subsequent printings are labeled 'Second Printing,' 'Third Printing,' etc. The actual name of the imprint is MFA Publications, identified as 'a division of the Museum of Fine Arts, Boston.' "

THE MUSEUM OF MODERN ART
1981 Statement: "First editions of our books are identified negatively. That is, we do nothing to say 'first edition' but we try to be quite careful about indicating on the copyright page 'Second printing', 'Third printing,' 'Revised Second Edition,' or whatever."
1988, 1994 Statements: *See* 1981 Statement

THE MUSEUM OF NEW MEXICO PRESS
1976 Statement: "Our title page imprint has the date of publication. The c/r page has the year of c/r & only second printings are indicated. '2nd ptg....., etc.' We don't have a steadfast rule as yet."
1981 Statement: "Our title page imprint does not include the date of publication. The c/r page has the year of c/r & only second printings are indicated."
1988 Statement: "Our title page imprint does not include the date of publication. The c/r page has the year (indicating year of publication) of c/r & only second printings (and thereafter) are indicated."
1994 Statement: "Our title page imprint does not include the date of publication. The c/r page has the year (indicating year of publication) of c/r and indicates number of edition in the following manner: 10 9 8 7 6 5 4 3 2 1. This method was instituted about five years ago."
2000 Statement: *See* 1994 Statement

MUSEUM PRESS, LTD. (UNITED KINGDOM)
1947 Statement: "In the case of first editions of all our books, the year of issue is placed under our imprint on the title page. In the case of subsequent editions the bibliography appears on the reverse of title."

MUSIC SALES CORP
2001 Statement: "We do not identify a first printing or any printing after the first printing on the copyright page. For a short time, in the mid-seventies, we identified a first printing with the letter string 'e d c b a' on the copyright page. Presence of the letter 'a' signifies a first printing."

BARROWS MUSSEY, INC.
1937 Statement: *See* 1937 Statement of Loring & Mussey, Inc.

MUSTANG PUBLISHING
1994 Statement: "We have always designated first printings by using the number series 10 9 8 7 6 5 4 3 2 1 at the bottom of the reverse of the title page. (We've been publishing since 1984). Subsequent printings delete the last number of the series."
2000 Statement: *See* 1994 Statement

MUTUAL PUBLISHING COMPANY
1995 Statement: "We state on the copyright the edition and indicate the printing by deleting a number in the series '0 1 2 3 4 5 6 7 8 9.' When a book sells very well we may spell out the number and dates of each printing."
2001 Statement: "We state on the copyright page the month and year first published in addition to a number series which also illustrates the printing. For example:

January 1999
November 1999
March 2000
November 2000
4 5 6 7 8 9."

MYCROFT AND MORAN
1947 Statement: *See* 1947 Statement of Arkham House

MYRIAD PRESS
2000 Statement: "Our first editions are marked by the fact that the copyright page bears *no* printing or edition notices whereas in subsequent editions the dates, and sometimes even the quantity of the printings, appear, as

First Printing, Month, Year
Second Printing, Month, Year, etc."

MYSTERIOUS PRESS
1988 Statement: "The Mysterious Press had its first book published in 1976 and it, as well as all subsequent books identified its first printing on the copyright page, employing the term 'First Edition' or 'First Printing.' The terms were used interchangeably, depending upon the typesetter. When second and later printings were called for, the words 'Second Printing' (or third, etc.) were added to the copyright page. In 1986, we adopted the policy of running numbers from 1 to 10 in addition to using the words 'First Edition' or 'First Printing.' The first printing begins the number sequence with number

'1,' the second printing retains the phrase 'First Edition' but the number sequence begins with the number '2' and so on.''
1993 Statement: *See* 1988 Statement
2000 Statement: *See* 2000 Statement of Warner Books, Inc.

MYSTERY HOUSE
1947 Statement: *See* 1947 Statement of Samuel Curl, Inc

MYSTIC SEAPORT MUSEUM
1988 Statement: "We normally designate the first edition of a work with a 'First Edition' line on the copyright page. Second editions are either so designated on the copyright page, or else implied with a multiple copyright date. We do not distinguish the different printings of an edition."
1995, 2000 Statements: *See* 1988 Statement

THE MYTHOLOGY COMPANY
1947 Statement: "The first edition of *This Was My Newport* may be recognized by a strange error occurring on page 160 line 20. The reading should be: 'The son of Dr. Parkman murdered by Dr. Webster.' "

N

N & A
2000 Statement: *See* 2000 Statement of The Nautical & Aviation Publishing Co.

NAG PRESS (UNITED KINGDOM)
1994, 2000 Statements: *See* 1994 Statement of Robert Hale Limited (United Kingdom)

NAGS HEAD ART
1995 Statement: "For the first printing of a first edition, we state 'first edition' at the bottom of the copyright or publisher's page. After this first edition, we drop any designation. Subsequent editions, therefore, always mean editions other than first edition, first printing."

THE NAIAD PRESS, INC.
1981 Statement: "We use FIRST EDITION as our mark. When we go into other printings we add SECOND PRINTING and so on. Thus, absence of any other marking is indication that it is first edition, first printing. We have always done this."
1988 Statement: "Everything is the same . . . . We try very hard to be very uniform about our habits on the verso of the title page recognizing that nothing in a book is so vital as that page of information."
1993, 2000 Statements: *See* 1988 Statement

NAL
See New American Library

NAL BOOKS
1988 Statement: *See* 1988 Statement of New American Library

NANTIER BEALL MINOUSTCHINE PUBLISHING INC.
1994 Statement: "For the last three years or so we have specifically identified reprints as '2nd printing' etc. without specific mention of first printing on the first one. For the most part now we include a countdown on the copyright page ('10 9 8 . . .') with the last digit seen being the number of the printing of that book. If we do not include that, it is because we do not anticipate going back to press with it. Prior to the last three years I must admit we were somewhat erratic in identifying different printings. Most reprints are identified as such, always on the copyright page. Those that aren't can be identified with updated information, addresses, etc."
2001 Statement: *See* 1994 Statement

NAPOLEON PUBLISHING/RENDEZ-VOUS PRESS (CANADA)
2001 Statement: "We identify the first printing of a first edition by the number line '05 04 03 02 01 54321' in the middle of the copyright page. In this example, the '1' would indicate the first printing of the first edition."

EVELEIGH NASH AND GRAYSON, LTD.
(UNITED KINGDOM)
(Became Grayson & Grayson, Ltd [United Kingdom].)
1928 Statement: "On the reverse of the title page:
First published in . . . .
Second printing.."

NATARAJ PUBLISHING
2000 Statement: *See* 2000 Statement of New World Library

NATION BOOKS
2001 Statement: *See* 2001 Statement of Avalon Publishing Group Incorporated

NATIONAL ACADEMY PRESS/JOSEPH HENRY PRESS
2001 Statement: "First printings can only be identified by the lack of any reference to a printing on the copyright page. Subsequent printings are identified, along with the month and year of that printing."

NATIONAL AERONAUTICS & SPACE
ADMINISTRATION (NASA)
1988 Statement: "All NASA publications are printed through the U. S. Government Printing Office, and are offered for sale by the U. S. Superintendent of Documents, Washington, DC. NASA publications are not protected by copyright and are in the public domain. The year of publication is often not indicated in a NASA publication. Reprints are not differentiated from original printings. No indication is given of first or subsequent editions."
1993 Statement: *See* 1988 Statement

NATIONAL ARCHIVES

1994 Statement: "We do not indicate a first printing of a first edition. When a book is reprinted, it is an exact duplicate of the first printing, with no statement like 'Second printing.' If we have revised a book, we will state on the verso title page 'Revised,' or 'Second edition.' "

2000 Statement: *See* 1994 Statement

NATIONAL BUS TRADER, INC.

1994, 2000 Statements: *See* 1994 Statement of Transportation Trails

NATIONAL COUNCIL OF TEACHERS OF ENGLISH

2001 Statement: "We do not identify a first printing or any printing after the first printing on the copyright page."

NATIONAL FOUNDATION PRESS

1947 Statement: "The National Foundation Press, a division of National Foundation for Education in American Citizenship, usually does not expressly identify first printings as such. Subsequent printings are identified as 'second printing,' and so on. Second editions are expressly identified. The first edition can in actuality be identified by the absence of any reference at all to the printing or edition."

NATIONAL GALLERY OF ART

1994 Statement: "We simply give date of publication. We seldom, if ever, publish 2nd editions. From time to time we may say 'revised edition.' "

2000 Statement: "We simply give the date of publication for the first edition. Subsequent editions are identified on the copyright page, as, e.g., 'Second printing.' If major changes are made in the text or in the illustration program, we may call it a 'revised edition.' "

NATIONAL GALLERY OF VICTORIA (AUSTRALIA)

1994 Statement: The first printing of a first edition is indicated by the line "Published by the National Gallery of Victoria, 180 St Kilda Road, Melbourne, Victoria, 3004" on the copyright page without any mention of subsequent printings or editions. This approach has been used for more than 15 years.

2000 Statement: "We have tended to change the identification of our first editions in recent times. We now tend to say

Published by the National Gallery of Victoria

Copyright symbol followed by National Gallery of Victoria with the year

"This Gallery has not changed its name since 1989 and we do not have any subsidiaries."

NATIONAL GEOGRAPHIC SOCIETY

1976 Statement: "The Society has no particular symbol or identification mark to indicate first printings. Most of our larger books contain a notice on the copyright page indicating whether the work is a first edition or a later printing. On some of the Society's other publications, the original copyright date, which coincides with the original publication date, and the dates of subsequent copyright registration and printings are marked on the copyright page.

"There is no simple way to ascertain whether early editions of the National Geographic Magazine are original editions or reprints. The best information relating to identification of original editions of the Magazine appears in Edwin Buxbaum's book *The Collector's Guide to the National Geographic Magazine.*

"In the late 1950s the Society reprinted the first 20 years of National Geographic Magazines. The word 'reprint' appears on the covers of these reprints."

1981, 1988, 2000 Statements: *See* 1976 Statement

NATIONAL LIBRARY OF AUSTRALIA (AUSTRALIA)

1988 Statement: "As a government authority the National Library follows guidelines set by the Australian Government Publishing Service.
First editions are identified by:
© (date) National Library of Australia
Subsequent editions are identified by:
© (date) National Library of Australia
First published (date)
Reprinted (date)
"We do not have any additional imprints and subsidiaries."

1994 Statement: *See* 1988 Statement

NATIONAL LIBRARY OF SCOTLAND (UNITED KINGDOM)

1994 Statement: "First editions of our publications simply bear the words 'First published [year]' on the reverse of title-page. Any subsequent reprints or new editions qualify this with an additional statement such as 'Reprinted [year].' "

2000 Statement: *See* 1994 Statement

NATIONAL LIBRARY OF WALES (WALES)

2001 Statement: "We do not identify a first printing; we do identify subsequent printings on the copyright page."

NATIONAL MUSEUMS OF SCOTLAND
(UNITED KINGDOM)

1994 Statement: "The first edition will contain 'Published by the National Museums of Scotland' with the copyright notice and date. Any subsequent edition will contain, e.g., 'First published 1988 by the National Museums of Scotland. Second edition 1990.' Straightforward reprints are identified as second, third impressions, etc."

In July, 1997, the National Museums of Scotland changed its name to NMS Publishing Limited (National Museums of Scotland)

THE NATIONAL MUSEUM OF WOMEN IN THE ARTS

1994 Statement: "Except in rare cases, we do not designate first printings and editions of our books per se. We do, however, designate second printings

and later editions on the verso of the title page. Thus, one can determine the first printing and edition of our publications by process of elimination."
2000 Statement: *See* 1994 Statement

THE NATIONAL TRUST (UNITED KINGDOM)
2001 Statement: "We identify only editions, not printings; a first edition is so identified on the copyright page."

NATIONAL WOODLANDS PUBLISHING COMPANY
1995 Statement: "Our first editions are identified as such on the back of the title page, followed by the date. For example, First Edition: April 1991. The number of the printing, e.g., First Printing, Second Printing, etc., followed by the date, is shown immediately below the information about the edition.

"We also use a numeric code at the bottom of the same page, but it does not designate what edition is being printed. The year of printing is the left-most set of years, e.g., 91 92 93 94 95; and the number of the printing is the right-most number, e.g., 5 4 3 2 1. In this example, the book is the first printing and was done in 1991."

This method has been in use since 1990.

NATIVE AMERICAN PUBLICATIONS
2000 Statement: *See* 2000 Statement of Council for Indian Education

NATUREGRAPH PUBLISHERS, INC.
1976 Statement: "Many of the early Naturegraph titles have been revised, sometimes 2 or 3 times. First editions are not designated as such, rather, revised editions are—e.g., 'Second revised and enlarged edition' accompanies copyright dates."
1981 Statement: "As we do not identify our books by designating them as a 'first printing,' 'second printing,' etc., all of our books are first editions until, if necessary, they are revised. A revised edition is always identified as such. The previous statement submitted by our company remains valid."
1988 Statement: "Our company hasn't changed practices in the way of identifying printings, and we are a small publisher without imprints and subsidiaries."
1993, 2000 Statements: *See* 1988 Statement

THE NAUTICAL & AVIATION PUBLISHING CO.
1988 Statement: "We don't make a point of designating first printings, but on second, third, etc., we mark the month and year.
E.g., *South to Java*:
     Second printing, December 1987
     Third printing, January 1988
"The information is included on the copyright page."
1993, 2000 Statements: *See* 1988 Statement

NAVAL INSTITUTE PRESS
1976 Statement: "The U.S. Naval Institute does not make a practice of identifying books as first editions. Most books don't go beyond a first edition.

Those that do are identified as 'Second Edition,' or whatever. So if there is nothing to indicate otherwise, one can be sure the book in hand is a first edition."

1981 Statement: "Like most publishers, the U.S. Naval Institute does not identify books as first editions, only second and succeeding editions. Similarly, the Institute does not identify first printings of first editions, only second and succeeding printings. Hence, if there is no mention of the edition on the title page, and there is also no mention of the printing on the copyright page, then the book is among the first printing of the first edition.

"Books published prior to 1971 carry the imprint of the U.S. Naval Institute; a few published since then do also. Most books published since 1971 carry the imprint of the Naval Institute Press. The U.S. Naval Institute and the Naval Institute Press are one and the same."

1988 Statement: "The [1981] statement is still correct. We do not identify first editions, only subsequent ones."

1993 Statement: "The U.S. Naval Institute does not identify books as first editions, only second and succeeding editions. Edition information is carried on the title page. However, since 1989, the Institute has identified first and subsequent printings with a string of numbers on the copyright page. Therefore, if the number 1 or the words 'first printing' appears on the copyright page, then the book is a first printing."

2000 Statement: *See* 1993 Statement

THE NAYLOR COMPANY

1976 Statement: "Only one date will appear on the copyright page and if it is a second or later edition it should be so stated."

NB (UNITED KINGDOM)

2000 Statement: *See* 2000 Statement of Yale University Press (United Kingdom)

NBM PUBLISHING COMPANY

2000 Statement: "A countdown is generally included under the © information. If the number '1' is there, that is the first printing."

THOMAS NELSON (UNITED KINGDOM)

2001 Statement: *See* 2001 Statement of Nelson Thornes Ltd (United Kingdom)

THOMAS NELSON & SONS, LTD. (UNITED KINGDOM)

1928 Statement: "We have used the following three phrases on the reverse of the title page in a number of our General and Fiction publications:

First Printed . . . .
First Published . . . .
First Impression . . . .

"When a second impression or a reprint is issued, we usually put the following in the same position:

First Impression . . . .
Second Impression . . . .

First Published . . . .
Reprinted . . . ."

1936 Statement: "We may say that the method we now use on the title page of our books is as follows:

First Published . . .
Reprinted . . ."

1947, 1994 Statements: *See* 1936 Statement

NELSON CANADA (CANADA)

1989 Statement: "Until the late 1970s, Nelson Canada had no established method for identifying first editions or printings. Usually the new edition of a book would be denoted on the cover, copyright page and title page as follows: *Nelson Math Second Edition.*

"The printing number would be indicated whether at the front or the back of the book by a print line which would also show the year of printing (see below).

"A standard was established in the late 1970s which now appears on the copyright page of all Nelson Canada titles. This information usually appears at the front of the book. However, occasionally it will appear at the back.

"The standard statement reads:

© Nelson Canada, A Division of
International Thomson Limited, YEAR.
Published in YEAR by
Nelson Canada
A Division of International Thomson Limited
1120 Birchmount Road
Scarborough, Ontario"

THOMAS NELSON PUBLISHERS

1994 Statement: "We identify all printings of Thomas Nelson books by placing a printing line on the copyright page. The print numbers are in ascending order on the left side and the year is in descending order on the right side. This represents print number and year printed.

"We used to spell out First Printing, etc. (around 1984)."

2001 Statement: *See* 1994 Statement

NELSON, FOSTER & SCOTT, LTD. (CANADA)

1976 Statement: "In reply to the above request we practice the following:

© The Author's name 1976
First edition 1976
Reprinted 1977."

NELSON-HALL PUBLISHERS

1976 Statement: Only those printings and/or editions after the first are indicated.

"Additional printings (or 'impressions') of the first edition are numbered and so identified on the copyright page.

"Subsequent editions (after the first) carry additional copyrights and are clearly identified on the copyright page. We have no secret codes."

These methods of designation do not differ from any previously used.

1981, 1988, 1993 Statements: *See* 1976 Statement

2000 Statement: "Nelson-Hall no longer exists." *See* Burnham Publishers Inc.

NESHUI PUBLISHING

2000 Statement: "It is our practice to indicate on the copyright page with a line thus: 'Second Printing, Third Printing' etc. This note does not appear on the first edition."

NET-WORKS (UNITED KINGDOM)

2000 Statement: *See* 2000 Statement of Take That Ltd. (United Kingdom)

NETHERLANDIC PRESS (CANADA)

1989 Statement: "The Netherlandic Press of Windsor, Ontario has no method for identifying first editions. We list all information on the copyright page. However when a book would be reprinted we would indicate this by adding the information 'Second Printing,' and the dates of both the first and second printing."

NEUGEBAUER

2001 Statement: *See* 2001 Statement of North-South Books Inc.

NEVADA PUBLICATIONS

2000 Statement: "First editions have no identifying statement; second and subsequent printings state so, viz: 'second printing. No number lines used.'"

NEW AMERICAN LIBRARY

1988 Statement: "New American Library clearly designates on the copyright page first printings of first editions in the imprints Signet, Signet Classic, Mentor, Onyx, Plume, Meridian, and NAL Books by the words:

First Printing, (date)

1 2 3 4 5 6 7 8 9

"Subsequent prints are denoted by the numbers on the above printing line.

"A revised edition would contain the words:

First Printing, Revised Edition, (date)

1 2 3 4 5 6 7 8 9

"When we reprint a book we indicate that it has been previously published by another publisher or by New American Library in another imprint by the following:

First (current imprint name) Printing, (date)

1 2 3 4 5 6 7 8 9"

(In 1993 New American Library became Dutton/Signet.)

NEW AMERICAN LIBRARY (AUSTRALIA)

2000 Statement: *See* 2000 Statement of Penguin Books Australia Ltd (Australia)

NEW AMSTERDAM BOOKS
1989 Statement: "Usually, we say 'First Printing.' Sometimes the hand of the potter shakes."
1994 Statement: *See* 1989 Statement
2001 Statement: *See* 2000 Statement of Ivan R. Dee and 2001 Statement of J. S. Sanders

NEW CITY PRESS
2001 Statement: "We do not identify a first printing; we do identify subsequent printings as such on the copyright page."

NEW CLASSICS LIBRARY
1994 Statement: "As with all our books, there [is] no designation of the first edition. However, it is easy to distinguish first editions because all subsequent editions state the number of the edition."

THE NEW DAWN PUBLISHING CO.
1994 Statement: "At The New Dawn Publishing Company, we designate the first printing by inserting on the copyright page the phrase 'First Edition,' as adopted in 1991, the year of our birth to the publishing business. Subsequent printings are differentiated by using the phrase 'Second Printing and year, plus year of First Edition.' "
2000 Statement: *See* 1994 Statement

NEW DIRECTIONS
1947 Statement: "Unfortunately for any collector, there is no standard way to tell a first printing of our books. The points vary in each case; they mainly consist of the use of a different color or type of cloth, and sometimes the absence of color printing, the use of offset printing, varying bulk of paper, etc., in later editions."
Statement for 1960: "Starting in 1970 a 'First published' line appears on the copyright page of New Directions books. In earlier years, the absence of a copyright page notice as to second, third etc. printing indicates that the book in hand is most likely a first printing. In the days when it was feasible to store sheets, there were second bindings, not always identical to the true first edition. Very few clothbound editions of New Directions books have ever gone into second printings."
1976 Statement: "There is no way to tell first printings of the early ND books . . . . A few years ago, we began putting SECOND PRINTING etc. on the copyright page of reprints."
1981 Statement: "The first editions of the early ND books were not identified in any way but since many of the books did not go into second printings most early ND books are first editions. In recent years all reprints are identifiable since 'Second Printing' and any further reprinting is noted on the copyright page."
1988, 1993 Statements: *See* 1981 Statement
2001 Statement: "New Directions' practice in regard to first and subsequent printings remains as stated in the 1981 version. We do not put 'First Printing'

on the copyright page, its absence being a sign that a first printing is in hand. We do put 'Second Printing' and any further reprint number on the copyright page when the occasion arises. We have no other imprints or subsidiaries."

NEW ENGLAND CARTOGRAPHICS, INC.

1995 Statement: "New England Cartographics standard is to print on the copyright page the following:

First Edition

First Printing 199(?) (year)

"Our company adopted this method in 1991."

2001 Statement: The copyright page carries the printing history plus a number/year line. The lowest printing number indicates the printing.

NEW ENGLAND PRESS, INC.

1988 Statement: "As of about 18 months ago I started using the words 'First Edition' on all initial printings of new works. After the first printing runs out, I simply delete those words and identify which printing it is and give the date, e.g., 'Second printing, October 1988.'

"Previously we had not designated first editions except by the lack of reprint information."

1993, 2000 Statements: *See* 1988 Statement

NEW ENGLISH LIBRARY LIMITED (UNITED KINGDOM)

1976 Statement: "When we first publish a book, we include on the copyright line the year of publication, and beneath 'first published by New English Library in 1976' and this date will coincide with the copyright notice. If on the other hand, we buy a book from the American publisher we will mention on the copyright page when and where it was first published. In this instance the year on the copyright line may differ from the English publishing date."

1981 Statement: *See* 1976 Statement

1989 Statement: "Our usual copyright page . . . is slightly different from our previous practice. The line 'First published in Great Britain 19—' shows when our company would first have published a book (it is, I think, unlikely for us to reissue a book in hardcover that has been previously published by another hardback company).

"The second half of our 1976 statement is still valid."

2000 Statement: *See* 1989 Statement. "New English Library is an imprint within the Hodder Headline Group."

See also Hodder Headline Group (United Kingdom)

NEW FALCON PUBLICATIONS

2000 Statement: "We identify the first printing of a first edition by the words 'First Edition (year).' Falcon Press is an earlier name for New Falcon. We changed it some years ago to avoid confusion with Falcon Publishing in Helena MT. Golden Dawn Publications was an imprint of New Falcon. It is no longer used."

NEW GLIDE PUBLICATIONS

1981 Statement: "We don't usually make a distinction."

NEW HARBINGER PUBLICATIONS INC.
1994 Statement: "Our first printings of first editions either say nothing or say 'first printing' and the date and number of copies. All subsequent printings are listed with the date of each printing, with the last listing being the current printing."

NEW HOLLAND PUBLISHERS LTD (UNITED KINGDOM)
2001 Statement: "We identify the first printing of a first edition by a number line on the copyright page; the lowest number indicates the printing."

THE NEW HUMANITY PRESS
2000 Statement: "We identify the first printing of a first edition by the following: 'First New Humanity Press Edition Published (Year).' "

NEW LEAF BOOKS
2000 Statement: *See* 2000 Statement of WigWam Publishing Co.

NEW LIFE MINISTRIES
2000 Statement: *See* LifeQuest

NEW NATIVE PRESS
1995 Statement: "All publications from 1979 to 1990 . . . carried this designation always on the copyright page in a variety of forms: 'First United States Printing' (in the case of translations), 'First Printing,' and 'Limited First Edition.' Since 1990 . . . the designation for all NNP books is now standard and reads: 'First Printing.' Subsequent printings are designated as 'Second Printing,' 'Third Printing,' etc."

NEW ODYSSEY
2001 Statement: *See* 2001 Statement of Truman State University Press

NEW ORCHARD EDITIONS (UNITED KINGDOM)
1994 Statement: *See* 1988 Statement of Cassell plc (United Kingdom)

NEW PARADIGM PRESS
2000 Statement: *See* 2000 Statement of Hope Publishing House

NEW PLAYWRIGHTS' NETWORK (UNITED KINGDOM)
2001 Statement: "New Playwrights' Network was formed in 1972. No bibliographical information was provided in the books at all. Since the change in ownership, in 1996, the title page verso gives date of publication. If the book is reprinted, the date of subsequent printings will be given. Only plays are published."

NEW POETS SERIES, INC.
1994 Statement: "The New Poets Series (which subsumes also the imprints Chestnut Hills Press and Stonewall) indicates first editions only by *not* making any specification of edition at all. Subsequent editions are signified 'Second Edition,' 'Third Edition,' whatever, in the applicable printings."
2000 Statement: *See* 2000 Statement of Brickhouse Books, Inc.

THE NEW PRESS

1994 Statement: "We have no special designation. We use: '9 8 7 6 5 4 3 2 1' in the first printing. In subsequent printings, we delete one number. We have always used this method."

2000 Statement: *See* 1994 Statement

THE NEW REPUBLIC BOOK CO., INC.

1976 Statement: "We have not—so far—designated our first editions or first printings in any special way.

"We would note a second or revised edition on the jacket and on the title page."

1981 Statement: "NRB (New Republic Books) became an 'imprint' (actually, it's a co-publishing arrangement) of Holt, Rinehart, & Winston in December, 1980. Their method of first edition designation will be ours, as they produce and publish all our books."

NEW REPUBLIC BOOKS

1993 Statement: *See* 1993 Statement of HarperCollins Publishers

NEW SCIENCE LIBRARY

1988 Statement: *See* 1988 Statement of Shambhala Publications, Inc.

2001 Statement: "The New Science Library imprint is inactive."

NEW SOCIETY PUBLISHERS

1994 Statement: "We don't identify the first edition."

THE NEW SOUTH COMPANY

1981 Statement: A first printing is not identified as such. However, all printings or editions after the first are indicated on the copyright page.

1988, 2000 Statements: *See* 1981 Statement

THE NEW SOUTH WALES UNIVERSITY PRESS LIMITED (AUSTRALIA)

1988 Statement: "We generally do not specify the first printing of a first edition—we simply append the year to the copyright convention e.g. © Keith Amos 1988. However, if the book is subsequently revised or reprinted more than once we sometimes provide more detail though we rarely include the month of publication."

(The name was changed to University of New South Wales Press Ltd in 1994.)

NEW STAR BOOKS (CANADA)

1988 Statement: "Since 1982, the usual form in which information regarding the edition and form of one of our titles has appeared on our copyright pages is as follows:

'Copyright © 1989 [for example] by [name of copyright holder]

'First Printing [month and year of first printing of first edition]

'1 2 3 4 5 93 92 91 90 89'

"When we reprint a book we opaque the lowest number on the left side of this bottom line. The lowest remaining number would indicate the printing number of a given book. Similarly, the number furthest right on that last line would be opaqued as necessary so that the right-hand number would be the year in which the copy of the book that you hold was printed.

"This convention was not generally used by us before 1982, but in almost all cases where a book was reprinted, this information was made known on the copyright page of the reprint.

"Previous to but not including 1989, no titles originated by New Star Books were reissued by us or by any other press in a revised edition.

"Previous to 1974, when the press's name was changed to New Star Books, titles published by the same press were issued under the imprint of 'Vancouver Community Press' or 'VCP,' and 'Georgia Straight Writing Series' or 'GSWS.' To my knowledge, none of the titles bearing these imprints was ever reprinted or issued by us in a new edition."

1993 Statement: *See* 1988 Statement

2000 Statement: "We do still follow the practice outlined in our last statement, with the exception of the 'First Printing (month and year of first printing of first edition)' line, which we now no longer include. Our imprints and subsidiaries do follow our practices."

NEW VICTORIA PUBLISHERS
1994 Statement: "We do not specifically designate first printings, but do designate subsequent printings."

2000 Statement: *See* 1994 Statement

NEW VIEW PUBLICATIONS
1995 Statement: "Up until now, we have had no particular way of designating first printings. However, second and revised printings are so noted on the copyright pages of our books. Beginning this year, we plan to use the 1 2 3 4 5 6 7 8 9 0 system for all our new books. When reprinted, we will delete figure 1, etc. and insert 2nd, 3rd, etc., printing on the copyright page."

2001 Statement: *See* 1995 Statement

NEW WOMEN'S PRESS LTD. (NEW ZEALAND)
1994 Statement: "First published 19—, Reprinted 19—, 19—, 19— appears on title page."

NEW WORLD LIBRARY
2000 Statement: "We identify the first printing of a first edition by 'First printing, Month Year' [and by] the following number line: 10 9 8 7 6 5 4 3 2 1."

NEW WORLD PAPERBACKS
2000 Statement: *See* 2000 Statement of International Publishers Co., Inc.

NEW YORK CULTURE REVIEW PRESS
1976 Statement:
" 'First Edition'
"Thereafter:

2nd Printing, Date
3rd Printing (Revised), Date
4th Printing, Date
5th Printing, # Copies in Print, Date."

NEW YORK GRAPHIC SOCIETY

1976 Statement: "We are now a part of Little, Brown and Company so we follow their style:

'First Edition' is printed on the copyright page, followed by a code, e.g.

'T 10/76' (Trade, October, 1976).

Alternatively the words 'First Printing' are used.

"Prior to our affiliation with Little, Brown we generally used the words 'First printing,' or in the case of books imported from foreign publishers, 'First published by . . . .' If the edition or printing is not specified it generally means the first edition, as subsequent printings are identified as 'Second printing,' etc."

1981 Statement: "We are now a part of Little, Brown and Company so we follow their style:

'First Edition' is printed on the copyright page.

Alternatively the words 'First Printing' are used.

"Prior to our affiliation with Little, Brown we generally used the words 'First printing,' or in the case of books imported from foreign publishers, 'First published by . . . .' 'First U.S. edition.' If the edition or printing is not specified it generally means the first edition, as subsequent printings are identified as 'Second printing, 19..,' etc."

1988 Statement: *See* 1988 Statement of New York Graphic Society Books/Little, Brown

NEW YORK GRAPHIC SOCIETY BOOKS/LITTLE, BROWN

1988 Statement: " 'First Edition' is printed on the copyright page. Alternatively the words 'First Printing' are used.

"In the case of books imported from foreign publishers, 'First published by ...,' 'First U.S. edition' is used. If the edition or printing is not specified it generally means the first edition, as subsequent printings are identified as 'Second printing, 19..,' etc."

1995 Statement: *See* 1995 Statement of Little, Brown & Company
2000 Statement: *See* 2000 Statement of Little, Brown & Company

NEW YORK UNIVERSITY PRESS

1994 Statement: "We use a line of numerals that represents the number of possible new impressions. The lowest number represents the present impression. Number 1 indicates the first printing of a first edition."
2000 Statement: *See* 1994 Statement

NEW YORK ZOETROPE

1989 Statement: "We designate our first editions by printing a statement on the copyright page, such as, 'First Edition' or 'First Printing' followed by the month and year. First and subsequent editions bear a '5 4 3 2 1' indicator, also on the copyright page."

1993 Statement: *See* 1989 Statement

NEWEST PRESS (CANADA)

2001 Statement: "At NeWest Press we currently identify the first printing of a first edition by the following number line: 1 2 3 4 5 04 03 02 01."

NEWNES

2000 Statement: *See* 2000 Statement of Butterworth-Heinemann

NEWNES (UNITED KINGDOM)

2000 Statement: *See* 2000 Statement of Butterworth-Heinemann

GEORGE NEWNES, LTD. (UNITED KINGDOM)

1928 Statement: "So far as this firm is concerned we have no fixed rule. It so happens that the greater part of our Book publishing work is concerned with the re-issue of books that have already appeared in library editions.

"In cases where we do publish original work ourselves, we do not mark our first editions in any way. On our second and subsequent editions or impressions we generally state on the page facing the title page the number of editions that have been published with the date of their publication, thus: 'First Impression May, 1928, Second Impression July 1928,' and so on."

1937 Statement: "We have no fixed rule. The greater part of our Book publishing work is concerned with the re-issue of books that have already appeared in library editions.

"In cases where we do publish original work ourselves, we usually print the word 'copyright' and the date of issue on the back of the title page of the first edition of a book. On our second and subsequent editions or impressions we generally state under this the number of editions that have been published with the date of their publication, thus: 'First Impression May, 1936, Second Impression July, 1936' and so on."

1947 Statement: "Our usual rule now is to insert on the back of the title page of every new book the date of publication, for example, 'First published . . . October 1947,' or sometimes the year only, as 'First published . . . . 1947.'

"Subsequent reprints or editions are noted as 'Second Edition . . . . December 1947,' or again, the year only.

"Also, on the back of the title page, we include the words 'copyright' and 'All rights Reserved.'

"The previous note which we sent to you does not now apply, as at that time we dealt chiefly with cheap reprints of novels.

"With the exception of two special Series, namely the 'WILLIAM' books and the 'SUDDEN' titles, we have now discontinued the issue of Fiction, and our Catalogue is devoted almost entirely to Technical works, dealing with Engineering, Electrical, Building, Radio, Automobile, etc. publications; also Children's Books.

"We publish too, a small number of General Books dealing with Literature, Art, etc."

NEXT DECADE, INC.
2000 Statement: "First printing is designated by the following: Copyright © 2000 by Next Decade, Inc or Author."

NEXUS (UNITED KINGDOM)
1994, 2000 Statements: *See* 1994 Statement of Virgin Publishing Ltd. (United Kingdom)

IVOR NICHOLSON & WATSON, LTD.
(UNITED KINGDOM)
(Successors to Elkin Mathews & Marrot, Ltd. [United Kingdom])
1936 Statement: "Our first editions are indicated by the words 'First published in 1936' on the title page verso. Subsequent issues and impressions are added below and the month of original publication is also included, i.e.:

> First Edition......May 1936
> Reprinted..........May 1936
> Reprinted..........June 1936

"This is now our invariable practice, although since the firm started in 1931 various methods have been used."
1947 Statement: *See* 1936 Statement

NGUOI DAN
2000 Statement: "No printing or edition notice on our first editions. Subsequent editions are marked: First reprint, Second reprint, etc . . . ."

NICOLAS-HAYS, INC.
2000 Statement: "Year: 07 06 05 04 03 02 01 00 Printing: 8 7 6 5 4 3 2 1. This indicates that this book was published in the year 2000. The number '1' shows the first [printing]. When we do a second printing the number '2' will be the number at the 'right' and the year will be selected from the [Year] list."

NICOLE GRAPHICS
1994 Statement: *See* 1994 Statement of Publishers Associates

NIGHT SKY BOOKS
2001 Statement: *See* 2001 Statement of North-South Books Inc.

NIGHTWOOD EDITIONS (CANADA)
1989 Statement: "None of our editions are reprinted—unless indicated on the copyright page as a second or subsequent printing."
1993 Statement: *See* 1989 Statement

NILGIRI PRESS
2001 Statement: "For our earliest books, we made no statement about edition. Soon our policy became to state it very clearly. We designate the first printing of the first edition on the copyright page either of these ways:
no statement about the edition or printing [OR] we identify it as the first printing.

"Subsequent printings and editions are always clearly identified with 'second edition' or 'third printing.' "

NIMROD PUBLICATIONS (AUSTRALIA)

1994 Statement: "All Nimrod Publications titles are first editions, but we have never designated any as such; we have never reprinted one! Babel Handbooks are also first editions, but in recent years we have published revised editions of a few. These are often re-titled . . . . Others are marked accordingly on the title-page, in a form such as 'Revised and Enlarged, 1992,' or 'Enlarged and Fully Revised, 1990' for a more complete reworking. In addition, where no change in title has occurred elucidation (including dates) of the relationship to the earlier edition is made on the verso.

"This practice has not varied since . . . 1965. Babel Handbooks began in 1980."

2001 Statement: "Nimrod Publications '*per se*' still publishes only first editions, and has never reprinted any of its books; these are mostly poetry, with a predictably small audience, The factual & literary critical works that we publish as *Babel Handbooks* are sometimes re-published, but always in a revised edition; this is always emphasised on the title-page and verso."

NINE MUSES BOOKS

1995 Statement: "We make no markings specifying first editions. Later editions would be marked as 2nd, 3rd, (etc.) edition, with the new date, and a statement of the date of the first edition. If it is not so marked, it is certainly a first edition. Sometimes several dates appear after the © sign. If it is not also marked 'second (or other) edition,' it is still a first edition. The date of publication usually also appears on the title page."

2000 Statement: *See* 1995 Statement but note that: "If a book is marked 'Second Printing' it is still a first edition from the same masters, unless it is also marked 'Second Edition.' "

NINETY-SIX PRESS

2000 Statement: "All of our titles are first editions and first printings, unless otherwise noted on the copyright page."

JAMES NISBET & CO., LTD. (UNITED KINGDOM)

1928 Statement: *See* 1937 Statement

1937 Statement: "It is our practice to insert the date of our First and subsequent Editions of general books on the reverse of the title page.

"We much regret that we cannot tell you when this practice commenced, but we have dated our editions over a considerable period."

1947, 2000 Statements: *See* 1937 Statement

NMS PUBLISHING LIMITED
(NATIONAL MUSEUMS OF SCOTLAND)
(UNITED KINGDOM)

2000 Statement: "The first edition will contain 'Published by NMS Publishing Limited (National Museums of Scotland)' with the copyright notice and date. Any subsequent edition will contain, e.g., 'First published 2000 by NMS Publishing Limited (National Museums of Scotland). Second edition 2001.' Straightforward reprints are identified as second, third impressions, etc.

"This company name change, from National Museums of Scotland to NMS Publishing Limited (National Museums of Scotland) has been effective since July 1997."

NO EXIT PRESS
2000 Statement: "The No Exit imprint does not mark its first editions in any way. It does indicate first, second printing and so on."

NO EXIT PRESS (UNITED KINGDOM)
2001 Statement: *See* 2001 Statement of Oldcastle Books Ltd. (United Kingdom)

NO STARCH PRESS
2000 Statement: "We identify the first printing of a first edition by the number line 1 2 3 4 5 6 7 8 9 10 appearing just below the line reading 'Printed in . . . ' on the copyright page. The number that appears on the far left is the number of the printing."

NOBLE PORTER PRESS
2000 Statement: "We do not designate 1st editions."

THE NONESUCH PRESS, LTD. (UNITED KINGDOM)
1928 Statement: *See* 1937 Statement
1937 Statement: "Our practice is to date our books, whether they be first or subsequent editions, upon the title page; and to record upon the back of the title page or elsewhere the particular impression to which the copy belongs.

"This has been our practice since the publication of our first book in 1923.
1948 Statement: "Our practice nowadays and since the early 1940s is to date the particular impression to which the copy belongs on the title page, and to record the date of the first edition on the title verso."

NONPAREIL BOOKS
1988, 2000 Statements: *See* 1988 Statement of David R. Godine, Publisher, Inc.

NOONDAY PRESS
1988, 2000 Statements: *See* 1988 Statement of Farrar, Straus & Giroux, Inc.

THE NOONTIDE PRESS
2000 Statement: "The practice of the Noontide Press and Institute for Historical Review has been to designate first printings as 'First Edition' or 'First English Edition.' A number line is not generally used."

NORD-SÜD VERLAG (SWITZERLAND)
2001 Statement: *See* 2001 Statement of North-South Books Inc.

NORMAN PUBLISHING
2001 Statement: "We do not identify a first printing or any printing after the first printing on the copyright page."

NORTH AMERICAN PRESS
1993 Statement: *See* 1993 Statement of Fulcrum Publishing

NORTH ATLANTIC BOOKS
1976 Statement: "No particular method is used to designate first editions. Second editions, of which we have not had any so far, will be marked as such. In the case of *Io*, it is more difficult, and a different system is needed for almost every issue. For instance, in number 7, only a small difference on the last page distinguishes first from second edition. Other *Io*'s like 1, 2, 3, 4, 5 state second edition. 6 is also difficult to tell. 8 is an enlarged edition. But if you are just asking about North Atlantic, there are none so far."

1981 Statement: "There is no special method of designating first editions for either North Atlantic Books or *Io*. Those issues of *Io* that have second editions are: 1, 2, 3, 4, 5, 6, 7, 8, 11, 24, and 25. In all cases except #7, there is some sort of double-dating or redating on the copyright page. Issue #4 also has a third edition, enlarged and revised.

"The North Atlantic Books that have second editions are: *Selected Poems* by Diane di Prima (enlarged, with different cover color and different dates on the cover) and *Ranger Volume I*, by Theodore Enslin, the second edition of which is pink instead of blue and extensively revised. *Essence of T'ai Chi Ch'uan*, the verse translation of the t'ai chi classics, has three going on four editions, and each of the later editions is marked by the edition number on the copyright page."

1988 Statement: "We often run second, third, etc., editions without any indication."

1994 Statement: "We just don't make edition specifications except in the case of revisions."

2001 Statement: *See* 1994 Statement

NORTH CAROLINA DIVISION OF ARCHIVES & HISTORY
2001 Statement: "We do not identify a first printing; we do identify subsequent printings on the copyright page."

NORTH CAROLINA WESLEYAN COLLEGE PRESS
1994 Statement: "Our first editions have no distinguishing marks unless the edition itself is a limited numbered and/or signed one, and then the designation 'first edition' appears on the colophon. We have followed this practice since the press was founded in 1987. None of our books has had a second printing. When that occurs, we plan to add 'second printing' to the copyright page."

NORTH POINT PRESS
1981 Statement: "We do not designate first printings. However we will designate subsequent printings, with a new slug on the copyright page indicating 'Second Printing,' 'Third Printing,' etc. This has not yet been necessary."

1988 Statement: "We do not designate first printings. However we will designate subsequent printings, with a new slug on the copyright page indicating 'Second Printing,' 'Third Printing,' etc."

2000 Statement: *See* 2000 Statement of Farrar, Straus & Giroux, Inc.

NORTH STAR PRESS OF SAINT CLOUD, INC.

1994 Statement: "North Star Press states: 'Copyright (the symbol) date and author's name.' This constitutes a first edition. In subsequent printings of the title, we list the printing number. I do not consider second printings to be first editions. This is the way we have always designated first printings."

2000 Statement: "Recently, especially cloth editions, we identify as 'First Edition.' Always, however, we clearly identify 'Second printing,' 'Third printing,' as needed, so some books with no print number are also first editions. [Number lines] are not frequently used, nothing recent."

NORTH WIND BOOKS

2000 Statement: *See* 2000 Statement of Harold Shaw Publishers

NORTHCOTE HOUSE PUBLISHERS LTD (UNITED KINGDOM)

2001 Statement: "We state: 'First Published in XXXX by Northcote House Publishers Ltd . . . ' etc. All further reprints and new editions are listed with year unless more than one reprint occurs in a single year when the month and year are included."

NORTHEASTERN UNIVERSITY PRESS

1988 Statement: "We print, below the line 'Manufactured in the United States of America,' a line of numbers showing the year of publication preceded by the next four or five years in descending order and followed by the numbers 5 through 1. For example:

94 93 92 91 90 89 5 4 3 2 1

"This shows that the book was first printed in 1989. When it is reprinted in, say, two years, the 90 and the 89 will be deleted by the printer, and the line will read:

94 93 92 91 5 4 3 2 —showing that the 2d printing was in 1991.

"A revised edition (very rare) is so noted by a new copyright notice: 'Revised edition © 1985 by Joe Doe.' (The row of numbers at this point would return to the full row, with '1' at the far right showing first printing of the revised edition)."

This method was adopted around 1984.

1993, 2000 Statements: *See* 1988 Statement

NORTHERN ILLINOIS UNIVERSITY PRESS

1976 Statement: "In answer to your questions, we have—so far—no second editions, so we haven't faced the problem of identifying subsequent editions. All books published by NIU Press, unless otherwise noted on the copyright page, are first editions. Second printings (not editions) are usually noted on the copyright page.

"The preceding paragraph does not constitute a formal statement of our policy; it is merely a description of our method of identifying editions and printings."

1981, 1988 Statements: *See* 1976 Statement

1994 Statement: "Second or revised editions and reprints are duly noted on the copyright page, if not on the title page."

2001 Statement: *See* 1994 Statement

NORTHFIELD PUBLISHING

2000 Statement: *See* 2000 Statement of Moody Press

NORTH-HOLLAND

1988 Statement: *See* 1988 Statement of Elsevier Science Publishing Company, Inc.

NORTHLAND PRESS

1976 Statement: "We have, since August, 1972, labeled all our books as first editions on the copyright page of each volume.

"Prior to August 1972 there was no such pattern. Some first editions were identified as such. Others were not.

"However, I know of no Northland Press title which when reprinted did not indicate such on the copyright page."

1981 Statement: *See* 1976 Statement

1988 Statement: "We do still follow the practice outlined in the 1981 statement, and all imprints bear the same sort of designation."

1993, 2000 Statements: *See* 1993 Statement of Northland Publishing

NORTHLAND PUBLISHING
(Previously Northland Press)

1993, 2000 Statements: *See* 1988 Statement of Northland Press

NORTH-SOUTH BOOKS (UNITED KINGDOM)

1988 Statement: *See* 1988 Statement of Blackie and Son Limited (United Kingdom)

NORTH-SOUTH BOOKS INC.

1994 Statement: The first printing of a first edition is indicated by the number line 10 9 8 7 6 5 4 3 2 1. The lowest number showing indicates the printing.

2001 Statement: *See* 1994 Statement

NORTH-SOUTH CENTER PRESS
AT THE UNIVERSITY OF MIAMI

2001 Statement: "We identify the first printing of a first edition by a number line on the copyright page; the lowest number indicates the printing."

NORTHSTONE PUBLISHING (CANADA)

2000 Statement: *See* 2000 Statement of Wood Lake Books (Canada)

NORTHWESTERN UNIVERSITY PRESS

1981 Statement: "The first editions of our books generally carry only the copyright date and notice on the copyright page. Subsequent reprints will carry the first printing and second printing, etc., notices and their respective dates. Although the Press has no official policy on this matter, I find this to be the case with almost all of our publications.

"Our Press has no other imprints; we do, however, sometimes distribute books which originate in other University departments, and we do import books from foreign publishers which will carry our imprint."

1988 Statement: "The first editions of our books carry the copyright date and notice on the copyright page. Subsequent editions include all printing notices and their respective dates. We have no other imprints."

1995 Statement: "The first editions of our books carry the copyright date and notice on the copyright page. Subsequent editions include all printing notices and their respective dates.

"Northwestern University Press publishes books under its own name and under two imprints as well: TriQuarterly Books/Northwestern University Press and Hydra Books/Northwestern University Press. The press has a new copublication arrangement with The Marlboro Press, under which books will be published under The Marlboro Press/Northwestern University Press."

2000 Statement: *See* 1995 Statement

NORTHWOODS PRESS

1988 Statement: "We do not designate first editions or first printings, but we do designate successive editions or printings."

1995 Statement: *See* 1995 Statement of Conservatory of American Letters

2000 Statement: "We do not have any method for designating a first edition, except it doesn't say anything. Subsequent editions and printings are designated simply, for example, 'Second printing, 2001', 'Second edition, 2001', 'Second printing of second edition, 2001' etc."

W. W. NORTON & COMPANY, INC.

1937 Statement: "On books when first published by us, we run a legend on the copyright page reading 'First edition.' On subsequent printings this legend is deleted, but we do not indicate second, third, etc., printings in the books."

1947 Statement: *See* 1937 Statement

1976 Statement: "Our method of identifying first impressions is shown by . . . the line of numbers across the bottom of the copyright page. When the second impression is made the number 1 will be dropped from the line; when the third impression is made the number 2 will be dropped, and so on."

1981, 1988, 1993 Statements: *See* 1976 Statement

NORTON COKER PRESS

2000 Statement: "We identify the first printing of a first edition by the following statement: © copyright 2000 Norton Coker Press."

NOVA SCIENCE BOOKS

2000 Statement: *See* 2000 Statement of Nova Science Publishers, Inc.

NOVA SCIENCE PUBLISHERS, INC.

1995 Statement: "We do not designate."
2000 Statement: *See* 1995 Statement

NUIT ISIS (UNITED KINGDOM)

1994 Statement: *See* 1994 Statement of Mandrake of Oxford (United Kingdom)
2000 Statement: *See* 2000 Statement of Mandrake of Oxford (United Kingdom)

NUMIDIA PRESS

1995 Statement: "We have no special way of designating first editions. Revisions are always noted."

NUNAGA PUBLISHING CO., LTD. (CANADA)

1976 Statement: *See* 1976 Statement of Antonson Publishing Ltd. (Canada)

NW EXPLORER

1995 Statement: *See* 1995 Statement of Cedar Bay Press

O

O!!ZONE

1995 Statement: "First edition is the last entry on the © page."
2000 Statement: "All O!!Zone publications are first editions."

OAK KNOLL BOOKS

1994 Statement: "We print 'published by Oak Knoll Books, 414 Delaware Street, New Castle DE 19720' in the first printing. Subsequent printings are designated thus:
    'Reprinted September 1992, August 1993,' etc.
  "We adopted this in 1992."

OAK KNOLL PRESS

2000 Statement: "We print 'published by Oak Knoll Press, 310 Delaware Street, New Castle, DE 19720' in the first printing. From 1996-1998, the address was 414 Delaware Street. Subsequent printings are designated thus: 'Reprinted September 1992, August 1993,' etc."

OAK PUBLICATIONS

2001 Statement: *See* 2001 Statement of Music Sales Corp

OAKHILL PRESS

1988 Statement: "Oakhill Press has adopted the convention of identifying edition and printing on the verso. If no edition statement appears on the verso, the book is a first edition. As regards printings within an edition, we identify the printing by using a string of sequential numbers, where the lowest number on the right is the printing number."

1995 Statement: "Our policy for identifying editions has changed only slightly since 1988. First editions will have 'First Edition' on the verso. Printings are still identified as noted in the 1988 statement."

THE OAKWOOD PRESS (UNITED KINGDOM)
1947 Statement: "All our first editions simply bear the imprint 'Published by' and the date, whereas further editions or reprints carry the imprint 'First published..second editions (or reprint)' Thus as far as our books are concerned the absence of a statement to the contrary in the front-papers stamps it as a first edition.

"This company has been in existence since 1936; before that date it was known as the Four O's Publishing Co. (1931)."
1994, 2000 Statements: *See* 1947 Statement

OASIS BOOKS (UNITED KINGDOM)
1976 Statement: "Oasis Books first editions are identified by the statement 'First published in (year) by Oasis Books, (address)' to be found on the reverse of the title page, or by the statement beginning 'First published in (month) (year) by Oasis Books (address) . . . ' to be found beneath our logotype on the page immediately following the last page of the book."
1981 Statement: "[The 1976 statement] is still an accurate description of the method by which Oasis Books designates its first editions. Perhaps the only rider to add to it is that the method used in Paragraph 1 is the most frequently used in the books produced since 1976.

"But this does not mean that the second method will never be used again, so that statement should stand as well. No other methods of designating first editions are likely to be used. Second editions always have the words 'second edition' and the date appended after the first statement."

OBELISK
1988 Statement: *See* 1988 Statement of E. P. Dutton & Co., Inc.

OBERLIN COLLEGE PRESS
1994 Statement: "All we do is say, FIRST EDITION on the copyright page."
2000 Statement: "Some, but not all, of our first editions have 'First Edition' on the verso."

OBOL INTERNATIONAL
2000 Statement: "No identifying marks on first editions; 2nd editions, 3rd editions & so on are marked thusly."

O'BRIEN EDUCATIONAL (REPUBLIC OF IRELAND)
1981, 1988 Statements: *See* 1981 Statement of The O'Brien Press (Republic of Ireland)

THE O'BRIEN PRESS (REPUBLIC OF IRELAND)
1981 Statement: "Normally we would do the following:
First published 1981
by The O'Brien Press

20 Victoria Road

Dublin 6, Ireland.

"You will note our new address. Previously it will have read 11 Clare Street, Dublin 2.

"Our other imprint, O'Brien Educational, is done in the same way except with the different imprint name."

1988 Statement: *See* 1981 Statement

OBSERVERS (UNITED KINGDOM)

2000 Statement: "The Observers are currently dormant and no new titles have been added for about 5 years. They would follow Penguin standard practice."

See also Frederick Warne (United Kingdom)

OCEAN PRESS

2000 Statement: "Our first editions bear no printing or edition notice. Subsequent editions identify themselves as second printing, third printing, etc."

OCEAN VIEW BOOKS

1995 Statement: "The first book issued under this imprint was Poly, again a split hardcover/paperback first edition. This book used, in addition to the 'first edition' statement, 1 2 3 4 5 etc. in anticipation of reprinting—however it has not been reprinted.

"All of our 20 or so books published since then have abandoned the use of 1 2 3 4 5 etc. and standardized on the use of the words 'first edition' on the copyright page which are then dropped from subsequent printings. It is our intention to maintain the use of this convention."

2000 Statement: "No change to our policy statement; however we have now published about 60 books. Documents of Colorado Art is an active imprint with more books currently in production; Ocean View Doubles is now inactive—there will be no new titles—however older titles are still in print under that imprint."

OCEAN VIEW DOUBLES

2000 Statement: *See* 2000 Statement of Ocean View Books

OCEAN VIEW PRESS
(Active 1981-1987)

Statement made in 1995: "During this period we published mostly literary chapbooks of very limited circulation (25 to several hundred copies). For all but one of these (*Co-Orbital Moons*), the first edition was so designated by the use of the phrase 'first edition' on the copyright page. When these Ocean View Press books were reprinted, the words 'first edition' were dropped.

"Through an oversight, in a few rare instances when nearly-out-of-print chapbooks were photocopied and bound in already-printed first edition covers in order to 'make up' more constituents of our popular slipcased sets, the 'first edition' statement was not always dropped.

"*Co-Orbital Moons* was our first book issued in hardcover and softcover, and entirely lacks the 'first edition' statement on both binding states. Both states are from the same print run, and the book has never been reprinted, so any copy found is a first edition."

OCEANA PUBLICATIONS, INC.

1976 Statement: "We make no distinction at the outset, either with regard to editions, or with regard to printings. If a book goes to a second printing (rare), we will sometimes indicate 'second printing' on the copyright page. If it goes to a second edition, we will usually indicate with 'second edition' on either the copyright or title pages, or both."

1981 Statement: "The [1976] statement concerning Oceana's method of designating the first printing of a first edition is still accurate. We have made no changes in our method."

1988, 1993 Statements: *See* 1981 Statement

THE OCTAGON PRESS LTD (UNITED KINGDOM)

2001 Statement: "We do not identify a first printing; we have identified subsequent printings since 1985 approximately. Earlier titles were sometimes treated differently."

THE OCTOPUS PUBLISHING GROUP PLC
(UNITED KINGDOM)

1989 Statement: "I apologise for the delay in responding; the Group's archive library is still in the process of being developed and until recently we did not have all the books relevant to your query.

"The Octopus Group comprises a number of publishers, the major ones being: the Heinemann Group; Secker & Warburg; Methuen; Octopus; and the Hamlyn Group. Smaller publishers coming under the Octopus umbrella include: Mitchell Beazley; Leo Cooper; Ginn; Brimax; Eyre & Spottiswoode; George Philip; and Osprey."

BRIMAX: "First printings have the statement 'published by Brimax Books . . . . 19—.' The absence of any note indicating subsequent printings will indicate first printing."

LEO COOPER: "Leo Cooper is an independent imprint of the Octopus Publishing Group. After leaving Warne, he became associated first with Secker & Warburg, then William Heinemann (both now part of the Octopus Group). First printings are indicated by the statement 'first published in 19—' and the absence of any note of subsequent printings."

COUNTRY LIFE: "Our archive copies only go back to 1903; from this date up to and including 1925 first printings are indicated by the date on the title page and no additional information on the title verso. From 1928 up to and including 1967 the statement on the title verso reads 'first published 19—' or 'first published in England 19—' (if previously published in another country). The absence of information about subsequent or earlier printings should indicate a first printing. From 1968 when Country Life became part of the Hamlyn Publishing Group, first printings follow the Hamlyn practice."

GINN: "First publication is indicated by the date in the copyright statement. Information about later editions or impressions is always included. Therefore, the absence of such information would indicate a first edition."

THE HAMLYN GROUP: "1960s, 70s and early 80s publications contain only a copyright line to indicate date of publication and first printing. From 1983 the statement on the title verso reads 'first published 19—.' For both periods the absence of additional information (earlier copyright dates as well as reprint or foreign printing details) should indicate a first printing. Other imprints such as Gondola, Spring and Rainbow follow the same practice. (Gondola and Spring are in fact almost totally reprint imprints.) Acquired companies such as Dean and Son usually follow the same practice from the date of acquisition. The Dean publishing company began at the turn of the nineteenth century. However first printings of the publications before the late 1960s will be extremely hard to identify as neither date of publication nor copyright line was included."

THE HEINEMANN GROUP: "From William Heinemann's first publication in 1890 up to and including 1921, first printings have just the year on the title page. Subsequent printings and editions would be indicated on the title verso. From 1923 to date the statement on the title verso reads 'first published, 19—' or 'first published in Great Britain 19—' (when it has previously been published in another country). In the absence of any note of subsequent reprintings or editions, it may be assumed that the book is a first printing. However, I have noticed that impressions in the same year as first publication were—very occasionally—not indicated."

METHUEN: "From the first publications in 1889 up to and including 1903, first printings have just the year on the title page. Subsequent editions are listed on the title verso or occasionally indicated on the title page. However, if words such as '43rd Thousand' appear on the title page the book is going to be a later edition despite no statement to that effect. From 1904 to the 1970s the statement on the title verso reads: 'first published in 19—.' 1980s publications (excepting children's) have the statement 'first published in Great Britain 198-' regardless of whether the work has been previously published in another country. If the work has been published previously by another company or in another language this will be indicated. In conclusion, the absence of printing history notes should indicate a first printing, however I have noticed that reprints and even different editions issued in the first year of publication are not always indicated in any way in the book itself.

"Methuen and Co. (the academic division of Methuen) was amalgamated with Routledge in 1986 when Associated Book Publishers bought Routledge. At the end of 1987, International Thomson bought out ABP and sold on Methuen London, Methuen Children's, Pitkin Pictorial, and Eyre & Spottiswoode to the Octopus Group. Methuen and Co. remained but lost the Methuen name (now with Octopus) and became absorbed into Routledge."

MITCHELL BEAZLEY: "First printings have a copyright statement and date; no statement as to 'first published.' Subsequent editions will be indicated but reprints are not always noted so identification of a first printing would be difficult."

OCTOPUS: "From the earliest books in 1972 to date, first printings are indicated by the statement 'first published (in) 19—.' An absence of any notes about subsequent printings or an earlier copyright will confirm first printing."

OSPREY: "First printings have the statement 'published in 19—.' The absence of any additional printing notes will indicate a first printing."

SECKER & WARBURG: "Our archive is incomplete for Secker & Warburg. Up to 1937, the date of publication appears on the title page. Note of subsequent printings is made on the title verso. During the 1940s and 1950s the statement appears on the title verso. It reads 'first published 19—.' From the early 1960s to date the statement reads 'first published in England [latterly 'Great Britain'] 19—' regardless of whether the work has been previously published in another country. Printing history notes are always included on the title verso, therefore their absence will indicate a first printing."

ODYSSEY AND VOYAGER PAPERBACKS
1995 Statement: *See* 1995 Statement of Harcourt Brace and Company

ODYSSEY CLASSICS
2001 Statement: *See* 2001 Statement of Harcourt, Inc.

THE ODYSSEY PRESS, INC.
1947 Statement: "We indicate every first edition of one of our books by printing the line, 'First Edition' just beneath the copyright notice of the book. In subsequent printings we change the line to read 'Second Printing,' 'Third Printing,' and so on. If the book is revised, the first edition of it is, in the same manner, called 'First Printing of Revised Edition,' and subsequent printings are labeled 'Second Printing of Revised Edition,' and so on."

OFFSET OFFSHOOTS
2000 Statement: *See* 2000 Statement of Ommation Press

OHARA PUBLICATIONS, INCORPORATED
1976 Statement: "We do not use any particular identifying statement to identify first editions. As the books move into second, third, etc. printings that is designated on the title page.

"If a book is a reprint that is explained in the publisher's foreword."

1981, 1988, 1994 Statements: *See* 1976 Statement

OHIO GENEALOGICAL SOCIETY
2000 Statement: "We do not designate first editions or first printings."

OHIO PSYCHOLOGY PRESS
1994 Statement: "We say 'First printing, 19—.' [This method was] adopted in 1982 and [we] have always used it."

OHIO STATE UNIVERSITY PRESS
1976 Statement: "The Ohio State University Press does not identify in any special way the first editions of the books that it publishes."

All printings of a first edition are indicated except for the very first. The absence of any statement would indicate the first printing of a first edition.

1981, 1988 Statements: *See* 1976 Statement

1993 Statement: "Since around 1989 the Ohio State University Press has been designating its first printings of first editions with a row of numbers set below the CIP data on the copyright page (i.e., 10 9 8 7 6 5 4 3 2 1). In subsequent printings the numbers would be deleted to reflect the number of the printing. We use this same designation for our imprint, Sandstone Books."

2000 Statement: *See* 1993 Statement, but note that Sandstone Books is no longer in operation.

OHIO UNIVERSITY PRESS

1988 Statement: "Ohio University Press does not designate its first printings in any way, but we note subsequent printings by printing number ('Second Printing') and date ('December 1999'). This has been our standard practice since 1965."

See also The Swallow Press, Inc.

1993 Statement: "Ohio University Press designates the year of the title's first printing and prints a dateline to indicate subsequent printings. Example:

First printing 1993

97 96 95 94 93 5 4 3 2 1

"This also applies for the Swallow Press. We began using this designation in 1991."

2000 Statement: *See* 1993 Statement

GEORGE OHSAWA MACROBIOTIC FOUNDATION

2000 Statement: "We identify the first edition by 'First Edition   Year'; we don't identify printings."

O'LAUGHLIN PRESS

1995 Statement: "Beginning with 1995 all first printings of first editions will carry the wording 'First Edition, first printing' on the title/copyright page. Prior to this date there has been no uniform indication of same, and many titles have been intended as one time printings only.

"From 1993-1995 the words 'original first edition' on the title page indicates First Edition, First Printing."

THE OLD FORT NIAGARA ASSOCIATION

1994 Statement: "We have no special manner of designating first editions."

2001 Statement: *See* 1994 Statement

THE OLD STILE PRESS (UNITED KINGDOM)

2001 Statement: "All our books are limited editions printed by hand. Each book has a colophon page at the back with details of the printing, the paper, the dates and signatures of author (where living) and artist (who is always contemporary) etc., but that will be all you will need because we do not reprint or do further editions (very occasionally we have had an arrangement with a trade publisher for a book to appear under another imprint based upon our original but it will have another publisher's name on it)."

428

OLD VICARAGE PUBLICATIONS (UNITED KINGDOM)
1994 Statement: "We print 'First published 19..' and then if needed 'Second edition 19..' etc."
2000 Statement: *See* 1994 Statement

OLD WEST PUBLISHING COMPANY
1995 Statement: "Old West Publishing Co. has been inactive since 1984 in that we have not done any publishing since then. Our publications are all first editions although not generally identified as such. We have never reprinted any book with the exception of the substantially revised *Life in the Rocky Mountains* by Warren Ferris (1940, 1983). The revised edition is clearly identified as such. Other titles such as *Trans-Missouri Stock Raising* have been first edited editions of very rare old books with which they could never be confused. The preceding applies only to trade titles. Our textbook line has been handled by Johnson Publishing in Boulder, CO, since 1976 and we have no record of how first editions of our textbooks were identified in the past or at the present."

OLDCASTLE BOOKS LTD. (UNITED KINGDOM)
1994 Statement: "We just use imprint number."
2001 Statement: *See* 1994 Statement

THE OLEANDER PRESS (UNITED KINGDOM)
2001 Statement: "Our first editions are identified on the title verso by the international copyright logo followed by the year, Author's Name and Publisher's Name. We have no other imprints or subsidiaries."

OLIVE BRANCH PRESS
2001 Statement: *See* 2001 Statement of Interlink Publishing Group Inc

OLIVER & BOYD
1976, 1981 Statements: *See* 1976, 1981 Statements of Longman Inc.

OLIVER & BOYD, LTD. (UNITED KINGDOM)
1937 Statement: "It is our practice to put the date of publication of any book on the title page itself. If the book is reprinted, the date of the reprint appears on the title page and a bibliographical description on the back of the title, e.g.
    First Edition 1922
    Reprinted 1923
    Second Edition 1924"
1947 Statement: "Our first editions are indicated by the words on the title page verso—'First Published—' or 'First Edition—' depending on whether the matter is completely new or whether it has appeared, or in part appeared, in some previous publication.

"It may or may not also appear on the title page, this being decided on the basis of appropriateness to the title page layout. Subsequent editions are added below on title page verso thus:

First Published   September 1944
Second Edition—Revised   May 1945
Reprinted   November 1945

"This is our current practice but there have naturally been many variations since our first publication in 1778."

OLIVER-NELSON BOOKS
1994 Statement: *See* 1994 Statement of Thomas Nelson Publishers

OM PUBLISHING (UNITED KINGDOM)
1994, 2000 Statements: *See* 1994 Statement of The Paternoster Press Ltd. (United Kingdom)

OMF INTERNATIONAL (IHQ) LTD (SINGAPORE)
1994 Statement: "All publications state when the first publication occurred, for example: 'First published . . . 1957.' Many are translated into other languages. Each foreign edition will also state: First published in English . . . . 1957.

"As far as we are aware, this convention has been followed consistently."

OMMATION PRESS
2000 Statement: "There is no special indication for 1st printing. Instead, subsequent printings are labeled as such (2nd printing, 3rd etc.)."

OMNIBUS BOOKS (AUSTRALIA)
1994 Statement: "Omnibus Books first began publishing children's books in 1982, and has always used the same method of designation.

"The first printing of a first edition says, simply 'First published [year].' A reprint of the first edition follows the first printing information with 'Reprinted [year],' and each further reprinting is indicated by the appropriate year. If a book is reprinted more than once in a single year, this is indicated after the appropriate year in parentheses: e.g., '(twice)' or '(three times).' When a hardback edition is released in paperback, the words 'First published in this edition [year]' or 'First published in paperback [year]' follow the first printing information.

"During our association with Penguin Books Australia, our first printing was designated 'First published by Omnibus Books in association with Penguin Books Australia Pty Ltd [year].' "

OMOHUMDRO INSTITUTE
OF EARLY AMERICAN HISTORY & CULTURE
2000 Statement: "Virtually all of our books are published through the University of North Carolina Press and follow their policy. Our self-published books, we tend not to reprint."
See also University of North Carolina Press

ON STREAM PUBLICATIONS (REPUBLIC OF IRELAND)
1994 Statement: "Our first printing of a first edition is designated thus and goes on the verso of the title page:

Published 199? by On Stream Publications Ltd.

Currabaha, Cloghroe, Blarney, Co. Cork, Ireland.

"Re-prints are called such and dated and the date of the first edition is also mentioned."

2001 Statement: *See* 1994 Statement, "but note that the word 'Blarney' would not appear in the address."

101 PRODUCTIONS

1976 Statement: "We state the printing date of reprints on our copyright page. Thus, any book without a printing date, only the copyright date, would be a first edition."

1981 Statement: *See* 1976 Statement

1988 Statement: "We are no longer publishing."

ONE WORLD

2001 Statement: *See* 2001 Statement of The Ballantine Publishing Group

ONTARIO FILM INSTITUTE (CANADA)

1981, 1988 Statements: *See* 1976 Statement of Associated University Presses

ONWORD PRESS

1994 Statement: *See* 1994 Statement of High Mountain Press

ONYX

1993, 2000 Statements: *See* 1993 Statement of Dutton Signet

OOLICHAN BOOKS (CANADA)

2001 Statement: "We do not make any specific identification of first editions unless the book is a special edition, in which case a letter or number and author's signature will appear on a colophon page at the end of the book. However, we do identify reprints and new editions on the copyright page."

OPC (UNITED KINGDOM)

2000 Statement: *See* 2000 Statement of Ian Allan Publishing (United Kingdom)

OPEN COURT PUBLISHING COMPANY

1981 Statement: "Open Court does not have fixed rules to apply to first editions. When a publication carries the copyright date only on its copyright page, it is an indication of a first edition. We usually designate second printings, second editions, etc."

1988 Statement: "Open Court does not have fixed rules that apply to first editions. When a publication carries the copyright date only on its copyright page, it is an indication of a first edition. Recently we have begun to include the words 'first printing' and the date of publication on the copyright page, where appropriate. We usually designate second printings, second editions, etc."

1995, 2000 Statements: *See* 1988 Statement

OPEN HAND PUBLISHING INC.

1994 Statement: "The first printing of our books says on the copyright page 'FIRST EDITION' followed by a series of dates and numbers which indicated the year and the print run. In subsequent printings numbers are deleted to correspond with the correct year and printing."

2001 Statement: *See* 1994 Statement

OPEN ROAD PUBLISHING

1993 Statement: *See* 1993 Statement of Cardoza Publishing

OPEN UNIVERSITY OF AMERICA PRESS

2000 Statement: "When no designation of edition or printing sequence appears on our copyright page, the book should be construed as the first edition and first printing.

"In the case of books which are a second or following edition, the information is given as part of the subtitle on the title page and then on the copyright page. The different ISBN and publication date further distinguish second and subsequent editions.

"In the case of books which are a second or following printing, the information appears on the copyright page, along with a new ISBN and publication date."

OPEN UNIVERSITY PRESS (UNITED KINGDOM)

1994 Statement: "The first printing of an Open University Press book would say: 'First Published' and then give the year of publication, e.g. '1994.' Any subsequent reprints will be listed on the following line, e.g. 'Reprinted 1995.'

"Second editions are indicated as such:

First published 1987

Reprinted 1988, 1991, 1993

First published in this second edition 1994

"This method of designation does not differ significantly from any previously used."

2000 Statement: *See* 1994 Statement

ORB

1994 Statement: *See* 1994 Statement of TOR

ORBIS BOOKS

1976 Statement: "We do not designate first editions. We indicate only those printings and/or editions after the first printing. This method is the only one we use and have ever used."

1981, 1988, 1993, 2000 Statements: *See* 1976 Statement

ORBIT (UNITED KINGDOM)

2001 Statement: *See* 2001 Statement of Little, Brown and Company (United Kingdom)

ORCHISES PRESS

1994 Statement: "On the verso of the title page of Orchises books appears a string of characters beginning with the letter G— G 6 E 4 C 2 A. This code

appears entire on the first print run of any book with a new ISBN. Later printings, if any, within that ISBN are indicated by removing the last letter from the string . . . . This device has been used for all books since Orchises was founded in 1983 except for a limited edition of C.K. Williams' *Helen*; since it was not to be reprinted, there was no reason to use the code."
2000 Statement: *See* 1994 Statement

OREGON HISTORICAL SOCIETY PRESS
1988 Statement: "No specific designation is made for first editions, although numbers 1 through 5 are often listed on the copyright page in anticipation of additional printings. Otherwise each new printing (e.g. 'second printing') or edition (e.g. 'second edition, revised') is listed on the copyright page."
1993 Statement: *See* 1988 Statement
2000 Statement: *See* 1988 Statement, but note: "Occasionally we include 'first edition' on the copyright page, but it is inconsistent."

OREGON STATE UNIVERSITY PRESS
1976 Statement: "We use no special means of identifying first impressions except that second printings and second editions are so indicated."
1981 Statement: *See* 1976 Statement
1988 Statement: "We use no special means of identifying first impressions, except that second and subsequent editions are so indicated."
1993, 2000 Statements: *See* 1988 Statement

ORIEL PRESS LTD. (UNITED KINGDOM)
1976 Statement: "Our practice is to state the date of first publication on the verso of the title page along with the date of copyright. Any reprintings, or subsequent editions are noted as such on the verso of the title page."
1981 Statement: *See* 1976 Statement
1988 Statement: "We are no longer publishing under the Oriel imprint, but the name is still with us."
See 1988 Statement of Associated Book Publishers (UK) Ltd. (United Kingdom)

O'REILLY & ASSOCIATES, INC.
1994 Statement: "We have a 'Print History' section on the copyright pages of our books. Entries have been streamlined to say:
    September 1994: First Edition.
Or, since the technical content of our books is constantly being revised:
    September 1995: Minor corrections."
2000 Statement: *See* 1994 Statement

ORION
1995 Statement: *See* 1995 Statement of Crown Publishers Inc.

ORION BOOKS (UNITED KINGDOM)
1994 Statement: *See* 1994 Statement of The Orion Publishing Group Ltd (United Kingdom)

ORION CHILDREN'S BOOKS (UNITED KINGDOM)

1994 Statement: *See* 1994 Statement of The Orion Publishing Group Ltd (United Kingdom)

THE ORION PUBLISHING GROUP LTD
(UNITED KINGDOM)

1994 Statement: "We don't appear to use any hard and fast system for designating a first edition. The actual first edition will state 'First published in Great Britain in (date) by (imprint).' The next impression should say '2nd impression' and so forth for subsequent editions. I gather from our production department that this sometimes gets overlooked when they are up against tight deadlines.

"First paperback editions, when published simultaneously with the first hardback, are not designated as such. Later editions in paperback will say something like 'First published in 1992 this paperback edition first published in 1994.'

"New editions of titles, where there are textual changes, will have a note to that effect on the copyright page.

"This system has been used in this form since our inception."

OSPREY (UNITED KINGDOM)

1989 Statement: *See* 1989 Statement of The Octopus Publishing Group PLC (United Kingdom)

1994 Statement: *See* 1994 Statement of Reed Consumer Books (United Kingdom)

2001 Statement: "Below is an example of a first edition, first printing copyright notice:

First published in 2000 by Osprey Publishing.
Elms Court, Chapel Way, Botley, Oxford OX2 9LP
© 2000 Osprey Publishing Limited.
Printed in China through World Print Ltd
00 01 02 03 04   10 9 8 7 6 5 4 3 2 1

"Any subsequent printings would be acknowledged by the dropping of a number (from the list of 10-1), and, if the printing was in a different year, the dropping of a date (from the list of 00-04). For example, the second printing in 2000 would drop the 1; the third printing, if it were to take place in 2001, would drop the 2, and the 00.

"Later editions would be identified as 'Revised Edition.' "

OTAGO HERITAGE BOOKS (NEW ZEALAND)

1994 Statement: "We have no cryptic method of identifying first editions. On all editions we state clearly the publishing date (usually the month and the year); and on all printings and editions subsequent to the first we state equally clearly the book's previous publishing history. That also applies when we publish reprints of titles not previously published by us. We have used that system from the time we began publishing, in 1978."

2000 Statement: *See* 1994 Statement

OUR CHILD PRESS
1995 Statement: First printings are not identified.
2001 Statement: *See* 1995 Statement

OUR POETS WORKSHOP
1995, 2001 Statements: *See* 1995 Statement of Longhouse

OUR SUNDAY VISITOR
1994 Statement: "We do not designate our first editions."
2000 Statement: *See* 1994 Statement

OUTDOOR PUBLISHERS
1988, 2000 Statements: *See* 1988 Statement of Cobblesmith

OUTER SPACE PRESS
2000 Statement: "We identify the first printing of a first edition by the following number line, 10 9 8 7 6 5 4 3 2 1, which appears in the copyright page just below the line that reads 'First Edition.' The first number on the right indicates which printing you have in hand. This statement applies to any edition."

OUTPOSTS PUBLICATIONS (UNITED KINGDOM)
1976 Statement: "All our publications are 'first editions' in your sense of the term, and all are collections of poetry. We do not make any identifying statements. We do give each title a number in the *OUTPOSTS MODERN POETS SERIES.*"
1981 Statement: *See* 1976 Statement

OUTRIDER PRESS
1995 Statement: "We would distinguish a second and subsequent edition on the back of the title page by saying second edition and indicating its date. This would be included with other copyright information, ISBN and Library of Congress information found on the same page."
2000 Statement: "An example of a 1st edition, 1st printing: 10 9 8 7 6 5 4 3 2 1."

OUTRIGGER PUBLISHERS (NEW ZEALAND)
2000 Statement: *See* 1994 Statement of Outrigger Publishers Limited (New Zealand)

OUTRIGGER PUBLISHERS LIMITED (NEW ZEALAND)
1994 Statement: "Since we have rarely gone beyond the first edition of anything, except for repeat printings, we have no marking on our books. For second editions, we do put down 'Second Edition.' "
2000 Statement: *See* 2000 Statement of Outrigger Publishers (New Zealand)

GEORGE OVER (RUGBY), LTD. (UNITED KINGDOM)
1928 Statement: "Our practice is to print date of publication only, and in case of later editions to state which."
1937, 1947 Statements: *See* 1928 Statement

THE OVERLOOK PRESS

1976 Statement: "We write 'first printing' on the copyright page. We've been doing this since we started five years ago."

1981 Statement: "Shortly after we wrote you, in 1976, we changed our policy; we no longer write 'first printing.' We write 'first published' or 'first edition' until we go back to press; we then add 'second printing' on the copyright page. On some books, we are happy to report, we add 'fifth printing.' "

1988 Statement: "We now print 'First published in (year) by The Overlook Press' and, as stated in our 1981 Statement, we add designations for each subsequent printing. On some books, we are happy to report, we add 'twenty-second printing.' "

1994 Statement: "We have begun using a '1 3 5 7 9 8 6 4 2' numeral system for our commercial books. Only with fiction do we notate 'First Edition' or 'First American Edition.' "

This method was adopted in 1993.

2000 Statement: "1. We use the numberline '1 3 5 7 9 8 6 4 2' to designate first editions.

"2. This is generally accompanied by the words 'First Edition', but not always.

"3. 'First Edition' is always used with fiction, but often also with non-fiction.

"4. We have over the years used 'First Edition' and simply dropped the number 1 to designate a second printing, but lately . . . we also drop the 'First Edition' and the number 1 to designate second printing.

"5. Sometimes we leave in 'First Edition' on the first paperback printing, but like the second hardcover printings, that practice [is no longer allowed] to continue. My method . . . is to clearly designate the first printing hardcover as the only true first edition, and thus labeled as such. It is a bit of a mess and case specific, but thankfully fiction has been consistent for all these years, to the best of my knowledge.

"Tusk Paperbacks and Elephant's Eye are our additional imprints. All practices, in terms of identifying first editions, also apply to these imprints."

THE OVERMOUNTAIN PRESS

2000 Statement: "We identify the first printing of a first edition by the following number line: 1 2 3 4 5 6 7 8 9 0 with the edition number being the first number on the left."

PETER OWEN LTD. PUBLISHERS (UNITED KINGDOM)

1976 Statement: "On all our first editions on the reverse of the title page there is marked 'first published by Peter Owen, followed by the year of publication.' If we reprint we state this below."

1981, 1988, 1994, 2000 Statements: *See* 1976 Statement

RICHARD C. OWEN PUBLISHERS INC.

2000 Statement: "We do not have a specific method of identifying a first edition. A second revised edition would be acknowledged on the inside front cover. We identify a first printing of a first edition by the following number line: 9 8 7 6 5 4 3 2 1. Subsequent printings would be identified by dropping the first number in the line beginning with 9."

OWL BOOKS
2000 Statement: *See* 2000 Statement of Henry Holt and Company, LLC

OXFORD ILLUSTRATED PRESS (UNITED KINGDOM)
1988, 1994, 2000 Statements: *See* 1988 Statement of Haynes Publishing (United Kingdom)

OXFORD POETS (UNITED KINGDOM)
2000 Statement: *See* 2000 Statement of Carcanet Press Limited (United Kingdom)

OXFORD PUBLISHING COMPANY (UNITED KINGDOM)
1988, 1994, 2000 Statements: *See* 1988 Statement of Haynes Publishing (United Kingdom)

OXFORD UNIVERSITY PRESS (NEW YORK)
1937 Statement: "In regard to the indicating of First and subsequent printings of books we use in general the system followed by our home office [in England]."

1947 Statement: "We now use in general the following procedure:

"The first edition of a book carries a single copyright line, bearing the date of the first printing. The dates of later printings and editions are given in additional lines under the original copyright line, and in the case of a new edition, the date is also added to the original copyright line. The imprint may then read:

Copyright 1945, 1947, by Oxford University Press,
New York, Inc.
Second printing, 1946
Second edition, revised and/or enlarged, 1947

"However, if the book is a first American edition of one that has been previously published in England or elsewhere, the copyright line bears the date of the original publication, and may read:

Copyright 1945 by the Oxford University Press,
New York, Inc.
First American edition, 1947
First published in England, 1945"

1988 Statement: "The first edition of a book carries a single copyright line, bearing the date of first publication. The dates of later editions are added to the original copyright line as appropriate.

"The current printing of the current edition is listed on a separate line near the foot of the copyright page:

Printing (last digit): 9 8 7 6 5 4 3 2 1

"For each subsequent reprint, the final digit is deleted. We began this designation in December 1980.

"Oxford University Press, Inc. has no subsidiaries."

1994 Statement: The first printing of a first edition is indicated by the number line 1 3 5 7 9 8 6 4 2. The lowest number showing indicates the printing. This method was initiated in 1990.

OXFORD UNIVERSITY PRESS (UNITED KINGDOM)

1928 Statement: "We never, I think, print *first edition* on any first edition. All our title pages are dated. For the information of the public we distinguish 'second edition' i.e. an issue embodying substantial alterations (whether reset or not) from 'second impression' i.e. an issue substantially (though not always identically) the same as the first. I know that this is not quite sound from a bibliographical point of view; but I think publishers in our position are bound to put the convenience of the public first. It is often important for a student to be sure he has the latest edition of a book; but it would be unfair to cause him to buy a mere reprint by calling it 'nth edition' simply."

1937 Statement: "We never, I think, print *first edition* on any first edition. All our title pages of first editions are dated, and so are the title pages of the first printing of editions which we distinguish as 'second,' 'third,' etc. For the information of the public we distinguish 'second edition,' i.e., an issue embodying substantial alterations (whether reset or not) from 'second impression,' i.e., an issue substantially (though not always identically) the same as the first. I know that this is not quite sound from a bibliographical point of view; but I think publishers in our position are bound to put the convenience of the public first. It is often important for a student to be sure he has the latest edition of a book; but it would be unfair to cause him to buy a mere reprint by calling it 'nth edition' simply.

"It is probably unnecessary to explain in this note our regular practice, when we produce an unaltered or corrected 'impression,' of taking the date off the title page and giving the necessary bibliographical information opposite the title page: with us, the absence of the date from the title page is a sign that the issue is not the first printing of an 'edition' in our sense of the term.

"We are afraid we cannot give you the date when we began using our present method of identifying first editions, but it was a good many years ago."

1947 Statement: *See* 1937 Statement

Statement for 1960: "As far as we know, the practice described to you in 1976 was already being followed in previous years, and it is still our practice."

1976 Statement: "Our normal practice is to give the date on the title page for the first edition of a book. On subsequent printings the date is transferred to the verso of the title page, where the dates of the succeeding impressions are given. If there is a new edition, the date is normally given on the title page and then for subsequent impressions transferred to the verso in the same manner as before."

1981, 1989 Statements: *See* 1976 Statement

1994 Statement: "On the first Impression of an Edition (First, Second) the date of publication will be carried on the title page. For subsequent Impressions of the same edition, information will be transferred to the title-verso, to read 'First published...,' 'Reprinted . . . .' An alternative system is now more frequently used, in that a line of Impression digits will be carried on the verso '1, 2, 3, 4, 5, 6, 7, 8, 9, 10.' If the figure 1 is displayed, then that book is from the first printing. If the figure 1 is not there the book is in its second impression, and so on."

2000 Statement: "As previously, a 'second *or later* edition' (but not the first edition) of a book will be so described on its title page; as will a 'revised', 'expanded', or otherwise altered edition. Since mid-1999 books published under the Oxford University Press imprint have not carried a date of publication on the title page, even for the first impression of an edition. The few books published each year under the Clarendon Press imprint continue to carry the year of publication on the title page for the first impression of an edition; this date is deleted from subsequent impressions. The title verso page now standardly states the year of first publication below the copyright line, where may also be noted peculiarities of individual reprints (such as significant corrections). The system of impression digits noted in the 1994 statement is now the norm. If a book is reissued in a different binding after its first publication, the full set of reprint digits will normally be restored, although there may be no change to the title page. The fact that this is not the first impression of an original edition ought to be clear from the publication history below the copyright line on the title verso.

"*In short*, the first impression of a first edition is to be distinguished by the lack of any edition number or descriptor on the title page, the lack of any qualifying information on the title verso, and the presence of a '1' in the list of reprint digits on the title verso."

OXFORD UNIVERSITY PRESS AUSTRALIA (AUSTRALIA)

1994 Statement: "The first printing of a first edition is shown in a separate line after the copyright notice [e.g., 'First published (date)']. Reprints and new editions are indicated as follows:

    First published 1988
    Reprinted 1990, 1991
    Revised edition 1992 or This edition 1992
    Paperback edition 1994 [Paperback editions also have a new ISBN]

"This method of imprint page has been in use for as long as anyone currently with Oxford can recall."

OXFORD UNIVERSITY PRESS CANADA (CANADA)

1988 Statement: "On the verso of the title page of the books we published in 1988 the following numbers appear: 1234 1098.

"The number 1 at the extreme left indicates this is a first impression and the number 8 at the extreme right indicates the first impression was published in 1988. If a second impression were produced in 1989 then this line would be changed to read: 234 109.

"This practice is followed by the Canadian division of Oxford University Press; I cannot speak with confidence of the policy followed by our other offices around the world.

"I don't know when we started using this method to designate first and subsequent impressions but I believe it's been in practice for some time."

OXMOOR HOUSE, INC.

1976 Statement: "In answer to your query: Oxmoor House does not identify a first edition or a first printing of a first edition of our ordinary books (cookbooks, quilt books, etc.). Our first printings are our first editions. Then we identify second printings as second editions on the copyright page.

"Now in our art books: *Jericho, The American Cowboy, A Southern Album, Southern Antiques and Folk Art*, we not only identify the first edition, we actually number each book of the first edition. Later editions are not numbered and are identified as later editions."

1981 Statement: *See* 1976 Statement

1988 Statement: "Oxmoor House does not now normally number its art books as we once did for first editions. Nothing else has changed."

2000 Statement: *See* 2000 Statement of Warner Books, Inc.

OYEZ

2000 Statement: "We identify the first printing of a first edition on copyright page by 'First Edition — First Printing,' then specify later printings."

JEROME S. OZER PUBLISHER INC.

1994 Statement: "We have no special way of designating the first printing of a first edition. This has been our practice since the beginning of our company."

2000 Statement: *See* 1994 Statement

P

P & R PUBLISHING

1994 Statement: "We indicate first editions simply by the year of copyright and the Library of Congress Cataloging-in-Publication Data, both on the copyright page. We generally do not indicate printing histories on the copyright page. Subsequent editions are indicated by a notice on the copyright page."

2000 Statement: *See* 1994 Statement

PAAMON PRESS

2001 Statement: *See* 2001 Statement of Mesorah Publications Ltd

PACIFIC BOOKS

1947 Statement: "Thus far I have made no special indication in a book that it is a first edition. It shows only the copyright date. But for future printings or second editions I have clearly indicated that fact by recording the date of the first printing or first edition and giving the dates of subsequent printings or editions."

1988 Statement: "The statement we supplied previously still is valid."

1993 Statement: *See* 1988 Statement

2000 Statement: "First editions of our books are not indicated as such. They show only the copyright date. Subsequent editions of a book note the copyright dates of the first edition and subsequent editions."

PACIFIC SEARCH PRESS
1981 Statement: "The copyright notice is the only indication of a first printing of a first edition. This is the only method that we have ever used."
1988 Statement: *See* 1981 Statement

PADRE PRODUCTIONS
1988 Statement: "Padre Productions is a publishing company which includes the following imprints: Bear Flag Books, The Countrywoman's Press, Helm Publishing, International Resources, The Press of MacDonald & Reinecke, as well as Padre Productions.

"Our first editions simply bear the copyright data, usually on the verso of the title page, but occasionally on the title page itself. Subsequent printings and editions (meaning printings with significant revisions), are so noted adjacent to the original copyright notice."
1994 Statement: "Heretofore we have not so designated First Editions, but we intend to do so commencing with several titles in 1994, especially those from The Press of MacDonald and Reinecke. We have indicated subsequent printings when there have been revisions of text, as Second Editions, etc. We will continue to do so. However, from now on we will use the words 'First Edition' on the copyright page."

L. C. PAGE & CO.
1928 Statement: "We use practically the same method as Doubleday, Page & Co., to designate our first editions. We print 'first impression' with the month and the year on the reverse of the title page. We do not, however, add the date on the title page."
1937 Statement: "We print 'first impression' with the month and the year on the reverse of the title page. We do not, however, add the date on the title page."
1947 Statement: *See* 1937 Statement

PALADIN PRESS
1994 Statement: "We have never established any policy regarding identification of first editions."
2000 Statement: *See* 1994 Statement

JOAN PALEVSKY IMPRINT IN CLASSICAL LITERATURE
2000 Statement: *See* 2000 Statement of University of California Press

PALGRAVE PUBLISHERS LTD (UNITED KINGDOM)
(formerly Macmillan Press Ltd (United Kingdom))
2000 Statement: *See* 2000 Statement of Macmillan Publishers Limited (United Kingdom)

PALLAS ATHENE (UNITED KINGDOM)
2001 Statement: "We identify each edition and printing on the copyright page. Our imprints include Pallas Guides, Pallas Editions, Wòl Guides, and Pallas Athene Arts."

PALLAS ATHENE ARTS (UNITED KINGDOM)
2001 Statement: *See* 2001 Statement of Pallas Athene (United Kingdom)

PALLAS EDITIONS (UNITED KINGDOM)
2001 Statement: *See* 2001 Statement of Pallas Athene (United Kingdom)

PALLAS GUIDES (UNITED KINGDOM)
2001 Statement: *See* 2001 Statement of Pallas Athene (United Kingdom)

PALM ISLAND PRESS
2000 Statement: "We identify the first printing of a first edition by the words 'First Edition.' Subsequent printings of the first edition are identified (i.e. 2nd printing, etc.)."

PALM TREE PUBLISHERS
2000 Statement: "We distinguish first editions from our other editions by marking our other editions as not first editions. For example, we regularly use 'Second Edition' and 'Third Edition' as part of the title of any new editions of previous works."

CECIL PALMER (UNITED KINGDOM)
(Out of business prior to 1937.)
1928 Statement: "The plan we have always adopted is to print on the back of the title page 'First Edition' and then the year of publication. In the event of further editions, we add to this information the following example:

First Edition	June 1927
Second Edition	September 1927
Third Edition	January 1928"

PAMPHLET ARCHITECTURE
2000 Statement: *See* 2000 Statement of Princeton Architectural Press

PAN (AUSTRALIA)
1994, 2001 Statements: *See* 1994 Statement of Pan Macmillan Australia (Australia)

PAN (UNITED KINGDOM)
1988 Statement: *See* 1988 Statement of Pan Books Ltd. (United Kingdom)

PAN BOOKS LTD. (UNITED KINGDOM)
1988 Statement: "I should like to point out to you that Pan Books is still predominantly a reprint house, issuing in paperback form books that have already been published in hard covers. At the moment, about fifteen per cent of our output is original material.
Pan Books Ltd, London
(including Pavanne, Picador, Piccolo and Piper)

"There are four sources for our books, each of which makes a small but significant difference to the way we set out the bibliographical details.

(a) Books first published in Great Britain as hard cover editions;

(b) Books first published elsewhere, then in Great Britain as hard cover editions;

(c) Books first published outside Great Britain, then by Pan Books directly;

(d) Original works.

"These are identified and printed as follows:

(a) First published 19.. by (name of British publisher)

(b) First published in Great Britain 19.. by (name of British publisher) This edition published 19.. by Pan Books Ltd

(c) First published (elsewhere) 19.. by (name of publisher) This edition first published in Great Britain 19.. by Pan Books Ltd

(d) First published 19.. by Pan Books Ltd"

"In each there then follows this information:

(i) Pan Books Address

(ii) A numerical indication of the impression number

(iii) The copyright symbol and the name of the copyright owner

(iv) The ISBN

"A note on (ii): up to about six years ago second and subsequent printings were designated as such by the addition of the legend '2nd printing,' '3rd Printing' and so on. Since then all printings have been indicated by a row of figures—9 down to 1, 19 to 10—with the lowest figure showing the current impression number.

"As far as I can ascertain from looking at books published by Pan in the late 1940s and early 1950s, Pan Books has always followed this pattern of designating the first and subsequent printings.

"A new edition of a book is shown as such, preferably with actual edition number—2nd, 3rd or whatever it is. A reprint with corrections is also specified, usually in cases where the changes are not sufficient to warrant its being called a new edition but with, possibly, a note from the author or publisher drawing the attention of the reader to the fact that advantage has been taken of the reprint to make minor but important changes.

"All the imprints in the Pan stable follow the same procedure."

1994 Statement: "Pan Books is part of Pan Macmillan and is an imprint of Macmillan Publishers Ltd. It began publishing in 1945. Other imprints used now or in the past are Picador, Piccolo, Piper and Pavanne.

"Where a book is a first edition, the bibliographical details state: 'First published 19.. by Pan Books Ltd,' together with a row of figures, 9 down to 1. A book which does not carry the figure 1 is not the first printing of its edition. Editions subsequent to the first are clearly identified. Until about 1982, the row of figures did not appear; instead there was the printing history, which makes clear whether a book is a first printing, or a subsequent printing or edition.

"A large proportion of Pan books are paperback reprints of works previously published elsewhere. In such cases, the words 'First published in

Great Britain [or wherever] by [name of publisher]' appear, followed by the date of Pan's publication. A first Pan printing can be identified by the method described in the preceding paragraph."

2000 Statement: *See* 1994 Statement

PAN MACMILLAN (UNITED KINGDOM)

1994 Statement: *See* 1994 Statement of Macmillan Publishers Limited (United Kingdom)

2000 Statement: *See* 2000 Statement of Macmillan Publishers Limited (United Kingdom)

PAN MACMILLAN AUSTRALIA PTY LTD (AUSTRALIA)

1994 Statement: "It is our practice to identify first printings as follows:
First published (year) in (imprint)
by Pan Macmillan Australia Pty Limited

"We have been using a similar statement for the past few years (minus the imprint) but have only just taken this up within the last few months following our name change.

"For your information we have no other subsidiaries."

2001 Statement: *See* 1994 Statement, but note: "our imprints are Macmillan, Pan, Picador, and Pancake Press."

PAN MACMILLAN CHILDREN'S BOOKS (AUSTRALIA)

1994 Statement: *See* 1994 Statement of Pan Macmillan Australia (Australia)

PANCAKE PRESS (AUSTRALIA)

2001 Statement: *See* 2001 Statement of Pan Macmillan Australia Pty Ltd (Australia)

PANJANDRUM BOOKS

1976 Statement: "On copyright page, it says first edition. Used to use a colophon in first 5-6 books I published, but dropped it. Also have poets/writers sign 25 copies, numbered, of first edition, for future collectors."

1981 Statement: "Books published 1971-5: On copyright page, it would state First Edition. Books published after 1975: On copyright page, it states First Printing. Subsequent printings are so stated.

"Colophon: Contained in poetry books published by us between 1971-4. Twenty-five copies of all poetry books published are signed and numbered by the author."

1988, 1993 Statements: *See* 1981 Statement

PANTHEON BOOKS, INC.

1947 Statement: "We *always* differentiate subsequent printings of a book by inserting '2nd printing' (or third, or fourth, as the case may be) on the copyright page.

"First printings are either specifically identified by inserting 'First Printing' on the copyright page, or *no mention* of printing or edition is made on copyright page. Whenever nothing to the contrary is mentioned, the edition is the first printing of the title."

1976, 1981 Statements: *See* 1976 Statements of Random House, Inc.
1988, 1993 Statements: *See* 1988, 1993 Statements of Schocken Books
2000 Statement: *See* 1993 Statement of Schocken Books, Inc.

PAPERFRONTS (UNITED KINGDOM)

1994, 2000 Statements: *See* 1994 Statement of Elliot Right Way Books, Publishers (United Kingdom)

PAPIER-MACHE PRESS

1994 Statement: "As of November 1994, we follow the Chicago Manual of Style with regard to impression identification.

Example: 04 03 02 01 00 99 98 97 96 95 94 10 9 8 7 6 5 4 3 2 1

"This line indicates that this book is a first impression and was printed in 1994."
2000 Statement: *See* 1994 Statement

PARA PUBLISHING

1994 Statement: "Our printing and revisions are fully described on our copyright pages because we always revise this page. A typical printing/revision notice can be found in *The Self-Publishing Manual*:

First Printing 1979
Second Printing 1980, revised
Third Printing 1984, completely revised
Fourth Printing 1986, revised
Fifth Printing 1989, completely revised
Sixth Printing 1991, revised
Seventh Printing 1993, revised
Eighth Printing 1994, revised

"Since we revise at each printing, each printing is a new edition. Each edition is either revised or completely revised depending upon the extent of the changes."
2000 Statement: *See* 1994 Statement

PARABOLA BOOKS

2000 Statement: "Our first editions are so identified on the copyright page of each book. This is the only identification we ever use."

PARACLETE PRESS

1994 Statement: "We identify the first printings of our books by inserting on the copyright page the phrase 'First Printing, month, year.' Subsequent printings are differentiated by adding the phrase 'Second Printing, month, year,' etc.

"On revised editions, we insert the following information on the copyright page: 'Original edition: # of last printing, year. Newly revised and updated edition: First Printing, month year.' Each time the revised edition is reprinted, we add the phrase 'Second Printing, month, year,' etc."
2000 Statement: "The first printing of our books can be identified by the following impression line: 1 2 3 4 5 6 7 8 9 10. Subsequent printings are differentiated by deleting the numerals in numerical order.

"On revised editions, we insert the following information on the copyright page; 'Original edition: year. Newly revised and updated edition: month, year.' "

PARADIGM PUBLICATIONS
1995 Statement: "We do not note first editions or first printings. However, it is possible to determine the edition and printings of most of our works through examination of the revision level."
2000 Statement: *See* 1995 Statement

PARADISE RESEARCH PUBLICATIONS, INC.
2000 Statement: "We do not identify the first printing of a first edition."

PARADOX PRESS
2000 Statement: *See* 2000 Statement of DC Comics

PARALLAX PRESS
2000 Statement: "We identify the first printing of a first edition by the following number line: 1 2 3 4 5 6 7 8 9 10 / 03 02 01 00. Some of our earlier books have no identification of first printing, but subsequent printings have had an impression line added."

PARENT AND CHILD (UNITED KINGDOM)
1989 Statement: *See* 1989 Statement of The Octopus Publishing Group PLC (United Kingdom)

PARENTING PRESS INC
2000 Statement: "We sometimes enter a statement of printing, e.g. 'First Printing.' But [we] are not consistent.

"All editions are first edition until they become second (or further) and are so identified, as in
'First edition © 1990
'Second edition © 1995.' "

PARENTS' MAGAZINE PRESS
1976 Statement: "Up to the present time, we have not had any method of designating first editions of the books we publish through our book publishing division, Parents' Magazine Press.

"However, beginning with our fall list (1977), we will be designating first and subsequent editions of our books with a line at the end of the copyright information (and preceding the Library of Congress Cataloging in Publication data) as follows:
10 9 8 7 6 5 4 3 2 1
and with each additional printing, one number at the right drops off to indicate edition."
1981, 1988 Statements: *See* 1976 Statement

PARK AVENUE
2001 Statement: *See* 2001 Statement of JIST Works Inc

PARK PLACE PUBLICATIONS

2000 Statement: "Our practice of designating our first editions is to place on the verso of the title page, First Edition, followed by the month and year."

PARK STREET PRESS

2000 Statement: *See* 2000 Statement of Inner Traditions International, Ltd.

PARKWAY PUBLISHERS, INC.

2000 Statement: "We identify 2nd and subsequent printings by a statement such as 'Second Printing [year].' Unfortunately, we were not consistent."

PARL-WIN PUBLISHING CO.

2001 Statement: "Our policy is to put no identification on first editions and to refer to reprints as second editions. We are not presently active."

PARNASSUS IMPRINTS

1988 Statement: "We print 'first edition' on the copyright page. Subsequent printings are designated as 2nd printing, 3rd printing, etc."

ERIC PARTRIDGE, LTD. (SCHOLARTIS PRESS)
(UNITED KINGDOM)

(Out of business prior to 1949. Oxford University Press took over some publications.)

1937 Statement: "It is our practice to put the date of the publication of any book on the title page itself. If the book is reprinted, the date of the reprint appears on the title page and a bibliographical description on the back of the title page, e.g.

First Edition	1922
Reprinted	1923
Second Edition	1924"

S. W. PARTRIDGE & CO. (UNITED KINGDOM)

1947 Statement: *See* 1947 Statement of A & C Black, Ltd. (United Kingdom)

PARTRIDGE PRESS (UNITED KINGDOM)

2001 Statement: *See* 2001 Statement of Transworld Publishers Ltd (United Kingdom)

PASSEGGIATA PRESS INC.

2000 Statement: "We generally specify a work as a first edition, but not always. We shall in the future do so. If the work is a 2nd or 3rd edition or later, we so state on the © page: p. iv."

PASSPORT PRESS INC.

1994 Statement: "First editions have current copyright year mentioned, and no other. Subsequent editions make reference to copyright years of previous editions, on the copyright page. This has been our practice since we began in business."

2000 Statement: *See* 1994 Statement

PAST & PRESENT (UNITED KINGDOM)

1994 Statement: *See* 1994 Statement of Silver Link Publishing Ltd (United Kingdom)

PATERNOSTER (UNITED KINGDOM)

2000 Statement: *See* 2000 Statement of The Paternoster Press Ltd. (United Kingdom)

THE PATERNOSTER PRESS LTD. (UNITED KINGDOM)

1976 Statement: "There is no difficulty about identifying first editions of our publications since a full bibliographical account appears on the verso of every book that we publish.

"In the absence of any indication to the contrary, it may be safely assumed that a book is a first edition."

1981, 1988, 1994, 2000 Statements: *See* 1976 Statement

PATHFINDER PRESS

1976 Statement: "Pathfinder Press uses the following form on the data pages of its books:

Copyright © 1976 by Pathfinder Press
All rights reserved
Library of Congress Catalog Card Number
00-00000
ISBN: 0-87348-000-0
Manufactured in the United States of America
First Edition, 1975

"Subsequent printings and editions are listed under the First Edition line, which is retained in all later printings and editions. In earlier years we did not list printings or editions and used only the copyright notice and year. We changed our practice after renewal of copyrights eliminated reference to the original year of publication."

1981, 1989, 1993, 2000 Statements: *See* 1976 Statement

PATHFINDER PUBLISHING OF CALIFORNIA

2000 Statement: "We do not differentiate a first edition."

PATHWAY PRESS
(Cleveland, Tennessee)

1994 Statement: "We do not use the designation 'First Edition.' If a book is reprinted, we use 'Second Edition' or 'Revised Edition' or 'Corrected Edition' as appropriate."

2001 Statement: *See* 1994 Statement

THE PATRICE PRESS

1995 Statement: "We do not identify first printings of any of our books. However, all subsequent editions are so noted on the copyright page. That includes the number of that edition, and the month and year of publication of all prior editions."

2000 Statement: *See* 1995 Statement

KEGAN PAUL, TRENCH, TRUBNER & CO., LTD.
(UNITED KINGDOM)

1947 Statement: "If there is no statement at all as to a second or later edition or impression, the assumption, of course, is that the book is a first edition. In the case of reprints, or new editions, we state this on the reverse of the title page.

"We regret we cannot tell you the date on which this method was started but it has been going on now for a very long period."

1976, 1981 Statements: *See* 1976, 1981 Statements of Routledge & Kegan Paul Ltd. (United Kingdom)

STANLEY PAUL (UNITED KINGDOM)

1994 Statement: *See* 1994 Statement of Ebury Press (United Kingdom)
2000 Statement: *See* 2000 Statement of The Random House Group Limited (United Kingdom)

PAULIST PRESS

1981 Statement: "Paulist Press does not designate first editions."
1988, 1993, 2000 Statements: *See* 1981 Statement

PETER PAUPER PRESS INC.

1947 Statement: "With one or two exceptions, any book of ours with a 'limitation notice' (i.e. number of copies printed) is a first edition or first printing. But in a large number of cases—in fact in all books of recent years—there has not appeared such a limitation notice. The absence of such a notice is therefore *not* an indication of a later edition or printing. In general there is not any such indication."
1988, 1993, 2000 Statements: *See* 1947 Statement

PAVANNE (UNITED KINGDOM)

1988 Statement: *See* 1988 Statement of Pan Books Ltd. (United Kingdom)

PAVEMENT SAW PRESS

2000 Statement: "Our way of designating first editions is by negative implication. In other words, our first editions usually bear no special designation. Only subsequent editions are marked clearly as such on the copyright page."

PAVILION BOOKS LTD. (UNITED KINGDOM)

1994 Statement: "We use 1234567890. When reprinted, we delete figure 1 etc., and leave it at that."
2000 Statement: "We use 10 9 8 7 6 5 4 3 2 1. When reprinted, we delete figure 1, etc."

PAVILION PRESS

1994 Statement: "We do not identify first editions. If there are subsequent printings of the same work, and the text and illustrations are unchanged, we print from the same negatives, with exactly the same information on the title and copyright pages. There is no way to identify the earlier printing. However, if there is any change in the text and illustrations, the copyright page carries the information that it is a 'Second Edition' (if there is a fairly large amount of changed material) or 'Second Printing' (if only correction of errors or minor changes)."

2000 Statement: "We do not identify first editions. If there are subsequent printings of the same work, and the text and illustrations are unchanged, we print from the same negatives, with exactly the same information on the title and copyright pages. There is no way to identify the earlier printing."

PAYBACK PRESS (UNITED KINGDOM)
2001 Statement: *See* 2001 Statement of Canongate Books Ltd (United Kingdom)

PAYSON & CLARKE, LTD.
(Became Brewer & Warren on Jan. 1, 1930, which later became Brewer, Warren & Putnam, Inc.; all three firms out of business prior to 1937.)
1928 Statement: "We do not put the actual words 'first edition' on the reverse of the title page for the first edition but when we go into the second printing we say 'first printing such and such a date,' 'second printing such and such a date,' therefore, all copies of a book which do not carry such designation may be taken as being 'firsts.' "

PEACHTREE JR
2000 Statement: *See* 2000 Statement of Peachtree Publishers, Ltd.

PEACHTREE PUBLISHERS, LTD.
1994 Statement: "Peachtree Publishers, Ltd. uses the countdown method to designate editions. The number series '10 9 8 7 6 5 4 3 2 1' is printed on the copyright page; these numbers reveal the edition of the text. A full countdown marks a first edition. The deletion of the '1' shows the text to be a second edition. In the same manner, the absence of '1' and '2' marks a third edition, and so on.

"Peachtree Publishers has used this countdown method for approximately seven years."
2000 Statement: *See* 1994 Statement

PEANUT BUTTER & JELLY PRESS
2000 Statement: "Our first editions are identified as such on the copyright page. Subsequent editions are also thus identified."

PEARL-WIN PUBLISHING COMPANY
1995 Statement: "We have not designated any of our first printings as first editions."

PEARL EDITIONS
2000 Statement: "Pearl Editions does not make any special identification of first editions. Subsequent printings or editions are noted on the copyright page ('second printing,' 'second edition,' etc.)."

J. MICHAEL PEARSON

1995 Statement: "We distinguish a first edition from subsequent editions by stating so on the back of the title page. We would say either 2nd edition, etc. or 2nd printing, etc."

PEARTREE

1995 Statement: "We designate the first printing by number on the bottom of the copyright page. Numbers are listed from right to left, (10 9 8 7 6 5 4 3 2 1), with 1 being the first number in the case of a first printing. When reprinted, the number 1 is deleted. We do not designate a first edition in our books."

2000 Statement: *See* 1995 Statement. This practice has been in use since 1985.

PEARTREE PUBLICATIONS (UNITED KINGDOM)

1994 Statement: "Second, subsequent or revised editions are so described on the reverse of the title page but we do not show whether it is a first or subsequent printing of that edition."

2000 Statement: *See* 1994 Statement

PEDESTAL PRESS

2000 Statement: "We identify the first printing of a first edition with the number line 1 3 5 7 9 10 8 6 4 2."

PEEL PRODUCTIONS INC

2000 Statement: "We generally do not indicate first edition or first printing."

PEERAGE (UNITED KINGDOM)

1989 Statement: *See* 1989 Statement of The Octopus Publishing Group PLC (United Kingdom)

PEERLESS PUBLISHING

2000 Statement: "We identify the first printing of a first edition by descending numbers to edition. 10 9 8 7 6 5 4 3 2 1 indicates a first edition."

PEGASUS (PUBLISHING)

1976 Statement: "First editions are designated on copyright page as first printing, second printing, etc."

1981 Statement: *See* 1981 Statement of Bobbs-Merrill Company, Inc.

PEGASUS PRESS LTD. (NEW ZEALAND)

1976 Statement: "Our usual method of identifying a first edition of our books is to state on the verso of the title page—First Published—and giving the year. In other cases if no date of a second printing or new edition is shown it can be taken that it is a first edition."

1981 Statement: "First editions of our books can be identified from the note normally printed on the verso of the title-page; this carries the words First Published, followed by the date. If no mention is made of a later edition or printing the book can be taken to be a first edition."

PELHAM BOOKS (UNITED KINGDOM)
1994 Statement: *See* 1994 Statement of Michael Joseph Ltd. (United Kingdom)

PELICAN BOOKS (UNITED KINGDOM)
1988, 2001 Statements: *See* 1988 Statement of Penguin Publishing Co Ltd. (United Kingdom)

PELICAN HISTORY OF ART (UNITED KINGDOM)
2000 Statement: *See* 2000 Statement of Yale University Press (United Kingdom)

PELICAN POND PUBLISHING
2000 Statement: *See* 2000 Statement of Blue Dolphin Publishing Inc.

PELICAN PUBLISHING COMPANY
1976 Statement: "Pelican has no standard method of identifying first editions. First edition may have no designation on copyright page, or it may read first printing. All subsequent editions or printings are so stated on the copyright page."
1981 Statement: *See* 1976 Statement
1988 Statement: "All Pelican first editions carry the copyright date only. Additional printings or editions are so designated.

"Our imprints and subsidiaries do follow our practices."
1993, 2000 Statements: *See* 1988 Statement

PELLA PUBLISHING CO
2000 Statement: "Since we seldom intend to reprint an edition, we do not identify first editions as such. We do, however, identify reprints and new editions."

PELLEGRINI & CUDAHY
1947 Statement: "Our first books came out this spring and to date we have not specified the first printing as such. Our subsequent printings have been so indicated, as:
    1st printing August, 1947
    2nd printing September, 1947 and so forth."

PEN & SWORD BOOKS LTD (UNITED KINGDOM)
2001 Statement: "First editions and reprints and new editions are all identified on the copyright page."

PEN QUILL PRESS
2000 Statement: *See* 2000 Statement of Jonathan David Publishers, Inc.

PEN ROSE PUBLISHING CO.
1994 Statement: "Our books include the words 'First Edition' on the copyright page. Subsequent printings include the words 'Second Printing,' etc. We adopted this method in 1992."

PENDRAGON PRESS
2000 Statement: "Our first editions and all unchanged reprints of our first editions are marked on p. iv, bottom line, with the year of publication, e.g. 'copyright 1983.' Any new edition is specified as such in the same place."

PENDULUM PUBLICATIONS, LTD. (UNITED KINGDOM)
1947 Statement: "No method is at present employed by us to identify first printings of our books, although most of them bear a date and when a second edition is produced, this fact is usually imprinted on the verso of the title page."

PENGUIN
1988 Statement: *See* 1988 Statement of Penguin Publishing Co Ltd (United Kingdom)

PENGUIN (AUSTRALIA)
1994, 2000 Statements: *See* 1994 Statement of Penguin Books Australia Ltd (Australia)

PENGUIN (NEW ZEALAND)
1994, 2000 Statements: *See* 1994 Statement of Penguin Books (N.Z.) Ltd (New Zealand)

PENGUIN BOOKS LTD (UNITED KINGDOM)
1988, 1994 Statements: *See* 1988 Statement of Penguin Publishing Co Ltd (United Kingdom)

PENGUIN BOOKS AUSTRALIA LTD (AUSTRALIA)
1988 Statement: *See* 1988 Statement of Penguin Publishing Co Ltd (United Kingdom)
1994 Statement: "Until 1990 Penguin Australia designated a first printing by including a statement, for example, 'First published in 1988' on the title page. Subsequent printings of that edition would carry advice on the title page that it was the 'second printing' or 'reprinted 1989' etc.

"From 1990 all new and reprinted books have carried a line of numbers e.g. '10 9 8 7 6 5 4 3 2 1' with the lowest number designating the printing. When the next impression is printed, the lowest number is deleted, enabling the reader to determine that if the lowest number in the series was '1,' they were holding a first edition, but if the lowest number was '6,' that copy represented the sixth printing. When a new edition is printed the numbering returns to '10 9 8 7 6 5 4 3 2 1.' This information covers all Penguin Group titles in Australia—Viking, Penguin, Puffin and McPhee Gribble."
See also Omnibus Books (Australia)
2000 Statement: *See* 1994 Statement, but note that,"As our imprints change from time to time, I suggest the final sentence finishes after the word 'Australia', although you may, if you wish, include our principle imprints which are Viking, Penguin and Puffin."

PENGUIN BOOKS CANADA LTD (CANADA)
1988 Statement: *See* 1988 Statement of Penguin Publishing Co Ltd (United Kingdom)
1993 Statement: "Since 1988 we have used the following designations for all books with all imprints produced by Penguin Canada. The former is for flush left designs and the latter for centred. When reprinting, one number is removed; thus the lowest number indicates the current edition.
    Published 19__   Published 19__
    10 9 8 7 6 5 4 3 2 1   1 3 5 7 9 8 6 4 2."
2001 Statement: *See* 1993 Statement, but note that "Published 19__" now reads "First published ____."

PENGUIN BOOKS (N.Z.) LTD (NEW ZEALAND)
1988 Statement: *See* 1988 Statement of Penguin Publishing Co Ltd (United Kingdom)
1994 Statement: "Our practice is as follows: on the imprint page we run a reprint number line using the numbers 1-10. The appearance of the number 1 in this line indicates that this is the first printing. With subsequent printings the number of the previous printing is deleted progressively. Thus the numbers 6-10 indicate that this is the sixth printing.

"We changed to this practice at the suggestion of our British parent company some five years ago. Previously our practice had simply been to indicate the year of publication and the subsequent year of each reprint.

"All of the imprints published by Penguin in New Zealand follow this practice: Penguin, Viking, Puffin, Picture Puffin."
2000 Statement: "On the imprint page we run a reprint number line using the numbers 1-10. The appearance of the number 1 in this line indicates that this is the first printing. With subsequent printings the number of the previous printing is deleted progressively. Thus the numbers 6-10 indicate that this is the sixth printing.

"All of the imprints published by Penguin in New Zealand follow this practice: Penguin, Viking, Puffin, Picture Puffin."

PENGUIN OVERSEAS LTD (UNITED KINGDOM)
1988 Statement: *See* 1988 Statement of Penguin Publishing Co Ltd (United Kingdom)

PENGUIN PUBLISHING CO LTD (UNITED KINGDOM)
1988 Statement: "Since we last corresponded the Penguin Group has introduced a new standard system for indicating the current impression of a book. This is now standard practice for all our imprints worldwide including Frederick Warne. I enclose a photocopy of an imprint page of one of our autumn titles from which you can see that we simply put the year of first publication followed by a row of numbers from 1 to 9 which indicates the impression number. As we reprint we knock off one number so that the lowest number shown is the number of the current impression. There is a slight variation according to whether the prelims are centred or ranged left. If they

are centred the numbers are as in the enclosed sample. If it is ranged left style then they are consecutive in descending order."

The sample provided shows:

First published 1988

1 3 5 7 9 8 6 4 2

2001 Statement: "Essentially we do still follow the practice outlined in our last statement.

"The slight change in our practice is that, although we still put the year of first publication and the publication number below, we now use one number only—the current impression number for that title. This is because, due to the latest technology, printers are now able to insert and delete this impression number as appropriate when a title reprints. We adopted this new practice in 2000.

"The three hardback imprints of Hamish Hamilton, Viking, and Michael Joseph have been combined in a new organizational structure within Penguin UK, and so they now follow the same practice on the imprint page.

"Where a book is published for the first time anywhere, we print:

First published 2000

1

whereby the figure '1' represents the first printing; for the second printing (or first impression) the figure '1' would be replaced by the figure '2'."

PENGUIN PUTNAM BOOKS FOR YOUNG READERS

2000 Statement: "While our standards remain exactly the same [as the 1993 statement of Grosset & Dunlap], our company name has changed. Grosset & Dunlap is a division of Penguin Putnam Inc. and publishes juvenile titles under the imprint Penguin Putnam Books for Young Readers."

See 1993 statement of The Putnam & Grosset Group

PENMAEN PRESS

1988 Statement: "Penmaen Press does not publish, and hasn't since 1985. Nevertheless, we designated our first editions by simply printing 'First Edition' on the copyright page next to the copyright material."

PENN PUBLICATIONS, INC.

1994 Statement: *See* 1994 Statement of Carstens Publications Inc.

THE PENN PUBLISHING COMPANY
(Succeeded by The William Penn Publishing Corporation.)

1928 Statement: "As we indicate first editions in none of our books, we are unable to give you any information regarding the subject about which you inquire."

1936 Statement: "The only way they can be distinguished from subsequent editions is by the fact that in later editions the words second, third, or fourth printing, with the date, will be found on the copyright page."

THE WILLIAM PENN PUBLISHING CORPORATION

1947 Statement: "We use no special mark to indicate first printings of new books. All our first printings merely bear the copyright information."

PENN STATE STUDIES
1988 Statement: *See* 1988 Statement of The Pennsylvania State University Press

PENNSYLVANIA HISTORICAL & MUSEUM COMMISSION
2000 Statement: "First editions are not specifically identified, but subsequent printings are noted by date on the copyright page."

THE PENNSYLVANIA STATE UNIVERSITY PRESS
1976 Statement: "This press identifies first editions only in the sense that the absence of a legend on the title page such as 'Revised and Enlarged Edition' or 'Third Edition' clearly implies that a book is in its original edition. The same is true of printings, since all printings after the first are so identified on the copyright page."
1981, 1988, 1994 Statements: *See* 1976 Statement

THE PENNYWORTH PRESS (CANADA)
1976 Statement: "1. First printings of first editions are not so marked—subsequent printings are, e.g. 'second printing' etc.

"2. First editions are so marked either on the title page or in the colophon on the last page."

PENOBSCOT PRESS
1994 Statement: *See* 1994 Statement of Picton Press

PENTAGRAM PRESS
1976 Statement: "Thus far most Pentagram 'first editions'—all we've had so far—have been more or less labeled as such by the wording of the colophon, usually to the effect of 'this edition is limited to 626 copies, 26 of which are lettered and signed by the author.' Because I usually am content to let the first printings sell out, there has been thus far no need to designate a book as either 2nd edition or 2nd printing. To my mind, tho, (& the way I'd do it should I need to) the 2nd printing of a book would exactly reproduce the contents of the first, while a 2nd edition would have the original contents either expanded, reduced, or otherwise edited . . . .

"Where I've included neither colophon nor the words 'first edition,' I do assume that people automatically take the book to be a first edition."
1981 Statement: "Only one Pentagram Press publication has gone into a second printing, due to confusion on the size of the initial pressrun. That second printing is so indicated on reverse of the title page, '700 copies July 1976/480 copies January 1978.'

"Pentagram is now issuing handset letterpressed books, each colophon states 'this edition is limited to 242 copies,' for example. I've no desire to re-issue a title once it's gone OP; the energy and spirit that went into the first edition could not be duplicated. Except for the offset-printed book noted above, all Pentagram books are first editions."
1988 Statement: *See* 1981 Statement

PENTATHOL PUBLISHING (UNITED KINGDOM)
2001 Statement: "We do not identify a first printing; we do identify subsequent printings on the copyright page."

PENTLAND PRESS, INC
2000 Statement: "We identify the first printing of a first edition by 'Copyright © 2000 Author's Name.' "

PENZLER BOOKS
1988 Statement: *See* 1988 Statement of Mysterious Press

THE PEOPLE'S PRESS
2000 Statement: "We do not annotate first editions. Subsequent editions are identified as revised, second, etc. on the copyright page and elsewhere as warranted."

THE PEQUOT PRESS, INC.
1976 Statement: "Our normal procedure is to put on the verso of the title page the words FIRST EDITION. With minimum or no changes we will list again the words FIRST EDITION and add the words, 'Second Printing.'

"When revisions are more than minimal we will list SECOND EDITION."
1988 Statement: *See* 1988 Statement of The Globe Pequot Press, Inc.

PEREGRINE BOOKS (UNITED KINGDOM)
1988 Statement: *See* 1988 Statement of Penguin Publishing Co Ltd (United Kingdom)

PETER PEREGRINUS LTD. (UNITED KINGDOM)
1994, 2000 Statements: *See* 1994 Statement of The Institution of Electrical Engineers (United Kingdom)

PERENNIAL
2001 Statement: *See* 2001 Statement of HarperCollinsPublishers

PERFORMANCE PUBLISHING
(Elgin, Illinois)
1976 Statement: "We do not maintain a system of identifying first editions of our publications."
1981 Statement: *See* 1976 Statement

PERGAMON PRESS LTD. (UNITED KINGDOM)
1976 Statement: "The only way in which we identify the first edition is the printing of the words 'First Edition 1976' on the verso of the title page along with the remainder of the copyright and bibliographic information.

"This has been our practice since 1965, prior to which the first edition was not identified in any way."
1981 Statement: "The statement as given in your letter describing how we designate the first printing of a first edition is still correct. However, we would like to add the following:

"In our school books, published under the imprint of Wheaton, we print 'First Published 1976' and subsequently add reprint notices with dates."
1988 Statement: "I confirm that the 1976 statement is still correct, but that the 1981 addition is no longer relevant."

PERIGEE BOOKS
1989 Statement: Printings are indicated by a sequence of numbers ranging from left to right on the copyright page:

1 2 3 4 5 6 7 8 9 10

The last number on the left indicates the number of the printing. In the example above, a first printing is indicated.

A Perigee edition of a book previously published in another edition is identified as the First Perigee Edition.
1995 Statement: *See* 1995 Statement of The Berkley Publishing Group
2000 Statement: *See* 2000 Statement of The Berkley Publishing Group

PERIGORD PRESS
1981 Statement: *See* 1981 Statement of William Morrow and Co. Inc.

PERIPLUS EDITIONS
2000 Statement: *See* 2000 Statement of Journey Editions

PERISCOPE PRESS (AUSTRALIA)
1994 Statement: *See* 1994 Statement of Roland Harvey Studios (Australia)

THE PERISHABLE PRESS LIMITED
1981 Statement: "There is no designation because, being a sort of glorified hobby press, doing small editions of usually 200, there is only one edition. We have never printed anything but as first edition."
1989 Statement: "As far as the 1981 statement goes, it is essentially still true. Since I have never re-printed anything, every edition from this press remains as the only edition."

PERIVALE PRESS
1981 Statement: "We use the designation 'First published in 19..' followed by 'Second printing,' etc. In one case we used 'Second printing corrected' instead of 'Second edition.' We have not yet gone into a second edition for any of our titles, nor has the method first used been changed. The imprints of our company, therefore, follow standard form."
1988, 2001 Statements: *See* 1981 Statement

THE PERMANENT PRESS
1981 Statement: "All Permanent Press books have a colophon at the back of the book which includes the words 'first edition,' and which gives the number of copies printed in both clothbound and paperback editions."
1988 Statement: "We do not designate first editions. We do designate as such all subsequent printings and editions."
1993 Statement: "Starting in December 1993, we will be including the words 'first edition' on our books as well as the date and number of copies printed."

2000 Statement: "The Permanent Press generally does a first printing between 1,000 and 2,000 copies that either say 'First Printing' on the copyright page, along with the month and year, or nothing at all. If a second printing is done, the books clearly state 'Second Printing.' "

PERSEA BOOKS, INC.
1976 Statement: "We print 'First Edition' on the copyright page. We had been using 'First Printing.' As soon as the book goes into a new printing, the designation becomes 'Second printing,' whether or not the book is the first edition of the work."
1981, 1988, 1993, 2000 Statements: *See* 1976 Statement

PERSEVERANCE PRESS
2001 Statement: *See* 2001 Statement of Fithian Press

PERSONHOOD PRESS
2000 Statement: *See* 2000 Statement of Jalmar Press

PERUGIA PRESS
2000 Statement: "All our books are first editions."

A. K. PETERS LTD.
2001 Statement: "We use the following number line to identify the first printing of a first edition: '02 01 00 99 98 10 9 8 7 6 5 4 3 2 1'. The lowest year number in the set of numbers on the left indicates the year of current printing. The lowest number in the set of numbers on the right indicates the current printing."

PEVSNER (UNITED KINGDOM)
2001 Statement: *See* 2001 Statement of Penguin Publishing Co Ltd (United Kingdom)

PHAIDON PRESS LIMITED (UNITED KINGDOM)
1947 Statement: "The second and following editions of our books are always marked: Second Edition or Third Edition and so on, whilst our first editions have no note at all to this effect."
Statement for 1960: "In [1960] we simply added the date of publication to the copyright notice, without any indication that it was a first edition. In general, we used the terminology:
© PHAIDON PRESS LTD. LONDON 1960"
1976 Statement: "I enclose a copy of our official copyright page which states that a book is first published in such and such a year. For reprints we always state 'second impression 19xx' and for a new edition we put 'first published 19xx' followed by 'second edition 19xx.' This is standard form for all Phaidon books."
1981 Statement: *See* 1976 Statement
1988 Statement: "Our company still follows the practice outlined in our last statement, and this applies to our other imprints."
1994 Statement: *See* 1988 Statement

PHILADELPHIA ART ALLIANCE PRESS
1976, 1981, 1993 Statements: *See* 1976 Statement of Associated University Presses

PHILADELPHIA MUSEUM OF ART
1994, 2001 Statements: "We do not identify first editions."

GEORGE PHILIP (UNITED KINGDOM)
1994 Statement: *See* 1994 Statement of Reed Consumer Books (United Kingdom)

GEORGE PHILIP LIMITED (UNITED KINGDOM)
(George Philip & Son Limited changed its name to George Philip Limited in April of 1988.)
1988 Statement: *See* 1976 Statement of George Philip & Son Limited (United Kingdom). Imprints of George Philip & Son Limited follow similar practices to those of the cartographic publishing.

GEORGE PHILIP & SON LIMITED (UNITED KINGDOM)
1976 Statement: "I can reply only about cartographic publications.

"We have no particular method of identifying first editions other than the biblio and the copyright date but these we have always taken considerable care to make and keep accurate. A second printing of a first edition is rare because we almost invariably make some corrections at every printing of an atlas and thus change the edition number. If there were to be a second printing without correction we would state this in the biblio thus 'reprinted, date.' "
1981 Statement: *See* 1976 Statement
1988 Statement: *See* 1988 Statement of George Philip Limited (United Kingdom)

PHILIPSBURG MANOR
1981 Statement: *See* 1981 Statement of Sleepy Hollow Press

S. G. PHILLIPS, INC.
1976 Statement: "Usually there is no designation of first editions. Later printings indicate number of printings and date."
1993, 2001 Statements: *See* 1976 Statement

PHILOMEL BOOKS
1988 Statement: *See* 1988 Statement of The Putnam & Grosset Group (Children's)
1993 Statement: *See* 1993 Statement of The Putnam & Grosset Group

PHILOMEL PRODUCTIONS LTD (UNITED KINGDOM)
2001 Statement: "We identify only editions, not printings; a first edition is so identified on the copyright page. We state 'Published' and the year, or 'First edition' and the year."

PHILOSOPHICAL LIBRARY, INC.
1947 Statement: "All subsequent editions are marked as such, 2nd., 3rd. edition, etc."

PHOENIX HOUSE (UNITED KINGDOM)
1994 Statement: *See* 1994 Statement of The Orion Publishing Group Ltd (United Kingdom)

PHOENIX PRESS
1947 Statement: "Printings are listed as first, second, etc."

PHOENIX PUBLISHING
(Canaan, New Hampshire)
1976 Statement: "We do not identify first editions as such but merely include the Copyright date, statement of rights and limited reproduction permitted, LC number, ISBN number, and names of printer, binder and designer. On subsequent reprintings or revisions we indicate first and second printings, etc."

1981 Statement: "We do not identify first editions as such but merely include the Copyright date, statement of rights and limited reproduction permitted, Library of Congress CIP data which includes LC number, ISBN number, and names of printer, binder and designer. On subsequent reprintings or revisions we indicate first and second printings, etc."

1994 Statement: "In virtually all our books the copyright year is identical with the year of first edition publication and the copyright notice, printed in conventional fashion below the Library of Congress Cataloging-in-Publication Data, serves as an identifier. Were this not the case, an additional line indicating a first edition and its month and year of publication would be included above the copyright notice. Additional printings are so noted with the month and year of publication in the same format position.

"Almost all the volumes we publish also carry a colophon, the first line of which always indicates the edition and usually the quantity of books printed."
2000 Statement: *See* 1994 Statement

PICA PRESS
1988 Statement: *See* 1988 Statement of Universe Books

PICADOR (AUSTRALIA)
1994, 2001 Statements: *See* 1994 Statement of Pan Macmillan Australia (Australia)

PICADOR (UNITED KINGDOM)
1988 Statement: *See* 1988 Statement of Pan Books Ltd. (United Kingdom)
1994 Statement: "We use a number system (9 through 1) on paperbacks and the same on hardcovers—after identifying a first edition by saying 'first published.' "
2000 Statement: *See* 2000 Statement of Pan Macmillan (United Kingdom)

PICAS SERIES (CANADA)
2000 Statement: *See* 2000 Statement of Guernica (Canada)

PICCADILLY BOOKS

1994 Statement: First printings are not identified.
2000 Statement: *See* 2000 Statement of Piccadilly Books, Ltd.

PICCADILLY BOOKS, LTD.

2000 Statement: *See* 1994 Statement of Piccadilly Books

PICADILLY PRESS (UNITED KINGDOM)

2001 Statement: "Picadilly Press was formed in 1983. In about 1997 we started to include the number string on the copyright page, the lowest number indicating the first printing. We also include bibliographical details in conjunction with the copyright line."

PICCOLO (UNITED KINGDOM)

1988, 1994 Statements: *See* 1988, 1994 Statements of Pan Books Ltd. (United Kingdom)

PICKERING & INGLIS LTD. (UNITED KINGDOM)

1976 Statement: "Our system is that in a first edition the date appears directly under our imprint on the title page, while on any reprints further editions appear on the reverse side of the title page."

1981 Statement: "Our present system is that any such information regarding editions is now printed on the reverse side of the title page. On the first edition we state 'First Printing' followed by the year and on any reprints we state 'First Published' followed by the year, and then 'Reprinted' followed by the year.

"We changed to this new method approximately four years ago."

1988 Statement: "Our current system is much the same as that used in 1981.

"All imprint information appears on the reverse of the title page. On the first edition, we state:

'First published in' followed by (year)

and on any reprints we state

'Reprinted: Impression number

88 89 90:   10 9 8 7 6 5 4 3 2

and delete as applicable.

"The above is standard to all our imprints."

PICKWICK PUBLICATIONS

2000 Statement: "The note 'First Edition' does not appear on the copyright page. We do, however, indicate 'Second Printing' or 'Third Printing.' "

PICTON PRESS

1994 Statement: "We make no designation of the first printing of the first edition. Instead, we designate all later printings with a month and year statement on the back of the title page, at which time we add the data for the first printing of the first edition. Example:

First printing March 1988

Second printing May 1993

"Similarly, a second edition will be identified thus on the back of the title page, at which time the first edition will be identified also with month and year. Example:

First edition May 1981

Second edition June 1991

"Not unexpectedly, there are certainly times when we have not consistently followed these practices."

PICTORIAL HISTORIES PUBLISHING CO. INC.

1994 Statement: "We simply list each printing as we reprint, i.e., 'First Printing: March, 1990,' 'Second Printing: March, 1992,' etc."

2000 Statement: *See* 1994 Statement

PICTURE CORGI (UNITED KINGDOM)

2001 Statement: *See* 2001 Statement of Transworld Publishers Ltd (United Kingdom)

PICTURE PUFFIN (NEW ZEALAND)

1994, 2000 Statements: *See* 1994 Statement of Penguin Books (N.Z.) Ltd (New Zealand)

PIG IRON PRESS

2001 Statement: "We do not identify the first printing of a first edition."

PILOT PRESS, PUBLISHERS, INC.

1947 Statement: "We have not adopted any system of identifying the first printings of our books."

PIMLICO (UNITED KINGDOM)

1994 Statement: *See* 1994 Statement of Random House UK Limited (United Kingdom)

2000 Statement: *See* 2000 Statement of The Random House Group Limited (United Kingdom)

PIÑATA BOOKS

1994, 2000 Statements: *See* 1994 Statement of Arte Público Press

PINE BARRENS PRESS

2000 Statement: "We do not identify first editions."

PINE CONE PRESS

1994 Statement: "We list all of our books . . . on the title page, with the year in which they were first printed, followed by years in which they were reprinted. This list includes the book in which this information is listed."

2000 Statement: *See* 1994 Statement

PINEAPPLE PRESS, INC.

1988 Statement: "We began publishing in 1982 in Englewood, Florida. Our first books do not indicate edition. Beginning in 1985, 'first edition' is printed on the copyright page of each first edition along with the numbers going backward from 10 to 1. At each subsequent printing a number is dropped so that the printing will be the last number appearing. Or some books just say 'third printing' or whichever.

"From 1988, place of publication is Sarasota, Florida."

1993, 2000 Statements: *See* 1988 Statement

PINNACLE BOOKS
1995, 2000 Statements: *See* 1995 Statement of Kensington Publishing Corp.

PIPER (UNITED KINGDOM)
1988, 1994 Statements: *See* 1988, 1994 Statements of Pan Books Ltd. (United Kingdom)

PITKIN GUIDES LTD (UNITED KINGDOM)
2001 Statement: *See* 2001 Statement of Pitkin Unichrome Ltd. (United Kingdom)

PITKIN PICTORIAL (UNITED KINGDOM)
1989 Statement: *See* the Methuen entry in the 1989 Statement of The Octopus Publishing Group PLC (United Kingdom)

PITKIN PICTORIALS LTD. (UNITED KINGDOM)
1994 Statement: "Pitkin guides carry a print code next to the ISBN (usually inside the back cover). The first digit(s) indicates which printing and the following two digits indicate the year; e.g. 1093/20 indicates the tenth printing was in 1993."

2001 Statement: *See* 2001 Statement of Pitkin Unichrome Ltd (United Kingdom)

PITKIN UNICHROME LTD (UNITED KINGDOM)
2001 Statement: "The company [Pitkin Pictorials Ltd.] changed its name twice since it was Pitkin Pictorials. The first time it was changed to Pitkin Guides Ltd in 1997. In March 1998, we merged with a company called Unichrome of Bath Ltd and we are now called Pitkin Unichrome Ltd.

"Our policy for ISBN has changed only slightly [from the 1994 Statement of Pitkin Pictorials Ltd]. We now show the edition and the year only. We do not show the print run as before. For example a new book for January 2001 would show as 1/01 and a reprint (say the fourth one) would be 4/01. The numbering is still shown on the inside back cover next to the ISBN."

PITMAN LEARNING, INC.
1981, 2001 Statements: *See* 1976 Statement of Pitman Publishing Corporation

PITMAN PUBLISHING (UNITED KINGDOM)
1994 Statement: "Three months ago we started using the 1 2 3 4 5 6 7 8 9 0 system, deleting the figure 1 when the book is reprinted for the first time, the figure 2 the second time etc. Up until this change we added the words 'Reprinted 19.. (the year of the reprint).' Books published under our M & E imprint are designated in the same way."

2001 Statement: "Our 1994 statement for Pitman Publishing remains the same, but please note that since 1999 our books are no longer published under the Pitman Publishing imprint; they are now published under the Financial Times Prentice Hall imprint except for law books which are published under the Longman imprint. We no longer use the M&E imprint."

PITMAN PUBLISHING CORPORATION

1976 Statement: "Pitman uses a printing line on the copyright page as follows.

10 9 8 7 6 5 4 3 2 1

"This is the way the line would appear on a first printing of the first edition. For each successive printing, one number would be removed at the right. Normally, after nine printings, we revise or substitute a new line with higher numbers."

1981 Statement: Pitman Publishing Corporation has changed its name to Pitman Learning, Inc.

See 1981 Statement of Pitman Learning, Inc.

PITTENBRUACH PRESS

1994 Statement: "We use 1 2 3 4 5 6 7 8 9 0. When reprinted, we delete figure 1, etc. and insert 2nd, 3rd, etc., printing on copyright page."

2000 Statement: "We say printing numbers 10 9 8 7 6 5 4 3 2 1 and remove the last number with each subsequent printing. We have been using this method (mostly) since our start-up in 1986."

THE PLACE IN THE WOODS

1995 Statement: "Up to last year (1994), all titles were First Editions. We did not designate First Editions or First Printings. Printings after the first were noted on the back of the title page (Acknowledgements page) as follows: 17th Printing—April 1993. Because our titles are historical, we are beginning this year (1995) to identify all printings and editions on the Acknowledgements page as follows: FIRST EDITION First printing—Jan. 1995."

2001 Statement: "Printings after the first are noted on the back of the title page (Acknowledgements page) as follows: 17th Printing—April 1993. Because our titles are historical, we identify all printings and editions on the Acknowledgements page as follows: FIRST EDITION First printing—Jan. 1995."

PLANET (UNITED KINGDOM)

2001 Statement: "Our copyright page indicates 'First published in . . . .' We identify only editions."

PLANET DEXTER

2000 Statement: *See* 2000 Statement of Price Stern Sloan

PLANTIN PUBLISHERS (UNITED KINGDOM)

2001 Statement: "© date represents 1st edition, 1st printing. Reprints [are] identified: Reprinted XYZA."

PLATT & MUNK

1976 Statement: *See* 1976 Statement of Questor Educational Products Company

1988 Statement: *See* 1988 Statement of The Putnam & Grosset Group (Children's)

1993 Statement: *See* 1993 Statement of The Putnam & Grosset Group

PLAYERS PRESS, INC.

1988 Statement: "No mention is made of any edition unless there is a Revised Edition, which is so indicated."

1993, 2000 Statements: *See* 1988 Statement

PLAYERS PRESS (CANADA)

2000 Statement: *See* 2000 Statement of Players Press, Inc.

PLAYERS PRESS A/Z LTD

2000 Statement: *See* 2000 Statement of Players Press, Inc.

PLAYERS PRESS LTD (UNITED KINGDOM)

2000 Statement: *See* 2000 Statement of Players Press, Inc.

PLAYLAND BOOKS

1988 Statement: *See* 1988 Statement of The Putnam & Grosset Group (Children's)

PLAYS, INC., PUBLISHERS

1976 Statement: "We don't designate first editions—second and others are stated second printing or second edition, etc."

1981 Statement: "The answer as typed is correct. We designate only editions after the first; the first edition simply bears the date of copyright.

"The only exception to this is an *import*, which may read:

First U.S. edition published by PLAYS, INC. 1981.

Formerly published by . . . . Ltd . . . London in 19..

"This information is also true for our other company, The Writer, Inc."

1988, 1993 Statements: *See* 1981 Statement

PLAYTIME PRESS (UNITED KINGDOM)

1989 Statement: *See* 1989 Statement of The Octopus Publishing Group PLC (United Kingdom)

PLAYWRIGHTS CANADA (CANADA)

1988 Statement: "The Playwrights Union of Canada, under the imprint Playwrights Canada, designates a first edition or first printing on the copyright page. A second printing will be designated as such, a printing and not an edition. Each subsequent printing will also be listed. A second edition will be listed only if the work has been revised or re-edited. Style is as follows:

First Edition: October 1988

Second Printing: November 1988

Third Printing: December 1988

(Or in the case of a revision of the work)

First Edition: October 1988
Second Printing: November 1988
Second Edition: December 1988
Second Printing: January 1989"

PLAYWRIGHTS CANADA PRESS (CANADA)

1993 Statement: *See* 1988 Statement of Playwrights Canada (Canada). Note that imprint would read Playwrights Canada Press rather than Playwrights Canada.
2001 Statement: *See* 1993 Statement

PLEASANT COMPANY PUBLICATIONS

1994 Statement: "The first 24 books in The American Girls Collection®—the six books each about Felicity, Kirsten, Samantha, and Molly—did not provide a way of distinguishing the first printing of the first edition. For the most recent books we've published—the books about Addy—we've included a conventional printing key on the copyright page to make this designation."
2000 Statement: "The first 24 books in The American Girls Collection®—the six books each about Felicity, Kirsten, Samantha, and Molly—did not provide a way of distinguishing the first printing of the first edition. Since 1994, we've included a conventional printing key on the copyright page to make this designation."

PLEIADES BOOKS, LTD. (UNITED KINGDOM)

1947 Statement: "Our present practice is as follows: In the case of the first edition we include in the prelims a statement to the effect that the book was 'First published 19...' In the case of a reprint: 'First published 19.., reprinted 19...' In the event of a second reprint: 'First published 19.., Reprinted 19.., Reprinted 19..,' and so on."

PLENUM PUBLISHING CORPORATION

1981 Statement: "Plenum Publishing company does not identify first editions or first printings in any positive way; however, editions other than the first will have an identifying statement on the title page, and printings other than the first will have an identifying statement on the copyright page. As far as I know this has always been our policy, and it applies to all the imprints under which we publish."
1994 Statement: *See* 1981 Statement
2001 Statement: *See* 2001 Statement of Kluwer Academic/Plenum Publishers (United Kingdom)

PLENUM TRADE (UNITED KINGDOM)

See 2001 Statement of Kluwer Academic/Plenum Publishers (United Kingdom) *and* 1994 Statement of Plenum Publishing Corporation

PLEXUS
(Texas)

2000 Statement: "We identify the first printing of a first edition by 'First Edition' [and the] following number line: '9 8 7 6 5 4 3 2 1.'"

PLEXUS PUBLISHING, INC.

2000 Statement: "We identify a specific edition of each book as part of that book's title, as registered with the ISBN Agency and the Library of Congress, and print the complete title on the copyright page. Our approach is that a new edition (whether second, third, fourth, etc.) is not merely a second (third, fourth, etc.) printing, but includes new or updated content from the preceding edition. We also include on the copyright page information about the specific printing, as follows: First Printing, [year of first printing]."

THE PLOUGH PUBLISHING HOUSE

1989 Statement: "We do not indicate in any way that a book is a first edition. In the absence of '2nd edition' etc., this can be assumed."

1994 Statement: "We designate first printings with © 1994 (the year of the first printing) Plough Publishing House on the copyright page. We have done this since we commenced operations in the U.S. in 1964. Subsequent printings will have © and the year. New editions will state 'Second Edition 1991.' "

2000 Statement: *See* 1994 Statement

THE PLOUGH PUBLISHING HOUSE (UNITED KINGDOM)

1994, 2000 Statements: *See* 1994 Statement of The Plough Publishing House

P. N. REVIEW (UNITED KINGDOM)

2000 Statement: *See* 2000 Statement of Carcanet Press Limited (United Kingdom)

PLUME

1988 Statement: *See* 1988 Statement of New American Library
1993, 2000 Statements: *See* 1993 Statement of Dutton Signet

PLUME (AUSTRALIA)

2000 Statement: *See* 2000 Statement of Penguin Books Australia Ltd (Australia)

PLYMOUTH PRESS/PLYMOUTH BOOKS

2000 Statement: "We identify the first printing of a first edition by 'First Printing' followed by date. We do not have a special method for identifying a first edition other than this statement. If further editions are needed, we add the line 'Second Edition', 'Third Edition' etc. If revised, we add the word 'Revised.' "

PLYMPTON PRESS INTERNATIONAL

1995 Statement: "On the copyright page we state 'First Edition 1995' (etc., as appropriate). We also use the numbers 10 9 8 7 6 5 4 3 2 1, deleting the 1 (etc.) when we reprint."

2001 Statement: *See* 1995 Statement

POCAHONTAS PRESS

1994 Statement: "On the page on the reverse of the full title page—page ii or iv—of each book we publish, we list the year of printing: 'First Printing 19__.' For reprints, we add the notation '2nd printing, 19__' after the 'First

Printing' notice . . . . We have identified our 'First Printing' in this way since 1984, when we began operation. When we publish a second edition—i.e., when the text has been significantly altered—we identify the new edition as 'Revised edition, 19__.'

"Our imprint (Manuscript Memories) does follow the same practice."

2001 Statement: *See* 1994 Statement

POCKET PARAGON

2000 Statement: *See* 2000 Statement of David R. Godine, Publisher, Inc.

POETRY AUSTRALIA (AUSTRALIA)

1988, 1994 Statements: *See* 1988 Statement of South Head Press (Australia)

POETRY BOOKSHOP (UNITED KINGDOM)
(Out of business prior to 1937.)

1928 Statement: "The First Editions of the Poetry Bookshop are generally designated by the words *on the back of title-page*: Published: month: year.

"For second and subsequent editions the words Reprinted or 2nd Impression, etc., are *added*.

"We would mention that this has only been a general rule heretofore, but it is certainly one we would be prepared to adopt in the case of future publications."

THE POETRY CENTER PRESS/SHOESTRING PRESS

2000 Statement: "We do not identify the first printing of a first edition. We do not reprint our limited editions which are each numbered (or given a letter) in the colophon. Books are hand numbered and signed."

POETRY HARBOR

2000 Statement: "We identify numbered first editions by sequential numbering of each copy (i.e. 10/500). Otherwise, only reprints are identified as such."

THE POETRY PLEÍADE

2000 Statement: *See* 2000 Statement of Carcanet Press Limited (United Kingdom)

POETRY WALES PRESS LTD. (WALES)

See Seren (Wales)

POETS WHO SLEEP

1995, 2001 Statements: *See* 1995 Statement of Longhouse

POGO PRESS, INCORPORATED

1995 Statement: "Of our fifteen titles published to this date, we have reprinted two. Each of these titles, however, were revised in various aspects, and contain new copyright dates and ISBN numbers. Accordingly, the copyright date, and/or the new, higher ISBN number contained therein will indicate the priority of the edition concerned."

2000 Statement: "Of our 27 titles published to this date, we have reprinted 3. Each of these titles were revised in various aspects, and contain new copyright dates and ISBN numbers. Accordingly, the copyright date, and/or the new, higher ISBN number contained therein will indicate the priority of the edition concerned. The third title was reprinted twice, in exactly the same form. There is no way to distinguish the printings."

POISONED PEN PRESS
2001 Statement: "We identify the first printing of a first edition by the words 'First Edition.' The first printing of a first edition is identified by the number line '10 9 8 7 6 5 4 3 2 1.' "

POLAR PUBLISHING (CANADA)
1995, 2000 Statements: *See* 1995 Statement of Townson Publishing Co., Ltd (Canada)

POLEBRIDGE PRESS
1994 Statement: The first printing of a first edition is indicated by the number line 10 9 8 7 6 5 4 3 2 1. The lowest number showing indicates the printing. This method has been in use since 1992; prior to 1992, the printing was not indicated.

POLYBOOKS LTD. (UNITED KINGDOM)
2000 Statement: *See* 2000 Statement of The Albyn Press (United Kingdom)

POLYGON (UNITED KINGDOM)
1994, 2000 Statements: *See* 1988 Statement of Edinburgh University Press (United Kingdom)

POLYGON AT EDINBURGH (UNITED KINGDOM)
2000 Statement: *See* 2000 Statement of Edinburgh University Press (United Kingdom)

POLYGONAL PUBLISHING HOUSE
1995 Statement: "We have not designated first printings in any way. We designate second editions as such. We have not yet had the occasion to do a second printing of a first edition. If and when this occurs, we'll designate the book as a second printing."
2001 Statement: *See* 1995 Statement

THE POMEGRANATE PRESS
1976 Statement: "We designate a first edition usually in the traditional colophon following the text of the book or broadside. We generally limit our publications to one printing."
1981 Statement: "We designate a first edition usually on the masthead (copyright) page and also in the colophon on a separate page at the end of the text. Here the explanation of paper, handprinting, graphic illustration and no. of copies are described. The books are numbered and limited number usually signed. Editions range from 200-900 copies."

POND FROG EDITIONS
2001 Statement: *See* 2001 Statement of Red Moon Press

THE POND-EKBERG COMPANY
1947 Statement: "There is no mark of identification on the first edition of any of the books we have published.

"We now have in process the first reprint of three of our books which will be so indicated on either the title page or the page immediately back of the title."

PONDEROSA PUBLISHERS
2000 Statement: "First printings of our books are all identified on the copyright page as 'First Edition' followed by the year. Second and additional same way."

POOLBEG PRESS LIMITED (REPUBLIC OF IRELAND)
1981 Statement: "Poolbeg Press's only method of designating first editions is in the printing of the preliminary pages. There we list the edition and the year and our own position, and when one of our own books goes into another edition we also list this in the same manner."
1988 Statement: "The Ward River Press is no more. Poolbeg now has no other imprints.

"Poolbeg designates first editions in the printing of the copyright page. We say 'First published [date]' and add 'Reprinted [date]' and so on (or 'New Edition/Revised Edition [date]') and so on."

POPULAR DOGS (UNITED KINGDOM)
1994 Statement: *See* 1994 Statement of Random House UK Limited (United Kingdom)
2000 Statement: *See* 2000 Statement of The Random House Group Limited (United Kingdom)

PORCEPIC BOOKS (CANADA)
1989 Statement: *See* 1989 Statement of Press Porcepic Ltd. (Canada)

THE PORPOISE PRESS (UNITED KINGDOM)
(Out of business prior to 1949.)
1928 Statement: "The first impressions of our ordinary issues bear on the back of the title, to which all bibliographical matter is relegated: 'First published in (date of year) by The Porpoise Press, 133a George Street, Edinburgh.' On the second and subsequent impressions, there is stated 'First impression (month and year); Second impression (month and year),' etc.

"Where special editions have also been issued, this fact is stated on the ordinary edition, and on the special edition itself there appears a statement as to the size of the edition, etc.: e.g., 'This edition, on hand-made paper, is limited to fifty signed and numbered copies. This copy is Number...' "
1937 Statement: *See* 1928 Statement

BERN PORTER BOOKS

1976 Statement: "All publications are marked first edition, second edition, etc. as reprinted.

"All publications being a first, second, third printing of a first edition are marked as such.

"As the oldest and largest small press in the world we have found it useful to be complete, consistent, accurate and non-changing in marks throughout the years.

note: should a later edition be revised over an earlier we also mark that.

note: all markings are on the back of the title page.

note: all signed numbered editions are dated firsts."—Bern Porter, Chairman of the Board, Bern Porter Books.

1981, 1989 Statements: *See* 1976 Statement

PORTER SARGENT PUBLISHERS INC

2000 Statement: "We identify subsequent printings on the copyright page by the statement 'second printing, 1952'; so only identify first editions by elimination."

PORTLAND PRESS LTD (UNITED KINGDOM)

2001 Statement: "We do not identify a first printing; we do identify subsequent printings as such on the copyright page."

POSSIBILITY PRESS

2001 Statement: *See* 2001 Statement of Markowski International Publishers

THE POST-APOLLO PRESS

1995 Statement: "Our policy, simply, has been to print the date of the first edition on the copyright page without further designation. The few times we have printed a second or third edition, the words second (or third) edition are added below the original date, usually with the print date of the new edition."

POTOMAC BOOKS, INC.

1976 Statement: Only those editions after the first are indicated. Printings of the first edition are indicated only after the first printing.

1981 Statement: *See* 1976 Statement

CLARKSON N. POTTER, INC.

1976 Statement: "Every printing after the first is listed with the edition on the copyright page (i.e. on the first edition, first printing, the c/r page says only first edition; on 2nd printing, '2nd printing' is added to first edition)."

1981, 1988 Statements: *See* 1981, 1988 Statements of Crown Publishers

1995 Statement: *See* 1988 Statement of Crown Publishers Inc.

T & A D POYSER (UNITED KINGDOM)

1994 Statement: "Under the management of its founding owners, first printings of T & A D Poyser books are identified on the history page by the wording *first published 19XX by T & A D Poyser Limited.* Second and subsequent printings are listed in the relevant copies giving the date and number of the printing concerned.

"This practise has been continued by the current owners, Academic Press Limited, a division of Harcourt Brace and Company."
2000 Statement: *See* 1994 Statement, but note that Harcourt Brace & Company changed their name to Harcourt Publishers Ltd in 1989."

PRACTICAL PRESS, LTD. (UNITED KINGDOM)
1947 Statement: *See* 1947 Statement of Rockliff Publishing Corporation, Limited (United Kingdom)

PRAEGER PUBLISHERS
1995, 2000 Statements: *See* 1995 Statement of Greenwood Publishing Group Inc.

PRAIRIE OAK PRESS INC
2000 Statement: "We identify the first printing of a first edition by the statement 'First edition, first printing.' "

PRAIRIE STATE BOOKS
2000 Statement: *See* 2000 Statement of The University of Illinois Press

PRAJNA PRESS
1981 Statement: *See* 1981 Statement of Shambhala Publications, Inc.
1988 Statement: This imprint no longer exists.

PRAKKEN PUBLICATIONS INC
2000 Statement: "No special wording. Date of copyright of 1st edition is date of first printing. Dates of *all* subsequent printings *and* subsequent editions are shown on reverse of title page."

PRB PRODUCTIONS
2000 Statement: "2nd, 3rd printings etc. carry the style second printing, third printing etc."

PRECEPT PRESS
1994, 2000 Statements: *See* 1994 Statement of Bonus Books Inc.

PRENTICE-HALL, INC.
1947 Statement: "Prentice-Hall is a very large organization, publishing both trade books and text books. The practice differs depending upon the division publishing the books involved.

"With trade books, we indicate the first edition by printing the words 'First Edition' on the copyright page of the book. On subsequent printings we delete that edition imprint, and substitute the number of the printing. We list all printings subsequent to the first on the copyright page, giving the month in which the printing was available for sale.

"When we publish a new textbook, the copyright page simply carries the year date of copyright and nothing else. When that book is reprinted, we generally include a statement below the copyright line reading:
First printing, January, 1947
Second printing, September, 1947

or whatever the case may be, and so on for subsequent printings.

"When we bring out new editions of both trade and textbooks, we indicate Second Edition, Third Edition, and so forth on both the title page and the cover of the book. And, of course, the copyright page carries the year date of all revisions. For instance, copyright, 1935, 1940, 1945, by Prentice-Hall, Inc.

"Of course, there are always exceptions to every rule, but the foregoing procedure is pretty much our general practice in both Trade and Textbook divisions."

1976 Statement: "We have no specific method of identifying first editions. We use a printing line of arabic numbers to designate how many printings a book has had:

"10 9 8 7 6 5 4 3 2 1 would be the line in the first printing of a first edition. Subsequent printings would drop a digit from the right. A revised edition would be so indicated either in the title or on the copyright page of a book.

"Before using the numeral printing line we used the words 'First printing,' 'Second printing,' etc."

1981 Statement: *See* 1976 Statement

PRENTICE HALL AUSTRALIA (AUSTRALIA)

1995 Statement: "Prentice Hall Australia identifies the first and subsequent printings of all locally-published material by using a string of numbers on the copyright page that initially covers five prints and five years. For a book first published in 1995 the string would appear as: 1 2 3 4 5 99 98 97 96 95. If reprinted that same year the number 1 would be deleted leaving the string at 2 3 4 5 99 98 97 96 95 to indicate it was the second printing in 1995, and so on for all reprints of that edition. Subsequent editions are treated independently, are clearly marked 'Second Edition' on their covers, title and copyright pages, and carry a new string to indicate their own printing history."

PRENTICE HALL UK (UNITED KINGDOM)

1994 Statement: "Prentice Hall identifies a first printing by inserting 'First published (date, e.g. 1994)' at the head of the copyright page. This date should be read in conjunction with the numerals '1 2 3 4 5 98 97 96 95 94' at the foot of the copyright page which are deleted accordingly to identify the impression and the year the impression was manufactured."

THE PRESERVATION PRESS

1976 Statement: "The Preservation Press has never identified first editions as such; subsequent editions (which are rare for us) are identified as 'second revised editions,' etc., as appropriate."

1981 Statement: "The Preservation Press has never identified first editions as such; subsequent reprintings are designated as such on the copyright page with the year of reprinting (e.g., Fourth printing, 1981). The few revised editions published are identified clearly on at least the title page."

1988 Statement: "We now use a numerical system, e.g.:
92 91 90 89 88 5 4 3 2 1."

1993 Statement: "We now use a numerical system on the © page to indicate reprintings, e.g.:

92 91 90 89 88 5 4 3 2 1.

"When publishing subsequent editions, we may use 'Revised Edition' or other designation, as appropriate."

PRESIDIO PRESS

1981 Statement: "Unless a book states on the copyright page that it is a second printing or second edition—or whatever number it may be—we assume that it will be recognized as a first edition.

"In other words, no special note is made of first editions."

1988, 1993, 2000 Statements: *See* 1981 Statement

THE PRESS AT CALIFORNIA STATE UNIVERSITY, FRESNO

See California State University Press

THE PRESS OF JAMES A. DECKER

(Including Compass Editions, Village Press, and Black Farm Press.)

1947 Statement: "We have not had second editions of our books due to the nature of the copy (poetry). Very rarely does an edition of poetry sell out, hence we have had no occasion to mark editions."

THE PRESS OF MacDONALD & REINECKE

1988, 1994 Statements: *See* 1988, 1994 Statements of Padre Productions

PRESS OF MORNINGSIDE BOOKSHOP

2000 Statement: *See* 2000 Statement of Morningside Bookshop

THE PRESS OF THE NIGHTOWL

2001 Statement: "Our books are limited editions, and not subject to reprinting. All of our publications are first printings."

PRESS PORCEPIC LTD. (CANADA)

1976 Statement: "We designate only those printings and/or editions after the first, and this method of identification does not differ from any previously used."

1981 Statement: "We designate only those printings and/or editions after the first, and this method of identification does not differ from any previously used.

"On books which we expect to reprint or revise we now print the following: 81 82 83 84 85 5 4 3 2 1 and opaque out the relevant numbers in subsequent printings."

1989 Statement: "Porcepic Books, or Press Porcepic Ltd., has never designated first printings or first editions."

(Note that Press Porcepic Ltd changed its name in June, 1991 to Beach Holme Publishing Limited.)

PRESSI SOLWAY (UNITED KINGDOM)

2000 Statement: *See* 2000 Statement of The Paternoster Press Ltd. (United Kingdom)

PRESSWORKS PUBLISHING INC.

1988 Statement: "It is our practice to print the words First Edition on the copyright page. We adopted this method of designation in 1980 and it does not vary from any previous method of designation."

PRICE MILBURN AND COMPANY LIMITED
(NEW ZEALAND)

1976 Statement: "We simply start with

First published 1967

on our first edition, and we continue to add

Reprinted 1968

or

New edition 1968

and so on, each time the book is printed again (on the back of the title page).

"I enclose a title page with verso from one of our books, and it proves me wrong—we often don't identify a first edition at all. But we add a publication history when it reprints."

1981 Statement: "My original answer still stands, though we have made a change in the light of offset litho printing from plates—where it is difficult and expensive to change the bibliographic information between printings. For our junior educational books we put

First published 1980. Reprinted regularly.

on all copies, so that a reader cannot tell whether the book in his hand is a first edition or not.

"When the printing plate that prints the verso of the title page wears out and has to be replaced, we bring the information up to date for the next printing."

PRICE STERN SLOAN

2000 Statement: "We now use a system of alternating numbers: (1 3 5 7 9 10 8 6 4 2) to be specific."

PRICE/STERN/SLOAN PUBLISHERS, INC.

1976 Statement: "Our form is to put FIRST PRINTING on the copyright page of the book."

1981 Statement: *See* 1976 Statement

1989 Statement: "Yes, we are still following the practice of putting the first printing of the first edition on the copyright page. However, we do it differently now: as you see by the xerox enclosed, [9 8 7 6 5 4 3 2], the descending numbers go down to 2 . . . this means this is the first edition. When we print the second edition, the number 2 will be omitted . . . the third edition, the number 3 will be omitted, and so on.

"Our imprints and subsidiaries do follow our practices."

1994 Statement: "Our first print line starts with 10 and ends with 1. . . . The descending numbers go down to 1 . . . . This means this is the first printing. When we print the second printing, the number 1 will be omitted."

2000 Statement: *See* 2000 Statement of Price Stern Sloan

PRIMA PUBLISHING
1994 Statement: The first printing of a first edition is indicated by the number line 94 95 96 97 98 RRD 10 9 8 7 6 5 4 3 2 1. The lowest number showing indicates the printing.
2000 Statement: "We now use a 2-letter code designation instead of 3. The first printing of a first edition is indicated by the number line 94 95 96 97 98 AA 10 9 8 7 6 5 4 3 2 1. The lowest number showing indicates the printing."

THE PRIMAVERA PRESS, INC.
(Out of business prior to 1949.)
1937 Statement: "Printings of our books following the first editions are so marked, i.e., 'Second Printing,' etc. This is true with one exception—the second printing of *Who Loves a Garden* is distinguished by the date on the title page '1935' being one year later than the date of copyright '1934.' "

PRINCETON ARCHITECTURAL PRESS
1994 Statement: "Until this year, Princeton Architectural Press did not designate first editions. We identified subsequent editions with 'second edition,' 'third edition,' etc. on the copyright page. Beginning this year, we will also include 'first edition' on the copyright page.

"We have always identified printings with a list of Arabic numerals in descending order (i.e., 5 4 3 2 1), with the number to the right being the number of the printing. This information is also located on the copyright page."
2000 Statement: *See* 1994 Statement

PRINCETON UNIVERSITY PRESS
1928 Statement: *See* 1937 Statement
1937 Statement: "Our only way of designating first editions is by negative implication. In other words, our first editions bear no special designation. If, however, a title is reprinted or reissued that fact is set forth on the copyright page.

"We have apparently always used our present method of designating first printings from subsequent ones. 'Always' in this case means for the approximate quarter of a century that we have been publishing."
1947 Statement: "Our only way of designating first editions is by negative implication. In other words, our first editions bear no special designation. If, however, a title is reprinted or reissued that fact is set forth on the copyright page.

"We seek to distinguish between a new edition and a new printing; a new edition implying a substantive change in the text, a new printing referring to a reissue of a book.

"We have apparently always used our present method of designating first printings from subsequent ones. 'Always' in this case means for the approximate three and a half decades that we have been publishing."
1976 Statement: "We do not identify first editions, but only subsequent editions."

1981 Statement: "We do not identify first printings, but only subsequent printings. Interested collectors may contact the Press for a more detailed printing history of Princeton University Press titles."

1988 Statement: *See* 1981 Statement

1994 Statement: "Since 1990, we have identified first printings by setting the numbers 1 2 3 4 5 6 7 8 9 10 at the bottom of the copyright page. With the second printing—by which we mean a reissue of the book—we remove the number 1, and so on for successive printings. We do not identify first editions, only subsequent ones—by which we imply that there has been a substantive change in the text. A subsequent edition is identified by the words Revised Edition or Second Edition, as appropriate, on the book's front jacket, title page, and copyright page."

2000 Statement: *See* 1994 Statement

PRINTED EDITIONS

1981 Statement: "Since we seldom intend to reprint an edition (like most very small presses), we don't identify our first editions as such."

PRISM PRESS

1988 Statement: "Our policy is to not make any special identification of first editions. However we do identify reprints and new editions so anything not identified as a reprint or new edition is a first edition."

PRODUCTIVE PUBLICATIONS (CANADA)

2001 Statement: "We are a 'just-in-time' publisher and there are no distinguishing characteristics between first and subsequent printings."

PROGRESS PRESS

1947 Statement: *See* 1947 Statement of Public Affairs Press

PROMETHEUS PRESS

1995 Statement: "All of our fine first limited editions are indicated so on the title page, and two portions of each edition are further demarcated—one by numbering (usually #1 through #148) and the other by lettering ('A' through 'Z' and 'AA' through 'ZZ'). Most lettered editions are hard-bound, while all trade and numbered editions are paper-bound."

PROMPT (UNITED KINGDOM)

2000 Statement: *See* 2000 Statement of Butterworth-Heinemann

PROSCENIUM PUBLISHERS INC

1988 Statement: "First printings of our books are all identified on the copyright page as 'First Limelight Edition' followed by the month and year of publication. Second printings are identified as 'Second Limelight Edition,' etc. It should be pointed out that since most of our books are paperback reprints, information about the original publication of a particular title almost always appears on the copyright page."

1993 Statement: *See* 1988 Statement

2000 Statement: *See* 2000 Statement of Limelight Editions

PROTEAN PRESS

2001 Statement: "We do not identify a first printing or any printing after the first printing on the copyright page. Protean Press is a letterpress shop that prints a single limited-sized edition of any of its books or broadsides. We do list copyright and ISBN."

PROVINCETOWN ARTS INC

2000 Statement: "First Edition is so identified on the copyright page. Subsequent printings are noted with date."

PRUETT PUBLISHING CO.

1976 Statement: "The only method that Pruett uses in designating first editions is by placing on the copyright page the following words:

First Edition
1 2 3 4 5 6 7 8 9

"Sometimes we do not even use the words 'First Edition,' and the numbers we use indicate the number of times an edition has been printed. For instance, if it is a second printing, the numbers will read '2 3 4 5 . . .' "

1981 Statement: *See* 1976 Statement

1988 Statement: "We usually identify a First Edition as such on the copyright page, followed by the string of numbers, used to indicate the number of times an edition has been printed. For instance, if it is a second printing, the numbers will read '2 3 4 5 . . .' "

1993 Statement: "We virtually never designate a first edition by printing 'First Edition' on the copyright page on books published after 1991. We print a string of numerals from 1 to 10 on the copyright page, which designates the number of times that particular edition has been printed (for the first printing of a first edition, for example, the string will begin with the numeral 1; for the second printing of a first edition, the string will begin with the numeral 2; and so on). Only in subsequent editions do we print the words 'Second (or Third, or Fourth, or whatever) Edition.' We began applying this method of designation with consistency in 1992, although some books we published earlier than 1992 may use it."

2001 Statement: "Please refer to the 1993 Statement to see how we identify first editions. The way we identify impressions has changed within the past two years. Other than that nothing else has changed. [Pruett now uses a number string "10 09 08 07 06 05 04 03 02 01   5 4 3 2 1' to identify impressions. The numbers on the left represent dates, those to the right, printings.] In this example, the first print run of the first edition was printed in 2001."

PSYCHOLOGY PRESS LTD. (UNITED KINGDOM)

2001 Statement: "LEA Ltd. [United Kingdom] is now part of The Taylor & Francis Group and has been re-named Psychology Press Ltd. New books have been published as Psychology Press since 1996. First editions carry no specific edition number, reprints state date of first printing and all subsequent reprints."

PSYCHOLOGY SOCIETY
2000 Statement: "We identify the first printing of a first edition by the following statement: 'Copyright 2000, First Printing of the First Edition.' "

PSYCHOSOCIAL PRESS
2000 Statement: *See* 2000 Statement of International Universities Press, Inc.

PUBLIC AFFAIRS PRESS
(Includes Progress Press.)
1947 Statement: "We haven't any differentiation."

PUBLISHERS ASSOCIATES
1994 Statement: "A first edition by any member press carries no markings unless it is a limited first edition and then it states so as well as the number of copies printed and which volume (number) it is on the back page.

"All subsequent editions are so noted on the title page and its verso (copyright page)."

PUCKERBRUSH PRESS
1976 Statement: "I use no designation for a first edition. I indicate only those printings/editions after the first. I've used no other methods of identification."
1988, 1993, 2000 Statements: *See* 1976 Statement

PUDDING HOUSE PUBLICATIONS
1995 Statement: "You know a first edition from Pudding House from lack of any second or thereafter edition (or printing) statement. If it says 'first edition' or says nothing, it is a first edition."
2000 Statement: *See* 1995 Statement

PUFFIN
1988 Statement: *See* 1988 Statement of Penguin Publishing Co Ltd (United Kingdom)

PUFFIN (AUSTRALIA)
1994, 2000 Statements: *See* 1994 Statement of Penguin Books Australia Ltd (Australia)

PUFFIN (NEW ZEALAND)
1994, 2000 Statements: *See* 1994 Statement of Penguin Books (N.Z.) Ltd (New Zealand)

PUFFIN BOOKS (UNITED KINGDOM)
1988 Statement: *See* 1988 Statement of Penguin Publishing Co Ltd (United Kingdom)
2001 Statement: "Essentially we do still follow the practice outlined in our last statement, although obviously that statement came from the adult division of the company, Penguin Publishing Co Ltd (UK).

"The slight change in our practice is that, although we still put the year of first publication and the publication number below, we now use one number only—the current impression number for that title. This is because, due to the latest technology, printers are now able to insert and delete this impression number as appropriate when a title reprints. We adopted this new practice in 2000 . . . our practice is always the same as the Penguin adult division . . . ."

PULP PRESS (CANADA)

1981 Statement: "Our first editions do not carry any notations. However, subsequent printings/editions carry the printing history on the © page."
All imprints use the same method.

PULSE-FINGER PRESS

1976 Statement: "We usually identify first editions and/or printings on the copyright page. Where no designation is used at the outset, subsequent editions/printings are identified.

"The methods of identification do not differ from those previously used."
1988 Statement: *See* 1976 Statement

THE PURCHASE PRESS

1995 Statement: "On new printings, we designate: 'Second printing, month and year; third printing, ditto, and so on.' This appears on copyright page, below 'FIRST EDITION, month and year,' which style continues in all printings."

PURDUE UNIVERSITY PRESS

1994 Statement: "In the past, the first printing had no designation as such at all, but subsequent printings were identified as second, third, etc., printed on the copyright page. In 1992, we switched over to the procedure recommended in the *Chicago Manual of Style*, with the series of dates and numbers on the copyright page. A second printing would just have the '1' and the date of the first printing opaqued out."

PURPLE FINCH PRESS

1995 Statement: "Purple Finch Press designates the first printing of first editions by writing: First Edition and the date. This method of designation was begun in 1992. This method is not different from any previously used. Subsequent printings say first edition, second printing, etc. The statement First Edition is found on the biblio on the reverse of the title page."
2001 Statement: *See* 1995 Statement

PURPLE MOUNTAIN PRESS, LTD.

1994 Statement: "About 70% of our books are original works and designated on the back of title page as first editions with the year. Subsequent printings are designated 'second printing,' etc. Some second printings note if minor corrections have been made. Second editions are designated 'revised edition' with the year (the year of the first edition is noted, also). A later printing of such would be designated 'revised edition, second printing.'

"The rest of our books are reprints which give the date of original issue on the back of the title page (when available, a publishing history has been included). It will then give the year of the reprint and be designated either 'first Purple Mountain Press printing' or 'first Purple Mountain Press edition.'

."Purple Mountain Press acquired Harbor Hill Books in 1990. About 95% of all Harbor Hill books under the old and new owners are reprints and bear the date of original issue on the title page or on the back of the title page followed by the year or by 'first (or second, etc.) printing' and year. The few original books published give only the copyright date. None of these has been reissued."

2000 Statement: "Beginning in 1996, on many of our titles we expect to reprint, we have been using the 5 4 3 2 1 designation for edition numbers."

PUSH/PULL PRESS
2000 Statement: *See* 2000 Statement of JSA Publications Inc.

PUSHCART PRESS
1981 Statement: "[A first printing] says so on the title page verso."
1988, 1993, 2000 Statements: *See* 1981 Statement

PUTNAM (AUSTRALIA)
2000 Statement: *See* 2000 Statement of Penguin Books Australia Ltd (Australia)

PUTNAM & COMPANY, LTD. (UNITED KINGDOM)
(Formerly G. P. Putnam's Sons, Ltd.)
1937, 1947 Statements: *See* 1928 Statement of G. P. Putnam's Sons, Ltd. (United Kingdom)

THE PUTNAM & GROSSET GROUP
1993 Statement: *See* 1988 Statement of The Putnam & Grosset Group (Children's). But note "Philomel Books and G. P. Putnam's Sons, also divisions of The Putnam & Grosset Group, carry a code in numbers and also the words: First Impression for all first editions. In the subsequent printings, the words are deleted and the lowest number in the code indicates the printing."

THE PUTNAM & GROSSET GROUP (CHILDREN'S)
1988 Statement: "Grosset & Dunlap is a division of The Putnam Publishing Group and now publishes juvenile titles under the imprint: The Putnam & Grosset Group.

"First editions are not identified in our books except that the copyright notice gives the year of publication. If a book is reprinted, there is no indication of which printing it is. Some of our books do carry a code in letters or numbers. For instance, under the copyright notice and other information (ISBN, LC number, manufacturing place) there may be the letters C D E F G H. It is obvious to those who are familiar with production codes that the book is in its third printing, because A and B are missing.

"If a second or third printing of a book contains new copyrightable material (new illustrations, editorial revisions, condensation) there will be a new copyright year in the notice, but the original copyright year must be included. There may or may not be a clue as to which printing it is.

"There are instances, in the case of classics (not public domain titles, but juvenile books that are in copyright and because of their popularity have never gone out of print) a line is included to show which printing it is. Our *Little Toot*, copyright 1939, © 1967 by Hardie Gramatky, states in a separate line: Twenty-seventh Impression. However, it does not give the year of the twenty-seventh impression.

"Many of our juvenile titles are imported from the countries in which they were published. In such cases, the original copyright year appears, and the copyright notice also indicates the year of the first United States edition. This is for copyright protection in the United States, not for first edition information, although the copyright year reveals the year of first printing.

"All of the imprints and subsidiaries of The Putnam & Grosset Group follow the practice mentioned."

1993 Statement: *See* 1993 Statement of The Putnam & Grosset Group

PUTNAM AERONAUTICAL BOOKS

2001 Statement: *See* 2001 Statement of Brassey's Inc.

G. P. PUTNAM'S SONS

1928 Statement: "Our system as to new publications does not usually include printing any entry on the back of the title page or otherwise indicating first edition.

"When a book is printed a second time, as a rule we print under the copyright notice the words 'First printed March 1927. Second printing April 1927, etc.' Where there is no note of this kind it may be assumed that the work is the first printing.

"It is always our intention not to use the word 'second edition' unless there is some distinct addition or change from the first edition. When that is the case, usually on the title page is the line 'second edition revised, or second edition corrected, or second edition revised, corrected and enlarged' or some such expression. A similar entry is often printed under the copyright notice.

"As to the date on the title page. This is supposed to be the date when the particular copy was printed. Reprints without change would generally have that title page, and when such reprint is made it would be the copyright entry which would tell by comparison that it was not first edition.

"For staple items that had been reprinted from year to year, as a rule that date is omitted from the title-page."

1937, 1947 Statements: *See* 1928 Statement

Statement for 1960: *See* 1976 Statement

1976 Statement: "Putnam's method of designating first editions is as follows: All editions other than the first one are distinguished by the words 'second (or third or fourth, etc.) impression' which appear on the copyright page. The first edition has no such designation."

1981 Statement: *See* 1976 Statement

1989 Statement: The printing is indicated by a sequence of numbers ranging from left to right on the copyright page:

1 2 3 4 5 6 7 8 9 10

The last number on the left indicates the printing. In the example above, a first printing is indicated.

A Putnam edition of a title previously published abroad is identified as the First American Edition on the copyright page.

1993 Statement: *See* 1993 Statement of The Putnam & Grosset Group

G. P. PUTNAM'S SONS, LTD. (UNITED KINGDOM)

1928 Statement: "Our English procedure for indicating first editions is as follows:

"On the reverse of the title page, we print the line

First published . . . .

followed by the month and year.

"When the book is reprinted, we retain the line, adding underneath it:

Reprinted . . . .

followed by the month and year.

"Further impressions are indicated in the same way. If, however, there is any definite alteration in matter or style, we indicate this by the words:

Second edition . . . .

followed by the month and year.

"The same procedure would apply for subsequent editions."

PYGMY FOREST PRESS

1995 Statement: "All books are first editions unless otherwise stated. On occasion there will be 'First Edition' stated. All 2nd and subsequent printings are stated as 2nd (or later) edition."

THE PYNE PRESS

1976 Statement: "We have no special or unusual way of listing first editions. We merely state somewhere on the page listing copyright, ISBN number, etc., that it is the first edition."

Q

QED PRESS

1994 Statement: The first printing of a first edition is indicated by the number line 10 9 8 7 6 5 4 3 2. The lowest number showing indicates the printing. The words "First Edition, (month) (year)" are also present. This method has been the only one used.

2000 Statement: *See* 1994 Statement

QUADRANGLE/THE NEW YORK TIMES BOOK CO., INC.

1976 Statement: "Our method of identifying editions is as follows:

"We put no identification on the first edition/first printing. Subsequent printings are marked second, third, etc.

"A second edition will usually be identified as 'revised edition' and will not have a printing identification, as with first editions."

1981 Statement: *See* 1976 Statement

QUAIL RIDGE PRESS

1994 Statement: "We identify the first printings of our books by inserting on the copyright page the phrase 'First Printing, month, year.' Subsequent printings are differentiated by using the phrase 'Second Printing, month, year,' etc."

THE QUAIL STREET PUBLISHING COMPANY

1976 Statement: "No designation = first printing, first edition. Other printings & editions are designated thusly:
2nd printing = 2nd printing of first edition
2nd edition, 2nd printing = the obvious."

QUEEN ANNE PRESS (UNITED KINGDOM)

1994, 2000 Statements: *See* 1994 Statement of Lennard Associates (United Kingdom)

QUERIDO, PUBLISHERS

1947 Statement: "No special identification."

QUEST BOOKS

1988, 1993 Statements: *See* 1988 Statement of The Theosophical Publishing House
2000 Statement: *See* 2000 Statement of The Theosophical Publishing House

QUESTAR PUBLISHERS INC.

1994 Statement: "We use 1 2 3 4 5 6 7 8 9 0 and change numerals upon reprinting."

QUESTOR EDUCATIONAL PRODUCTS COMPANY

1976 Statement: "Thank you for contacting us re our method of identifying first editions. Unfortunately, we have none at this time. We plan to institute one, however, for our 1977 list and all future books."

QUICK FOX

1981 Statement: "We make no notation of printings—first or second, or whatever."

QUICKSILVER PRODUCTIONS

1995 Statement: "Reprints are indicated by number on the bottom of the copyright page. The numbers are listed from left to right with the first number indicating the printing . . . . These methods do not differ from any previously used."

QUILL

2001 Statement: *See* 2001 Statement of HarperCollinsPublishers

QUILL & BRUSH

1995 Statement: "Quill & Brush states 'First Edition' on the copyright page. Second and revised printings are so designated. Limited editions are identified on a colophon page. Chapbooks are issued in only one printing."

QUILL DRIVER BOOKS

1995 Statement: "We designate the first printing by stating 'First Edition' on the copyright page."

2001 Statement: *See* 1995 Statement

QUILL TRADE PAPERBACKS

1994 Statement: *See* 1994 Statement of Tambourine Books

QUILLER PRESS LTD (UNITED KINGDOM)

2001 Statement: "We designate by: 'First published' with date then 'reprinted' with dates. Quiller Press Ltd was formed in January 1980."

QUINCANNON PUBLISHING GROUP

2000 Statement: "In 1999, the newly established Quincannon Publishing Group acquired Tory Corner Editions but keeps it as an individual imprint.

"Prior to 1995, each Tory Corner Editions first edition book was clearly labeled with FIRST PRINTING. By the same token, each successive edition was also marked SECOND PRINTING, etc.

"Beginning in 1995, the first printing of a first edition is no longer notated as such; notations on the copyright page begin with the SECOND PRINTING. Further notes concerning printing history and revisions can also be found on the copyright page.

"If a book has gone through a title change, that is noted on the title page where the original title is given in parentheses under the new title. Such a notation appears only on the first printing of the title change; the notation is dropped from subsequent printings since the new title will have been established. [This] holds true for all Quincannon imprints."

QUIXOTE

1976 Statement: "We indicate second and third printings of first editions and second editions, but not first edition or first printing. Also everything we print we try to have as an issue of our magazine *QUIXOTE*, so volume number and issue number usually show something about the time/edition. For something we really like, too, we do a preface or second preface as the case may be, but we have only had a few second or third printings and only two I think second editions so far."

1981 Statement: "We have made no essential changes in our indications of first editions—they are indicated by default, since we only indicate 2d editions, second printings, or revised editions. I have now had about eight second editions or revisions and several third editions and printings. Since I have talked to you about it, I have been thinking about indicating first edition at the bottom of the title page of all our work."

QUORUM BOOKS

1995, 2000 Statements: *See* 1995 Statement of Greenwood Publishing Group Inc.

QUOTA PRESS (NORTHERN IRELAND)

1947 Statement: "In the case of first edition the date is usually put on title page or the book is described:

First Published.........................

"In the case of a new impression or edition this is stated below, e.g.

First Published........................ November 1930

Second Impression........................ December 1930

"This practice was not always adhered to during the war years."

R

R & E PUBLISHERS

1995 Statement: "We do not specify that it is the first printing or the first edition. If we go into the second printing or update information in a book, we state that on the copyright page and/or the cover. This has been done since we have been in business (28 years)."

RABETH PUBLISHING COMPANY

1995 Statement: "[We publish] mostly first editions, with only the date of the copyright on the back of the title page. Those we have published as second editions have the date of the first copyright then 'Second edition Copyright, date.' As of [1995] we shall adopt the policy of printing the words, 'FIRST EDITION' before the copyright date."

RADIANT SUMMIT

1995 Statement: *See* 1995 Statement of Blue Dove Press

2000 Statement: "Our imprint, Radiant Summit, is now called Laurel Creek Press."

See also 1995 Statement of Blue Dove Press

RADIUS (UNITED KINGDOM)

1988 Statement: *See* 1988 Statement of Century Hutchinson Publishing Group Limited (United Kingdom)

RAGWEED PRESS (CANADA)

1995 Statement: "We have no particular way of designating first printings, other than to show the year of publication in the copyright holder statement(s). Second and subsequent printings are noted and dated, on the copyright page."

2000 Statement: *See* 1995 Statement

RAINBIRD (UNITED KINGDOM)

1988 Statement: *See* 1988 Statement of Penguin Publishing Co Ltd (United Kingdom)

RAINBOW (UNITED KINGDOM)

1989 Statement: *See* 1989 Statement of The Octopus Publishing Group PLC (United Kingdom)

RAINBOW BOOKS INC.
1994 Statement: "All subsequent editions are titled as such: 2nd printing, 3rd, etc." This method has been in use since 1979.
2000 Statement: *See* 1994 Statement

RAINCOAST BOOKS (CANADA)
2001 Statement: "We do not identify first editions, but only subsequent editions."

RAINTREE PUBLISHERS INC.
1976 Statement: "Printings are designated by a line of numbers on the copyright page. One-digit numbers indicate the printing; two-digit numbers indicate the year of the printing.
1 2 3 4 5 6 7 8 9 0 85 84 83 82 81
"On the first printing of a first edition, the number 1 will appear on the left, and the two-digit number will agree with the last two digits of the copyright year. There will be no reference to first edition."
1981 Statement: *See* 1976 Statement

RAINTREE/STECK-VAUGHN PUBLISHERS
1994 Statement: "We use 1 2 3 4 5 6 7 8 9 98 97 96 95 94 and delete figure 1 and the year as reprints are published."

RAM PUBLISHING COMPANY
1994 Statement: "We are publishers of books pertaining to the use of metal detection equipment, both for treasure hunting and for security purposes. In addition to books telling how to use such equipment effectively, we publish books that suggest the locations of buried treasure that might be recovered with a metal detector.
"Our First Editions are noted by the words 'First Printing' on the copyright page. Subsequent editions of each volume are noted by such indications as 'Second Printing,' 'Third Printing,' etc."

RAMDIL
1995 Statement: "We do not have 2nd and subsequent editions."

RAMPARTS PRESS, INC.
1976 Statement: "Ramparts Press now prints 'First Edition' on the copyright page of the first printing of each of our books."
1981 Statement: *See* 1976 Statement
1988 Statement: "We usually follow the practice of printing 'First Edition' on the copyright page of the first printing of our new books."

RAND McNALLY & COMPANY
1937 Statement: "We are sorry to tell you that the first editions of our publications have no marks to distinguish them from later editions, except in a few cases you will find the letters 'MA' in the lower righthand corner of the copyright page. The 'M' before the 'A' has no connection with the edition, but the 'A' does signify that the book is a first edition. Sometimes this 'A' is

omitted on the first edition, but 'B' appears on the second edition, 'C' on the third edition, etc.''

1947 Statement: ''It has been our practice in recent years to use the letter 'A' on the copyright page, or on the last page of text to indicate the first printing. Subsequent printings are marked 'B,' 'C,' 'D' to identify them. In our earlier Rand McNally publications, however, this system was not consistently used, and very often there is nothing to identify a first printing except the copyright date.''

1976 Statement: ''As to how Rand McNally trade books are identified, the copyright page carries all pertinent information, including the line 'First printing,' 'First paperback printing,' or whatever appropriate wording is necessary, followed by the month and year of the edition. Previously, Rand McNally used letter identification for various editions, with 'A' being the first.''

1981 Statement: ''As to how Rand McNally trade books are identified, the copyright page carries all pertinent information, including the line 'First printing,' 'First paperback printing,' or whatever appropriate wording is necessary, followed by the year of the edition. The month is not indicated unless two editions are printed within the same calendar year.''

1988 Statement: ''Rand McNally's principal publications are world atlases and maps; educational atlases, wall maps, and globes; road atlases, and state and city maps; and marketing atlases and directories. These publications are identified on the copyright page which carries all pertinent information. The first printing of a new edition carrying a new copyright will not include the line, 'First Printing' or 'First Edition.'

''Subsequent printings of the unrevised publication will carry the line, 'Second Printing,' etc. If revisions have been made, but not sufficient to warrant a new copyright, the statement will be, 'Revised Edition' or 'Revised Printing.' These statements will be preceded or followed by the year. The month is not indicated unless there are more than two printings within the same calendar year.

''This practice is followed by all of our divisions.''

1993 Statement: *See* 1988 Statement

See also 1993 Statement of Checkerboard Press, Inc.

RANDOM HOUSE, INC.

1928 Statement: ''Since Random House only publishes limited editions, all of the necessary information that you require is contained in the colophon, i.e., as far as we are concerned, there is only one edition, the first.''

1936 Statement: ''As far as Random House first editions are concerned, with the exception of limited editions where all the necessary information is contained in the colophon, all books are plainly marked 'first edition' on the copyright page.''

1947 Statement: *See* 1936 Statement

1976 Statement: ''All of the first editions of Random House, Pantheon, and A. A. Knopf books carry the words 'FIRST EDITION' in small caps on the copyright page. These first editions are by our definition also first printings.

This practice has not been uniformly adhered to during the entire history of all these imprints, but in recent years it has."

1981, 1988, 1993 Statements: *See* 1976 Statement

2001 Statement: "This [1976] statement is absolutely true for Random House and Villard. We can't speak for Knopf and Pantheon, which have their own management."

RANDOM HOUSE AUSTRALIA (AUSTRALIA)

2000 Statement: "We have changed our practices for first editions. We simply add a line that records 10 9 8 7 6 5 4 3 2 1, and we delete a number starting at 1 for first reprint. The numbers remain intact starting at 1 for first print."

See also 2000 Statement of Transworld Publishers (Australia)

RANDOM HOUSE AUSTRALIA PTY LTD (AUSTRALIA)

1994 Statement: "We simply insert 'First published . . . ' on the imprint page, and then add 'Reprinted . . . ' if and as necessary. This has always been our standard form."

2000 Statement: *See* 2000 Statement of Random House Australia (Australia)

RANDOM HOUSE BUSINESS BOOKS (UNITED KINGDOM)

1994 Statement: *See* 1994 Statement of Random House UK Limited (United Kingdom)

2000 Statement: *See* 2000 Statement of The Random House Group Limited (United Kingdom)

THE RANDOM HOUSE GROUP LIMITED (UNITED KINGDOM)

2000 Statement: "The Company has changed to The Random House Group Limited since 1999. The Random House Group Limited still follows the practice outlined in the last [1994 Statement of Random House UK Limited] statement. In designating first printings, the imprints do follow the same practice."

See 1994 Statement of Random House UK Limited (United Kingdom)

RANDOM HOUSE (NZ) LTD (NEW ZEALAND)

1995 Statement: "We have no particular way [of identifying first printings of first editions] except for noting subsequent reprints or editions."

RANDOM HOUSE TRADE BOOKS

2001 Statement: *See* 2001 Statement of Random House, Inc.

RANDOM HOUSE UK LIMITED (UNITED KINGDOM)

1994 Statement: "Random House UK Limited standardised the copyright pages of the various imprints two years ago.

"We identify when each book is first published on the copyright page and identify each impression using 1 3 5 7 9 10 8 6 4 2, deleting '1' when we first reprint, '2' at the second reprint, etc."

2000 Statement: *See* 2000 Statement of The Random House Group Limited (United Kingdom)

RANGER INTERNATIONAL PRODUCTIONS

1995 Statement: "Imprint 'First Edition' begun in 1969, along with each book signed and numbered."

HARRY RANSOM HUMANITIES RESEARCH CENTER

1994 Statement: "The Harry Ransom Humanities Research Center does not identify its books as first editions, since the Center does not issue second editions or printings. Press runs are small (less that 500 normally), and all books since about 1980 have been issued simultaneously as numbers of the Center's quarterly journal, *The Library Chronicle*. Special double issues have often appeared as books, but not always. Only with the first issue (a double number) of the fall/winter 1993-94 volume (number 24) has the book issue been identified as originally appearing as a number of the *Chronicle*. Books printed in this way carry their own titles rather than that of the journal."

2001 Statement: *See* 1994 Statement

RARACH PRESS

1995 Statement: "Rarach Press is a small bibliophilic imprint which does nothing but first editions, printed by hand in letterpress with original art-work."

RAVAN PRESS (PTY) LTD (REPUBLIC OF SOUTH AFRICA)

1981 Statement: "We designate a first edition by the words 'first impression,' followed by the date. Books published 1978-79 often cite the month as well as the year, whereas books from 1980 onwards cite only the year.

"Collectors are warned that our imprint practices have not been consistent."

RAVEN ROCKS PRESS

2001 Statement: "No printing designation is given."

SHANNON RAVENEL BOOKS

2001 Statement: *See* 2001 Statement of Algonquin Books of Chapel Hill

RAVEN'S RIDGE

2000 Statement: *See* 2000 Statement of Baker Book House

RAWSON ASSOCIATES

1993 Statement: *See* 1993 Statement of Macmillan, Inc.

RAWSON, WADE PUBLISHERS, INC.

1981 Statement: "We identify the first printing of a first edition with the words 'First Edition' on the copyright page. In subsequent printings this is replaced with, for instance, 'Second Printing' and the date of the printing, month and year. That's how we've always done it."

R D R BOOKS

2000 Statement: "We don't identify 1st printings."

THE READER'S DIGEST ASSOCIATION, INC.

1988 Statement: "The Reader's Digest Association, Inc. (the imprint of titles published by the General Books division), does not identify first printings as such. We do, however, identify subsequent printings by stating, at the bottom of the copyright page, the number of the printing and the month and year of its publication. And if there are later editions (as distinguished from printings), we state that fact in a line that runs above the copyright information for the new edition.

1993 Statement: *See* 1988 Statement

2000 Statement: "Our policy remains the same [as the 1988 statement]. Only one correction . . . please change General Books to Illustrated Reference Books."

READERS DIGEST CHILDREN'S PUBLISHING, INC.

2001 Statement: "We identify the first printing of a first edition by a number line, the lowest number indicates the printing."

READER'S DIGEST CONDENSED BOOKS

1988 Statement: "As a rule, Reader's Digest Condensed Books are only published and printed once and are designated 'First Edition' on the copyright page."

1993 Statement: *See* 1988 Statement

REAKTION BOOKS LTD (UNITED KINGDOM)

2001 Statement: "We state on the copyright page 'First edition' and identify only editions, not printings."

THE REAL COMET PRESS

1988 Statement: "Regarding the manner we designate the first printing of a first edition: We have adopted a standard formula for identifying first printings which easily identifies subsequent printings as well as the first;

First Edition 1987 (year optional)
87 88 89 90 10 9 8 7 6 5 4 3 2 1

"Thus, this reads that the first printing was in 1987. If there are two printings in the same year we would only drop the number 1, to read that the second printing was in 1987."

1995 Statement: "The Real Comet Press designates its first editions on the copyright page. Most of our titles have a series of numbers with the year on the left and the printing on the right: 93 94 95 96 97 98 99 10 9 8 7 6 5 4 3 2 1.

"As each printing is issued, numbers are deleted in order to indicate the printing and the year in which it was made: 91 92 93 94 95 10 9 8 7 6 5 4 3. Some titles specify first edition. All editions indicate if the title is an original publication or a reprint. If, in a reprint, there are changes from the original, or if the book is a second or subsequent edition, the copyright page will indicate so."

2001 Statement: *See* 1995 Statement

REAL PEOPLE PRESS

1976 Statement: "So far, none of our books has been altered in subsequent printings. The first printing is indicated on the © page thusly:

1 2 3 4 5 6 Printing 76 75 74

"The second printing has the '1' deleted:

2 3 4 5 6 Printing 76 75 74."

1981 Statement: The 1976 statement is still accurate. However, not all of their books have remained unaltered in subsequent printings.

1988 Statement: *See* 1981 Statement

2001 Statement: "The [previous statements] are still correct. It is very rarely that we alter a book in a subsequent printing, and then the changes are very minor updates."

RECOLLECTIONS (UNITED KINGDOM)

2001 Statement: *See* 2001 Statement of George Mann Books (United Kingdom)

RECTOR PRESS LTD.

1994 Statement: The first printing of a first edition is indicated by the number line 1 2 3 4 5 6 7 8 9 10. The lowest number showing indicates the printing.

2001 Statement: *See* 1994 Statement

RED CRANE BOOKS

1994 Statement: "We designate first editions by stating that on the copyright page. The copyright page also notes subsequent printings, for example, Second Printing, etc."

2000 Statement: "We designate first editions on the copyright page. The copyright page also notes subsequent printings, for example, Second Printing, etc."

RED DEER COLLEGE PRESS (CANADA)

1995 Statement: "Red Deer College Press designates first printings numerically with: 5 4 3 2 1. These numbers are found on the copyright page. When a book is reprinted we delete the last number in the series. This method of designating first printings has been in use since 1993. Prior to that time, we used no consistent method for designating first printings."

2001 Statement: *See* 2001 Statement of Red Deer Press (Canada)

RED DEER PRESS (CANADA)

2001 Statement: "Red Deer Press designates first printings numerically with: 5 4 3 2 1. These numbers are found on the copyright page. When a book is reprinted we delete the last number in the series."

RED DRAGON PRESS

2001 Statement: "We state 'First printing' on the copyright page."

RED DUST, INC.

1976 Statement: "Every Red Dust Book is a first edition. We have no special way of designating it—if it ran to a second edition—we would say second possibly on copyright page."

1981 Statement: "We have recently reprinted *The Libera Me Domine* and *Passacaglia*, Pinget 500 copies each and also *The Park*, Sollers. We did not mark these new editions 2nd edition. Otherwise all our other books are still in their first edition. Next time we reprint I will try to remember to put 2nd edition in."

1988 Statement: "We reprinted *The Third Wedding*. In it we put: Paperback edition: 1986 (First edition 1971)."

1993 Statement: "We have had no reprints since 1988. We will mark any reprints 2nd edition."

2000 Statement: "First editions are not marked but reprinted editions will be marked: 2nd, 3rd, etc. Reprintings are very small, about 500 copies. Initial printings never exceed 1000.

"*Third Wedding* has been reprinted in the paper edition so that it is now in its 2nd paper edition

"*The Nature of Things,* Francis Ponge, translated by Lee Fahnestock is being reprinted 1000 copies. It is marked as a second edition. The *Libera Me Domine* and *Passacaglia*, Robert Pinget, will soon be reprinted in their first paperback edition. (They have already been reprinted in hard cover once.) *Someone* and *Fable,* Pinget, will be reprinted in their first paperback edition—they were never reprinted in hard cover."

RED EYE PRESS, INC.

2001 Statement: "Red Eye Press, Inc. uses a descending string that ends with the current printing, such as: 20, 19, 18, 17, 16, 15 which indicates that this book is from the 15th printing. First editions are not identified as such, but first editions and printings are indicated by the following string: 10, 9, 8, 7, 6, 5, 4, 3, 2, 1 preceded by the words: First printing, month, year. Titles with subsequent editions are listed as such with each edition listed accompanied by the year of publication such as:

First edition ©1982
Second edition ©1988
Third edition ©1997

(and)

9 8 7 6 5 4 3 printing, 3rd edition,
42nd printing all editions

"We've changed this a number of times and seem to have settled on this format last year, 2000."

RED FOX (UNITED KINGDOM)

1994 Statement: *See* 1994 Statement of Random House UK Limited (United Kingdom)

2000 Statement: *See* 2000 Statement of The Random House Group Limited (United Kingdom)

RED HEN PRESS

2000 Statement: "We include on the copyright page the words 'First Edition' only. All subsequent editions are identified second, third etc. No statement is made to identify a first printing; however subsequent printings are identified (second, third . . .) and reference is made to the date of the first printing in all subsequent printings."

THE RED HERRING POETS

1994 Statement: "Since we only print first editions—we have no special way to designate first printings."

RED MOON PRESS

2001 Statement: "We do not identify a first printing; we do identify subsequent printings as such on the copyright page."

THE RED ROSE STUDIO

1994 Statement: "We do not indicate whether it is a first printing. However, any future printings of *Pennsylvania Profiles* will indicate 'First Printing,' etc."

RED WAGON BOOKS

2001 Statement: *See* 2001 Statement of Harcourt, Inc.

REDBIRD PRESS, INC.

1995 Statement: "Redbird Press prints on the copyright page: First edition, followed by: —printing—month—year."

REDWORDS (UNITED KINGDOM)

2001 Statement: *See* 2001 Statement of Bookmarks Publications (United Kingdom)

REED BOOKS AUSTRALIA (AUSTRALIA)

1995 Statement: "Reed Books Australia titles are not distinguished in any particular manner at first editions."

REED BOOKS PTY., LTD. (AUSTRALIA)

1989 Statement: "The company you have listed as A. H. & A. W. Reed Pty. Ltd. is now the holding company, the operating company being Reed Books Pty. Ltd.

"Our designation of first printings has not changed and all imprints follow this practice."

See 1981 Statement of A. H. & A. W. Reed Pty., Ltd. (Australia)

REED CHILDREN'S BOOKS (NEW ZEALAND)

2000 Statement: *See* 2000 Statement of Reed Publishing (NZ) Ltd (New Zealand)

REED CONSUMER BOOKS (UNITED KINGDOM)

1994 Statement: "Reed Consumer Books is a division of Reed International Books and includes the following imprints: *Hamlyn; Mitchell Beazley; George Philip; Osprey; William Heinemann; Methuen; Secker & Warburg; Sinclair-Stevenson.*

"Children's publications include the following imprints and usually state 'imprint of Reed Children's Books' (Reed Children's Books is a subdivision of Reed Consumer Books): *Hamlyn Children's Books; Heinemann Young Books; Methuen Children's Books.* Some Heinemann Children's books carry the *William Heinemann* imprint.

"All imprints should carry the words 'First published in Great Britain in [year];' this combined with the absence of reprint or subsequent edition information should indicate a first printing."

REED FOR KIDS (NEW ZEALAND)

1994 Statement: *See* 1994 Statement of Reed Publishing (NZ) Ltd (New Zealand)

A. H. & A. W. REED PTY., LTD. (AUSTRALIA)

1981 Statement: "This company designates the first edition of any book simply by giving the date of publication on the Imprint Page. Any subsequent reprinting or revised edition is notified by adding further date(s) in the same place."

1989 Statement: *See* 1989 Statement of Reed Books Pty., Ltd. (Australia)

REED PUBLISHING (NZ) LTD (NEW ZEALAND)

1994 Statement: "Our first editions may be identified by a statement similar to the following:

First published 1994 by Reed Books,
a division of Reed Publishing (NZ) Ltd.

"Reprints or revised editions may be identified by way of separate statements such as:

Reprinted 1994

or

Second edition 1994

"Other divisions and imprints within the company follow a similar practice. These include Heinemann New Zealand, Reed for Kids, Minerva NZ, Mandarin NZ, Secker & Warburg (NZ).

"I think this way of designating first editions has been in force for more than twenty years."

2000 Statement: "The information [in the 1994 Statement] is still correct though we do not publish under Minerva NZ, Mandarin NZ, Secker & Warburg (NZ) or Reed For Kids. Our local children's imprint is Reed Children's Books."

REFERENCE PUBLICATIONS, INC.

1994 Statement: "We have no statement designating first printings. Second or revised printings are so annotated; therefore editions with the copyright date and no other identification are first editions."

2000 Statement: *See* 1994 Statement

REFERENCE SERVICE PRESS

2000 Statement: "We identify the first printing of a first edition by the number line 10 9 8 7 6 5 4 3 2 1."

REFLECTED IMAGES PUBLISHERS

1994 Statement: *See* 1994 Statement of Webb Research Group
2000 Statement: *See* 2000 Statement of Webb Research Group Publishers

REGAN BOOKS
2001 Statement: *See* 2001 Statement of HarperCollinsPublishers

JUDITH REGAN BOOKS
1993 Statement: *See* 1993 Statement of HarperCollins Publishers
2001 Statement: *See* 2001 Statement of Regan Books

REGENCY
1994 Statement: *See* 1994 Statement of Thomas Nelson Publishers

REGENT HOUSE, PUBLISHERS, INC.
1947 Statement: "All titles carry the statement on the title page: FIRST EDITION."

REGENT PRESS
2001 Statement: "We're inconsistent in how we indicate first editions. Usually, we don't say anything, but then, in later editions say second, third, etc. Sometimes, we'll say 'First Edition' on the copyright page."

THE REGENTS PRESS OF KANSAS
1976 Statement: "The first printing does not say 'First printing.' The later printings are so labeled on © page.

"We label a second printing as 'Second printing (date).' It is not considered a new edition, even if a few corrections have been made."
1981 Statement: *See* 1976 Statement
1988 Statement: *See* 1988 Statement of University Press of Kansas

HENRY REGNERY COMPANY
1976 Statement: "The Henry Regnery Company does not have a method of designating first editions or first printings of first editions.

"A few Regnery books carried a printing code in 1974:
1 2 3 4 5 6 7   PY   9 8 7 6 5 4. The '1' in the printing row would be deleted in the second printing 2 3 4 5 6 7   PY   9 8 7 6 5 4. The code has been dropped and we do not intend to use it again."
1988 Statement: *See* 1988 Statement of Regnery Gateway, Inc.

REGNERY GATEWAY, INC.
1988 Statement: "We do not identify 'first editions' when we print them, although we will identify subsequent printings.

"Regnery Gateway, Inc. was formerly named Henry Regnery Co. The name change occurred in 1976."
1993 Statement: "Regnery Gateway, Inc. identifies first printings with a uniform code placed on each title's copyright page.
10 9 8 7 6 5 4 3 2 1
"When a book is reprinted for the first time, we will delete the '1' from the end of the line. The same method is used for all subsequent printings.

"Occasionally, we will also include a line indicating successive years in which the reprinting occurs. Years are deleted as necessary."
2000 Statement: *See* 2000 Statement of Regnery Publishing

REGNERY PUBLISHING
2000 Statement: *See* 1993 Statement of Regnery Gateway, Inc.

REGNUM (UNITED KINGDOM)
2000 Statement: *See* 2000 Statement of The Paternoster Press Ltd. (United Kingdom)

REGULAR BAPTIST PRESS
1994 Statement: "We have no special way to designate first printings. We indicate revisions with the words 'Revised Edition.' We indicate further printings with the identification of the number and the year (e.g., Third printing—1994). This information appears on the same page as our copyright information."

2000 Statement: *See* 1994 Statement. "Make one small change [in the second sentence]: We indicate *major* revisions with the words 'Revised Edition.' "

THE REILLY & LEE CO., INC.
1937 Statement: "In the future we intend to put 'First Printing' on the copyright page and when that edition is exhausted the 'First Printing' will be removed and no other mark will be put in its place."

1947 Statement: "We put 'First Printing' on the copyright page and when that edition is exhausted the 'First Printing' will be removed and no other mark will be put in its place."

MAX REINHARDT (UNITED KINGDOM)
1988 Statement: *See* 1988 Statement of The Bodley Head Limited (United Kingdom)

REINHARDT BOOKS (UNITED KINGDOM)
1994 Statement: "We normally say: First published, with the dates of the year—and that is the important statement, usually followed by the copyright notice of either the author or ourselves—it is usually the same year."

RELEASE PRESS
1976 Statement: "We distinguish our first editions with the statement 'first printing' on the verso of the title page. We have not had occasion to go into any printings or editions beyond the first, so anyone obtaining any of our 11 books is assured of a first ed."

RELIGIOUS EDUCATION PRESS
1995 Statement: "We identify the first printing of a first edition with the following number line: 10 9 8 7 6 5 4 3 2 1. Subsequent printings delete the number from the right to the left.

"No additional statement is listed for first editions. The copyright information is also listed."

2000 Statement: *See* 1995 Statement

RELIGIOUS RESEARCH PRESS
1994 Statement: First printings are not identified.

RELIGIOUS TRACT SOCIETY (UNITED KINGDOM)
See The Lutterworth Press (United Kingdom)

RENAISSANCE HOUSE PUBLISHERS
1988 Statement: "Renaissance House Publishers makes no specific statement of first edition status unless the book is published as a limited edition. In that event, we state on the copyright page:

This edition limited to XXXX (signed and numbered)
copies, of which this is number XXXX.

"It can be assumed that our books are first editions unless noted otherwise on the copyright page. Subsequent editions are always noted by an addition to the copyright page that reads in the manner of this example:

First printing, February 1985
Second printing April, 1985
Third printing March, 1988

"The above example refers to subsequent printings where the text is substantially unaltered. Should there be extensive revisions, we would indicate (e.g.): Revised edition April, 1988."

1993 Statement: "We also use the declining number system to show which printing a book is in. If . . . all numbers (1-10) [are present] on the copyright page, that would indicate a first edition."

RENDEZ-VOUS PRESS (CANADA)
2001 Statement: *See* 2001 Statement of Napoleon Publishing/Rendez-vous Press (Canada)

REPRINT CO. PUBLISHERS
1994 Statement: "We do identify the edition of the original printing from which we work. In the instance of a new, or original publication, we state on the copyright page that this is 'an original edition and the date.' "
2001 Statement: *See* 1994 Statement

THE RESEARCH INSTITUTE FOR INNER ASIAN STUDIES
1994 Statement: "Our volumes list the year of printing, and, if reprinted, that year as well."
2001 Statement: *See* 1994 Statement

RESEARCH PRESS
1994 Statement: "We designate the first printing of a book by number and by year of that printing of the copyright page.

5 4 3 2 1 94 95 96 97 98

"This indicates that the book is in its first printing, which was in 1994.

"When a book is revised, the copyright page states 'Revised Edition' with the year of the revised edition's publication."
2000 Statement: *See* 1994 Statement

RESEARCH PUBLISHING COMPANY
1947 Statement: "We have not given the matter any consideration whatsoever and there is nothing in any of our publications to indicate whether first

or other printing. We, ourselves, identify the various printings by color of cloth or some such matter."

RESOURCE PUBLICATIONS, INC.

1994 Statement: "A first printing of a Resource Publications, Inc. book may be identified by the following line printed on the copyright page:

YR YR YR YR YR / 5 4 3 2 1

"We started using this method in 1987. Previously, there was no way to tell which printing a book represented, unless a person knew of any text corrections from earlier printings, or unless the copyright date was updated.

"We have no imprints or subsidiaries at this time.

"Subsequent *editions* of a book may be identified by display type on the cover announcing a revised edition and by the printing history printed on the copyright page."

2000 Statement: *See* 1994 Statement

RESOURCES FOR THE FUTURE

1994 Statement: "We do not identify first editions *per se*, but number successive reprintings."

2000 Statement: "We do not identify first printings, but number successive reprintings. We do not provide new reprint numbers for print-on-demand copies."

FLEMING H. REVELL COMPANY

1947 Statement: "Formerly, we identified first editions of our books, but more recently we have not done so, except that the jacket of the second and subsequent editions are so indicated so that around the office and generally through the trade, a Revell Company book that has no edition indicated is a first edition."

Statement for 1960: First printings are not so marked.

1976 Statement: "We do not indicate on a First Edition that it is the first edition."

1981, 2000 Statements: *See* 1976 Statement.

See also Baker Book House

REVIEW AND HERALD PUBLISHING ASSOCIATION

1994 Statement: "We print the figures 1 2 3 4 5 6 7 8 9 0 on the copyright page. For the first reprint we remove the one, and so on consecutively. The first figure remaining indicates the number of printing. This is mostly for identification within the trade. For purposes of promotion we may occasionally add, 'Fifth printing,' etc. We have no subsidiaries."

2000 Statement: *See* 1994 Statement

REYNAL AND HITCHCOCK, INC.
(Merged with Harcourt, Brace and Co., Inc., January 2, 1948.)

1937 Statement: "For some time now The John Day Company has adopted the following method of distinguishing first editions: On the first printing copyright page appears only the copyright notice: Copyright, 1936, by John Doe, and the usual printer's imprint: Printed in the United States of America by The John Smith Printing Company. Lately we have included a paragraph: All rights reserved, including the right to reproduce this book or portions thereof in any form. However, all other printings of the same book may be distinguished by: Second printing, Jan. 1936. Third printing, February 1936, et cetera, with the proper month inserted.

"You will notice that 'John Day & Co.' is no longer used; when the book is wholly owned by The John Day Company 'The John Day Company, New York' appears on the title page.

"The same method applies to Reynal and Hitchcock; that is, no notice of first printing appears on the first edition, but notices of second, third, and fourth printings being added as is the case. In 1935, The John Day Company was associated with Reynal and Hitchcock, and on the title page of books published under this new association you will find the imprint: 'a John Day Book, Reynal and Hitchcock, New York.' This method of imprinting our books is similar to The Atlantic Monthly Press and Little, Brown & Co., with which you may be familiar. On the copyright page of books put out under the joint imprint you will find on both first printing and subsequent printings the words: Published by John Day in association with Reynal and Hitchcock. However, this has no bearing on the edition printings."

1947 Statement: "On a first printing we carry only the copyright line (Copyright, author or Reynal & Hitchcock, as the case may be, date) and the usual short paragraph about 'all rights reserved, etc.'

"On a second printing we add a line saying simply 'Second Printing.' And on subsequent printings we change this line each time to read 'Third Printing' or 'Fourth Printing' and so on.

"John Day Company books are no longer published in association with Reynal & Hitchcock."

1948 Statement: "Reynal and Hitchcock books will from time to time appear under that imprint and will carry a Reynal and Hitchcock copyright line and a Reynal and Hitchcock title page with the sometime exception of a book appearing with a Harcourt, Brace title page but with the following annotation: A Reynal and Hitchcock book.

"Reynal and Hitchcock books will no longer be identified with respect to their first printings according to the method formerly used. Both Reynal and Hitchcock books and Harcourt, Brace books will be identified with respect to first printings according to Harcourt, Brace's 1947 statement."

RFF PRESS
2000 Statement: *See* 2000 Statement of Resources for the Future

RIBA PUBLICATIONS (UNITED KINGDOM)
1994 Statement: "We do not specifically indicate first printings or first editions. A list of all editions and reprints with updates is produced on the reverse of the title page, along with the other bibliographic details. The company has always operated this dating policy."

RICCARDI PRESS (UNITED KINGDOM)

1937 Statement: *See* 1937 Statement of Medici Society, Limited (United Kingdom)

RICE UNIVERSITY PRESS

1988 Statement: "First editions are indicated as such on the copyright page along with the year of publication, as are subsequent printings. Sometimes additional numeric sequence appears on the copyright page to indicate impressions."

1993 Statement: *See* 1988 Statement

2001 Statement: Rice University Press ceased operations December 31, 1996.

RICH & COWAN, LIMITED (UNITED KINGDOM)

1937 Statement: "It is our custom now to put 'first printing 1936' 'second printing—such and such a date.' In special occasions, as with H. V. Morton, we put the number printed of the first edition.

"Our early system was to include the month of publication."

1947 Statement: "Owing to war-time production conditions we have had to omit dating our books and we are not yet reverting to the pre-war practice. The system shown on our previous statement was, of course, in use up to 1940."

RICHARDS PRESS, LTD. (UNITED KINGDOM)

1928 Statement: "It may be taken that any book published by us is the first edition unless there appears a note on the back of the title page indicating more than one printing. It is possible that in a few cases the fact that the book is not a first edition may be indicated by the words 'cheap edition' or 'new edition' on the title page itself."

1937, 1947 Statements: *See* 1928 Statement

RIDER (UNITED KINGDOM)

1988 Statement: *See* 1988 Statement of Century Hutchinson Publishing Group Limited (United Kingdom)

1994 Statement: *See* 1994 Statement of Random House UK Limited (United Kingdom)

2000 Statement: *See* 2000 Statement of The Random House Group Limited (United Kingdom)

THE RIDGE PRESS, INC.

1976 Statement: Ridge Press does not designate first editions and never has.

LYNNE RIENNER PUBLISHERS INC.

1994 Statement: "We do not denote first editions—we do indicate second and third printings, etc., on the © pages of our books, and subsequent editions on the front covers and title pages."

2000 Statement: *See* 1994 Statement

RIGBY HEINEMANN (AUSTRALIA)
1994 Statement: "We do not distinguish first editions in any particular way
. . . and we do not intend to designate first editions in a particular manner at
present."

RIGBY LIMITED (AUSTRALIA)
1976 Statement: "In answer to your question, we do not have any particular
method of identifying first editions apart from a line on the imprint page
reading 'First published in Australia 19..' If the book is reprinted, this line
would be followed by others giving the year of reprint. We have not used any
method apart from this."
1981 Statement: *See* 1981 Statement of Rigby Publishers Limited (Australia)

RIGBY PUBLISHERS LIMITED (AUSTRALIA)
1981 Statement: "In answer to your question, we have not changed our
method of indicating first impressions and editions of a book."
See 1976 Statement of Rigby Limited (Australia)
1988 Statement: *See* 1988 Statement of Kevin Weldon & Associates Pty.
Ltd. (Australia)

RIGHT WAY (UNITED KINGDOM)
1994, 2000 Statements: *See* 1994 Statement of Elliot Right Way Books,
Publishers (United Kingdom)

RINEHART & COMPANY, INC.
1947 Statement: "Rinehart first printings can be identified by the colophon
of an 'R' enclosed in a circle which appears immediately above the copyright
line in all first printings of our books. On subsequent printings the colophon
does not appear. The present colophon was adopted when our name was
changed from Farrar and Rinehart, Inc., to Rinehart and Co., Inc., on January
1st, 1946."

THE RIO GRANDE PRESS, INC.
1976 Statement: "Our books are all reprints of rare or scarce books.

"We identify all of our first editions (all of our EDITIONS, really) by a
comment just above our logo on the title page—on The Rio Grande Press title
page. We indicate whether this is a first printing, a second printing, third,
fourth etc.

"Where we have not done this, as in the very beginning (1962), there would
be an indication of a subsequent printing. For instance, in some of our very
first reprints, we indicated the year of the reprint, but after a year or so of
business, we began inserting the print designation. So if there is no indication
other than the date, it is one of our first editions. Since the latter part of 1963,
all of our editions have referred to the 'printing' by its chronology."
1981 Statement: "From 1962 (when The Rio Grande Press, Inc., started in
business), thru 1963, we designated the year of publication just above our
logo on the copyright page of our edition. During those two years, we did not
identify the edition any further than that, so any of our editions that read 1962

or 1963 above our logo on the copyright page would be a 'first edition' of TRGP.

"However, commencing in 1964, we began to identify an edition by indicating 'First Printing 1964,' or 'Second Printing 1971,' etc. Any title we published after (including) 1964 would indicate what printing it was, i.e., second, third, fourth, etc.

"But not many of our titles go into subsequent printings. Our title *Turquois*, for instance, did go into 10 printings. *Black Range Tales* has had several printings, as have *Navajo Weaving, Hopi Katcinas, Navajo Shepherd and Weaver*, and others.

"But if the imprint above the logo on the title page says 1963 or 1964, then yes, it is one of our 'first editions.' "

1988 Statement: "All editions since 1963 are identified on the title page above our logo—

1st, 2nd, 3rd, 4th, etc."

1993 Statement: *See* 1988 Statement

RISING MOON

2000 Statement: *See* 2000 Statement of Northland Publishing

RISING TIDE PRESS

1995 Statement: "All of our first editions include the words 'First Edition' or 'First Printing.' We then follow with the year of publication, all of this on the Copyright Page. Our imprints and subsidiaries as a rule follow this procedure. Generally, there are no exceptions. Subsequent printings are differentiated by using the phrase 'Second Printing' followed by the year. All these procedures began in 1954."

2000 Statement: *See* 1995 Statement

RIVER CITY PRESS

2001 Statement: *See* 2000 Statement of Black Belt Press

RIVERCROSS PUBLISHING, INC.

1995 Statement: "We are book publishers who identify the first publication of a book as 'First Edition' on the copyright page. When that title goes back to press for a second printing, we add a line to the copyright page which reads, 'Second Printing.' We change the number for subsequent printings.

"If a title has substantial revisions or additions, not simply corrections of typos, it is designated as a Second or Revised or Enlarged Edition, and usually a combination of those terms to indicate as closely as possible what changes have been made."

THE RIVERDALE CO.

1995 Statement: The first printing is not identified.

RIVERHEAD (AUSTRALIA)

2000 Statement: *See* 2000 Statement of Penguin Books Australia Ltd (Australia)

RIVERHEAD BOOKS
1995 Statement: *See* 1995 Statement of The Berkley Publishing Group
2000 Statement: *See* 2000 Statement of The Berkley Publishing Group

RIVEROAK PUBLISHING
2001 Statement: "We do not identify a first printing; we do identify subsequent printings on the copyright page."

RIVERRUN PRESS INC.
1994 Statement: "We will begin using number lines in 1995. They will read '1 2 3 4 5 6 7 8 9' with a three-letter printer's code centered below the number line.

> First published in the United States in [year]
> by Riverrun Press, Inc.,
> 1170 Broadway,
> New York, NY 10001

"If a book was initially acquired in the U.K., substitute 'in Great Britain' for 'the United States'; below will appear 'and in the United States in [year] by . . . .' "

RIVERSIDE BOOK CO. INC.
1994 Statement: First printings are not identified.

RIVERSIDE PUBLISHING COMPANY
1993 Statement: *See* 1993 Statement of Clarion Books
2000 Statement: "Riverside Publishing is a subsidiary of Houghton Mifflin, as is Clarion Books. However, there is no direct connection between Riverside and Clarion. Please change reference to Houghton Mifflin."
See 2000 Statement of Houghton Mifflin Company

RIVERSWIFT (UNITED KINGDOM)
1994 Statement: *See* 1994 Statement of Random House UK Limited (United Kingdom)
2000 Statement: *See* 2000 Statement of The Random House Group Limited (United Kingdom)

RIZZOLI INTERNATIONAL PUBLICATIONS, INC.
1981 Statement: "On copyright page:
First edition:

> First published in the United States of America in 1981 by
> Rizzoli International Publications, Inc.
> 712 Fifth Avenue, New York, NY 10019

"Any subsequent edition:

> First published in the United States of America in 1981 by
> Rizzoli International Publications, Inc.
> 712 Fifth Avenue, New York, NY 10019
> Second impression (or second edition) 1982
> Third impression (or third revised (if so) edition) 1983

1988 Statement: *See* 1981 Statement. Note that publisher's address will now read 597 Fifth Avenue, New York, NY 10017.
1993 Statement: *See* 1988 Statement

ROADMASTER PUBLISHING (UNITED KINGDOM)
2001 Statement: "We do not identify a first printing; we do identify subsequent printings as such on the copyright page."

SKELTON ROBINSON (UNITED KINGDOM)
(Formerly Citizen Press, Ltd.)
1947 Statement: "Not marked on first editions, but in cases of second impressions and editions, printed on reverse of bastard title-page."

ROC
1993, 2000 Statements: *See* 1993 Statement of Dutton Signet

THE ROCK SPRING COLLECTION
OF JAPANESE LITERATURE
2000 Statement: *See* 2000 Statement of Stone Bridge Press

ROCKBRIDGE PUBLISHING CO.
1994 Statement: "On copyright page we print First Edition (or subsequent edition) and list numbers 1 through 10. The lowest number indicates which printing it is."
2000 Statement: "Titles by Rockbridge Publishing, an imprint of Howell Press Inc., are first edition, first printing, unless explicitly stated otherwise on the copyright page."

ROCKLIFF PUBLISHING CORPORATION, LIMITED
(UNITED KINGDOM)
(Practical Press, Ltd. and Art Trade Press, Ltd., associates.)
1947 Statement: "We follow the custom as given in *Rules for Compositors and Readers* of the Oxford University Press, namely the edition is indicated on the reverse of the title page. The first edition includes the date of the copyright only. All subsequent editions and impressions are indicated under the copyright line."

ROCKPORT PRESS, INC.
1947 Statement: "The words FIRST EDITION appear on the copyright page of all first editions, in small caps.

"Subsequent printings of first editions will bear proper identification in italics on the copyright page, i.e. 'Second Printing,' etc."

ROCKY MOUNTAIN BOOKS (CANADA)
1995 Statement: "First editions can be identified by there being no statement of edition on the copyright page. Further printings or new editions will always have a statement to that effect on the copyright page."
2001 Statement: *See* 1995 Statement

ROCKY MOUNTAIN CREATIVE ARTS JOURNAL & BOOKS
2000 Statement: *See* 2000 Statement of The Academic & Arts Press

ROD & STAFF PUBLISHERS INC.
2000 Statement: "We identify the first printing of a first edition by the following number line:

Code no. 99-1

"The '99' would indicate the year first printed, the '1' would indicate that it was a first printing. For reprints, the line would show:

Code no. 79-4-91

"The '79' would indicate the year first printed, the '4' indicates the fourth printing, the '91' indicates the year last printed."

RODALE PRESS
(Successor to Rodale Publications, Inc.)

1947 Statement: "At the present time we have no way of identifying the first printings of our books."

1976 Statement: "We here at Rodale Press identify our first editions by indicating on the copyright page what printing that particular edition is. Obviously if the book has 'First Printing', it is the first edition. If it has 'Second Printing', 'Third Printing', etc. it is a later printing. Also if a book is a first edition, we sometimes make no note at all on the copyright page as to what printing the book is in."

1981 Statement: "We don't use the system described to you in 1976, but I really can't pinpoint exactly when we changed. On the copyright page, our books have a line of numbers, which we call the reprint line. It looks like this:

2 4 6 8 10 9 7 5 3 1

"The lowest number represents the number of the printing. If the number 1 is there, you have a copy from the first printing, if the line is:

6 8 10 9 7 5

you have a copy from the fifth printing.

"I don't know how pertinent this is for a book about first editions, but we have many books that go through multiple—10 or 20 or 30—printings. So after the tenth printing, a new reprint line is used:

12 14 16 18 20 19 17 15 13 11

"And so on into higher and higher numbers of printings."

1988 Statement: *See* 1981 Statement

1993 Statement: *See* 1981 Statement, but with one addition. "These [number] lines end with the term 'hardcover' or 'paperback' to designate the version, as some of our first printings are in paperback. [There was] probably a more deliberate effort to include [this] with each title since 1988."

GEORGE RONALD PUBLISHER LTD (UNITED KINGDOM)
1994 Statement: "George Ronald first started publishing in the 1940s as a general publisher. Until the late 1960s there was no house style and it is difficult to identify first editions unless they have 'FIRST EDITION' printed on them. However, few of the titles during the 1950s and 1960s were reprinted. In the early 1950s some George Ronald books have the address 2

Alfred Street, Oxford and others are marked Wheatley, Oxford. In the late 1950s and early 60s George Ronald was based in London.

"Our house style, which dates back to the early 1970s, for the back of the title page is:

George Ronald, Publisher
46 High Street, Kidlington, Oxford OX5 2DN
© [Author], [date]
All rights reserved

"If a book has been reprinted, the date of the original printing is given followed by the dates of reprints."

2000 Statement: *See* 1994 Statement

RONIN PUBLISHING, INC.

1995 Statement: "We use 1 2 3 4 5 6 7 8 9 0. When reprinted, we delete figure 1, etc. and insert '2nd, 3rd, etc. printing' on copyright page."

2000 Statement: First editions have not been designated since 1997.

RONSDALE PRESS (CANADA)

2001 Statement: "We give no indication of the first printing of a first edition, but we do indicate second and third printings on the copyright page."

THE ROSE & NEFR PRESS

1994 Statement: "We are a very small press, and usually do not distinguish between different printings of the same book. If substantive changes have been made we will append 'revised and corrected' to the title; if the changes are large, we will say 'second edition.'

"When we do distinguish between printings, it is by a line of numbers: 1 2 3 4 5 6 7 8 9 0. The lowest number remaining is the printing."

ROSENDALE PRESS LTD. (UNITED KINGDOM)

1994 Statement: "Rosendale Press titles simply list the date of first publication on the imprint page, and subsequent printings are listed underneath."

BERTRAM ROTA (PUBLISHING) LTD
(UNITED KINGDOM)

1989 Statement: "With one solitary exception all the books we have published have been first editions and we have never reprinted them. The solitary new edition bore its own date and the date of the original edition on the verso of the title-page.

"London Limited Editions, by definition, publishes only first printings."

1995, 2001 Statements: *See* 1989 Statement

ROTH FAMILY FOUNDATION BOOK IN AMERICAN MUSIC

2000 Statement: *See* 2000 Statement of University of California Press

ROTOVISION

2000 Statement: *See* 2000 Statement of Butterworth-Heinemann

ROUGH GUIDES (AUSTRALIA)
2000 Statement: *See* 2000 Statement of Penguin Books Australia Ltd (Australia)

ROUGH GUIDES LTD. (UNITED KINGDOM)
1994 Statement: "We use a pretty standard form to designate editions:
   This first edition published MONTH/YEAR
   by Rough Guides Ltd,
followed by our address.

"For subsequent editions, we replace first with second, etc.

"Pre-1992 editions of the guides have different forms, as they were published by Harrap Columbus in the UK and Prentice Hall in the US, and pre-1987, worldwide by Routledge & Kegan Paul."

2001 Statement: "The 1994 statement is still correct, as far as it goes. In order to cover what happens when we reprint . . . the statement may be corrected to read:
   'This first edition published MONTH/YEAR' by Rough Guides Ltd, followed by our address. Any reprints are recorded by the addition of 'Reprinted in MONTH/YEAR,' following the company address."

THE ROUND HALL PRESS (REPUBLIC OF IRELAND)
1994 Statement: *See* 1994 Statement of Irish Academic Press Limited (Republic of Ireland)

ROUNDHOUSE PRESS
2000 Statement: *See* 2000 Statement of Heyday Books

ROUNDHOUSE PUBLISHING LTD. (UNITED KINGDOM)
1994 Statement: "We print the year of publication above our name and address on the title verso with the number sequence 5 4 3 2 1 shown immediately below. The lowest number in the sequence indicating the edition, which is then supplemented by the inclusion of a line indicating *Reprinted 1994*—or whatever date. The same applies to our imprint Roundhouse Reference Books, and has been the adopted method of designation used since the company was formed in 1991."

2000 Statement: *See* 1994 Statement

ROUNDHOUSE REFERENCE BOOKS (UNITED KINGDOM)
1994, 2000 Statements: *See* 1994 Statement of Roundhouse Publishing Ltd. (United Kingdom)

THE ROUNDWOOD PRESS (1978) LIMITED
(UNITED KINGDOM)
1981 Statement: "The Roundwood Press (Publishers) Limited ceased to trade in April 1978 and a new company, The Roundwood Press (1978) Limited, took over all the responsibilities of the old company including the publishing side.

"Our method of designating the first printing of a first edition is unchanged [since the 1976 statement of The Roundwood Press (Publishers), Ltd.]."

See also 1976 Statement of The Roundwood Press (Publishers), Ltd. (United Kingdom)

THE ROUNDWOOD PRESS (PUBLISHERS), LTD.
(UNITED KINGDOM)

1976 Statement: "Our practice is as follows: The imprint on the verso of the title page, with the copyright symbol, will show whether the book is a first edition. If the book has been reprinted it will say as much on this page, i.e. 'second impression' or similar. If there is nothing else on this page, then it may be safely assumed that it is the first printing of a first edition.

"Actually, our books are usually the first printing of a first edition, or alternatively an updated edition of a work long out of print, and we always give the most explicit information to this effect."

1981 Statement: *See* 1981 Statement of The Roundwood Press (1978) Limited (United Kingdom)

ROUTLEDGE

1988, 1994 Statements: *See* 1988 Statement of Routledge, Chapman and Hall, Inc.

ROUTLEDGE (UNITED KINGDOM)

1988 Statement: *See* 1988 Statement of Associated Book Publishers (UK) Ltd. (United Kingdom)

1994 Statement: A first printing will carry the statement "First published (date)" on the copyright page.

2000 Statement: See 1994 Statement, but note that Routledge is now an imprint of the Taylor & Francis Group.

ROUTLEDGE, CHAPMAN AND HALL, INC.

1988 Statement: "Methuen, Inc. has changed its name to Routledge, Chapman and Hall, Inc. and now publishes under the two imprints of Routledge, and of Chapman and Hall.

"New editions are identified by the statement 'first published 1988/first published in the USA 1988.' Subsequent printings are designated either by 'reprinted 1987, 1988' or 'second impression 1988.' "

ROUTLEDGE, CHAPMAN, AND HALL
(UNITED KINGDOM)

1988 Statement: *See* 1988 Statement of Associated Book Publishers (UK) Ltd. (United Kingdom)

ROUTLEDGE & KEGAN PAUL LTD. (UNITED KINGDOM)

1976 Statement: "Our present practice is to put on the back of the title page the words 'First published 1977 by Routledge & Kegan Paul Ltd.' and any reprint would have, lower down, the words 'Reprinted in 1978.'

"Previously, our methods were more slovenly, particularly in the last century, where finding the date of an impression is a matter of guesswork and comparing our London and American addresses.

"This information applies equally to George Routledge & Sons Ltd., and Kegan Paul, Trench, Trubner."

1981 Statement: *See* 1976 Statement

ROUTLEDGE & KEGAN PAUL OF AMERICA LTD.

1981 Statement: "For books printed in the USA, the phrase: 'first published (date)' will appear on the copyright page. For a first edition, the date will correspond to the copyright date.

"Any subsequent printings are indicated on [the copyright] page as reprints. This procedure is the same for all our imprints."

GEORGE ROUTLEDGE & SONS, LTD.
(UNITED KINGDOM)

1947 Statement: "If there is no statement at all as to a second or later edition or impression, the assumption, of course, is that the book is a first edition. In the case of reprints, or new editions, we state this on the reverse of the title page.

"We regret we cannot tell you the date on which this method was started but it has been going on now for a very long period."

1976 Statement: *See* 1976 Statement of Routledge & Kegan Paul Ltd. (United Kingdom)

GEORGE ROUTLEDGE & SONS, LTD., KEGAN PAUL, TRENCH, TRUBNER & CO., LTD.
(UNITED KINGDOM)

1928 Statement: *See* 1937 Statement

1937 Statement: "If there is no statement at all as to a second or later edition or impression, the assumption, of course, is that the book is a first edition. In the case of reprints, or new editions, we state this on the reverse of the title page.

"We regret we cannot tell you the date on which this method was started but it has been going on now for a very long period."

ROWLAND WARD LIMITED (UNITED KINGDOM)

1976 Statement: "As far as Rowland Ward's publications is concerned we publish only our own work on Big Game, and as this is rather a limited field we only handle one printing of each edition which is now published every two years.

"The work you are probably interested in is Rowland Ward's *Records of Big Game* of which the first edition was published in 1892 and the latest, the XVI Edition published last year."

1981 Statement: *See* 1976 Statement

ROWMAN & LITTLEFIELD PUBLISHING GROUP

2000 Statement: *See* 2000 Statement of Lexington Books

ROY PUBLISHERS

1947 Statement: "Our procedure has varied in the past, but we have now determined on the following course. First editions will not be marked in any way. Second editions will have the phrase 'Second Printing' under the author's name on the title page, and, on the back of the title page, the phrases 'First Printing, date' and 'Second Printing, date' will appear under the copyright statement."

ROYAL COLLEGE OF GENERAL PRACTITIONERS (UNITED KINGDOM)

1994 Statement: "We indicate first publications on the reverse of the title page as follows:

First published in 19..

Exeter Publications Office, Royal College of General Practitioners

9 Marlborough Road, Exeter, Devon EX2 4TJ

"Any future editions or impressions are indicated as follows: Second edition [month, year]."

2000 Statement: "We indicate first publications on the reverse of the title page as follows:

First published in 20..

Publications Network, Royal College of General Practitioners, 14 Princes Gate, Hyde Park, London SW7 1PU

"Any future editions or impressions are indicated as follows: Second edition."

ROYAL FIREWORKS PRESS

1994 Statement: "After its first 8 books, Royal Fireworks Printing Co., Inc. has stated which printing each book is from, beginning with the first printing. For the first 8 titles, all editions after the first are designated."

2000 Statement: "After its first 8 books, Royal Fireworks Printing Co., Inc. has stated which printing each book is from, beginning with the second printing. For the first 8 titles, all editions after the first are designated."

ROYAL FIREWORKS PRINTING CO.

See Royal Fireworks Press

ROYAL HISTORICAL SOCIETY (UNITED KINGDOM)

1988 Statement: *See* 1988 Statement of Boydell & Brewer, Ltd. (United Kingdom)

ROYAL HOUSE PUBLISHING CO. INC.

1994 Statement: "The first printing of a first edition is identified by 'First Edition' or 'First Printing.' "

THE ROYAL SOCIETY (UNITED KINGDOM)

1994 Statement: "The Royal Society is a publisher of scientific journals, books and reports. Although it has no way of designating first printings specifically, second or revised printings, impressions and editions are so noted in the biblio on the reverse of the title page. Thus it is possible to identify first editions by a process of elimination."

2000 Statement: *See* 1994 Statement

ROYAL SOCIETY OF CHEMISTRY (UNITED KINGDOM)

1994 Statement: "In our books we do not specify first edition or first printing. However, a second edition is specified in the title, and a second printing is specified on the verso page."
2000 Statement: *See* 1994 Statement

WILLIAM EDWIN RUDGE

1928 Statement: "Up to the present time we have never included anything in these limited editions of ours that would indicate that they were first editions though ninety per cent of the books we issue are first editions.

"In the future we will carry this information on the copyright page."
1948 Statement (by William Edwin Rudge, Jr.): "As in the case of my father, I can state that most books bearing my name are first editions but no effort has been made so far in thus identifying them. In the future, I will endeavor to identify first editions bearing my name as William Edwin Rudge, Publisher at The Elm Tree Press, Woodstock, Vermont."

THE RUNA PRESS (REPUBLIC OF IRELAND)

1976 Statement: "We have no method of identifying first editions."
1988 Statement: *See* 1976 Statement

THE RUNAWAY SPOON PRESS

1994 Statement: "My press does nothing to indicate that a particular copy of one of our books is a first edition nor do we indicate whether it's a first or a later printing. However, if one of our books is revised or added to in any significant way and then reprinted, its being a second edition, or third, etc., will be indicated by the words, 'Second, Revised Edition,' or the like on the cover and on the title page. This has always been the Runaway Spoon policy."
2001 Statement: *See* 1994 Statement

RUNESTONE PRESS

1993 Statement: *See* 1993 Statement of Lerner Publications Company
2000 Statement: *See* 2000 Statement of Lerner Publishing Group

RUNNING PRESS

1976 Statement: "Running Press has had no particular method of identifying first editions. We list our printings and their dates on the copyright page."
1981 Statement: Running Press indicates its printings by the use of both the copyright date and by a string of numbers from 1 through 9. A first printing would have both the copyright date and the number 1 present.
1994 Statement: "Our company follows the same practice for identifying first editions as was outlined in our 1981 statement with the following addition: Running Press Miniature Editions™ printed before 1992 contain printing numbers on their copyright pages. Those printed after 1992 contain no printing numbers."
2000 Statement: *See* 1994 Statement

RUNNING PRESS MINIATURE EDITIONS™

1994, 2000 Statements: *See* 1994 Statement of Running Press

RUTGERS CENTER OF ALCOHOL STUDIES

1993 Statement: "The initial printing of our publications make no mention of their edition—it is assumed to be the first. Subsequent editions *would* state 'Second printing 1994,' etc. immediately above the copyright date."
2001 Statement: *See* 1993 Statement

RUTGERS UNIVERSITY PRESS

1976 Statement: "The first edition of a Rutgers University Press book is identifiable as such when the edition is not indicated on the copyright page. If we have a second or succeeding editions, we indicate 'second', 'third', etc."
1981, 1988, 1994, 2000 Statements: *See* 1976 Statement

RUTHERFORD HOUSE (UNITED KINGDOM)

2000 Statement: *See* 2000 Statement of The Paternoster Press Ltd. (United Kingdom)

RUTLEDGE HILL PRESS

2000 Statement: "We identify the first printing of a first edition by the following number line: 10 9 8 7 6 5 4 3 2 1. The lowest number indicates the printing. A second edition would be acknowledged on the cover and title page as 'new, revised edition' and on copyright page as 'second edition' under the copyright notice; the numbering would return to original: 10 9 8 7 6 5 4 3 2 1."

S

S. B. PUBLICATIONS (UNITED KINGDOM)

1994 Statement: "We designate the first printing of a first edition as follows:
'First published in 1994 (or other date) by S. B. Publications.'
[This method was] adopted when first commencing publications in 1987."
The only imprint, Brompton Publications, was purchased in 1992 and follows the same procedure.
2000 Statement: *See* 1994 Statement

SABRE PRESS

1995, 2000 Statements: *See* 1995 Statement of Momentum Books Ltd.

SADDLE MOUNTAIN PRESS

2000 Statement: *See* 2000 Statement of The Bacchae Press

SAFARI PRESS INC.

1994 Statement: "After 1986 we designated all first printings of a first edition as 'First Edition.' Subsequent printings either have no designation or say 'second edition' or 'imprint.' If the book has no designation on the copyright page, this means that we were not the first to print it, but rather we acquired the rights to reprint the book. All our books are published under the name Safari Press, Inc. We have no imprints."

2000 Statement: " . . . we have added 10 9 8 7 6 5 4 3 2 1 where 1 means the first imprint. If it is then removed, it means we are on the second imprint, if the 2 is removed we are on the third imprint, etc., etc."

SAGE BOOKS, INC.

1947 Statement: "The policy of this firm is as follows:

1) First printings of any title are not numbered.

2) Subsequent printings identical in matter with the first printing (that is, printings from the same type or plates as the first printing, or printings by photo offset from the original printing) will be numbered on the copyright page, as second printing, third printing, etc.

3) Any book re-set or the matter changed in some way so that subsequent printings would not be identical matter with the first printing, will at that time be designated a subsequent edition, as second edition, third edition, etc.

4) Printings will be numbered within editions, as second edition, second printing, etc."

RUSSELL SAGE FOUNDATION

1937 Statement: "The Russell Sage Foundation has been issuing books and pamphlets in the general social field since 1908. In general our practice has been to indicate on the copyright page the year of first publication and the copyright. If nothing else appears on this page the volume concerned is a first printing of a first edition. Subsequent printings and subsequent editions are all entered on this page in clear form with the inclusion of the date of the first edition or printing. We distinguish between printings and editions on the basis of textual changes. If they are very numerous, the edition is called a new edition. If they are slight, or if no changes are made, the new issue is called a new printing."

1947 Statement: *See* 1937 Statement

1976 Statement: "Unless the word 'Reprinted' and the date appear on the copyright page, the buyer may assume the Russell Sage Foundation book in question is a first edition."

1981 Statement: *See* 1976 Statement

1995 Statement: "We have printing information encoded: [10 9 8 7 6 5 4 3 2 1] since 1983."

SAGE PUBLICATIONS LTD. (UNITED KINGDOM)

1994 Statement: "In books published by Sage Ltd, first editions are identified by the line: First published (date). Subsequent reprints carry this line, plus the reprint history: Reprinted (date)."

2000 Statement: *See* 1994 Statement

THE SAINT ANDREW PRESS (UNITED KINGDOM)

1976 Statement: "The Saint Andrew Press uses 'First published 1975 by,' followed by our name and address, the copyright notice, and the International Standard Book Number. Supposing that this particular book sells out by 1980 and we decide to reprint it, without an alteration of any kind then at the new printing the phrase 'reprinted 1980' is added.

"In a second or revised edition, the date is omitted from the opening line which now simply reads 'Published by' and the edition details and dates are given below the copyright line.

"In all honesty I cannot say that any utterly consistent method has been followed since the foundation of The Saint Andrew Press in its present form in 1954 but the scheme outlined above is certainly the one currently followed."

1981, 1989, 1994, 2000 Statements: *See* 1976 Statement

ST ANTHONY MESSENGER PRESS
2000 Statement: "We do not differentiate first editions. If it is a revised edition, we note that, but nothing for a first edition."

SAINT BEDE'S PUBLICATIONS
1994 Statement: "When we first started in 1978, we put a notation on the bottom of the copyright page such as 'First Printing, 1978,' followed by subsequent printings and the year. More recently, we have adopted the method of using digits that can be stripped out by the printer on subsequent printings, e.g., '94 93 92 1 2 3.' We began using this method around 1989."

2000 Statement: *See* 1994 Statement

ST. BOTOLPH PUBLISHING CO., LTD.
(UNITED KINGDOM)
1947 Statement: "We have so far, as a new Company, not had occasion to have second printings of any of our books. Should we do so, however, we propose to indicate the number of the printing on the back of the title page in the place usually adopted for naming series of printings and editions."

ST. HERMAN OF ALASKA BROTHERHOOD
1994 Statement: "Our general policy is that on the reverse of the true title page we print:

Copyright 199x,

St. Herman of Alaska Brotherhood

and below against left margin justification in about the middle of the page in caps, we print:

FIRST EDITION.

"The second identification has not been used uniformly on our books. Subsequent editions are denoted by either: Second Printing year or: Second Edition year following underneath the original copyright information.

"Our imprints do not uniformly follow this procedure, especially in regards to saddle stitch books, which, due to the nature of our manifold work, have been infrequent. Additionally, xerox editions of out-of-print books have not uniformly followed these guidelines as they tend to be executed by someone other than the editor—Monk Damascene Christiansen, author of the recently published *Not of This World*, published by the Fr. Seraphim Rose Foundation. This imprint did use the practice outlined above which is considered at present normative for our work."

ST. JAMES PRESS

1988 Statement: "A St. James Press publication is a first edition unless stated otherwise. It is also a first printing unless stated otherwise."
1993 Statement: *See* 1988 Statement

ST. MARTIN'S PRESS (AUSTRALIA)

1994 Statement: *See* 1994 Statement of Pan Macmillan Australia (Australia)

ST. MARTIN'S PRESS, INCORPORATED

1976 Statement: "We very rarely designate first editions per se. A revised version of a book can be 'second' or 'third' edition, and sometimes we will add 'fifth printing' etc. on the copyright page. But not always."
1988 Statement: *See* 1976 Statement

ST. MARY'S COLLEGE PRESS

(As of 1980, the name was changed to Saint Mary's Press.)
1976 Statement: "We use nothing to designate a first edition in our publication. We do, however, indicate on the copyright page printings other than the first.

"Earlier we did not indicate subsequent printings."
1981 Statement: *See* 1981 Statement of Saint Mary's Press

SAINT MARY'S PRESS

1981, 1988, 1993, 2000 Statements: *See* 1976 Statement of St. Mary's College Press

ST. PAUL BOOKS & MEDIA

1995 Statement: "We use 1 2 3 4 5 6 7 8 9 0; when reprinted, we delete 1, etc. Revised editions are noted with a statement 'Revised edition.' "

ST. PAUL'S HOUSE (UNITED KINGDOM)

1994 Statement: "We have always distinguished a first edition from subsequent editions by stating so, most always on the back of the title page. We would say either 2d edition, etc or reprinted 19... etc."
2000 Statement: *See* 2000 Statement of St. Paul's Publishing (United Kingdom)

ST. PAUL'S PUBLISHING (UNITED KINGDOM)

2000 Statement: *See* 1994 Statement of St. Paul's House (United Kingdom)

ST. WILLIBRORD'S PRESS

1993 Statement: *See* 1993 Statement of The Borgo Press
2000 Statement: *See* 2000 Statement of The Borgo Press

SALEM HOUSE PUBLISHERS LTD.

1988 Statement: "Salem House does not identify the first edition of a publication; subsequent editions are identified as such.

"The method of designation has not changed since Salem House was founded."

THE SALTIRE SOCIETY (UNITED KINGDOM)

1988 Statement: "Up until about 1982 publications of the Saltire Society were described as First Edition 1947, Reprinted 1974 or First Published 1951, Enlarged Edition 1983 or First Published 1951, Reprinted 1974. On one occasion, we have Fourth Edition (1977), Reprinted 1982.

"Since 1982, the year of publication appears on the title page below the name of the publisher (The Saltire Society). The year of publication is also recorded in the copyright note, usually on the verso of the title page."

1994 Statement: "For some time after 1982, the year of publication appeared on the title page below the name of the publisher (The Saltire Society), as well as being recorded in the copyright note, usually on the verso of the title page. The practice of putting the date on the title page has, however, ceased since 1991, and it now appears only in the copyright note. The new title page carries only the Saltire logo.

"The new book-size productions, which are often reprints, are variously described as 'Published in 1992 by Saltire Society, 9, Fountain Close, High Street, Edinburgh EH1 1TF'; 'First published 1977 by (e.g.) Paul Harris Publishing. This paperback edition published 1993 by The Saltire Society, 9, Fountain Close, 22, High Street, Edinburgh EH1 1TF.' "

SAMISDAT

1976 Statement: "Normally SAMISDAT does not designate first printings of first editions. We do make an exception, however, when we expect one of our books to be subsequently reprinted by someone else. Then the title page of our first printing, first edition, includes the words 'First Edition,' usually near our logo & copyright notice. I think we've done this twice, maybe three times, in our 55 publications to date.

"We do designate all printings & editions after the first, again on the title page.

"Most of our first editions do exist in several states, since we often run covers in several different colors of paper, and since we usually use paper plates, which tend to break down during long or difficult runs. (We make new plates for second & third printings, & haven't yet printed anything a 4th time.)"

1981 Statement: "Normally SAMISDAT does not designate first printings of first editions. We do make an exception, however, when we expect one of our books to be subsequently reprinted by someone else. Then the title page of our first printing, first edition, includes the words 'First Edition,' usually near our logo & copyright notice. I think we've done this twice, maybe three times, in our 115 publications to date.

"We do designate most printings & editions after the first, again on the title page. We missed once, with the 2nd printing of Dorothea Condry's poetry collection *The Latter Days*, where we used the same plates as for the first printing. The first printing bore yellow covers, however, while the 2nd bears gold.

"Most of our first editions do exist in several states, since we often run covers in several different colors of paper and since we usually use paper plates, which tend to break down during long or difficult runs. (We make new plates for second & third printings, & haven't yet printed anything a 4th time.)

"We might note that the Avon paperback edition of Tom Suddick's novel *A Few Good Men* purports to be a first; in fact, we published the first edition, long out of print, during November, 1974, 4 full years earlier, and the original title page notes 'first edition' along with the copyright information."

1988 Statement: *See* 1981 Statement

SAN DIEGO STATE UNIVERSITY PRESS

1994 Statement: "A first edition will either state those words on the copyright page or have no mention of edition or printing. A second edition is listed as such on the copyright page, although a second printing may not be distinguished. Our imprints and subsidiaries follow the same practices."

2000 Statement: *See* 1994 Statement

SAN FRANCISCO BOOK COMPANY, INC.

1976 Statement: "Our method of designating first editions is to print the numbers from 10 backwards to 1 on the copyright page, as follows: 10 9 8 7 6 5 4 3 2 1. If all the numbers from 10 to 1 are there, that edition is a first edition. If the number 1 is deleted, it is a second edition; if the number 2 is gone, a third edition; and so on up to 10 editions. Naturally, if the book were to go into multiple editions, a further explanation might be included."

1981 Statement: *See* 1976 Statement

SAN FRANCISCO PRESS, INC.

1988 Statement: "We specifically designate a first edition only when we publish a preliminary version of the book (such as our *ELECTRON MICRO-SCOPY SAFETY HANDBOOK*), of which the definitive version will be identified as a second edition and will have a similar format but in a different color. The First Edition imprint is on the cover and on the title page."

1994, 2001 Statements: *See* 1988 Statement

SANDCASTLE BOOKS

1988 Statement: *See* 1988 Statement of The Putnam & Grosset Group (Children's)

J. S. SANDERS & CO.

2001 Statement: "In the past, J. S. Sanders has marked first editions a few different ways. Some are designated as such (for example, 'First J. S. Sanders & Co. edition published 1998'). First editions can also be noted because the printing year matches the copyright year (for example, 'This edition copyright 1992' and '1992 printing'). Other first editions are designated with the year of the edition (for example, 'J. S. Sanders 1993 edition'). If there is no subsequent printing information, this is also the first printing. If there have been subsequent printings, they are noted (for example, 'Second printing 1996, Third printing 1998').

"From 2000 forward, we will not be designating subsequent printings of books. J. S. Sanders is now an imprint of Ivan R. Dee, Publisher. Other imprints include New Amsterdam Books and Elephant Paperbacks."

THE SANDHILL CRANE PRESS INC.

1994 Statement: "Unless otherwise stated on the copyright (& CIP) page, our books are first editions. Second editions or second printings are identified on that page when these printings occur, along with new date for these printings or editions. We have very few second editions due to the very specialized nature of our books."

2001 Statement: "Sandhill Crane Press, Inc. is no longer in business. Our books are part of CRC Press."

SANDSTONE BOOKS

1993 Statement: *See* 1993 Statement of Ohio State University Press
2000 Statement: Sandstone Books is no longer in operation.

SAPPHIRE (UNITED KINGDOM)

2000 Statement: *See* 2000 Statement of Virgin Publishing Ltd (United Kingdom)

SARTO

2001 Statement: "We identify the first printing by 'First Printing — Month Year', e.g. 'First Printing — April 1998.' We don't identify editions, but only printings. Subsequent printings would say 'Second (or Third or Fourth) Printing — Month, Year', e.g. 'Third Printing May 1997.' This holds for most titles published after the mid-80s."

THE SAUNDERSTOWN PRESS

1995 Statement: "We do not mark first editions with any special symbol."
2000 Statement: "We do not identify first editions. But, second, third editions, etc. have been so marked on the title page."

SAUVIE ISLAND PRESS (OREGON)

See Cedar Bay Press

SAVOYARD

1988 Statement: *See* 1988 Statement of Wayne State University Press

SCARBOROUGH HOUSE

2000 Statement: *See* 2000 Statement of Madison Books

THE SCARECROW PRESS, INC.

1976 Statement: "We do not designate first editions in any special manner, nor do we designate subsequent printings of first editions. All revised or other editions are noted as such on the title page."
1981, 1988, 1993, 2000 Statements: *See* 1976 Statement

SCARLET PRESS (UNITED KINGDOM)

1994 Statement: "We do not designate our first printing; subsequent printings say 'second printing' etc."
2001 Statement: *See* 1994 Statement

SCARTHIN BOOKS (UNITED KINGDOM)

1994 Statement: "Our treatment of the verso of the title page is consistent. The phrase '© Heather and John Hurley 1989,' for instance, indicates the year of first publication. Above this we print 'Published 1989' and under this 'Reprinted 1992' or 'Revised 1991.' Our title pages are inconsistent, sometimes giving no date, sometimes the date of the first edition, sometimes the date of the current edition. We never print the words 'first edition.' "

2000 Statement: "This [1994 Statement] seems ok, tempted as I might be to insert a 'normally' or a 'usually.' "

SCEPTER PUBLISHERS

1994 Statement: "We don't use number lines. We normally state the second edition."

2000 Statement: *See* 1994 Statement

SCHENKMAN BOOKS, INC.

1995 Statement: "We do not designate the first printing of our first editions."

SCHIRMER BOOKS

1993 Statement: *See* 1993 Statement of Macmillan, Inc.

SCHOCKEN BOOKS, INC.

1947 Statement: "First printings of our books are not designated in any way. Second printings, and all subsequent printings, are so noted on the copyright pages of our publications."

1976 Statement: "We do not specifically indicate that any book is a first edition. We do indicate on the copyright page of books for which we have purchased the rights from other publishers, either domestic or foreign, the year in which the book was first published by Schocken Books. We also give the printing number after the first printing."

1981 Statement: "Our practice has changed since 1976. We indicate on the copyright page of every book we publish—whether it originates with us or we have purchased rights from another publisher (either domestic or foreign) the year in which the book was first published by Schocken Books. We also give the printing number, beginning with the first printing.

"These changes were initiated in 1978, Schocken Books has no imprints."

1988 Statement: "Schocken Books was purchased by Random House in 1987 and is now publishing in coordination with Pantheon Books, a division of Random House. It is the policy of both Pantheon and Schocken to designate books First Edition, First Paperback Edition, or First American Edition where appropriate. Reprint editions are designated using a system of numbers. Pantheon and Schocken are two separate houses and have no imprints."

1993 Statement: "For first printings we either say simply 'First Edition' and nothing else, or we run the 987654321 line under 'First Edition.'

"Subsequent printings can be identified by the lowest visible number on the printing line."

2000 Statement: *See* 1993 Statement

SCHOLAR PRESS (UNITED KINGDOM)

2000 Statement: *See* 2000 Statement of Gower Publishing Limited (United Kingdom)

SCHOLARS BOOKS

1994 Statement: *See* 1994 Statement of Publishers Associates

SCHOLARS' FACSIMILES & REPRINTS

1994 Statement: The first printing of a first edition is indicated by the statement "First Printing 19xx."
   "Second and subsequent printings are listed. E.g.,
      First Printing 1965
      Second Printing 1994."

SCHOLARS PRESS

1988 Statement: "Scholars Press does not normally designate either first editions or first, and subsequent, printings. If, however, the Press reprints a title that was originally published by another company, we will indicate the year in which the Scholars Press edition was originally published on the copyright page."
1993 Statement: *See* 1988 Statement

SCHOLARTIS PRESS (UNITED KINGDOM)

See Eric Partridge, Ltd. (Scholartis Press) (United Kingdom)

SCHOLASTIC AUSTRALIA (AUSTRALIA)

2001 Statement: "Our company name [is no longer] Ashton Scholastic but is now simply Scholastic Australia. The rest of the [1994] Statement [of Ashton Scholastic (Australia)] is correct. One further check is the number stamp at the bottom of the imprint."
See 1994 Statement of Ashton Scholastic Australia

SCHOLASTIC INC.

1995 Statement: "The information provided in that 1981 statement [of Scholastic Magazines, Inc.] is still used today, but it is only one of several ways in which we indicate first printings."

SCHOLASTIC MAGAZINES, INC.

1981 Statement: "Attached is a Xerox of a copyright page from a recently published textbook, at the bottom of which appears our Printing History code and beneath which I have explained the code.
      12 11 10 9 8 7 6 5 4 3 2 1   1 1 2 3 4 5 6/8
      Printed in U.S.A.
      [The numbers on the left (1 through 12) indicate the printings.]
      Number of printings, reading from right to left.
      This example represents First Printing.
      (For Second Printing, the '1' would be deleted— and so on up to Twelfth Printing—without plate change) [The number in the middle (1) indicates the month of first printing.]
      Month of First Printing. This example is January. Appears only on First

Printing.

(At Second Printing it is deleted—without plate change)

[The numbers on the right (1 through 6/8) indicate the year of printing.]

Year of Printing.

This example is 1981

(Numbers are deleted from the left for subsequent printings— without plate change)

"We have been using this code since 1975. Prior to that we used a number code (e.g., 1/811, meaning January 1981, First Printing), which meant resetting for each printing, patching the film, and remaking the plate.

"The current code enables us to do twelve printings over a six-year period by simply deleting numbers and without any remaking of plates.

"We use this method of identification on all our [Textbook Division and] Book Club titles."

HENRY SCHUMAN, INC.

1947 Statement: "We do not make any special identification for a first edition of our publications. The means of identification would be the usual one of the copyright date on the manufacturing notice page. On further printings of our books (we are just now issuing our first 'trade list') we would doubtless follow the usual practice of naming the number of the printing and the date. For example,

Copyright 1947 by Henry Schuman, Inc.

First Printing, November, 1947

Second Printing, January, 1948

"In the case of an entirely new edition we would, of course, follow what I believe to be the customary practice of citing the fact that sufficient changes have been made in the text of the first edition of any work to warrant the inscription of a Second or Third Edition to be carried on the title page of a new edition and on the manufacturing page."

SCIVISION

2001 Statement: *See* 2001 Statement of Academic Press, A Harcourt Science and Technology Company

SCIENTIFIC PUBLISHERS, INC.

1994 Statement: "Our scientific books do not state first edition. On subsequent printings, we state 'Second printing' etc. Trade books may also have a number sequence where first editions have all numbers present, as 10 9 8 7 6 5 4 3 2 1. Subsequent printings of such trade books will have the next lower number deleted, thus 10 9 8 7 6 5 4 3 2 for a second printing."

2000 Statement: *See* 1994 Statement

SCM PRESS (UNITED KINGDOM)

2000 Statement: "Our main aim is to make the publishing history of the book quite clear. First impressions are identifiable by the absence of any reference to subsequent impressions.

"In 1998 SCM Press was incorporated into a larger publishing group and is now a division of SCM-Canterbury Press Ltd, which is a subsidiary of Hymns Ancient & Modern Ltd. At that time our imprint changed from SCM Press Ltd to SCM Press."

SCM PRESS LTD (UNITED KINGDOM)

1988 Statement: "Our main aim is to make the publishing history of the book quite clear."

Sample pages provided show the following:

First published 1988
by SCM Press Ltd
26-30 Tottenham Road, London N1 4BZ

First published 1977
by SCM Press Ltd
26-30 Tottenham Road, London N1 4BZ
Second Edition 1981
Second impression 1984

First published in English 1982
by SCM Press Ltd, 26-30 Tottenham Road, London, N1 4BZ
Sixth impression 1988

First published 1957
by The University of Chicago Press, Chicago 60637
First published in Great Britain 1957
by James Nisbet & Co Ltd
This edition first published 1978
by SCM Press Ltd
26-30 Tottenham Road, London N1 4BZ
Second impression 1984

1994 Statement: *See* 1988 Statement
2000 Statement: *See* 2000 Statement of SCM Press (United Kingdom)

SCM-CANTERBURY PRESS LTD (UNITED KINGDOM)

See SCM Press (United Kingdom)

ANDREW SCOTT PUBLISHERS

2000 Statement: "First editions are listed as 'First Printing.' "

WILLIAM R. SCOTT, INC.

1937 Statement: "Our policy will be to mark seconds, thirds, etc., clearly on the copyright page; marking firsts or not as the spirit moves us."
1947 Statement: "Since sending you information regarding our policy on First Editions, back in 1937, we have had to change, due to manufacturing difficulties.

"All our books are printed by offset. To indicate a first or subsequent printing, the entire black plate for the whole book would have to be made over. Therefore, our books are not marked at all, and won't be, until such time as we print by letter press, if we ever do."

SCOTTISH ACADEMIC PRESS LIMITED
(UNITED KINGDOM)

1988 Statement: "We do not specially indicate the first printing of the first edition on that edition. Subsequent printings or new editions are always indicated together with a note of the date of the first edition."

1994 Statement: "We indicate on the reverse of the Title Pages the dates of the first, and additionally also subsequent, editions as applicable."

2000 Statement: *See* 1994 Statement

SCOTTISH LIBRARY ASSOCIATION PUBLICATIONS
(UNITED KINGDOM)

2001 Statement: "We do not give printing designation on a first edition of any publication. We do not state 'First edition' on any publication, although the date of publication is shown on the title page. Subsequent editions are shown as 'Second edition', 'Third edition', etc and the date of publication of that edition is shown on the title page."

SCOUT WORKSHOP

1995, 2001 Statements: *See* 1995 Statement of Longhouse

SCOW BAY BOOKS

2000 Statement: *See* 2000 Statement of The Bacchae Press

CHARLES SCRIBNER'S SONS

1928 Statement: "We have no fixed plan for designating our first editions of general publications. If a book runs to more than one printing we usually print somewhere in the 'front matter' Second Printing, Third Printing, Fourth Printing, whatever it might be. From this it might be assumed that a copy containing no such printing notice might be considered the first edition."

1937 Statement: "There is no sure way of telling in most cases what is a first edition of a book printed previously to 1930 except that in most cases in the front matter a second printing or any later printing is usually so indicated in the front matter. On books published since 1930 first editions are indicated with a capital 'A' on the copyright page."

1947 Statement: *See* 1937 Statement

1976 Statement:

   "E - 9.66 [H]

"E is the fifth printing, 9.66 the date of that printing H the manufacturer.

   1 3 5 7 9 11 13 15 17 19 H/C 20 18 16 14 12 10 8 6 4 2

"After 1972 the keyline was changed to the above system where the lowest number indicates which printing, the first letter in the center, the manufacturer, and the second letter the edition (i.e. cloth or paper)."

1981 Statement: *See* 1976 Statement

1989 Statement: "In 1984, Scribner's became part of Macmillan and now follows Macmillan's procedure of indicating printings at the bottom of the

copyright page: the *lowest numeral* in the sequence generally indicates the printing for that copy."
See also 1989 Statement of Macmillan Publishing Co., Inc.
1993 Statement: *See* 1993 Statement of Macmillan, Inc.

CHARLES SCRIBNER'S SONS, LTD. (UNITED KINGDOM)

1928 Statement: "In response to your inquiry as to the method followed by my firm distinguishing first editions, I do not think that there is any absolute hard and fast rule laid down which would apply in every case. The rule generally followed is to note on the reverse of the title page under the copyright notice the dates when the book has been reprinted. The words 'First Edition' or 'First Printing' do not usually appear on first editions, but if the copyright date and the date on the title page are in agreement, and there is no further note, the assumption is that the copy is a first edition. Taking half a dozen books at random I note the following details:

Edward Bok. *The Americanization of Edward Bok.*
New York
Charles Scribner's Sons
1927

on the reverse—Copyright 1920, 1922 by Charles Scribner's Sons. First Edition September 1920, Second Edition November 1920, Third Edition December 1920, and so on down to 24th Edition August 1923, 25th Edition (Popular Edition) August 1923, and so on down to 34th Edition (Popular Edition) March 1924. In the meantime a different edition known as the Library Edition was published in February 1924 which goes down to the 40th Edition March 1927.

Will James. *Smoky*
Charles Scribner's Sons
New York—London
1927

Copyright 1926 by Charles Scribner's Sons. Published September 1926. Reprinted September, October, twice in November, five times in December, 1926, once in February 1927; August 1927. Popular Edition published August 1927.

Pupin. *From Immigrant to Inventor*
Charles Scribner's Sons
New York—London
1924

Copyright 1922, 1923 by Charles Scribner's Sons. Published September 1923, Reprinted November 1923, January, March, July, October 1924. In this case the copyright notice of 1922 indicates prior publication of part of the book in the Magazine, but here the actual publication date is mentioned.

"The assumption is that unless otherwise stated on the reverse of the title page the book may be considered as a first edition. Of course it does not take into account such questions as issues. A mistake might be discovered while the presses were running and an alteration made in later copies. There would naturally be nothing on the book to indicate such a change."

1936 Statement: "Charles Scribner's Sons, Ltd., are associated, as you doubtless understand, with Charles Scribner's Sons, New York. As far as editions which we import from America are concerned, the rule for distinguishing first editions is naturally the same as that adopted by the New York house of Charles Scribner's Sons. In future any books published separately here will bear on the title page 'First Published in . . . .,' and if this coincides with the date on the title page, and there is no reprint notice, the book may be assumed to be a first edition."

1947 Statement: *See* 1936 Statement

CHARLES SCRIBNER'S SONS REFERENCE
1993 Statement: *See* 1993 Statement of Macmillan, Inc.

THE SCRIMSHAW PRESS (CALIFORNIA)
1976 Statement: "To the best of my recollection, we have never indicated an edition as being the first. We have, in fact, generally assumed that the first would be the last.

"On the other hand, we have been quite consistent, I think, in indicating second and subsequent printings and even to the point of resetting some of our colophons when the printer or some other major supplier changed between one printing and another. I am reasonably sure that the verso of the title page, at least, will tell the true story: no indication of printing means first edition; any subsequent printings are named as such. Anyone who wishes may verify this with us on specific titles."

SCRIPTURE PRESS PUBLICATIONS, INC.
1994 Statement: "Victor Books indicates the first edition of a book by using a Printing/Year line on the copyright page. An example is as follows: 1 2 3 4 5 6 7 8 9 10 Printing/Year 98 97 96 95 94.

"This method allows us to update information for subsequent printings (through the 10th) without resetting copy; we merely opaque out the previous printing number and the year of reprint (if necessary).

"Victor Books adopted this method of designation about five or six years ago. Prior to that, the only indication that a book was the first edition was the fact that it did not bear a reprint notice on the copyright page."

SCRIVENER PRESS
2000 Statement: *See* 2000 Statement of JSA Publications Inc.

SCROOGE'S LEDGER
2000 Statement: *See* 2000 Statement of The Academic & Arts Press

THE SEA HORSE PRESS
(New York, New York)
1981 Statement: "Sea Horse Press doesn't in any way note a first edition. Because we are a small press with rather large first printings—i.e. 2000–3000; we only note a printing if it is beyond a first printing. Then we note the months and year of the printings as follows:

First printing March, 1978
Second printing September 1978
Third Printing June 1980 etc.

which is taken from the only one of our books to have received a smaller (1000 copy) first printing: and subsequently received two more.

"This is standard for us since we began publishing. Thus every Sea Horse book is a first printing unless it says otherwise."

SEABURY PRESS

1988 Statement: *See* 1988 Statement of Crossroad/Continuum

SEAFLOWER BOOKS (UNITED KINGDOM)

2001 Statement: *See* 2001 Statement of Ex Libris Press (United Kingdom)

SEAGULL BOOKS (UNITED KINGDOM)

1988 Statement: *See* 1988 Statement of The Book Guild Limited (United Kingdom)

1994, 2000 Statements: *See* 1988 Statement

SEAL BOOKS (CANADA)

1989 Statement: Seal hardcover first editions are not designated in any particular manner.

1993, 2000 Statements: *See* 1989 Statement

SEAL PRESS

1989 Statement: "Our books designate the printing number by a series of numbers: 10 9 8 7 6 5 4 3 2 1. The current printing is indicated by the final number to the right.

"The first printing of a first edition also indicates the month and year: First edition, March 1989."

1993 Statement: *See* 1989 Statement

2000 Statement: "Our books designate the printing number by a series of numbers: 10 9 8 7 6 5 4 3 2 1. The current printing is indicated by the final number to the right.

"The first printing of a first edition also indicates the month and year: First printing, March 1989."

SEARCH PRESS LTD (UNITED KINGDOM)

1994 Statement: "Search Press has always used the following designation for new books and reprints:

First published in Great Britain 19XX."

SEASTAR BOOKS

2001 Statement: *See* 2001 Statement of North-South Books Inc.

MARTIN SECKER, LTD. (UNITED KINGDOM)

1928 Statement: "Bibliographical entry on the reverse of the title page."

See also Martin Secker & Warburg, Ltd. (United Kingdom)

See also 1989 Statement of The Octopus Publishing Group PLC (United Kingdom)

SECKER & WARBURG (NZ) (NEW ZEALAND)
1994 Statement: *See* 1994 Statement of Reed Publishing (NZ) Ltd (New Zealand)

SECKER & WARBURG (UNITED KINGDOM)
1994 Statement: *See* 1994 Statement of Reed Consumer Books (United Kingdom)
2000 Statement: *See* 2000 Statement of The Random House Group Limited (United Kingdom)

MARTIN SECKER & WARBURG, LTD.
(UNITED KINGDOM)
(Formerly Martin Secker, Ltd.)
For statement of practice from 1937 through 1989, see 1989 Statement of The Octopus Publishing Group PLC (United Kingdom).
1937 Statement: "Bibliographical entry on the reverse of the title page.

"Above is the new style of the firm. No alteration in policy of differentiating reprints, which has been in existence since the business began."
1947 Statement: "We still continue to differentiate between new editions reprints and first editions in the bibliographical information given on the verso of the title page of our books."
1976 Statement: "Our first editions, and indeed first printings, bear:

First published in England 19.. by

Martin Secker & Warburg Limited

14 Carlisle Street, London W1V 6NN

"Second and further impressions add below:

Reprinted 19..

Reprinted 19..

"Occasionally older books carry the words 'Second impression 19..,' but this convention is no longer followed.

"Re-issues are similarly treated (by a re-issue we mean a reprint of a book which has been out of print a sufficiently long time—a year or more; it is not a new edition, there is no new material):

Re-issued 19..

"Second and further editions follow in the same vein with the addition of Second edition 19.."
1981 Statement: The 1976 statement is still correct. However, Martin Secker & Warburg Limited have moved. The address on the copyright page will now read:

54 Poland Street, London W1V 3DF
and not:

14 Carlisle Street, London W1V 6NN
1988 Statement: "The information on Martin Secker & Warburg still stands, and our practice is as described. However, we have moved again. Volumes published since January 1988 bear the following address on the copyright page: Michelin House, 81 Fulham Road, London SW3 6RB."
See also 1989 Statement of The Octopus Publishing Group PLC (United Kingdom)

SECOND CHANCE PRESS
1988, 1993, 2000 Statements: *See* 1988, 1993, 2000 Statements of The Permanent Press

SECOND COMING PRESS, INC.
1981 Statement: "Second Coming Press, despite its many titles, remains a small press publisher, and therefore 100% of our book line is a first edition, ranging in print runs of 500 to 2000 copies. A second edition, would be a reprinting of the first print run, something we have never done, though tempted to on two of our best sellers."

SECOND STORY PRESS (CANADA)
1995 Statement: "We have no particular way of designating first printings. Obviously second or revised printings are so noted and in this way we have a key to first editions by the process of elimination."

LISA SEE ENDOWMENT
IN SOUTHERN CALIFORNIA HISTORY
2000 Statement: *See* 2000 Statement of University of California Press

SEE SHARP PRESS
2000 Statement: "We identify the first printing of a first edition by the words 'First Printing' or 'First Edition' on copyright page; either indicates a true first."

SEELEY, SERVICE & CO., LTD. (UNITED KINGDOM)
1937 Statement: "The following has been and is our present practice: We used to put the date on the title page of the first edition, and generally altered it, in the same position, to the date of any reprint which might follow.

"Now we sometimes follow the above practice and if not, we insert the date of printing after the printer's name at the end of the book."
1947 Statement: *See* 1937 Statement
See also Seeley, Service & Cooper Ltd. (United Kingdom)

SEELEY, SERVICE & COOPER LTD. (UNITED KINGDOM)
1976 Statement: "The Leo Cooper imprint has existed only since 1969 and I think it can be safely said that the bibliographical details given on the verso title provide all the information necessary.

"Our sister company, Seeley, Service & Co. were in the past exceedingly lax about including such information in their publications, and I can say no more than if you have any specific queries regarding books published under this imprint we would be happy to let you have whatever information we can find from such files as remain."
1981 Statement: "Since you last wrote to us there has been a change in ownership and we are now owned by Frederick Warne Ltd. Leo Cooper & Seeley Service books are still published under those imprints by Frederick Warne and I see no reason to alter what we said in the first edition of your book except to say that on the spine and title page of the books it now says either a Leo Cooper book or a Seeley Service book published by Warne."

SELF-COUNSEL PRESS INC. (CANADA AND USA)
1994 Statement: "Self-Counsel Press simply designates first editions by stating so on the copyright page, for example,

First edition: September, 1994

"We use both month and year, because the specific time of publication is important for many of our books that contain fast-changing legal information. In subsequent editions, we retain the listing of previous editions and reprints so that a history can be followed, until after the tenth edition when we summarize the history by listing the first, tenth, fifteenth, twentieth, etc."
2000 Statement: *See* 1994 Statement

SELWYN & BLOUNT, LTD. (UNITED KINGDOM)
1928 Statement: "We always show our first editions by the words 'First Printed . . . .' and the date. On all further editions the words 'Reprinted . . . .' and the date, are added. These words are printed on the back of the half title page."
1936 Statement: "The system as originally stated has not been adhered to during the past two or three years."
1947 Statement: "As a rule, we adhere to the procedure outlined in our 1928 statement, but there may have been some unfortunate occasions during the War when the rule was not strictly kept.

"This also applies to our Associate Company, Messrs. Denis Archer."

SEPHER-HERMON PRESS, INC.
1976 Statement: "We do not put any designation on our first editions designating them as such.

"Subsequent editions are designated as 'second edition,' 'third edition' etc."
1981, 1988 Statements: *See* 1976 Statement

SEPORE
1994 Statement: *See* 1994 Statement of Publishers Associates

SEREN (WALES)
2000 Statement: "Our policy remains the same [as the 1988 Statement of Seren Books (Wales)]. Please note we have dropped the 'Books' and are called simply Seren. Seren is the imprint of Poetry Wales Press, but we're generally known as Seren now, and PWP is just the limited company name."

SEREN BOOKS (WALES)
1988 Statement: "We show second impression on the title verso. New editions have always been revised and expanded in the past, so we make this clear on the book cover. This is the practice which we have always followed."
1994 Statement: *See* 1988 Statement
2000 Statement: *See* 2000 Statement of Seren (Wales)

SERENDIPITY
1989 Statement: *See* 1989 Statement of Price/Stern/Sloan Publishers, Inc.
2000 Statement: *See* 2000 Statement of Price Stern Sloan

SERGEANT KIRKLAND'S PRESS

2000 Statement: "We identify the first printing of a first edition by the number line 1 2 3 4 5 6 7 8 9 10."

SERIF BOOKS (UNITED KINGDOM)

1949 Statement: "The first edition of each book which we publish carries the words 'First Published in 19..,' usually on the reverse of the title page. Subsequent printings have added below this 'Second Printing, Third Printing, etc.,' and the appropriate date. In the event of a new edition being produced this is stated in some such formula as 'New And Revised Edition' or simply 'New Edition' again with the appropriate date.

"We have standardised on this method since our first book. This firm was founded in 1947."

SERPENT'S TAIL

1994 Statement: "We use 10 9 8 7 6 5 4 3 2 1. When reprinted, we delete the number 1. We also print 'First US edition year' at the top of the copyright page."

SERPENT'S TAIL (UNITED KINGDOM)

1994 Statement: The date of publication is listed on the title verso, i.e., "First published 1994."

SERVANT BOOKS

1994, 2000 Statements: *See* 1994 Statement of Servant Publications

SERVANT PUBLICATIONS

1994 Statement: "Servant Publications first editions can be determined by examining the copyright line. First editions have only one date, the original date of publication. Successive editions are identified by adding the dates of subsequent editions to the copyright line.

"For example, 'Copyright © 1975, 1982, 1990 by H. John Doe' indicates the book is in its third edition, the first published in 1975, the second in 1982, and the third in 1990.

"A reprint designation is noted on the copyright page as follows (beginning with the copyright year): 93 94 95 96 97 10 9 8 7 6 5 4 3 2 1. With each reprint, one number from the far right is omitted; the year indicated at the far left of the reprint designation indicates the year in which the reprint was produced.

"For example, a designation that reads, '94 95 96 10 9 8 7 6' indicates that the sixth and most recent reprint was produced in 1994.

"All our subsidiaries, including Vine Books, Charis Publications, and Servant Books, use this designation."

This method was adapted in the mid-1980s.
2000 Statement: *See* 1994 Statement

SEVEN STAR COMMUNICATIONS

1994 Statement: "We use the words 'first printing' and follow it with the month and year. Subsequent printings are designated 'second printing,' 'third printing,' etc. also with the month and year. Subsequent editions are denoted

similarly and also identified as 'second edition' or 'revised edition,' i.e.: 'Second Edition, first printing,' etc."
2000 Statement: *See* 1994 Statement

SEVERN HOUSE PUBLISHERS (UNITED KINGDOM)
2001 Statement: "We identify only editions, not printings; a first edition is so identified on the copyright page."

SEVERN HOUSE PUBLISHERS INC
2000 Statement: "We identify the first printing of a first edition by the statement: 'This first world edition published xxxx (year) by Severn House Publishers.' "

SHAAR PRESS
2001 Statement: *See* 2001 Statement of Mesorah Publications Ltd

SHADOW MOUNTAIN
2000 Statement: *See* 2000 Statement of Deseret Book Company

SHAKESPEARE HEAD PRESS (UNITED KINGDOM)
1988, 2000 Statements: *See* 1988 Statement of Basil Blackwell Limited (United Kingdom)

SHAMBHALA PUBLICATIONS, INC.
1976 Statement: "Early Shambhala titles were marked first printing or first edition on the copyright page, later printings being marked second, third, etc.

"For the past two-three years we have stopped making marks in our books to distinguish first editions or printings. However, subsequent editions are marked so if any substantial changes have been made in the text or if a book has been changed from cloth to paper."
1981 Statement: "Our statement of designating editions and printings is still accurate with our current practices. Therefore, I suggest you leave the entry as it stands. This procedure does also apply to our subsidiary, the Great Eastern Book Co., and its imprints: Great Eastern and Prajna Press."
1988 Statement: "Early Shambhala titles were marked 'first printing' or 'first edition' on the copyright page, with subsequent printings marked numerically as second, third, etc. Current titles are marked 'first edition' on the copyright page, with subsequent editions identified numerically.

"Great Eastern Book Company and Prajna Press titles are governed by the same designation guidelines. (However, these imprints no longer exist.) New Science Library is presently the only imprint of Shambhala Publications and follows the same guidelines.

"These guidelines went into effect in approximately January of 1988."
1993, 2000 Statements: *See* 1988 Statement. Note that New Science Library imprint is inactive.

M E SHARPE INC
2000 Statement: "We identify the first printing of a first edition by the following number line: MV(C) 10 9 8 7 6 5 4 3 2 1. [The first two letters are

a printer code, the second letter refers to case (binding); the numbers are a print generation line.]

SHARPE PROFESSIONAL
2000 Statement: *See* 2000 Statement of M E Sharpe Inc

SHARPE REFERENCE
2000 Statement: *See* 2000 Statement of M E Sharpe Inc

HAROLD SHAW PUBLISHERS
1994 Statement: The first printing of a first edition is indicated by the number line 10 9 8 7 6 5 4 3 2 1. The lowest number showing indicates the printing. "First printing, (month, year) [was also used] on older books."

2000 Statement: "The information regarding first edition lines is the same. We are still called Harold Shaw Publishers but we are now an imprint of WaterBrook Press. Shaw was bought out by WaterBrook Press in January 2000. WaterBrook is a division of Random House. Imprints of Shaw follow the same first edition practice of all Shaw books. North Wind and the Wheaton Literary Series are still imprints of Harold Shaw Publishers. Please add Fisherman Bible Studyguides to our list of imprints as well."

SHEARWATER BOOKS
2000 Statement:; *See* 2000 Statement of Island Press

SHEED AND WARD, INC.
1937 Statement: "Whenever we reprint a book we note this fact on the reverse of the title page. If this is not indicated, the reader is generally safe in assuming that the book is a first edition. Occasionally we explicitly state the fact that the book is a first edition, but more often we do not indicate it."

1947 Statement: *See* 1949 Statement

SHEED & WARD, INC.
1976 Statement: *See* 1976 Statement of Sheed Andrews and McMeel, Inc.
1995 Statement: "First printing date is assumed to be same as year of copyright. Subsequent printings are indicated: Second printing, 1992, etc."

SHEED AND WARD, LIMITED (UNITED KINGDOM)
1937 Statement: "Our usual method of indicating first editions from subsequent printings, is to add to the bibliographical note on the reverse of the title-page, the number and date of the impression. For instance the bibliographical note of the first edition will have the name and address of the printer, our name and address, and 'first published September 1936,' and reprints will have '2nd impression September 1936' added beneath 'first published.' In the case of a new *edition* '2nd edition October 1936.'

"This method applies only to books published by us in England."

1947 Statement: *See* 1937 Statement

SHEED ANDREWS AND McMEEL, INC.
1976 Statement: "Although we have, this year, once issued a book in a thoroughly revised edition which was identified as 'Second edition, revised,'

in the normal course of things we do not consider minor changes sufficient to refer to a new printing as a new edition. Thus, I will refer to first printings and second printings rather than first editions and second editions.

"We have no special identifying mark for a first printing. It has become the practice of some publishers to run the numbers one to ten on their copyright page and knock off the initial number on subsequent printings. We have not adopted this policy as yet, although it might be a good one for us to follow. The only way one could tell a first printing would be the absence of information on subsequent printings and even this can be misleading because until this year Sheed and Ward had no consistent policy of introducing a line on the copyright page indicating that the book was in a second printing, third printing, etc. Our present policy is as follows: When a book goes into a second printing we then introduce on to the copyright page the words 'First printing' and the date and 'Second printing' and the date. A new line is added for each subsequent printing. Thus, as I said, a first printing is actually identified by the lack of such a line. Because our company has a rather complicated history, having changed management a few years ago, changed location given on our title page last year, and changed our name this year, production records on some of the old Sheed and Ward books have gone astray and it is not possible even for us to identify what printing a very old book might be in. In such cases, new printings are being identified as 'A Sheed and Ward Classic' and the logo of Sheed Andrews and McMeel and our Kansas City address is being carried on the title page, to identify the book from previous printings."

1981 Statement: *See* 1981 Statement of Andrews and McMeel, Inc.

THE SHEEP MEADOW PRESS

2000 Statement: "We do not indicate the first printing of our first editions. In the rare cases of limited first editions, we would inscribe something on the copyright page. Otherwise, we make no special distinction for them. We do, however, distinguish new editions and reprints. If the book has been previously published, we mention the name, place, and date of the original publisher and printer on the copyright page."

SHEFFIELD ACADEMIC PRESS (UNITED KINGDOM)

1994 Statement: "Our first printing is designated on the copyright page. Subsequent printings are shown by date on the same page. If the edition has been revised it states 2nd edition."

2001 Statement: *See* 1994 Statement

SHEFFIELD PUBLISHING COMPANY

2000 Statement: "A first edition of a Sheffield Publishing Company book would simply have a title and no edition listed. The first printing would be indicated by the following: 7 6 5 4 3 2 1. Successive printings are indicated by deletions of previous numbers."

SHELDON PRESS (UNITED KINGDOM)

1937, 1947 Statements: *See* 1937 Statement of Society for Promoting Christian Knowledge (United Kingdom)

1976 Statement: "We identify first editions by the following statement:
First Published in Great Britain in 19.. by Sheldon
Press Marylebone Road, London, NW1 4DU
"Subsequent printings are always identified as such."
1981 Statement: "SPCK [Society for Promoting Christian Knowledge], our parent company, incorporated from January, 1980. All imprints mention SPCK." *See* 1976 Statement
See also Society for Promoting Christian Knowledge (United Kingdom)
2000 Statement: *See* 1981 Statement

SHENGOLD PUBLISHERS, INC.
1976 Statement: "With regard to designating a first edition, we do not use any. We do designate subsequent editions (e.g. Second Edition) which appears on the title pages and in some instances, such as our Encyclopedia, also on the copyright page. This is the same method we have always used."
1981 Statement: *See* 1976 Statement

SHEPHEARD-WALWYN (PUBLISHERS) LIMITED
(UNITED KINGDOM)
1976 Statement: "Our normal wording on a first edition is:—'First published 19.. by Shepheard-Walwyn (Publishers) Limited.' We do not at this stage identify it as the first printing. However, where the same edition is re-printed we would state 'Reprinted 19..' and we would build up the printing history, as we went into other printings of the same edition.

"Although we have published new editions of works previously published by other houses, we have not yet published second editions of works we originally published. It is therefore a little difficult to give you firm information as to how we would designate second editions, but I think it is safe to assume that we would simply say 'First published 19... Second edition published 19...' "
1981, 1994, 2000 Statements: *See* 1976 Statement

SHERIDAN HOUSE, INC.
1947 Statement: "Ordinarily when the first edition is printed, it carries nothing but the usual copyright notice. Should there be a second, third and fourth printing, we generally mark these printings on the copyright page. On the other hand, when a book sells very rapidly, it is not always practical to change the printings and we leave it without any further identification other than that which appears in the original edition. Unless there are changes made in the book, we don't see that it would make any difference whether the book is first, second or third printing."
Statement for 1960: *See* 1947 Statement
1976 Statement: "No new publishing."
1982 Statement: "Same as 1947. Also, books first published in the U.S. are clearly marked 'First published in the United States 1982.' Reprints of books long out of print are marked 'Reprinted 1982.' "
1988, 1993, 2000 Statements: *See* 1982 Statement

SHERWIN BEACH PRESS

2001 Statement: "All our books are done in a single, limited edition, with the number in the edition and total edition size printed on the colophon."

SHETLAND LIBRARY (UNITED KINGDOM)

2001 Statement: "We do not identify first printings but we do identify subsequent printings as such on the copyright page. Normally our publications are only produced for one print run and on the occasions where we have a reprint or a new edition we always make this very clear on the copyright page details."

SHIRE PUBLICATIONS LTD. (UNITED KINGDOM)

1994 Statement: "First editions are distinguished by the information on the verso in the copyright panel, which always gives first publication date; subsequent editions and imprints are similarly identified. For very early Shire titles, refer to *30 Years of Shire Publications—a bibliography for collectors 1962-91.*"

2000 Statement: *See* 1994 Statement

SHOAL CREEK PUBLISHERS, INC.

1976 Statement: "We prefer no designation for first editions, but have on several occasions at authors request put 'First Edition' on the copyright page.

"For all subsequent editions we do put date of first and subsequent editions."

1981 Statement: *See* 1976 Statement

1988 Statement: "Shoal Creek Publishers Inc. is no longer actively publishing."

SHOESTRING PRESS
(California)

2000 Statement: *See* 2000 Statement of The Poetry Center Press/Shoestring Press

THE SHOE STRING PRESS, INC.

1976 Statement: "Although we try to be exceedingly careful when we do reprints as to who did the original edition or the edition used for reprinting, we have not had a special policy with respect to identifying first editions of original works.

"We do, however, identify subsequent editions although not necessarily impressions if there have been no changes."

1981 Statement: *See* 1976 Statement

1988 Statement: "We no longer publish reprints, as a general rule, but the 1976 statement is valid to the extent any policy applies."

1993, 2000 Statements: *See* 1988 Statement

SHORELINE (CANADA)

2001 Statement: "We do not identify a first edition as such. Subsequent editions or printings are labeled accordingly."

SHORTLAND PUBLICATIONS LIMITED (NEW ZEALAND)

1994 Statement: "Since 1992 we have printed

99 98 97 96 95 94

10 9 8 7 6 5 4 3 2 1

on our copyright page. The bottom line identifies the printing, and the top line identifies the year of the printing. E.g., for a second printing in 1995, 94 would be deleted from the top line and 1 would be deleted from the bottom line. From second printing on there is no indication of date of first printing. Prior to 1992, the copyright page carried the book's first published date and which printing it was. We have never identified first editions."

SHOWCASE SUBSIDIARIES

2000 Statement: *See* 2000 Statement of Players Press Inc.

GEORGE SHUMWAY, PUBLISHER

1976 Statement: "Usually we provide a statement on the back of the title page such as:

1500 copies this First Edition October 1976

2000 copies this Second Edition January 1978."

1981 Statement: "You have my permission to use my previous reply about how we designate a first edition of our books.

"In practice, however, we have not always followed this format. Our most recent publication, *Rifles of Colonia*, carries the following:

Published 1980

2800 copies casebound, standard edition

200 copies specially casebound and numbered, deluxe edition

"This of course is not so specific, and there is no particular reason for it— I just didn't think about first editions when making up the copyright page. Now that you have jogged my memory, I suppose I should be more specific on future books."

1988 Statement: *See* 1976 Statement

SIDEWINDER

(Formerly Sun Dance Press)

1993 Statement: *See* 1993 Statement of The Borgo Press

2000 Statement: *See* 2000 Statement of The Borgo Press

SIDGWICK & JACKSON (AUSTRALIA)

1994 Statement: *See* 1994 Statement of Pan Macmillan Australia (Australia)

SIDGWICK AND JACKSON, LTD. (UNITED KINGDOM)

1928 Statement: "We do not designate our first editions at all, except by the negative method of there being no second or later edition or impression indicated on the back of the title page. Occasionally we state 'Second Impression,' or so on, on the front of the title page."

1935 Statement: "If there is no indication, either on the front or the back of the title-page of any of our publications, that the issue is a second or later edition or impression, it must be taken to be the only, and therefore the first, edition or impression.

"We have employed this method from the start of this business in 1909."

SIDGWICK & JACKSON LIMITED (UNITED KINGDOM)
1976 Statement: "In answer to your query about whether we have any particular method of identifying first editions, we can say that if the book does not bear a reprint line, then it is of the first printing."
1981, 1988 Statements: *See* 1976 Statement
2000 Statement: *See* 1976 Statement. *See also* 2000 Statement of Macmillan Publishers Limited (United Kingdom)

SIERRA CLUB BOOKS
1994 Statement: "We designate the first printing by number on the bottom of the copyright page. We list the numbers from left to right, with 1 being the first number in the case of a first printing. We do not designate a first edition in our books."
2000 Statement: *See* 1994 Statement

ELISABETH SIFTON BOOKS
1988 Statement: *See* 1988 Statement of Penguin Publishing Co Ltd. (United Kingdom)

SIGMA BOOKS, LTD. (UNITED KINGDOM)
1947 Statement: "We always identify the first edition of a new book published by ourselves by the words 'first published . . . .' on the verso of the title page. Reprints are distinguished by having the words 'reprinted . . . .' or 'new edition . . . .' followed by the date, in addition to the date of the first publication."

SIGNET
1988 Statement: *See* 1988 Statement of New American Library
1993, 2000 Statements: *See* 1993 Statement of Dutton Signet

SIGNET (AUSTRALIA)
2000 Statement: *See* 2000 Statement of Penguin Books Australia Ltd (Australia)

SIGNET CLASSICS
1988 Statement: *See* 1988 Statement of New American Library
1993, 2000 Statements: *See* 1993 Statement of Dutton Signet

SILES PRESS
2000 Statement: *See* 2000 Statement of Silman-James Press

SILHOUETTE (UNITED KINGDOM)
2000 Statement: *See* 2000 Statement of Harlequin Mills & Boon Limited (United Kingdom)

SILHOUETTE BOOKS (CANADA)
1994, 2000 Statements: *See* 1994 Statement of Harlequin Enterprises Limited (Canada)

SILMAN-JAMES PRESS
2000 Statement: "We identify the first printing of a first edition by 'First Edition' which is printed on the copyright page, above the number line '10 9 8 7 6 5 4 3 2 1.' "

SILVER BURDETT & GINN
1988 Statement (but *see also* the following Note on the 1988 Statement): "Recently Ginn and Company has been joined by Silver Burdett into a new company, Silver, Burdett & Ginn. We are generally following the most recent copyright notification practices of Ginn and Company.

"First editions of Ginn publications could usually be detected by a single line on the last page of each publication that would begin by a series of letters (e.g., ABCDEFGH). If 'A' was the first letter, the book was a first impression; if 'B' were the first letter, the book was a second impression, etc.

"The copyright notice provides information about revisions. If only one year appears, the book is not a revision of an earlier copyright. If two years appear (e.g., Copyright 1985, 1982) the book is a revision of the earlier copyright.

"In the past, Ginn and Company inserted a number following the copyright notice. An example is 840.1 which indicated that the book was published in August (the eighth month) in the year 1940. The number after the decimal indicated that the book was a first impression.

"There is no date when the system changed from one to the other. In fact, for many years both systems were used on a seemingly arbitrary basis."

Note on the 1988 Statement: In a 1999 letter to the editors of this volume, Richard Wunderlich, Ph.D., of The College of Saint Rose in Albany, New York, wrote:

"I am writing in appreciation of your work, *First Editions,* and its importance for bibliographic research . . . . Unfortunately, I discovered the first edition of your book too late to help me very much with my *Pinocchio Catalogue* (published 1988). I referenced your assistance with Scholastic Book Services, but I am truly indebted to you for interpreting the Harper Brothers printing mark (which I could not use because that part of the catalogue was already completed for printing). I created the Catalogue so I could explore how, when, and possibly why Collodi's *Pinocchio* was changed in the United States over this century. I also needed to know whether the original novel was popular here in the first place, or whether it did not become popular until after it had been changed. To do all that I had to find every variation of the story possible and I had to create a printing history. The Catalogue reflects about 2 decades of work searching out libraries and collections throughout the country (as best as my resources would permit). I am now in the process of developing a book discussing these changes in the story . . . .

"I go into all of this for a purpose, I find that your third edition catches up with Ginn and Company and I have good reason to believe that the source is incorrect about interpreting their older printing mark . . . .

"In the early 1980s I had lengthy correspondence with Catherine Simeone in Ginn's Copyright Department, and while she was able to provide a great deal of information about their various productions of *Pinocchio*, she was unable to locate any information about the printing mark, and informed me that she could find no one at Ginn who could read it and that the records deciphering it simply were no longer extant. Based on suggestions by various librarians (particularly Catherine de Saint-Rat of Miami University, Oxford, Ohio) and the examination of many, many Ginn editions (*Pinocchio* and several other titles) I devised and tested [an interpretation], and have concluded that the printer's mark provides no interpretation about whether a volume is a first edition or not. I should also add that I have collected and examined many more Ginn editions since the Catalogue was published.

"Ginn is correct in identifying the printing year. But the number to the left of the year does not indicate the month, and more importantly for your purposes, the number to the right of the decimal does not indicate the impression (so that a 1 following the decimal does not reflect a first impression or printing). I do not know what the numbers to the left of the year signify, but I am quite certain that the numbers to the right of the decimal do indicate the month.

"One way to test whether a 1 to the right of the decimal signifies a first printing is to examine what are reasonably known to be actual first editions. My work provides two tests. Ginn's first edition of *Pinocchio* was released in September, 1904, and the printing mark on the copyright deposit copy (Library of Congress) is 44.7, which I interpret as July, 1904, but it is not 44.1. In 1911 Ginn released *Pinocchio in Africa*. The copyright deposit copy is marked 811.4; it is not 811.1.

"Ginn shows an active record of reprints because many of its books were meant for use by elementary schools. I do not claim to have captured all Ginn reprints, but I have captured enough to demonstrate, I believe, that the number to the right of the decimal does not indicate a printing, but more likely denotes the month."

SILVER DAGGER MYSTERIES
2000 Statement: *See* 2000 Statement of The Overmountain Press

SILVER LINK PUBLISHING LTD (UNITED KINGDOM)
1994 Statement: "On all books published by Silver Link since its establishment in 1985, and all those of its only other imprint, Past & Present, first editions will be recognised by the statement 'First published in (month) (year)' with no other printing history. Subsequent editions and reprints have the above followed by 'Reprinted (month) (year)' or 'New revised edition (month) (year),' or similar."

SILVER MOUNTAIN PRESS
1995 Statement: "In response to your query regarding first editions, all Silver Mountain Press books use 1 2 3 4 5 6 7 8 9 0 on the copyright page to mark the number of the edition. The first number to appear on the left indicates the edition. The only exception is the 1994 novel *Isla Grande* by Richard Hughes.

The first editions of *Isla Grande* do not use the 1 2 3 4 5 6 7 8 9 0 markings and can be identified by the misspelled name of the press on the copyright page: Silver Mounatin Press. The second and following editions of this novel use the 1 2 3 4 5 6 7 8 9 0 system and have the correct spelling of the press.''

SILVER PIXEL PRESS

2000 Statement: "A first printing of a first edition is not specifically designated. If a book goes into a subsequent printing or a subsequent edition, these are clearly designated by the words 'xxxth Printing' or 'xxxth Edition' after the year in the copyright line. If these extra words do not appear, it may be presumed the book is a first printing of a first edition.''

SILVER QUILL PRESS

2000 Statement: *See* 2000 Statement of Down East Enterprise

SILVER WHISTLE

2001 Statement: *See* 2001 Statement of Harcourt, Inc.

SILVERFISH REVIEW PRESS

1995 Statement: "First printing is designated by the following: Copyright © 1993 by Silverfish Review Press.''

SIMMONS-BOARDMAN PUBLISHING CORPORATION

1937 Statement: "We print on the copyright page the date of each revised edition of our books. Each revised edition is copyrighted as to its new material.''

1947 Statement: "Our entry is unchanged. You might add that the number of the reprint of an edition is also added on the copyright page.''

SIMON AND SCHUSTER

1928 Statement: "Our first editions are marked by the fact that the copyright page bears *no* printing or edition notice, whereas in subsequent editions the dates, and sometimes even the quantity of the printings appear, as

First Printing, April 1927

Second Printing, May 1927, etc.''

1937 Statement: "Our first editions are marked by the fact that the copyright page bears *no* printing or edition notices whereas in subsequent editions the dates, and sometimes even the quantity of the printings, appear, as

First Printing, April 1936

Second Printing, May 1936, etc.

"The date is not always used nor is the phrase 'First Printing' but second and subsequent editions are always marked.''

1947 Statement: *See* 1937 Statement

1976 Statement: "Simon and Schuster indicates which printing a book is in by a string of numbers on the copyright page, which appears just below the line that reads, 'Manufactured in . . . .' If you look at the first number on the *left*, you will know which printing you have in hand. Thus if the first number you see is 1, you have a first printing; if the first number you see is 3, you have a third printing. This system of indicating the printing is fairly common in the industry. The only difference of opinion seems to be whether to run the numbers from left to right or vice versa.

"The number system was adopted here over three years ago. We do, however, make an occasional exception to this style and go back to our earlier custom of spelling out: First Printing. Some of our books have carried the date of the printing: First Printing, 1964. The custom of spelling out the printing was, as far as I have been able to determine, the only method of identifying printings prior to mid-1973.

"It should be noted that we use the word 'edition' two ways: (1) to distinguish the style of binding, i.e. a book may be available in both a case-bound edition and a paperback edition; (2) to indicate the version of the text. We do not use 'edition' to mean 'impression' or 'printing.' Therefore one may find certain books in which the first number of the string is 1, but the title page and/or the copyright page indicates that the book is a revised (or second, or third, etc.) edition."

1981 Statement: "The entry you enclosed for Simon and Schuster is still accurate, with one exception. We continue to indicate the number of the printing on the copyright page, but it isn't always the first number on the left. We sometimes will print the numbers like this:

1 3 5 7 9 10 8 6 4 2

Regardless of which system we use, the correct printing is always the lowest number shown."

1989 Statement: "Simon and Schuster indicates which printing a book is in by a string of numbers on the copyright page, which appears just below the line that reads, 'Manufactured in . . . .' If you look at the lowest number you will know which printing you have in hand. Thus if the lowest number you see is 1, you have a first printing; if the lowest number you see is 3, you have a third printing. This system of indicating the printing is fairly common in the industry. The only difference of opinion seems to be whether to run the numbers from left to right, vice versa, or centered as in 1 3 5 7 9 10 8 6 4 2."

1994 Statement: *See* 1989 Statement

SINCLAIR-STEVENSON (UNITED KINGDOM)

1994 Statement: "A first impression would be designated as 'First published in Great Britain by Sinclair-Stevenson' etc. A second impression would be indicated by 'First reprint' and the year. If there are subsequent impressions in the same year, this would be shown by, for example, 'Reprinted twice in 1994,' or 'Reprinted three times in 1994.' A subsequent paperback edition, using the same type, would be indicated as follows, e.g.: 'This paperback edition by Sinclair-Stevenson in 1994.' Sinclair-Stevenson is an imprint of Reed Consumer Books, and the method of designation accords with the one used by Reed."

SINGING BONE PRESS

2000 Statement: *See* 2000 Statement of Ibbetson St. Press

SINGULAR SPEECH PRESS

1994 Statement: "A very small-scale publisher of poetry, we have published 30 titles, more or less, of which 20 remain in print. Of these, but one is a second edition, so designated on the copyright page. All others are and must be construed as first editions, having nowhere any indication to the contrary. We have always done so, since our start eighteen years ago."

2000 Statement: *See* 1994 Statement

SIR PUBLISHING (NEW ZEALAND)

1994 Statement: "Rarely do we get into first/second, etc. editions and hence have no policy at this stage. Where we have reprinted . . . we have not mentioned this in the title page."

SIXTEENTH CENTURY ESSAYS & STUDIES

2001 Statement: *See* 2001 Statement of Truman State University Press

SIXTEENTH CENTURY JOURNAL PUBLISHERS INC.

1994 Statement: "We have always put the date of original publication on the copyright page. Any subsequent reprinting or new edition is so marked on that page."

2001 Statement: *See* 2001 Statement of Truman State University Press

SKEFFINGTON & SON, LTD. (UNITED KINGDOM)

1937 Statement: "It is not our practice to insert the date of publication on the title page of our new books. In cases where they are reprinted, second, third, or fourth impressions, are printed on the title page and where new editions are issued, the words 'New Edition' are also printed.

"Our first editions are therefore quite easy to identify as the title page appears without date and no reference to any edition."

1948 Statement: "It is not our present practice to include dates in our publications. In the case of books which are reprinted, we state 'Second Impression,' 'Third Impression' and so on, as appropriate."

CHARLES SKILTON LTD. (UNITED KINGDOM)

1994, 2000 Statements: *See* 1947 Statement of The Albyn Press (United Kingdom)

SKOOB BOOKS LTD (UNITED KINGDOM)

2000 Statement: "Our specifications for copyright details remain pretty much as in our 1994 Statement [of Skoob Books Publishing Ltd (United Kingdom)]. There is one change to make to the overall company name . . . 'Publishing' no longer appears. The change took place in 1996."

SKOOB BOOKS PUBLISHING LTD (UNITED KINGDOM)

1994 Statement: "Broadly speaking all books are designated as:

First Published 199- by Skoob Books etc.

"This appears on the copyright page. The method may vary from time to time, depending on the design of this page and the nature of the material being published. Where the book is a first paperback edition we will credit the first publication."

SKOOB ESOTERICA (UNITED KINGDOM)

1994 Statement: *See* 1994 Statement of Skoob Books Publishing Ltd (United Kingdom)

2000 Statement: *See* 2000 Statement of Skoob Books Ltd (United Kingdom)

SKOOB PACIFICA (UNITED KINGDOM)

1994 Statement: *See* 1994 Statement of Skoob Books Publishing Ltd (United Kingdom)

2000 Statement: *See* 2000 Statement of Skoob Books Ltd (United Kingdom)

SKOOB SERIPH (UNITED KINGDOM)

1994 Statement: *See* 1994 Statement of Skoob Books Publishing Ltd (United Kingdom)

2000 Statement: *See* 2000 Statement of Skoob Books Ltd (United Kingdom)

SKY PUBLISHING CORP

2000 Statement: "We do not differentiate first editions."

SKYLIGHT PATHS

2000 Statement: *See* 1994 Statement of Gemstone Press

SLAVICA PUBLISHERS, INC.

1994 Statement: "Slavica does not differentiate a first printing from reprints in any way, unless the reprint has been revised or changed in some way, in which case the later year of copyright will also appear on the copyright page (we never have had more than one printing in a single calendar year)."

SLEEPY HOLLOW PRESS

1981 Statement: *See* 1976 Statement of Sleepy Hollow Restorations

SLEEPY HOLLOW RESTORATIONS

1976 Statement: "First editions of books published by Sleepy Hollow Restorations may be identified by the appearance of the words 'First Printing' on the copyright page of the book.

"Reprints of the first edition of one of our books will be identified by the words 'Second Printing,' 'Third Printing,' etc., with the date of the printing, on the copyright page of the book.

"Subsequent or revised editions will be identified by the words 'Revised Edition,' 'Second Edition,' etc., on the copyright page of the book."

1981 Statement: *See* 1981 Statement of Sleepy Hollow Press

WILLIAM SLOANE ASSOCIATES, INC.

1947 Statement: "The only distinguishing marks are carried on the copyright notice. First editions are marked 'First Printing' and subsequent printings carry the number of that particular printing: second, third, and so on."

JAQUI SMALL (UNITED KINGDOM)

2000 Statement: *See* 2000 Statement of Aurum Press (United Kingdom)

SMALL HELM PRESS

2000 Statement: "[Edition] statement [is] only on subsequent editions. We identify the first printing of a first edition by the number line '10 9 8 7 6 5 4 3 2 1.' "

THE SMITH

1976 Statement: "We simply print, on the copyright page, 'First Edition,' followed by the month and the year."

1981 Statement: *See* 1976 Statement

1988 Statement: "We use the same method of reporting First Editions that we have always used, though we do not indicate month of publication— only the year of copyright."

1993, 2000 Statements: *See* 1988 Statement

GIBBS SMITH, PUBLISHER

1988 Statement: "First editions are so designated on the copyright page. Subsequent printings of the first edition are so noted.

"We print as the first words of the copyright page 'First Edition.' Following that comes the line of numbers, then the copyright notice. As far as I know, this is the way we have always done it.

"Please note that the current and correct name of our company is Gibbs Smith, Publisher. Our books all carry the Peregrine Smith Books imprint."

1993 Statement: "First editions are so designated on the copyright page.

"We print as the first words of the copyright page 'First Edition.' Following that comes the line of numbers, then the copyright notice. A number is deleted each time the book is reprinted."

2000 Statement: *See* 1993 Statement. Note that, "Since about 1998, our books no longer carry the Peregrine Smith Imprint."

HARRISON SMITH, INC.

(Became Harrison Smith & Robert Haas, Inc., in March, 1932.)

1937 Statement: "Although no strict rule was followed, in general it will be found that unless books are marked 'Second printing,' they are first editions."

HARRISON SMITH & ROBERT HAAS, INC.

(Organized in March, 1932. Out of business.Merged with Random House, Inc. on April 1, 1936.)

1937 Statement: "Although no strict rule was followed, in general it will be found that unless books published by us are marked 'Second printing,' they are first editions."

PEREGRINE SMITH, INC.

1976 Statement: "Peregrine Smith, Inc. does not have a particular or unique method of identifying first editions at this time. We do note second (and subsequent) or revised editions on the copyright page of the edition so designated, however; this notation being used when there have been textual changes, additions or alterations in the book. Printing runs have seldom (if ever) been noted on Peregrine Smith, Inc. books."

1981 Statement: "Until 1980 first editions had no distinguishing mark or imprint. The date on the title page and copyright page correspond to the first publication of the book. If the book was reprinted, this would usually be noted by either a date change on the title page or the notation '2nd printing' etc. on the copyright page. Any revisions or alterations would be acknowledged by the notation 'Revised.' Since 1980, our policy has been to print 'First edition' on the copyright page of the book, this to be replaced by '2nd printing'.. etc., if the book returned to press."

1988, 1993 Statements: *See* 1988, 1993 Statements of Gibbs Smith, Publisher

2000 Statement: *See* 2000 Statement of Gibbs Smith, Publisher

PETER SMITH, INC.
1937 Statement: "Date of edition is always indicated on title page."
1947, 2000 Statements: *See* 1937 Statement

RICHARD R. SMITH
(Including Margent Press.)
1947 Statement: "Since I have been publishing under my sole individual imprint, which was in December 1935, I have placed the date of publication both on the title page and on the copyright page which backs it up. In the event that a book is reprinted, I change the date on the title page but not, of course, on the copyright. I also add to the copyright page the dates of the various reprints. It is true, however, that if a reprint happened to be required very hurriedly as was the case with some of my books during the war, we may have failed to change the date on the title page.

"Margent Press is a subsidiary imprint of mine and is used primarily for fiction, poetry, and books in the occult field."

URE SMITH (AUSTRALIA)
1976 Statement: "In answer to your question regarding the method of identifying first editions, in the majority of cases since 1960 a first edition can be identified by the words FIRST EDITION *or* First published in (date) . . . ."
1981 Statement: *See* Lansdowne Press (Australia)
1988 Statement: *See* 1988 Statement of Kevin Weldon & Associates Pty. Ltd. (Australia)

SMITH AND DURRELL, INC.
(October 1, 1947, name changed to Oliver Durrell, Inc.)
1947 Statement: *See* Oliver Durrell, Inc.

SMITH & KRAUSE INC PUBLISHERS
2000 Statement: "We identify the first printing of a first edition by:
    First edition: (date of publication)
    10 9 8 7 6 5 4 3 2 1."

SMITH GRYPHON LIMITED (UNITED KINGDOM)
1994 Statement: "Our first editions say:

'First published in Great Britain in (year)
by Smith Gryphon Ltd.'
"Any subsequent impressions will give the date of the first and all later impressions or editions."

SMITH SETTLE LIMITED (UNITED KINGDOM)

1994 Statement: "Since our inception in 1986 all our books have the date of first publication on the imprint page; subsequent reprints or revised editions are also listed on the imprint page. First editions would thus be those books which do not have any reprints or revised editions on the imprint page."

2000 Statement: "Since we published our first book in 1988, all our books have had the date of first printing on the imprint page. Revised editions are sometimes also listed, but not always. Reprints are not usually listed on the imprint page."

SMITHSONIAN INSTITUTION PRESS

1976 Statement: "We do not designate first editions. Yes, we indicate only those printings or editions after the first. Thus, it may be safely assumed that any book bearing the Smithsonian Institution Press imprint is a first edition, unless otherwise indicated."

1981 Statement: *See* 1976 Statement

1988 Statement: "This year we began designating editions by means of a range of numbers listed on the copyright page. The last number on the right-hand side designates the edition, so that a first edition would bear the numerals ten, or in some cases five, through one. In some cases we follow the same format for year dates, e.g.: 93 92 91 90 89 5 4 3 2 1."

1993 Statement: *See* 1988 Statement

2000 Statement: "We designate editions by means of a range of numbers listed on the copyright page. The last number on the right-hand side designates the edition, so that a first edition would bear the numerals five through one. We follow the same format for year dates, e.g.: 93 92 91 90 89 5 4 3 2 1. We do not change edition numbers for short-run, 'on-demand' reprints of less than 100 copies."

SMYRNA PRESS

2000 Statement: "Our first editions bear no distinguishing printing or edition notice. Subsequent editions identify themselves as second printing, third printing, etc. Almost all second editions have a change of paper weight or some other physical change. There is only one edition of Bill Plympton's *Tube Strips*. Published for $2.50, it now brings $100 per copy."

COLIN SMYTHE LIMITED, PUBLISHERS (UNITED KINGDOM)

1976 Statement: "First editions normally have the statement 'First published in . . . .' Reprints always are indicated 'Reprinted . . . .' If ours is not the first publication, we normally give as much bibliographical information as possible."

1981 Statement: "I think the [1976] entry could possibly be expanded to read:

"First editions normally have the statement

'First published in . . . .

second edition published in . . . .'

"Reprints are indicated by a statement to that effect. If ours is not the first publication, we normally give as much bibliographical information as possible.

"By second edition, I mean the bibliographical second edition, where new material has been added, the old revised, or when the book has been reset, not just the CIP definition of a rewrite. If a book is a photographic reproduction of an earlier edition from a different publisher, such information is normally indicated in the book. Normally we only issue straight photographic reprints in paperback format. Regrettably I am not as consistent in my descriptions as I should be. When I started publishing I tried to give even the publication day in my description, but printers' delays so often made a nonsense of this that I had to give it up."

1988 Statement: "My 1976 statement remains unchanged. I have not found any reason for making changes.

"As to Dolmen Press, we bought the books but not the imprint or logo. We have made new contracts with many of the authors and should we reprint any of the titles, they will appear with our imprint. The Dolmen ISBN prefix 0-85105 will continue to be used for those publications for the foreseeable future. I will of course also use our own system of providing bibliographical information for Dolmen titles in future."

1994, 2000 Statements: *See* 1988 Statement

SOCIAL ECOLOGY PRESS

2000 Statement: *See* 2000 Statement of Dog-Eared Publications

SOCIETY FOR INDUSTRIAL & APPLIED MATHEMATICS

1994 Statement: "We identify the first printing of a first edition by the following number line: 10 9 8 7 6 5 4 3 2 1."

The lowest number indicates the printing.

2000 Statement: *See* 1994 Statement

SOCIETY FOR PROMOTING CHRISTIAN KNOWLEDGE (UNITED KINGDOM)

1937 Statement: "It is our practice to put the date of the publication of any book on the title-page itself. If the book is reprinted, the date of the reprint appears on the title-page and a bibliographical description on the back of the title-page, e.g.

First Edition 1922

Reprinted 1923

Second Edition 1924

"If only slight corrections are made we put Second Impression: and Second Edition when changes in the text are important."

1947, 1989, 2000 Statements: *See* 1937 Statement

SOFFIETTO EDITIONS
2001 Statement: *See* 2001 Statement of Red Moon Press

SOFTBABCKS (UNITED KINGDOM)
1994 Statement: *See* 1994 Statement of ABC (United Kingdom)

SOHNEN–MOE ASSOCIATES
1995 Statement: "We distinguish a first edition from subsequent editions by stating the actual edition on the back of the title page. We identify the printings with the date, such as 'First published 1988,' 'Seventh Printing January 1995,' and 'Second Edition June 1991.' "

THE SOHO BOOK COMPANY LTD. (UNITED KINGDOM)
1988 Statement: "Our first editions carry the statement
'Published by the Soho Book Company Ltd,
1/3 Brewer Street, London W1
19...'
"Later editions add: '2nd Edition 19...'
"Later impressions add: '2nd impression 19...' "

SOHO CRIME
2000 Statement: *See* 2000 Statement of Soho Press Inc.

SOHO PRESS INC.
1988 Statement: "We carry the term 'FIRST EDITION' on the copyright page of every book and have done so consistently. Additional printings are likewise noted as they occur."
1993 Statement: "We now carry numbers, from 10 to 1, on the copyright page and drop numbers as subsequent editions are printed."
2000 Statement: *See* 1993 Statement

SOM PUBLISHING
1994 Statement: "First editions are noted on the copyright page of each publication by the original copyright date (month and year). Subsequent printings are noted below the original copyright date with the appropriate printing edition and its month and year; i.e., 'Second Printing, May, 1994.' "
2000 Statement: *See* 1994 Statement

SONO NIS PRESS (CANADA)
1995 Statement: "Our first editions are identified on the reverse of the title page, by the year of copyright. Subsequent editions are listed below the Canadian Cataloguing in Publication Data thus: First printing November 1982 Tenth printing January 1993."
2000 Statement: *See* 1995 Statement

SOPHIA INSTITUTE PRESS
1994 Statement: "Prior to 3/94 we used 2 4 6 8 10 9 7 5 3 1. When reprinted we deleted the figure 1, etc. on the copyright page. Now we use 94 95 96 97 98 99 10 9 8 7 6 5 4 3 2 1. When reprinted, we delete figure 1, etc. and the year as appropriate."

2000 Statement: *See* 1994 Statement

SORIN BOOKS

2000 Statement: "Sorin Books does not identify first editions. Once a book reaches 25,000 copies in print, a printing history is included on the copyright page. This history indicates the date of the first printing, the date and number of the current printing, and the number of copies in print."

SOS PUBLICATIONS

1995 Statement: "A second edition . . . is stated as Copyright, new date, Title, 2nd edition; Title, 1st edition, date."
2000 Statement: *See* 1995 Statement

SOUND VIEW PRESS

1994 Statement: "All of our books are first editions."
2000 Statement: *See* 1994 Statement

SOUTH END PRESS

1994 Statement: The first printing of a first edition is indicated by a number line on the copyright page. The lowest number showing indicates the printing.
2000 Statement: *See* 1994 Statement

SOUTH HEAD PRESS (AUSTRALIA)

1988 Statement: "South Head Press does not particularly identify First Edition printings. The date of printing set forth in each book is the way Editions are identified.

"The same applies to books published as issues of Poetry Australia."
1994 Statement: *See* 1988 Statement

SOUTH JETTY BOOKS

2000 Statement: *See* 2000 Statement of The Bacchae Press

SOUTHBOUND PRESS

1995 Statement: "First edition lacks reference to additional printings; second and third printings, etc. include reference to first edition with 'First Printing (date) month, year.' "
2001 Statement: *See* 1995 Statement

SOUTHERN ILLINOIS UNIVERSITY PRESS

1976 Statement: "We do not indicate first printing of a first edition, but do indicate number—and give date—of subsequent printing(s). We note revised edition on title page and on copyright page."
1981 Statement: "Southern Illinois University Press has made only one change in designating printings and editions, a change effective just this month [January, 1981]. In printings after the first, we indicate the printing and date of the most recent printing and no longer indicate the date of printings prior to the current one."
1988 Statement: "We now indicate printing and year by numbers on [the] © page:

91 90 89 88 4 3 2 1

"This is a first printing in 1988.

"Subsequent printings [are] similarly indicated by removing [the] number

91 90 89 4 3

"[This is a] third printing in 1989."

1993, 2000 Statements: *See* 1988 Statement

SOUTHERN IMAGES

2000 Statement: *See* 2000 Statement of Wyrick & Co.

SOUTHERN METHODIST UNIVERSITY PRESS

1976 Statement: "We do not designate a first edition, but we do designate each subsequent printing and edition. Therefore it may be assumed that if any one of our books has simply the copyright date it is a first edition. A subsequent printing will have below that line on the copyright page 'Second Printing 1975' or whatever the year may be. And this will continue with each subsequent printing. A second edition carries a similar line. For example, *John C. Duval, First Texas Man of Letters* by J. Frank Dobie has the copyright date 1939 and then below it 'Second Edition, 1965.' We have used these methods of identification from the earliest days of our press."

1981 Statement: *See* 1976 Statement

1988 Statement: "In May 1987 we began to designate first editions 'First Edition 1987' or whatever the year may be, and we continue to designate each subsequent printing or edition ('Second Printing 1988' or 'Second Edition 1988').

"For books published prior to May 1987, see 1976 Statement."

1993 Statement: *See* 1988 Statement

2001 Statement: "We state 'First edition, date' on the copyright page. A number string is used to identify printings: '10 9 8 7 6 5 4 3 2 1.' "

SOUTHWEST PRESS

(Succeeded by Turner Company in 1935.)

THE SOUTHWORTH PRESS

1947 Statement: *See* 1947 Statement of The Anthoensen Press

SOUTHWORTH-ANTHOENSEN PRESS

(Name changed to The Anthoensen Press, in 1947.)

1947 Statement: *See* 1947 Statement of The Anthoensen Press

SOUVENIR PRESS LIMITED (UNITED KINGDOM)

1976 Statement: "We do not differentiate specifically on our various editions except to have the words, 'this edition first published by Souvenir Press Limited in the year of publication it is.' I hope this gives you sufficient information. We tend to put in the next reprint underneath whenever such a happy event occurs, which actually with our books is quite often."

1981 Statement: *See* 1976 Statement

1988 Statement: "I am astonished at how pertinent the statement we made in 1976 still is today. We do continue to have many reprints happily."

2000 Statement: *See* 1988 Statement

SPARROW PRESS

1988 Statement: *See* 1988 Statement of Vagrom Chap Books

SPCK PUBLISHING (UNITED KINGDOM)

See Society for Promoting Christian Knowledge (United Kingdom)

NEVILLE SPEARMAN PUBLISHERS (UNITED KINGDOM)

1994, 2000 Statements: *See* 1994 Statement of The C.W. Daniel Company Ltd (United Kingdom)

THE SPEECH BIN

1995 Statement: "The Speech Bin, Inc. does not distinguish the first printing of first editions. Second and subsequent editions are so described."
2000 Statement: *See* 1995 Statement

ROBERT SPELLER PUBLISHING CO.

(The 1949 edition of Boutell's "First Editions of Today and How to Tell Them" incorrectly identified this company as being "out of business.")
1937 Statement: "Each book published by us carries, on the copyright page, the words FIRST EDITION. Subsequent editions are marked thus: Second Printing, Third Printing, etc."
See Statement for 1960 of Robert Speller & Sons, Publishers, Inc.

ROBERT SPELLER & SONS, PUBLISHERS, INC.

Statement for 1960: "Robert Speller Publishing Co. did not go out of business in 1938. Book sales distribution were handled by Elliott Publishing Co. in 1938-39. Elliott is out of business as far as we know.

"Robert Speller Publishing Co. changed its name to Robert Speller & Sons, Publishers, Inc. in 1957. All books are distributed by us. We have been in business since 1930.

"First impressions were identified by the words, 'First edition, 2nd printing, etc.' "
1976, 1982, 1994, 2000 Statements: *See* Statement for 1960

SPHERE BOOKS

2001 Statement: "Today Sphere Books is part of Little, Brown and Co (Publishers). The Sphere imprint is rarely used.

"We do not in fact follow the numbering procedure. When books are reprinted we state the year in which they are. If a book is reprinted more than once a year we simply state this in brackets, i.e.:
Reprinted in 2001 (three times)."

SPHERE BOOKS LIMITED (UNITED KINGDOM)

1988 Statement: "The publication date and record of each new impression and new edition is entered on the copyright page. This has been the practice since Sphere Books Ltd was formed twenty-one years ago in 1967. Our Abacus and Cardinal imprints use the same method."
(In late 1988, the Penguin Group changed its method of designating a first edition. For a book published in the latter part of 1988, see 1988 Statement of Penguin Publishing Co Ltd [United Kingdom].)

SPHINX PRESS INC
2000 Statement: *See* 2000 Statement of International Universities Press, Inc.

SPHINX PUBLISHING
1994 Statement: "On the copyright page we state first edition and the year. The next printing would state First edition, second printing and the year, etc. For second and subsequent editions we note this on the title page.

"On our early books we did not mention the edition, only the printing and the month and year. We also used to call every press run a printing. Now, if no changes have been made to the text we do not call it a new printing. The reason for this is that we use a just-in-time inventory system and print our books in small quantities as we need them."

SPINDLEWOOD (UNITED KINGDOM)
1994 Statement: "We always designate:
'First published in Great Britain by Spindlewood.'
"If we reprint this is always stated—and a date will be given for the reprint.
"We do publish synchronised co-editions from time to time—if we are not the originating publisher we designate:
'Published in Great Britain by Spindlewood (date)' and underneath,
'First published in New Zealand, Australia' etc.
"The above would signify a first UK edition."

SPINIFEX PRESS (AUSTRALIA)
1994 Statement: "Our first editions are indicated by the phrase: First published by Spinifex Press 199__. This designation was adopted in 1991 when we established the company. Co-productions or takeovers include the name of the originating publisher. Second editions or printings are designated as: Second edition published 199__ and Reprinted 199__."
2000 Statement: *See* 1994 Statement

SPINSTERS/AUNT LUTE BOOK CO.
1988 Statement: "We indicate a first edition on the copyright page by indicating printings as follows:
10 - 9 - 8 - 7 - 6 - 5 - 4 - 3 - 2 - 1
"Each subsequent printing has one number deleted. 'Second Editions' are so named with a new number sequence.
"1982 was the year we adopted this method. It differs from previous years when we did nothing. We have no imprints or subsidiaries."

SPINSTERS INK
1993 Statement: "We indicate a first edition on the copyright page by indicating printings as follows:
10 - 9 - 8 - 7 - 6 - 5 - 4 - 3 - 2 - 1
"Each subsequent printing has one number deleted. 'Second Editions' are so named with a new number sequence.
"1982 was the year we adopted this method."

SPIRE BOOKS
2000 Statement: *See* 2000 Statement of Fleming H. Revell Company

SPIRITUAL SCIENCE LIBRARY
1988 Statement: *See* 1988 Statement of Garber Communications Inc.

E. & F. N. SPON LTD. (UNITED KINGDOM)
1976 Statement: "We do not use any particular method to identify first editions of our books. There is a simple statement on the biblio page of when the book was first published. If there is no additional information on either reprints or new editions then the book is a first edition."

1981 Statement: "It remains true to say that we make no special announcement in the first edition of any of our titles. The absence of any information about re-printing or revision can be taken as an indication that the book in question is indeed a first edition."

1988 Statement: *See* 1988 Statement of Associated Book Publishers (UK) Ltd. (Scientific and Technical Division) (United Kingdom)

THE SPOON RIVER PRESS
1977 Statement: "All books published by The Spoon River Press bear the publishing history on the title page verso. First printings are designated by the phrase 'First published (month) (year).' Later printings are noted below this line. We have always followed this practice."

1983, 1989, 1995, 2001 Statements: *See* 1977 Statement

SPORTS ILLUSTRATED BOOKS
2000 Statement: *See* 2000 Statement of Madison Books

SPOTLIGHT BOOKS
2000 Statement: *See* 2000 Statement of Empire Publishing Service

SPRING (UNITED KINGDOM)
1989 Statement: *See* 1989 Statement of The Octopus Publishing Group PLC (United Kingdom)

SPRING CREEK PRESS
1988 Statement: *See* 1988 Statement of Johnson Publishing Company, Inc.
1995, 2000 Statements: *See* 1995 Statement of Johnson Books

SPRING PUBLICATIONS INC.
1995 Statement: "We now say 'First printing' (Second printing) etc. plus the date on the copyright page (verso of title page)."
2000 Statement: *See* 1995 Statement

SPRINGER PUBLISHING COMPANY, INC.
1994 Statement: The first printing of a first edition is indicated by the number line 93 94 95 96 97/5 4 3 2 1. The lowest number showing indicates the printing.
2000 Statement: *See* 1994 Statement

SPRINGER-VERLAG NEW YORK INC.

1994 Statement: The first printing of a first edition is indicated by the number line 10 9 8 7 6 5 4 3 2 1. The lowest number showing indicates the printing.
2000 Statement: *See* 1994 Statement

SPRINGHOUSE CORPORATION

1994 Statement: "At Springhouse Books, we incorporate each edition after the first edition into the title of the book; for example, *Illustrated Manual of Nursing Practice, Second Edition.* The first edition is unlabeled as such. On all editions, we signify printings through a code of six numbers on the copyright page, beginning with 0, followed by the number of the printing, then the month, then the year. For example, 010893 indicates a first printing in August of 1993. We have used this coding system since 1980."

2000 Statement: "For Springhouse Corporation books, we incorporate each edition after the first edition into the title of the book; for example, *Illustrated Manual of Nursing Practice, Third Edition.* The first edition in unlabeled as such. For software products, we signify printings through a code of six numbers on the copyright page, beginning with 0, followed by the number of the printing, then the month, then the year. For example, 010800 indicates a first printing in August of 2000. For all other products, we use a code of single letters that each represent a month of the year. We also use two additional codes, the first a series of double digit numbers that each represent a year and the second a series from 10 to 1 that represent the number of the printing. Each of these codes is obscured so that the last number or letter on the right represents the month, year, and number of the printing, respectively.

"For example, a code of:

D N O S

02 01 00   10 9 8 7 6

indicates a 6th printing in September of 2000. We have used this coding system since 1999."

SPRINGHOUSE EDITIONS

2000 Statement: *See* 2000 Statement of White Pine Press

SPS STUDIOS, INC.

2001 Statement: "We identify the first printing of a first edition by the statement 'First Printing: (month/year).' Subsequent printings are identified as 'Second, Third,' etc. Printing."

SR BOOKS

1994 Statement: "At SR Books, we designated our first and subsequent editions as follows:

© 1985 by Norman A. Graebner

All rights reserved

First published 1985

Second printing 1989

Printed and bound in the United States of America

"The method shown above does not differ from any previously used."

2001 Statement: *See* 1994 Statement

STACKPOLE BOOKS

1976 Statement: "I'm sorry to say that we don't have any method of identifying first editions. Generally, our books do not contain this information, since many of our publications are quality paperback titles. We may, however, put printing and edition information in the front matter of a select few of our titles in the near future."

1981 Statement: "Stackpole now identifies its second, third, fourth, etc., editions. We do not identify first editions. Thus, if one of our books is without an edition designation in the front matter, that book may be assumed to be a first edition.

"This, I understand has been our policy for a couple of years or so now."

1988 Statement: "Stackpole identifies its second, third, fourth, and subsequent editions. We have been identifying our first editions in some books and expect to do so in most of our future books. If one of our books is without an edition designation in the front matter, that book may be assumed to be a first edition.

"In 1987 we began designating the number of the printing within each edition by a row of numbers on the copyright page: 10 9 8 7 6 5 4 3 2 1. In copies from the first printing of any edition, all the numbers appear. For each successive printing, one number is removed. So, if the farthest-right number is 2, that copy of the book is from the second printing of the designated edition."

1993 Statement: "Our practice has not changed since 1988, with the minor exception that Stackpole identifies first editions in all its books."

2000 Statement: *See* 1993 Statement

STACKPOLE SONS

1937 Statement: "The lack of notice of additional printings shows a Stackpole Sons first edition. There is one exception—*Caleb Catlum's America*. The first printing of this book is marked 'First Edition' at the bottom of the verso of the title page.

"The Telegraph Press has adhered to no strict policy in the past, though usually its first printings have been marked 'First Edition'; but hereafter it will follow the same method as that used by Stackpole Sons, and its first printings will be identified by the lack of notice of subsequent reprintings."

1947 Statement: "The lack of notice of additional printings shows a Stackpole Sons first edition. There is one exception—*Caleb Catlum's America*. The first printing of this book is marked 'First Edition' at the bottom of the verso of the title page."

STAINER & BELL LTD. (UNITED KINGDOM)

1976 Statement: "We as publishers have no particular method of identifying first editions. Unless it states otherwise (i.e. 'second revised edition') then our book is a first edition—but not necessarily a 'first printing' of a first edition.

"I'm afraid we have no other more definite method of identification."

1981, 1988 Statements: *See* 1976 Statement

2001 Statement: "For our book publications, the first edition indicates 'First Published (year).' Any subsequent edition or reprint will be indicated on the history page. If no further printing information appears then it will be a first edition. This does not apply to our sheet music publications where no printing history is recorded in the copy.

"The majority of titles that were in the Augener, Galliard, Weekes and Joseph Williams catalogues come under the sheet music category. Nothing new is now produced under these imprints but any reprints of 'books' would be treated in the same way as Stainer & Bell publications. The imprint 'Belton' is also no longer used and nothing remains in print using it."

STANDARD PUBLISHING
1994 Statement: "When a book is first published, we list the publishing date + seven years and five printings on the copyright page. For example:
00 99 98 97 96 95 94 5 4 3 2 1
When the book is reprinted, we delete figure 1, etc., and whatever date(s) is past.

"If we publish a second edition of a book, it is usually changed enough that it would carry a revised copyright and would start over again with the numbering system described above.

"Instead of this method, we used to state the number of the printing, followed by the year, on the copyright page: Second printing, 1995."

STANFORD MARITIME (UNITED KINGDOM)
1988 Statement: *See* 1988 Statement of George Philip Limited (United Kingdom)

STANFORD UNIVERSITY PRESS
1928 Statement: *See* 1937 Statement
1937 Statement: "Our method of indicating our first editions is the negative one of not mentioning reprinting or revision. Editions or printings subsequent to the first edition or printing carry on the copyright page both
'First published, 19—'

and

'Second Printing, 19—'

or

'Second (Revised) Edition'
"We believe we have followed this practice since we issued our first books in 1925."
1947 Statement: *See* 1937 Statement
Statement for 1960: "The [1976] statement for Stanford University Press holds for all Stanford University Press books from 1928 to the present."
1976 Statement: "We do not have any particular method of identifying first editions. I believe it is correct to say, however, that a Stanford book is unquestionably a first edition if its copyright page (1) does not specify 'Second printing' or the like, and (2) does not carry a line reading 'Last figure below indicates year of this printing,' followed by a line of two-digit numbers."

1981 Statement: "Your current write-up for Stanford University Press still accurately describes our practice. I may add that it is also our practice to include the year of publication on the title page in a first printing, and to eliminate it in second and subsequent printings. This practice has been unvarying since 1956, to the best of my knowledge."

1988 Statement: "Your current write-up for Stanford University Press still accurately describes our practice. I may add that it is also usually our practice to include the year of publication on the title page in a first printing and to eliminate it in second and subsequent printings."

1993 Statement: *See* 1988 Statement

2000 Statement: "Stanford University Press indicates the year of the 'original' or first printing in a notation set below the Library of Congress data, which until this year was placed at the end of the book and as of early in 2000 has been incorporated into the copyright page. The year of original 'publication on the title page is set at the designer's discretion and may or may not be removed on subsequent printings.' "

STANTON AND LEE

1947 Statement: *See* 1947 Statement of Arkham House

STANTON & LEE PUBLISHERS, INC.

1981 Statement: "The first printing of any book we publish carries the notice 'First Edition' on the copyright page; any subsequent printing carries the number of that printing only: second printing, October 1980; or third printing, January 1981 and so on. Our imprints use the same procedure."

STANWIX HOUSE INCORPORATED

1976 Statement: "Stanwix House does not mark First Editions in any way. In the area of our professional books, we do mark each printing after the first. Subsequent editions can be distinguished by their newer copyright."

1981 Statement: *See* 1976 Statement

C & J STAPLES SOUTH WEST REGION PUBLICATIONS FUND (AUSTRALIA)

2000 Statement: *See* 2000 Statement of University of Western Australia Press (Australia)

STAR PUBLISHING

1988 Statement: "Currently first editions are not especially designated. However, the terms 'revised edition,' 'second edition,' etc., appear when appropriate. Indications of which printing are usually not coded in the book."

1993 Statement: "Indications of which printing are usually coded in the book."

2000 Statement: *See* 1993 Statement

STARBOOK PRESS

1995 Statement: *See* 1995 Statement of Woldt Publishing Group

2000 Statement: *See* 2000 Statement of Starbooks Press

STARBOOKS PRESS
2000 Statement: "We would distinguish a first edition from subsequent editions by stating so on the copyright page. We would say 2nd Edition.

"Our Florida Literary Foundation imprints are all first editions. Wherever they are found they are first editions."

STARMONT HOUSE, INC.
1993 Statement: *See* 1993 Statement of The Borgo Press
2000 Statement: *See* 2000 Statement of The Borgo Press

STARRHILL PRESS
2000 Statement: *See* 2000 Statement of Black Belt Press

STARSEED PRESS
1994 Statement: *See* 1994 Statement of H J Kramer Inc.
2000 Statement: *See* 2000 Statement of New World Library

STATE HISTORICAL SOCIETY OF WISCONSIN (THE SOCIETY PRESS)
1976 Statement: The absence of any identifying statement would indicate the first printing of a first edition.

"Subsequent printings of an edition are indicated on the copyright page."
1981, 1988, 2001 Statements: *See* 1976 Statement

STATE HOUSE PRESS
1994 Statement: "Our reprint editions of earlier non-State House Press works normally do not carry any designation of first printing or first edition. On the copyright page will be an indication of when the book was first printed by the original publisher.

"On State House Press original publications we sometimes use the designation of first edition or first printing on the copyright page. However, on at least ten of our original publications there is no indication of their being first printings; for these, however, they can be assumed to be first printings since none, as of this date, have been reprinted."

STATE UNIVERSITY OF NEW YORK PRESS
1976 Statement: "In response to your inquiry, any book published by this Press may be considered a first edition, first printing, unless otherwise indicated on the verso of the title leaf.

"Our books seldom require recomposition and, hence, nearly all of them are 'first editions.' Second and third printings, first paperback printings, etc. are so indicated as noted above."
1988, 1995 Statements: *See* 1976 Statement
2000 Statement: "Any title published by the State University of New York Press may be considered a first edition, unless otherwise stated within the subtitle. Our books seldom require recomposition; therefore, nearly all are 'first editions.'

"Subsequent printings are specified by the reprint line located at the bottom of the Library of Congress Cataloging-in-Publication Data Page."

STEAM PRESS

1988 Statement: "First editions bear no identification. Subsequent editions are marked 'second printing 19..' or 'revised edition . . . ' on the copyright page. We do not note reprints on subsequent editions on our Vinyl Shower books."

STEIN AND DAY, PUBLISHERS

1976 Statement: "If the copyright page does not say 'second printing,' then the book is a first edition. There are no special marks identifying first or second editions."

1981 Statement: "The [1976] information on Stein and Day is still correct." Stein and Day does indicate first printings of a first edition by the notation "First published in (date)." Second printings will also have the notation SECOND PRINTING, (date).

First printings of a book first published abroad have the notation "First published in the United States of America in (date)."

1988 Statement: Stein and Day was not publishing in 1988.

STEINER BOOKS

1988 Statement: *See* 1988 Statement of Garber Communications Inc.

RUDOLF STEINER PUBLICATIONS

1988 Statement: *See* 1988 Statement of Garber Communications Inc.

STEMMER HOUSE

1981 Statement: The practice we follow with respect to designating first editions is as follows:

"The first printing of a book originated by Stemmer House is designated First Edition on the copyright page. If the book was originally published by a foreign publisher, our own book bears the words First American Edition.

"When we go back to press for a new printing, unrevised, we delete the words First Edition and substitute Second Printing, along with the month and year of this printing. Subsequent printings are listed under this line, e.g.:

    Second Printing July 1979

    Third Printing October 1980

"However, when the text is revised, the words Second Edition are substituted for the original First Edition line."

1988 Statement: "The practice we follow with respect to designating first editions is as follows:

"The first printing of a book originated by Stemmer House is designated First Edition on the copyright page. If the book was originally published by a foreign publisher, our own book bears the words First American Edition.

"When we go back to press for a new printing, unrevised, we delete the words First Edition and substitute First Printing with the date of this printing, and add Second Printing, along with the year of this printing. Subsequent printings are listed under this line, e.g.:

    Second Printing 1979

    Third Printing 1980

"When the text is revised, the words Second Edition are substituted for the original First Edition line."
1993, 2000 Statements: *See* 1988 Statement

STEMMER HOUSE PUBLISHERS INC
1988, 1993, 2000 Statements: *See* 1988 Statement of Stemmer House

STEPHEN-PAUL PUBLISHERS
1947 Statement: "In all our publications, first printings or editions are designated as such. Subsequent printings read—'second (or third) printing.' In the case of two of our publications this year, which slipped by without the designation 'First Edition,' second printings will be designated."

PATRICK STEPHENS LIMITED PUBLISHERS (UNITED KINGDOM)
1976 Statement: "We merely put on the verso of the title page of a new book, 'First published in (date).' This follows the usual copyright notice. If there is a second edition, we add the words 'Second edition (date).' "
1988 Statement: *See* 1988 Statement of Thorsons Publishing Group Ltd. (United Kingdom)
1994, 2000 Statements: *See* 1994 Statement of Haynes Publishing (United Kingdom)

STERLING PUBLISHING COMPANY, INC.
1976 Statement: "We merely put the copyright date in without any reference that it is a first edition. Should we print again without revisions, we add 'Second Printing' etc. We have always used this particular wording. If revisions are made, we obtain a new copyright, and add this © date."
1981 Statement: *See* 1976 Statement
1988 Statement: "We merely put the copyright date in without any reference that it is a first edition. However, we insert a numerical impression series, normally 1 through 10, above the copyright notice at the time of first publication. The presence of '1' indicates the first impression. At the second run, the '1' is opaqued, and so on. If revisions are made and are sufficient to do so, we obtain a new copyright, add this © date, and a new numerical sequence of impressions begins."
1994 Statement: *See* 1988 Statement, but note that a paperback previously published in hardcover will say "First paperback edition published in—" and carry a new impression series.

GARETH STEVENS PUBLISHING
2000 Statement: "Here is an example of a first edition, first printing notice that is listed on the copyright page in our books:
This edition first published in 2000 by
Gareth Stevens Publishing
A World Almanac Education Group Company
330 West Olive Street, Suite 100
Milwaukee, WI 53212 USA
This edition © 2000 by Gareth Stevens, Inc.

Printed in the United States of America
1 2 3 4 5 6 7 8 9 05 04 03 02 01 00

"Any further printings would be acknowledged by the dropping of numbers. For example, the second printing would drop the 1 on the left and the last number on the right would reflect the new print date."

GEORGE W. STEWART, PUBLISHER, INC.

1947 Statement: "With few accidental exceptions our second and subsequent printings and editions are so marked on the copyright pages. All others are first editions."

ROBERT STEWART BOOKS/SCRIBNER'S

1993 Statement: *See* 1993 Statement of Macmillan, Inc.

STILL WATERS PRESS

1994 Statement: "We identify first editions of our books by placing the words 'First Edition' on the copyright page. Subsequent printings are so identified by the phrase 'Second Edition' (or 'Third' or 'Fourth,' etc.), followed by the month and year of publication of the subsequent printing.

"This is the method we have used since Still Waters Press was founded in 1989."

2000 Statement: *See* 1994 Statement

STIPES PUBLISHING CO

2000 Statement: "We only indicate editions by noting if it is a later edition, i.e., 2nd or 3rd. If a first edition has corrections we also indicate that."

STOBART & SON LTD. (UNITED KINGDOM)

See Stobart Davies Limited (United Kingdom)

STOBART DAVIES LIMITED (UNITED KINGDOM)

1994 Statement: "Stobart Davies first editions will read on the title verso: Published 1989 (or other date) by Stobart Davies Ltd; reprints will read the original date (e.g., 1989) then the reprinted date, thus: Published 1989, reprinted, 1991, 1993 (etc).

"Prior to 1989, Stobart Davies titles (i.e. ISBN prefix 085442) were published with the imprint Stobart & Son Ltd and followed the same printing information as for Stobart Davies. As (older) Stobart & Son Ltd imprint titles come up for reprint or new edition the imprint is changed to read Stobart Davies."

2000 Statement: *See* 1994 Statement

ELLIOT STOCK (UNITED KINGDOM)

1928 Statement: "The first editions of our publications are marked with the date thereof upon the title page. All later editions carry the record, *i.e.*, the date of the first edition, and of the subsequent editions or reprints as the case may be."

1937 Statement: *See* 1928 Statement

STODDART PUBLISHING CO. LIMITED (CANADA)

2001 Statement: "I can only speak for Stoddart . . . , as we have a number of imprints (House of Anansi Press, Cormorant Press, Stoddart Kids, Boston Mills Press) that may do things differently . . . .

"Until recently, we identified the first printing of any edition by including the following line of type on the copyright page:

03 02 01 00 99 1 2 3 4 5

"The descending two-digit numbers indicate the year, and the ascending single-digit numbers indicate the number of the printing. So in the above example, the first printing of the book was in 1999. For the second printing, taking place, for example, in the year 2000, the numbers '99' and '1' would be removed, so the line would read as follows:

03 02 01 00 2 3 4 5

"Recently, we found this system to be lacking in that it did not accommodate more than five printings or five years. So now we are not identifying the year of subsequent printings specifically, but include the following line to indicate only the number of the printing:

10 9 8 7 6 5 4 3 2 1

"First editions are not explicitly identified as such on the copyright page; a hardcover first edition will simply bear the copyright line 'Copyright 2001 by The Author' and the print line above. The first trade paperback edition will bear the same copyright notice ('Copyright 2001 by The Author'), but also the lines 'Published in (for example) 2002 by Stoddart Publishing Co. Limited' and 'First published in hardcover in 2001,' as well as a brand new print line.

"Revised trade paperback editions will bear the copyright line 'Copyright 2001, 2003 by The Author' (when the revised edition is published in 2003), along with a new print line and the lines 'Published in 2003 by Stoddart Publishing Co. Limited' and 'Published in hardcover in 2001' and (if applicable) 'First trade paperback edition published in 2001.' "

FREDERICK A. STOKES CO.

(Sometime between 1937 and 1949, Stokes publications were acquired by Lippincott, which publishes Stokes juveniles under the Stokes imprint.)

1928 Statement: "To date we have omitted putting any special mark or distinction upon first printings of any of our books, but in general these can very readily be distinguished from succeeding printings by the fact that on the Copyright Page (reverse of Title) no printing notice appears. After first printings we generally put the date of publication and the words 'Second Printing' and date of such printing."

1937 Statement: *See* 1928 Statement

STONE BRIDGE PRESS

2000 Statement: "The edition number is the lowest # in the sequence on the © page. The date (year) is the lowest year in the sequence (usually adjacent to the edition # line)."

STONE WALL PRESS, INC.

1988 Statement: "This is more or less what we do:
Copyright [date] by Stone Wall Press, Inc.
First Printing, November [date]
Second Printing, January [date]"

1993 Statement: "First edition and first printing information is clearly designated on © page."

2000 Statement: "We no longer publish 'special editions' and will not designate/differentiate between printings. If we do a 'revised edition' we will so state on the copyright page."

STONEWALL SERIES

1994 Statement: *See* 1994 Statement of New Poets Series, Inc.

2000 Statement: *See* 2000 Statement of Brickhouse Books, Inc.

STOREY COMMUNICATIONS, INC.

1988 Statement: "We publish how-to books on a variety of topics; not the type of books that will have value to collectors in later years. It is not generally our policy to designate first editions unless it is a big and important book in which case the copyright page would list both First Edition and the month and year of the first printing.

"The copyright page will list the number of the printing, and the month and year, regardless of what printing it is.

"When a title has 25 percent (or more) of new material, it then becomes a revised edition. Such will be printed on the cover and title page and the book will be issued a new ISBN number and will no doubt be reintroduced to the trade as a revised edition.

"Storey Communications, Inc., has two imprints: Garden Way Publishing and Storey Publishing."

1993 Statement: *See* 1988 Statement

STOREY PUBLISHING

1988, 1993 Statements: *See* 1988 Statement of Storey Communications, Inc.

STORM PUBLISHERS

1947 Statement: "Our printings are to be identified on the copyright page. Notes to that effect appear there irregularly in the case of first printings and systematically in the case of later printings. Storm books are hence *princeps* editions when they are identified as such and when they are not identified at all. We do not expect ever to deviate from this procedure."

STORMLINE PRESS INC.

1988 Statement: "We do not designate first printings of any editions. We do specify 2nd printing, 3rd printing, etc."

2000 Statement: *See* 1988 Statement

STORY LINE PRESS

1994 Statement: "Founded in 1985, Story Line Press has varied in its designation of a first printing of a first edition. From 1990, however, we have traditionally indicated a first edition with the phrasing, 'First American Printing.' If the edition number is not indicated, it may be assumed the work is a first edition. All subsequent editions are indicated in the same format, i.e. 'Second American Printing.' "

2000 Statement: *See* 1994 Statement

STRAWBERRY HILL PRESS

1981 Statement: "The only manner in which we *normally* indicate a first edition (first printing) is by stating on the copyright page the first printing information (for example: First Printing, June, 1981).

1988 Statement: "We do not show first printing notices at all—rather, when a book is *reprinted*, the new printing information only is noted on the copyright page (e.g.: Second Printing, February, 1988). When we issue a new edition of a book, as opposed to simply another printing, that is stated on the front cover and title page of the book, as: New Edition, Revised and Expanded.

"This policy applies to our imprints and subsidiaries (we do have both)."

1994 Statement: *See* 1988 Statement

STREET & MASSEY, LTD. (UNITED KINGDOM)
(Out of business prior to 1949.)

1937 Statement: "It is our rule to place on the title page of each book the year in which the book is last printed. On the back of the title page we clearly state:

First published in January, 1936

"This indicates the initial printing. After this:

Second Impression March, 1936
Third Impression June, 1936
Second Edition (Revision) January, 1937
Fifth Impression June, 1937

"We have adopted the use of the word revision in brackets after every new edition. Collectors are quite aware that a new edition is (or should be) a revision, but the general public is not so sure and we prefer to emphasize the fact."

STRETHER AND SWANN, PUBLISHERS

1976 Statement: "Our first editions are designated as such by the words First Edition on the copyright page. Subsequent printings are designated by number."

1981 Statement: *See* 1976 Statement

STRIVERS ROW

2001 Statement: *See* 2001 Statement of Random House, Inc.

PAUL A. STRUCK, INC.

1947 Statement: "Our First Editions are just marked as such."

LYLE STUART, INC.

1976 Statement: "We have no policy about first editions. Sometimes we so identify them and at other times the only way that someone would know that a book is not a first edition is to find first printing and second printing dates and quantities on the copyright page."

1981 Statement: *See* 1976 Statement

1988 Statement: "We continue to follow the practice indicated in our 1976 statement. Frequently we use 2 through 10 numbers on a first printing and then drop a number in subsequent editions."

1995 Statement: *See* 1995 Statement of Carol Publishing Group

STUDIO 4 PRODUCTIONS

2000 Statement: "We do not have a special method for designating a first edition. However, we do identify 2nd edition and subsequent editions by stipulating on the front cover."

THE STUDIO LIMITED (UNITED KINGDOM)

1947 Statement: "Studio books always have the first year of publication printed on the back of their title pages, and subsequent reprints are noted thereunder with their respective year of publication. If, however, a book is re-set or revised, with new material added, it is our custom to list it as a 'new and revised edition,' but the notation to this effect still appears on the back of the title page under the previous listings of first publication and reprintings."

STUDIO PRESS

1994 Statement: "We do not identify first editions."

STUDIO PUBLICATIONS, INC.

1947 Statement: "We do not state Edition in first edition. Subsequent editions carry notation '2d. Edition,' etc."

STUDIO VISTA (UNITED KINGDOM)

1988, 1994 Statements: *See* 1988 Statement of Cassell plc (United Kingdom)

SUFFOLK RECORDS SOCIETY (UNITED KINGDOM)

1988 Statement: *See* 1988 Statement of Boydell & Brewer, Ltd. (United Kingdom)

GEORGE SULLY AND CO.
(Out of business prior to 1937.)

1928 Statement: "We do not mark the first editions of our books in any particular manner."

SULZBERGER & GRAHAM PUBLISHING CO. LTD.

1994 Statement: "We do not designate first printings. Subsequent printings are designated on the copyright page."

This method does not differ from any previously used.

SUMMIT BOOKS

1981 Statement: "The first printing of a Summit book is identified on the copyright page, either by the words 'First Edition' or by the number '1' on the printing number line. This has been our practice since Summit Books began publishing in 1977."

1988 Statement: *See* 1981 Statement

SUMMIT BOOKS (AUSTRALIA)

1976, 1981 Statements: *See* 1976, 1981 Statements of Lansdowne Press (Australia)

1988 Statement: *See* 1988 Statement of Kevin Weldon and Associates Pty Ltd (Australia)

SUN (AUSTRALIA)

1994 Statement: *See* 1994 Statement of Pan Macmillan Australia (Australia)

SUN & MOON CLASSICS

1988, 1993 Statements: *See* 1988 Statement of Sun & Moon Press

SUN & MOON PRESS

1988 Statement: "Sun & Moon Press designates both first editions and first printings. First editions are designated by the words FIRST EDITION on the copyright page. Second and further editions are designated in the same way, by the words SECOND EDITION and so on.

"Printings are designated by the line of numbers, from 10 to 1, running across the lower part of the copyright page. A first printing is designated by a complete series, from 10 to 1; each subsequent printing drops a number, e.g. a second printing bears the numbers 10-2, having dropped the '1.'

"Sun & Moon Press has used this method since 1980. Our imprints all use the same method."

1993 Statement: *See* 1988 Statement

SUN HILL PRESS

2001 Statement: "We do not identify a first printing; we do identify subsequent printings. Special editions carry pertinent information on colophon page at the end of the book."

SUN PUBLISHING COMPANY

1976 Statement: "We do not have any particular method of identifying first editions."

All printings of a first edition are indicated.

1981 Statement: "First printings say: 'First Sun Books Printing: (Date).' "

1988 Statement: "All printings of a first edition are indicated."

1993 Statement: *See* 1988 Statement

SUN RIVER PRESS

1976 Statement: "Sun River Press does not identify first editions—we do not identify first printing either."

The state of a book is never indicated.

1981 Statement: Sun River Press is no longer active.

SUNBELT PUBLICATIONS
2000 Statement: "On the verso of the title page (the copyright page), we state 'first edition' and year. On subsequent editions we state 'second [edition]' or 'third edition' and year. We [also use] the following number line: 10 9 8 7 6 5 4 3 2 1. Subsequent printings are acknowledged by dropping a number. A second edition would drop the 1, a third edition would drop the 2, etc."

SUNBIRD PUBLICATIONS (UNITED KINGDOM)
1994 Statement: *See* 1994 Statement of Ladybird Books Ltd (United Kingdom)

SUNBURST BOOKS
1988, 2000 Statements: *See* 1988 Statement of Farrar, Straus & Giroux, Inc.

SUNDIAL (UNITED KINGDOM)
1989 Statement: *See* 1989 Statement of The Octopus Publishing Group PLC (United Kingdom)

SUNDIAL BOOKS
1976, 1981, 1988 Statements: *See* 1976, 1981 and 1988 Statements of The Sunstone Press

SUNFLOWER BOOKS (UNITED KINGDOM)
1994 Statement: "The first edition of any book published by Sunflower Books carries a statement on the verso title page stating 'First published (year) by Sunflower Books.' If there is no further qualifying statement (e.g. 'Revised printing . . . ,' 'Reprinted . . . ' or 'Second Edition . . . ') then it is a first edition. This has been our practice since the company's inception."

SUNFLOWER UNIVERSITY PRESS
1995 Statement: "We do not designate first editions, though we do designate reprinting and occasionally revised or expanded editions."
2001 Statement: *See* 1995 Statement

SUNNYSIDE
1981 Statement: *See* 1981 Statement of Sleepy Hollow Press

SUNRISE LIBRARY
2000 Statement: *See* 2000 Statement of Theosophical University Press

SUNSET BOOKS
1981, 1988 Statements: *See* 1981, 1988 Statements of Lane Publishing Co.
2001 Statement: *See* 2001 Statement of Sunset Publishing Corporation

SUNSET PUBLISHING CORPORATION
1993 Statement: "Lane Publishing Company became Sunset Publishing Corporation in 1990. Our policy regarding first editions of books has not changed [from the 1988 Statement of Lane Publishing Co]. The words first edition appear immediately following the copyright statement on the copyright page of all our books."

2001 Statement: "Sunset Books/Sunset Publishing Corporation prints the words 'first edition' on the copyright/masthead page. We list the numbers 1 through 10 to indicate which printing; so if the number 1 appears it also indicates it to be a first edition."

SUNSINGER BOOKS
2000 Statement: *See* 2000 Statement of The University of Illinois Press

THE SUNSTONE PRESS
1976 Statement: "The Sunstone Press uses no distinguishing marks or symbols to identify first editions. As a general rule no edition statement is used at all for first editions. (Alas, there are one or two exceptions when 'First Edition' has been printed on the verso of the title page). Second editions carry the publishing history of the book on the verso of the title page as follows:

First Edition 1974

Second Edition 1976

"Being a small regional press we do not frequently produce more than one edition of a work. A second or third printing is so indicated on the verso of the title page. When reprinting an older title from another publisher we so indicate. If the printing has added material, illustrations, etc., we designate it a new edition and print the publishing history as above."

1981 Statement: "Yes, our methods have changed since we were last contacted by you. We now do state that a book is a first edition on the copyright page. The words First Edition appear in caps. At the bottom of the same page it will also state that the book is either a Sunstone Press title or a new imprint of ours, Sundial Books. Sundial Books are ones that we produce and distribute, but they are often published by other companies and individuals.

"In addition to the above, we also print a limited edition of each of our trade first edition books. In the back of these, usually on the last page in the book, there appears a colophon, which I am enclosing so you can see how we do it. For example:

> *RURAL ARCHITECTURE OF*
> *NORTHERN NEW MEXICO*
> *AND SOUTHERN COLORADO*
> Five hundred copies
> in a limited edition
> signed by the author
> of which this is number. . .

"And finally, our practice of stating second, third or fourth printings follows the same pattern described above in my first paragraph."

1988 Statement: "All books have edition statements. Most books are indicated as

First Edition

"For subsequent editions or reprintings, the printing history is given, i.e.,

First Edition, 1985

Second Edition, 1987

or

First Edition, 1985
Reprinted, 1987

"We no longer print limited editions of our trade books. If a limited edition of a title is printed, it is so noted."

1993 Statement: "The words First Edition appear in caps. At the bottom of the same page it will also state that the book is either a Sunstone Press title or a new imprint of ours, Sundial Books. Sundial Books are ones that we produce and distribute, but they are often published by other companies and individuals.

"In addition to the above, we sometimes print a limited edition of each of our trade first edition books. In the back of these, usually on the last page in the book, there appears a colophon. For example:

RURAL ARCHITECTURE OF
NORTHERN NEW MEXICO
AND SOUTHERN COLORADO
Five hundred copies
in a limited edition
signed by the author
of which this is number. . ."

2000 Statement: *See* 1993 Statement

SUNSTONE PUBLICATIONS

1994 Statement: "We do not use any special designation."

SUPERIOR PUBLISHING COMPANY
(Seattle, Washington)

1947 Statement: "First printings of our books so far have had no identifying mark. On subsequent printings we include the words 'Second Printing,' 'Third Printing,' etc., as the case may be, directly under the copyright notice on the back of the title page."

1976 Statement: "We usually label our first editions on page 4 of our books and this would be our first printing also, on future printings the First Edition is taken off."

1981 Statement: *See* 1976 Statement

SURREY BOOKS INC.

1994 Statement: The first printing of a first edition is indicated by the number line 1 2 3 4 5 6 etc. The lowest number showing indicates the printing.

2000 Statement: *See* 1994 Statement

SUSQUEHANNA UNIVERSITY PRESS

1988, 2000 Statements: *See* 1988 Statement of Associated University Presses

SUSSEX UNIVERSITY PRESS (UNITED KINGDOM)

1976 Statement: "Readers may assume that all our books are first editions unless we specify on the copyright page that the book has been reprinted or is published in a new edition. The date after the copyright sign normally indicates when the book was first published."

SUTTON COURTENAY PRESS (UNITED KINGDOM)
1994 Statement: *See* 1994 Statement of Appleford Publishing Group (United Kingdom)

ALAN SUTTON PUBLISHING LIMITED
(UNITED KINGDOM)
1988 Statement: "The first edition would have the words 'First published 198-.' Subsequent editions would have the words 'Second edition 198-' and so on. If the text of a book has been revised, the word 'revised' is also inserted."
1994 Statement: *See* 1988 Statement

SUTTONHOUSE LTD.
1937 Statement: "Please note that all first printings of Suttonhouse Ltd., in the past have been identified by the appearance of the same date on both the title and the copyright page, unless 'second printing' appeared on the copyright page.

"In the future, however, 'first edition' will appear on the copyright page, so that there will be no confusion whatsoever. This means that all books published after May 1, 1936, will carry this marking. The second printings will have no such marking."

SWALLOW PRESS
1947 Statement: "First printings of our books carry only the copyright notice, except in a few instances the line
　　'FIRST PRINTING (month—year)'
below the copyright notice.

"All subsequent printings are marked 'Second Printing, Third Printing, Fourth Printing' as the case may be, and new editions of the book are clearly marked. A distinction should be made between an edition and a printing, edition having some material change in the text or format of the publication."

SWALLOW PRESS
(Imprint of Ohio University Press)
1982, 1988 Statements: *See* 1982 Statement of The Swallow Press, Inc.
1993, 2000 Statements: *See* 1993 Statement of Ohio University Press

THE SWALLOW PRESS, INC.
1976 Statement: Both editions and printings are so indicated.
1981 Statement: *See* 1976 Statement
1982 Statement: "The Swallow Press, Inc., is now an imprint of Ohio University Press. The title pages will read either The Swallow Press or
　　The Swallow Press
　　Ohio University Press
　　Athens, Chicago, London
"The copyright page carries the Statement that 'Swallow Press/Sage books are published by Ohio University Press.'

572

"I believe that when the Press began in 1946 the name was Alan Swallow. The name may have changed to The Swallow Press, Inc., in 1966 or 1967, after the death of Alan Swallow.

"Ohio University Press took on the Swallow Press as an imprint in 1979.

"We mark the edition on subsequent printings on the copyright page."
1988 Statement: *See* 1988 Statement of Ohio University Press

SWALLOW'S TALE PRESS
1995 Statement: *See* 1995 Statement of Livingston Press
2000 Statement: *See* 2000 Statement of Livingston Press

SWAN HILL PRESS (UNITED KINGDOM)
1994, 2000 Statements: *See* 1994 Statement of Airlife Publishing Limited (United Kingdom)

SWEDENBORG FOUNDATION, INC.
1976 Statement: "Since our concern is exclusively with Swedenborgian theology and we have a copy of *A Bibliography of the Works of Emanuel Swedenborg* (743 pages) by the Rev. James Hyde, published in 1906 and containing a complete list and description of all these works in the original Latin and translations published prior to that date, we can easily identify any of these. We occasionally mention the date of original Latin publication, and the ordinal number of the particular reprint of ours, on the respective title page, but not always. Many of these works and extracts are also published by the Swedenborg Society, Ltd., London, which follows a similar practice."
1981, 1988, 1993, 2000 Statements: *See* 1976 Statement

SYCAMORE ISLAND BOOKS
2000 Statement: *See* 2000 Statement of Paladin Press

SYDNEY UNIVERSITY PRESS (AUSTRALIA)
1976 Statement: "We have no particular method of identifying first edition printings, other than the stated year in which the book is first published and the copyright notice and date on the verso of the title page."
1981 Statement: *See* 1976 Statement
1988 Statement: Sydney University Press was inactive after 31 March 1988.

SYLVAN PRESS, INC.
1947 Statement: "First Editions of all of our books are (1) limited, (2) numbered by hand."

SYLVAN PRESS, LIMITED (UNITED KINGDOM)
1947 Statement: "We fall in line with the majority of established English publishers by printing the month and year of first publication on the back of the title page.

"The same imprint is used on reprints, retaining the date of the first edition and printing the date of reprint underneath.

"In the last twelve to fifteen months we have been obliged to abandon temporarily the insertion of the month in our imprint, production and binding delays being so acute; also, from the commercial standpoint, should a book be first published say in November, bearing the imprint of the previous April or May, this is liable to influence sales adversely.

"We are only too anxious to revert to the practice of including the month of publication as soon as production difficulties are more under control and timing can be fairly assessed."

SYRACUSE UNIVERSITY PRESS

1976 Statement: "The Syracuse University Press places the following information on the copyright page of the first edition:

Copyright notice

All rights reserved

First edition

"On subsequent editions, we add the new copyright date and indicate the number of the edition (second edition, etc.).

"The later printings give the number of the printing. i.e.:

1st

First Edition

2nd

First Edition

Second printing, 1976

3rd

First Edition

Third printing, 1977

etc."

1981 Statement: *See* 1976 Statement

1988 Statement: "In 1987 we did begin to use a new format to designate our first editions. However, in a few cases when we are relatively certain that a book will not require a second edition, we do still use the previous format.

"The Syracuse University Press places the following information on the copyright page of the first edition:

Copyright notice

First published 1987

All Rights Reserved

First Edition

97 96 95 94 93 92 91 90 89 88 87 6 5 4 3 2 1

"The above line of numbers refers to the year and the number of a particular reprint.

"If the book is the first edition of the paperback (that is, the book was initially published in cloth only), then it is designated as follows:

Copyright notice

First published 1986

All Rights Reserved

First paperback edition 1988

97 96 95 94 93 92 91 90 89 88 87 6 5 4 3 2 1

"On subsequent editions, we add the new copyright date and indicate the number of the edition (and other information as necessary), please see the following example:

Copyright notice
All Rights Reserved
First Edition 1984
Revised, Second Edition 1987
97 96 95 94 93 92 91 90 89 88 87 6 5 4 3 2 1
"We do not have any subsidiaries [or] imprints."

1993 Statement: "Syracuse University Press places the following notice on the copyright page of a first edition:
Copyright © 1993
All Rights Reserved
First Edition 1993
93 94 95 96 97 98 99 6 5 4 3 2 1"

T

TABB HOUSE (UNITED KINGDOM)

1988 Statement: "Our policy is to print the year of a book's first edition at the top of the copyrights page, followed in chronological order by the years of further reprints or new editions."

2001 Statement: "Our policy is to print the year of a book's first Tabb House edition at the top of the copyright page, followed in chronological order by the years of previous editions, if any, and of further reprints or new editions."

TAFFORD PUBLISHING, INC.

1994 Statement: "All Tafford first editions are identified by the phrase 'First Edition' on the copyright page. Subsequent printings of a first edition are not identified as a first edition."

2000 Statement: *See* 1994 Statement

TAHRIKE TARSILE QUR'AN, INC.

1994 Statement: "We simply state in the publication which edition it is along with the year it is being published."

TAKE THAT LTD. (UNITED KINGDOM)

1994 Statement: "We have no formal method of identification. On the copyright page we usually have the line 01234 . . . 9; with the intention of removing the zero, then 1, etc. with subsequent reprints. However, the production manager usually forgets in the rush to reprint!"

2000 Statement: *See* 1994 Statement

TALBOT PRESS LIMITED (REPUBLIC OF IRELAND)

1976 Statement: "In the case of Talbot Press books the incidence of first edition is usually recognized by the year appearing at the foot of the title page following the imprint. Also on the verso of the title page you will invariably find reference to 'First published . . . .' "

1981 Statement: *See* 1976 Statement

TRUMEN TALLEY BOOKS
1988 Statement: *See* 1988 Statement of E. P. Dutton & Co., Inc.

TALLIS PRESS LTD. (UNITED KINGDOM)
2000 Statement: *See* 2000 Statement of The Albyn Press (United Kingdom)

TALON BOOKS LTD. (CANADA)
1976 Statement: "We're primarily a literary publisher and we publish poetry, plays, fiction and short stories. For most books of poetry, they only have one printing, which sometimes is dated by the month that the book was printing, but, more recently, only by the copyright date. Second printings usually are noted with an updated copyright page, on which it says, 'Second printing,' then the date. Our plays often go into numerous printings and these are noted on the copyright page, but only as the latest printing, i.e., the printing history is not given, although the original copyright date remains the same. Ditto for the fiction. If we do a second edition or a revised first edition, this too is noted, but as a continuum, i.e., 'Second printing (revised),' then the date. The third printing of a revised edition is noted only as 'Third printing,' however, the revision having earlier taken place."

1981 Statement: *See* 1976 Statement

1994 Statement: "First printings of first editions are described as 'First printing, (month), (date)' on the copyright page.

"In the case of new format editions in which the text remains basically the same, the description for revised editions in the 1976 statement remains true. In the case of extensively revised texts, there is a new copyright date indicated on the copyright page for first and subsequent printings of the revised edition. Each printing is indicated on the copyright page as a revised printing with the date: e.g. 'Seventh Revised Printing, (month), (date).' "

TAMAR PRESS
2001 Statement: *See* 2001 Statement of Mesorah Publications Ltd

TAMARACK BOOKS, INC.
1995 Statement: "Tamarack Books, Inc. published its first book in January, 1993. At that time, no special designation was given to the first edition. After that for later printings, we began listing printings and dates (First printing, January, 1993, etc.). In 1994, we began to use the numbering system 10 9 8 7 6 5 4 3 2 1, and mark the editions as first, second, etc."

2001 Statement: *See* 1995 Statement

TAMARACK PRESS
1981 Statement: A first printing is designated by the statement "First printing (year)" on the page bearing the copyright.

1988 Statement: "Tamarack Press is no longer involved in book publishing."

TAMBOURINE BOOKS
1994 Statement: "Since Tambourine's inception in 1991, all our copyright notices have featured a number string in the form of

1 2 3 4 5 6 7 8 9 10 (when body text is set flush right),
1 3 5 7 9 10 8 6 4 2 (with centered text), or
10 9 8 7 6 5 4 3 2 1 (with text flush left).
With each successive reprint we delete a digit so that the lowest remaining number represents the appropriate printing. The words 'First edition,' 'First US edition,' or 'First Tambourine edition' remain on all reprints except in the case of books that have been substantially reset, reillustrated, or redesigned."

TANDEM PRESS (NEW ZEALAND)
1994 Statement: The first printing of a first edition is designated by the phrase "First published (date)" on the copyright page. Reprints are noted on the copyright page.
2001 Statement: *See* 1994 Statement

TANDEM PRESS, INC.
1976 Statement: "We identify our first editions by merely printing our Library of Congress and our ISBN numbers. Any edition following the first edition is then named as: Second edition and the date; third edition, date and so forth. This has been our policy and no other method was previously used."
1981, 1989 Statements: *See* 1976 Statement

TANGELWÜLD PRESS
1994 Statement: *See* 1994 Statement of Publishers Associates

THE TANTIVY PRESS (UNITED KINGDOM)
1947 Statement: "We send herewith a marked catalogue which may help, as our practice has varied greatly in the dating of our books, as a result of war-time difficulties.*

"At the outset it was often necessary to have the same book set up several times by different printers, in order to get paper. We were feeling our way and experimented with different methods of marking editions and impressions. We seem to have stabilized at the moment, however, in the method of indicating an edition or impression by a datemark in Roman characters within a bibliographical note at the foot of the verso of the title page.

"Often our first editions have several different kinds of binding, owing to the shortage of cloth, but there are so many variations here that to detail same would require a day's work and, frankly, we cannot afford that. We leave it to the eventual scholar with his university grant! And it will be an interesting job."

*According to the catalogue all first editions of books published by this Press carry the bibliographical details on the verso of the title page or of the bastard, except the following five titles, which carry the date on the title page: *The Pioneers, Satirical Verses, Representative Lyrics, Indiscretions of an Infant, Tubers and Taradiddle.*
1988 Statement: *See* 1947 Statement, but note that the company no longer publishes original works of a literary nature.
1994 Statement: *See* 1988 Statement

S. MARK TAPER FOUNDATION IMPRINT
IN JEWISH STUDIES
2000 Statement: *See* 2000 Statement of University of California Press

TAPLINGER PUBLISHING CO., INC.
1976 Statement: "Our current and continuing practice for designating all first printings of our original titles is to cite FIRST EDITION on the copyright page. Subsequent printings are so stated, as 'Second Printing,' 'Third Printing,' and so on.

"We also import a number of foreign titles (usually from England or Australia). These normally constitute a first American Edition although our copyright page rarely says so. These titles can usually be distinguished from our own original titles from the notice 'First published in the United States in . . . by Taplinger Publishing Company.' We often do subsequent printings of these books here in the United States, but not always; however, when we do, the copyright page will note the particular printing.

"I am sorry that I cannot verify if this has been standard policy or whether it does differ from previous methods in the company's early days. But of course we do indicate revised editions, printings with corrections and so forth."

1981, 1988, 1993, 2000 Statements: *See* 1976 Statement

TARA PUBLICATIONS (REPUBLIC OF IRELAND)
1994 Statement: *See* 1994 Statement of Irish Academic Press Limited (Republic of Ireland)

TARBORO BOOKS
2000 Statement: *See* 2000 Statement of Wyrick & Co.

TARCHER (AUSTRALIA)
2000 Statement: *See* 2000 Statement of Penguin Books Australia Ltd (Australia)

J. P. TARCHER, INC.
1976 Statement: "To answer your question as to how we identify first editions: We identify it by the absence of any designation such as 'first edition.' In subsequent editions we designate it by 'revised edition' or '(title) No. 3' (or whatever edition).

"As for printings in each edition, we list the numbers 1 2 3 4 5 6 7 8 9 0 on the copyright page of our books and delete the number corresponding to the printing each time we reprint."

1981 Statement: "We have indeed changed the method of identifying first editions and printings:

"As of May 1979, J. P. Tarcher, Inc. identifies first editions by placing the designation 'First Edition' on the copyright page. In subsequent editions we do not indicate the edition on the copyright page but may place 'Revised edition' on the cover or jacket.

"We indicate the printings of an edition by listing '10 9 8 7 6 5 4 3 2 1' on the copyright page and deleting numbers so that the lowest number showing is the number of the printing.

"We also place a letter code before the printing numbers to help us quickly identify the manufacturer.

"These procedures apply to all our imprints."

1988 Statement: *See* 1988 Statement of Jeremy P. Tarcher, Inc.

JEREMY P. TARCHER, INC.

1988 Statement: As of 1985, Jeremy P. Tarcher, Inc. ceased placing a *letter* code before the printing number.

"Additionally, since *around* 1983 (nobody here is exactly sure of the date) the company name became Jeremy P. Tarcher as opposed to J. P. Tarcher. Certainly all books from 1984 on have that name on the title page."

1993 Statement: *See* 1993 Statement of G.P. Putnam's Sons

TARQUIN BOOKS (UNITED KINGDOM)

2000 Statement: *See* 2000 Statement of Tarquin Publications (United Kingdom)

TARQUIN PUBLICATIONS (UNITED KINGDOM)

1994 Statement: "We designate the first edition simply by the copyright notice: e.g. © 1992. Usually there are several printings and we do not modify this statement. A new edition, including substantial modifications is designated: This edition © 1989. Previous edition © 1982, etc."

2000 Statement: "We designate the first edition simply by the copyright notice: e.g. © 1992. Usually there are several printings and we do not modify this statement. A new edition, including substantial modifications or not is designated: This edition © 1989. Previous edition © 1982, etc.

"We alter the date at each new printing whether there are substantial modifications or not. Only if we reprinted twice in the same year would we not alter it."

TATSCH ASSOCIATES

1976 Statement: "We leave first editions unmarked, on the assumption that if no edition number is specified the reader will know that it is the first. Likewise, for the first printing of the first edition.

"These methods of identification do not differ from any previously used."

1981, 1988 Statements: *See* 1976 Statement

THE TAUNTON PRESS

1988 Statement: "We indicate a first printing with the words 'first printing, month, year' on the copyright page. Subsequent printings would be listed underneath that in the same manner. This has been our practice since 1978 when we first began publishing books. We have only one imprint, but if we ever create others or subsequent ones, they would follow the same practice."

1993 Statement: *See* 1988 Statement

TAXATION PUBLISHING COMPANY (UNITED KINGDOM)
1994 Statement: *See* 1994 Statement of Tolley Publishing Co. Ltd. (United Kingdom)

TAYLOR PUBLISHING COMPANY
1994 Statement: "Taylor Publishing Company uses 10 9 8 7 6 5 4 3 2 1 to identify first printings. When the book is reprinted, we delete figure 1, etc. No other method has ever been used.

"However, Taylor's trade division was established in 1981 and it did not adopt a method for identifying first printings until after its first few years. As a result, some early books have no printing designation."

TCG
See Theatre Communications Group, Inc.

TELEGRAPH PRESS
1947 Statement: "The Telegraph Press has adhered to no strict policy in the past, though usually its first printings have been marked 'First Edition'; but hereafter it will follow the same method as that used by Stackpole Sons, and its first printings will be identified by the lack of notice of subsequent reprintings."

TELEOS
2000 Statement: *See* 2000 Statement of LP Publications

THOMAS TELFORD PUBLICATIONS (UNITED KINGDOM)
1994 Statement: "Our statement is valid for publications of the Institution of Civil Engineers, London, as we are the Publications Division of their company Thomas Telford Services Limited. We publish both as Thomas Telford and on behalf of the Institution of Civil Engineers.

"First editions before around 1985 bear no statement at all. Reprints and later editions bear the printing history as follows:
'First published 19XX
Reprinted 19XY, 19XZ'
etc. on the verso of the title page. Since then, first editions should all bear the wording 'First published 19XX' on the verso of the title page. Later prints or editions bear the printing history as before."
2001 Statement: *See* 1994 Statement

TELL-A-STORY (UNITED KINGDOM)
1994 Statement: *See* 1994 Statement of Random House UK Limited (United Kingdom)
2000 Statement: *See* 2000 Statement of The Random House Group Limited (United Kingdom)

TEMPEST
2001 Statement: *See* 2001 Statement of HarperCollinsPublishers

C. & J. TEMPLE, LTD. (UNITED KINGDOM)

1947 Statement: "We usually give the required information on the reverse of the title page, together with the colophon of the printer.

"In the case of a first edition of a new book we print: 'First published by C. J. Temple, Ltd., etc. 1947.' In the case of subsequent reprints we add the words 'reprinted in 1948.'

"When we publish a new edition of a classic, or a new edition of a novel published by some other firm or firms in the past, we print: 'This edition was first published by etc., 194—.' "

TEMPLE HOUSE BOOKS (UNITED KINGDOM)

1988 Statement: *See* 1988 Statement of The Book Guild Limited (United Kingdom)
1994, 2000 Statements: *See* 1988 Statement

TEMPLE UNIVERSITY PRESS

1988 Statement: "If we are publishing a book for the first time, the following information is inserted on the copyright page:

Temple University Press, Philadelphia 19122

Copyright (year) by Temple University. All rights reserved

Published (year)

Printed in the United States of America

(Any necessary acknowledgements)

(Library of Congress Cataloging in Publication Data box)

"If our book does *not* say 'Revised Edition,' 'Second Edition,' 'Third Edition,' etc., it is the first edition.

"We do not indicate second, third, etc. printings."
1993 Statement: *See* 1988 Statement

TEMPLEGATE PUBLISHERS

1988 Statement: "We adopt the same method to identify the first printings of our books as that employed by other leading publishers. The first edition would have the words 'First published 198-' and subsequent editions would have the words 'Second edition 198-' and so on. If the text of a book has been revised the word 'revised' is also inserted."
1993 Statement: *See* 1988 Statement

TEN PENNY PLAYERS, INC.

1994 Statement: "Ten Penny Players, Inc.'s letterpress books are designated as Limited Edition with each book in a run being numbered. Subsequent letterpress, xeroxed or offset editions are noted as second printing, third printing, etc.

"All Ten Penny Players, Waterways Project or Bard Press publications printed by xerography or offset do not designate that the work is a first edition. Reprints of books offered for sale would be designated as second printing, etc.; reprints of books or magazines intended for distribution to schools or students without charge would not carry a printing designation."
2000 Statement: *See* 1994 Statement

TEN SPEED PRESS

1976 Statement: "We have no special designation for first editions. We do sometimes indicate 'Tenth Printing' but not always, so that you cannot assume the lack of such identification means a first edition."

1981 Statement: *See* 1976 Statement

1988 Statement: "We now indicate the first printing with a number code from '1' and a year code, so the entry would come out

88 89 90 91 9 8 7 6 5 4 3 2 1

to indicate a first printing in 1988."

1995 Statement: "As of this year, 1995, we have implemented a standard 'first printing' line on the imprint page above the print code bar. So it reads, say

First printing, 1995
95 96 97 98 99 — 5 4 3 2 1."

2000 Statement: *See* 1995 Statement

TEXAS A&M UNIVERSITY PRESS

1976 Statement: "We identify first editions by the statement 'First edition' on the copyright page. Subsequent printings are likewise identified: 'Second printing,' 'Third printing' and so on. This does not differ from any previous practice here."

1981 Statement: *See* 1976 Statement

1988 Statement: "Concerning first editions our press still follows the practice outlined in our last statement. The only difference involves second and following printings; we now add the year following the printing notice, as 'Second printing 1988.' "

1993 Statement: *See* 1988 Statement

TEXAS CHRISTIAN UNIVERSITY PRESS

1988 Statement: "We do not designate first printings as such, but simply put the copyright date on the copyright page. On subsequent printings that page also indicates second or third or whatever printing. This is not a policy adopted at any point in time by the press but a practice that has been followed over the years.

"We have no imprints other than our own and no subsidiaries."

1993, 2000 Statements: *See* 1988 Statement

TEXAS MONTHLY PRESS

1981 Statement: "The way we indicate the edition of a particular title is on the copyright page. [The phrase 'First Edition, (month) (year)' would be printed on the copyright page.] This has always been our practice. Also, we do not have any imprints.

"Starting [in the fall of 1980], we started indicating editions by setting on the copyright page, 'A B C D E F G H.' When a book goes back for a second printing, we ask the printer to scratch out the 'A' Therefore, a 'B' indicates a second printing, a 'C' indicates a third printing, etc."

TEXAS STATE HISTORICAL ASSOCIATION

1994 Statement: The first printing of a first edition is indicated by the number line 10 9 8 7 6 5 4 3 2 1. The lowest number showing indicates the printing.
2000 Statement: *See* 1994 Statement

TEXAS TECH UNIVERSITY PRESS

1988 Statement: "We do not explicitly designate first editions or first printings. Second and subsequent editions are designated by 'Second edition; first edition 1972.' This represents no change in our practice since 1971, and it holds for all imprints under our control."

TEXAS WESTERN PRESS

1988 Statement: "Texas Western Press does not print the phrase 'first edition' in its books but does, on the verso of the title page, in the space which includes copyright data, indicate if a printing is anything but a first. We use the phrase 'second printing,' followed by the year, for a new printing of a book that is unaltered from the first, and 'second edition' for any book that is changed—added to, updated, etc.—in any significant way.

"This has not, however, been a consistent rule over the 35-year history of this press. The late J. Carl Hertzog, an eminent typographer and book designer, who was founder of this press, occasionally did print 'First Edition' in some of his elegant limited edition books and monographs.

"I would say the present practice has been consistently followed since about 1980."
1993 Statement: *See* 1988 Statement and the following: "From 1986 forward, 'First Edition' has been used consistently, on the copyright page. Any subsequent printings or editions are indicated as stated above."
2000 Statement: "Texas Western Press does not print the phrase 'first edition' in its books but does, on the verso of the title page, in the space which includes copyright data, indicate if a printing is anything but a first. We use the phrase 'second printing,' followed by the year, for a new printing of a book that is unaltered from the first, and 'second edition' for any book that is changed—added to, updated, etc.—in any significant way.

"This has not, however, been a consistent rule over the 50-year history of this press. The late J. Carl Hertzog, an eminent typographer and book designer, who was founder of this press, occasionally did print 'First Edition' in some of his elegant limited edition books and monographs.

"I would say the present practice has been consistently followed since about 1980."

TEXTWORD PRESS

2001 Statement: *See* 2001 Statement of Mesorah Publications Ltd

THAMES & HUDSON LTD. (UNITED KINGDOM)

2000 Statement: "Firstly, since 1999, we have been using the imprint Thames & Hudson, rather than Thames and Hudson. This applies to all new publications and reprints of existing titles. Our present policy is to provide:
  a) the date of first publication in the UK

b) (in the case of translations or books bought from American publishers) the copyright date of the original edition

c) the date of the first paperback edition (where this applies)

d) the year of current reprint (if this applies)

"I cannot guarantee that this policy applies to all Thames & Hudson books in print, since we are a backlist publisher that sometimes keeps inventory available for many years, but it does register the situation for all new books and all reissues of existing books."

THAMES AND HUDSON INC.

1981 Statement: First printings are indicated on the copyright page by the copyright date and the words "First published in (year corresponding to copyright year)."

"Subsequent printings are indicated by numbers at the bottom of the copyright page (e.g. 3 4 5 6 7 8 9 0).

"But—looking over a number of our books, there are exceptions and inconsistencies."

1988 Statement: "We do not make any special identification of first editions. On the other hand, we do indicate any edition which is a reprint. The result is that any of our books which do not have a reprint line can be taken to be first editions."

1994 Statement: *See* 1988 Statement

THAMES AND HUDSON LTD. (UNITED KINGDOM)

1976 Statement: "We do not make any special identification of first editions. On the other hand, we do indicate any edition which is a reprint. The result is that any of our books which do not have a reprint line can be taken to be first editions."

1981, 1988, 1994 Statements: *See* 1976 Statement

2000 Statement: *See* 2000 Statement of Thames & Hudson Ltd. (United Kingdom)

THAMES AND HUDSON (AUSTRALIA) PTY LTD.
(AUSTRALIA)

1994 Statement: *See* 1976 Statement of Thames and Hudson Ltd. (United Kingdom)

2000 Statement: *See* 2000 Statement of Thames & Hudson Ltd. (United Kingdom)

THEATRE ARTS BOOKS

1947 Statement: "Over the years Theatre Arts has published various volumes as they came up, and no consistent device was used to indicate first editions. Usually, however, the absence of any information in regard to the edition or the printing meant that the volume was a first edition."

1976 Statement: "Theatre Arts Books does not designate first editions. We do designate subsequent printings, so one can assume a book not so designated to be a first edition."

1981 Statement: *See* 1976 Statement

1988 Statement: "Theatre Arts Books, now an imprint of Routledge, does not identify first editions."
1993 Statement: *See* 1988 Statement

THEATRE COMMUNICATIONS GROUP, INC.

1994 Statement: "Since 1984, with the expansion of our book program, all original titles published by TCG list 'First Edition, month, year' as the last line on the copyright page. Subsequent printings of each title follow below the first edition entry line. Reprints of books originally published by other publishers would cite original publication information and would read 'First TCG Edition, month, year.' "

THEMIS BOOKS (UNITED KINGDOM)

2000 Statement: *See* 2000 Statement of Green Books Ltd (United Kingdom)

THEOSOPHICAL HERITAGE CLASSICS

1993 Statement: *See* 1988 Statement of The Theosophical Publishing House

THE THEOSOPHICAL PUBLISHING HOUSE

1976 Statement: "We designate our first editions with a statement on the copyright page similar to the one below.

" 'First Quest Book edition 1975 published by the Theosophical
Publishing House, Wheaton, Illinois, a department of
The Theosophical Society in America.' "

1981 Statement: *See* 1976 Statement
1988 Statement: "The edition statement you list from 1976 is now obsolete. As of 1980 we started to develop a new format which currently encompasses two different types of Quest Books. For a title that has not been published before and thus is originated from Quest, our statement reads: 'A Quest Original. First Edition 19__.' If the book is a reprint, previously published by another publisher, then our statement will read: 'First Quest Edition 19__.' "
1993 Statement: *See* 1988 Statement
2000 Statement: "Quest Books currently uses the following statement in first editions: First Quest Edition 2000."

THEOSOPHICAL UNIVERSITY PRESS

1994 Statement: The first printing of a first edition is indicated by the statement "First Edition."
2000 Statement: *See* 1994 Statement

THIRD SIDE PRESS, INC.

1994 Statement: "Our first books were produced in 1991, and our imprinting of information on first editions has been consistent since then. The very bottom of the copyright page bears this notice:

First edition, May 1991 (or other date)
10 9 8 7 6 5 4 3 2 1

"Subsequent printings of the first edition bear the same lines, but with printing numbers removed to indicate the printing. For example, the following would indicate the second printing of a book still in its first edition (which would probably include very minor corrections from the first printing):

First edition, May 1991

10 9 8 7 6 5 4 3 2

"We're about to print our first non-first edition, and its copyright page will contain the following information to distinguish it:

First edition, May 1991

Second edition, April 1994

10 9 8 7 6 5 4 3 2

"The printing numbers do not change when the edition changes. Should we someday print more than 10 printings of a title (we hope!), we'll add a new printing line with the next 10 numbers."

2000 Statement: *See* 1994 Statement

THISTLEDOWN PRESS LTD. (CANADA)

1989 Statement: "Most of our titles are published in a first edition only, and many are not reprinted. We are therefore not in the habit of indicating first editions in any way. We do, however, indicate second and subsequent printings and we also indicate if the book is a second edition. One can assume, then, that if there is no edition statement that the book in hand is a first printing of a first edition. This has been our practice throughout Thistledown's history.

"Thistledown Press is an independently owned company without subsidiaries or other imprints."

1993 Statement: *See* 1989 Statement

CHARLES C. THOMAS, PUBLISHER

1988 Statement: "We list on the Copyright Page each new edition but not reprintings."

1993 Statement: *See* 1988 Statement

PETER & DONNA THOMAS

2001 Statement: "We do not identify First editions as such, but all edition information is included on the colophon page, and if the book were a subsequent edition, it would be mentioned there."

S. EVELYN THOMAS (UNITED KINGDOM)

1947 Statement: "The first editions of my books are either not marked at all with the edition reference or they are marked 'First Edition.' All editions after the first have the edition number shown thereon."

THOMASSON-GRANT PUBLISHERS

1994 Statement: "We do not explicitly designate 'First edition' or 'First printing' on the copyright page of our books. We use numbers to indicate 1st, 2nd, 3rd printing, etc., and the year in which the printing took place. For example, if the numbers 99 98 97 96 95 94 followed by 5 4 3 2 1 appear on the copyright page of the book, the book is in its first printing and was first published in 1994. Each time the book is reprinted, we delete a number from each group as appropriate, so that the last number on the right in each group corresponds to the last printing and the date that printing took place. The numbers 99 98 97 96 95 5 4 3 2 would indicate that the second printing of the book occurred in 1995. We have always used this method of designation."

THORNDIKE PRESS

1981 Statement: "We do not designate a first edition in any way, except that 2nd printings (and so on) will say, sometimes, '2nd Printing.' "

1988 Statement: "Thorndike Press no longer does first editions of any kind. We are exclusively a large print *reprint* house, and purchase those rights from other publishers."

1993 Statement: *See* 1988 Statement

2000 Statement: "The 1988 Statement is still correct. Thorndike Press now has an imprint called Five Star (since 1996). Five Star publishes first edition titles and they are designated as such by:

'Five Star First Edition . . . .'

The blank indicates the series: Five Star First Edition Western Series, Five Star First Edition Mystery Series [or] Five Star First Edition Romance Series. If there is a second printing, it is designated with an additional line:

'First Edition, second printing.' "

NELSON THORNES LTD
(UNITED KINGDOM)

2001 Statement: "Stanley Thornes (Publishers) Ltd acquired the UK educational assets of Thomas Nelson in June last year and we are now one company called Nelson Thornes Ltd and we are based in Cheltenham.

"Our practice is [as follows]:

First published in 1997 by Stanley Thornes (Publishers) Ltd.

Second edition published in 2001 by:

Nelson Thornes Ltd

[address block follows]

01 02 03 04 05 / 10 9 8 7 6 5 4 3 2 1

ISBN."

THORSONS (UNITED KINGDOM)

1988 Statement: *See* 1988 Statement of Thorsons Publishing Group Ltd. (United Kingdom)

THORSONS PUBLISHERS LIMITED (UNITED KINGDOM)

1981 Statement: "The administration of Turnstone is now run by Thorsons.

"The statement which appeared in [1976] for Turnstone Press still holds good although we differ slightly as you will see when comparing the final sentence.

"I have, therefore, set below the complete statement ready for publication.

"Our policy is to put 'First published 1981' as an indication for first editions of a book which we originate. 'First published in the United Kingdom 1981' would identify the first edition of a book which originated in America or elsewhere. 'This Edition first published 1981' would identify a title which has already appeared in another edition. Subsequent editions which have undergone updating, revision and resetting would appear as 'This Edition, completely revised and reset, 1981' and subsequent printings would appear as 'Fifth Impression 1981.' "

1988 Statement: *See* 1988 Statement of Thorsons Publishing Group Ltd. (United Kingdom)

THORSONS PUBLISHING GROUP LTD.
(UNITED KINGDOM)

1988 Statement: "Thorsons Publishing Group comprises the following imprints:

THORSONS
GRAPEVINE
AQUARIAN PRESS
CRUCIBLE BOOKS
PATRICK STEPHENS LTD (PSL)
EQUATION

All these imprints adopt the following rules:

" 'First published 1988' indicates a first edition of a book which we have originated.

" 'First published in the United Kingdom 1988' will identify the first edition of a book which was originated in America or other English language markets.

" 'This edition first published 1988' indicates a title which has already appeared in another edition; e.g. a trade paperback edition of a title first published in hardback.

" 'This edition completely revised and reset 1988' indicates a subsequent edition which has been completely updated, revised and reset.

"We now use the rub-off method to indicate the reprint history of a book."

THREE CONTINENTS PRESS, INC.

1976 Statement: "In all our publications to date, we state very clearly at the top of our copyright page, 'First Edition' and we expect to continue to do so in future books.

"A second printing of the first edition will read: First Edition, 2nd printing (or 3rd or 4th etc. as appropriate).

"For us, a second edition signifies a basic change (one or more pgs. from the original first ed.) & 2nd printings of a second edition would be—2nd Ed-2nd printing."

1981 Statement: "As far as our statement is concerned, it still stands as is, with our imprints also."

1989, 1993 Statements: *See* 1981 Statement

THUNDER'S MOUTH PRESS

1988 Statement: "Subsequent to a first edition, the later editions of a book are so designated on the copyright page by its ordinal number and date (e.g. 'Seventh Printing April 1988'). This has been our policy since we began publishing in fall of 1981.

"We have no imprints or subsidiaries."

1993 Statement: "Our first editions are indicated 'First Edition, First printing, (Year)' on our copyright page. Subsequent editions are indicated by a printing history line on the copyright page. We have been in this practice since November 1992."

2001 Statement: *See* 2001 Statement of Avalon Publishing Group Incorporated

THURMAN PUBLISHING LTD (UNITED KINGDOM)
1989 Statement: *See* 1989 Statement of Price/Stern/Sloan Publishers, Inc.

TIA CHUCHA PRESS
1994 Statement: "In the past, we had not designated a first edition in our books. If it went into a second printing, we would say so on the copyright page as thus: Second printing (and then the year)."

2001 Statement: *See* 1994 Statement

TICKNOR & FIELDS
1988 Statement: "We use reverse numbers: e.g., '10 9 8 7 6 5 4 3 2 1' designates a first edition. For the second the '1' would be omitted, and so on. If we use up all 10, we start over using '20' through '11.'

"This is what our parent, Houghton Mifflin, does."

1993, 2000 Statements: *See* 1988 Statement

TIDEWATER PUBLISHERS
1976 Statement: *See* 1976 Statement of Cornell Maritime Press, Inc.

1981, 1988, 1993, 2000 Statements: *See* 1981 Statement of Cornell Maritime Press, Inc.

TIGERS (UNITED KINGDOM)
2000 Statement: *See* 2000 Statement of Andersen Press Limited (United Kingdom)

TILBURY HOUSE, PUBLISHERS
1994 Statement: "We always print on the copyright page the words First Printing for the first printing of a book. As far as I know, everyone of our books has carried this designation since we began publishing books under the Tilbury House, Publishers imprint in 1990."

2001 Statement: "Harpswell Press titles are all identified for editions on the copyright page. First editions are marked as such; subsequent printings, revised editions, etc., are noted. In 1990, the Harpswell Press merged with the Dog Ear Press and took the name Tilbury House, Publishers. All new titles have been identified as above under the Tilbury House name, and new printings of old Harpswell Press titles are identified as above under the Tilbury House name." *See also* 1994 Statement

TIME-LIFE BOOKS INC.
1981 Statement: "Before I explain how we designate first printings of first editions, a brief history is in order.

"Time-Life Books started as a division of Time Inc. 21 years ago. From the very beginning we have published books primarily in series. To date, we have published 28 series with a total of 620 titles. And now to the particulars about the manner in which we designate first printings of first editions.

"With the first series, LIFE WORLD LIBRARY, which started in September 1960 we designated first printings by a small hourglass symbol [⌛] published on the last page of the book. Second printings of the same title carried two hourglasses; third printings, three hourglasses, etc. This hourglass designation was used for all series through 1975. The book series that carried this hourglass design during that time were:

LIFE WORLD LIBRARY	....	 1960
LIFE NATURE LIBRARY	....	 1961
TIME READING PROGRAM	....	 1962
LIFE HISTORY OF THE U.S.	....	 1963
LIFE SCIENCE LIBRARY	....	 1963
GREAT AGES OF MAN	....	 1965
TIME-LIFE LIBRARY OF ART	....	 1966
TIME-LIFE LIBRARY OF AMERICA		 1967
FOODS OF THE WORLD	....	 1968
THIS FABULOUS CENTURY	....	 1969
LIFE LIBRARY OF PHOTOGRAPHY		 1970
T-L ENCYCLOPEDIA OF GARDENING		 1971
THE AMERICAN WILDERNESS	....	 1972
THE EMERGENCE OF MAN	....	 1972
THE ART OF SEWING	....	 1973
THE OLD WEST...	....	 1973
WORLD'S WILD PLACES	....	 1973
HUMAN BEHAVIOR	....	 1974
TIME-LIFE LIBRARY OF BOATING		 1975

"Starting in 1976 Time-Life Books no longer used the hourglass designation and in its place designated the particular printings of all books (even those that originally carried an hourglass and subsequently had additional printings starting in 1976) on the copyright page. The Time-Life book series that carry this latest designation since 1976 are:

THE GREAT CITIES	....	 1976
HOME REPAIR AND IMPROVEMENT		 1976
WORLD WAR II...	....	 1976
THE ENCYCLOPEDIA OF GARDENING		 1978
THE SEAFARERS	....	 1978
THE GOOD COOK	....	 1979
CLASSICS OF THE OLD WEST	....	 1980
THE EPIC OF FLIGHT	....	 1980
LIBRARY OF HEALTH	....	 1981

"Over our 21 year history, Time-Life Books has also published 84 single titles. The hourglass design was also used on these books through 1975 and the first printing designated on the copyright page was employed starting in 1976."

1988 Statement: *See* 1981 Statement. Note, though, that the following titles should be added to the post-1976 publication list:

COLLECTOR'S LIBRARY OF THE CIVIL WAR	 1982
PLANET EARTH.	 1982

590

"On both series and single titles from Time-Life Books, the printing number is always designated on the copyright page, and for printings other than the first, the date of the latest revision is shown."

1993 Statement: *See* 1988 Statement. Note, though that the following titles should be added to the post-1976 publication list:

2000 Statement: *See* 2000 Statement of Warner Books, Inc.

TIME WARNER

2000 Statement: *See* 2000 Statement of Warner Books, Inc.

TIMES BOOKS

1976, 1981 Statements: *See* 1976, 1981 Statements of Quadrangle/The New York Times Book Co., Inc.

1988 Statement: "Our method of identifying editions is as follows:

"The first edition/first printing is marked 'First Edition.' Subsequent printings are marked 2, 3, etc.

"A second edition will usually be identified as 'revised edition' and will have a printing identification, as with first editions."

1993 Statement: *See* 1988 Statement

TIMES CHANGE PRESS

2000 Statement: "We identify the first printing of a first edition by the statement 'First Printing.' "

TITAN BOOKS LTD. (UNITED KINGDOM)

1994 Statement: "Our first editions can be identified by '10 9 8 7 6 5 4 3 2 1.' When we reprint, we simply delete the figure '1' for the second edition, the figure '2' for the third edition, and so on. As far as I am aware this is the only system we have used."

2000 Statement: *See* 1994 Statement

TOAD HALL, INC.

2000 Statement: "All first printings (and subsequent printings) appear on the copyright page, along with the month and year of each printing. This appears in all our imprints: Toad Hall Press, Belfry Books, The Bradford Press, and Hands & Heart Books."

TOAD HALL PRESS

2000 Statement: *See* 2000 Statement of Toad Hall, Inc.

TOLLEY PUBLISHING CO. LTD. (UNITED KINGDOM)

1994 Statement: "This company designates first printings of first edition as follows:

Published by
Tolley Publishing Company Ltd
Tolley House
2 Addiscombe Road
Croydon, Surrey CR9 5AF
0181-686 9141

"This method of designation does not differ from any previously used."

TOLLEY (UNITED KINGDOM)

2000 Statement: *See* 2000 Statement of Butterworths Tolley (United Kingdom)

TONGG PUBLISHING CO.

1947 Statement: "No special marks. Other than first editions carry indications of later printing."

TOR

1994 Statement: "All first editions are indicated with a legend which identifies the publication month, i.e., 'First Edition: March 1994.' This is true for hardcovers and mass market editions. In mass market reprint editions, the legend identifies first edition and first mass market printing, with the dates, i.e., 'First Edition, April 1993. First mass market printing: March 1994.' Later printings can be identified by the number at the end of a series appearing at the bottom of the copyright page: '0 9 8 7 6 5 4 3 2' would indicate that this was the second printing. Our Limited Edition books are the first books off the press from the first printing of a given title. There is no legend on the copyright page which distinguishes the Limited First Edition from the standard first edition; however, most such editions have a tipped in signature sheet which includes the edition number, and states that the book is a first edition."

TORY CORNER EDITIONS

1994 Statement: "On the copyright page of each first edition book, FIRST PRINTING is clearly labeled. By the same token, each successive edition is also marked SECOND PRINTING, THIRD PRINTING, etc.

"If a book has gone through a title change, that is noted on the title page where the original title is given in parentheses under the new title. Further notes concerning original publishers, author arrangements, copyright holders, et al, will then appear on the copyright page or, if necessary, be given an expanded explanation in a Foreword or Publisher's Note."

2000 Statement: *See* 2000 Statement of Quincannon Publishing Group

THE TOUCHSTONE PRESS

1976 Statement: "Touchstone does not have a special way of identifying first editions . . . . We do identify different printings with the simple statement 'second printing' etc."

1981 Statement: *See* 1976 Statement

TOWN HOUSE AND COUNTRY HOUSE
(REPUBLIC OF IRELAND)

1994 Statement: "All our imprint information appears on the title verso. We would always distinguish a first edition by including the following information on our imprint page:

First published in (year)

"In the event of a reprint, we would add 'Reprinted, (year),' and we would add to this each time the book was reprinted.

"If it was a second edition, we would print 'Second edition (year).' "

TOWNSON PUBLISHING CO. LTD (CANADA)

1995 Statement: "Townson Publishing and its imprints, ABZ Books and Polar Publishing, use figures 1 2 3 4 5 6 7 8 9 0. When reprinted, we delete figure 1, etc. and insert Second, Third, (etc.) Printing on the Copyright Page."

2000 Statement: *See* 1995 Statement. Note that there is now one additional imprint, Journal.Ca.

TRABUCO BOOKS

2000 Statement: *See* 2000 Statement of Wheat Forders Press

TRAIL'S END PUBLISHING CO.

1947 Statement: "*All* my books have the edition, year, etc., plainly printed on the copyright page. Second, third, etc., are likewise imprinted."

TRANSACTION BOOKS

1976 Statement: "Since we demarcate second and third editions, and second and third printings on the title page, the simplest way of identifying an original edition is that it will simply have the year of publication and the conventional Library of Congress markings."

1981 Statement: "The only revision I would make to [the 1976 Statement] is to note that the demarcation between editions now lists ISBN numbers.

"Since we demarcate second and third editions, and second and third printings on the title page, the simplest way of identifying an original edition is that it will have the year of publication, the ISBN listings, and the conventional Library of Congress markings."

1989, 1993 Statements: *See* 1981 Statement

2001 Statement: *See* 2001 Statement of Transaction Publishers

TRANSACTION PUBLISHERS

2001 Statement: "Upon reflection, I would add to my previous statements of 1976, 1981, 1989, and 1993 [for Transaction Books], the following sentence: 'In order to reduce any ambiguity for public and professional use, we will indicate the title of the original edition on boilerplate pages.' "

TRANSATLANTIC ARTS, INC.

1947 Statement: "We identify first printings of our titles by the words:

First American Edition, 1900

"We identify second (and subsequent) printings of the same work by repeating the first line above and adding, beneath it:

Second Printing, 1900

"If a subsequent second or other printing is revised, instead of the immediate phrase reprintings, we note, beneath the last line of data:

Second American Revised Edition, 1900

"All the preceding apply to imported imprint editions that are not subject to copyright. On domestically produced titles, we follow the same plan but add the word 'Copyright' preceding the year for the first editions and revised editions. On every edition, we include all editions and all printings."

1982, 1993 Statements: *See* 1947 Statement

TRANSPORTATION TRAILS

1994 Statement: "Two books (*The Woodstock and Sycamore Traction Co.,* and *Days of the North Shore Line*) were published at our old Delavan, Wisconsin address by our parent Company, National Bus Trader, Inc. Following books were published at Polo, Illinois under the Transportation Trails imprint. The procedure under both names is the same.

"For us a first printing and a first edition are the same thing. To verify, simply turn to the title/copyright/CIP page at the front of the book. All first editions will list only a first printing with a date; usually a month and a year. It is company policy that second and subsequent printings/editions are *always* listed on this page, usually in the format 'Second Printing: month, year.' Hence, if you only see a first printing listed, you can rest assured that you have a first edition from Transportation Trails."

2000 Statement: *See* 1994 Statement

TRANSWORLD PUBLISHERS (AUSTRALIA)

2000 Statement: "Transworld Publishers has now merged with Random House Australia Pty Ltd, but we have retained the two separate publishing divisions of Transworld Publishers (previously Transworld Publishers (Australia) Pty Limited); and Random House Australia.

"The two divisions have slightly different imprint information but both basically state the year in whihc the title is first published and any new editions. For both divisions, reprints are indicated by an impression line at the base of the copyright page (numbers 10 descending to 1) of which the smallest number is deleted with each reprint.

Transworld Publishers Division—standard imprint information:

> First published in Australia and New Zealand in 20XX by Bantam (or) Doubleday
> a division of Random House Australia Pty Ltd
> 20 Alfred Street, Milsons Point, NSW 2061
> 10 9 8 7 6 5 4 3 2 1 (impression line for reprints)

Random House Division—standard information for Random House Australia imprint:

> Published by
> Random House Australia Pty Ltd
> 20 Alfred Street, Milsons Point, NSW 2061
> First published by Random House Australia 20XX
> 10 9 8 7 6 5 4 3 2 1 (impression line for reprints)

Random House Division—standard information for Vintage or Arrow imprints:

> A Vintage (or) Arrow Book
> Published by
> Random House Australia Pty Ltd
> 20 Alfred Street, Milsons Point, NSW 2061
> First published by (insert name of original local
> imprint or overseas publisher, if appropriate) 20XX
> This Arrow (or) Vintage edition first published 20XX
> 10 9 8 7 6 5 4 3 2 1 (impression line for reprints)."

TRANSWORLD PUBLISHERS (AUSTRALIA) PTY LIMITED (AUSTRALIA)

1988 Statement: "[This is] a copy of our standard imprint information which states the year in which the title is first published, subsequent reprints and new editions:

> First published in Australasia in 19xx by
> Doubleday, a division of Transworld Publishers (Aust.) Pty Ltd
> 15-23 Helles Avenue, Moorebank NSW 2170."

2000 Statement: *See* 2000 Statement of Transworld Publishers (Australia)

TRANSWORLD PUBLISHERS LTD (UNITED KINGDOM)
2001 Statement: "We identify the printing of a first edition by a number line, the lowest number indicating the printing. [This] applies to all Transworld imprints: Bantam Press, Bantam, Black Swan, Corgi, Doubleday etc."

TRAVEL KEYS
1994 Statement: "We do not designate First Printing."
2000 Statement: *See* 1994 Statement

TRAVEL LINE
2000 Statement: *See* 2000 Statement of Passport Press Inc.

TRAVELLER'S PRESS (UNITED KINGDOM)
1989 Statement: *See* 1989 Statement of The Octopus Publishing Group PLC (United Kingdom)

TREACLE PRESS
1988, 2000 Statements: *See* 1988 Statement of McPherson & Company

TREASURE PRESS (UNITED KINGDOM)
1989 Statement: *See* 1989 Statement of The Octopus Publishing Group PLC (United Kingdom)

TREEHAUS COMMUNICATIONS, INC.
1994 Statement: "We identify the first printings of our books by inserting on the copyright page the phrase 'First Printing, month, year.' Subsequent printings are differentiated by using the phrase 'Second Printing, month, year,' etc."
2000 Statement: *See* 1994 Statement

TREND HOUSE
1976 Statement: "First edition does not have any distinguishing features except that the single copyright line is an indication that it is a first edition. Later we use 'second printing' if no substantial editing or recopyright it in the event there is significant editing."
1981 Statement: *See* 1976 Statement

TRIAD EDITIONS
1947 Statement: *See* 1947 Statement of Falmouth Publishing House, Inc.

TRIANGLE (UNITED KINGDOM)
2000 Statement: *See* 2000 Statement of Society for Promoting Christian Knowledge (United Kingdom)

TRICYCLE PRESS
2000 Statement: *See* 2000 Statement of Ten Speed Press

TRIGON PRESS (UNITED KINGDOM)
1988 Statement: "All title pages say 'first published in . . . (year).' If [there are] 2nd or subsequent editions, then

596

'1st published . . . [date]
2nd edition published . . . [date]
3rd edition published . . . '
etc."
1994 Statement: *See* 1988 Statement

TRILLIUM PRESS
1994 Statement: "Has never designated a first edition or first printing, but subsequent ones are designated. Hence first editions are obvious by the omission."

THE TRINITY FOUNDATION
2000 Statement: "The first printing of a first edition is indicated only by a single copyright notice and date, and the absence of any language such as 'second printing,' etc."

TRINITY PRESS INTERNATIONAL
2000 Statement: "We do not have a specific method to show first editions. In a second edition, 'Second Edition, (year)' is noted on the copyright. In a second printing, the second printing is noted in the number line. So, a second printing that was printed in 2000 would look like this: 00 01 02 03 04 10 9 8 7 6 5 4 3 2."

TRIQUARTERLY BOOKS/NORTHWESTERN
UNIVERSITY PRESS
1995, 2000 Statements: *See* 1995 Statement of Northwestern University Press

TRIUMPH BOOKS
(Chicago)
1994, 2000 Statements: "We do not identify first editions or first printings in any way. We are in no way associated with Ligouri Publications or their Ligouri/Triumph imprint."

TRIUMPH BOOKS
1994 Statement: *See* 1994 Statement of Liguori Publications
2000 Statement: *See* 2000 Statement of Liguori Publications

TROITSA BOOKS
2000 Statement: *See* 2000 Statement of Nova Science Publishers, Inc.

TROUBADOR PRESS, INC.
1976 Statement: "We have had various methods for identifying first editions of our publications. 1) On most of our hard cover books we use the phrase 'first edition' on the © page. 2) On some of our paperback books we use the code '1 2 3 4 5 6 7 8 9 0,' erasing from the plate the last digit remaining on the left at each reprint. 3) Only when it seemed important, we've printed the edition number on reprints; esp. *The Fat Cat Coloring and Limerick Book* in which we printed 'Fourteenth printing' when that occasion arose. Another method of identifying editions of our books is the change of copy on the ad

page (last page) in most of our books. This changes almost every reprinting, but there is no indication of sequence other than noting the increased prices (i.e. you never know, necessarily, from the ad page which edition came before the other)."

1981 Statement: *See* 1976 Statement

1989 Statement: *See* 1989 Statement of Price/Stern/Sloan Publishers, Inc.

2000 Statement: "Troubador has been discontinued."

TROUT CREEK PRESS

1995 Statement: "Trout Creek Press has not identified first editions in any way. Subsequent printings are so noted on the reverse of the title page, i.e. Second printing (month - year). Beginning in 1995 first editions will state: First published (month - year)."

2000 Statement: *See* 1995 Statement

TRUMAN STATE UNIVERSITY PRESS

2001 Statement: *See* 1994 Statement of Thomas Jefferson University Press. "Thomas Jefferson University Press changed its name to Truman State University Press in July 1999. We've changed the imprint New Odyssey Press to the series New Odyssey series. It is poetry only. We use the same methods of production as the rest of our books.

"We also publish The Sixteenth Century Essays & Studies series, which was owned by Sixteenth Century Journal Publishing Co., Inc. until Jan. 1998. At that time, this monograph series was transferred to our press, but The Sixteenth Century Journal remains as the only publication of Sixteenth Century Journal Publishing Co., Inc."

TRUE CRIME (UNITED KINGDOM)

1994 Statement: *See* 1994 Statement of Virgin Publishing Ltd. (United Kingdom)

TSG ENTERPRISES PUBLICATIONS

1994 Statement: "We do not state in the book when it is the first printing. When we have a second printing, then we will state: First Printing—date—; Second Printing——date——, etc."

TUART HOUSE (AUSTRALIA)

2000 Statement: *See* 2000 Statement of University of Western Australia Press (Australia)

TUBA PRESS (UNITED KINGDOM)

2001 Statement: "We identify only editions, not printings; a first edition is so identified on the copyright page. The term 'reprinted' will be used if the mode of printing is changed."

TUCKAMORE BOOKS (CANADA)

2001 Statement: *See* 2001 Statement of Creative Book Publishing (Canada)

TUCKWELL PRESS LTD (UNITED KINGDOM)
2001 Statement: " 'First published in Great Britain in (year) by Tuckwell Press' (followed by Tuckwell Press address) and then, if appropriate, 'this second edition published in (date).' We identify only editions, not printings; a first edition is so identified on the copyright page."

TUFTS UNIVERSITY
1988, 1993 Statements: *See* 1988 Statement of University Press of New England

TUMBLEWEED PRESS
1993 Statement: *See* 1993 Statement of Regnery Gateway, Inc.

TUNDRA BOOKS (CANADA)
2001 Statement: "Although we do not place the words 'first edition' on the copyright page of our titles, we occasionally specify 'first Tundra edition' if the book has a publishing history elsewhere. This publishing history is usually indicated on the copyright page. Similarly, we may indicate 'first Canadian edition' if we are the co-publishers of a particular title.

"Generally speaking, all titles published by Tundra Books and Tundra Books of Northern New York contain count-down numbers and the last two digits of the year of publication. While a '1' indicates a first edition, a '2' reflects the second printing of the original edition, a '3' the third printing, and so on. If a new format reprint is published, it is considered a new edition and the numbering starts with '1.' As you can see . . . our company name changed in 1996, when Tundra moved from Montreal to Toronto."

TUNDRA BOOKS OF MONTREAL (CANADA)
1976 Statement: "We designate the edition only after the first. The only time we show it as a first is when it is a limited numbered edition. If there is only one entry—ex. © 1975, William Kurelek, it can be assumed it is the first edition."
1981, 1988 Statements: *See* 1976 Statement
1994 Statement: "Subsequent editions of our works now generally contain count-down numbers, the last number being '2,' although a '1' would indicate a first edition. In many instances, the count-down numbers are not added until the second edition of a book. The count-down numbers were introduced in approximately 1989."
2001 Statement: *See* 2001 Statement of Tundra Books (Canada)

TUNDRA BOOKS OF NORTHERN NEW YORK
1976 Statement: "We don't have a special way of designating first editions, except where we say 'This first edition is limited to—copies.' But since we always indicate in *later* editions the dates of previous editions, where there is no such listing, it can be assumed that the edition is the first."
1981 Statement: *See* 1976 Statement
1988 Statement: "We don't have a special way of designating first editions, except where we say 'This first edition is limited to—copies.' But since we

always indicate in *later* editions the date of the first edition, where there is no such listing, it can be assumed that the edition is the first."
2001 Statement: *See* 2001 Statement of Tundra Books (Canada)

TUPPER AND LOVE, INC.
1947 Statement: "We do not make any difference between first and subsequent printings of our books. If there are changes in the manuscript, we show first or subsequent editions—but not printings of the same editions."

TURNER COMPANY
1937 Statement: "We purchased the assets of the Southwest Press in 1935 and continue to publish all titles formerly published by that concern.

"Since 1935 we use the following plan to differentiate first from subsequent printings of our books: On all editions except the first we run a line on the copyright page stating the number of printing, second printing, third printing, etc., as the case may be."
1947 Statement: *See* 1937 Statement

TURNER PUBLISHING, INC.
1994 Statement: "We use '10 9 8 7 6 5 4 3 2 1' on the copyright page. When reprinted, we delete figure 1, and so on with each subsequent printing.

"With each new edition, we insert 'Second edition' (or Third, etc.).

"If we print a softcover edition of a hardcover book, we insert: 'First hardcover edition (Month, Year). First softcover edition (Month, Year).' "

TURNSTONE PRESS (CANADA)
2001 Statement: "Simply stated, we do not identify first editions, but only subsequent editions. We do not identify first printings, but only subsequent printings."

TURNSTONE PRESS LIMITED (UNITED KINGDOM)
1976 Statement: "Our policy is to put 'First published 1976' as an indication for first editions of a book which we originate. 'First published in Great Britain 1976' would identify the first edition of a book which originated in America or elsewhere. 'This edition first published 1976' would identify a title which had already appeared in another edition. Subsequent editions or printings in addition to the foregoing have 'Revised edition 1976' '5th printing 1976.' "
1981 Statement: *See* 1981 Statement of Thorsons Publishers Limited (United Kingdom)
1988 Statement: *See* 1988 Statement of Thorsons Publishing Group Ltd. (United Kingdom)

TUROE PRESS
1981 Statement: *See* 1981 Statement of Arlen House: The Women's Press (Republic of Ireland)

TURTON & ARMSTRONG PTY LTD (AUSTRALIA)

1994 Statement: "We follow the traditional British method of printing this information on the back of the title page. First editions and printings may be recognised by the absence of any additional information on this page."

2000 Statement: *See* 1994 Statement

TUSK PAPERBACKS

2000 Statement: *See* 2000 Statement of The Overlook Press

CHARLES E. TUTTLE CO., INC.

1976 Statement: "We normally indicate on the reverse of the title page for any book we publish, that this is the first printing. If we do not make this particular statement on a new printing, we do say 'second printing.'

"In other words, I think you can assume that anything we publish is a first edition, if it actually says so, or if there is no indication on the back that it is a second, third, fourth, etc. printing."

1981, 1988 Statements: *See* 1976 Statement

TUTTLE PUBLISHING

2000 Statement: *See* 2000 Statement of Journey Editions

TWAYNE PUBLISHERS, INC.

1976 Statement: "Twayne has never designated a 'first edition.' Where a title does have a revised or second edition ('revised' indicates changes of 10% or less; 'second' indicates changes of more than 10% and usually nearly complete rewriting) the new editions are marked 'Revised Edition' on half-title and title pages; a new copyright covering the new material is entered; and a preface indicates the nature of changes.

"As for 'printings' it was only in 1976 that Twayne introduced the line *'First Printing'* on the copyright page; this line is deleted on subsequent printings. Otherwise, to identify a first printing of a first edition of a Twayne book is almost a book-by-book task that is complicated by the fact that until 1974, the common practice was to print twice as many copies as were first bound (e.g., print 2000, bind 1000), so there are variant bindings. Now we bind all copies."

1994 Statement: *See* 1976 Statement

TWENTIETH CENTURY FUND

1947 Statement: "We don't mark our first printings in any special way. The first printing is usually indicated as follows, on the copyright page:

    Copyright 1939 by the Twentieth Century Fund

"Subsequent printings bear the following legends on the copyright page:

    First published April 1942

    Reprinted April 1942

    Third printing April 1942

    Fourth printing June, 1942, etc."

1994 Statement: *See* 1947 Statement

TWENTY-THIRD PUBLICATIONS INC.
1994 Statement: "We identify the first printing of a first edition by saying nothing about the printing. All subsequent printings are listed by year:
Second printing 1990
Third printing 1992, etc."
2000 Statement: *See* 1994 Statement

TWO BYTES PUBLISHING, LTD.
1995 Statement: "We identify our first printing by inserting on the copyright page 'First Printing, month, year.' Subsequent printings are listed below the first printing in the same manner. When we do book collector editions, we use a slightly different wording: 'Limited Edition: First Printing, month, year.' We also have a colophon which indicates a book's copy number and the signature of the author."

TWO LANE PRESS INC.
1994 Statement: The first printing of a first edition is indicated by the number line 10 9 8 7 6 5 4 3 2 1 93 94 95 96 97. The lowest number showing indicates the printing.
2001 Statement: "No longer in business."

TYCOOLY PUBLISHING (UNITED KINGDOM)
1988 Statement: *See* 1988 Statement of Cassell plc (United Kingdom)

TYCOOLY PUBLISHING USA
1994 Statement: "We do not really designate first editions as such. However, we usually put 9 8 7 6 5 4 3 2 1 on copyright page. Last number in series indicates edition/printing number."

TYNDALE HOUSE PUBLISHERS INC.
1995 Statement: The first printing of a first edition is indicated by the number line 99 98 97 96 95 6 5 4 3 2 1. The lowest number showing indicates the printing.
2000 Statement: *See* 1995 Statement

TYPOGRAPHEUM
1994 Statement: "I have no common practice for [designating first editions/reprints] for the reason that everything I do is, in one way or another, a first appearance. So far I have not reprinted anything I have done earlier."
2000 Statement: "All books published by us may be assumed to be first editions, unless stated."

U

UBC PRESS (CANADA)
1993 Statement: "The name of the press has been altered somewhat; it is now shown as UBC Press on our books rather than written out in full, though it is not incorrect to use the full form. The information given in the [1988

Statement of University of British Columbia Press (Canada)] is ok except that we would put 'UBC Press' and the year of publication after the ©.

"If we sell rights, co-publishers generally follow the same practice of indicating first printings simply by the copyright symbol and the publisher name and year of publication. Reprints also are generally indicated on the copyright page, on a separate line below a line saying 'All rights reserved.' That line appears right below the main copyright line."

2000 Statement: "We use UBC Press rather than write out the Press's name in full, though it is not incorrect to use University of British Columbia Press. Although sometimes copyright is registered in an author's name, usually the copyright line has the copyright symbol followed by UBC Press and the year of publication.

"If we sell rights, copublishers usually follow the same practice of putting the copyright symbol followed by publisher name and year of publication. Reprints are indicated on the copyright page, on a separate line below the main copyright line and before a paragraph that says 'All rights reserved. No part of this publication may be reproduced, stored in a retrieval system, or transmitted, in any form or by any means, without prior written permission of the publisher.' "

UCCB PRESS (CANADA)
See University College of Cape Breton Press (Canada)

UCL PRESS (UNITED KINGDOM)
1994 Statement: "The first printings of our first editions are designated on the copyright page thus:
    First published in YEAR by UCL Press
  "A second printing would be designated thus:
    First published in YEAR by UCL Press
    Second impression YEAR
  "A second edition would be designated thus:
    First published in YEAR by UCL Press
    Second edition YEAR
  "A second printing of a second edition would be designated thus:
    First published in YEAR by UCL Press
    Second edition YEAR
    Second impression YEAR."
2000 Statement: "UCL Press no longer continues as an imprint."

UGLYTOWN
2001 Statement: "We identify the first printing of a first edition by the statement 'First Edition.' We identify the first printing of a first edition by the number line '10 9 8 7 6 5 4 3 2 1."

ULTRAVIOLET LIBRARY
2001 Statement: *See* 2001 Statement of Circlet Press

ULYSSES PRESS

1994 Statement: "On the copyright page of each book there is a sequence of numbers—10 9 8 7 6 5 4 3 2 1. The last number indicates the printing. If that number is 1, then the book is the first printing of the first edition."

ULYSSES TRAVEL GUIDES (CANADA)

2001 Statement: "Our policy is to not make any special identification of first editions. However we identify new editions so anything not identified as second or third edition or else is a first edition."

UNDERWOOD-MILLER

1988 Statement: "All Underwood-Miller and Brandywyne Books editions, since 1976, are noted First Edition, or First Hardcover Edition if the book is a reprint with only a previous paperback incarnation, or First Deluxe Edition if it is a special, limited signed edition of a title which has appeared elsewhere. Later printings are noted by 'Second' or 'Third' Printing, or nothing at all listed on the copyright page."

FREDERICK UNGAR BOOKS

1988 Statement: "The identifications for first editions or first printings in our books are the usual copyright line giving the year of publication plus the year of the printing at the top of the copyright page. We never use the words 'first edition' or 'first printing.' We do add 'second printing,' 'third printing,' and so on, whenever such printings are done.

"When a book is revised, enlarged, or substantially changed, we will include on the title page and/or the copyright page, either 'second edition,' 'enlarged edition,' etc., plus the year of this edition at the top of the copyright page. If these editions are reprinted, we also add 'second printing,' 'third printing,' etc.

"We have some reprints on our list. In such books the copyright information is different, depending on whether the book was in the public domain. These reprints or republications are, of course, not first editions, though they may have a new copyright line if we have added an introduction.

"[We] started printing the year at the top of the copyright page on 1 January 1986."

FREDERICK UNGAR PUBLISHING CO.

1947 Statement: "Our method of identifying the various printings of our books is to add the words 'Second Printing' or 'Third Printing' etc. on the copyright page.

"Revisions are indicated on the title page by 'Revised Edition' or a similar wording."

Statement for 1960: *See* 1982 Statement

1976 Statement: *See* 1982 Statement

1982 Statement: "The only identification for first editions or first printings in our books is the usual copyright line giving the year of publication. We never use the words 'first edition' or 'first printing.' We do add 'second printing,' 'third printing' and so on, whenever such printings are done.

"When a book is revised, enlarged, or substantially changed, we will include on the title page and/or the copyright page, either 'second edition,' 'enlarged edition,' etc. If these editions are reprinted, we also add second printing, 'third printing,' etc.

"We have some reprints on our list. In such books the copyright information is different, depending on whether the book was in the public domain. These reprints or republications are, of course, not first editions, though they may have a new copyright line if we have added an introduction."

1988 Statement: *See* 1988 Statement of Frederick Ungar Books

UNICORN & SON, PUBLISHERS
1993 Statement: *See* 1993 Statement of The Borgo Press
2000 Statement: *See* 2000 Statement of The Borgo Press

UNICORN PRESS (UNITED KINGDOM)
*(Incorporating John Heritage, Publisher. Taken over
by Richards Press, Ltd.)*

1937 Statement: "It is our practice to put the date of publication of any book on the verso of the title-page. If the book is reprinted, the date of the reprint appears on the verso of the title-page under the original insertion. It should read so:

First printed February 1935

"In the case of a reprint, as above, but with the following appended:

Reprinted May 1935"

UNICORN PRESS, INC.
1976 Statement: "The editions (e.g., signed, numbered, cloth, etc.) of our hand-printed books are described on the colophon pages of each book, accompanied often by the names of the persons who typeset, printed, bound them. For our larger books, which are usually machine-printed but hand-bound, the info. you are interested in is on the © page."

1981, 1988 Statements: *See* 1976 Statement

UNITED NATIONS
1976 Statement: "All United Nations publications carry sales number identification on both the back of the title page and in the tag line at the bottom of either the last page of text or the back cover. In the event of reprint of a publication, a statement to this effect is also indicated on the tag line."

1981, 1988, 1993 Statements: *See* 1976 Statement

UNITY PRESS
1976 Statement: "We have no special designation for indicating first editions. Subsequent printings would not be so indicated. Should there be a revised edition of a work, it would be so indicated on the copyright page."

1981 Statement: "All 'First Editions' now carry the nomenclature on the copyright page. Subsequent editions are indicated by the lowest number appearing in a series located on the same page under the nomenclature 'Printed in the United States.' This practice was begun a couple of years ago."

UNIVERSE BOOKS
1976 Statement: "First printing contains no identification. Subsequent printings and editions are always stated."
1981 Statement: "In 1980 we changed our procedure. We now print the following type of line on the copyright page: 80 81 82 83 84 / 10 9 8 7 6 5 4 3 2 1. In reprints we drop the year (if necessary) and the number of the previous printing(s). Thus, a reprint of a 1980 book might contain the altered line: 81 82 83 84 / 10 9 8 7 6 5 4 3 2. A new book published in 1981 would contain the figures: 81 82 83 84 85 / 10 etc."
1988 Statement: *See* 1981 Statement

UNIVERSE PUBLISHING
1994 Statement: *See* 1981 Statement of Universe Books

UNIVERSITY ART MUSEUM
(CALIFORNIA STATE UNIVERSITY, LONG BEACH)
1994 Statement: "We publish only exhibition catalogues and do not reprint them."

UNIVERSITY BOOKS, INC.
1976 Statement: "We show no designation for a first edition, but additional printings are identified."
1981, 1988 Statements: *See* 1976 Statement
1995 Statement: *See* 1995 Statement of Carol Publishing Group

UNIVERSITY CLASSICS, LTD.
1994 Statement: "We do not make any special designation of first editions in our publications other than the year of printing. We decided on this method the year we published our first book—1981. A second printing carries both the new and the original printing.

"We have no subsidiaries."

UNIVERSITY COLLEGE OF
CAPE BRETON PRESS (CANADA)
1995 Statement: The first printing of the first edition is indicated by the following statement on the copyright page:
University College of Cape Breton Press
First published in (date)
2000 Statement: *See* 1995 Statement

THE UNIVERSITY OF ALABAMA PRESS
1988 Statement: "The Press does not use any special designation to identify first editions. First editions and first printings can be assumed unless the copyright page carries a notice that the book is either a second or subsequent printing, or a second or subsequent edition.

"This method of designation does not differ from any previously used."
1994 Statement: *See* 1988 Statement

UNIVERSITY OF ALASKA PRESS

1988 Statement: "We have various ways of designating first printings, editions and reprints. On an unrevised reprint of another publisher's material we print 'Reprinted by the University of Alaska Press date' on the title page. On an original printing of our material we state 'First printing' on the back of the title page under the copyright date or year printed. For a second printing, we would so state 'Second Printing date.' In some cases [we] will do the first book printing of revised material and will note this on the back of title page as 'Revised Edition, Originally Published As: date.' For other revised editions, we would state on the back of title page, 'Revised Edition, date,' etc."

1994 Statement: *See* 1988 Statement

UNIVERSITY OF ARIZONA PRESS

1976 Statement: "At our Press, a book which carries only the copyright date as *the* date information on the back of the title page is a first printing. All subsequent printings will carry an additional line showing the year of the printing (as well as the copyright date itself, of course)."

1981 Statement: *See* 1976 Statement

1988 Statement: "At the University of Arizona Press, a first edition carries the copyright date only. Subsequent editions carry an additional line giving the year and number of the printing.

"The policy applies equally to our imprints."

2000 Statement: "At the University of Arizona Press, the first printing of the first edition includes the phrase 'First printing' on the copyright page, which also includes a line giving the date of publication and the printing sequence (e.g., 06 05 04 03 02 01 6 5 4 3 2 1). Subsequent printings include only the line of numbers. The policy applies equally to our imprints. We began this method in 1998."

THE UNIVERSITY OF ARKANSAS PRESS

1988 Statement: "Until 1986 our first editions were distinguished only by the lack of any notation as to printing, which was added for subsequent printings. We now indicate the first printing of a first edition by serial notation, e.g.

92 91 90 89 88 5 4 3 2 1

dropping the single and double digits from the right as additional printings occur and years pass."

1993, 2000 Statements: *See* 1988 Statement

UNIVERSITY OF BRITISH COLUMBIA PRESS (CANADA)

1976 Statement: "In those titles which we have reprinted, we indicate the dates of the reprints on the copyright page."

1981 Statement: *See* 1976 Statement

1988 Statement: "Readers may assume that all our books are first editions unless we specify on the copyright page (page iv) that the book has been reprinted or is published in a new edition. The copyright line starts with the c in a circle symbol and is followed by 'The University of British Columbia Press' and the year of publication. Information about a reprint is put on a separate line below the original copyright year line, and consists of the word 'Reprinted' and the year in which the reprint was done.

"UBC Press adopted this method of designation when it was established in 1971. We have no subsidiaries."

1993 Statement: *See* 1993 Statement of UBC Press (Canada)

2000 Statement: *See* 2000 Statement of UBC Press (Canada)

UNIVERSITY OF CALGARY PRESS (CANADA)

1988 Statement: "The University of Calgary Press does not identify first printings in any particular way. Second or subsequent printings and/or revised editions are indicated on the copyright page. The UCP has followed this procedure since it was established in 1982."

1993, 2000 Statements: *See* 1988 Statement

UNIVERSITY OF CALIFORNIA INTERNATIONAL STUDIES

1995 Statement: "[We] have no particular way of identifying a first or subsequent printing. A second or subsequent edition or revision is so identified in the volume and is assigned a new ISBN."

THE UNIVERSITY OF CALIFORNIA PRESS

1937 Statement: "The few books that have gone into a second edition have had printed on the verso of the title page 'Second Edition' or 'Third Edition.' Such a notice will be printed on all editions after the first."

1947 Statement: "All new printings and revised editions are identified on the verso of the title page by a notice such as 'Second Edition,' 'Revised Edition,' or 'Third Printing.' A careful distinction is made between printings and editions."

1976 Statement: "We do not use any sort of identifying statement to designate first editions of our books. We print only a copyright date.

"We do print a line to indicate such things as second, third, revised, paperback, etc. editions, although the wording may vary according to particular circumstances.

"In the past, we did add a new printing line every time a book was reprinted ('Second printing, 1968' or 'Fourth printing, 1972'), but as that practice has been largely discontinued the absence of such a line no longer assures a first edition."

1981 Statement: "The numbers 1 to 9 are now included in the copyright statement to indicate the printing of the book. The lowest number appearing indicates the printing of the book."

1988 Statement: "Our process for identifying printings and editions remains the same as in our 1976 and 1981 statements."

1993 Statement: *See* 1988 Statement

2000 Statement: "The previous statements remain accurate. We now also include a series of two-digit numbers of which the lowest number indicates the year of the most recent printing.

"There are certain names identified as imprints in University of California Press Books, usually as a means of identifying a source of sponsorship whose financial support has made publication of titles in a specific subject area possible. These 'imprints' include: Philip E. Lilienthal Asian Studies; Centennial books; Ahmanson Murphy Fine Arts Imprint; George Gund Foundation Imprint in African-American Studies; S. Mark Taper Foundation Imprint in Jewish Studies; Lisa See Endowment in Southern California History; Joan Palevsky Imprint in Classical Literature; and Roth Family Foundation Book in American Music.

"The method of identification of first editions on the copyright page would be the same for each of these 'imprints' as for any other book published by University of California Press."

UNIVERSITY OF CENTRAL FLORIDA
(Orlando)
1981, 1988 Statements: *See* 1981, 1988 Statements of University Presses of Florida

THE UNIVERSITY OF CHICAGO PRESS
1928, 1937 Statements: *See* 1947 Statement
1947 Statement: "You will notice that the publication date, and record of each new impression and new edition, is entered on the copyright page. Unless notice happens to be made in an occasional new preface, no other record is made in the book. This method has been used for at least thirty-one years."
Statement for 1960: *See* 1982 Statement
1976 Statement: "We have traditionally identified second and subsequent printings of a book, as well as second or later editions, on the verso of the title page. So if no such indication appears there, the reader can assume that the book is the first printing of the first edition.

"Currently, for some books, especially titles we expect to reprint frequently, we use a double sequence of numbers, the last of which indicates the year and number of the impression. That is, for the first impression of a book published in 1976 the sequence is as follows:

$$80\ 79\ 78\ 77\ 76\ \ 9\ 8\ 7\ 6\ 5\ 4\ 3\ 2\ 1$$

Then as new printings are ordered, numbers are removed from the plate or negative."
1982 Statement: "We have traditionally identified second and subsequent printings, as well as second or later editions, on the copyright page. If no such identification appears there, the reader can assume that the book is the first printing of the first edition.

"In recent years we have been indicating the year and number of the impression by means of a double sequence of numerals on the copyright page. These are easily altered to show subsequent impressions. The first impression of an edition published, for example, in 1980 would carry the following line:

$$87\ 86\ 85\ 84\ 83\ 82\ 81\ 80\ \ 54321$$

"For a second impression in 1982, the line would be altered to read as follows:

$$87\ 86\ 85\ 84\ 83\ 82\ \ 5432$$

"Second or later editions are identified as such on the copyright page and carry a new set of impression numbers."

1988 Statement: "The Press's practice for indicating edition and impression number remains as it last appeared in your publication."
1993, 2000 Statements: *See* 1988 Statement

UNIVERSITY OF CONNECTICUT
1988, 1993 Statements: *See* 1988 Statement of University Press of New England

UNIVERSITY OF DELAWARE PRESS
1976, 1981, 1988, 1993, 2000 Statements: *See* 1976 Statement of Associated University Presses

UNIVERSITY OF FLORIDA
(Gainesville)
1976, 1981, 1988 Statements: *See* 1976, 1981, 1988 Statements of University Presses of Florida

THE UNIVERSITY OF GEORGIA PRESS
1976 Statement: "We do not use any specific identification; however, on later editions we designate them as second edition, third edition, and so on.

"Later printings are designated: Second Printing, 1976; Third Printing, 1980, etc.

"If there has been a revision of the book, the designation will be: second edition, 1976, etc."
1981 Statement: *See* 1976 Statement
1988 Statement: "In 1984 we changed our method designating editions and now uniformly use a line of numbers with years and editions for all new books. We block out numbers as required on subsequent editions.

"For our books published before 1984, we follow our older method of designation."
1993, 2000 Statements: *See* 1988 Statement

THE UNIVERSITY OF HAWAII PRESS
1988 Statement: "The University of Hawaii Press uses a numerical system to designate first and subsequent printings. For example:

First printing in 1988:   92 91 90 89 88 1 2 3 4 5
Second printing in 1990: 92 91 90 2 3 4 5
Third printing in 1991:   92 91 3 4 5

"We began this system in 1988. The information appears on the copyright page."
1993 Statement: "We use the same system [as in 1988], but we arrange the numbers slightly differently depending on the design of the copyright page. E.g.: 93 94 95 96 97 98 5 4 3 2 1."

THE UNIVERSITY OF HULL PRESS (UNITED KINGDOM)
1994 Statement: "The [1989 Statement of Hull University Press (United Kingdom)] appears to be acceptable as the same practice as outlined then continues.

"The name of the Press was changed in 1993 to The University of Hull Press and in 1991 we commenced publishing books of local interest and less academic content under the imprint of The Lampada Press. The same printing procedures apply to both Presses."

2000 Statement: "The University of Hull and Lampada Press closed [in 1999]."

UNIVERSITY OF IDAHO PRESS

2001 Statement: "We do not identify first printings but only subsequent printings with numbers on the copyright page."

THE UNIVERSITY OF ILLINOIS PRESS

1976 Statement: "In general, books from this Press which do not indicate otherwise are first editions. Succeeding printings, impressions, revised editions, etc., are so indicated, either on the title page (occasionally) or on the back of the title page along with the copyright notice. There undoubtedly have been some lapses, but this has been the policy since 1950. For titles published during the years 1918-50, the earliest publication date is almost certain to indicate the first and only printing or impression in that year."

1981 Statement: *See* 1976 Statement

1988 Statement: "Since 1981 we have also included a printing code on the copyright page, which indicates which printing of *our* edition is the current one. This code will change with each reprinting, of course, and is relevant only for *our* edition (i.e. the *first* edition may have been published by another press—information that will also be clearly indicated on the copyright page, however)."

1993, 2000 Statements: *See* 1988 Statement

UNIVERSITY OF IOWA PRESS

1976 Statement: "Our press has no unusual method of identifying first editions of the works it publishes. Second printings and second editions are identified as such."

1981 Statement: *See* 1976 Statement

1988 Statement: "Since 1985 on our copyright page for first editions, we have stated, e.g. 'First edition, 1985.'

"Our imprints and subsidiaries follow our practices."

1993 Statement: "In 1993, to make reprinting easier, we switched to this system: 96 95 94 93 92 C 5 4 3 2 1."

2000 Statement: *See* 1993 Statement

UNIVERSITY OF KANSAS
MUSEUM OF NATURAL HISTORY

1994 Statement: "We do not identify first printings of our books on natural history. Second or revised printings are so noted on the reverse title page, and thus give identity to first printings."

THE UNIVERSITY OF MASSACHUSETTS PRESS

1976 Statement: "We do not provide a specific statement to the effect that the volumes we publish are first editions.

"Printings are not identified. We identify only revised editions."
1981, 1988, 1993, 2000 Statements: *See* 1976 Statement

UNIVERSITY OF MICHIGAN
MUSEUM OF ANTHROPOLOGY

1994 Statement: "To my knowledge, we've never issued a second edition, and rarely a second printing, so designating the first is not very important to us. On the few books we've reprinted, we have sometimes said '2nd impression' or some such on the copyright page. But sometimes not. We have no official policy on this—it would be at the discretion of the editor."

2001 Statement: "The 1994 Statement is accurate except that we now have issued a second edition . . . . If we actually changed text before we reprinted something—or changed anything that might be noticed, like paper quality—we would identify the impression. But this is not usually the case."

THE UNIVERSITY OF MICHIGAN PRESS

1988 Statement: "The first edition is not so stated. The copyright statement and the printing number and year indicate the printing history.

"Subsequent editions are designated in a statement preceding the copyright notice. The statement contains the edition and year, and the year is added to the copyright statement when necessary. The statement might be worded in the following ways:

Revised Edition
Second Edition
New Edition
First Paperback Edition
First Edition as a Paperback."

1993 Statement: *See* 1988 Statement

UNIVERSITY OF MINNESOTA PRESS

1937 Statement: "University Press books, as you know, are usually published in small editions and, with no exception that I can think of, the *absence* of the words 'Second Edition' is enough identification for a first edition of our books. We do, however, make a distinction between a second edition and a second printing of the first edition, and almost invariably add the line 'Second Printing,' 'Third Printing' etc., under the copyright notice."

1947 Statement: *See* 1937 Statement

Statement for 1960: "Our 1976 statement on the identification of first editions applies to books published by this Press for the years between 1949 and 1976. The same statement also holds for the identification of impressions."

1976 Statement: "First editions of books published by this Press are not identified as such in the books themselves and may be distinguished from subsequent editions by the fact that the latter are identified as such. The same holds true for impressions."

1981 Statement: *See* 1976 Statement

1988 Statement: "The practice previously outlined (in 1976) for identifying editions and impressions stands without change. We have no other imprints or subsidiaries."

1993 Statement: *See* 1988 Statement

2000 Statement: "First editions of books published for the first time by the University of Minnesota Press are not explicitly identified as such; subsequent and revised editions are clearly indicated as such on the title page and cover of the book (as well as in promotional and catalog copy for the book). Reprints and translations published by the University of Minnesota Press provide publication and copyright information of the original publication on the copyright page; the copyright page of reprints also includes a line stating that the book is the 'first University of Minnesota Press edition' of the work.

"This designation of first editions has been in effect since 1997. The Press does not have imprints or subsidiaries. We have not changed our name since 1995."

UNIVERSITY OF MISSOURI PRESS

1976 Statement: "We rarely do second or third editions of books (that is, with significant changes or revisions from the first). We do, however, reprint books as we run out of stock.

"The best way to determine the printing or edition of one of our books is to look at the copyright page. If there is no indication to the contrary, you probably have a book from the first printing. The appropriate information should be supplied in any other case."

1981, 1988 Statements: *See* 1976 Statement

1993 Statement: "In 1990 we began to use drop numbers on the copyright page to indicate the most recent printing of each book. Thus, for a book published in 1994, the numbers appear as 5 4 3 2 1 98 97 96 95 94 to indicate that the book was first printed in 1994. If a second printing was done in the same year, the number 1 would be dropped so that the lowest number (2) would indicate the number of the printing; if the second printing was in a later year, the digits for the years would be dropped up to the appropriate one. When a new edition is prepared, the full set of numbers is provided, with an indication on the title page of the nature of the edition and information on the copyright page concerning the publication history of the book.

"In books first published before 1989, the number of the printing will be given on the copyright page. Any book that does not indicate it is a second or later printing would be a first printing."

UNIVERSITY OF MONTANA
U M O P L—LINGUISTICS LABORATORY

1994 Statement: The first printing of a first edition is indicated by the statement "First Published in (Month), (Year)."

"We started doing so in April 1991, with the seventh volume of our series."

UNIVERSITY OF NEBRASKA PRESS

1976 Statement: "The University of Nebraska Press does not identify the first printing of a work as a first edition. However, subsequent printings are

identified as such on the copyright page. Thus, the absence of an edition statement indicates a first edition."
1981, 1988, 1994, 2000 Statements: *See* 1976 Statement

UNIVERSITY OF NEW HAMPSHIRE
1988, 1993 Statements: *See* 1988 Statement of University Press of New England

THE UNIVERSITY OF NEW MEXICO PRESS
1976 Statement: "It is presently our practice to use the words FIRST EDITION on the copyright page of each book. This is the verso of the title page, of course.

"Subsequent printings of the first edition usually carry the word *reprinted* and a date. A revised or enlarged edition has the words that so state. We do not use any alphabetical or numerical symbols such as A B C D, etc., or 1 2 3 4, etc.

"This press has been in existence since 1930 under a succession of directors, designers, and production managers. Regrettably, the words FIRST EDITION were not always used on earlier books. Seldom was a book reprinted within the same year, so the date of copyright would therefore indicate a first edition if there was no mention of a reprint with a later date.

"Our staff realizes that while the term 'edition' refers to an edition whose text remains unchanged, and may go through several printings, the average reader usually thinks of 'first edition, first impression, first issue, first state' as all the same thing. So we now state 'First edition' and add 'reprinted 1976' even if it remains unchanged, or if changed from cloth to paperback we will state this as well."
1981 Statement: "We identify a first edition by using the words *first edition* on the copyright page of each new book we publish. This practice seems to have been standard procedure since sometime in the late 1950s. Since we have generally indicated subsequent printings or editions on the copyright page (though not always by one particular method), any University of New Mexico Press book carrying only a copyright date can be identified reliably as first edition."
1988, 1993, 2000 Statements: *See* 1981 Statement

UNIVERSITY OF NEW SOUTH WALES PRESS LTD (AUSTRALIA)
1994, 2000 Statements: *See* 1988 Statement of The New South Wales University Press Limited (Australia)

THE UNIVERSITY OF NORTH CAROLINA PRESS
1937 Statement: "We do not have any general rule by which a first edition of one of our books may be distinguished from a later edition.

"We sometimes reprint from type within a few weeks after the first printing, without distinguishing in any way the second from the first printing. We may indicate on the back of the title page, after the first printing, the dates of various subsequent printings, but we do not always do this.

"Whenever we publish a new edition of a work, we usually secure a copyright to cover the new matter. Both the new and the old dates will appear on the back of the title page."

1947 Statement: "We do not have any general rule by which a first edition of one of our books may be distinguished from a later edition.

"When we reprint without revising, we usually indicate on the copyright page, after the first printing, the dates of various subsequent printings. Whenever we publish a revised edition of a work, we secure a copyright to cover the new matter. Both the new and the old dates will appear on the copyright page."

Statement for 1960: "The UNC Press does not have any method of identifying first editions. Unless one of our books is clearly designated as either a second edition or a revised edition, the reader and bibliographer may assume that they are dealing with a first edition.

"This statement applies before and after 1976."

1976 Statement: "The Press does not have any method of identifying first editions. Unless one of our books is clearly designated as either a second edition or a revised edition, the reader and bibliographer may assume that they are dealing with a first edition."

1981, 1988, 1994, 2000 Statements: *See* 1976 Statement

UNIVERSITY OF NORTH FLORIDA
(Jacksonville)

1976, 1981, 1988 Statements: *See* 1976, 1981, 1988 Statements of University Presses of Florida

UNIVERSITY OF NOTRE DAME PRESS

1976 Statement: "We have no method of designating a first edition."
1981, 1988, 1995, 2000 Statements: *See* 1976 Statement

UNIVERSITY OF OKLAHOMA PRESS

1937 Statement: "All of our books contain on the copyright page a statement of the day, month, and year of first publication. This usually takes the following form: 'Set up and printed at Norman, Oklahoma, by the University of Oklahoma Press, Publishing Division of the University. First edition May 18, 1936.' If a second printing is issued, this information is always added to the material on the copyright page, though the day of second printing is usually not given. Notice of second printing is almost uniformly carried on our jackets as well. We have employed this method of differentiating first from subsequent printings since the founding of the Press in 1928."

1947 Statement: "The copyright pages on our books now customarily carry information arranged according to the following form: 'Copyright 1947 by the University of Oklahoma Press, Publishing Division of the University. All rights reserved. Set up and printed at Norman, Oklahoma, U.S.A., by the University of Oklahoma Press. First edition.' If a second printing is issued, we further particularize the information about the first edition and add the date for the second printing as follows: 'First edition, August, 1947. Second printing, October, 1947.' We frequently carry information about printings beyond the first on our jackets. This general method of differentiating first from subsequent printings as here described has been in use by the Press since its founding nearly twenty years ago. It is of particular importance that our colophon page, which always appears at the end of volume, be read in connection with the copyright page, especially for any notation of limited edition."

Statement for 1960: "The wording used to designate first printings in 1960 is as follows:

Copyright 1960 by the University of Oklahoma Press,
Publishing Division of the University. Composed and printed at Norman, Oklahoma, U.S.A., by the University of Oklahoma Press. First edition."

1976 Statement: "From the year, 1976, on, the form shown in new books will be:

Copyright 19—by the University of Oklahoma Press,
Publishing Division of the University. Manufactured in the U.S.A. First edition.

"At the time of the Press's founding, the form used was the following:

Copyright 1932 by the University of Oklahoma Press
All rights reserved
Manufactured in the United States of America. Set up and printed by the University of Oklahoma Press at Norman. First printed January, 1932

"The form used from the early 1940s until 1976 was the following: Copyright 1975 by the University of Oklahoma Press, Publishing Division of the University. Composed and printed at Norman, Oklahoma, U.S.A., by the University of Oklahoma Press. First edition."

1981 Statement: *See* 1976 Statement

1988 Statement: "As of January 1, 1988, the University of Oklahoma Press copyright statement for the first printing of a new title reads as follows:

Copyright © 1988 by the University of Oklahoma Press,
Norman, Publishing Division of the University. All rights reserved. Manufactured in the U.S.A. First edition.

"The changes in this statement were made in the interval between 1981 (the date of your last statement) and the present: the addition of ©, the addition of 'Norman' after the name of the Press, the addition of 'All rights reserved,' and the change from 'Composed and printed at Norman, Oklahoma, U.S.A., by the University of Oklahoma Press' to 'Manufactured in the U.S.A.'

"We have no subsidiaries; our imprints (titles in series) carry the same copyright statement."

1993 Statement: *See* 1988 Statement but note that beginning in 1992, the words "First Edition" no longer appear.

UNIVERSITY OF OTAGO PRESS (NEW ZEALAND)

1994 Statement: "We state 'First published in (year)' and list dates of reprints."

2000 Statement: *See* 1994 Statement

UNIVERSITY OF OTTAWA PRESS (CANADA)

2001 Statement: "The University of Ottawa Press does not make any special identification of first editions. However, we identify reprints and new editions so anything not identified as a reprint or new edition is a first edition."

UNIVERSITY OF PENNSYLVANIA PRESS

1937 Statement: "All titles published by us are first printings unless otherwise noted on the copyright page. In the case of second and subsequent printings, we give the date of publication and the dates of further printings."

1947 Statement: *See* 1937 Statement

1976 Statement: "If our book does not say 'Revised Edition,' 'Second Edition,' 'Third Edition,' etc., it is the first edition."

1981, 1988, 1993 Statements: *See* 1976 Statement

UNIVERSITY OF PITTSBURGH
LATIN AMERICAN ARCHAEOLOGY PUBLICATIONS

1994 Statement: "We publish bilingual (English/Spanish) monographs on the results of archaeological research in Latin America for a professional audience. Any edition not designated as a second or revised edition is a first edition. The second printing of a first edition would also be noted on the copyright page.

"This has been the practice at UPLAAP since its founding in 1989."

2001 Statement: *See* 1994 Statement

UNIVERSITY OF PITTSBURGH PRESS

1947 Statement: "We indicate second and third printings of our books as follows:

    Copyright 1937
    University of Pittsburgh Press
    Published 1937
    Second Printing 1940
    Third Printing 1947"

1976 Statement: "If we are publishing a book for the first time, the following information is inserted on the copyright page:

    'Copyright © (date), University of Pittsburgh Press
    (or author)
    All rights reserved
    Feffer & Simons, Inc., London
    Manufactured in the United States of America
    (Library of Congress Cataloging in Publication Data box)
    (Any necessary acknowledgements)'

We do not indicate that it is the first edition or first printing.

"If we reprint the first edition, we add: 'Second printing (date)', 'Second printing (date) / Third printing (date),' etc.

"If we reprint a cloth book in paper, we add: 'First printing, (date) / Paperback reissue, (date).'

"If we have bought the American rights of a British book, the usual wording is: 'First published in Great Britain (date) by (publishers) / Published in the U.S.A. (date) by the University of Pittsburgh Press.'

"I do not believe we have ever published a second edition.

"I do not believe the procedures are different from earlier ones, although minor aspects such as punctuation may vary."

1981, 1988, 1993 Statements: *See* 1976 Statement

UNIVERSITY OF QUEENSLAND PRESS (AUSTRALIA)

1981 Statement: "We don't actually designate that our books are the first printing of the first edition in any way. But their lack of identification marks them as such. All subsequent reprints or later editions are indicated as such, for example 'Second reprint of third edition.'

"Our imprints are not always the same. Our usual style is for the copyright line to read: Copyright University of Queensland Press. This is because our contracts assign the rights to us. However, there has grown up a loose tradition with creative writers that they always have copyright in their name, which legally speaking is incorrect."

1988 Statement: "All University of Queensland Press titles should carry both the year of first publication as well as the year any particular edition has been printed. If only one date is mentioned on the copyright page, and this is the date of first publication, then that clearly identifies the book as a first printing of a first edition. Should a reprint be issued in the same year, then the word 'reprinted' will also appear on the copyright page."

1994 Statement: "We don't actually designate that our books are the first printing of the first edition in any way. But their lack of identification marks them as such. All subsequent reprints or later editions are indicated as such, for example 'Second reprint of third edition.' "

2000 Statement: *See* 1988 Statement

UNIVERSITY OF RHODE ISLAND

1988, 1993 Statements: *See* 1988 Statement of University Press of New England

UNIVERSITY OF ROCHESTER PRESS

1994 Statement: "We do not actually state that a work is a first printing or edition *per se*, but in all subsequent printings or editions we specify whether the work is a second edition or second printing etc . . . on the copyright page."

2000 Statement: *See* 1994 Statement

UNIVERSITY OF SOUTH CAROLINA PRESS

1976 Statement: "Our first editions are identified on the copyright page with 'First Edition' and the date. All subsequent printings or revised editions are also identified on the copyright page. In short, we normally give all publishing information, including joint publishers abroad, if any."

1981 Statement: *See* 1976 Statement

1988 Statement: "Since about 1985, we have done an increasing number of simultaneous hard and paperback printings that do not indicate the first edition

618

since this procedure is tantamount to two first editions. We do however, indicate 'First Edition' in books initially published in hardback only.

"In all cases we do indicate the previous publishing history including copyrights, original publisher if other than the University of South Carolina Press, printing history, joint publishers, if any, and where published."

1994 Statement: "Since about 1990 we do not identify first editions on the copyright page. We do always indicate previous publishing history including copyrights, original publisher if other than USC Press, printing history and where published."

THE UNIVERSITY OF SOUTH DAKOTA PRESS

1988 Statement: "We never explicitly note the appearance of a first edition. Some books are printed in editions signed and numbered by the author, but these are infrequent. This information is carried on the copyright page."

(The Dakota Press at the University of South Dakota was renamed The University of South Dakota Press.)

UNIVERSITY OF SOUTH FLORIDA
(Tampa)
1976, 1981, 1988 Statements: *See* 1976, 1981, 1988 Statements of University Presses of Florida

THE UNIVERSITY OF TENNESSEE PRESS

1976 Statement: "On the copyright page of most of our books we carry the words 'First Edition' in addition to the customary copyright information. As a general rule we do not add 'First Edition' to the information given in scientific or technical studies; however, if the copyright page does not indicate that the volume is a 'Second' or 'Third Printing,' etc., bibliographers and book collectors can be assured that the volume is a first edition. If a title is a 'Second' or 'Third Edition' (a revision) that information is also noted on the copyright page."

1981, 1988, 1993 Statements: *See* 1976 Statement

UNIVERSITY OF TEXAS PRESS

1976 Statement: "We do not state that a book is a first edition. The date in the copyright notice indicates the year of first publication. Subsequent printings are marked 'Second Printing, date,' 'Third Printing, date,' etc. on the copyright page. A revised edition would be so identified on the title page. Paperback editions not published at the same time as the clothbound editions are identified as 'First Paperback Printing, date,' 'Second Paperback Printing, date' etc. on the copyright page."

1981 Statement: "Our new policy, effective 1/1/81, is to put 'First Edition' and the year on the copyright page. Subsequent printings and revised editions will be indicated as before."

1988, 1993 Statements: *See* 1981 Statement

2000 Statement: *See* 1981 Statement, "but we now lowercase 'edition' and 'printing' in most cases."

UNIVERSITY OF TORONTO PRESS (CANADA)

1976 Statement: "We don't normally indicate that books are first editions. The date of publication is shown in the copyright notice, and if there are further printings or further editions the dates are listed on the copyright page. So that, as you suggest, when no designation is made, it may be assumed that it is a first printing and edition."

1981 Statement: *See* 1976 Statement

1988 Statement: "We do not designate first editions. Subsequent editions or printings are so indicated. It may be safely assumed that any book bearing the University of Toronto Press imprint is a first edition, unless otherwise indicated.

"This has always been the case.

"We have no subsidiary imprints."

2000 Statement: *See* 2000 Statement of University of Toronto Press Incorporated (Canada)

UNIVERSITY OF TORONTO PRESS INCORPORATED (CANADA)

2000 Statement: *See* 1988 Statement of University of Toronto Press (Canada)

UNIVERSITY OF UTAH PRESS

1976 Statement: "The University of Utah Press does not have a specific statement for identifying first editions. We do, however, identify a printing as a 2d, 3rd, etc., or as a 2d, 3rd, etc., edition. This information appears on the copyright page, usually beneath the copyright and rights statements, simply as: Second printing, 1976, or Second edition. Of course, subsequent editions beyond the first would have applicable copyright dates."

1981, 1988, 1993 Statements: *See* 1976 Statement

2000 Statement: "The University of Utah Press printings and years:
06 05 04 03 02 01 00
6 5 4 3 2 1

"Editions are listed 1st edition, 2nd edition, etc."

UNIVERSITY OF VERMONT

1988, 1993 Statements: *See* 1988 Statement of University Press of New England

UNIVERSITY OF WALES PRESS (WALES)

1988 Statement: "Where only one date of publication appears on the title page and/or the copyright page, it can be taken that the book is a first edition. Details of any subsequent editions or impressions are carried on the copyright page. (The Press was founded in 1922, and we cannot give an absolute guarantee that this was the invariable practice in the earlier years.)

"This information applies to all our imprints (University of Wales Press; Gwasg Prifysgol Cymru; GPC Books)."

1994, 2000 Statements: *See* 1988 Statement

UNIVERSITY OF WASHINGTON PRESS

1976 Statement: "This Press does not identify first editions as such. We do list reprintings and revised editions on the copyright page, so that the complete printing history of the book is given there."

1981, 1988, 1993, 2000 Statements: *See* 1976 Statement

UNIVERSITY OF WEST FLORIDA
(Pensacola)

1976, 1981, 1988 Statements: *See* 1976, 1981, 1988 Statements of University Presses of Florida

UNIVERSITY OF WESTERN AUSTRALIA PRESS
(AUSTRALIA)

2000 Statement: "Our company name is now styled 'University of Western Australia Press' (note no definite article) or abbreviated as 'UWA Press.'

"Our practice is unchanged since 1988. The only alteration is . . . we now have several imprints. Our trade title imprint 'Tuart House', our children's title imprint 'Cygnet Books', and our regional imprint 'C & J Staples South West Region Publications Fund'; all adopt the same method."

See 1988 Statement of The University of Western Australia Press (Australia)

THE UNIVERSITY OF WESTERN AUSTRALIA PRESS
(AUSTRALIA)

1988 Statement: "Our customary method is to indicate on the verso of the title page, in addition to the standard copyright notice and National Library of Australia Cataloguing-in-publication data (C.I.P.), that the book was 'First published in (year).' Reprints are noted thereunder as 'Reprinted (year),' or 'Reprinted with revisions/amendments (year).' A completely revised edition is treated as a new book with new ISBN number and C.I.P. data.

"Where a book is co-published we state 'First published in Australia (year).'

"This method has been unchanged (apart from the fairly recent innovation of the C.I.P. data) since the first book to be published under the imprint in 1954. Our trade title imprint 'Cygnet Books' adopts the same method."

THE UNIVERSITY OF WISCONSIN PRESS

1976 Statement: "The copyright page of each new title contains the year of publication and the words 'first printing.' Previous to 1970, the year of publication appeared on the title page. The copyright page of each reprint contains the year of first publication and the years of the subsequent printings."

1981 Statement: *See* 1976 Statement

1988 Statement: "With our Fall 1988 list the University of Wisconsin Press has instituted the practice of designating printings by a series of numbers in descending order from left to right:

5 4 3 2 1

"The number at the right represents the number of the printing.

"First editions are not labeled as such. Later editions are identified."

1993 Statement: "If the copyright page has a centered design, the numbers are arranged so that, when a number is deleted, the centering effect remains, thus: 2 4 5 3 1. The lowest number represents the number of the printing. First editions are not labeled as such. Later editions are identified. This method was first used in 1992."

UNIVERSITY PRESS OF AMERICA INC.
1994 Statement: "We do not identify first printings; we only differentiate if it is a revised or second edition."

UNIVERSITY PRESS OF COLORADO
1994 Statement: "We . . . do not distinguish first editions by any particular wording. We do, however, indicate on the copyright page whether a title is revised or whether it is a successive edition. On the copyright page, we print 10, 9, 8, 7, 6, 5, 4, 3, 2, 1, and each time a book is reprinted we delete the far-most right numeral."
2000 Statement: *See* 1994 Statement

UNIVERSITY PRESS OF FLORIDA
1993 Statement: "Printings: On the copyright page we now carry five double-digit numbers in addition to the book's year of publication. And we carry the numbers 6, 5, 4, 3, 2, 1 to designate most recent printing.

"With subsequent printings, we delete 1, leaving 2 on the copyright page; if the year also changes, we delete the double digits so the current printing corresponds with the year in which it took place.

"Editions: If an original clothbound work is reprinted and bound in paper covers, it is designated 'first paperback edition' (with the year noted) on the book's copyright page. If a work is revised by 20 percent or more, it is called 'revised edition.' "
2000 Statement: *See* 1993 Statement

THE UNIVERSITY PRESS OF HAWAII
1976 Statement: "Editions and printings after the first are so indicated."
1981 Statement: *See* 1976 Statement
1988 Statement: *See* 1988 Statement of The University of Hawaii Press

UNIVERSITY PRESS OF KANSAS
1988 Statement: The Regents Press of Kansas changed its name to University Press of Kansas in June of 1982.

"The first printing does not say 'First printing.' The later printings are so labeled on © page.

"We label a second printing as 'Second printing (date).' It is not considered a new edition, even if a few corrections have been made."
1993 Statement: "Effective 1988 or thereabouts, the first and subsequent printings are indicated in the reprint line on the copyright page. The last number designates the printing."

THE UNIVERSITY PRESS OF KENTUCKY

1976 Statement: "Since the vast majority of our books appear in only one edition, we have had no occasion to develop a statement identifying first editions. Often when a book is reprinted we correct errors discovered too late in the first printing. But we have never to my knowledge identified such a reprint as a new edition, although I suppose that technically it is that."

The individual printings of a first edition are not identified.

1981 Statement: "Normally a book appears in only one edition, one printing; we do not identify it as a first edition, nor are the individual printings usually identified, although in one instance a corrected reprinting was so marked on the copyright page. Revised editions are identified as such."

1988 Statement: *See* 1981 Statement

1995 Statement: *See* 1981 Statement, but note that "Second or revised editions are identified as such."

UNIVERSITY PRESS OF MISSISSIPPI

1976 Statement: "First editions contain our normal copyright and imprint while later editions carry special notices such as 'second printing: (date).' "

1981 Statement: *See* 1976 Statement

1988 Statement: "[The] 1976 statement regarding first editions is still correct. In addition, we often use the five number/five date method—all five numbers and years indicate first printing; lowest remaining number and year indicates successive printing dates. (This method was begun in 1986; we do not use it for every book.)

"Imprints and subsidiaries follow this practice."

2000 Statement: *See* 1988 Statement

UNIVERSITY PRESS OF NEW ENGLAND

1976 Statement: "Our identification of a first edition is in our copyright notice. The first edition contains only the copyright year. Subsequent editions are identified by the added notice: 'Second edition, copyright—. Third edition, copyright—.' "

1981 Statement: *See* 1976 Statement

1988 Statement: "Our 1981 Statement . . . is correct. However, during 1987 we began to phase in a new method of identifying printings on new books as well as most backlist titles that happened to reprint during this period. Under the new system, we place a series of numbers (5 4 3 2 1) toward the bottom of the copyright page. The printing is indicated by the lowest number in the string. Thus '5 4 3 2 1' is the first printing in an edition, '5 4 3' would be a third printing, and so on. We will be using this system on all our imprints."

1993 Statement: *See* 1988 Statement

THE UNIVERSITY PRESS OF VIRGINIA

1976 Statement: "Our first editions, first printings carry: *First published 19*— on the copyright page.

"A second printing would add: *Second printing 19*— to the above notice, or, in some cases, merely *Reprinted 19*—.

"A second edition would add: *Second edition 19*— to the above notice, and carry *Second edition* or some other qualifying statement on the title page."

1981, 1988, 1993, 2000 Statements: *See* 1976 Statement

UNIVERSITY PRESS OF WASHINGTON, D.C.

1988 Statement: *See* 1988 Statement of Larlin Corporation

2000 Statement: *See* 2000 Statement of Cherokee Publishing Co

UNIVERSITY PRESSES OF FLORIDA

Florida A & M University (Tallahassee), Florida Atlantic University (Boca Raton), Florida International University (Miami), Florida State University (Tallahassee) University of Central Florida (Orlando), University of Florida (Gainesville), University of North Florida (Jacksonville), University of South Florida (Tampa), University of West Florida (Pensacola)

To determine which of the following statements applies to the above universities, please refer to the individual entries for each of the universities.

1976 Statement: "Printings. There is no designation as such in a first printing. Subsequently we carry on the copyright page 'Second Impression,' 'Third Impression,' etc. Quantities and dates are not indicated.

"*Editions.* First editions have no special identity. If a work is revised it is designated 'Revised Edition' on the title page and on the copyright page. A *second* revision is called 'Third Edition.'

"The foregoing has been our practice for at least ten years."

1981 Statement: *See* 1988 Statement. The 1981 Statement previously provided was erroneous.

1988 Statement: The 1981 Statement was erroneous. The corrected statement reads as follows:

"*Printings.* There is no designation of a first or subsequent printing.

"*Editions.* First editions have no special identity. If a work is revised it is designated 'Revised Edition' on the title page and on the copyright page. A *second* revision is called 'Third Edition.'

"The foregoing has been our practice for at least ten years."

UNIVERSITY SOCIETY, INC.

1976 Statement: "The copyright date has always been the key to identifying first editions (our Company was founded in 1896). Our older anthologies generally indicated subsequent editions with new copyright dates, plus a note referring to earlier editions from which material was taken. There was no clear-cut method of identification, however.

"Today we use code numbers for each printing of a particular multivolume anthology. For example, 'Pub. No. 1001' on the copyright page means that the volume in question is a first edition, '1002' a second printing, etc. The reason we do this is because in a 17 volume anthology, for example, the individual volumes are reprinted on a stagger system to accommodate our bindery. It would not do to have a set of books with one volume labeled 'third printing' and another volume labeled 'fourth printing;' yet sets with volumes from various printings do appear. The code is to prevent our customers from becoming alarmed at any apparent discrepancy.

"In the case of single volumes, we merely indicate 'First Edition' or 'Second Edition' on the copyright page."

UNWIN HYMAN, INC.

1988 Statement: "We do not identify first printings as such but identify all subsequent printings: 'Second printing, 1988,' and so on. This has been standard procedure for as long as I am aware. I believe that our imprints and subsidiaries follow this same practice, though to be honest, I cannot guarantee it.

"Please note that we have changed our name to: Unwin Hyman, Inc. We are the wholly owned subsidiary of Unwin Hyman Ltd of Great Britain, which now publishes titles under the former imprints of George Allen & Unwin, Allen & Unwin, Bell & Hyman, and Hutchinson."

UNWIN HYMAN LIMITED (UNITED KINGDOM)

1988 Statement: "1. First editions are designated by the line 'First published in Great Britain by . . . ' followed by the date, then the copyright line. Second and subsequent printings or editions contain an additional line so stating.

"2. This method has been in use for a number of years.

"3. Imprints and subsidiaries should follow the same practice."

W.E. UPJOHN INSTITUTE FOR EMPLOYMENT RESEARCH

2000 Statement: "We do not identify first editions."

UPWARD TRENDS

1995 Statement: *See* 1995 Statement of Cedar Bay Press

UQP (AUSTRALIA)

2000 Statement: *See* 2000 Statement of University of Queensland Press (Australia)

URBAN & SCHWARZENBERG, INC.

1988 Statement: "First Printing is indicated by © date on the © page. This method was adopted in 1866. It does not differ from methods previously used. Subsidiary companies follow this practice."

URBAN INSTITUTE PRESS

1976 Statement: "The Urban Institute uses a code on the copyright page which shows the printing, year of printing, and the quantity printed. Thus, 'A/76/1 M' would translate 'First printing, 1976, 1000 copies,' and 'B/78/1 M' would translate as 'Second Printing, 1978, 1000 copies.' In that case, the date of the original printing is verified by the copyright notice."

1981 Statement: *See* 1976 Statement

1989 Statement: "The Urban Institute no longer has any special designation for a first printing."

1993 Statement: *See* 1989 Statement

URIZEN BOOKS, INC.

1981 Statement: "First printing on our first editions means first edition, further printings are indicated and it is also indicated whether revisions have been made by saying Revised New Edition on the title page. In the event we enter the reprint market we will write the book's past history on the copyright page."

U. S. GAMES SYSTEMS, INC.

1994 Statement: "U.S. Games Systems, Inc. identifies first editions in one of two ways:

10 9 8 7 6 5 4 3 2 1

or

First Printing

"Either one of the above appears on the copyright page."

U. S. NAVAL INSTITUTE

1976, 1981, 1988 Statements: *See* 1976, 1981, 1988 Statements of Naval Institute Press

UWA PRESS (AUSTRALIA)

2000 Statement: *See* 2000 Statement of University of Western Australia Press (Australia)

V

VAGROM CHAP BOOKS

1976 Statement: "Our first editions have all been, so far, 'only' editions. We would only designate those editions after the first with proper numbering and information, to distinguish from first 'only' editions. All our issues may be taken as first editions."

1988 Statement: *See* 1976 Statement

VALLENTINE, MITCHELL AND COMPANY LIMITED (UNITED KINGDOM)

1994 Statement: *See* 1988 Statement of Frank Cass Publishers (United Kingdom)

VAN CORTLANDT MANOR

1981 Statement: *See* 1981 Statement of Sleepy Hollow Press

VAN DER PLAS PUBLICATIONS

2001 Statement: *See* 2001 Statement of Bicycle Books, Inc.

VAN NOSTRAND REINHOLD

1993 Statement: "Since 1970, a numerical sequence, usually 16 through 1, has been used to indicate printings of a first edition. If the number 1 is present, the book in question is the first printing of a first edition. The words 'first edition' are not used.

"Second editions are noted and the numerical sequence is restarted, with 1 indicating a first printing."

VAN NOSTRAND REINHOLD COMPANY

1976 Statement: "Since 1970, a numerical sequence, usually 16 through 1 has been used to indicate printings of a first edition. If the number 1 is present, the book in question is the first printing of a first edition. The words 'first edition' are not used.

"Second editions are noted and the sequence is started over again as well."

1981, 1988 Statements: *See* 1976 Statement

("Name was changed to Van Nostrand Reinhold approximately 1989.")

THE VAN PETTEN COMPANY

1994 Statement: "We designate the first printing of a first edition by stating the print dates of each printing. We have always used this method of designation. We have no imprints or subsidiaries."

VANCOUVER COMMUNITY PRESS (CANADA)

See 1988 Statement of New Star Books (Canada)

VANDAMERE PRESS

1994 Statement: "Vandamere Press provides all edition and printing information on the Verso page of our books. A first printing of a first edition will contain only the copyright date. Subsequent printings will appear below the copyright date with month and year of the printing.

"If a book is revised, it will receive a new copyright date with a full printing history of all previous editions that we published. In the event that the previous edition was published by another publisher, that information and the original copyright date are included. In the case of guide books which are revised frequently, only the current edition number and the new copyright date are provided. This practice applies to all published Vandamere Press titles."

2000 Statement: *See* 1994 Statement

VANDERBILT UNIVERSITY PRESS

1976 Statement: Editions and printings are indicated only after the first.

1981, 1988 Statements: *See* 1976 Statement

1993 Statement: "We plan to change our former practice regarding the identification of first editions on the copyright page of each book we publish. Beginning with 1994 titles, first editions whether in hardcover or paperback will be specifically indicated:

First Edition 1994

94 95 96 97 98 99 5 4 3 2 1."

2000 Statement: *See* 1993 Statement

THE VANGUARD PRESS

1937 Statement: "The Vanguard Press uses no special mark or wording to indicate its first editions, but states on the copyright page when a book is in any but the first printing."

1947 Statement: *See* 1937 Statement

1976 Statement: "Actually, there is no way to determine whether our books of the past were first editions or not. Some, not all, had second edition notices in them. However, if there was a rush to publication for a second edition or later this was often omitted. Thus, one could not tell the difference between the first edition and later printings. Presently, we do differentiate by numbering the edition on the copyright page with the numerals: 1 2 3 4 5 6 7 8 9 0. As each new edition is printed, the preceding number is deleted. Thus a second edition would bear the number 2, a third 3, etc."

1981 Statement: *See* 1976 Statement

1988 Statement: *See* 1937 Statement

VANWELL PUBLISHING LIMITED (CANADA)

1995 Statement: "We use 1 2 3 4 5 6 7 8 9 0. When reprinted, we delete figure 1, etc., insert 2nd, 3rd, etc., printing on copyright page, change copyright year to Roman numerals."

VARIORUM (UNITED KINGDOM)

2000 Statement: *See* 2000 Statement of Ashgate Publishing Limited (United Kingdom)

VCH PUBLISHERS INC.

1995 Statement: The first printing of a first edition is indicated by the number line 10 9 8 7 6 5 4 3 2 1. The lowest number showing indicates the printing.

VCP (CANADA)

See 1988 Statement of New Star Books (Canada)

VEDANTA PRESS

1976 Statement: "Our early titles simply had the copyright date for the first edition. Later editions would be so marked, i.e., '2nd printing, 1976.'

"Lately, we have been marking our books to designate the first edition, i.e., 'First Edition, 1976.' "

1981, 1988, 1993 Statements: *See* 1976 Statement

VELOCE PUBLISHING PLC (UNITED KINGDOM)

1994 Statement: "Veloce Publishing Plc denotes a first edition by the statement 'First published in (date) by Veloce Publishing . . . .' Should a reprint occur, we would add the words 'Reprinted (date).' "

2000 Statement: *See* 1994 Statement

THE VENDOME PRESS

1994 Statement: "We don't do anything special about first editions. Generally we don't have a second edition, and if we do we don't do anything to identify it."

VENTURE PRESS

(See Simon and Schuster, Inc., who in 1945 added this as an imprint for work by beginning authors, as well as for first work in a new form by established authors.)

VERBA MUNDI

2000 Statement: *See* 2000 Statement of David R. Godine, Publisher, Inc.

VERBATIM BOOKS

1994 Statement: "I am well aware that some publishers want to make sure that book buyers are informed that subsequent *editions* of the work in question will follow . . . despite the fact that some of them have never gone into a second edition. (I always found that practice a little odd, but could well understand the commercial purpose in it.)

"We have not followed such a practice at Verbatim, however. Our *Grammar of the English Language* has been printed seven times, and each of those printings and its date is listed on the copyright page."

2001 Statement: "Perhaps I should change the 1994 Statement in view of the embarrassing fact that we recently reprinted the *Grammar* (for the eighth time) and someone forgot to make the addition or change on the copyright page. Alas, the same thing happened for the (recent) reprint of *Colonial American English,* so I guess I'd better not make any statement at all . . . and keep out of trouble.

"In any event, the first part of my earlier statement doesn't make much sense unless the reader is aware that it referred to the practice of (certain) publishers I know (who shall remain nameless), to put 'First Edition' prominently on the first edition of a book. In other words, I was commenting on the practices of others, not ours. My position is that one publishes a book. Period. If subsequent editions are published, they should be marked 'Second Edition,' etc. till the cows come home."

VERITAS PRESS
(Bought by Julian Messner in 1945.)

VERMILION (UNITED KINGDOM)
1994 Statement: *See* 1994 Statement of Ebury Press (United Kingdom)
2000 Statement: *See* 2000 Statement of The Random House Group Limited (United Kingdom)

VERTIGO
2000 Statement: *See* 2000 Statement of DC Comics

THE VESTAL PRESS LTD
1988 Statement: "We do not provide a statement in a first edition but we do identify subsequent editions and subsequent printings."
1993 Statement: *See* 1988 Statement

VICTOR BOOKS
1995 Statement: *See* 1995 Statement of Scripture Press Publications, Inc.

VICTORIA UNIVERSITY PRESS (NEW ZEALAND)
1994 Statement: "Our practice is to print on the title page verso, beneath our name and address and notification of the author's copyright: 'First published 19XX.' Reprints are identified by a line immediately below, e.g.: 'Reprinted 1991 (twice), 1992.' When significant changes have been made, a new line might read: 'New edition 1994.' This method has been used since the Press's formal inception in 1979, although perhaps not with complete rigour."

VIET NAM GENERATION
1994 Statement: "We do not designate first edition. We do designate reprints, however, so any book not marked as a reprint is a first edition."

VIKING
1988 Statement: *See* 1988 Statement of Penguin Publishing Co Ltd (United Kingdom)

VIKING (AUSTRALIA)
1994, 2000 Statements: *See* 1994 Statement of Penguin Books Australia Ltd (Australia)

VIKING (NEW ZEALAND)
1994, 2000 Statements: *See* 1994 Statement of Penguin Books (NZ) Limited (New Zealand)

VIKING (UNITED KINGDOM)
1988 Statement: *See* 1988 Statement of Penguin Publishing Co Ltd (United Kingdom)
1994 Statement: "At Viking we indicate first editions by printing 'First edition' as part of the print history on the copyright page. In addition, 1 2 3 4 5 6 7 8 9 0 appears on the same page. On each reprinting, a digit is removed to indicate a further printing."
2001 Statement: *See* 2001 Statement of Penguin Publishing Co Ltd (United Kingdom)

VIKING KESTREL
1988 Statement: *See* 1988 Statement of Penguin Publishing Co Ltd (United Kingdom)

VIKING KESTREL (UNITED KINGDOM)
1988 Statement: *See* 1988 Statement of Penguin Publishing Co Ltd (United Kingdom)

VIKING PENGUIN INC.
1989 Statement: "Our 1982 Statement is still accurate. We use a line of figures and strike out one of them with each new printing. Our subsidiaries (Viking Studio Books) follow this practice."
See also 1988 Statement of Penguin Publishing Co Ltd (United Kingdom)

THE VIKING PRESS INC.
1928 Statement: *See* 1937 Statement
1937 Statement: "Our first editions can be distinguished by the fact that there is no indication to the contrary on the copyright page. That is, we indicate the date and number of each reprinting.

"This has always been our method and we shall continue it until further notice.

"The Viking Press and B. W. Huebsch, Inc., merged in August, 1925, to be known as The Viking Press Inc.

"The policy of B. W. Huebsch, regarding first editions, was the same as the present policy of The Viking Press."

1947 Statement: *See* 1937 Statement

1976 Statement: The usual practice is to have no printing line in the first printing of a book, and to add "second printing," etc., on reprints.

1981 Statement: *See* 1976 Statement

1982 Statement: "Our system of printing lines remains pretty much the same, but sometimes we add a line of figures (5 4 3 2 1, e.g.) and strike out one of them with each new printing."

1989 Statement: *See* 1989 Statement of Viking Penguin Inc.

VIKING STUDIO BOOKS

1989 Statement: *See* 1989 Statement of Viking Penguin Inc.

VILLAGE GREEN PRESS

1947 Statement: *See* M. Barrows and Company, Inc.

VILLAGE PRESS

1947 Statement: *See* 1947 Statement of The Press of James A. Decker

VILLARD BOOKS

1988, 1993, 2001 Statements: *See* 1976 Statement of Random House, Inc.

VINE BOOKS

1994, 2000 Statements: *See* 1994 Statement of Servant Publications

VINTAGE (AUSTRALIA)

2000 Statement: *See* 2000 Statement of Transworld Publishers (Australia)

VINTAGE (UNITED KINGDOM)

2000 Statement: *See* 2000 Statement of The Random House Group Limited (United Kingdom)

VINTAGE BOOKS

1988, 1993 Statements: *See* 1976 Statement of Random House, Inc.

VINYL SHOWER

1988 Statement: *See* 1988 Statement of Steam Press

VIRAGO PRESS LIMITED (UNITED KINGDOM)

1988 Statement: "We currently put, and have always put, on the title verso 'Published by Virago Press Limited 19—,' giving the date of first publication by ourselves.

"Should the book be reprinted, we keep the above line, but insert a further one saying 'Reprinted 19—' together with the word Twice or Three Times if necessary! So any book without an indication of a reprint is thus a first edition.

"We have no imprints or subsidiaries of a very separate nature, just different series within our whole list, and this practice is used on all the books we published and always has been."

1994 Statement: *See* 1988 Statement

VIRAGO (UNITED KINGDOM)

2001 Statement: *See* 2001 Statement of Little, Brown and Company (United Kingdom)

VIRGIN (UNITED KINGDOM)

1994 Statement: *See* 1994 Statement of Virgin Publishing Ltd (United Kingdom)

VIRGIN PUBLISHING LTD (UNITED KINGDOM)

1994 Statement: "First printings of our first editions can generally be identified by the first lines of information on the imprint page ('First published in Great Britain in 1992 by Virgin Books, an imprint of Virgin Publishing Ltd' etc), together with the absence of any information about reprints or previous editions. Whenever an edition is reprinted, that information is given as follows: 'Reprinted 1993 (twice), 1994.' A second, revised edition might be designated as follows: 'This revised edition published in 1994 by Virgin Books' etc, followed by details of the book's previous publishing history. The precise wording and details may vary from time to time, but the general principle is as described here."

2000 Statement: "The company name is now Virgin Publishing rather than Virgin Books. In 1989, the company name was W.H. Allen. It became Virgin Publishing in 1990.

"First printings of our first editions can generally be identified by the first lines of information on the imprint page ('First published in Great Britain in 1992 by Virgin Publishing Ltd' etc.), together with the absence of any information about reprints or previous editions. Whenever an edition is reprinted, that information is given as follows: 'Reprinted 1993 (twice), 1994.' A second, revised edition might be designated as follows: 'This revised edition published in 1994 by Virgin Publishing Ltd' etc, followed by details of the book's previous publishing history. The precise wording and details may vary from time to time, but the general principle is as described here.

"All our four imprints (Black Lace, Nexus, Idol and Sapphire) replace 'by Virgin Publishing Ltd' with the name of the imprint (directly followed by the address). For example, they might read 'First published in Great Britain in 1996 by Black Lace' etc."

VIRGINIA CENTER FOR THE CREATIVE ARTS

1988 Statement: *See* 1988 Statement of Associated University Presses

VIRGINIA STATE LIBRARY AND ARCHIVES

1994 Statement: "The Virginia State Library and Archives has not followed any consistent pattern in indicating first editions. Rarely, until now, has the designation 'first edition' appeared in a State Library publication, although second and subsequent editions are always marked as such. Revised editions are often, although not always, so indicated. Beginning this year, all Virginia State Library and Archives publications will carry a statement concerning edition number, including the first, below the copyright line on the reverse of

the title page. First, second, and subsequent printings will also be indicated, when possible."
2000 Statement: *See* 2000 Statement of Library of Virginia

VISA BOOKS (AUSTRALIA)
1981 Statement: *See* 1981 Statement of Widescope International Publishers Pty. Ltd. (Australia)

VISION BOOKS INTERNATIONAL
1994 Statement: "We insert the words 'first printing' and/or 'first edition' on our copyright page. Subsequent editions indicate printing sequence, such as 'first edition, second printing,' etc. This policy was adopted in 1991."

VOLTAIRE FOUNDATION LTD. (UNITED KINGDOM)
2001 Statement: "We do not identify a first printing; we do identify subsequent printings on the copyright page."

VOYAGER BOOKS
2001 Statement: *See* 2001 Statement of Harcourt, Inc.

VOYAGEUR PRESS
1994 Statement: The first printing of a first edition is indicated by the number line 5 4 3 2 1. The lowest number showing indicates the printing.
2000 Statement: *See* 2000 Statement of Voyageur Press Inc.

VOYAGEUR PRESS INC.
2000 Statement: *See* 1994 Statement of Voyageur Press

W

W H & O INTERNATIONAL
1994 Statement: "We identify the first printing of a first edition by
    First Edition
then
    First Edition, 2nd printing, (etc.)."

WADSWORTH
2000 Statement: *See* 2000 Statement of The Wadsworth Group

THE WADSWORTH GROUP
(A Division of Thomson Learning, Inc.)
2000 Statement: "Our name was changed to The Wadsworth Group, a division of Thomson Learning, Inc. in 2000."
See 1981 Statement of Wadsworth Publishing Company, Inc.

WADSWORTH PUBLISHING COMPANY
1994 Statement: *See* 1976 Statement of Wadsworth Publishing Company, Inc.

WADSWORTH PUBLISHING COMPANY, INC.

1976 Statement: "EDITIONS

First Editions. Usually no designation is given in the title. Only designate editions after the first.

Subsequent *editions.* Ordinarily designated in the title as Second Edition, Third Edition, etc. Sometimes designated as Revised Edition, College Edition, etc.

PRINTINGS

The particular printing of any edition of any book is currently designated by a printing line on the copyright page. The line looks like this:

1 2 3 4 5 6 7 8 9 10—80 79 78 77 76

The first number on the left indicates the printing (first printing in this case) and the last two digits on the right indicate the year the printing was made (1976 in this example). We did use a different method of indicating printings a number of years ago. We wrote it out (First printing: 1976)."

1981 Statement: "EDITIONS

First Editions. Usually no designation is given in the title. Only designate editions after the first.

Subsequent editions. Ordinarily designated in the title as Second Edition, Third Edition, etc. Sometimes designated as Revised Edition, International Edition, College Edition, etc.

PRINTINGS

The particular printing of any edition of any book is currently designated by a printing line on the copyright page. The line may look like this:

1 2 3 4 5 6 7 8 9 10—80 79 78 77 76

The first number on the left indicates the printing (first printing in this case) and the last two digits on the right indicate the year the printing was made (1976 in this example). Or the line may look like this:

10 9 8 7 6 5 4 3 2 1

The last digit on the right indicates the printing (first printing in this case). The year the printing was made is not indicated at all. We did use a different method of indicating printings a number of years ago. We wrote it out (First printing: 1976)."

WAKE FOREST UNIVERSITY PRESS

1989 Statement: "When we first publish a title, we indicate the publication date with the other copyright information. If the book will appear in England or Ireland before our edition is available, that publication date is usually mentioned as well. When a book is reprinted, the original date is included in the copyright information."

1994 Statement: *See* 1989 Statement

WAKE-BROOK HOUSE

1976 Statement: "Our first editions always state that they are first editions on the verso of the title page. Reprints are identified as such. We have not changed our practice in this since our founding in 1946."

1981, 1988 Statements: *See* 1976 Statement

WAKEFIELD EDITIONS
1993 Statement: *See* 1993 Statement of Christian Classics, Inc.

WALES TOURIST BOARD (WALES)
1995 Statement: "First editions . . . are not clearly identified by us as such. All titles published feature our imprint and date of production together with our ISBN. All subsequent editions are updated with the date and a new ISBN."
2000 Statement: *See* 1995 Statement

WALKER AND COMPANY
1994 Statement: "Walker and Company identifies first editions on the copyright page (p. iv), following the title page, of each book. The standard line reads: First published in the United States of America in [year] by Walker Publishing Company, Inc. In addition, we use a 'print line'—the numbers 1 through 10—at the bottom of the copyright page. The numeral 1 is dropped at the time of the second printing, and so on."
2000 Statement: *See* 1994 Statement

WALLAROO BOOKS
2001 Statement: *See* 2001 Statement of BkMk Press, University of Missouri-Kansas City

WALNUT HILL BOOKS
1988 Statement: *See* 1988 Statement of Strawberry Hill Press

THE WARBURG INSTITUTE (UNITED KINGDOM)
2001 Statement: "We do not identify a first printing; we do identify subsequent printings as such on the copyright page."

EDMUND WARD (UNITED KINGDOM)
1947 Statement: "As a general rule, first editions of our books can be identified by the fact that no date or 'history' is shown on the title-page, verso of the titles, or opposite the title. Should a second edition or reprint be published then a 'history' such as:

First Edition October, 1947
Reprinted November, 1947

will be included on the verso of the title-page. It follows, therefore, that if no 'history' appears, then the book is a first edition."

WARD HOUSE BOOKS
2001 Statement: *See* 2001 Statement of Higginson Book Co.

WARD LOCK (UNITED KINGDOM)
1994 Statement: *See* 1988 Statement of Ward Lock Limited (United Kingdom)

WARD, LOCK & CO. LIMITED (UNITED KINGDOM)
1928 Statement: "We have no fixed method of designating our first editions."

1935 Statement: "Generally speaking, at the present time we are placing on the back of the title page:

First published in . . . ."
1947 Statement: *See* 1935 Statement
1988 Statement: *See* 1988 Statement of Ward Lock Limited (United Kingdom)

WARD LOCK LIMITED (UNITED KINGDOM)
1988 Statement: "Generally speaking, at the present time we are placing on the back of the title page:

First published in . . . ."
2000 Statement: "There have been several changes at Ward Lock Ltd. Since 1999, Ward Lock has been known as Cassell & Co. Our practices remain unchanged [from the 1988 Statement]. *See* 1988 Statement

FREDERICK WARNE (AUSTRALIA)
2000 Statement: *See* 2000 Statement of Penguin Books Australia Ltd (Australia)

FREDERICK WARNE (UNITED KINGDOM)
1988 Statement: *See* 1988 Statement of Penguin Publishing Co Ltd (United Kingdom)
1995 Statement: *See* 1994 Statement of Penguin Books Ltd (United Kingdom). "However, there is one exception to the general rule and that is the original 123 little books of Beatrix Potter's. These reprint so frequently that the numbers system is far too unwieldy. What we therefore do is to print a 4 digit code at the bottom right hand side of the imprint page which denotes the month and year of each printing.

"You might also want to note that Frederick Warne Inc. no longer publishes anything itself since all Warne books are originated and produced in the United Kingdom. If they happen to manufacture anything locally then the prelims follow the United Kingdom style."
2000 Statement: *See* 1995 Statement

FREDERICK WARNE & CO., INC.
Statement for 1960: "In answer to your question, in the year 1960, we were not printing any information in our book to actually denote first printing so that, in other words, a book that did not state what the printing number was would actually be a first printing. If the book went into any subsequent printings then the legend 'First printing 1960' [was] followed by the legends 'Second printing 1962,' 'Third printing 1965,' etc. This would show which printing that particular volume came from."
1976 Statement: "We identify the first edition of our books by the following symbolic system on the copyright page.

1 2 3 4 5 6 7 8 9 10

"Each time we reprint, we eliminate the appropriate number—i.e. for the second edition, the symbol looks as follows:

2 3 4 5 6 7 8 9 10."

1981 Statement: "About our method of designating the first printing of a first edition: we have changed our method (this was done in the fall of 1978) and the entry should read as follows:

"We identify the first edition of our books by the following symbolic system on the copyright page:

1 2 3 4 5 85 84 83 82 81

"Each time we reprint we eliminate the appropriate numbers—i.e. for the second printing the symbols might be:

2 3 4 5 85 84 83

"The first digit represents that this is a second printing and the last digits represent the year of that second printing."

FREDERICK WARNE & CO., LTD. (UNITED KINGDOM)
1928 Statement: "We did at one time mark first editions of our publications with a private mark, but we are afraid the habit has been discontinued over a number of years now, and we have even lost trace of the private marks."
1937, 1947 Statements: *See* 1928 Statement

WARNER (UNITED KINGDOM)
2001 Statement: *See* 2001 Statement of Little, Brown and Company (United Kingdom)

WARNER BOOKS, INC.
1981 Statement: "Warner First Editions are easily distinguished; they carry a line on the copyright page: first printing with date. Underneath that is a set of numbers from 10 down to one; the last number on the right is the number of the printing in your hand. This is the method we use for our mass market books, our trade paper backs and our hardcover publications. The hardcover edition is usually the first publication in any form in this country. Paperbacks are reprints unless they are marked as originals.

"We've been using this system for quite some time, but I couldn't tell you exactly when this first began."
1988, 1994, 2000 Statements: *See* 1981 Statement

WARNER VISION
2000 Statement: *See* 1981 Statement of Warner Books, Inc.

THE WARTBURG PRESS
1947 Statement: "The policy which we are now following for identification of printings of our books is to enter the number of the printing on the copyright page, thus, 'Second Printing,' 'Third Printing,' etc.

"This plan is not operative until the second printing—the original edition carries only the copyright notice, giving the year of the edition.

"With many of our older books, say those of five or more years ago, no identification of printings is possible. It would be difficult or even impossible to identify the original edition."

IVES WASHBURN INC.
1928 Statement: *See* 1937 Statement

1937 Statement: "We print the date of publication on the title page and on the reverse run a copyright date line but do not print 'first edition' or 'first printing' beneath it. When we make a second printing, we change the date on the title page, provided it is done in a subsequent year; otherwise, it remains the same.

"In making a second printing, whether new material is added to the book or not, we always print beneath the copyright date line on the reverse of the title page in italics the words 'first printing' followed by the month and year, and below 'second printing' with month and year, and so on for subsequent printings. In other words, unless we give this information on the reverse of the title page the buyer may know that he has bought the first editions of our books.

"We have used this method since 1927."

1947 Statement: "Our policy has changed somewhat. We print the year of publication on the copyright page but do not print 'first edition' or 'first printing' beneath it. When we make a subsequent printing we add the number, the month, and the year to the copyright page."

WASHINGTON RESEARCHERS PUBLISHING
1994 Statement: The first printing is identified by "Edition 1."

WASHINGTON STATE UNIVERSITY PRESS
1994 Statement: "We distinguish a first edition with the words 'First Printing' and the 'year' in which it is published."
2000 Statement: *See* 1994 Statement

WATER ROW PRESS
1988 Statement: "First printings are identified with 'First Edition.' [This method was] adopted [in] 1981."
1993, 2000 Statements: *See* 1988 Statement

WATERFRONT BOOKS
1994 Statement: "We designate our first printings by inserting on copyright page the phrase 'First Printing, impression and the year.' "

WATERLINE (UNITED KINGDOM)
1994, 2000 Statements: *See* 1994 Statement of Airlife Publishing Limited (United Kingdom)

WATERMARK PRESS
1994 Statement: "Most all of our printings are limited first editions only. If a printing is not the first edition, it will be stated on the copyright page."
2001 Statement: *See* 1994 Statement

THE WATERWAYS PROJECT
1994, 2000 Statements: *See* 1994 Statement of Ten Penny Players, Inc.

WATSON-GUPTILL PUBLICATIONS

1976 Statement: "Please note that we identify the first publication following the copyright. We follow this practice whether first published by ourselves or by someone else prior to our publication.

"Subsequent printings are identified at the bottom of the front matter by 1st printing, 1972, second printing, 1972, third printing, 1974, etc."

1981 Statement: *See* 1976 Statement

G. HOWARD WATT
(Out of business prior to 1949.)

1937 Statement: "On second printings we always mention the fact that it is the second edition. That is our only distinguishing mark."

FRANKLIN WATTS

1993 Statement: *See* 1981 Statement of Franklin Watts, Inc.

2000 Statement: "On the copyright page the numbers 9 8 7 6 5 4 3 2 1 are printed. The 1 indicates that it is only the first printing. This has always been our method for the various imprints we have used. Obviously, as each new printing run is done, we drop the number of the printing that has gone before it. We also list the years and remove the appropriate one at reprint."

FRANKLIN WATTS, INC.

1947 Statement: "We now have no distinguishing mark for first editions. When we publish books where there may be first edition interest we shall mark them 'first edition.' "

1981 Statement: "On the copyright page the numbers 5 4 3 2 1 are printed. The 1 indicates that it is only the first printing. This has always been our method for the various imprints we have used. Obviously, as each new printing run is done, we drop the number of the printing that has gone before it."

1988 Statement: *See* 1981 Statement

(Changed the name to Franklin Watts in 1993.)

WAVERLY HOUSE

1947 Statement: "We have no special method for identification of first printings."

WAYNE STATE UNIVERSITY PRESS

1976 Statement: The first edition is not designated. The first printing of a first edition is not designated. All editions and printings after the first are indicated on the copyright page. These methods are not new.

1981 Statement: "The first edition is not designated as such. The title page carries the year of publication, indicating that the book is a first edition. All editions and printings after the first are indicated as such on the copyright page."

1988 Statement: *See* 1981 Statement

1993 Statement: "The first edition is not designated as such. All editions and printings are indicated as such on the copyright page."

WAYNEBOOKS
1988 Statement: *See* 1981 Statement of Wayne State University Press

WEATHERHILL
1994 Statement: The first printing of a first edition is indicated by the statement "First edition, (date)" and by the use of a number line showing the year of publication and the number of printings, e.g., 96 95 94 93 8 7 6 5 4 3 2 1.

THE WEBB PUBLISHING COMPANY
(Including Itasca Press and Midland House.)
1947 Statement: "In the case of fiction and general nonfiction, our practice is to indicate first printings by the statement 'First Edition' in a small italic on the copyright page. In the case of text books and technical books this is not always done, although in most cases the month of publication is indicated on the copyright page and subsequent printings are listed in the editions as issued.

"The Midland House imprint appears only in those titles which we took over from the Midland House of Iowa City. Although we are privileged to use this imprint we do not contemplate doing so at the present time. We use, instead, The Itasca Press imprint."

WEBB RESEARCH GROUP
1994 Statement: "We make no mention of first editions but determine the edition by date of copyright. If there is an update to the first book then added copyright dates also appear. As: 1988, 1992, 1994. If we merely reprint a book without any changes, there is a statement '2nd printing' or whatever number it is on verso of title page. But in some of the earlier books, a 2nd printing would not be noted . . . . On the original 6 of our Oregon Trail diaries, the 2nd printings were shown only on the bottom of outside back cover near the price and ISBN. This was simply expedient because we did not have time and would not spend the money to change the plate inside merely to add the phrase '2nd printing.' "
2000 Statement: *See* 2000 Statement of Webb Research Group Publishers

WEBB RESEARCH GROUP PUBLISHERS
2000 Statement: "We make no mention of first editions."

WEE SING
2000 Statement: *See* 2000 Statement of Price Stern Sloan

WEEKES (UNITED KINGDOM)
2001 Statement: *See* 2001 Statement of Stainer & Bell Ltd. (United Kingdom)

WEIDENFELD & NICOLSON (UNITED KINGDOM)
1994 Statement: *See* 1994 Statement of The Orion Publishing Group Ltd (United Kingdom)

GEORGE WEIDENFELD & NICOLSON LIMITED
(UNITED KINGDOM)

1976 Statement: "We do not have any particular way of identifying first editions, except by the date and no mention of any edition. Subsequent editions state that they are reprints, second editions, or whatever."

1981, 1989 Statements: *See* 1976 Statement

WEIDENFELD PAPERBACKS (UNITED KINGDOM)

1994 Statement: *See* 1994 Statement of The Orion Publishing Group Ltd (United Kingdom)

SAMUEL WEISER, INC.

1988 Statement: "First editions carry the notice: 'First published in 1988 (or whatever year) by Samuel Weiser, Inc.' Subsequent printings carry a printing history such as 'third printing, 1988' or whatever the accurate printing history is for the title. The information about second or more printings is listed under our address."

1993 Statement: "We still identify any additional printings but . . . a new program was started in 1993.

We do: 99 98 97 96 95 94 93
     10 9 8 7 6 5 4 3 2 1

This list appears on copyright page, so if we reprint the book in 1995 and it is the 7th printing, we will remove the incorrect data and the copyright page will look like:

99 98 97 96 95
10 9 8 7

"We always carry the original publication data on the book. If we take on a book and change its title, we always carry the original title on the copyright page."

2000 Statement: *See* 1993 Statement

ROBERT WELCH PUBLISHING CO.

1948 Statement: "We differentiate between first printings and subsequent printings by stating on the copyright page of the subsequent printings the particular number that printing may be, such as, 'Second Printing' or 'Third Printing,' etc. In the case of First Printings the copyright page is left blank as to this information."

KEVIN WELDON AND ASSOCIATES PTY LTD
(AUSTRALIA)

1988 Statement: "From September 1988 we will use the following imprint format for all new books.

A Kevin Weldon Production
Published by Kevin Weldon & Associates Pty Limited
372 Eastern Valley Way, Willoughby, NSW 2068, Australia
First published 1988
© Author

"For reprints and subsequent editions of books published by Weldon Publishing we would use the format as above with the addition of:

First published 1988

Reprinted 1989

"If a reprint has been first published by Ure Smith, Lansdowne Press or Rigby Publishers, we will keep the name and change the details on the imprint page as follows:

A Kevin Weldon Production

Published by Ure Smith

Lansdowne Press   use name appropriate to reprint

Rigby Publishers

a division of Kevin Weldon & Associates Pty Limited

372 Eastern Valley Way, Willoughby, NSW 2068, Australia

© Author

First published 1974

Reprinted 1975 (twice), 1976, 1988

"We will still continue to print some of our new titles under the Lansdowne Press and Rigby imprints.

"Limited editions are published under the imprint Lansdowne Editions. The print run and the number of the book are printed on a verso page in the preliminary pages."

WELLINGTON LANE PRESS (AUSTRALIA)

2000 Statement: *See* 2000 Statement of Chapter & Verse/Wellington Lane Press (Australia)

WELLSPRING

2001 Statement: *See* 2001 Statement of The Ballantine Publishing Group

WESCOTT COVE PUBLISHING CO.

1994 Statement: "Wescott Cove makes no designation of a first printing or a first edition. Subsequent printings and subsequent editions are listed by date on the title page. Subsequent editions are featured on the cover and the title of the book. We do not have a verso page.

"This method has varied slightly during the 27 years we've been publishing. Some of our earlier editions did not acknowledge subsequent printings where nothing changed. New editions, incorporating updated information, have always been acknowledged, both on the cover and the title page."

2000 Statement: *See* 1994 Statement, "but note that we have now been publishing for 33 years."

WESLEYAN UNIVERSITY PRESS

1981 Statement: "As a rule, a 'printing' and an 'edition' are one and the same in Wesleyan books, and the fact that one is a first edition is so indicated on the copyright page."

1988 Statement: "While there has been some inconsistency in the past, 'printing' and 'edition' do not mean the same thing. 'Edition' is usually 'First Edition,' which is first printing. Later printings usually omit this and add:

First printing, 19__; third printing, 19__. All of our poetry is published originally simultaneously in cloth and paper; usually (collected works often excepted) reprintings are in paper. Most of our nonfiction books, after 1982, have been published in cloth first, paperback later and these latter are designated, 'Wesleyan Paperback, first printing, 19__.' Most (but not all) reprintings of these titles are in paper only.

"Since 1984 we have been publishing a number of reissues of books out of print at their original publishers, usually in paper only (but in 1987 and 1988 in cloth also). In our *Books in Print* these are designated with original date bracketed. Copyright pages list the original publisher and also: 'Wesleyan Paperback, first printing, 19__.'

"We have no *imprints* as such, but several series, all with the Wesleyan name, such as Wesleyan Poetry, Wesleyan Paperback, Wesleyan Edition of the Works of Henry Fielding (co-published with Clarendon Press, Oxford), of which only the novels are in both cloth and paper."

1993 Statement: "A first edition is the first printing of a given edition. Later printings of a given edition indicate only printings: First printing, 19__; third printing, 19__. Most of our poetry is published originally simultaneously in cloth and paper; reprintings are in paper. Most of our nonfiction books have been published in cloth first, paperback later."

WEST COAST CRIME
2000 Statement: *See* 2000 Statement of Blue Heron Publishing

WEST COAST POETRY REVIEW PRESS
1976 Statement: "We only designate edition and printings after the first— 'First Printing, May, 1975/Second Printing, July, 1976' etc."
1981, 1989 Statements: *See* 1976 Statement

WEST END PRESS
1994 Statement: The first printing of a first edition is indicated by the statement "First edition, (month), (date)."
2000 Statement: *See* 1994 Statement

WEST, SCHIRMER, AND DUXBURY
2000 Statement: *See* 2000 Statement of The Wadsworth Group

WESTCLIFFE PUBLISHERS INC.
1994 Statement: "We do not designate first or subsequent printings."
2000 Statement: *See* 1994 Statement

WESTERN PRODUCER PRAIRIE BOOKS (CANADA)
1989 Statement: "Regarding your inquiry about how our company designates the first printing of a first edition, up until now it has been indicated simply by giving the date of publication on the copyright page. Subsequent printings have been indicated by stripping in a new line: e.g. Second printing 1987. The original date of publication remains on the top line: e.g. Copyright © 1986 by Cora Taylor.

"Beginning with our spring 1989 books, however, we are starting a new system. A first printing will be indicated thusly: 10 9 8 7 6 5 4 3 2 1. The second printing will have the 1 deleted, the third, the 2 etc. The original date of publication will remain on the top line of the copyright page.

"Subsequent editions, as opposed to printings, are indicated by an edition statement plus year on the copyright page.

"We do not have any subsidiaries but in the case of co-publications, each publisher generally supplies its own copyright page and the style and form of these do not necessarily follow our practices."

WESTERN PUBLISHING COMPANY, INC.

1976 Statement: "First editions at Golden Press, which publishes children's books, cookbooks, craft books and science guides are never designated as first editions. Our printing code is shown on the last page or inside back cover of each book. First printings (first editions) bear the code ABCDE etc. Second prints then eliminate the letter A and so on."

1981 Statement: "The Western Publishing entry is basically correct, with a few minor changes:

"First editions at Golden Books, which publishes children's books, cookbooks, craft books and science guides are never designated as first editions. Our printing code is shown on the copyright page, the last page, or inside back cover of each book. First printings (first editions) bear the code ABCDE etc. Second printings then eliminate the letter A and so on."

1988 Statement: "First editions at Golden Books, which publishes children's books, cookbooks, craft books, and science guides, are never designated as first editions. Our printing code is shown on the copyright page, the last page, or inside back cover of each book. First printings (first editions) bear the code

ABCDEFGHIJKLMN

"Second printings then eliminate the letter A and so on.

"Our imprints and subsidiaries follow the same practice."

1994 Statement: "Each copyright page at Golden Books contains a code that distinguishes the first edition from subsequent printings. The letter 'A' plus the year of publication in Roman numerals indicates the first edition. Reprint printings eliminate the letter 'A' and the Roman numeral is updated on an annual basis. When a book is reissued, the letter 'R' is used with the year of publication in Roman numerals for the first printing. Subsequent printings eliminate the letter 'R' and the Roman numeral is updated on an annual basis. Whenever a book title is changed, the new title page clearly states: 'Formerly titled *The Original Title.*' Our imprints and subsidiaries follow the same practice."

WESTERNLORE BOOKS

1976 Statement: "Westernlore first editions are undesignated as such. Unless subsequent editions are typographically so noted it is a first edition."

WESTERNLORE PRESS

1988 Statement: First editions are not designated.
1994 Statement: *See* 1988 Statement

JOHN WESTHOUSE (PUBLISHERS) LIMITED
(UNITED KINGDOM)

1947 Statement: "We generally use the phrase—'First published in . . . .' in the preliminary pages of our first editions."

WESTLAND PUBLICATIONS

1994 Statement: "We have no special method of identifying first editions. However, they can easily be identified, as subsequent editions contain the information, on the back of the title page, that the particular monograph or book was reprinted."

THE WESTMINSTER PRESS

1947 Statement: "We do not attempt to identify first printings of all of our books. However, those which have a distinctly scholarly use and which are possibly changed from edition to edition or printing to printing are identified on the copyright page by 'First Printing,' 'Second Printing,' etc."

Statement for 1960: *See* 1976 Statement

1976 Statement: "Prior to 1974 there was no way to distinguish one printing from another on most Westminster Press publications.

"Starting in 1974 all but the first printings are identified on the copyright page with the printing and the year of the printing, i.e., Second Printing, 1974."

1981 Statement: "To the information you have, please add that starting in 1977 Westminster Press first printings are identified with a line of figures 9 through 1.

"The lowest figure is deleted on all future printings so that the printing may be identified by the lowest number showing. The date of the printing is not shown."

1988 Statement: *See* 1988 Statement of Westminster/John Knox Press

WESTMINSTER/JOHN KNOX PRESS

1988 Statement: "Starting January 1, 1989, titles from The Westminster Press and from the John Knox Press will bear the same imprint: Westminster/John Knox Press, and the city will be Louisville, Kentucky.

See 1981 Statement of The Westminster Press

("On June 1, 1994 the name was changed to Westminster John Knox Press [without a slash].")

WESTMINSTER JOHN KNOX PRESS

1994 Statement: "First editions of Westminster John Knox Press books are identified by the words 'First Edition,' which appear in italics after the design credits on the copyright page. If it is not a first edition, no reference to edition will appear. The number of the edition is shown in the CIP data following the author's name. The number and year of the printing are identified by a line of figures. Numbers 9 through 1 indicate the number of printings. Numbers 94 (for year 1994) through 04 (year 2004) indicate the years in which the printing took place. In both cases the lowest number showing applies. On June 1, 1994 our imprint changed from Westminster/John Knox Press (with a

slash) to Westminster John Knox Press (without a slash). The city is Louisville, Kentucky."
2000 Statement: *See* 1994 Statement

WESTVIEW PRESS
1993 Statement: *See* 1993 Statement of HarperCollins Publishers

WESTVIEW PRESS, INC.
1976 Statement: "We in no way designate a first edition or a first printing of a first edition. Only if it *isn't* a first edition do we say anything at all."
1981 Statement: *See* 1976 Statement
1988 Statement: "Westview Press does not label its first editions as such; however, the reader is notified of a second (or any subsequent) edition on both the copyright page and the title page. As to printings of a given edition, the copyright page carries a series of numbers descending from 10 to 1 or from 6 to 1. A second printing lacks the number '1' in that sequence, a third printing lacks numbers '2' and '1,' and so on."
1995 Statement: *See* 1988 Statement

WESTWATER PRESS
1988 Statement: *See* 1988 Statement of Howe Brothers

WETLANDS PRESS
2000 Statement: *See* 2000 Statement of R D R Books

WHALESBACK BOOKS
1994 Statements: *See* 1994 Statement of Howells House
2000 Statement: *See* 2000 Statement of The Compass Press. *See also* 1994 Statement of Howells House

WHARNCLIFFE PUBLISHING LTD (UNITED KINGDOM)
2001 Statement: "First editions and reprints and new editions are all identified on the copyright page."

WHEAT FORDERS PRESS
1995 Statement: "We have identified first printings of first editions . . . with the statement 'First published in (date)' placed just below the copyright notice, or with the statement 'First American edition' at the very bottom of the copyright page."
2000 Statement: *See* 1995 Statement

WHEATON (UNITED KINGDOM)
1981 Statement: *See* 1981 Statement of Pergamon Press Ltd. (United Kingdom)

WHEATON LITERARY SERIES
2000 Statement: *See* 2000 Statement of Harold Shaw Publishers

WHEATSHEAF BOOKS LIMITED (UNITED KINGDOM)
1988 Statement: *See* 1988 Statement of The Harvester Press Ltd. (United Kingdom)

J. WHITAKER & SONS, LTD. (UNITED KINGDOM)

1988 Statement: "We do not identify first editions. We do identify second and subsequent editions, reprints and so forth, by a statement on the history page (verso of title page)."

1994 Statement: *See* 1988 Statement

WHITCOMB AND BARROWS

(Early name [1904-?] of M. Barrows and Company, Inc.)

WHITE COCKADE PUBLISHING (UNITED KINGDOM)

1994 Statement: "Our first editions simply say on the reverse of the title page 'Published by White Cockade Publishing' followed by our address, and the copyright line giving the date. Subsequent editions will say 'First published in *date*. Reprinted in paperback *date*' or whatever. The exception is our first book which gives White Cockade Publishing and the address, followed by the copyright line from which the date, which was 1988, was omitted in error!"

2000 Statement: *See* 1994 Statement

WHITE MANE BOOKS

1994 Statement: *See* 1994 Statement of White Mane Publishing Co., Inc.

WHITE MANE PUBLISHING CO., INC.

1994 Statement: "We do not identify first or following printings unless we revise the book or add substantial new material. This . . . does not differ from any previously used."

WHITE PINE PRESS

1988 Statement: "We use no special designation for first editions but mark subsequent printings as such."

1993, 2000 Statements: *See* 1988 Statement

WHITEHORSE PRESS

1994 Statement: "Whitehorse Press does not mark its first editions in any distinguishing way. However, subsequent printings and editions are identified as such on the copyright page, making first editions identifiable by the absence of notations to the contrary."

2000 Statement: *See* 1994 Statement

WHITMAN

1988 Statement: *See* 1988 Statement of Western Publishing Company, Inc.

ALBERT WHITMAN & CO.

1947 Statement: "The only way that our books are marked is the printing date on the title page and the copyright date on the reverse side, which must agree in order for the book to be the first edition. All extra printings are marked underneath the copyright. Any book that carries the second printing with the year of date would not be the first edition. Where this does not appear the book would be the first edition if printed by us."

Statement for 1960: "Our first edition has no special marking but subsequent printings are indicated by a note (e.g., Second Printing 1960) above or below the copyright notice. Revised editions are identified as such when they occur."

1976 Statement: "Our first edition has no special marking but subsequent printings are indicated by a note (e.g., Second Printing 1976) above or below the copyright notice. Revised editions are identified as such when they occur."

1981 Statement: *See* 1976 Statement

1988 Statement: *See* 1988 Statement of Albert Whitman & Company

ALBERT WHITMAN & COMPANY

1988 Statement: "For each first edition, a row of numbers is printed beneath the copyright notice in descending order from 10 through 1. With each reprinting, the number of the previous printing is deleted from the row. The number of the printing will be the lowest number in the row.

"We began using the method of designation in 1984.

"We do not have other imprints or subsidiaries."

1993, 2001 Statements: *See* 1988 Statement

WHITMAN GOLDEN LTD. (CANADA)

1988 Statement: *See* 1988 Statement of Western Publishing Company, Inc.

THE WHITNEY LIBRARY OF DESIGN

1976 Statement: "I'm afraid we have no special way of designating a first edition. The copyright page simply says 'Copyright (©) 1976 by Watson Guptill Publications,' or whoever the copyright holder may be. This is then followed by a line that says: 'first published in the United States 1974 by Watson-Guptill Publications' or 'by the Whitney Library of Design.' "

1981 Statement: *See* 1976 Statement

WHITSTON PUBLISHING COMPANY

1989 Statement: "1st Printing—copyright date.

"Second printings have new date added to the page, i.e.:
Second printing 1989."

1993, 2000 Statements: *See* 1989 Statement

WHITTLESEY HOUSE

1937 Statement: "The first printing of the first edition of Whittlesey House books has the words 'first edition' under the statement of copyright, which, of course, includes the year of publication. Subsequent printings have 'second printing,' 'third printing,' etc. Considerably revised editions are designated 'second edition,' 'third edition,' etc. This statement is run on the verso of the title page of all Whittlesey House books."

1947 Statement: "The first printing of the first edition of Whittlesey House books has no indication of edition or printing anywhere in the book. The first edition may be identified only in a negative manner. Subsequent printings have 'second printing,' and subsequent editions 'second edition,' etc., on the verso of the title page under the copyright statement."

WIDESCOPE INTERNATIONAL PUBLISHERS PTY., LTD. (AUSTRALIA)

1981 Statement: "Our imprint details always commence with the notation 'First published 19....' with the dates of reprints or other subsequent editions shown in chronological order.

" 'First published' means the first Australian edition. We rarely republish in Australia books first published abroad although, when we do, we do not indicate the book's foreign publishing record.

"We have not changed our method of designation except by adding the Cataloguing in Publication data supplied by the National Library of Australia.

"This information applies to the following four imprints: Commemorative Editions, Visa Books, Cavalier Press and Widescope Publishers."

WIGWAM PUBLISHING CO.

2000 Statement: "We do not use a special method for designating a first print edition. The copyright symbol and year designates both a first edition and first printing. Any subsequent editions or printings are identified by the addition of 'Second edition' or 'Second printing' to the copyright notice."

WILD & WOOLLEY PTY. LIMITED (AUSTRALIA)

1981 Statement: "Most of our books—we've published 45 so far—have had only one edition. Those that have had additional printings are: *WRAPPINGS* by Vicki Viidikas. 1 was cloth, 2nd paperback. *Cobb Book* by Ron Cobb 6th or 7th printing, I'm not sure. First printing had a poor reproduction of the back cover cartoon, which we corrected in the 2nd printing when we located the original. *Cobb Again* by Ron Cobb. Uses form 5 4 3 2 1 to denote printing.

"That's about all I can tell you. I've tried to standardise with the 5 4 3 2 1 style, but it seems silly when you know there'll only be the one printing."
1988 Statement: *See* 1981 Statement

WILD GOOSE PUBLICATIONS (UNITED KINGDOM)

2001 Statement: "We usually have a statement on the reverse of the title page saying 'First published (year) by Wild Goose Publications', etc. Further printings and/or editions are identified beneath this."

W. A. WILDE COMPANY

1947 Statement: "We do not have any specific method of identifying our first printing of a book but refer you to a sample copyright page for the method employed in additional printings:

Copyright 1945
W. A. WILDE COMPANY
All rights reserved
Sixth Edition
Fourth Printing
MADE IN THE UNITED STATES OF AMERICA"

WILDERNESS PRESS

1976 Statement: "A first edition of ours is indicated by the fact that it does not say 'Xth revised edition' or 'Xth revised printing' or 'Xth printing.' When it is a revised edition, a revised printing or a subsequent printing, the copyright page says so."

1981, 1988 Statements: *See* 1976 Statement

1995 Statement: "We designate the first printing of a first edition merely by showing the copyright year. Succeeding printings of the first edition show the copyright year of the first edition plus the month and year of the additional printing(s). We have always used this method."

2000 Statement: *See* 1995 Statement

WILDSTORM

2000 Statement: *See* 2000 Statement of DC Comics

JOHN WILEY & SONS (AUSTRALIA)

1994 Statement: *See* 1994 Statement of Jacaranda Wiley (Australia)

JOHN WILEY & SONS, INC.

1976 Statement: "There is no designation of our first edition titles. Only subsequent editions carry a designation. To my knowledge, this has always been our practice.

"As for the printing, since 1969 we have placed the numbers from 10 through 1 on the bottom line of the copyright page. If all of these numbers appear it is the initial printing; if the 1 has been deleted, it is the first printing; the 2, the second printing, etc. Prior to 1969 the system called for specifically spelling out the printing. The absence of a printing designation should indicate that it is the first printing. How diligent we have been in following this routine over the years, I can't be certain. For the past fifteen years, I know for certain that we have emphasized the need to follow this system and I *suspect* such has been the case all along."

1981, 1993 Statements: *See* 1976 Statement

JOHN WILEY & SONS, LTD. (UNITED KINGDOM)

1994 Statement: *See* 1976 Statement of John Wiley & Sons, Inc.

2000 Statement: *See* 2000 Statement of John Wiley & Sons Australia, Ltd. (Australia)

JOHN WILEY & SONS AUSTRALIA, LTD. (AUSTRALIA)

2000 Statement: "Our company has changed its name since your last edition in 1995. We are now known as John Wiley & Sons Australia, Ltd.

"Since 1999 John Wiley & Sons Australia, Ltd has designated the first edition of a book at the top of the imprint page by the words 'First published XXXX by John Wiley & Sons Australia, Ltd.' The numbers 10 9 8 7 6 5 4 3 2 1 at the foot of the imprint page show that the book is a first printing. We delete the last digit each time we reprint the book. We indicate second and subsequent editions by the words 'Second edition published XXXX by . . . ' at the top of the imprint page. We still own the Jacaranda Press imprint."

WILLETT, CLARK & COLBY
(Became Willett, Clark & Company on Oct. 22, 1930.)
See Willett, Clark & Company

WILLETT, CLARK & COMPANY

1937 Statement: "Any book published by Willett, Clark & Company that goes into a second edition has the designation 'second edition' under the copyright notice or at least on that page. The first edition is never given any distinctive marking of any kind, therefore, any book not designated as second, third, or fourth edition is a first edition."

1947 Statement: *See* 1937 Statement

JOSEPH WILLIAMS (UNITED KINGDOM)

2001 Statement: *See* 2001 Statement of Stainer & Bell Ltd. (United Kingdom)

WILLIAMS & NORGATE LTD. (UNITED KINGDOM)

1937 Statement: "Our usual practice, adopted a good many years ago, is to put the date of original publication and particulars of any reprint on the back of the title page. Thus:

First printed in Great Britain in 1934
Second impression (or) Reprinted
Third (revised) edition, 1935

"Very occasionally the date appears on the title page itself."

1947 Statement: *See* 1937 Statement

WILLIAMS & WILKINS

1994 Statement: "First printings of first editions are identifiable by the lack of an edition number in the title, and by the appearance of the 1 in the string of successive numbers from 1 to 10 that appears on our copyright page. These numbers indicate in which printing the book is, and as we reprint, we delete a number as necessary. Thus, for the fourth printing of a title, the string of numbers would start at 4."

WILLIAMSON PUBLISHING CO.

1994 Statement: "At Williamson Publishing, we use 1 2 3 4 5 6 7 8 9 0 on the bottom of the copyright page. When reprinted, we delete figure 1, and so on for each subsequent printing, so that the first number on the left is the number of that printing.

"We have used this procedure for all books we have printed since 1983. We have no special indications for first printing of first edition."

2000 Statement: *See* 1994 Statement

WILLING PUBLISHING CO.

1947 Statement: "Printings are listed on copyright page."

WILSON & HORTON LTD (NEW ZEALAND)

1994 Statement: "This company is no longer in the paperback book publishing business. When it was, there was no policy on designating first printings; in fact I cannot remember ever seeing a book being described as a first edition."

THE WOODROW WILSON CENTER PRESS

1994 Statement: The first printing of a first edition is indicated by the number line 9 8 7 6 5 4 3 2 1. The lowest number showing indicates the printing. This method was introduced in 1987.

B. L. WINCH & ASSOCIATES

2000 Statement: *See* 2000 Statement of Jalmar Press

WINCHESTER PRESS

1976 Statement: "It is not the practice of Winchester Press to differentiate between or among first and subsequent editions. If there is no indication on the title page, the work is a first printing, however; other printings are identified by number."

1981 Statement: "We have changed our methods and the [1976] statement is no longer accurate. The new practice was begun in Jan. 1980.

"Winchester Press does indicate Revised Edition on the copyright page of any such book. A printing history line also runs on the copyright page and is revised with each reprint. This line will indicate a first printing."

1988 Statement: *See* 1981 Statement

THE WINDRUSH PRESS (UNITED KINGDOM)

1994 Statement: A first printing is indicated by the line "First published in Great Britain in (date)."

"Second editions that are not revised or do not have a new ISBN are indicated by adding the new year date to the author's copyright line.

"Revised later editions are indicated by stating 'Second edition with revisions published in Great Britain, etc.' followed by the new year of publication, and the year is also added to author's copyright line.

"Sometimes a Printing History is also added when necessary, stating years, types of edition, etc."

2000 Statement: *See* 1994 Statement

WINDSWEPT HOUSE

1994 Statement: "We print '1-2-3-4-5-6-7-8-9-10' on the copyright page of our books. When reprinted, we delete the figure 1; for the third printing we delete the figure 2, and so on. Our imprint, Windswept Too, follows the same practice.

"We have been using this method since 1989; previously, we would have '1st printing,' or '2nd printing,' etc. printed on the copyright page."

WINDSWEPT PRESS

1988 Statement: *See* 1988 Statement of Heart of the Lakes Publishing

WINDSWEPT TOO

1994 Statement: *See* 1994 Statement of Windswept House

WINDWARD HOUSE

(Out of business prior to 1949.)

1937 Statement: "All books published under this imprint are trade editions. Unless they are new editions of Derrydale Press books, they are first editions

of the text, though this is not stated in the book. In the case of a second edition this is so stated on the back of the title page."
See also The Derrydale Press, Inc.

WINDWARD PUBLISHING INC.

1994 Statement: "We identify the first printing of a first edition by the following number line: 1 3 5 7 9 10 8 6 4 2 or 1 3 5 7 9 11 13 15 17 19 20 18 16 14 12 10 8 6 4 2.

"Later editions will have 'Second Edition,' 'Third Edition,' etc printed on the title page. We have always used this type of printing code."

ALLAN WINGATE (PUBLISHERS), LIMITED (UNITED KINGDOM)

1947 Statement: "With reference to your letter, I can supply you with the following information. When any of our titles is first published, it is printed on the imprint page in the following manner—

'First Published in MCMXLVII
by Allan Wingate, Publishers, Ltd.,
64 Great Cumberland Place,
London, W. 1'

and when the title is reprinted, the second impression is mentioned in this manner—

'First Published in MCMXLVII,
second impression February MCMXLVIII
by Allan Wingate, Publishers, Ltd.,
64 Great Cumberland Place, London, W. 1' "

WINGBOW PRESS

1976 Statement: "Any second printing or second edition is always clearly marked."

1981 Statement: "A first edition is noted by either 'First edition,' or 'First printing,' followed by the date."

1988, 1993 Statements: *See* 1981 Statement. "Wingbow Press publishes only under its own imprint and has no subsidiaries."

WINSLOW (UNITED KINGDOM)

1994 Statement: "A first printing of a Winslow title states 'First published in (year) by Winslow Press Ltd, Telford Road, Bicester, Oxon OX6 0TS, United Kingdom' on the reverse of the title page. When reprinted, the line below states 'Reprinted (year),' with further years added at each subsequent reprint."

2000 Statement: *See* 1994 Statement

JOHN C. WINSTON CO.

1928 Statement: "We publish books in a number of different classes and have private marks on some of our editions, notably on our text-books, which give us the date of each edition for our own information.

"We have not, however, made a practice of marking the first editions of our trade publications and should we decide to do so we will probably adopt a symbol which would not mean anything to the public, as I can think of at least one good reason why it might not be desirable to have first editions indicated.

"I must confess that this is undesirable from a book collector's standpoint but other considerations unfortunately outweigh this to such an extent that we are not as yet prepared to establish a permanent system of marking our first editions."

1937 Statement: *See* 1928 Statement

1948 Statement: "We have realized now for some time the importance of distinguishing first editions of trade books, and are endeavoring to include the notification on the copyright page of every new book we publish. If it does not appear in all publications issued from 1948 on, it is an oversight, and not a change in policy."

WINSTON-DEREK PUBLISHERS, INC.
(Became Winston-Derek Publishers Group, Inc. in 1993.)

1988 Statement: "We do not use any specific identification; however, on later editions we designate them as second edition, third edition, and so on.
  Second Printing, 1989;
  Third Printing, 1990, etc."

WINSTON-DEREK PUBLISHERS GROUP, INC.

1993 Statement: *See* 1988 Statement of Winston-Derek Publishers, Inc.

WISCONSIN HOUSE, LTD.

1976 Statement: "At present, Wisconsin House merely indicates a First Edition with the statement 'First Edition' on the copyright page. Subsequent editions carry the number of each printing."

WM. H. WISE & CO., INC.

1976 Statement: "We do not especially designate first editions."

1981 Statement: *See* 1976 Statement

WISHART AND CO., LTD. (UNITED KINGDOM)

1928 Statement: "The title page carries the date of the edition. On the back of the title page there are the words 'First published in . . . .' The date of the second and subsequent editions and impressions is printed below this. First editions are therefore not specifically marked as such."

1935 Statement: "We do not print any bibliographical information on the back of the title page, unless the book goes into a second impression, in which case we give details as to date. The absence of such information implies therefore that the copy is a first edition."

1948 Statement: "Wishart Books Ltd. (formerly Wishart and Co., Ltd.), although technically still in existence has not actually carried on any publishing business for the last eight or nine years, and no titles have been published. Any information given you in 1939 would hold good since there have been no further publications after that date."

H. F. & G. WITHERBY, LTD. (UNITED KINGDOM)

1937 Statement: "Our usual practice is always to give a full biblio on the reverse of the title page. In certain cases the date appears in the title page, but more usually the date of publication appears on the biblio."

1947 Statement: *See* 1937 Statement

WITHERBY & COMPANY LIMITED (UNITED KINGDOM)

1994 Statement: "We identify all first printings of our titles by the words First Edition followed by the date. Subsequent editions would be Second Edition, Third Edition followed by the date etc.

"Similarly reprints would be denoted by: First Reprinted followed by the date, i.e., Eighth Reprint 1987.

"With certain technology sensitive information the Edition may be prefixed by the date/month, such as Fourth Edition, May 1991."

2000 Statement: *See* 1994 Statement

WITTENBORN ART BOOKS, INC.

1981 Statement: "No method is used. Only the reprint/reissue date is noted."

1988 Statement: "[We] have no special mark for first edition. [We] do note later printings."

WIZARDS BOOKSHELF

1988 Statement: "We specialize in 19th century scholarly reprints, but have done a number of first editions. In most we state in the introductory note to the book that it is the first edition, or the first translation. There is no immediate obvious way to determine it is a first edition, and we have never thought this an important point, since our runs are 2,000 copies, and we don't have enormous turnover as popular novels might.

"We have a few heavily annotated reprints such as the *Zohar*, which has undergone extensive revisions to the notes, in which case we put '2nd edition,' or '3rd edition' on the title page.

"We have no subsidiaries."

1994 Statement: *See* 1988 Statement

THE WOBURN PRESS (UNITED KINGDOM)

1994 Statement: *See* 1988 Statement of Frank Cass Publishers (United Kingdom)

ALAN WOFSY FINE ARTS

1988 Statement: "There will usually be an indication on the copyright page for printings or editions after the first."

WOL GUIDES (UNITED KINGDOM)

2001 Statement: *See* 2001 Statement of Pallas Athene (United Kingdom)

WOLDT PUBLISHING GROUP

1995 Statement: "For our STARbooks Press imprints, we would distinguish a first edition from subsequent editions by stating so on the copyright page. We would say 2nd Edition.

"Our Florida Literary Foundation imprints are all first editions. Wherever they are found they are first editions."

2000 Statement: Woldt Publishing Group is now Starbooks Press.
See 2000 Statement of Starbooks Press

HELEN & KURT WOLFF BOOKS

1995 Statement: *See* 1995 Statement of Harcourt Brace and Company

WOLFHOUND PRESS (REPUBLIC OF IRELAND)

1981 Statement: "Wolfhound Press has only one imprint to date, Wolfhound Press. First editions from Wolfhound Press can be identified by reference to the verso of the title page. The copyright date given will be the date of the first edition unless a statement to the contrary is contained on that page. Reprints in the same year as the first edition have not to date been separately identified but reprints in the year after that of the first edition carry that information on the title verso page. First Wolfhound editions of previously published works include the relevant bibliographical information."

1988, 1994 Statements: *See* 1981 Statement. Wolfhound Press now has two imprints: Wolfhound Press and Monarch Line.

WOLSAK AND WYNN PUBLISHERS LTD. (CANADA)

2001 Statement: "Wolsak and Wynn Publishers Ltd. are publishers of poetry exclusively. We publish original poetry collections, books of selected and new poetry, and, occasionally, poetry anthologies. We do not designate our first editions as such, but identify second, third, and further printings on the copyright page. We do not differentiate between second printings and second editions, except if substantive editing is involved."

THE WOMAN'S PRESS

1947 Statement: "When we have a revised edition of a book, we state the number of the edition and the year, for example, 'First Edition, 1945,' 'Second Edition, 1947.'

"The first printing of a book is not specifically designated, although the copyright is stated. Usually our second printing is marked 'Second Printing.' In other words, first printings of any of our books are not so designated, but subsequent printings are designated from the first printings."

WOMEN'S EDUCATIONAL PRESS (CANADA)

1995 Statement: "We use a numbering system. The first printing would be 1 2 3 4 5 1999 1998 1997 1996 1995. So the first number on the left is the printing and the last number on the right is the year.

"The second printing would read 2 3 4 5 1999 1998 1997 1996 for example."

This method was initiated in 1989. Previously, no indication was given.

WONDER/TREASURE BOOKS

1989 Statement: *See* 1989 Statement of Price/Stern/Sloan Publishers, Inc.

KAYE WOOD PUBLISHING

1994 Statement: "We do not differentiate between printings; revisions are noted by an 'R' following the ordering code on the front cover."

WOOD LAKE BOOKS INC. (CANADA)

1988 Statement: "We tend to publish in very small quantities, since our market is a) religious, and b) entirely Canadian. Therefore we rarely expect to go into second or subsequent printings.

"When we do have a second printing, we identify it on the credits page (verso of title page) with the notation, Second Printing 1989. Or Third, etc.

"We don't have any plans for changing the system."

1993 Statement: *See* 1988 Statement

2000 Statement: "All books include an edition statement on the CIP page (verso of title page) as follows: Printing 10 9 8 7 6 5 4 3 2 1. If it is a first printing, the number 1 will still be showing. If it is a second printing, the 1 will be absent and the series will start with the number 2, and so forth for subsequent printings. This change was made for both Wood Lake Books and Northstone Publishing titles in the spring of 1997. Prior to spring 1997, both . . . followed the 1988 statement of practice.

"In 1995, Wood Lake Books . . . started a new imprint called Northstone Publishing. Both Wood Lake Books and Northstone titles are now distributed throughout North America, and foreign language rights are often sold."

WOODBINE HOUSE

1994 Statement: "Ever since Woodbine House was founded in 1985, we have identified the printing with a series of numbers at the bottom of the copyright page. Until 1992, we listed the numbers 1-10 in ascending order and then deleted numbers from the left, as appropriate, to indicate the printing. Since 1992, we have listed the numbers 1-10 in descending order and deleted numbers from the right to indicate the printing. We have no imprints or subsidiaries."

2001 Statement: *See* 1994 Statement

WOODBINE PRESS

1994 Statement: "All Woodbine Press first editions were printed from letterpress. It is obviously detectable from some subsequent editions which were printed from the offset process. From 1990 to present Left Hand Books imprint editions have letterpress covers with 'Woodbine Press' printed at bottom of cover in gold ink. No Left Hand Books second editions have letterpress covers."

WOODBRIDGE PRESS PUBLISHING COMPANY

1976 Statement: "First Edition if no indication otherwise.

"Subsequent editions and/or printings identified by No."

1981 Statement: *See* 1976 Statement

1988 Statement: "First Edition if no indication otherwise.

"Subsequent editions and/or printings identified by number and/or date."

1993, 2000 Statements: *See* 1988 Statement

WORD DANCER PRESS
1995, 2001 Statements: *See* 1995 Statement of Quill Driver Books

WORDSONG/BOYDS MILLS PRESS
1995 Statement: *See* 1995 Statement of Boyds Mills Press

WORDSWORTH EDITIONS LIMITED
(UNITED KINGDOM)
1994 Statement: "Our First Editions all state: © Wordsworth Editions Limited followed by the year of first publication by us. Where we license an edition, the copyright attribution is that of the copyright owner and the year of the edition we have licensed is given."
2000 Statement: *See* 1994 Statement

WORKSHOP
1995 Statement: *See* 1995 Statement of Longhouse

THE WORLD BANK
1994 Statement: The first printing of a first edition is indicated by the statement "First Printing (month) (year)."

WORLD LEISURE CORPORATION
1994 Statement: "We do not annotate the first printing of a first edition. So far, with our travel books, we have not had second printings of editions, but have printed several editions each with changes and updates.

"When we begin with additional printings, it will be noted on the verso page of each title."

WORLD RESOURCES INSTITUTE
1994 Statement: "WRI does not specifically identify first editions, but we do identify reprints (Reprinted: month, year)."

WORLD SCIENTIFIC PUBLISHING CO.
1994 Statement: "If there is a second or third printing, we will print this line on the © page: Reprinted (year)."

WORLD WILDLIFE FUND
1994 Statement: "World Wildlife Fund does not make any designation of the first printing of a first edition primarily because we seldom publish subsequent editions. We are a noncommercial publisher and do not have any subsidiaries or imprints."

WORLDWIDE LIBRARY (CANADA)
1989 Statement: "First printings of Worldwide Library books are designated:

A Worldwide Library Book / (month and year of publication)

"Worldwide Library also holds a number of imprints, including Worldwide Mysteries, Worldwide Science Fiction and Gold Eagle Books. First printings of Worldwide Mysteries are designated:

A Worldwide Mystery / (month and year of publication)

"Worldwide Science Fiction is designated in the same manner as the general Worldwide Library publications.

"Books in the Gold Eagle imprint, which are all paperback originals, are designated:

First edition (month and year of publication)."

1993 Statement: "Worldwide Library holds a number of imprints, including Worldwide Mystery and Gold Eagle Books. First printings of Worldwide Mystery are designated:

A Worldwide Mystery/(month and year of publication)

"Books in the Gold Eagle imprint, which are all paperback originals, are designated:

First edition (month and year of publication)."

2000 Statement: *See* 1993 Statement

WORLDWIDE MYSTERIES (CANADA)

1989, 1993, 2000 Statements: *See* 1989, 1993 Statements of Worldwide Library (Canada)

WORLDWIDE SCIENCE FICTION (CANADA)

1989 Statement: *See* 1989 Statement of Worldwide Library (Canada)

WORMWOOD BOOKS

1995 Statement: "We do not reprint, so all of our publications represent first printings of first-appearance work. Each publication is individually numbered and on last page is a statement indicating size of edition and the number of signed copies. This has been a consistent practice since 1964."

WRIGHT

2000 Statement: *See* 2000 Statement of Butterworth-Heinemann

WRIGHT (UNITED KINGDOM)

1988 Statement: *See* 1988 Statement of Butterworth Scientific, Ltd. (United Kingdom)

2000 Statement: *See* 2000 Statement of Butterworth-Heinemann

JOHN WRIGHT OF BRISTOL (UNITED KINGDOM)

See 1988 Statement of Wright (United Kingdom)

WRITE WAY PUBLISHING

1995 Statement: "We put on the copyright page: First Edition: (date). We also presently indicate the first print-run as: 1 2 3 4 5 6 7 8 9 10. Should we run second or third printings, we will designate them by starting with the number 2 (etc.), and then 3 (etc.), and will take out the words 'First Edition: (date).' "

2000 Statement: *See* 1995 Statement

THE WRITER, INC.

1981, 1988, 1994 Statements: *See* 1981 Statement of Plays, Inc., Publishers

WRITERS AND THEIR WORK (UNITED KINGDOM)

2001 Statement: *See* 2001 Statement of Northcote House Publishers Ltd (United Kingdom)

WYCHWOOD PRESS (UNITED KINGDOM)

2001 Statement: *See* 2001 Statement of Jon Carpenter Publishing (United Kingdom)

A. A. WYN, INC.

1947 Statement: "First printings of our books may be identified by the fact that the copyright page carries no reference to the printing. Subsequent printings are identified by the number, as 'Second Printing,' 'Third Printing,' etc.

"A. A. Wyn, Inc. is distributor for books published under the imprints of Current Books, Inc., A. A. Wyn, Inc. and The L. B. Fischer Publishing Corporation. Since the L. B. Fischer Corporation was purchased by A. A. Wyn, the imprint will not be used on any further printings of Fischer books."

WYNWOOD PRESS

2000 Statement: *See* 2000 Statement of Baker Book House

WYRICK & CO.

1994 Statement: "We do not make special note of the first printing. Subsequent printings will bear a numerical code such as 9 8 7 6 5 4 3 2."

2000 Statement: "We do not make special note of the first printing on non-fiction. Fiction titles are marked 'First Edition.' Subsequent printings might bear a numerical code such as 9 8 7 6 5 4 3 2."

X

XANADU PUBLICATIONS LIMITED (UNITED KINGDOM)

1988 Statement: "We do not designate editions. At this point most of our reprints are indistinguishable from our first editions, due to the cost of making that alteration. However, we hope to indicate new editions and reprints for book clubs and the like by changing the date. For the foreseeable future we will not be attempting anything more sophisticated."

Y

Y LOLFA CYF (WALES)

2001 Statement: "We state 'First edition' and 'First printing' on the copyright page."

YACHTING

1947 Statement: "Yachting Publishing Company has only three active titles at present. They are: *The Gaff Rigged Yachtsman* by Darrell McClure;

Gadgets and Gilhickies by Ham deFontaine; *Ocean Racing* by Alfred F. Loomis.

"Second and third printings of the above, if any, are so noted.

"Books published by Kennedy Brothers, later Yachting Publishing Corporation, are now published by Dodd, Mead and Company."

YALE CENTER FOR BRITISH ART

1994 Statement: "We have no special method of identifying first editions. However, it should be clear from the back of the title page if a publication belongs to a reprinted or revised edition."

YALE ENGLISH MONARCHS (UNITED KINGDOM)

2000 Statement: *See* 2000 Statement of Yale University Press (United Kingdom)

YALE UNIVERSITY PRESS

1928 Statement: "We do not print the words 'First Edition' in any of our books, but on the reverse of the title-page, under the copyright notice, we indicate the subsequent printings as follows:

First Published, 1915.

Second Printing 1916.

Third Printing, 1919.

Second and Enlarged Edition, 1922.

Third Edition with Many New Chapters, 1924.

"It is therefore safe to assume that any of our publications which have no designation below the copyright notice are first editions."

1936 Statement: "The statement of method as used by us is correct as far as it goes. In the case of some of our earlier books, we ran a line under the copyright line reading, 'First published January 1921.' In most cases, and on all books which we are now publishing, the first edition simply carries the copyright line, but some first editions carry a second line as indicated above."

1947 Statement: *See* 1936 Statement

1976 Statement: "We do not identify first editions as such, but any edition except the first has that fact displayed on the title page or the copyright page or both. Second and subsequent printings of a first edition contain a line stating which printing it is on the copyright page. This method of identification has not changed over the years."

1981, 1988 Statements: *See* 1976 Statement

1994 Statement: "Prior to 1981, later printings of Yale U.P. books were identified on the copyright page by 'second printing,' 'third printing,' etc.

"In 1981, we began to set the numerals 10 9 8 7 6 5 4 3 2 1 on the copyright page and to opaque the numeral representing previous printings. Thus the printing number will be the lowest numeral shown."

YALE UNIVERSITY PRESS (UNITED KINGDOM)

1994, 2000 Statements: *See* 1994 Statement of Yale University Press

YANKEE, INC.
1976 Statement: "Usually we simply include the words FIRST EDITION on the title or colophon page."
Printings of a first edition may not be distinguished.
1981 Statement: "Now that our books have gone into a number of printings and continue to do so, we have changed our policy as follows:

"For the first printing of the first edition of any book, usually we simply include the words FIRST EDITION on the title or colophon page. Successive printings of a first edition are distinguished by the number of the printing underneath the words 'First Edition,' i.e.:
FIRST EDITION
2nd Printing
"I would say roughly that this practice has been our habit for the past three years."

YE GALLEON PRESS
1988 Statement: "This is a small book deal working in the university-college-public library market. Most of my list is reprint material, mildly scarce to excessively rare, going down in some cases to one known original copy.

"We rarely reprint hard case books. When we do it is usually in a different format and different typesetting. This is especially the case with limited, numbered editions. We have not had a special policy of identification of first and second editions, but we could watch this and put in a printed explanation. We have sometimes printed a facsimile edition and then later reset the title and printed in a different format.

"However, we do reprint booklets where there is continued demand. Sometimes we have reset the booklet and sometimes not. Some of the booklets are backlist and have been printed several times but it is rare to reprint hard cased material.

"We could easily have a policy of designating second or third printings on the reverse of the title page with an explanation of reset type or other changes but have not had such a policy as hard case material has rarely been reprinted."

YELLOW HOOK PRESS
1995 Statement: "First printing of the first edition just says 'first edition' on the reverse of the title page—subsequent printings say 'first edition, second printing,' etc."

YELLOW JERSEY (UNITED KINGDOM)
2000 Statement: *See* 2000 Statement of The Random House Group Limited (United Kingdom)

YMAA PUBLICATION CENTER
1995 Statement: "To date, YMAA Publication Center has not published a second edition of any of our titles. Most of our titles designate a first printing, second printing, etc., by the words 'First Printing' with the year on the copyright page. Our 3 children's story books have no such designation. Where

subsequent printings are not indicated by the above, the designation will be as the following example:

First Printing 1985
10, 10, 3, 3

This means that the first printing for this title was 10,000 copies: second printing, 10,000; third printing, 3,000; and fourth printing, 3,000."

2000 Statement: "We have published five second editions. Titles are designated as: 10 9 8 7 6 5 4 3 2 1. The print quantity is not identified in the book."

JANE YOLEN BOOKS

1995 Statement: *See* 1995 Statement of Harcourt Brace and Company

YORKTOWN MUSIC PRESS

2001 Statement: *See* 2001 Statement of Music Sales Corp

BRIGHAM YOUNG UNIVERSITY PRESS

1976 Statement: A line similar to the following appears on the copyright page:

76 2M 12735

On initial printings, the last two digits of the copyright date agree with the number at the left.

1981 Statement: A line similar to the following appears on the copyright page:

8/76   12735
(month/year) (job number)

On initial printings, the last two digits of the copyright date agree with the second number at the left (following the slash).

YOUNG CORGI (UNITED KINGDOM)

2001 Statement: *See* 2001 Statement of Transworld Publishers Ltd (United Kingdom)

YOUNG SCOTT BOOKS

1937, 1947 Statements: *See* 1937, 1947 Statements of William R. Scott, Inc.

YOUR DOMAIN

2001 Statement: *See* 2001 Statement of JIST Works Inc

YUCCA TREE PRESS

1994 Statement: "First editions say 'First edition and the date.' "
2000 Statement: *See* 1994 Statement

Z

Z–FAVE

1995 Statement: *See* 1995 Statement of Kensington Publishing Corp.

Z PRESS

1988 Statement: "Z Press does not identify a first edition as such. On the colophon page, the date of printing and the size of the edition, as well as the number of signed copies (usually twenty-six, A to Z) are specified. The year of each printing appears on the title page, and is changed in case of subsequent printings. In one case (*3 Plays*, by John Ashbery), in the second printing, the colophon page was dropped, and the information regarding first and second printing appeared on the copyright page. But this is an exception. The tradition of the colophon page continues, and began with *Miltie Is a Hackie* by Edwin Denby, the first Z Press book, in 1973."

ZEBRA

1995, 2000 Statements: *See* 1995 Statement of Kensington Publishing Corp.

ZENOBIA PRESS

2000 Statement: *See* 2000 Statement of R D R Books

ZEPHYR PRESS

1995 Statement: "In all original publications of Zephyr Press, we have included the words, 'First edition' on the copyright page. If there has been a subsequent printing, we have always designated it 'Second Printing' on the copyright page.

"However, five of the six travel titles we have published during the past four years, have instead used the statement, 'First published in (year) . . . ' Some of these were not Zephyr originals (i.e., were acquired from a foreign publisher).

"We publish a work of Russian literature in translation in 1995 which did not carry the statement 'First edition' on the copyright page, but instead listed the work's previous publication history, in Russian and French editions."
2000 Statement: *See* 1995 Statement

ZEPHYRUS PRESS, INC.

1981 Statement: "On the copyright page we specify that it is the first edition and the first printing. Reprintings are labeled as such, e.g., second printing. New editions are labeled as such and have a second copyright date."

MARK V. ZIESING

1994 Statement: The first printing of a first edition is indicated by the statement "First Edition."

ZIFF DAVIS, LIMITED (UNITED KINGDOM)

1947 Statement: "Our bibliographical notices follow the usual English practice, namely:—
    "First printing will be identified:—
        First published . . . .
    "Subsequent printings will be identified with the different number of impressions as follows:—
        First published . . . .
        New impression . . . ."

ZIFF-DAVIS PUBLISHING COMPANY

1947 Statement: "Our first printings and first editions have no marks to distinguish them as such. Second and subsequent printings are referred to on the copyright page as SECOND PRINTING, THIRD PRINTING, etc. Second or revised editions are mentioned as such on either the title page or the copyright page.

"The above applies to both Ziff-Davis and Alliance books."

ZIGGURAT PRESS

1995 Statement: "The colophon indicates the date of publication and other pertinent information concerning our books. On the rare occasion of a second edition, the colophon will so clearly indicate, with the new date. This method has been used from the first year of publication, 1985."

ZOILUS PRESS (UNITED KINGDOM)

2001 Statement: "Zoilus Press was founded in 1993 and we published our first title the same year. Generally speaking we designate a first printing by 'First published in Great Britain by Zoilus Press, (year)' or 'First published in (year) by Zoilus Press.' There is no logic behind these differences—that's just the way it turned out. However, there are one or two titles where the fact that it is a first edition is not explicitly stated, but it should be reasonably obvious from an examination of the book that this is the case. At the time of writing (2001) all our titles are first editions. We have no imprints or subsidiaries."

ZOLAND BOOKS INC.

1994 Statement: "We identify the first printing of a first edition by the following number line: 00 99 98 97 96 95 94 7 6 5 4 3 2 1. This would be for 1994 . . . .

"The first printing of a book says 'FIRST EDITION.' For further editions the date would be changed and the number 1 dropped etc."
2000 Statement: *See* 1994 Statement

ZONDERVAN PUBLISHING HOUSE

1947 Statement: "We have no particular method of differentiating between various printings and editions of our publications. We indicate the edition on the title page whenever an edition is printed."
1976 Statement: "As new editions are printed (or new printings are scheduled) we indicate the number of the printing on the copyright page.

"This does not differ markedly from our previous practice. On certain books, where the printing history is rather overwhelming (such as *Halley's Bible Handbook*), we do indicate a complete printing history on a separate page."
1981, 1988 Statements: *See* 1976 Statement
1993 Statement: "We include a 'printing history' line at or toward the bottom of the copyright page. This line includes two series of figures, one series indicating the number of the printing and the other indicating the year of publication. The lowest number in each series is the designating figure; the

presence of a '1' denotes a first edition. (The line also usually includes a two-letter code devised by the publishing house to denote the printery.)

For example, the following line means that the book in hand was published in 1993, was printed at Color House Graphics, and is a first edition:

93 94 95 96 97 98 / CH / 10 9 8 7 6 5 4 3 2 1

"I should explain also that the printing history continues uninterrupted when the book changes format, as from hardcover to softcover; that is, a book that had two hardcover printings and then was issued in softcover would have a '3' at the end of the line."

2000 Statement: *See* 1993 Statement

IDENTIFYING BOOK CLUB EDITIONS

We have included this brief summary of book club edition identification practices in response to readers' queries regarding techniques for differentiating a book club edition from the trade edition. Generally, book club editions do not attract the interest of collectors; neither are they usually the true first edition, though there are exceptions.

A book club edition is a book issued by a book club to its members. The book club edition may or may not be part of a special edition. Because some book club editions are taken from the first printing of the trade edition, it is not uncommon for a book club edition to be mistaken for a first printing of the trade edition. For example, a book club edition may be marked as a first edition or first printing. In other cases, it may seem to be such by the absence of any identifying marks to the contrary. The collector, then, needs to ensure that the book at hand is indeed a first printing from the trade edition, and not a first printing issued as a book club edition.

IDENTIFYING BOOK-OF-THE-MONTH CLUB® EDITIONS

Probably the most well-known of the major book clubs in the United States, the Book-of-the-Month Club offers to its members several books each month. Among these offerings, books by a number of collected modern authors inevitably appear. All of the following points relate to the identification of Book-of-the-Month Club editions, though some of the points relate also to the identification of editions issued by other book clubs.

- Look at the lower right-hand corner of the back cover board of the book. Book-of-the-Month Club editions can usually be identified by a small circle, square, or other geometric form on the lower right-hand corner of the back cover board. In past years, this mark was printed on the cover cloth. Later, however, the mark was indented, or debossed.
- Look in the gutter of the last few pages of the book. Editions of the Book-of-the-Month Club are now said to be marked by a alphanumeric code string here (e.g., MP6Z).
- Check the dust jacket for reference to a book club. A book club edition is sometimes identified as such at the top and/or the bottom of the front or back jacket flap. For example, a Book-of-the-Month Club edition may be identified as "A Selection of the Book-of-the-Month Club."
- Does the dust jacket carry a price? Book club editions sometimes carry no price on the dust jacket.
- Does the book have headbands? These are the small decorative bands, usually of cloth, fastened inside the top and sometimes also the bottom of the back, or spine, of a book. Generally, Book-of-the-Month Club editions lack headbands.
- Are the top edges of the pages stained, or colored? On Book-of-the-Month Club editions, the top page edges usually are not stained.

- Book club editions also often feel lighter. Because of the use of paper stocks and cover stocks that are different from those used for the trade edition, book club editions may weigh less.

There are, of course, exceptions to all of the above general guidelines.

IDENTIFYING LITERARY GUILD EDITIONS

Literary Guild editions state "Literary Guild" on the title page and spine.

IDENTIFYING EDITIONS OF OTHER BOOK CLUBS IN THE UNITED STATES

Many book clubs, especially the smaller book clubs, buy their books from the publisher's general run. On receiving the books, they sell them directly to their members, making no changes whatsoever to the books or their jackets. These books are indistinguishable from the publisher's books sold, say, through a retail trade outlet such as a general bookstore. In gathering information on the identification of book club editions, we queried all of the book clubs in the United States, Canada, and England.

1988 General Responses: The following book clubs in the United States responded, in 1988, that the titles issued by them were bought from the publisher's general run and not marked as a book club edition in any way: Aviators Guild, Books of Light, The Computer Book Club, Computer Professionals Book Society, Dance Book Club, Electronics Book Club, Electronics Engineers and Designers Book Club, Evangelical Book Club, How-To Book Club, Intercultural Book Club, Interior Design Book Club, The Jewish Book Club, Mechanical Engineers' Book Club, Thomas More Book Club, Music Book Society, Mystic Arts Book Society, Performing Arts Book Club, Prevention Book Club, Publisher's Choice Book Club, Semontodontics, Inc., The Troll Book Club, Writer's Digest Book Club.

1995 General Responses: The following book clubs in the United States responded, in 1995, that the titles issued by them were bought from the publisher's general run and not marked as a book club edition in any way: Dance Book Club, Graphic Design Book Club, Publisher's Book Club, Woodworker's Book Club, Writer's Digest Book Club.

The following book clubs in the United States responded with more specific information.

EPISCOPAL BOOK CLUB

1988 Statement: In the years 1980 to 1984, books from the trade edition served as club editions, with the publisher's price on them. The book usually carried a club emblem and corporate name inside the dust jacket. This also sometimes appeared on the front cover, along with the words "Selection of the Episcopal Book Club."

FRAGGLE ROCK BOOK CLUB

1988 Statement: "As you can see, we:
-identify Weekly Reader Books on the back cover, the spine and copyright page
-do not have an ISBN
-do not have a retail price
-are a different size
-use different paper and cover stock

"This same method holds true for all of our book clubs and in some we even print Weekly Reader Books on the end pages. As far as I know, we have been doing this type of identification as long as we have had book clubs and book club editions (about 35 years)."

GUIDEPOSTS

1988 Statement: "On most of our Book Club and Book Service selections we use a cross enclosed in a circle on the spine of the book itself, as well as on the dust jacket. And the Guideposts registered name along with the words 'Carmel, New York 10512,' are often printed on the back of the dust jacket.

"As far as I've been able to determine, we've been using the Guideposts cross inside a circle at least since 1953. I can not say what methods were used to designate our Book Club and Book Service selections prior to that year, however."

MUPPET BABIES BOOK CLUB

1988 Statement: *See* 1988 Statement of Fraggle Rock Book Club

WEEKLY READER CHILDREN'S BOOK CLUB

1988 Statement: *See* 1988 Statement of Fraggle Rock Book Club

IDENTIFYING EDITIONS OF BOOK CLUBS IN THE UNITED KINGDOM

Among queried book clubs in the United Kingdom, the following offered helpful statements:

THE ARTISTS BOOK CLUB LTD. (UNITED KINGDOM)

1988 Statement: "The Artists' Book Club is a small specialist Club and as such, rarely buys 'own editions' from its suppliers, but rather smaller quantities which are either extra to the originating publisher's print-run, if the book is a new title, or from publisher's stock for a backlist item. In these cases, nothing distinguishes the Club editions from the trade one.

"In the case where the quantity ordered (currently 1500 copies in the UK, though renegotiations of the Book Club Regulations will put the maximum for an exclusive Book Club Edition up to 3500) is sufficient to warrant the extra cost, the two editions are distinguished in that
a) the Book Club colophon appears on the jacket spine and possibly on the spine of the binding;
b) the Book Club name appears on the title page in the position usually occupied by the Publisher's name;

c) the Book Club is sometimes mentioned in the verso of the title page with a separate ISBN number.

"This has been a practice used widely in the UK from at least the late '60s onwards."

BOOKMARX CLUB (UNITED KINGDOM)

1988 Statement: "We almost always use the regular trade edition. Stickers were applied to some early titles, with Bookmarx Club on them. Nowadays we don't usually bother."

THE POETRY BOOK SOCIETY (UNITED KINGDOM)

1988 Statement: "We do not have special book club editions. Books are not distinguished from trade editions."

W9-BWD-348

Planets
Beyond

Wiley Science Editions

The Search for Extraterrestrial Intelligence, by Thomas R. McDonough

Seven Ideas That Shook the Universe, by Bryan D. Anderson and Nathan Spielberg

The Naturalist's Year, by Scott Camazine

The Urban Naturalist, by Steven D. Garber

Space: The Next Twenty-Five Years, by Thomas R. McDonough

The Body in Time, by Kenneth Jon Rose

Clouds in a Glass of Beer, by Craig Bohren

The Complete Book of Holograms, by Joseph Kasper and Steven Feller

The Scientific Companion, by Cesare Emiliani

Starsailing, by Louis Friedman

Mirror Matter, by Robert Forward and Joel Davis

Gravity's Lens, by Nathan Cohen

The Beauty of Light, by Ben Bova

Cognizers: Neural Networks and Machines That Think, by Colin Johnson and Chappell Brown

Inventing Reality: Physics as Language, by Bruce Gregory

Planets Beyond: Discovering the Outer Solar System, by Mark Littmann

The Starry Room, by Fred Schaaf

The Weather Companion, by Gary Lockhart

To the Arctic: An Introduction to the Far Northern World, by Steven Young

Ozone Crisis: The 15-Year Evolution of a Sudden Global Emergency, by Sharon Roan

The Endangered Kingdom, by Rober DiSilvestro

Serendipity: Accidental Discoveries in Science, by Royston M. Roberts

Sense and Sensibilities, by Jillyn Smith

The Atomic Scientists: A Biographical History, by Henry Boorse, Lloyd Motz, and Jefferson Weaver

The Starflight Handbook: A Pioneer's Guide to Intellerstellar Travel, by Eugene Mallove and Gregory Matloff

Levitating Trains and Kamikaze Genes: Technological Literacy for the 1990s, by Richard P. Brennan

The House of Science, by Philip R. Holzinger

Reality's Mirror: Exploring the Mathematics of Symmetry, by Bryan Bunch

Planets Beyond

Discovering the Outer Solar System

Updated and Revised

Mark Littmann

Wiley Science Editions

John Wiley & Sons, Inc.

New York • Chichester • Brisbane • Toronto • Singapore

Library of Congress Cataloging-in-Publication Data

Littmann, Mark. 1939—
　　Planets beyond: discovering the outer solar system / Mark Littmann.
　Littmann.
　　　p.　　cm　　　— (Wiley science editions)
　　Bibliography : p. 271
　　ISBN 0-471-61128-X　ISBN 0-471-51053-X (pbk)
　　1. Uranus (Planet) 2. Neptune (Planet) 3. Pluto (Planet)
　I. Title. II. Series.
　QB681.L58　1988　　　　　　　　　　　　　　　　　　　88-20498
　523.4'7—dc19　　　　　　　　　　　　　　　　　　　　　　CIP

Printed in the United States of America

90 91 10 9 8 7 6 5 4 3 2 1

*For Peggy
with love*

Preface

I hope you like this story. The discoveries of Uranus, Neptune, and Pluto were among the first sagas I encountered when I began to read about astronomy. They stuck fast to my sense of drama and irony and I wanted someday to retell them, ideally with the power with which they struck me.

Now might be an appropriate time to try. NASA's *Voyager 2* spacecraft, having succeeded magnificently at Jupiter, Saturn, and Uranus, has just completed its 12-year Grand Tour of the giant outer planets by an encounter with Neptune in August 1989. The great legacy of *Voyager 2* data from Neptune has just begun to be evaluated.

And although no spacecraft is planned to visit Pluto, Pluto has come part way to visit us. From 1979 to 1999 it is closer to the Sun than Neptune. In 1989 it was closer to us than at any other time in its 248-year orbit. At the same time, Pluto and its moon Charon were engaged in a rare frenzy of mutual eclipses. Pluto's closeness and eclipses are allowing astronomers to extract from the ninth planet more information than ever before possible.

It used to be that Uranus, Neptune, and Pluto each received a vague paragraph in astronomy textbooks. Not much of interest. Not much was known. Now each is a world surrounded by worlds with unique and fascinating stories to tell us about their evolution and, because they have been less changed by the Sun, about the formation of the solar system itself. These geologic worlds have stories as worthy of recounting as their discoveries.

Thus, in part, this book is a progress report—a way to know what is known and suspected so that we can better appreciate what is being discovered.

Here is a history of long-ago events; here are modern events that are shaping history.

In these pages are striking personalities and high drama; profound confirmations of universal scientific laws; human arrogance and stupidity; intellectual courage and perseverance; triumph, humor, irony, and tragedy. Here are scientific discoveries as they were made and modern scientific research as it bounds and staggers forward with uncertainty and brilliance.

Acknowledgments

Spend a moment here, please.

My name is on the cover, but this book would not have happened or had what quality you find in it without some very special and generous people.

It is an extensive list because wherever I turned in need, a leading professional was graciously willing to provide me with information, ideas, and encouragement. These experts, despite their busy schedules, went far beyond what I ever would have thought possible or proper to request. Previously they had my admiration as scholars. Now they also have my admiration as human beings.

They saved me from many a misstatement and flawed explanation. They even saved me on occasion from my writing style.

The errors that remain in this book are mine. (Let me know what you find; I hope to have the chance to fix them.)

When in this book you find the names of people never fully identified anywhere else, when you find the phrasing precise, you know you have encountered the touch of Ruth S. Freitag of the Library of Congress. She has at her fingertips the most amazing information. It was she who contributed the vignette on the automatic asteroid finder. Her encyclopedic knowledge and unfailing good spirits make me very fortunate indeed to have her as a friend and mentor. She and Don Yeomans are currently writing a wonderful book on comets, to be published by Wiley.

Two noted scientists (and authors) read my entire manuscript and offered extremely helpful suggestions for improvements together with warm encouragement. My sincere thanks to Dr. Thomas R. McDonough, California Institute of Technology, Dr. Andrew Szentgyorgyi, Columbia University, and Dr. Robert S. Harrington, U.S. Naval Observatory.

Several distinguished scientists and engineers who made major discoveries or who work at the heart of major projects have contributed vignettes to *Planets Beyond.* By their graciousness, these researchers have provided us with special insight into the progress of science and technology. They are:

James W. Christy, Hughes Aircraft Corporation
Dr. Gary A. Flandro, Georgia Institute of Technology
William J. O'Neil, Jet Propulsion Laboratory
Rex Ridenoure, Jet Propulsion Laboratory
Dr. E. Myles Standish, Jr., Jet Propulsion Laboratory
Professor Clyde W. Tombaugh, New Mexico State University
Dr. Donald K. Yeomans, Jet Propulsion Laboratory.

Christy, Flandro, Standish, Tombaugh, and Yeomans also helped me greatly with portions of the manuscript in which I tried to tell of their
discoveries and research.

A number of very generous scientists and engineers found time to read
and provide very significant improvements for one or several chapters.
To them, too, I am very grateful:

Dr. Robert Hamilton Brown, Jet Propulsion Laboratory
Dr. Marc W. Buie, University of Hawaii
Dr. Robert J. Cesarone, Jet Propulsion Laboratory
Dr. Dale P. Cruikshank, NASA Ames Research Center
Candace J. Hansen, Jet Propulsion Laboratory
Dr. Charles Kohlhase, Jet Propulsion Laboratory
Dr. William B. McKinnon, Washington University
Dennis Rawlins, Loyola College
Dr. Mark V. Sykes, University of Arizona.

Planets Beyond could not have included a chapter on the search for
a tenth planet without the enthusiastic explanations and candid advice
of the researchers in this field. I sincerely appreciate their help:

Dr. John Anderson, Jet Propulsion Laboratory
Dr. Thomas J. Chester and Michael Melnyk, Jet Propulsion Laboratory
Dr. Robert S. Harrington, U.S. Naval Observatory
Charles T. Kowal, Space Telescope Science Institute
Dr. Conley Powell, Teledyne-Brown Engineering
Dr. Thomas C. Van Flandern, VF Associates
Dr. Daniel P. Whitmire and Dr. John J. Matese, University of
    Southwestern Louisiana.

Often, I had questions to ask—many questions—about articles that I
read, about differing interpretations, about ways to explain difficult concepts. What a privilege it was to be able to call on experts. They were
terrific:

Dr. Edward Bowell, Lowell Observatory
Dr. J.E.P. Connerney, NASA Goddard Space Flight Center
Dr. Donald L. Gray, Jet Propulsion Laboratory
Dr. William B. Hubbard, University of Arizona

Dr. Andrew P. Ingersoll, California Institute of Technology
Dr. Stanley L. Jaki, Seton Hall University
Dr. Torrence V. Johnson, Jet Propulsion Laboratory
Dr. William S. Kurth, University of Iowa
Dr. Jack J. Lissauer, State University of New York at Stony Brook
Dr. Brian Marsden, Smithsonian Astrophysical Observatory
Dr. Ellis D. Miner, Jet Propulsion Laboratory
Dr. Philip D. Nicholson, Cornell University
Dr. Carolyn C. Porco, University of Arizona
Dr. Harold J. Reitsema, Ball Corporation Aerospace Systems Group
Dr. P. Kenneth Seidelmann, U.S. Naval Observatory
Dr. Eugene M. Shoemaker, U.S. Geological Survey
Dr. Bradford A. Smith, University of Arizona
Dr. Laurence A. Soderblom, U.S. Geological Survey
Dr. David J. Stevenson, California Institute of Technology
Dr. Richard Terrile, Jet Propulsion Laboratory
Dr. David J. Tholen, University of Hawaii
Dr. Peter Thomas, Cornell University
Dr. Laurence M. Trafton, University of Texas
Dr. Scott D. Tremaine, University of Toronto
Dr. Jack Wisdom, Massachusetts Institute of Technology.

Many people went far out of their way to help me with information, illustrations, and special resources for this book. I am very grateful to:

Dr. Roy M. Batson, U.S. Geological Survey
Richard Berry, *Astronomy* magazine
Gail Cleere, U.S. Naval Observatory
Brenda Corbin, U.S. Naval Observatory
James A. DeYoung, U.S. Naval Observatory
Dr. Owen Gingerich, Harvard University
Dr. Dieter B. Herrmann, Archenhold Observatory, German Democratic
    Republic
Thomas Jaqua and Althea Washington, NASA
Ruth Leerhoff, San Diego State University Library
Tony Moller, U.S. Naval Observatory
Adam J. Perkins, Royal Greenwich Observatory
Venetia Burney (Mrs. E. Maxwell) Phair of Epsom, England
Jurrie van der Woude, Jet Propulsion Laboratory
James W. Young, Table Mountain Observatory, California Institute of
    Technology.

To the staffs of the Loyola College, Towson State University, and Baltimore County Libraries, you were wonderful and considerate and efficient. I wish I could thank you all by name here.

The people listed above helped to get this work down on paper. Then the professionals at John Wiley & Sons and G&H SOHO turned it into a book. You are reading *Planets Beyond* because of the dedication and skill of Andrew Hoffer, Ruth Greif, and Corine McCormick at Wiley, David Sassian and Claire McKean at G&H SOHO, and Dr. Charles Messing, who very artfully provided the diagrams for this book.

A most special note of thanks to David Sobel, editor of this work and of all the Wiley Science Editions, for his enthusiasm and confidence and wise suggestions.

Finally, there are certain generous and talented souls who contributed in unique and deeply appreciated ways:

Muriel Littmann, my mother
Lewis Littmann, my father, who saw this project started and whom we all miss deeply
Beth and Owen Littmann, my children
David and Esther Littmann
Carl Littmann
Ann and Paul Rappoport
Jane Littmann
Bea and Tom Owens
Anita and David Carstens
Sara Althoff
Frank Bigger

and most especially, my wife, Peggy, to whom this book is lovingly dedicated.

Contents

Planets
Beyond

CHAPTER 1

The Discovery of Uranus

". . . it was that night its turn *to be discovered."*
William Herschel describing his discovery of Uranus

". . . very different from any comet I ever read any description of or saw."
Nevil Maskelyne, Astronomer Royal, April 1781

On March 13, 1781, amateur astronomer William Herschel discovered a new planet. It was completely unexpected.

For as long as anyone could remember, for the thousands of years of recorded history, the solar system ended at Saturn. Mercury, Venus, Mars, Jupiter, Saturn, the Sun, and the Moon slowly shifted their positions against the background stars. That was why the Greeks had named these objects *planētes asteres*—"wandering stars." The telescope, invented early in the seventeenth century, showed some previously invisible features and moons of the known planets. But still no one suspected that planets lay beyond Saturn.

That's why it came as such a surprise to Herschel when he saw a small disk in his telescope on the evening of Tuesday, March 13, 1781. The quality of his eyes and his instrument told him that this was not one of the "fixed stars." When he checked this location between the horns of Taurus and one foot of Gemini on his charts, they did not show a star. Four nights later, when the weather again made observations possible, Herschel saw that his strange object had moved slightly among the stars. Celestial bodies that behaved like this were discovered from time to time. They were called comets. So Herschel published an announcement of this comet, although he noted it was unusual in that it had no tail and showed a distinct rather than a fuzzy disk.

So the actual discovery of this new planet was an accident. That it happened to Herschel was no accident at all.

William Herschel at the age of 46 (1784), three years after his discovery of Uranus (from a crayon copy of an oil painting by L. T. Abbott in the National Portrait Gallery, London)
Courtesy of Special Collections, San Diego State University Library

1

Resourcefulness

William Herschel was born on November 15, 1738, as Friederich Wilhelm Herschel in Hanover, Germany, the third surviving child of an oboist in the Hanoverian Guards military band. Isaac, the father, saw to it that all four of his sons and, when his wife, Anna, wasn't looking, both his daughters not only received excellent musical training but partook of his interest in scientific and cultural matters as well.

William was recognized early as a fine musician. He was admitted as an oboist and violinist to his father's band at age 14.

In 1756, at the onset of the Seven Years' War, the Hanoverian Guards, including the band—father Isaac, older brother Jacob, and William among them—were posted to England for about nine months. Prussia and Austria were the principal adversaries in this war. France allied itself with Austria, so Great Britain, France's worldwide rival in the quest for colonies, sided with Prussia.

As a French attack on Hanover became more likely, the Hanoverian Guards were called home. The band was needed for combat duty to provide the patriotic inspiration and the disciplined beat that encouraged soldiers into battle. William was present on July 26, 1757, during the disastrous Battle of Hastenbeck. The Hanoverian forces were routed. William escaped from the battlefield and rejoined his shattered unit, but the danger, confusion, and the long forced marches in the days ahead convinced him that he was not cut out for army life. His father agreed and arranged for his discharge from the band.[1] William and his older brother Jacob escaped just in time. The retreating Hanoverian Guards were finally trapped and forced to surrender in September. For the next two years, while they occupied Hanover, the French held the Guards captive—band and all—in a military encampment. Isaac was essentially lost to his family for that period and never recovered his health.

Late in 1757, William, at the age of 19, and his brother Jacob left Germany for England. There William copied music while Jacob gave lessons and performed as opportunities permitted. Two years later, upon the defeat of the French, Jacob returned to a musical career in Germany. William stayed on in England. He gave music lessons to the Durham Militia band for two years and then became an itinerant musician, performing in concerts, teaching, and composing in the style of Haydn. He anglicized his name to William. By 1762 he was doing so well that he could send money home to help support his family. But this kind of musical career was too precarious. He sought more secure employment.

Organs were just being installed in English churches, and organist-choir directors were needed. There was one obstacle: William had never played the organ. He began to practice wherever possible, and then he applied for the post of church organist in Halifax. The competition was stiff, in-